Get Ahead of the Curve

P9-DBR-327

Personalized Learning

In MyEconLab you are treated as an individual with specific learning needs.

Auto-Graded Tests and Assignments

- MyEconLab comes with two pre-loaded sample tests for each chapter so you can self-assess your understanding of the material.

Personalized Study Plan

- A study plan is generated based on your results on sample tests and instructor assignments. You can clearly see which topics you have mastered and, more importantly, which topics you need to work on!

Practice Problems

- Use the study plan exercises to get practice where you need it. To check how you're doing, click "results" to get an overview of all your scores.

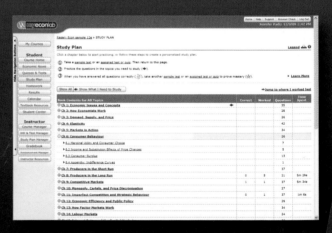

Save Time. Improve Results. www.myeconlab.com

THIRTEENTH CANADIAN EDITION

MACROECONOMICS

CHRISTOPHER T.S.
RAGAN
McGILL UNIVERSITY

RICHARD G.
LIPSEY
SIMON FRASER UNIVERSITY, EMERITUS

THIRTEENTH CANADIAN EDITION
MACROECONOMICS

Pearson Canada
Toronto

Library and Archives Canada Cataloguing in Publication

Ragan, Christopher
    Macroeconomics/Christopher T.S. Ragan, Richard G. Lipsey.— 13th Canadian ed.

Includes index.
Authors' names in reverse order on Canadian 10th ed.
ISBN 978-0-321-60655-6

1. Macroeconomics—Textbooks.   2. Macroeconomics—Canada—Textbooks.
I. Lipsey, Richard G., 1928–   II. °Lipsey, Richard G., 1928– . Macroeconomics.   III. Title.

HB172.5.R35 2011   339   C2009-904726-8

ISBN 978-0-321-60655-6

Vice-President, Editorial Director: Gary Bennett
Editor-in-Chief: Nicole Lukach
Acquisitions Editor: Claudine O'Donnell
Sponsoring Editor: Don Thompson
Marketing Manager: Leigh-Anne Graham
Developmental Editor: Maurice Esses
Production Editor: Marisa D'Andrea
Production Coordinator: Andrea Falkenberg
Copy Editor: Valerie Adams
Proofreader: Dawn Hunter
Indexer: Belle Wong
Permissions and Photo Researcher: Terri Rothman
Compositor: MPS Limited, A Macmillan Company
Art Director: Julia Hall
Cover and Interior Designer: Quinn Banting
Cover Image: Dietrich Rose/Corbis

    2 3 4 5   14 13 12 11

Printed and bound in the United States of America.

Brief Contents

Contents

List of Boxes

Applying Economic Concepts

Lessons from History

Extensions in Theory

Additional Topics on MyEconLab (www.myeconlab.com)

To the Instructor

Economics is a living discipline, changing and evolving in response to developments in the world economy and in response to the research of many thousands of economists throughout the world. Through thirteen editions, *Macroeconomics* has evolved with the discipline. Our purpose in this edition, as in the previous twelve, is to provide students with an introduction to the major issues facing the world's economies, to the methods that economists use to study those issues, and to the policy problems that those issues create. Our treatment is everywhere guided by three important principles:

1. Economics is *scientific,* in the sense that it progresses through the systematic confrontation of theory by evidence. Neither theory nor data alone can tell us much about the world, but combined they tell us a great deal.

2. Economics is *useful* and it should be seen by students to be so. An understanding of economic theory combined with knowledge about the economy produces many important insights about economic policy. Although we stress these insights, we are also careful to point out cases where too little is known to support strong statements about public policy. Appreciating what is not known is as important as learning what is known.

3. We strive always to be *honest* with our readers. Although we know that economics is not always easy, we do not approve of glossing over difficult bits of analysis without letting readers see what is happening and what has been assumed. We take whatever space is needed to explain why economists draw their conclusions, rather than just asserting the conclusions. We also take pains to avoid simplifying matters so much that students would have to unlearn what they have been taught if they continue their study beyond the introductory course. In short, we have tried to follow Albert Einstein's advice:

Everything should be made as simple as possible, but not simpler.

Current Economic Issues

In writing the thirteenth edition of *Macroeconomics,* we have tried to reflect the major economic issues that we face in the early twenty-first century.

Living Standards and Economic Growth

One of the most fundamental economic issues is the determination of overall living standards. Adam Smith wondered why some countries become wealthy while others remain poor. Though we have learned much about this topic in the past 235 years since Adam Smith's landmark work, economists recognize that there is still much we do not know.

Technological change also plays a central role in our discussions of long-run economic growth in Chapters 25 and 26. We explore not only the traditional channels of saving, investment, and population growth, but also the more recent economic theories that emphasize the importance of increasing returns and endogenous growth.

We are convinced that no other introductory economics textbook places as much emphasis on technological change and economic growth as we do in this book. Given the importance of continuing growth in living standards and understanding where that growth comes from, we believe this emphasis is appropriate. We hope you agree.

Financial Crisis and Recession

The collapse of U.S. housing prices in 2007 led to a global financial crisis the likes of which had not been witnessed in a century, and perhaps longer. A deep recession, experienced in many countries, followed quickly on its heels. These dramatic events re-awakened many people to two essential facts about economics. First, modern economies *can and do* go into recession. This essential fact had perhaps been forgotten by many who had become complacent after more than two decades of economic prosperity. Second, financial markets are crucial to the operation of modern economies. Like an electricity system, the details of financial markets are a mystery to most people, and the system itself is often ignored when it is functioning properly. But when financial markets cease to work smoothly, and interest rates rise while credit flows decline, we are all reminded of their importance. In this sense, the financial crisis of 2007–2008 was like a global power failure for the world economy.

The financial crisis had micro causes and macro consequences. It affected the Canadian banking system, discussed in Chapter 27, and led to some "unconventional" actions by the Bank of Canada, as discussed in Chapter 29. Moreover, as the global financial crisis led to a deep recession worldwide, Canadian fiscal policy was forced to respond, as we review in Chapters 24 and 32. Finally, as has happened several times throughout history, the recession raised the threat of protectionist policies, as we examine in Chapter 34.

Globalization

Enormous changes have occurred throughout the world over the last few decades. Flows of trade and investment between countries have risen so dramatically that it is now common to speak of the "globalization" of the world economy. Today it is no longer possible to study any economy without taking into account developments in the rest of the world.

Throughout its history, Canada has been a trading nation, and our policies relating to international trade have often been at the centre of political debates. International trade shows up in many parts of this textbook, but it is the focus of two chapters. Chapter 33 discusses the theory of the gains from trade; Chapter 34 explores trade policy, with an emphasis on NAFTA and the WTO, especially its round of negotiations that began in Doha.

With globalization and the international trade of goods and assets come fluctuations in exchange rates. In recent years there have been substantial changes in the Canada–U.S. exchange rate—a 15-percent depreciation followed the Asian economic crisis in 1997–1998, and an even greater appreciation occurred in the 2002–2008 period. Such volatility in exchange rates complicates the conduct of economic policy. In Chapters 28 and 29 we explore how the exchange rate fits into the design and operation of Canada's monetary policy. In Chapter 35 we examine the debate between fixed and flexible exchange rates.

The forces of globalization are with us to stay. In this thirteenth edition of *Macroeconomics*, we have done our best to ensure that students are made aware of the world outside Canada and how events elsewhere in the world affect the Canadian economy.

The Role of Government

Between 1980 and 2008, the political winds had shifted in Canada, the United States, and many other countries. Political parties that previously had advocated a greater role for government in the economy began to argue the benefits of limited government. But the political winds shifted again with the arrival of the financial crisis and global recession in 2008, which led governments the world over to take some unprecedented actions. Many soon argued that we were observing the "end of laissez-faire" and witnessing the return of "big government." But was that really true?

Has the *fundamental* role of government changed significantly over the past 30 years? In order to understand the role of government in the economy, students must understand the benefits of free markets as well as the situations that cause markets to fail. They must also understand that governments often intervene in the economy for reasons related more to equity than to efficiency.

In this thirteenth edition of *Macroeconomics*, we continue to incorporate the discussion of government policy as often as possible. Here are but a few of the many examples that we explore:

- fiscal policy (in Chapters 22 and 24)
- policies related to the economy's long-run growth rate (in Chapter 26)
- monetary policy (in Chapters 28, 29, and 30)
- policies that affect the economy's long-run unemployment rate (in Chapter 31)
- the importance of debt and deficits (in Chapter 32)
- trade policies (in Chapter 34)
- policies related to the exchange rate (in Chapter 35)

The Book

Economic growth, financial crisis and recession, globalization, and the role of government are pressing issues of the day. Much of our study of economic principles and the Canadian economy has been shaped by these issues. In addition to specific coverage of growth and internationally oriented topics, growth and globalization appear naturally throughout the book in the treatment of many topics once thought to be entirely "domestic."

Most chapters of *Macroeconomics* contain some discussion of economic policy. We have two main goals in mind when we present these discussions:

1. We aim to give students practice in using economic theory, because applying theory is both a wonderfully effective teaching method and a reliable test of students' grasp of theory.

2. We want to introduce students to the major policy issues of the day and to let them discover that few policy debates are as "black and white" as they often appear in the press.

Both goals reflect our view that students should see economics as useful in helping us to understand and deal with the world around us.

Structure and Coverage

Our treatment of macroeconomics is divided into six parts. We make a clear distinction between the economy in the short run and the economy in the long run, and we get quickly to the material on long-run economic growth. Students are confronted with issues of long-run economic growth *before* they are introduced to issues of money and banking. Given the importance of economic growth in driving overall living standards, we feel this is an appropriate ordering of the material; but for those who prefer to discuss money before thinking about economic growth, the ordering can be easily switched without any loss of continuity.

The first macro chapter, Chapter 19, introduces readers to the central macro variables, what they mean, and why they are important. The discussion of national income accounting in Chapter 20 provides a thorough treatment of the distinction between real and nominal GDP, the distinction between GDP and GNP, and a discussion of what measures of national income *do not measure.*

Part 8 develops the core short-run model of the macro economy, beginning with the fixed-price (Keynesian Cross) model in Chapters 21 and 22 and then moving on to the *AD/AS* model in Chapter 23. Chapter 21 uses a closed economy model with no government to explain the process of national-income determination and the nature of the multiplier. Chapter 22 extends the setting to include international trade and government spending and taxation. Chapter 23 rounds out our discussion of the short run with the *AD/AS* framework, discussing the importance of both aggregate demand and aggregate supply shocks. We place the Keynesian Cross before the *AD/AS* model to show that there is no mystery as to where the *AD* curve comes from and why it is downward sloping; the *AD* curve is derived directly from the Keynesian Cross model. In contrast, books that begin their analysis with the *AD/AS* model are inevitably less clear about where the model comes from. We lament the growing tendency to omit the Keynesian Cross from introductory macroeconomics textbooks; we believe the model has much to offer students in terms of economic insights.

Part 9 begins in Chapter 24 by showing how the short-run model evolves toward the long run through the adjustment of factor prices—what we often call the Phillips curve. We introduce potential output as an "anchor" to which real GDP returns following *AD* or *AS* shocks. This chapter also addresses issues in fiscal policy, including the important distinction between automatic stabilizers and discretionary fiscal stabilization policy. Chapter 25 is a short chapter that contrasts short-run with long-run macroeconomics, emphasizing the different typical causes of output changes over the two time spans. Using Canadian data, we show that long-run changes in GDP have their root causes in changes in factor supplies and productivity, whereas short-run changes in GDP are more closely associated with changes in the factor utilization rate. With this short-run/long-run distinction firmly in place, we are well positioned for the detailed discussion of long-run economic growth that appears in Chapter 26. Our treatment of long-run growth, which we regard as one of the most important issues facing Canada and the world today, goes well beyond the treatment in most introductory texts.

Part 10 focuses on the role of money and financial systems. Chapter 27 discusses the nature of money, various components of the money supply, the commercial banking system, and the Bank of Canada. In Chapter 28 we review the determinants of the demand for money. We then turn to a detailed discussion of the link between the money supply and other economic variables such as interest rates, the exchange rate, national income, and the price level. This chapter builds directly on the material in Chapters 23 and 24, with an emphasis on the distinction between short-run and long-run effects. In Chapter 29 we discuss the Bank of Canada's monetary policy, including a detailed discussion of inflation targeting. The chapter ends with a review of Canadian monetary policy over the past 30 years. This provides some important historical context for policy discussions later in the book, as well as an opportunity to draw some general conclusions about the operation of monetary policy.

Part 11 deals with some of today's most pressing macroeconomic policy issues. It contains separate chapters on inflation, unemployment, and government budget deficits. Chapter 30 on inflation examines the central role of expectations in determining inflation, and the importance of credibility on the part of the central bank. Chapter 31 on unemployment examines the determinants of frictional and structural unemployment and discusses likely reasons for increases in the NAIRU over the past few decades. Chapter 32 on budget deficits stresses the effect of deficits on long-term economic growth.

Virtually every macroeconomic chapter contains at least some discussion of international issues. However, the final part of *Macroeconomics* focuses primarily on international economics. Chapter 33 gives the basic treatment of international trade, developing both the traditional theory of static comparative advantage and newer theories based on imperfect competition and dynamic comparative advantage. Chapter 34 discusses both the positive and normative aspects of trade policy, as well as the WTO and NAFTA. Chapter 35 introduces the balance of payments and examines exchange-rate determination. Here we also discuss three important policy issues: the desirability of current-account deficits or surpluses, whether there is a "right" value for the Canadian exchange rate, and the costs and benefits of Canada's adopting a fixed exchange rate. Chapter 36W discusses the main impediments to economic development and the current debates about development policies.

We hope you find this menu both attractive and challenging; we hope students find the material stimulating and enlightening. Many of the messages of economics are complex—if economic understanding were only a matter of common sense and simple observation, there would be no need for professional economists and no need for textbooks like this one. To understand economics, one must work hard. Working at this book should help readers gain a better understanding of the world around them and of the policy problems faced by all levels of government. Furthermore, in today's globalized world, the

return to education is large. We like to think that we have contributed in some small part to the understanding that increased investment in human capital by the next generation is necessary to restore incomes to the rapid growth paths that so benefited our parents and our peers. Perhaps we may even contribute to some income-enhancing accumulation of human capital by some of our readers.

Substantive Changes to This Edition

We have revised and updated the entire text with guidance from an extensive series of formal reviews and other feedback from both users and nonusers of the previous editions of this book. As always, we have strived very hard to improve the teachability and readability of the book. We have focused the discussions so that each major point is emphasized as clearly as possible, without the reader being distracted by non-essential points. We have removed some material from the textbook and placed it in the *Additional Topics* section of the book's MyEconLab (www.myeconlab.com), which also includes new material that has been written especially for this edition. (A complete listing of the *Additional Topics* on MyEconLab is provided following the Contents after the List of Boxes.) As in recent editions, we have kept all core material in the main part of the text. Three types of boxes (Applying Economic Concepts, Lessons from History, and Extensions in Theory) are used to show examples or extensions that can be skipped without fear of missing an essential concept. But we think it would be a shame to skip too many of them, as there are many interesting examples and policy discussions in these boxes.

What follows is a brief listing of the main changes that we have made to the textbook.

Microeconomics Introduction

Part 1: What Is Economics? In Chapter 1, we have brought forward the discussion of money and markets. And in the discussion of the "great debate" regarding the choice between market and planned economies, we have added a short discussion of the experience of the transition economies following the

collapse of the Soviet Union. In Chapter 2, we have streamlined our treatment of theories and models, and we have added a new Study Exercise so students can practise the creation of an index number.

Part 2: An Introduction to Demand and Supply
In Chapter 3, which develops the basic model of demand and supply, we now explain why we choose a "boring" product like carrots to demonstrate the model—because unlike many more "interesting" products like iPods and cell phones, it satisfies the conditions required for the model to be applicable. We have streamlined the discussion of the various factors that lead to shifts in demand and supply curves, and we have added *perception of product quality* to the list of supply shifters.

Part 7: An Introduction to Macroeconomics
Chapter 19 now contains many references to the recent financial crisis and the current recession, thus improving the chapter's relevance for the typical student reader. We have added a new discussion of interest rates and credit flows, motivated by recent events. In the chapter's closing passages, we add a discussion regarding the debate over the government's role in developing new technologies, an important issue for long-run growth. In Chapter 20, we now mention the concept of *chain weighting* in the box on real and nominal GDP. At the end of the chapter where we discuss the connection between GDP and living standards, we have added a citation of the online *Additional Topic* "What Makes People Happy?"

Part 8: The Economy in the Short Run
Chapter 21 presents the basic model of the Keynesian Cross. The discussion on self-fulfilling prophesies has been expanded to include the decline in business and consumer confidence observed in the current recession. In Chapter 22, which adds government and foreign trade to the basic macro model, we have shortened our opening discussion of the government's budget balance, and we have improved and expanded our treatment of fiscal stabilization policy. Chapter 23 introduces the *AD/AS* model. We have reworked the explanation for why the *AD* curve is downward sloping. When introducing shifts in the *AS* curve, we now explain clearly that we are focusing on exogenous shifts in the *AS* curve (the endogenous shifts coming from wage adjustments are discussed in the next chapter).

Part 9: The Economy in the Long Run
In Chapter 24, we have redesigned the first table to better explain the various aspects of the three macro states—the short run, the adjustment process, and the long run. We have added a new box discussing how the intrinsic dynamics of the business cycle help to return real GDP to potential GDP. This is especially important for recessions when the wage-adjustment process is very weak. Our discussion of the limitations of discretionary fiscal policy has been strengthened by discussing some of the problems encountered by the federal government in its 2009 budget. We have added a new box discussing the current recession and how it motivated the fiscal actions taken in the Canadian federal budget of 2009.

In Chapter 25, we have added two new numerical Study Exercises requiring students to work through the short-run and long-run changes in GDP as they are discussed in the chapter. Chapter 26 examines long-term economic growth. We have added a new box on climate change and economic growth in the chapter's final section, where we discuss the possible limits to economic growth.

Part 10: Money, Banking, and Monetary Policy
In Chapter 27 on money and banking, we have enriched our discussion of the Bank of Canada by mentioning some of the unusual actions taken during the recent financial crisis. A new section on the "provision of credit," motivated by recent economic events, helps to explain the role played by commercial banks. We also have a citation to a new online *Additional Topic* on "The U.S. Housing Collapse and the Financial Crisis of 2007–2008."

In Chapter 28, we have expanded and improved our explanation of the different stages of the monetary transmission mechanism. In Chapter 29, we have added a new box discussing "unconventional" monetary policy actions during the recent financial crisis, including the possible actions of quantitative easing and credit easing. In the chapter's final section, we have added a substantial discussion on monetary policy since the beginning of the financial crisis.

Part 11: Macroeconomic Problems and Policies
In Chapter 30, which examines the details of inflation in the *AD/AS* model, we have clarified the explanation of a constant inflation, with nominal interest rates being held constant by two equal but opposing forces (monetary expansion versus rising wages and prices leading to a rise in money demand).

We have added a new box discussing the potential danger of deflation, and we have added a second new box examining whether the NAIRU is really a "razor's edge" as assumed by the standard macro model. The old box on the "death of inflation" has been removed.

In Chapter 31 on the NAIRU and unemployment fluctuations, we have clarified the discussion of New Classical theory in the existing box. We now illustrate the concept of structural unemployment with reference to changes in Canada between 2002 and 2008, driven largely by rising energy and commodity prices. In the discussion of policies to reduce structural unemployment, we discuss the recent government support provided to GM and Chrysler. Chapter 32 examines budget deficits and debt. With the significant turnaround in Canadian government budgets since 2008, this chapter has been updated throughout, although the basic structure of the chapter is unchanged.

Part 12: Canada in the Global Economy

Chapter 33 examines the theory of the gains from trade. We have added a new box that works through two numerical examples of absolute and comparative advantage, as well as a new discussion of human capital as one of the sources of comparative advantage. In the section discussing whether comparative advantage is obsolete, we have added some mention of government successes and failures in trying to create comparative advantage. Finally, we have added a new box on the concept of global supply chains and *integrative trade*.

In Chapter 34, we have added a new box discussing how recession usually leads to an increase in trade protection, with references to the Great Depression and the current economic situation. And in Chapter 35, we have improved our presentation of the demand and supply of foreign exchange, including a more intuitive figure.

* * *

If you are moved to write to us (and we hope that you will be!), please do. You can send any comments or questions regarding the text (or any of the supplementary material, such as the *Instructor's Manual*, the *Study Guide*, the *TestGen*, or the web-based *Additional Topics*) to:

Christopher Ragan
Department of Economics
McGill University
855 Sherbrooke St. West
Montreal, Quebec H3A 2T7
e-mail: christopher.ragan@mcgill.ca

To the Student

Welcome to what is most likely your first book about economics! You are about to encounter what is for most people a new way of thinking, which often causes people to see things differently than they did before. But learning a new way of thinking is not always easy, and you should expect some hard work ahead. We do our best to be as clear and logical as possible, and to illustrate our arguments whenever possible with current and interesting examples.

You must develop your own technique for studying, but the following suggestions may prove helpful. Begin by carefully considering the Learning Objectives at the beginning of a chapter. Read the chapter itself relatively quickly in order to get the general run of the argument. At this first reading, you may want to skip the boxes and any footnotes. Then, after reading the Summary and the Key Concepts (at the end of each chapter), reread the chapter more slowly, making sure that you understand each step of the argument.

With respect to the figures and tables, be sure you understand how the conclusions that are stated in boldface at the beginning of each caption have been reached. You should be prepared to spend time on difficult sections; occasionally, you may spend an hour on only a few pages. Paper and pencil are indispensable equipment in your reading. It is best to follow a difficult argument by building your own diagram while the argument unfolds rather than by relying on the finished diagram as it appears in the book.

The end-of-chapter Study Exercises require you to practise using some of the concepts that you learned in the chapter. These will be excellent preparation for your exams. To provide you with immediate feedback, we have posted Solutions to Selected Study Exercises on MyEconLab (www.myeconlab.com). The end-of-chapter Discussion Questions require you to apply what you have studied. We advise you to outline answers to some of the questions. In short, you should seek to understand economics, not to memorize it.

The red numbers in square brackets in the text refer to a series of mathematical notes that are found starting on page M-1 at the end of the book. For those of you who like mathematics or prefer mathe-matical argument to verbal or geometric exposition, these may prove useful. Others may disregard them.

In this edition of the book, we have incorporated many elements to help you review material and prepare for examinations. A brief description of all the features in this book is given in the separate section that follows.

We encourage you to make use of the brand new MyEconLab that accompanies this book (www.myeconlab.com) at the outset of your studies. MyEconLab contains a wealth of valuable resources to help you. MyEconLab provides Solutions to Selected Study Exercises. It also includes many additional practice questions, some of which are modelled on Study Exercises in the book. In the book, the MyEconLab icon **myeconlab** directs you to online discussions of *Additional Topics*—these represent material written especially for this textbook and include many interesting theoretical, empirical, and policy discussions. You can also find animations of some of the key figures in the text, as well as an electronic version of the textbook. For more details about the MyEconLab, please see the description at the very beginning of this book.

We strongly suggest you make use of the excellent *Study Guide* written expressly for this text. The *Study Guide* is closely integrated with the book. In fact, special references in the margins of the textbook will direct you to appropriate practice questions and exercises in the *Study Guide*. They will test and reinforce your understanding of the concepts and analytical techniques stressed in each chapter of the text and will help you prepare for your examinations. Explanations are provided for the answers to many of the Multiple-Choice Questions to facilitate your independent study. The ability to solve problems and to communicate and interpret your results are important goals in an introductory course in economics. The *Study Guide* can play a crucial role in your acquisition of these skills.

Over the years, the book has benefited greatly from comments and suggestions we have received from students. Please feel free to send your comments to christopher.ragan@mcgill.ca. Good luck, and we hope you enjoy your course in economics!

Features of This Edition

We have made a careful effort with this edition to incorporate features that will facilitate the teaching and learning of economics.

- A set of **Learning Objectives** at the beginning of each chapter clarifies the skills and knowledge to be learned in each chapter. These same learning objectives are used in the chapter summaries, as well as in the Study Guide.

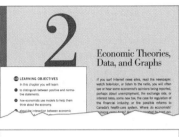

- **Major ideas** are highlighted with a yellow background in the text.
- **Key terms** are boldfaced where they are defined in the body of the text and they are restated with their definitions in the margins. In the index at the back of the book, each key term and the page reference to its definition are boldfaced.
- **Weblinks** to useful Internet addresses are given in the margins. Each weblink presents a URL address, along with a brief description of the material available there. Some links are to government home pages where much data can be obtained. Other links are to organizations such as OPEC, the UN, and the WTO.
- **Study Guide** references in the margin direct students to appropriate questions in the *Study Guide* that reinforce the topic being discussed in the text.

- The **colour scheme for Figures** consistently uses the same colour for each type of curve. For example, all demand curves are blue, whereas all supply curves are red.
- **A caption for each Figure and Table** summarizes the underlying economic reasoning. Each caption begins with a boldfaced statement of the relevant economic conclusion.

- **Additional Topics on MyEconLab** (www.myeconlab.com) are referenced in special boxes inserted at the appropriate place in the body of the relevant chapter. The *Additional Topics* include the entire online Chapter 36W, "Challenges Facing the Developing Countries."
- **Applying Economic Concepts** boxes demonstrate economics in action, providing examples of how theoretical material relates to issues of current interest.
- **Extensions in Theory** boxes provide a deeper treatment of a theoretical topic that is discussed in the text.
- **Lessons from History** boxes contain discussions of a particular policy debate or empirical finding that takes place in a historical context.
- **Photographs with short captions** are interspersed throughout the chapters to illustrate some of the arguments.

- **Chapter Summaries** are organized using the same numbered heading as found in the body of the chapter. The relevant learning objectives (LO) numbers are given in dark blue next to each heading in the summary.
- **Key Concepts** are listed near the end of each chapter.
- A set of **Study Exercises** is provided for each chapter. These often quantitative exercises require the student to analyze problems by means of computations, graphs, or explanations.

- A set of **Discussion Questions** is also provided for each chapter. These questions require the student to synthesize and generalize. They are designed especially for discussion in class.

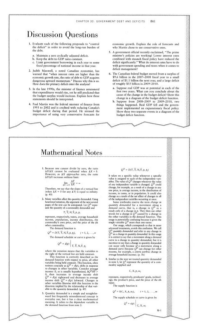

- A set of **Mathematical Notes** is presented in a separate section near the end of the book. Because mathematical notation and derivations are not necessary to understand the principles of economics but are more helpful in advanced work, this seems to be a sensible arrangement. References in the text to these mathematical notes are given by means of red numbers in square brackets.

- A **Timeline of Great Economists,** running from the mid-seventeenth century to the late-twentieth century, is presented near the end of the book. Along this timeline we have placed brief descriptions of the life and works of some great economists, most of whom the reader will encounter in the textbook. Along this timeline we have also listed some major world events in order to give readers an appreciation for when these economists did their work.

- **Economists on Record,** given on the inside of the back cover, quotes some classic excerpts that are relevant to the study and practice of economics.
- For convenience, a list of the **Common Abbreviations Used in the Text** is given on the inside of the front cover.

Supplements

A comprehensive set of supplements has been carefully prepared to assist students and instructors in using this new edition.

Study Guide

A robust *Study Guide*, written by Paul T. Dickinson and Gustavo Indart, is available as split volumes for microeconomics (978-0-321-68523-0) and macroeconomics (978-0-321-69496-6). It is designed for use either in the classroom or by students on their own. The *Study Guide* offers additional study support and reinforcement for each text chapter. It is closely integrated with the textbook. Special notes in the margins of the textbook direct students to appropriate practice exercises in the *Study Guide*. To facilitate independent study, we have now provided explanations for about 70 percent of the answers to the Additional Multiple-Choice Questions. For each chapter, the *Study Guide* provides the following helpful material:

- Learning Objectives matching those in the textbook
- Chapter Overview
- Hints and Tips
- Chapter Review consisting of Multiple-Choice Questions, organized into sections matching the numbered sections in the textbook
- Short-Answer Questions
- Exercises
- Extension Exercises
- Additional Multiple-Choice Questions
- Solutions to all of the Questions and Exercises above
- Explanations for the answers to at least 70 percent of the Additional Multiple-Choice Questions

Instructor's Resource CD-ROM

The *Instructor's Resource CD-ROM* (978-0-321-67477-7) for this new edition contains the following items:

- An Instructor's Manual (in both Word and PDF format) written by Christopher Ragan. It includes full solutions to all the Study Exercises and suggested answers to all the Discussion Questions.

- A **Computerized Testbank (Pearson TestGen)** prepared by Ingrid Kristjanson and Christopher Ragan. The testbank consists of 4000 multiple-choice questions, with an emphasis on applied questions (as opposed to recall questions) and quantitative questions (as opposed to qualitative questions). Approximately 60 percent of the questions test applied skills, about 20 percent of the questions are quantitative, and about 20 percent of the questions have a graph or table. All the questions have been carefully checked for accuracy. For each question, the authors have provided the correct answer, identified the relevant section number in the textbook chapter, specified the concept being tested, assigned a level of difficulty (easy, moderate, or challenging), identified the skill tested (recall or applied), noted whether the question is qualitative or quantitative, and noted whether the question involves a graph or table. *TestGen* enables instructors to search for questions according to any of these attributes and to sort questions into any order desired. With *TestGen,* instructors can easily edit existing questions, add questions, generate tests, and print the tests in a variety of formats. *TestGen* also allows instructors to administer tests on a local area network, have the tests graded electronically, and have the results prepared in electronic or printed reports.
- **PowerPoint® Slides** prepared by Christopher Ragan. Instructors can readily adapt these slides for lecture presentations.
- **Clicker Questions,** consisting of more than 600 questions in PowerPoint format, that can be used with any Personal Response System.
- **An Image Library,** consisting of all the Figures and Tables from the textbook in gif format. These files can easily be imported into PowerPoint slides for class presentation.
- **Additional Topics,** written by Christopher Ragan, offer optional topics on a wide variety of economic subjects, all cited in the textbook and found on MyEconLab (www.myeconlab.com).

MyEconLab

MyEconLab (www.myeconlab.com) provides students with personalized Study Plans and the opportunity for unlimited practice. It also provides instructors with ready-to-use assignments that can be graded electronically. MyEconLab also includes Pearson eText, a robust electronic version of the textbook that enables students and instructors to highlight sections, add notes, share notes, and magnify any of the images or pages without distortion.

Pearson's Technology Specialists work with faculty and campus course designers to ensure that Pearson technology products, assessment tools, and online course materials are tailored to meet your specific needs. This highly qualified team is dedicated to helping students take full advantage of a wide range of educational resources, by assisting in the integration of a variety of instructional materials and media

formats. Your local Pearson Canada sales representative can provide you with more details about this service program.

CourseSmart eTextbook

CourseSmart eTextbook represents a new way for instructors and students to access textbooks online anytime from anywhere. With thousands of titles across hundreds of courses, CourseSmart helps instructors choose the best textbook for their class and give their students a new option for buying the assigned textbook as an eTextbook at a lower cost. For more information, visit www.coursesmart.com.

Acknowledgments

It would be impossible to acknowledge here by name all the teachers, colleagues, and students who contributed to the development and improvement of this book over its previous twelve editions. Hundreds of users have written to us with specific suggestions, and much of the credit for the improvement of the book over the years belongs to them. We can no longer list them individually but we thank them all sincerely.

For the development of this thirteenth edition, we are grateful to the many people who offered informal suggestions. We would also like to thank the following instructors who provided us with formal reviews of the textbook. Their observations and recommendations were extremely helpful.

- Iris Au (University of Toronto Scarborough)
- Yolina Denchev (Camosun College)
- Sacha Des Rosiers (Dawson College)
- Zuzana Fromm (British Columbia Institute of Technology)
- Viktoriya Galushko (University of Regina)
- Robert Gateman (University of British Columbia)
- David Gray (University of Ottawa)
- Robert Jefferson (Wilfrid Laurier University)
- Sunil Kaplash (University of Victoria)
- Ambrose Leung (Bishop's University)
- Roberto Martínez-Espiñeira (St. Francis Xavier University)
- Vettivelu Nallainayagam (Mount Royal College)
- A. Gyasi Nimarko (Vanier College)
- Manish Pandey (University of Winnipeg)
- Mathieu Provencher (McGill University)
- Don Reddick (Kwantlen Polytechnic University)
- Charlene Richter (British Columbia Institute of Technology)
- Kevin Richter (Douglas College)
- Neil Roberts (Kwantlen Polytechnic University)
- Duane Rockerbie (University of Lethbridge)
- John Saba (McGill University)
- Avinash S. Samboo (John Abbott College)
- Chandan Shirvaikar (Red Deer College)
- Peter Sinclair (Wilfrid Laurier University)
- Brennan Thompson (Ryerson University)
- Andrew Wong (Grant MacEwan College)

We would like to express our thanks to the many people at Pearson Canada involved in the production of this textbook. Through several editions, we have been privileged to work closely with Gary Bennett (Vice-President, Editorial), Don Thompson (Sponsoring Editor), Maurice Esses (Developmental Editor), and Marisa D'Andrea (Production Editor), and are grateful for their experience, professionalism, and diligence and care in guiding this book through the publication process. Leigh-Anne Graham joined the team on this edition as the Marketing Manager and has brought a great deal of energy, enthusiasm, and creativity to this project. These individuals have been a pleasure to work with each step along the way and we are deeply grateful for their presence and their participation, and delighted to consider them friends as well as professional colleagues.

Our thanks also to the many people at Pearson with whom we work less closely but who nonetheless toil behind the scenes to produce this book, including Andrea Falkenberg, Julia Hall, Quinn Banting, and Terri Rothman.

Thanks also to Valerie Adams for copyediting, Ron Kessler for the technical review, and to Dawn Hunter for proofreading, all of whom provided an invaluable service with their attention to detail.

In short, we realize that there is a great deal more involved in producing a book than *just* the writing. Without the efforts from all of these dedicated professionals, this textbook simply would not exist. For their assistance with the MyEconLab, we'd like to thank Andrew Naaum, Michael Padbury, and Jessica Courtney. Our sincere thanks to all of you.

Finally, we would like to express our appreciation to Ingrid Kristjanson, who is deeply involved in all stages of the revision of the textbook. She discusses the revision ideas, reviews and edits first and second drafts, and carefully handles the often-complex transcription process. In addition, for the past two editions she has played a leading role in the rewriting and expansion of the electronic testbank. Without her, the revision of the textbook would be far less pleasant and efficient than it now is.

Christopher Ragan
Richard Lipsey

Economic Issues and Concepts

1

If you want a litre of milk, you go to your local grocery store and buy it. When the grocer needs more
milk, he orders it from the wholesaler, who in turn
gets it from the dairy, which in its turn gets it from
the dairy farmer. The dairy farmer buys cattle feed
and electric milking machines, and he gets power to
run all his equipment by putting a plug into a wall
outlet where the electricity is supplied as he needs
it. The milking machines are made from parts manufactured in several different places in Canada, the
United States, and overseas. The parts themselves
are made from materials mined and smelted in a
dozen or more different countries.

   As it is with the milk you drink, so it is with
everything else that you buy. When you go to the
appropriate store, what you want is normally on the
shelf. Those who make these products find that all
the required components and materials are available
when they need them—even though these things
typically come from many different parts of the world
and are made by many people who have no direct
dealings with one another.

🔵 LEARNING OBJECTIVES

In this chapter you will learn

❶ to view the market economy as self-organizing
in the sense that coordination and order
emerge from a large number of decentralized
decisions.

❷ the importance of scarcity, choice, and
opportunity cost, and how all three concepts
are illustrated by the production possibilities boundary.

❸ about the circular flow of income and
expenditure.

❹ that all actual economies are mixed
economies, having elements of free markets,
tradition, and government intervention.

1.1 The Complexity of the Modern Economy

Your own transactions are only a small part of the remarkably complex set of transactions that takes place every day in a modern society. Shipments arrive daily at our ports, railway terminals, and airports. These shipments include raw materials, such as iron ore, logs, and oil; parts, such as automobile engines, transistors, and circuit boards; tools, such as screwdrivers, lathes, and digging equipment; perishables, such as fresh flowers, coffee beans, and fruit; and all kinds of manufactured goods, such as washing machines, computers, and personal DVD players. Railways and trucking lines move these goods among thousands of different destinations within Canada. Some go directly to consumers. Others are used by local firms to manufacture their products—some of which will be sold domestically and some exported to other countries.

Most people who want to work can find work. They spend their working days engaging in the activities just described. In doing so, they earn incomes that they then spend on goods and services produced by others. Some people own firms that employ workers to assist in the many activities described above, such as importing, producing, transporting, and selling things. They earn their incomes as profits from these enterprises.

economy A system in which scarce resources are allocated among competing uses.

An **economy** is a system, typically a very complex one, in which scarce resources—such as labour, land, and machines—are allocated among competing uses. Decisions must be made about which goods are produced and which are not; who works where and at what wage; and who consumes which goods at what times. Although each of these individual decisions may seem simple, the entire combination is remarkably complex, especially in modern societies.

The Self-Organizing Economy

Early in the development of modern economics, thoughtful observers wondered how such a complex set of dealings gets organized. Who coordinates the whole set of efforts? Who makes sure that all the activities fit together, providing jobs to produce the things that people want and delivering those things to where they are wanted? The answer is, surprisingly, no one!

> The great insight of economists is that an economy based on free-market transactions is *self-organizing*.

A market economy is self-organizing in the sense that when individual consumers and producers act independently to pursue their own self-interests, responding to prices determined in open markets, the collective outcome is coordinated—there is a "spontaneous economic order." In that order, literally thousands of millions of transactions and activities fit together to produce the things that people want within the constraints set by the resources that are available to the nation.

The great Scottish economist and political philosopher Adam Smith (1723–1790),[1] who was the first to develop this insight fully, put it this way:

---

[1] Throughout this book, we encounter many great economists from the past whose ideas shaped the discipline of economics. At the back of the book you will find a timeline, beginning in the 1600s, that contains brief discussions of many of these thinkers and places them in their historical context.

It is not from the benevolence of the butcher, the brewer, or the baker, that we expect our dinner, but from their regard to their own interest. We address ourselves, not to their humanity but to their self-love, and never talk to them of our own necessities but of their advantages.

Smith is not saying that benevolence is unimportant. Indeed, he praises it in many passages. He is saying, however, that the massive number of economic interactions that characterize a modern economy cannot all be motivated by benevolence. Although benevolence does motivate some of our actions, often the very dramatic ones, the vast majority of our everyday actions are motivated by self-interest. Self-interest, not benevolence, is therefore the foundation of economic order.

Adam Smith wrote An Inquiry into the Nature and Causes of the Wealth of Nations *in 1776. Now referred to by most people simply as* The Wealth of Nations, *it is considered to be the beginning of modern economics.*

Efficient Organization

Another great insight, which was hinted at by Smith and fully developed over the next century and a half, was that this spontaneously generated economic order is relatively *efficient*. Loosely speaking, efficiency means that the resources available to the nation are organized so as to produce all the goods and services that people want to purchase and to produce them with the least possible amount of resources.

An economy organized by free markets behaves almost as if it were guided by "an invisible hand," in Smith's now-famous words. This does not literally mean that a supernatural presence runs a market economy. Instead it refers to the relatively efficient order that emerges spontaneously out of the many independent decisions made by those who produce, sell, and buy goods and services. The key to explaining this market behaviour is that these decision makers all respond to the same set of prices, which are determined in markets that respond to overall conditions of national scarcity or plenty. Much of economics, and this book, is devoted to a detailed elaboration of how this market order is generated and to how efficiently that job is done.

Main Characteristics of Market Economies

The main characteristics of market economies that produce this spontaneous self-organization are as follows:

SELF-INTEREST. Individuals pursue their own self-interest, buying and selling what seems best for them and their families.

INCENTIVES. People respond to incentives. Sellers usually want to sell more when prices are high; buyers usually want to buy more when prices are low.

MARKET PRICES AND QUANTITIES. Prices and quantities are determined in free markets in which would-be sellers compete to sell their products to would-be buyers.

INSTITUTIONS. All these activities are governed by a set of institutions largely created by government. The most important are private property, freedom of contract, and the rule of law. The natures of private property and contractual obligations are defined by laws passed by legislatures and enforced by the police and the courts.

1.2 Scarcity, Choice, and Opportunity Cost

All the issues discussed so far would not matter much if we lived in an economy of such plenty that there was enough to satisfy all of everyone's wants. But such an economy is impossible. Why?

The short answer is because we live in a world of *scarcity*. Compared with the known desires of individuals for such products as better food, clothing, housing, education, holidays, health care, and entertainment, the existing supplies of resources are clearly inadequate. They are sufficient to produce only a small fraction of the goods and services that people desire. This scarcity gives rise to the basic economic problem of choice. If we cannot have everything we want, we must choose what we will and will not have.

One definition of *economics* comes from the great economist Alfred Marshall (1842–1924), whom we will encounter at several points in this book: "Economics is a study of mankind in the ordinary business of life." A more penetrating definition is the following:

> **Economics is the study of the use of scarce resources to satisfy unlimited human wants.**

Scarcity is inevitable and is central to economic problems. What are society's resources? Why is scarcity inevitable? What are the consequences of scarcity?

Resources

A society's resources are often divided into the three broad categories of land, labour, and capital. *Land* includes all natural endowments, such as arable land, forests, lakes, crude oil, and minerals. *Labour* includes all mental and physical human resources, including entrepreneurial capacity and management skills. *Capital* includes all manufactured aids to production, such as tools, machinery, and buildings. Economists call such resources **factors of production** because they are used to produce the things that people desire. We divide what is produced into goods and services. **Goods** are tangible (e.g., cars and shoes), and **services** are intangible (e.g., haircuts and education).

People use goods and services to satisfy many of their wants. The act of making them is called **production**, and the act of using them to satisfy wants is called **consumption**. Goods are valued for the services they provide. An automobile, for example, helps to satisfy its owner's desires for transportation, mobility, and possibly status.

Scarcity and Choice

For almost all of the world's 6.8 billion people, scarcity is real and ever present. As we said earlier, relative to people's desires, existing resources are inadequate; there are enough to produce only a fraction of the goods and services that are wanted.

But aren't the advanced industrialized nations rich enough that scarcity is nearly banished? After all, they have been characterized as affluent societies. Whatever

factors of production Resources used to produce goods and services; frequently divided into the basic categories of land, labour, and capital.

goods Tangible commodities, such as cars or shoes.

services Intangible commodities, such as haircuts or medical care.

production The act of making goods or services.

consumption The act of using goods or services to satisfy wants.

affluence may mean, however, it does not mean the end of the problem of scarcity. Canadian families that earn $72 000 per year, the average Canadian family after-tax income in 2007 but a princely amount by *world* standards, have no trouble spending it on things that seem useful to them and they would certainly have no trouble convincing you that their resources are scarce relative to their desires.

Because resources are scarce, all societies face the problem of deciding what to produce and how much each person will consume. Societies differ in who makes the choices and how they are made, but the need to choose is common to all. Just as scarcity implies the need for choice, so choice implies the existence of cost. A decision to have more of something requires a decision to have less of something else. The less of "something else" can be thought of as the cost of having the more of "something."

> **Scarcity implies that choices must be made, and making choices implies the existence of costs.**

Opportunity Cost To see how choice implies cost, we look first at a trivial example and then at one that affects all of us; both examples involve precisely the same fundamental principles.

FIGURE 1-1   Choosing Between Pizza and Beer

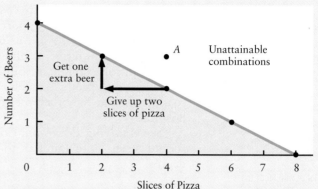

Limited resources force a choice among competing alternatives. Given a total of $16 to spend on $2 slices of pizza and $4 beers, some choices are unattainable, such as point *A*. The five points on the green line show all combinations that are attainable by spending the $16. If it were possible to buy parts of a beer and parts of a slice of pizza, then *all* combinations on the line and in the green area would be attainable. If the entire $16 is to be spent, the choice between more pizza and more beer involves an opportunity cost. The *slope* of the green line reflects opportunity costs. The opportunity cost of one extra slice of pizza is half of a beer; the opportunity cost of one extra beer is two slices of pizza.

Consider the choice David faces on a Saturday night when he goes out for pizza and beer with his friends. Suppose that he has only $16 for the night and that each beer costs $4 and each slice of pizza costs $2. Since David is both hungry and thirsty, he would like to have 4 slices of pizza and 3 beers, but this would cost $20 and is therefore unattainable given David's scarce resources of $16. There are several combinations, however, that are attainable: 8 slices of pizza and 0 beers; 6 slices of pizza and 1 beer; 4 slices of pizza and 2 beers; 2 slices of pizza and 3 beers; and 0 slices of pizza and 4 beers.

David's choices are illustrated in Figure 1-1, which graphs the combinations of beers and slices of pizza that David considers buying. The numbers of slices of pizza are shown on the horizontal axis; the numbers of beers are shown on the vertical axis. The downward-sloping line connects the five possible combinations of beer and pizza that use up all of David's resources—$16. Notice that point *A* shows a combination—4 slices of pizza and 3 beers—that lies outside the line because its total cost is more than $16. Point *A* is *unattainable* to David. If David could buy fractions of a beer and of a slice of pizza, *all* points that lie on or inside the line would be *attainable* combinations.

In this setting David can ask himself, "What is the cost of one beer?" One answer is that the cost is $4. An equivalent answer, assuming that he wanted to spend all of this $16 on these two items, is that the cost of one beer is the two slices of pizza he must give up to get it. In fact, we say in this case that two slices of pizza is the *opportunity cost* of one beer since it is the opportunity David must give up to get one extra beer.

Practise with Study Guide
Chapter 1, Exercise 3.

Every time a choice is made, opportunity costs are incurred.

opportunity cost The cost of using resources for a certain purpose, measured by the benefit given up by not using them in their best alternative use.

Practise with Study Guide Chapter 1, Exercise 4.

The idea of opportunity cost is one of the central insights of economics. Here is a precise definition. The **opportunity cost** of using resources for a certain purpose is *the benefit given up by not using them in the best alternative way*. That is, it is the cost measured in terms of other goods and services that could have been obtained instead. If, for example, resources that could have produced 20 km of road are best used instead to produce one hospital, the opportunity cost of a hospital is 20 km of road; looked at the other way round, the opportunity cost of 20 km of road is one hospital.

See *Applying Economic Concepts 1-1* for an example of opportunity cost that should seem quite familiar to you: the opportunity cost of getting a university degree.

---

myeconlab   ADDITIONAL TOPICS

Economists use graphs to illustrate theories and to show data. If you need a quick refresher about how to use graphs, look for **A Brief Introduction to Graphing** in the *Additional Topics* section of this book's MyEconLab.

www.myeconlab.com

Production Possibilities Boundary Although David's choice between pizza and beer may seem to be a trivial consumption decision, the nature of the decision is the same whatever the choice being made. Consider, for example, the choice that any country must face between producing military and civilian goods.

If resources are fully and efficiently employed, it is not possible to have more of both. However, as the government cuts defence expenditures, resources needed to produce civilian goods will be freed up. The opportunity cost of increased civilian goods is therefore the forgone military output. Or, if we were considering an increase in military output, the opportunity cost of increased military output would be the forgone civilian goods.

The choice is illustrated in Figure 1-2. Because resources are scarce, some combinations—those that would require more than the total available supply of resources for their production—cannot be attained. The negatively sloped curve on the graph divides the combinations that can be attained from those that cannot. Points above and to the right of this curve cannot be attained because there are not enough resources; points below and to the left of the curve can be attained without using all of the available resources; and points on the curve can just be attained if all the available resources are used efficiently. The curve is called the **production possibilities boundary**. (Sometimes the word "boundary" is replaced with "curve" or "frontier.") It has a negative slope because when all resources are being used efficiently, producing more of one good requires producing less of others.

production possibilities boundary A curve showing which alternative combinations of commodities can just be attained if all available resources are used efficiently; it is the boundary between attainable and unattainable output combinations.

A production possibilities boundary illustrates three concepts: scarcity, choice, and opportunity cost. Scarcity is indicated by the unattainable combinations outside the boundary; choice, by the need to choose among the alternative attainable points along the boundary; and opportunity cost, by the negative slope of the boundary.

APPLYING ECONOMIC CONCEPTS 1-1

The Opportunity Cost of Your University Degree

As discussed in the text, the opportunity cost of choosing one thing is what must be given up as the best alternative. Computing the opportunity cost of a college or university education is a good example to illustrate which factors are included in the computation of opportunity cost. You may also be surprised to learn how expensive your university degree really is!*

Suppose that a bachelor's degree requires four years of study and that each year you spend $6000 for tuition fees—approximately the average at Canadian universities in 2009—and a further $1500 per year for books and materials. Does this mean that the cost of a university education is only $30 000? Unfortunately not; the true cost of a university degree is much higher.

The key point is that the opportunity cost of a university education does not just include the out-of-pocket expenses on tuition and books. You must also take into consideration *what you are forced to give up* by choosing to attend university. Of course, if you were not studying you could have been doing any one of a number of things,

but the relevant one is *the one you would have chosen instead*—your best alternative to attending university.

Suppose that your best alternative to attending university was to get a job. In this case, the opportunity cost of your university degree must include the earnings that you would have received had you taken that job. Suppose that your (after-tax) annual earnings would have been $20 000 per year, for a total of $80 000 if you had stayed at that job for four years. To the direct expenses of $30 000, we must therefore add $80 000 for the earnings that you gave up by not taking a job. This brings the true cost of your university degree—the opportunity cost—up to $110 000!

Notice that the cost of food, lodging, clothing, and other living expenses did not enter the calculation of the opportunity cost in this example. The living expenses must be incurred in either case—whether you attend university or get a job.

If the opportunity cost of a degree is so high, why do students choose to go to university? Maybe the students simply enjoy learning and thus are prepared to incur the high cost to be in the university environment. Or maybe they believe that a university degree will significantly increase their future earning potential. (In Chapter 14 we will see that this is true.) In this case, they are giving up four years of earnings at one salary so that they can invest in their own skills in the hope of enjoying many more years in the future at a considerably higher salary.

Whatever the reason for attending college or university, the recognition that a post-secondary degree is very expensive should convince students to make the best use of their time while they are there. Read on!

The opportunity cost to an individual completing a university degree in Canada is large. It includes the direct cost of tuition and books as well as the earnings forgone while attending university.

---

*This box considers only the cost *to the student* of a university degree. For reasons that will be discussed in detail in Part 6 of this book, provincial governments heavily subsidize post-secondary education in Canada. Because of this subsidy, the cost *to society* of a university degree is generally much higher than the cost to an individual student.

The shape of the production possibilities boundary in Figure 1-2 implies that an increasing amount of civilian production must be given up to achieve equal successive increases in military production. This shape, referred to as *concave* to the origin, indicates that the opportunity cost of either good increases as we increase the amount of it that is produced. A straight-line boundary, as in Figure 1-1, indicates

FIGURE 1-2 A Production Possibilities Boundary

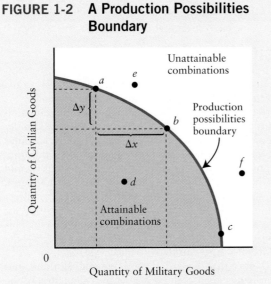

The negatively sloped boundary shows the combinations that are attainable when all resources are efficiently used. The production possibilities boundary separates the attainable combinations of goods, such as *a*, *b*, *c*, and *d*, from unattainable combinations, such as *e* and *f*. Points *a*, *b*, and *c* represent full and efficient use of society's resources. Point *d* represents either inefficient use of resources or failure to use all the available resources. If production changes from point *a* to point *b*, an opportunity cost is involved. The opportunity cost of producing Δ*x* more military goods is the necessary reduction in the production of civilian goods equal to Δ*y*.

that the opportunity cost of one good stays constant, no matter how much of it is produced.

The concave shape in Figure 1-2 is the way economists usually draw a country's production possibilities boundary. The shape occurs because each factor of production is not equally useful in producing all goods. To see why differences among factors of production are so important, suppose we begin at point *c* in Figure 1-2, where most resources are devoted to the production of military goods, and then consider gradually shifting more and more resources toward the production of civilian goods. We might begin by shifting nutrient-rich land that is particularly well suited to growing wheat. This land may not be very useful for making military equipment, but it is very useful for making certain civilian goods (like bread). This shift of resources will therefore lead to a small reduction in military output but a substantial increase in civilian output. Thus, the opportunity cost of producing a few more units of civilian goods, which is equal to the forgone military output, is small. But as we shift more and more resources toward the production of civilian goods, and therefore move along the production possibilities boundary toward point *a*, we must shift more and more resources that are actually quite well suited to the production of military output, like aerospace engineers or the minerals needed to make gunpowder. As we produce more and more civilian goods (by having more and more resources devoted to producing them), the amount of military output that must be forgone to produce one *extra* unit of civilian goods rises. That is, the opportunity cost of producing one good rises as more of that good is produced.

Practise with Study Guide Chapter 1, Exercises 1 and 2.

Four Key Economic Problems

Modern economies involve millions of complex production and consumption activities. Although this complexity is important, many of the basic types of decisions that must be made are not very different from those made in primitive economies in which people work with few tools and barter with their neighbours. Whatever the economic system, whether modern or primitive, there are four key economic questions.

resource allocation The allocation of an economy's scarce resources of land, labour, and capital among alternative uses.

What Is Produced and How?

This question concerns the *allocation* of scarce resources among alternative uses. This **resource allocation** determines the quantities of various goods that are produced. Choosing to produce a particular combination of goods means choosing a particular allocation of resources among the industries or regions producing the goods. What determines which goods are produced and which ones are not?

Furthermore, because resources are scarce, it is desirable that they be used efficiently. Hence, it matters which of the available methods of production is used to produce each of the goods. What determines which methods of production get used and which ones do not? Any economy must have some mechanism by which these decisions about resource allocation are made.

What Is Consumed and by Whom? Economists seek to understand what determines the distribution of a nation's total output among its people. Who gets a lot, who gets a little, and why?

If production takes place on the production possibilities boundary, then how about consumption? Will the economy consume exactly the same goods that it produces? Or will the country's ability to trade with other countries permit the economy to consume a different combination of goods?

> Questions relating to what is produced and how, and what is consumed and by whom, fall within the realm of microeconomics. Microeconomics is the study of the causes and consequences of the allocation of resources as it is affected by the workings of the price system and government policies that seek to influence it.

Why Are Resources Sometimes Idle? Sometimes many workers who would like to have jobs are unable to find employers to hire them. At the same time, the managers and owners of offices and factories could operate at a higher level of activity—that is, they could produce more goods and services. For some reason, however, these resources—land, labour, and factories—lie idle. Thus, in terms of Figure 1-2, the economy is operating inside its production possibilities boundary.

Why are resources sometimes idle? Should governments worry about such idle resources, or is there some reason to believe that such occasional idleness is necessary for a well-functioning economy? Is there anything that the government could do to reduce such idleness?

Is Productive Capacity Growing? The capacity to produce goods and services grows rapidly in some countries, grows slowly in others, and actually declines in others. Growth in productive capacity can be represented by an outward shift of the production possibilities boundary, as shown in Figure 1-3. If an economy's capacity to produce goods and services is growing, some combinations that are unattainable today will become attainable in the future. What are the determinants of growth? Are there some undesirable side effects of growth? Can governments do anything to influence economic growth?

> Questions relating to the idleness of resources and the growth of productive capacity fall within the realm of macroeconomics. Macroeconomics is the study of the determination of economic aggregates, such as total output, total employment, the price level, and the rate of economic growth.

FIGURE 1-3   The Effect of Economic Growth on the Production Possibilities Boundary

Economic growth shifts the boundary outward and makes it possible to produce more of all products. Before growth in productive capacity, points *a*, *b*, and *c* were on the production possibilities boundary and points *e* and *f* were unattainable. After growth, points *e* and *f* and many other previously unattainable combinations are attainable.

microeconomics The study of the causes and consequences of the allocation of resources as it is affected by the workings of the price system.

macroeconomics The study of the determination of economic aggregates such as total output, the price level, employment, and growth.

1.3 Who Makes the Choices and How?

So choices have to be made, but who makes them and how are they made?

The Flow of Income and Expenditure

Figure 1-4 shows the basic decision makers and the flows of income and expenditure that they set up. Individuals own factors of production. They sell the services of these factors to producers and receive payments in return. These are their incomes. Producers use the factor services that they buy to make goods and services. They sell these to individuals, receiving payments in return. These are the incomes of producers. These basic flows of income and expenditure pass through markets. Individuals sell the services of the factor that they own in what are collectively called *factor markets*. When you get a part-time job during university, you are participating in the factor market. Producers sell their outputs of goods and services in what are collectively called *goods markets*. When you purchase a haircut or a new pair of shoes, for example, you are participating in the goods market.

The prices that are determined in these markets determine the incomes that are earned. People who get high prices for their factor services earn high incomes; those who get low prices earn low incomes. The *distribution of income* refers to how the nation's total income is distributed among its citizens. This is largely determined by the price that each type of factor service receives in factor markets.

Maximizing Decisions Consumers and producers are the basic decision makers in a market economy. To these two groups we will shortly add a third, the government. The important assumption that economists usually make about how these two groups make their decisions is that everyone tries to do as well as possible for himself or herself. In the jargon of economics, people are assumed to be *maximizers*. When individuals decide how many factor services to sell to producers and how many products to buy from them, we assume that they make choices designed to maximize their well-being, or *utility*. When producers decide how many factor services to buy from individuals and how many goods to produce and sell to them, we assume that they make choices designed to maximize their *profits*.

Marginal Decisions Firms and consumers who are trying to maximize usually need to weigh the costs and benefits of their decisions *at the margin*. For example, when you consider buying an additional CD, you know the *marginal cost* of the CD—that is, how much you must pay to get one extra CD—and you

FIGURE 1-4   The Circular Flow of Income and Expenditure

The red line shows the flows of goods and services; the blue line shows the payments made to purchase these. Factor services flow from individuals who own the factors (including their own labour) through factor markets to firms that use them to make goods and services. These goods and services then flow through goods markets to those who consume them. Money payments flow from firms to individuals through factor markets. These payments become the income of individuals. When they spend this income buying goods and services, money flows through goods markets back to producers.

need to weigh it against the *marginal benefit* that you will receive—the *extra* satisfaction you get from that CD. If you are trying to maximize your utility, you will buy that CD only if you think that the benefit to you in terms of extra utility exceeds the marginal cost.

Similarly, a producer attempting to maximize its profits and considering whether to hire an extra worker must evaluate the *marginal cost* of the worker—the extra wages and benefits that must be paid—and weigh it against the *marginal benefit* of the worker—the increase in sales revenues that will be generated by the extra worker. A producer interested in maximizing its profit will hire the extra worker only if the benefit in terms of extra revenue exceeds the cost in terms of extra wages.

Consumers and producers who are maximizers make marginal decisions—whether to buy or sell a little bit more or less of the many things that they buy and sell.

Voting in an election is an example in which decisions are *not* made on a marginal basis. When you vote in a Canadian federal election, you have only one vote and you must support one party over the others. When you do, you vote for everything that party stands for, even though you may prefer to pick and choose elements from each party's political platform. You cannot say "I vote for the Liberals on issue A and for the Conservatives on issue B." You must make a total, rather than a marginal, decision.

The Complexity of Production

Producers decide what to produce and how to produce it. Production is a very complex process in any modern economy. A typical car manufacturer assembles a product out of thousands of individual parts. It makes some of these parts itself. Most are subcontracted to parts manufacturers, and many of the major parts manufacturers subcontract some of their work out to smaller firms. This kind of production displays two characteristics noted long ago by Adam Smith—*specialization* and the *division of labour*.

Specialization In ancient hunter–gatherer societies, and in modern subsistence economies, most people make most of the things they need for themselves. However, from the time that people first engaged in settled agriculture and some of them began to live in towns, people have specialized in doing particular jobs. Artisan, soldier, priest, and government official were some of the earliest specialized occupations. Economists call this allocation of different jobs to different people the **specialization of labour**. There are two fundamental reasons that specialization is extraordinarily efficient compared with universal self-sufficiency.

First, individual abilities differ, and specialization allows each person to do what he or she can do relatively well while leaving everything else to be done by others. Even when people's abilities are unaffected by the act of specializing, the economy's total production is greater when people specialize than when they all try to be self-sufficient. This is true for individuals, but it is also true for entire countries, and it is one of the most fundamental principles in economics: the principle of *comparative advantage*. A much fuller discussion of comparative advantage is found in Chapter 33, where we discuss the gains from international trade.

The second reason that specialization is more efficient than self-sufficiency concerns changes in people's abilities that occur *because* they specialize. A person who concentrates on one activity becomes better at it than could a jack-of-all-trades. This is

specialization of labour
The specialization of individual workers in the production of particular goods or services.

called *learning by doing*, and it was a factor much stressed by early economists; research shows that it is important in many modern industries.

The Division of Labour Throughout most of history each artisan who specialized in making some product made the whole of that product. Over the last several hundred years, many technical advances have made it efficient to organize production methods into large-scale firms organized around what is called the **division of labour**. This term refers to specialization *within* the production process of a particular product.

division of labour The breaking up of a production process into a series of specialized tasks, each done by a different worker.

MASS PRODUCTION. In a mass-production factory, work is divided into highly specialized tasks by using specialized machinery. Each individual repeatedly does one or a few small tasks that represent only a small fraction of those necessary to produce any one product.

ARTISANS AND FLEXIBLE MANUFACTURING. Two recent changes have significantly altered the degree of specialization found in many modern production processes. First, individual artisans have recently reappeared in some lines of production. They are responding to a revival in the demand for individually crafted, rather than mass-produced, products. Second, many manufacturing operations are being reorganized along new lines called *lean production* or *flexible manufacturing*, which was pioneered by Japanese car manufacturers in the mid-1950s. It has led back to a more craft-based form of organization within the factory. In this technique, employees work as a team; each employee is able to do every team member's job rather than only one very specialized task at one point on the assembly line. However, even these workers are practising the division of labour—but the division is not as fine as it is in mass production.

Markets and Money

People who specialize in doing only one thing must satisfy most of their wants by consuming things made by other people. In early societies the exchange of goods and services took place by simple mutual agreement among neighbours. In the course of time, however, trading became centred on particular gathering places called *markets*. For example, the French markets or trade fairs of Champagne were well known throughout Europe as early as the eleventh century. Even now, many small towns in Canada have regular market days. Today, however, the term *market* has a much broader meaning, referring to any institutions that allow buyers and sellers to transact with each other, possibly by meeting physically or possibly by communicating on the Internet. For example, eBay represents one of the modern forms that an Internet-based market can take. Also, we use the term *market economy* to refer to a society in which people specialize in productive activities and meet most of their material wants through voluntary market transactions with other people.

> Specialization must be accompanied by trade. People who produce only one thing must trade most of it to obtain all the other things they want.

barter An economic system in which goods and services are traded directly for other goods and services.

Early trading was by means of **barter**, the trading of goods directly for other goods. But barter is costly in terms of time spent searching out satisfactory exchanges. If a farmer has wheat but wants a hammer, he must find someone who has a hammer and wants wheat. A successful barter transaction thus requires what is called a *double coincidence of wants*.

Money eliminates the cumbersome system of barter by separating the transactions involved in the exchange of products. If a farmer has wheat and wants a hammer, he merely has to find someone who wants wheat. The farmer takes money in exchange. Then he finds a person who wants to sell a hammer and gives up the money for the hammer.

Money greatly facilitates specialization and trade.

Globalization

Market economies constantly change, largely as a result of the development of new technologies. Many of the recent changes are referred to as *globalization*, a term often used loosely to mean the increased importance of international trade. International trade is, however, a very old phenomenon. The usual pattern over most of the last 200 years was manufactured goods being sent from Europe and North America to the rest of the world, with raw materials and primary products being sent in return. What is new in the last few decades is the globalization of manufacturing. Assembly of a product may take place in the most industrialized countries, but the hundreds of component parts are manufactured in dozens of different countries and delivered to the assembly plant "just in time" for assembly.

The revolution in shipping and in computer technology has drastically reduced communication and transportation costs. This reduction in costs lies at the heart of globalization.

Two major causes of globalization are the rapid reduction in transportation costs and the revolution in information technology that have occurred in the past 50 years. The cost of moving products around the world fell greatly over the last half of the twentieth century because of containerization and the increasing size of ships. Our ability to transmit and analyze data increased even more dramatically, while the costs of doing so decreased, equally dramatically. For example, today $1500 buys an ultra-slim laptop computer that has the same computing power as one that in 1970 cost $10 million and filled a large room. This revolution in information and communication technology has made it possible to coordinate economic transactions around the world in ways that were difficult and costly 50 years ago and quite impossible 100 years ago.

Globalization is as important for consumers as it is for producers. For example, as some tastes become universal to young people, spread by ever-increasing access to foreign television stations and global Internet chat lines, we can see the same clothes and hear the same music in virtually all big cities. And as tastes have become more universal, many *corporations* have globalized and have become what economists call **transnational corporations (TNCs).** McDonald's restaurants are as visible in Moscow or Beijing as in London, New York, Vancouver, or Montreal. Many other brands are also known around the world, such as Calvin Klein, Nike, Coca-Cola, Kellogg's, Heinz, Nestlé, Molson, Toyota, Rolls-Royce, Sony, and Mitsubishi.

transnational corporations (TNCs) Firms that have operations in more than one country. Also called *multinational enterprises (MNEs).*

Through the ongoing process of globalization, national economies are ever more linked to the global economy, in which an increasing share of jobs and incomes is created.

The word *globalization* has recently become a focal point for an important and contentious set of policy debates and public protests. These debates are often very confusing to the observer. See *Applying Economic Concepts 1-2* for a brief outline of the key issues.

APPLYING ECONOMIC CONCEPTS 1-2

The Globalization Debate

Over the past several years, large public "globalization protests" have occurred in many cities around the world, from Seattle and Quebec City to Washington, D.C., and Athens. These protests often occur when political leaders from many countries gather to discuss and negotiate agreements regarding international trade or finance. What are these protests about? What are the key issues?

The protesters, who generally refer to themselves as "anti-globalization activists," have two main arguments. First, they argue that increases in the flow of international trade and investment have been responsible for increasing global income inequality and worsening poverty in developing countries. Second, they argue that such organizations as the World Trade Organization (WTO), the World Bank, and the International Monetary Fund (IMF) operate in an undemocratic fashion and hold their meetings behind closed doors, out of view of and without critical input from the people whose lives their policies are so dramatically influencing. A related concern is that global economic agreements appear to give power to transnational corporations, taking power out of the hands of citizens. The anti-globalization activists are in favour of slowing down the process of globalization and reforming (if not eliminating) these international organizations.

On the other side of the barricades are the defenders of globalization and a rules-based approach to international trade. They argue that the process of globalization, far from being the cause of poverty in developing countries, is the best bet for *reducing* such poverty. They claim that freer trade between countries has been responsible for enormous advances in living standards over the past century, and that the developing countries of today will be much better off if trade is further liberalized. For example, the dramatic transformation of much of China and India into industrial nations with quickly rising living standards is based mainly on international trade. Indeed, some defenders of globalization argue that one of the problems has been the developed countries' unwillingness to permit genuinely free international trade with the developing countries—especially for such products as agricultural commodities and textiles in which the developing countries have a comparative advantage. According to this view, the biggest contributor to poverty in developing countries is too *little* trade, not too much!

Defenders of globalization also point out that the meetings held by the WTO and other international organizations are voluntary meetings held between the democratically elected leaders of the member countries; no agreements are legal until each of the member countries ratifies them in its parliament. Thus, they say, the process is democratic.

Is there a middle ground in this debate? On the democratic issue, the defenders of globalization are probably correct, at least literally. The agreements do not come into force until they are passed by the respective parliaments. The political challenge for all countries involved is to improve communications so that these complicated international agreements—which often run thousands of pages in length—are made clear enough that they can be effectively debated in the respective parliaments. With effective political debates within each member country, citizens will be more involved in the policy-making process.

The more subtle issue is the relationship between globalization and poverty. Most economists would argue, for reasons that we will explore in Chapters 33 and 34, that freer trade leads to increases in *average* living standards within both developed and developing countries. A typical empirical finding is that an economy whose trade share increases from 20 percent to 40 percent of its GDP can expect to experience a 10-percent increase in per capita income. But there is no guarantee that, within any particular country, these gains in living standards will be shared among the various segments of society in what their citizens regard as a socially just way. Quite often while the manufacturing sector prospers, the agricultural sector languishes. Although no one may be actually made worse off, the rising disparity between growing incomes in the manufacturing sector and static ones in agriculture often create social tensions. One of the crucial challenges faced by governments negotiating international economic agreements is to ensure that the benefits from such agreements are spread throughout the population, thus increasing their public acceptability.

1.4 Is There an Alternative to the Market Economy?

In this chapter we have discussed the elements of an economy based on free-market transactions—what we call a *market economy*. But are there any alternatives to this type of economy? The answer is no in one sense and yes in another. We answer no because the modern economy has no *practical* alternative to reliance on market determination for many of its transactions. We answer yes because not all transactions take place in free markets even in the most market-oriented society. To go further we need to identify various types of economic systems.

Types of Economic Systems

It is helpful to distinguish three pure types of economies, called *traditional, command,* and *free-market economies.* These economies differ in the way in which economic decisions are coordinated. But no actual economy fits neatly into one of these three categories—all real economies contain some elements of each type.

Traditional Economies
A **traditional economy** is one in which behaviour is based primarily on tradition, custom, and habit. Young men follow their fathers' occupations. Women do what their mothers did. There is little change in the pattern of goods produced from year to year, other than those imposed by the vagaries of nature. The techniques of production also follow traditional patterns, except when the effects of an occasional new invention are felt. Finally, production is allocated among the members according to long-established traditions.

> **traditional economy**
> An economy in which behaviour is based mostly on tradition.

Such a system works best in an unchanging environment. Under such static conditions, a system that does not continually require people to make choices can prove effective in meeting economic and social needs.

Traditional systems were common in earlier times. The feudal system, under which most people in medieval Europe lived, was a largely traditional society. Peasants, artisans, and most others living in villages inherited their positions in that society. They also usually inherited their specific jobs, which they handled in traditional ways.

Command Economies
In command economies, economic behaviour is determined by some central authority, usually the government, which makes most of the necessary decisions on what to produce, how to produce it, and who gets it. Such economies are characterized by the *centralization* of decision making. Because centralized decision makers usually create elaborate and complex plans for the behaviour that they want to impose, the terms **command economy** and *centrally planned economy* are usually used synonymously.

> **command economy** An economy in which most economic decisions are made by a central planning authority.

The sheer quantity of data required for the central planning of an entire modern economy is enormous, and the task of analyzing it to produce a fully integrated plan can hardly be exaggerated. Moreover, the plan must be continually modified to take account not only of current data but also of future trends in labour supplies, technological developments, and people's tastes for various goods and services. This is a notoriously difficult exercise, not least because of the unavailability of all essential, accurate, and up-to-date information.

Thirty years ago, more than one-third of the world's population lived in countries that relied heavily on central planning. Today, after the fall of the Berlin Wall and the collapse of the Soviet Union, the number of such countries is small. Even in countries in which central planning is the proclaimed system, as in Cuba, increasing amounts of market determination are being quietly permitted.

Free-Market Economies In the third type of economic system, the decisions about resource allocation are made without any central direction. Instead, they result from innumerable independent decisions made by individual producers and consumers. Such a system is known as a **free-market economy** or, more simply, a *market economy*. In such an economy, decisions relating to the basic economic issues are *decentralized*. Despite the absence of a central plan, these many decentralized decisions are nonetheless coordinated. The main coordinating device is the set of market-determined prices—which is why free-market systems are often called *price systems*.

free-market economy An economy in which most economic decisions are made by private households and firms.

In a pure market economy, all these decisions are made by buyers and sellers acting through unhindered markets. The state provides the background of defining property rights and protecting citizens against foreign and domestic enemies but, beyond that, markets determine all resource allocation and income distribution.

Mixed Economies Economies that are fully traditional or fully centrally planned or wholly free-market are pure types that are useful for studying basic principles. When we look in detail at any real economy, however, we discover that its economic behaviour is the result of some mixture of central control and market determination, with a certain amount of traditional behaviour as well.

mixed economy An economy in which some economic decisions are made by firms and households and some by the government.

> In practice, every economy is a mixed economy in the sense that it combines significant elements of all three systems in determining economic behaviour.

Furthermore, within any economy, the degree of the mix varies from sector to sector. For example, in some planned economies, the command principle was used more often to determine behaviour in heavy-goods industries, such as steel, than in agriculture. Farmers were often given substantial freedom to produce and sell what they wanted in response to varying market prices.

When economists speak of a particular economy as being centrally planned, we mean only that the degree of the mix is weighted heavily toward the command principle. When we speak of one as being a market economy, we mean only that the degree of the mix is weighted heavily toward decentralized decision making.

Although no country offers an example of either system working alone, some economies, such as those of Canada, the United States, France, and Hong Kong, rely much more heavily on market decisions than others, such as the economies of China, North Korea, and Cuba. Yet even in Canada, the command principle has some sway. Crown corporations, legislated minimum wages, rules and regulations for environmental protection, quotas on some agricultural outputs, and restrictions on the import of some items are just a few examples.

The Great Debate

As we saw earlier, in 1776 Adam Smith was one of the first people to analyze the operation of markets, and he stressed the relative efficiency of free-market economies. A century later, another great economist and political philosopher, Karl Marx (1818–1883), argued that although free-market economies would indeed be successful in producing high levels of output, they could not be relied on to ensure that this output would be justly distributed among citizens. He argued the benefits of a centrally planned system in which the government could ensure a more equitable distribution of output.

Beginning with the Soviet Union in the early 1920s, many nations adopted systems in which conscious government central planning replaced the operation of the free market. For almost a century, a great debate then raged on the relative merits of command economies versus market economies. Along with the Soviet Union, the countries of Eastern Europe and China were command economies for much of the twentieth century. Canada, the United States, and most of the countries of Western Europe were, and still are, primarily market economies. The apparent successes of the Soviet Union and China in the 1950s and 1960s, including the ability to mobilize considerable resources into heavy industries, suggested to many observers that the command principle was at least as good for organizing economic behaviour as the market principle. Over the long run, however, planned economies proved to be a failure of such disastrous proportions that they seriously depressed the living standards of their citizens.

During the last decade of the twentieth century, most of the world's centrally planned economies began the difficult transition back toward freer markets. These transitions occurred at different paces in different countries, but in most cases the initial few years were characterized by significant declines in output and employment. Twenty years later, however, most of the "transition" economies are experiencing growth rates above the ones they had in their final years as centrally planned economies. Living standards are on the rise.

Lessons from History 1-1 discusses in more detail why the centrally planned economies failed. This failure suggests the superiority of decentralized markets over centrally planned ones as mechanisms for allocating an economy's scarce resources. Put another way, it demonstrates the superiority of mixed economies with substantial elements of market determination over fully planned command economies. However, it does *not* demonstrate, as some observers have asserted, the superiority of completely free-market economies over mixed economies.

There is no guarantee that completely free markets will, on their own, handle such urgent matters as controlling pollution, providing public goods (like national defence), or preventing financial-market disasters, such as occurred in 2008 and 2009. Indeed, as we will see in later chapters, much economic theory is devoted to explaining why free markets often *fail* to do these things. Mixed economies, with significant elements of government intervention, are needed to do these jobs.

Furthermore, acceptance of the free market over central planning does not provide an excuse to ignore a country's pressing social issues. Acceptance of the benefits of the free market still leaves plenty of scope to debate the most appropriate levels and types of government policies directed at achieving specific social goals. It follows that there is still considerable room for disagreement about the degree of the mix of market and government determination in any modern mixed economy—room enough to accommodate such divergent views as could be expressed by conservative, liberal, and modern social democratic parties.

Karl Marx argued that free-market economies could not be relied on to ensure an equitable distribution of income. He advocated a system of central planning in which government owns most of the means of production.

So, the first answer to the question about the existence of an alternative to the market economy is no: There is no practical alternative to a mixed system with major reliance on markets but some government presence in most aspects of the economy. The second answer is yes: Within the framework of a mixed economy there are substantial alternatives among many different and complex mixes of free-market and government determination of economic life.

(X) myeconlab   ADDITIONAL TOPICS

The debate regarding the appropriate roles of governments and free markets figures prominently in discussions of how today's developing countries can best bring about improvements in their citizens' living standards. For a detailed discussion of the **Challenges Facing the Developing Countries,** see the *Additional Topics* section of this book's MyEconLab.

www.myeconlab.com

LESSONS FROM HISTORY 1-1

The Failure of Central Planning

The fall of the Berlin Wall in November 1989 was the beginning of the end of the Soviet system of central planning.

The Bolshevik Revolution in 1917 in Russia brought the world its first example of a large-scale communist society. With the rise to power of Joseph Stalin and the creation of the Soviet Union in 1922, communism and central economic planning began their spread throughout Eastern and Central Europe. This spread of central planning was accelerated by the Soviet Union's role following the Second World War in "liberating" several countries from Nazi domination, thus creating the group of countries that became known as the Eastern Bloc or the Soviet Bloc.

Despite the successful geographic spread of communism, the Soviet system of central economic planning had many difficulties. By 1989, communism had collapsed throughout Central and Eastern Europe, and the economic systems of formerly communist countries began the difficult transition from centrally planned to market economies. Although political issues surely played a role in these events, the economic changes generally confirmed the superiority of a market-oriented price system over central planning as a method of organizing economic activity. The failure of central planning had many causes, but four were particularly significant.

Failure of Coordination

In the centrally planned economies, a body of planners attempted to coordinate all the economic decisions about production, investment, trade, and consumption that were likely to be made by producers and consumers throughout the country. Without the use of prices to signal relative scarcity and abundance, central planning generally proved impossible to do with any reasonable degree of success. Bottlenecks in production, shortages of some goods, and gluts of others plagued the Soviet economy for decades.

Government in the Modern Mixed Economy

Market economies in today's advanced industrial countries are based primarily on voluntary transactions between individual buyers and sellers. Private individuals have the right to buy and sell what they want, to accept or refuse work that is offered to them, and to move where they want when they want.

> Key institutions are private property and freedom of contract, both of which must be maintained by active government policies. The government creates laws of ownership and contract and then provides the institutions, such as police and courts, to enforce these laws.

In modern mixed economies, governments go well beyond these important basic functions. They intervene in market transactions to correct what economists call *market failures*. These are well-defined situations in which free markets do not work well. Some products, called *public goods*, are usually not provided at all by markets because

Failure of Quality Control

Central planners could monitor the number of units produced by any factory, reward plants that exceeded their production targets, and punish those that fell short. Factory managers operating under these conditions would meet their quotas by whatever means were available, and once the goods passed out of their factory, what happened to them was someone else's headache.

In market economies, poor quality is punished by low sales, and retailers soon give a signal to factory managers by shifting their purchases to other suppliers. The incentives that obviously flow from such private-sector purchasing discretion were generally absent from centrally planned economies, where purchases and sales were organized by the body of planners and prices and profits were not used to signal customer satisfaction or dissatisfaction.

Misplaced Incentives

In market economies, relative wages and salaries provide incentives for labour to move from place to place, and the possibility of losing one's job provides an incentive to work diligently. This is a harsh mechanism that punishes job losers with loss of income (although social programs provide floors to the amount of economic punishment that can be suffered). In centrally planned economies, workers usually had complete job security. Industrial unemployment was rare, and even when it

did occur, new jobs were usually found for all who lost theirs. Although the high level of security was attractive to many people, it proved impossible to provide sufficient incentives for reasonably hard and efficient work under such conditions.

Environmental Degradation

Fulfilling production plans became the all-embracing goal in centrally planned economies, to the exclusion of most other considerations, including the environment. As a result, environmental degradation occurred in the Soviet Union and the countries of Eastern Europe on a scale unknown in advanced Western nations. A particularly disturbing example (only one of many) occurred in central Asia, where high quotas for cotton output led to indiscriminate use of pesticides and irrigation. Birth defects became very common, and the vast Aral Sea has been more than three-quarters drained, causing major environmental effects.

This failure to protect the environment stemmed from the pressure to fulfill production plans and the absence of a "political marketplace" where citizens could express their preferences for the environment. Imperfect though the system may be in democratic market economies—and in some particular cases it has been quite poor—their record of environmental protection has been vastly better than that of the centrally planned economies.

their use cannot usually be restricted to those who pay for them. Defence and police protection are examples of public goods. In other cases, private transactors impose costs called *externalities* on those who have no say in the transaction. This is the case when factories pollute the air and rivers. The public is harmed but plays no part in the transaction. In yet other cases, financial institutions, such as banks, mortgage companies, and investment houses, may indulge in risky activities that threaten the health of the entire economic system. These market failures explain why governments sometimes intervene to alter the allocation of resources.

Also, important equity issues arise from letting free markets determine people's incomes. Some people lose their jobs because firms are reorganizing to become more efficient in the face of new technologies. Others keep their jobs, but the market places so little value on their services that they face economic deprivation. The old and the chronically ill may suffer if their past circumstances did not allow them to save enough to support themselves. For many reasons of this sort, almost everyone accepts some government intervention to redistribute income. Care must be taken, however, not to kill the goose that lays the golden egg. By taking too much from higher-income people, we risk eliminating their incentives to work hard and produce income, some of which is to be redistributed to those in need.

These are some of the reasons that all modern economies are mixed economies. Throughout most of the twentieth century in advanced industrial societies, the mix had been altering toward more and more government participation in decisions about the allocation of resources and the distribution of income. In the past three decades, however, there has been a worldwide movement to reduce the degree of government participation. The details of this shift in the market/government mix, and the reasons for it, are some of the major issues that will be studied in this book.

Summary

1.1 The Complexity of the Modern Economy   🔵 ❶

- A market economy is self-organizing in the sense that when individual consumers and producers act independently to pursue their own self-interest, responding to prices determined in open markets, the collective outcome is coordinated.

1.2 Scarcity, Choice, and Opportunity Cost   🔵 ❷

- Scarcity is a fundamental problem faced by all economies. Not enough resources are available to produce all the goods and services that people would like to consume. Scarcity makes it necessary to choose. All societies must have a mechanism for choosing what goods and services will be produced and in what quantities.
- The concept of opportunity cost emphasizes the problem of scarcity and choice by measuring the cost of obtaining a unit of one product in terms of the number of units of other products that could have been obtained instead.

- A production possibilities boundary shows all the combinations of goods that can be produced by an economy whose resources are fully and efficiently employed. Movement from one point to another along the boundary requires a reallocation of resources.
- Four basic questions must be answered in all economies: What is produced and how? What is consumed and by whom? Why are resources sometimes idle? Is productive capacity growing?

1.3 Who Makes the Choices and How?

- The interaction of consumers and producers through goods and factor markets is illustrated by the circular flow of income and expenditure. Individual consumers sell factor services to producers and thereby earn their income. Similarly, producers earn their income by selling goods and services to individual consumers.
- Individual consumers are assumed to make their decisions in an effort to maximize their well-being or utility.

Producers' decisions are assumed to be designed to maximize their profits.
- Modern economies are based on the specialization and division of labour, which necessitate the exchange (trading) of goods and services. Exchange takes place in markets and is facilitated by the use of money.
- Driven by the ongoing revolution in transportation and communications technology, the world economy is rapidly globalizing.

1.4 Is There an Alternative to the Market Economy?

- We can distinguish three pure types of economies: traditional, command, and free-market. In practice, all economies are mixed economies in that their economic behaviour responds to mixes of tradition, government command, and price incentives.
- In the late 1980s, events in Eastern Europe and the Soviet Union led to the general acceptance that the system of fully centrally planned economies had failed to produce minimally acceptable living standards for its

citizens. All these countries are now moving toward greater market determination and less state command in their economies.
- Governments play an important role in modern mixed economies. They create and enforce important background institutions such as private property and freedom of contract. They intervene to correct market failures. They also redistribute income in the interests of equity.

Key Concepts

The self-organizing economy
Scarcity and the need for choice
Choice and opportunity cost
Production possibilities boundary

Resource allocation
Specialization
The division of labour
Globalization

Traditional economies
Command economies
Free-market economies
Mixed economies

Study Exercises

SAVE TIME. IMPROVE RESULTS.

Visit MyEconLab to practise Study Exercises and prepare for tests and exams. MyEconLab also offers a variety of other study tools to help you succeed.
www.myeconlab.com

1. What is the difference between microeconomics and macroeconomics?

2. List the four main types of economic systems and their main attributes.

3. Explain the three economic concepts illustrated by the production possibilities boundary.

4. Consider an economy that produces only food and clothing. Its production possibilities boundary is shown below.

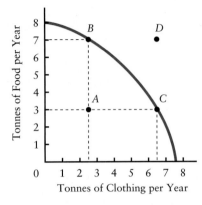

a. If the economy is at point *A*, how many tonnes of clothing and how many tonnes of food are being produced? At point *B*? At point *C*?
b. What do we know about the use of resources when the economy is at point *A*? At point *B*? At point *C*?
c. If the economy is at point *B*, what is the opportunity cost of producing one more tonne of food? What is the opportunity cost of producing one more tonne of clothing?
d. What do we know about the use of resources at point *D*? How would it be possible for the economy to produce at point *D*?

5. State and explain two reasons why the specialization of labour is more efficient than universal self-sufficiency.

6. Choiceland has 250 workers and produces only two goods, *X* and *Y*. Labour is the only factor of production, but some workers are better suited to producing *X* than *Y* (and vice versa). The table below shows the maximum levels of output of each good possible from various levels of labour input.

Number of Workers Producing X	Annual Production of X	Number of Workers Producing Y	Annual Production of Y
0	0	250	1300
50	20	200	1200
100	45	150	900
150	60	100	600
200	70	50	350
250	75	0	0

a. Draw the production possibilities boundary for Choiceland on a scale diagram, with the production of *X* on the horizontal axis and the production of *Y* on the vertical axis.

b. Compute the opportunity cost of producing an extra 15 units of *X* if the economy is initially producing 45 units of *X* and 600 units of *Y*. How does this compare to the opportunity cost if the economy were initially producing 60 units of *X*?
c. Suppose now that the technology associated with producing good *Y* improves, so that the maximum level of *Y* that can be produced from any given level of labour input increases by 10 percent. Explain (or show in a diagram) what happens to the production possibilities curve.

7. Explain why a technological improvement in the production of one good means that a country can now produce more of *other* goods than it did previously. Hint: Draw a country's production possibilities boundary to help answer this question.

8. Consider your decision whether to go skiing for the weekend. Suppose transportation, lift tickets, and accommodation for the weekend cost $300. Suppose also that restaurant food for the weekend will cost $75. Finally, suppose you have a weekend job that you will have to miss if you go skiing, which pays you $120 (after tax) for the one weekend day that you work. What is the opportunity cost of going skiing? Do you need any other information before computing the opportunity cost?

9. Suppose you and a friend go wilderness camping for a week and must find your own food to survive. From past experience, you know that you and your friend have different abilities in fishing and hunting. If each of you were to work for one day either catching fish or trapping rabbits, the number of fish and rabbits that you could catch is given in the following table:

	Fish	Rabbits
You	6	3
Your friend	8	2

You and your friend decide that you should each specialize so that one person catches fish while the other traps rabbits. But who should do which task?

a. What is the opportunity cost for you to catch an additional rabbit? What is your friend's opportunity cost of catching an extra rabbit?
b. Assuming that you and your friend specialize, what allocation of tasks maximizes total output for your one day of joint effort?
c. Suppose you both decide to work for two days according to the allocation in part (b). What is the total amount of output? What would it have been had you chosen the reverse allocation of tasks?

Discussion Questions

1. What is the difference between scarcity and poverty? If everyone in the world had enough to eat, could we say that food was no longer scarce?

2. Evidence accumulates that the use of chemical fertilizers, which increases agricultural production greatly, damages water quality. Analyze the choice between more food and cleaner water involved in using such fertilizers. Use a production possibilities curve with agricultural output on the vertical axis and water quality on the horizontal axis. In what ways does this production possibilities curve reflect scarcity, choice, and opportunity cost? How would an improved fertilizer that increased agricultural output without further worsening water quality affect the curve? Suppose a pollution-free fertilizer were developed; would this mean that there would no longer be any opportunity cost in using it?

3. Discuss the following statement by a leading economist: "One of the mysteries of semantics is why the government-managed economies ever came to be called planned and the market economies unplanned. It is the former that are in chronic chaos, in which buyers stand in line hoping to buy some toilet paper or soap. It is the latter that are in reasonable equilibrium—where if you want a cake of soap or a steak or a shirt or a car, you can go to the store and find that the item is magically there for you to buy. It is the liberal economies that reflect a highly sophisticated planning system, and the government-managed economies that are primitive and unplanned."

4. Consider the market for doctors' services. In what way has this market taken advantage of the specialization of labour?

5. "It is not from the benevolence of the butcher, the brewer, or the baker, that we expect our dinner, but from their regard to their own interest. We address ourselves, not to their humanity but to their self-love, and never talk to them of our own necessities but of their advantages." Do you agree with this quotation from Adam Smith's classic, *The Wealth of Nations*? How are "our dinner" and "their self-interest" related to the price system? What does Smith assume to be the motives of firms and households?

6. In the chapter we used a simple idea of a production possibilities boundary to illustrate the concepts of scarcity, choice, and opportunity cost. We assumed there were only two goods—call them X and Y. But we all know that any economy produces many more than just two goods. Explain why the insights illustrated in Figure 1-2 on page 8 are more general, and why the assumption of only two goods is a useful one.

Economic Theories, Data, and Graphs

LO LEARNING OBJECTIVES

In this chapter you will learn

1. to distinguish between positive and normative statements.

2. how economists use models to help them think about the economy.

3. about the interaction between economic theories and empirical observation.

4. to identify several types of economic data, including index numbers, time-series and cross-sectional data, and scatter diagrams.

5. that the slope of a line on a graph relating two variables shows how one responds to a small change in the other.

If you surf Internet news sites, read the newspaper, watch television, or listen to the radio, you will often see or hear some economist's opinions being reported, perhaps about unemployment, the exchange rate, or interest rates; some new tax; the case for regulation of the financial industry; or the possible reforms to Canada's health-care system. Where do economists' opinions come from? Are they supported by hard evidence, and if so, why do economists sometimes disagree with each other over important issues?

Economics is a social science, and in this chapter we explore what it means to be "scientific" in the study of economics. Along the way we will learn much about theories, predictions, data, testing, and graphing—economists use all of these tools and techniques in their attempt to understand the economic world. We begin with the important distinction between positive and normative statements.

2.1 Positive and Normative Advice

Economists give two broad types of advice, called *normative* and *positive*. For example, they sometimes advise that the government ought to try harder to reduce unemployment. When they say such things, they are giving normative advice; in this case, they are making judgements about the value of the various things that the government could do with its limited resources and about the costs and benefits of reducing unemployment. Advice that depends on a value judgement is normative—it tells others what they *ought* to do.

Another type of advice is illustrated by the statement, "If the government wants to reduce unemployment, reducing unemployment insurance benefits is an effective way of doing so." This is positive advice. It does not rely on a judgement about the value of reducing unemployment. Instead, the expert is saying, "If this is what you want to do, here is a way to do it."

Normative statements depend on value judgements and cannot be evaluated solely by a recourse to facts. In contrast, **positive statements** do not involve value judgements. They are statements about matters of fact and so disagreements about them are appropriately dealt with by an appeal to evidence. The distinction between positive and normative is fundamental to scientific progress. Much of the success of modern science depends on the ability of scientists to separate their views on *what does happen* in the world from their views on *what they would like to happen*. For example, until the eighteenth century almost everyone believed that Earth was only a few thousand years old. Evidence then began to accumulate that Earth was billions of years old. This evidence was hard for most people to accept since it ran counter to a literal reading of many religious texts. Many did not want to believe the evidence. Nevertheless, scientists, many of whom were religious, continued their research because they refused to allow their feelings about what they wanted to believe to affect their scientific search for the truth. Eventually, all scientists and most members of the public came to accept that Earth is about 4 billion years old.

Distinguishing what is actually true from what we would like to be true requires distinguishing between positive and normative statements.

Examples of both types of statements are given in Table 2-1. All five positive statements in the table are assertions about the nature of the world in which we live. In

normative statement
A statement about what ought to be as opposed to what actually is.

positive statement
A statement about what actually is (was or will be), as opposed to what ought to be.

Practise with Study Guide Chapter 2, Short-Answer Question 1.

TABLE 2-1 Positive and Normative Statements

Positive	Normative
A Raising interest rates encourages people to save.	F People should be encouraged to save.
B High rates of income tax encourage people to evade paying taxes.	G Governments should arrange taxes so that people cannot avoid paying them.
C Lowering the price of tobacco leads people to smoke less.	H The government should raise the tax on tobacco to discourage people from smoking.
D The majority of the population would prefer a policy that reduced unemployment to one that reduced inflation.	I Unemployment is a more important social problem than inflation.
E Government financial assistance to the auto sector is ineffective at preventing job losses.	J Government should not spend taxpayers' money on supporting firms in the auto sector.

contrast, the five normative statements involve value judgements. Notice two things about the positive/normative distinction. First, positive statements need not be true. Statement *C* is almost certainly false. Yet it is positive, not normative. Second, the inclusion of a value judgement in a statement does not necessarily make the statement itself normative. Statement *D* is a positive statement about the value judgements that people hold. We could conduct a survey to check if people really do prefer low unemployment to low inflation. We could ask them and we could observe how they voted. There is no need for the economist to rely on a value judgement to check the validity of the statement itself.

We leave you to analyze the remaining eight statements to decide precisely why each is either positive or normative. Remember to apply the two tests. First, is the statement only about actual or alleged facts? If so, it is a positive one. Second, are value judgements necessary to assess the truth of the statement? If so, it is normative.

Disagreements Among Economists

Economists often disagree with each other in public discussions, frequently because of poor communication. The adversaries fail to define their terms or their points of reference clearly, and so they end up "arguing past" each other, with the only certain result being that the audience is left confused.

Another source of disagreement stems from some economists' failure to acknowledge the full state of their ignorance. There are many things on which the evidence is far from conclusive. Informed judgements are required to take a position on even a purely positive question. In such cases, a responsible economist will make clear the extent to which his or her view is based on judgements about the relevant facts.

Many other public disagreements are based on the positive/normative distinction. Different economists have different values, and these normative views play a large part in most discussions of public policy. Many economists stress the importance of individual responsibility and argue, for example, that lower employment insurance benefits would be desirable because people would have a greater incentive to search for a job. Other economists stress the need for a generous "social safety net" and argue that higher employment insurance benefits would be desirable

Economists often disagree with each other in the press or at conferences, but their debates are more often about normative issues than positive ones.

because human hardship would be reduced. In such debates, and there are many in economics, it is the responsibility of the economist to state clearly what part of the proffered advice is normative and what part is positive.

Because the world is complex and because no issue can be settled beyond any doubt, economists rarely agree unanimously on an issue. Nevertheless, there is an impressive amount of agreement on many aspects of how the economy works and what happens when governments intervene to alter its workings. A survey published in the *American Economic Review*, perhaps the most influential economics journal, showed strong agreement among economists on many propositions, including "Rent control leads to a housing shortage" (85 percent yes), "Tariffs usually reduce economic welfare" (93 percent yes), "Large government budget deficits have adverse effects on the economy" (83 percent yes), and "A minimum wage increases unemployment among young workers" (79 percent yes). Notice that all these are positive rather than normative statements. Other examples of these areas of agreement will be found in many places throughout this book.

2.2 Economic Theories

Economists seek to understand the world by developing *theories* and *models* that explain some of the things that have been seen and to predict some of the things that will be seen. What is a theory and what is a model?

Theories

Theories are constructed to explain things. For example, economists may seek to explain what determines the quantity of eggs bought and sold in a particular month in Manitoba and the price at which they are sold. Or they may seek to explain what determines the quantity of petroleum bought and sold around the world on a particular day and the price at which it is traded. As part of the answer to such questions as these, economists have developed theories of demand and supply—theories that we will study in detail in the next three chapters. These and all other theories are distinguished by their *variables*, *assumptions*, and *predictions*.

Variables The basic elements of any theory are its variables. A **variable** is a well-defined item, such as a price or a quantity, that can take on different possible values.

In our theory of the egg market, the variable *quantity of eggs* might be defined as the number of cartons of 12 Grade A large eggs. The variable *price of eggs* is the amount of money that must be given up to purchase each carton of eggs. The particular values taken on by those two variables might be 2000 cartons at a price of $2.55 on July 1, 2009; 1800 cartons at a price of $2.75 on July 1, 2010; and 1950 cartons at a price of $2.95 on July 1, 2011.

There are two broad categories of variables that are important in any theory. An **endogenous variable** is one whose value is determined within the theory. An **exogenous variable** influences the endogenous variables but is itself determined outside the theory. To illustrate the difference, the price of eggs and the quantity of eggs are endogenous variables in our theory of the egg market—our theory is designed to explain them. The state of the weather, however, is an exogenous variable. It may well affect the number of eggs consumers demand or producers supply but we can safely assume that the state of the weather is not influenced by the market for eggs.

Assumptions A theory's assumptions concern motives, directions of causation, and the conditions under which the theory is meant to apply.

MOTIVES. The theories we study in this book make the fundamental assumption that everyone pursues his or her own self-interest when making economic decisions. Individuals are assumed to strive to maximize their *utility*, while firms are assumed to try to maximize their *profits*. Not only are they assumed to know what they want, but we also assume that they know how to go about getting it within the constraints they face.

DIRECTION OF CAUSATION. When economists assume that one variable is related to another, they are usually assuming some causal link between the two. For example,

variable Any well-defined item, such as the price or quantity of a commodity, that can take on various specific values.

endogenous variable A variable that is explained within a theory. Sometimes called an *induced variable* or a *dependent variable*.

exogenous variable A variable that is determined outside the theory. Sometimes called an *autonomous variable* or an *independent variable*.

when the amount of eggs that producers want to supply is assumed to increase when the price of their chicken feed falls, the causation runs from the price of chicken feed to the supply of eggs. Producers supply more eggs because the price of chicken feed has fallen; they are not assumed to get cheaper chicken feed because of their decision to supply more eggs.

CONDITIONS OF APPLICATION. Assumptions are often used to specify the conditions under which a theory is meant to hold. For example, a theory that assumes there is "no government" usually does not mean literally the absence of government but only that the theory is meant to apply when governments are not significantly affecting the situation being studied.

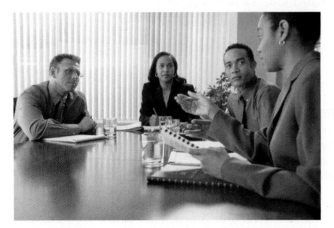

A key assumption in economics is that firms make decisions with the goal of maximizing their profits.

Although assumptions are an essential part of all theories, students are often concerned about those that seem unrealistic. An example will illustrate some of the issues involved. Much of the theory that we are going to study in this book uses the assumption that owners of firms attempt to make as much money as they can—that is, to maximize their profits. The assumption of profit maximization allows economists to make predictions about the behaviour of firms, such as "firms will supply more output if the market price increases."

Profit maximization may seem like a rather crude assumption. Surely, for example, the managers of firms sometimes choose to protect the environment rather than pursue certain highly polluting but profitable opportunities. Does this not discredit the assumption of profit maximization by showing it to be unrealistic?

The answer is no; to make successful predictions, the theory does not require that managers be solely and unwaveringly motivated by the desire to maximize profits at all times. All that is required is that profits be a sufficiently important consideration that a theory based on the assumption of profit maximization will lead to explanations and predictions that are substantially correct. It is not always appropriate to criticize a theory because its assumptions seem unrealistic. A good theory abstracts in a useful way; a poor theory does not. If a theory has ignored some genuinely important factors, its predictions will usually be contradicted by the evidence.

All theory is an abstraction from reality. If it were not, it would merely duplicate the world in all its complexity and would add little to our understanding of it.

Predictions A theory's predictions are the propositions that can be deduced from it. They are often called *hypotheses*. For example, a prediction from our theory of the egg market is that "if the price of chicken feed falls, producers will want to sell more eggs." Another prediction from the same theory is that "if the price of eggs declines, consumers will want to purchase more eggs."

Models

economic model A term used in several related ways: sometimes for an abstraction designed to illustrate some point but not designed to generate testable hypotheses, and sometimes as a synonym for theory.

Economists use the term **economic model** in two different but related ways.

First, a model may be primarily an illustrative abstraction, designed to help us organize our thinking and gain crucial insights. At the same time, it may lack the detail or precision necessary to generate testable predictions. The circular flow of income and expenditure and the production possibilities boundary discussed in Chapter 1 are each models of this type. In some ways, models of this sort are like political caricatures. Their value is in the insights they provide; insights that help us to understand key features of the much more complex real world.

Second, the term *model* is used as a synonym for a theory, as when economists speak of the demand-and-supply model of the Manitoba egg market that we discussed earlier. Sometimes economists use *model* to refer to a specific quantitative version of a theory. In this case, specific numbers are attached to the mathematical relationships embodied in the theory. The result is that the predictions are more precise. For example, rather than such a prediction as "a decrease in the price of chicken feed will lead to an increase in the quantity of eggs supplied," the prediction from the more specific model might be "a 10-percent reduction in the price of chicken feed will lead to an 8-percent increase in the number of eggs supplied."

2.3 Testing Theories

A theory is tested by confronting its predictions with evidence. For example, is a decrease in the price of chicken feed *actually* followed by an increase in the number of eggs supplied by producers? A theory ceases to be useful when it cannot predict better than an alternative theory. When a theory consistently fails to predict better than an available alternative, it is either modified or replaced.

The old question "Which came first: the chicken or the egg?" is often raised when discussing economic theories. In the first instance, it was observation that preceded economic theories; people were not born with economic theories embedded in their minds. However, once economics was established as a scientific line of inquiry, theories and evidence interacted with each other. It has now become impossible to say that one precedes the other. In some cases, empirical evidence may suggest inadequacies that require the development of better theories. In other cases, an inspired guess may lead to a theory that has little current empirical support but is subsequently found to explain many observations. This interaction between theory and empirical observation is illustrated in Figure 2-1.

> The scientific approach is central to the study of economics: Empirical observation leads to the construction of theories, theories generate specific predictions, and the predictions are tested by more detailed empirical observation.

ⓧ myeconlab ADDITIONAL TOPICS

Economists sometimes disagree about the usefulness of a theory or model. For a glimpse of one such debate between two Nobel Laureates, Milton Friedman and Ronald Coase, look for **How Economists Choose Their Theories** in the *Additional Topics* section of this book's MyEconLab.

www.myeconlab.com

FIGURE 2-1   The Interaction Between Theory and Empirical Observation

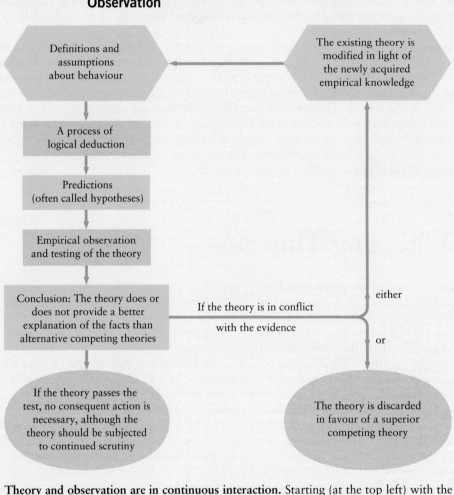

Theory and observation are in continuous interaction. Starting (at the top left) with the assumptions of a theory and the definitions of relevant terms, the theorist deduces by logical analysis everything that is implied by the assumptions. These implications are the predictions or the hypotheses of the theory. The theory is then tested by confronting its predictions with evidence. If the theory is in conflict with facts, it will usually be amended to make it consistent with those facts (thereby making it a better theory), or it will be discarded, to be replaced by a superior theory. The process then begins again: The new or amended theory is subjected first to logical analysis and then to empirical testing.

Rejection Versus Confirmation

An important part of the scientific approach consists of creating a theory that will explain some observation. A theory designed to explain observation X will typically generate a prediction about some other observable variables, Y and Z. The prediction about Y and Z can be tested and may be *rejected* by the data. If the prediction is rejected, the value of the theory is brought into question.

The alternative to this approach is to create a theory and then look for *confirming* evidence. Such an approach is hazardous because the world is sufficiently complex that some confirming evidence can be found for any theory, no matter how unlikely the theory may be. For example, flying saucers, the Loch Ness monster, fortune telling, and astrology all have their devotees who can quote confirming evidence in spite of the failure of many attempts to discover systematic, objective evidence of these things.

Statistical Analysis

Most theories generate a prediction of the form "if X increases, then Y will also increase." Another example is "if X falls, then Z will rise." Statistical analysis can be used to test such predictions and to estimate the numerical values of the function that describes the relationship. In practice, the same data can be used simultaneously to test whether a relationship exists and, if it does exist, to provide an estimate of the magnitude of that relationship.

Because economics is primarily a non-laboratory science, it lacks the controlled experiments central to such sciences as physics and chemistry. Economics must therefore use millions of uncontrolled "experiments" that are going on every day in the marketplace. Households are deciding what to purchase given changing prices and incomes, firms are deciding what to produce and how, and governments are involved in the economy through their various taxes, subsidies, and regulations. Because all these activities can be observed and recorded, a mass of data is continually being produced by the economy.

The variables that interest economists—such as the level of employment, the price of a DVD, and the output of automobiles—are generally influenced by many forces that vary simultaneously. If economists are to test their theories about relations among specific variables, they must use statistical techniques designed for situations in which other things *cannot* be held constant.

Fortunately, such techniques exist, although their application is usually neither simple nor straightforward. Later in this chapter we provide a discussion of some graphical techniques for describing data and displaying some of the more obvious relationships. Further examination of data involves techniques studied in elementary statistics courses. More advanced courses in econometrics deal with the array of techniques designed to test economic hypotheses and to measure economic relations in the complex circumstances in which economic evidence is often generated.

Correlation Versus Causation

Suppose you want to test your theory's prediction that "if X increases, Y will also increase." You are looking for a *causal* relationship from X to Y, because a change in X is predicted to *cause* a change in Y. When you look at the data, suppose you find that X and Y are positively correlated—that is, when X rises, Y also tends to rise. Is your theory supported? It might appear that way, but there is a potential problem.

A finding that X and Y are positively correlated means only that X and Y tend to move together. This correlation is *consistent* with the theory that X causes Y, but it is *not* direct evidence of this causal relationship. The causality may be in the opposite direction—from Y to X. Or X and Y may have no direct causal connection but may instead be jointly caused by some third variable, Z.

Here is an example. Suppose your theory predicts that individuals who get more education will earn higher incomes as a result—the causality in this theory runs from

Practise with Study Guide
Chapter 2, Short-Answer
Question 3.

education to income. In the data, suppose we find that education and income are positively correlated. This should not, however, be taken as direct evidence for the (causal) prediction. The data are certainly consistent with that theory, but they are also consistent with others. For example, individuals who grow up in higher-income households may "buy" more education, just as they buy more clothes or entertainment. This is a case of "reverse causality": income causes education, rather than the other way around. Another possibility is that education and income are positively correlated because the personal characteristics that lead people to become more educated—ability and motivation—are the same characteristics that lead to high incomes. In this case, the *causal* relationship runs from personal characteristics to both income and education.

> **Most economic predictions involve causality. Economists must take care when testing predictions to distinguish between correlation and causality. Correlation can establish that the data are consistent with the theory; establishing the likelihood of causality usually requires advanced statistical techniques.**

2.4 Economic Data

For data on the Canadian economy and many other quantifiable aspects of Canadian life, see Statistics Canada's website: **www.statcan.gc.ca**

Economists use real-world observations to test their theories. For example, did the amount that people saved last year rise—as the theory predicts it should have—when a large tax cut increased their after-tax incomes? To test this prediction we need reliable data for people's incomes and their savings.

Political scientists, sociologists, anthropologists, and psychologists often collect for themselves the data they use to formulate and test their theories. Economists are unusual among social scientists in mainly using data collected by others, often government statisticians. In economics there is a division of labour between collecting data and using it to test theories. The advantage is that economists do not need to spend much of their scarce research time collecting the data they use. The disadvantage is that they are often not as well informed about the limitations of the data collected by others as they would be if they had collected the data themselves.

After data are collected, they can be displayed in various ways, many of which we will see later in this chapter. They can be laid out in tables. They can be displayed in various types of graphs. And when we are interested in relative movements rather than absolute ones, the data can be expressed in *index numbers*. We begin with a discussion of index numbers.

Index Numbers

index number An average that measures change over time of such variables as the price level and industrial production; conventionally expressed as a percentage relative to a base period, which is assigned the value 100.

Economists frequently look at data on prices or quantities and explore how specific variables change over time. For example, they may be interested in comparing the time paths of output in two industries: steel and newsprint. The problem is that it may be difficult to compare the time paths of the two different variables if we just look at the "raw" data.

Table 2-2 shows some hypothetical data for the volume of output in the steel and newsprint industries. Because the two variables are measured in different units, it is not immediately clear which of the two variables is more volatile or which, if either, has an upward or a downward trend.

It is easier to compare the two paths if we focus on *relative* rather than *absolute* changes. One way to do this is to construct some **index numbers**.

How to Build an Index Number We start by taking the value of the variable at some point in time as the "base" to which the values in other periods will be compared. We call this the *base period*. In the present example, we choose 2001 as the base year for both series. We then take the output in each subsequent year, called the given year, and divide it by the output in the base year, and then multiply the result by 100. This gives us an index number for the output of steel and a separate index number for the output of newsprint. For each index number, the value of output in the base year is equal to 100. The details of the calculations are shown in Table 2-3.

An index number simply expresses the value of some series in any given year as a percentage of its value in the base year. For example, the 2011 index of steel output of 122.5 tells us that steel output in 2011 was 22.5 percent greater than in 2001. In contrast, the 2011 index for newsprint output of 93.8 tells us that newsprint output in 2011 was only 93.8 percent of the output in 2001—that is, output was 6.2 percent lower in 2011 than in 2001. The results in Table 2-3 allow us to compare the relative fluctuations in the two series. It is apparent from the values in the table that the output of steel has shown significantly more percentage variability than has the output of newsprint. This is also clear in Figure 2-2.

TABLE 2-2   Volume of Steel and Newsprint Output

Year	Volume of Steel (thousands of tonnes)	Volume of Newsprint (thousands of rolls)
2001	200	3200
2002	210	3100
2003	225	3000
2004	215	3200
2005	250	3100
2006	220	3300
2007	265	3100
2008	225	3300
2009	255	3100
2010	230	3200
2011	245	3000

Comparing the time paths of two data series is difficult when absolute numbers are used. Since steel output and newsprint output have quite different absolute numbers, it is difficult to detect which time series is more volatile.

TABLE 2-3   Constructing Index Numbers

Year	Steel Procedure	Index	Newsprint Procedure	Index
2001	$(200/200) \times 100$ =	100.0	$(3200/3200) \times 100$ =	100.0
2002	$(210/200) \times 100$ =	105.0	$(3100/3200) \times 100$ =	96.9
2003	$(225/200) \times 100$ =	112.5	$(3000/3200) \times 100$ =	93.8
2004	$(215/200) \times 100$ =	107.5	$(3200/3200) \times 100$ =	100.0
2005	$(250/200) \times 100$ =	125.0	$(3100/3200) \times 100$ =	96.9
2006	$(220/200) \times 100$ =	110.0	$(3300/3200) \times 100$ =	103.1
2007	$(265/200) \times 100$ =	132.5	$(3100/3200) \times 100$ =	96.9
2008	$(225/200) \times 100$ =	112.5	$(3300/3200) \times 100$ =	103.1
2009	$(255/200) \times 100$ =	127.5	$(3100/3200) \times 100$ =	96.9
2010	$(230/200) \times 100$ =	115.0	$(3200/3200) \times 100$ =	100.0
2011	$(245/200) \times 100$ =	122.5	$(3000/3200) \times 100$ =	93.8

Index numbers are calculated by dividing the value in the given year by the value in the base year and multiplying the result by 100. The 2011 index number for steel tells us that steel output in 2011 was 22.5 percent greater than in the base year, 2001. The 2011 index number for newsprint tells us that newsprint output in 2011 was 93.8 percent of the output in the base year, 2001.

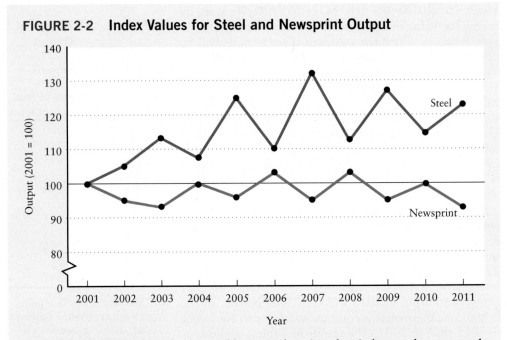

FIGURE 2-2 Index Values for Steel and Newsprint Output

Comparing the time paths of two variables is much easier when index numbers are used. Since both index numbers are equal to 100 in the base year, relative volatility and trends become clear. Steel output is clearly more volatile in percentage terms than newsprint output. Steel output also has an upward trend, whereas newsprint output appears to have little or no trend.

The formula of any index number is:

$$\text{Value of index in any given period} = \frac{\text{Absolute value in given period}}{\text{Absolute value in base period}} \times 100$$

Care must be taken, however, when using index numbers. The index number always tells you the percentage change compared with the base year, but when comparing an index number across non-base years, the percentage change in the index number is *not* given by the absolute difference in the values of the index number. For example, if you want to know how much steel output changed from 2005 to 2007, we know from Table 2-3 that the index number for steel output increased from 125.0 to 132.5. But this is not an increase of 7.5 percent. The *percentage* increase in steel output is computed as $(132.5 - 125.0)/125.0 = 7.5/125.0 = 0.06$, or 6 percent.

More Complex Index Numbers

Perhaps the most famous index number used by economists is the index of average prices—the consumer price index (CPI). This is a price index of the *average* price paid by consumers for the typical basket of goods that they buy. The inclusion of the word "average," however, makes the CPI a more complex index number than the ones we have constructed here.

With what you have just learned, you could construct separate index numbers for the price of beef, the price of coffee, and the price of orange juice. But to get the

Practise with Study Guide
Chapter 2, Exercise 1.

consumer price index, we need to take the *average* of these separate price indexes (plus thousands of others for the goods and services we have ignored here). But it cannot be a simple average. Instead, it must be a *weighted* average where the weight on each price index reflects the relative importance of that good in the typical consumer's basket of goods and services. For example, since the typical consumer spends a tiny fraction of income on sardines but a much larger fraction of income on housing, the weight on the "sardines" price index in the CPI will be very small and the weight on the "housing" price index will be very large. The result is that even huge swings in the price of sardines will have negligible effects on the CPI, whereas much more modest changes in the price of housing will have noticeable effects on the CPI.

We will spend much more time discussing the consumer price index when we study macroeconomics beginning in Chapter 19. For now, keep in mind the usefulness of the simple index numbers we have constructed here. They allow us to compare the time paths of different variables.

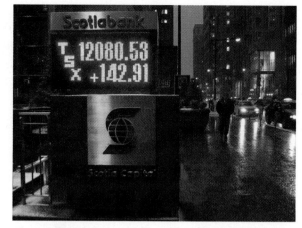

The S&P/TSX is one of the best-known index numbers in Canada. Its fluctuations reflect changes in the market value of the largest publicly traded companies in Canada.

---

myeconlab ADDITIONAL TOPICS

Another famous index that is reported every day on the news is the S&P/TSX, an index number showing the average market value of a specific set of companies traded on the Toronto Stock Exchange. For more information about the S&P/TSX index, look for **What the S&P/TSX Really Measures** in the *Additional Topics* section of this book's MyEconLab.

www.myeconlab.com

Graphing Economic Data

A single economic variable, such as unemployment, national income, or the average price of a house, can come in two basic forms.

Cross-Sectional and Time-Series Data The first is called **cross-sectional data**, which means a number of different observations on one variable all taken in different places at the same point in time. Figure 2-3 shows an example. The variable in the figure is the average selling price of a house. It is shown for each of the ten Canadian provinces in May 2009.

The second type of data is called **time-series data**. It refers to observations of one variable at successive points in time. The data in Figure 2-4 show the unemployment rate for Canada from 1978 to 2009. (Note that the Canadian unemployment rate is simply a weighted average of the ten provincial unemployment rates, where the weight for each province is that province's labour force as a fraction of the total Canadian

cross-sectional data A set of observations made at the same time across several different units (such as households, firms, or countries).

time-series data A set of observations made at successive periods of time.

FIGURE 2-3   A Cross-Sectional Graph of Average House Prices for Ten Canadian Provinces, 2009

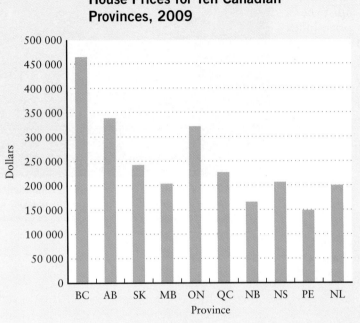

(*Source:* Adapted from MLS® Statistics © 2009 The Canadian Real Estate Association; www.crea.ca/public/news_stats/statistics.htm.)

labour force.) Time-series graphs are quite useful in economics because we often want to know how specific economic numbers are changing over time. As is clear in Figure 2-4, the Canadian unemployment rate is relatively volatile over long periods of time, but in recent years it has been low by historical standards.

Scatter Diagrams Another way in which data can be presented is in a **scatter diagram.** It is designed to show the relation between two different variables, such as the price of eggs and the quantity of eggs purchased. To plot a scatter diagram, values of one variable are measured on the horizontal axis and values of the second variable are measured on the vertical axis. Any point on the diagram relates a specific value of one variable to a corresponding specific value of the other.

The data plotted on a scatter diagram may be either cross-sectional data or time-series data. An example of a cross-sectional scatter diagram is a scatter of the price of eggs and the quantity sold in

FIGURE 2-4   A Time-Series Graph of the Canadian Unemployment Rate, 1978–2009

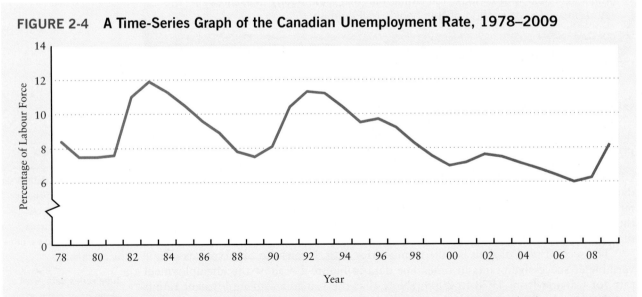

(*Source:* Annual average of monthly, seasonally adjusted data from Statistics Canada, CANSIM database, V2062815 Canada; unemployment rate; both sexes; 15 years and over.)

FIGURE 2-5   A Scatter Diagram of Household Income and Saving

Household	Annual Income	Annual Saving
1	$ 70 000	$10 000
2	30 000	2 500
3	100 000	12 000
4	60 000	3 000
5	80 000	8 000
6	10 000	500
7	20 000	2 000
8	50 000	2 000
9	40 000	4 200
10	90 000	8 000

Saving tends to rise as income rises. The table shows the amount of income earned by ten selected households together with the amount they saved during the same year. The scatter diagram plots the income and saving for the ten households listed in the table. The number on each dot refers to the household in the corresponding row of the table.

July 2010 at two dozen different places in Canada. Each dot refers to a price–quantity combination observed in a different place at the same time. An example of a scatter diagram using time-series data is the price and quantity of eggs sold in Thunder Bay for each month over the last ten years. Each of the 120 dots refers to a price–quantity combination observed at the same place in one particular month.

The table in Figure 2-5 shows data for the income and saving of ten households in one particular year and these data are plotted on a scatter diagram. Each point in the figure represents one household, showing its income and its saving. The positive relation between the two stands out. The higher the household's income, the higher its saving tends to be.

scatter diagram A graph of statistical observations of paired values of two variables, one measured on the horizontal and the other on the vertical axis. Each point on the coordinate grid represents the values of the variables for a particular unit of observation.

myeconlab   ADDITIONAL TOPICS

If you need a quick refresher course on graphing, look for **A Brief Introduction to Graphing** in the *Additional Topics* section of this book's MyEconLab.

www.myeconlab.com

2.5 Graphing Economic Theories

Theories are built on assumptions about relationships between variables. For example, the quantity of eggs demanded is assumed to fall as the price of eggs rises, and the total amount an individual saves is assumed to rise as his or her income rises. How can such relations be expressed?

Functions

When one variable, *X*, is related to another variable, *Y*, in such a way that to every value of *X* there is only one possible value of *Y*, we say that *Y* is a *function* of *X*. When we write this relation down, we are expressing a *functional relation* between the two variables.

Here is a specific but hypothetical example. Consider the relation between an individual's annual income, which we denote by the symbol *Y*, and the amount that person spends on goods and services during the year, which we denote by the symbol *C* (for consumption). Any particular example of the relation between *C* and *Y* can be expressed several ways: in words, in a table or schedule, in a mathematical equation, or in a graph.

VERBAL STATEMENT. When income is zero, the person will spend $800 a year (either by borrowing the money or by consuming past savings), and for every extra $1 of income the person will increase expenditure by 80 cents.

SCHEDULE. This table shows selected values of the person's income and consumption.

Annual Income	Consumption	Reference Letter
$ 0	$ 800	*p*
2 500	2 800	*q*
5 000	4 800	*r*
7 500	6 800	*s*
10 000	8 800	*t*

MATHEMATICAL EQUATION. $C = \$800 + 0.8Y$ is the equation of the relation just described in words. As a check, you can first see that when *Y* is zero, *C* is $800. Further, you can see that every time *Y* increases by $1, the level of *C* increases by 0.8($1), which is 80 cents.

FIGURE 2-6   Income and Consumption

Consumption expenditure rises as income rises. The figure graphs the schedule and the equation for the hypothetical functional relation discussed in the text.

GRAPH. Figure 2-6 shows the points from the preceding schedule and the line representing the equation given in the previous paragraph.

Comparison of the values on the graph with the values in the schedule, and with the values derived from the equation just stated, shows that these are alternative expressions of the same relation between *C* and *Y*. All four of these modes of expression refer to the same relation between the person's consumption expenditure and income.

More Detail About Functions Let us look in a little more detail at the mathematical expression of this relation between income and consumption. To state the expression in general form, detached from the specific numerical example above, we use a symbol to express the dependence of one variable on another. Using *f* for this purpose, we write

$$C = f(Y) \qquad (2\text{-}1)$$

This is read, "*C* is a function of *Y*." Spelling this out more fully, we would say, "The amount of consumption expenditure depends on the person's income."

The variable on the left-hand side is the dependent variable, since its value depends on the value of the variable on the right-hand side. The variable on the right-hand side is the independent variable, since it can take on any value. The letter *f* tells us that a functional relation is involved. This means that a knowledge of the value of the variable (or variables) within the parentheses on the right-hand side allows us to determine a unique value of the variable on the left-hand side. Although in this case we have used *f* (as a memory-aid for "function"), any convenient symbol can be used to denote the existence of a functional relation.

Functional notation can seem intimidating to those who are unfamiliar with it. But it is helpful. Since the functional concept is basic to all science, the notation is worth mastering.

Functional Forms   The equation $C = f(Y)$ states that *C* is a function of *Y*. It says nothing about the *form* of this function. The term *functional form* refers to the specific nature of the relation between the variables in the function. Earlier, we gave one specific functional form for this relation:

$$C = \$800 + 0.8Y \qquad (2\text{-}2)$$

Equation 2-1 expresses the general assumption that consumption expenditure depends on the consumer's income. Equation 2-2 expresses the more specific assumption that *C* is equal to $800 when *Y* is zero and rises by 80 cents for every $1 that *Y* rises. An alternative assumption would be $C = \$600 + 0.9Y$. You should be able to say in words the behaviour implied in this relation. There is no reason why either of these assumptions must be true; indeed, neither may be consistent with the facts. But that is a matter for testing. What we do have in each equation is a precise statement of a particular assumption.

Notice that Equation 2-2 also specifies a *linear* consumption function—the relationship between *C* and *Y* is shown as a straight line in Figure 2-6. This is a very special case. Another possibility is that the relationship between *C* and *Y* is *non-linear*—so that the consumption function when graphed is not a straight line. This possibility takes us to our next discussion, of linear and non-linear functions, and of how to measure and interpret the *slopes* of functions.

Graphing Functional Relations

Different functional forms have different graphs, and we will meet many of these in subsequent chapters. Figure 2-6 is an example of a relation in which the two variables move together. When income goes up, consumption goes up. In such a relation the two variables are *positively related* to each other.

Figure 2-7 gives an example of variables that move in opposite directions. As the amount spent on reducing pollution goes up, the amount of remaining pollution goes down. In such a relation the two variables are *negatively related* to each other.

FIGURE 2-7   Linear Pollution Reduction

Pollution as a linear function of clean-up expenditure. Between points *A* and *B* it costs $2000 to reduce pollution by 1000 tonnes. The cost of pollution reduction is the same elsewhere on the line. The slope of the line, −0.5, indicates that any $1 expenditure on pollution clean-up reduces the amount of pollution by 0.5 tonnes.

Both of these graphs are straight lines. In such cases the variables are *linearly related* to each other (either positively or negatively).

Practise with Study Guide
Chapter 2, Exercise 2.

The Slope of a Straight Line   Slopes are important in economics. They show you how much one variable changes as the other changes. The slope is defined as the amount of change in the variable measured on the vertical axis per unit change in the variable measured on the horizontal axis. In the case of Figure 2-7 it tells us how many tonnes of pollution, symbolized by P, are removed per dollar spent on reducing pollution, symbolized by E. Consider moving from point A to point B in the figure. If we spend $2000 more on clean-up, we reduce pollution by 1000 tonnes. This is 0.5 tonnes per dollar spent. On the graph the extra $2000 is indicated by ΔE, the arrow indicating that E rises by 2000. The 1000 tonnes of pollution reduction is indicated by ΔP, the arrow showing that pollution falls by 1000. (The Greek uppercase letter delta, Δ, stands for "the change in.") To get the amount of pollution reduction per dollar of expenditure, we merely divide one by the other. In symbols this is $\Delta P/\Delta E$.

> If we let X stand for whatever variable is measured on the horizontal axis and Y for whatever variable is measured on the vertical axis, the slope of a straight line is $\Delta Y/\Delta X$. [1][1]

The equation of the line in Figure 2-7 can be computed in two steps. First, note that when $E = 0$, the amount of remaining pollution, P, is equal to 6 (thousand tonnes). Thus, the line meets the vertical axis ($E = 0$) when P equals 6. Second, we have already seen that the slope of the line, $\Delta P/\Delta E$, is equal to –0.5, which means that for every one-unit increase in E, P falls by 0.5 unit. We can thus state the equation of the line as

$$P = 6 - (0.5)\,E$$

where both P and E are expressed as thousands of units (tonnes and dollars, respectively).

Non-linear Functions   Although it is sometimes convenient to simplify a real relation between two variables by assuming them to be linearly related, this is seldom the case over their whole range. Non-linear relations are much more common than linear ones. In the case of reducing pollution, it is usually quite cheap to eliminate the first units of pollution. Then, as the environment gets cleaner and cleaner, the cost of further clean-up tends to increase because more and more sophisticated and expensive methods need to be used. As a result, Figure 2-8 is more realistic than Figure 2-7. Inspection of Figure 2-8 shows that as more and more is spent, the amount of pollution reduction for an additional $1 of clean-up expenditure gets smaller and smaller. This is shown by the diminishing slope of the curve as we move rightward along it. For example, as we move from point A to point B, an increase in expenditure of $1000 is required to reduce pollution by 1000 tonnes. Thus, each tonne of pollution reduction costs $1. But as we move from point C (where we have already reduced pollution considerably) to point D, an extra $6000 must be spent in order to reduce pollution by 1000 tonnes. Each tonne of pollution reduction therefore costs $6.

Economists call the change in pollution when a bit more or a bit less is spent on clean-up the *marginal* change. The figure shows that the slope of the curve at each

---

[1] Red numbers in square brackets indicate mathematical notes that are found in a separate section at the back of the book.

FIGURE 2-8   Non-linear Pollution Reduction

Pollution as a non-linear function of clean-up expenditure. The slope of the curve changes as we move along it. Between points A and B, it costs \$1000 to reduce pollution by 1000 tonnes. Between points C and D, it costs \$6000 to reduce pollution by 1000 tonnes. At point Z, the slope of the curve is equal to the slope of the straight line tangent to the curve at point Z. The slope of the tangent line is $-0.75/1.75 = -0.43$.

point measures this marginal change. It also shows that, in the type of curve illustrated, the marginal change per dollar spent is diminishing as we spend more on reducing pollution. There is always a payoff to more expenditure over the range shown in the figure, but the payoff diminishes as more is spent. This relation can be described as *diminishing marginal response*. We will meet such relations many times in what follows, so we emphasize now that diminishing marginal response does not mean that the *total* response is diminishing. In Figure 2-8, the total amount of pollution continues to fall as more and more is spent on clean-up. But diminishing marginal response does mean that the amount of pollution reduced per dollar of expenditure gets less and less as the total expenditure rises.

Figure 2-9 shows a graph in which the marginal response is increasing. The graph shows the relationship between annual production costs and annual output for a firm that makes hockey sticks. Notice that the more hockey sticks produced annually, the higher the firm's costs. This is shown by the positive slope of the line. Notice also that as more and more hockey sticks are produced, the extra amount that the firm must pay to produce each extra hockey stick rises. For example, as the firm moves from point A to point B, annual costs rise by \$30 000 in order to increase its annual output by 10 000 hockey sticks. Each extra hockey stick costs \$3 (\$30 000/10 000 = \$3). But when the firm is producing many more hockey sticks, such as at point C, its factory is closer to its capacity and it becomes more costly to increase production. Moving from point C to point D, the firm's annual costs increase by \$150 000 in order to increase its annual output by 10 000 hockey sticks. Each extra hockey stick then costs \$15 (\$150 000/10 000 = \$15). This figure illustrates a case of *increasing marginal cost*, a characteristic of production that we will see often in this book.

Figures 2-8 and 2-9 show that with non-linear functions the slope of the curve changes as we move along the curve. For example, in Figure 2-8, the slope of the curve

FIGURE 2-9   Increasing Production Costs

Production costs increase at an increasing rate as annual output rises. From point A to point B, an extra annual output of 10 000 hockey sticks increases annual costs by $30 000. Each extra hockey stick costs $3. From point C to point D, an extra output of 10 000 hockey sticks increases annual costs by $150 000. Each extra hockey stick then costs $15. This is a case of increasing marginal cost. At point Z, the slope of the curve is equal to the slope of the straight line tangent to the curve at point Z. The slope of the tangent line is $65/8 = 8.1$.

falls as the expenditure on pollution clean-up increases. In Figure 2-9, the slope of the curve increases as the volume of production increases.

How, exactly, do we measure the slope of a curved line? The answer is that we use the slope of a straight line *tangent to that curve* at the point that interests us. For example, in Figure 2-8, if we want to know the slope of the curve at point Z, we draw a straight line that touches the curve *only* at point Z; this is a tangent line. The slope of this line is $-0.75/1.75 = -0.43$. Similarly, in Figure 2-9, the slope of the curve at point Z is given by the slope of the straight line tangent to the curve at point Z.

> For non-linear functions, the slope of the curve changes as X changes. Therefore, the marginal response of Y to a change in X depends on the value of X.

Functions with a Minimum or a Maximum

So far, all the graphs we have shown have had either a positive or a negative slope over their entire range. But many relations change directions as the independent variable increases. For example, consider a firm that is attempting to maximize its profits and is trying to determine how much output to produce. The firm may find that its unit production costs are lower than the market price of the good, and so it can increase its profit by producing more. But as it increases its level of production, the firm's unit costs may be driven up because the capacity of the factory is being approached. Eventually, the firm may find that extra output will actually cost so much that its profits will be *reduced*. This is a relationship that we will study in detail in later chapters, and it is illustrated in Figure 2-10. Notice that when profits are maximized at point A, the slope of the curve is zero (because a tangent to the curve at point A is horizontal) and so the *marginal response* of profits to output is zero.

Now consider an example of a function with a minimum. You probably know that when you drive a car, the fuel consumption per kilometre depends on your speed. Driving very slowly uses a lot of fuel per kilometre travelled. Driving very fast also uses a lot of fuel per kilometre travelled. The best fuel efficiency—the lowest fuel consumption per kilometre travelled—occurs at a speed of approximately 95 kilometres per hour. The relationship between speed and fuel consumption is shown in Figure 2-11 and illustrates a function with a minimum. Note that at point A the slope of the curve is zero (because a tangent to the curve at point A is horizontal) and so the *marginal response* of fuel consumption to speed is zero.

> At either a minimum or a maximum of a function, the slope of the curve is zero. Therefore, at the minimum or maximum, the marginal response of Y to a change in X is zero.

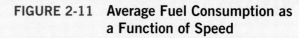

FIGURE 2-10   **Profits as a Function of Output**

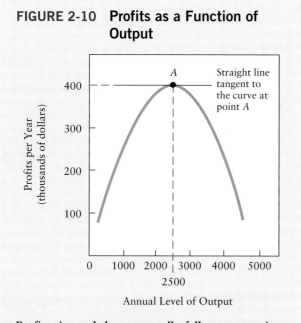

Profits rise and then eventually fall as output rises. When the firm is producing fewer than 2500 units annually, the marginal response of profit to output is positive—that is, an increase in output leads to an increase in profit. Beyond 2500 units annually, the marginal response is negative—an increase in output leads to a reduction in profit. At point *A*, profits are maximized and the marginal response of profit to output is zero. Because the tangent at point *A* is horizontal, the slope of the curve is zero at that point.

FIGURE 2-11   **Average Fuel Consumption as a Function of Speed**

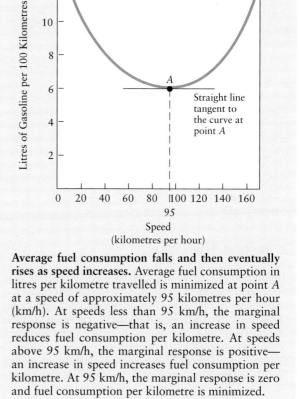

Average fuel consumption falls and then eventually rises as speed increases. Average fuel consumption in litres per kilometre travelled is minimized at point *A* at a speed of approximately 95 kilometres per hour (km/h). At speeds less than 95 km/h, the marginal response is negative—that is, an increase in speed reduces fuel consumption per kilometre. At speeds above 95 km/h, the marginal response is positive—an increase in speed increases fuel consumption per kilometre. At 95 km/h, the marginal response is zero and fuel consumption per kilometre is minimized.

A Final Word

We have done much in this chapter. We have discussed why economists use theory and how they build economic models. We have discussed how they test their theories and how there is a continual back-and-forth process between empirical testing of predictions and refining the theoretical model. Finally, we have devoted considerable time and space to exploring the many ways that data can be displayed in graphs and how economists use graphs to illustrate their theories.

Many students find themselves intimidated when they are first confronted with all the details about graphing. But try not to worry. You may not yet be a master of all the graphing techniques that we have discussed in this chapter, but you will be surprised at how quickly it all falls into place. And, as is true for most skills, there is no substitute for practice. In the next three chapters we will encounter many graphs. But we will start simply and then slowly attempt more complicated cases. We are confident that in the process of learning some basic economic theories you will get enough practice in graphing that you will very soon look back at this chapter and realize how straightforward it all is.

Summary

2.1 Positive and Normative Advice

- A key to the success of scientific inquiry lies in separating positive statements about the way the world works from normative statements about how one would like the world to work.

2.2 Economic Theories

- Theories are designed to explain and predict what we see. A theory consists of a set of definitions of the variables to be employed, a set of assumptions about how things behave, and the conditions under which the theory is meant to apply.
- A theory provides predictions of the type "if one event occurs, then another event will also occur."

- The term *model* is often used as a synonym for *theory*. It is also used to describe an illustrative abstraction that is used to organize our thinking even though it may not generate testable hypotheses.

2.3 Testing Theories

- Theories are tested by checking their predictions against evidence. In some sciences, these tests can be conducted under laboratory conditions in which only one thing changes at a time. In economics, testing is almost always done using the data produced by the world of ordinary events.
- Economists make use of statistical analysis when testing their theories. They must take care to make the distinction between correlation and causation.

- The progress of any science lies in finding better explanations of events than are now available. Thus, in any developing science, one must expect to discard some existing theories and replace them with demonstrably superior alternatives.

2.4 Economic Data

- Index numbers express economic series in relative form. Values in each period are expressed in relation to the value in the base period, which is given a value of 100.
- Economic data can be graphed in three different ways. Cross-sectional graphs show observations taken at the same time. Time-series graphs show observations on one variable taken over time. Scatter diagrams show many points, each one of which refers to specific observations on two different variables.

2.5 Graphing Economic Theories

- A functional relation can be expressed in words, in a schedule giving specific values, in a mathematical equation, or in a graph.
- A graph of two variables has a positive slope when they both increase or decrease together and a negative slope when they move in opposite directions.
- The marginal response of a variable gives the amount it changes in response to a change in a second variable.

When the variable is measured on the vertical axis of a diagram, its marginal response at a specific point on the curve is measured by the slope of the line at that point.
- Some functions have a maximum or minimum point. At such points, the marginal response is zero.

Key Concepts

Positive and normative statements
Endogenous and exogenous variables
Theories and models
Variables, assumptions, and
  predictions

Correlation versus causation
Functional relations
Positive and negative relations between
  variables

Positively and negatively sloped curves
Marginal responses
Maximum and minimum values

Study Exercises

> ✗ **myeconlab**   **SAVE TIME. IMPROVE RESULTS.**
>
> Visit MyEconLab to practise Study Exercises and prepare for tests and exams.
> MyEconLab also offers a variety of other study tools to help you succeed.
> **www.myeconlab.com**

1. In the following examples, identify the exogenous (or independent) variable and the endogenous (or dependent) variable.

   a. The amount of rainfall on the Canadian prairies determines the amount of wheat produced in Canada.
   b. When the world price of coffee increases, there is a change in the price of your cup of coffee at Tim Hortons.
   c. If student loans were no longer available, there would be fewer students attending university.
   d. An increase in the tax on gasoline leads people to drive more fuel-efficient vehicles.

2. Use the appropriate graph—time-series, cross-sectional, or scatter diagram—to illustrate the economic data provided in each part below.

   a. Canada's prime interest rate in 2008:

January	5.75
February	5.75
March	5.25
April	4.75
May	4.75
June	4.75
July	4.75
August	4.75
September	4.75
October	4.00
November	4.00
December	3.50

   b. A comparison of average household expenditures across provinces and territories in 2007:

British Columbia	$72 621
Alberta	85 912
Saskatchewan	63 944
Manitoba	63 303
Ontario	76 654
Quebec	57 308
New Brunswick	58 205
Nova Scotia	59 987
Prince Edward Island	55 574
Newfoundland and Labrador	69 946
Yukon Territory	76 997
Northwest Territories	89 075
Nunavut	73 747

   c. Per capita growth rates of real GDP and investment rates for various countries, averaged over the period 1970–1990:

Country	Average Growth Rate (% per year)	Average Investment Rate (% of GDP)
Canada	2.6	22.0
Austria	2.6	25.5
Japan	3.6	31.0
United States	1.7	18.7
United Kingdom	2.1	18.2
Spain	2.5	23.0
Norway	3.2	28.2

3. Use the following figure to answer the questions below.

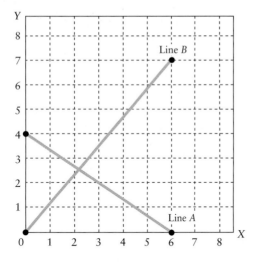

a. Is the slope of Line *A* positive or negative? Line *B*?
b. Calculate the slope of Line *A*. Write the equation describing the line in the form $Y = mX + b$ where *m* is the slope of the line and *b* is a constant term.
c. Calculate the slope of Line *B*. Write the equation describing the line in the form $Y = mX + b$ where *m* is the slope of the line and *b* is a constant term.

4. Suppose the relationship between the government's tax revenue (*T*) and national income (*Y*) is represented by the following equation: $T = 10 + 0.25Y$. Plot this relationship on a scale diagram, with *Y* on the horizontal axis and *T* on the vertical axis. Interpret the equation.

5. Consider the following three specific functional forms for a functional relation between *X* and *Y*:

i) $Y = 50 + 2X$
ii) $Y = 50 + 2X + 0.05X^2$
iii) $Y = 50 + 2X - 0.05X^2$

   a. For the values of *X* of 0, 10, 20, 30, 40, and 50, plot *X* and *Y* on a scale diagram for each specific functional form. Connect these points with a smooth line.
   b. For each functional form, state whether the slope of the line is constant, increasing, or decreasing as the value of *X* increases.
   c. Describe for each functional form how the marginal change in *Y* depends on the value of *X*.

6. Suppose you want to create a price index for the price of a particular physics textbook over ten years in your university bookstore. The price of the book on September 1 of each year is as follows:

Year	Price ($)	Year	Price ($)
2000	85	2006	120
2001	87	2007	125
2002	94	2008	127
2003	104	2009	127
2004	110	2010	130
2005	112		

a. The base year is 2000. Construct a physics textbook price index.
b. What is the percentage increase in the price of the book between the base year and 2005?
c. What is the percentage increase in the price of the book from 2007 to 2010?
d. Are the data listed above time-series or cross-sectional data? Explain why.

7. Suppose you want to create a price index for the price of pizza across several Canadian university campuses, as of March 1, 2010. The data are as follows:

University	Price per Pizza
Dalhousie	$6.50
Laval	5.95
McGill	6.00
Queen's	8.00
Waterloo	7.50
Manitoba	5.50
Saskatchewan	5.75
Calgary	6.25
UBC	7.25
Victoria	7.00

a. Using Calgary as the "base university," construct the Canadian university pizza price index.
b. At which university is pizza the most expensive, and by what percentage is the price higher than in Calgary?
c. At which university is pizza the least expensive, and by what percentage is the price lower than in Calgary?
d. Are the data listed above time-series or cross-sectional data? Explain why.

8. For each of the functional relations listed below, plot the relations on a scale diagram (with X on the horizontal axis and Y on the vertical axis) and compute the slope of the line.

i) $Y = 10 + 3X$
ii) $Y = 20 + 4X$
iii) $Y = 30 + 5X$
iv) $Y = 10 + 5X$

9. Suppose we divide Canada into three regions: the West, the Centre, and the East. Each region has an unemployment rate, defined as the number of people unemployed, expressed as a fraction of that region's labour force. The table that follows shows each region's unemployment rate and the size of its labour force.

Region	Unemployment Rate	Labour Force
West	5.5%	5.3 million
Centre	7.2%	8.4 million
East	12.5%	3.5 million

   a. Compute an unemployment rate for Canada using a simple average of the rates in the three regions. Is this the "right" unemployment rate for Canada as a whole? Explain why or why not.

   b. Now compute an unemployment rate for Canada using weights that reflect the size of that region's labour force as a proportion of the overall Canadian labour force. Explain the difference in this unemployment rate from the one in part (a). Is this a "better" measure of Canadian unemployment? Explain why.

10. Draw three graphs in which the dependent variable increases at an increasing rate, at a constant rate, and at a diminishing rate. Then draw three graphs in which it decreases at an increasing, constant, and diminishing rate. For each of these graphs state a real relation that might be described by it—other than the ones given in the text of this chapter.

Discussion Questions

1. What are some of the positive and normative issues that lie behind the disagreements in the following cases?

   a. Economists disagree on whether the government of Canada should try to stimulate the economy in the next six months.

   b. European and North American negotiators disagree over the desirability of reducing European farm subsidies.

   c. Economists argue about the merits of a voucher system that allows parents to choose the schools their children will attend.

   d. Economists debate the use of a two-tier medical system in Canada (whereby health care continues to be publicly provided, but individuals are permitted to be treated by doctors who bill the patient directly—"extra billing").

   e. Economists debate the costs of global climate change and the relative merits of carbon taxes and other policies to reduce greenhouse gas emissions.

   f. Policymakers disagree about the extent to which financial markets need to be regulated.

2. Much recent public debate has centred on the pros and cons of permitting continued unrestricted sale of cigarettes. Proposals for the control of cigarettes range from increasing excise taxes to the mandatory use of plain packaging to an outright ban on their sale. Discuss the positive and normative assumptions that underlie the national mood to reduce the consumption of tobacco products.

3. Economists sometimes make each of the following assumptions when they construct models. Discuss some situations in which each of these assumptions might be a useful simplification in order to think about some aspect of the real world.

   a. Earth is flat.
   b. There are no differences between men and women.
   c. There is no tomorrow.
   d. There are only two periods: this year and next year.
   e. A country produces only two types of goods.
   f. People are wholly selfish.

4. Untestable statements can often be reworded so that they can be tested by an appeal to evidence. How might you do this for each of the following assertions?

   a. Free-market economic systems are the best in the world.

   b. Unemployment insurance is eroding the work ethic and encouraging people to become wards of the state rather than productive workers.

   c. Robotics ought to be outlawed because it will destroy the future of working people.

   d. Laws requiring equal pay for work of equal value will make women better off.

   e. Free trade improves the welfare of a country's citizens.

5. There are hundreds of eyewitnesses to the existence of flying saucers and other UFOs. There are films and eyewitness accounts of Nessie, the Loch Ness monster. Are you convinced of their existence? If not, what would it take to persuade you? If you are already convinced, what would it take to make you change your mind?

3

Demand, Supply, and Price

LEARNING OBJECTIVES

In this chapter you will learn

1. the determinants of "quantity demanded," the amount of some product that consumers want to purchase.

2. to distinguish between a shift in a demand curve and a movement along a demand curve.

3. the determinants of "quantity supplied," the amount of some product that producers want to sell.

4. to distinguish between a shift in a supply curve and a movement along a supply curve.

5. about the forces that drive market price to equilibrium, and how equilibrium price is affected by changes in demand and supply.

We are now ready to study the important question of how markets work. The answer leads us to develop a simple model of supply and demand. And though there is much more to economics than just demand and supply (as many following chapters will illustrate), this is an essential starting point for understanding how a market, and thus a market economy, functions.

As a first step, we need to understand what determines the demand for and the supply of particular products. Then we can see how demand and supply together determine the prices of products and the quantities that are bought and sold. Finally, we examine how the price system allows the economy to respond to changes in demand and supply. The concepts of demand and supply help us to understand the price system's successes and failures, and the consequences of many government policies.

This chapter deals with the basic elements of demand, supply, and price. In the next two chapters we use the demand-and-supply apparatus to discuss such issues as cigarette taxes, legislated minimum wages, rent controls, and the burden of payroll taxes.

3.1 Demand

What determines the demand for any given product? How have Canadian consumers responded to the recent declines in the prices of personal computers and cell phones? How will they respond to the next sudden change in the price of gasoline or coffee? We start by developing a theory designed to explain the demand for some typical product.

Quantity Demanded

The total amount of any particular good or service that consumers want to purchase in some time period is called the **quantity demanded** of that product. It is important to notice two things about this concept.

First, quantity demanded is a *desired* quantity. It is the amount that consumers want to purchase when faced with a particular price of the product, other products' prices, their incomes, their tastes, and everything else that might matter. It may be different from the amount that consumers actually succeed in purchasing. If sufficient quantities are not available, the amount that consumers want to purchase may exceed the amount that they actually purchase. (For example, think of standing in line to purchase tickets to a show, only to find out that the show is sold out before you get to the head of the line.) To distinguish these two concepts, the term *quantity demanded* is used to refer to desired purchases, and such phrases as *quantity bought* or *quantity exchanged* are used to refer to actual purchases.

Second, quantity demanded refers to a *flow* of purchases. It must therefore be expressed as so much per period of time: 1 million units per day, 7 million per week, or 365 million per year. For example, being told that the quantity of new television sets demanded (at current prices) in Canada is 50 000 means nothing unless you are also told the period of time involved. For a country as large as Canada, 50 000 TVs demanded per day would be an enormous rate of demand, whereas 50 000 per year would be a very small rate of demand. The important distinction between *stocks* and *flows* is discussed in *Extensions in Theory 3-1*.

The total amount of some product that consumers in the relevant market want to buy in a given time period is influenced by the following important variables: [2]

- Product's own price
- Consumers' income
- Prices of other products
- Tastes
- Population
- Expectations about the future

We will discuss the separate effects of each of these variables later in the chapter. For now, we focus on the effects of changes in the product's own price. But how do we analyze the distinct effect of changes in one variable when all are likely to be changing at once? Since this is difficult to do, we manage it in two stages. First, we consider the influence of the variables one at a time. To do this, we hold all but one of them constant. Then we let the selected variable vary and study how its change affects quantity demanded. We can do the same for each of the other variables in turn, and in this way we can come to understand the importance of each. Second, we combine the separate influences of the variables to discover what happens when several things change at the same time—as they often do.

quantity demanded
The amount of a good or service that consumers want to purchase during some time period.

EXTENSIONS IN THEORY 3-1

The Distinction Between Stocks and Flows

An important conceptual issue that arises frequently in economics is the distinction between *stock* and *flow* variables. Economic theories use both, and it takes a little practice to keep them straight.

As noted in the text, a flow variable has a time dimension—it is so much *per unit of time*. For example, the quantity of Grade A large eggs purchased in Edmonton is a flow variable. No useful information is conveyed if we are told that the number purchased was 2000 dozen eggs unless we are also told the period of time over which these purchases occurred. Two thousand dozen eggs per hour would indicate a much more active market in eggs than would 2000 dozen eggs per month.

In contrast, a stock variable is a variable whose value has meaning *at a point in time*. Thus, the number of eggs in the egg producer's warehouse on a particular day—for example, 20 000 dozen eggs on September 3, 2010—is a stock variable. All those eggs are there at one time, and they remain there until something happens to change the stock held in the warehouse. The stock variable is just a number at a point in time, not a rate of flow of so much per unit of time.

The terminology of stocks and flows can be understood in terms of an analogy to a bathtub. At any moment, the tub holds so much water. This is the *stock*, and it can be measured in terms of the volume of water, say, 100 litres. There might also be water flowing into the tub from the tap; this *flow* is measured as so much water per unit time, say, 10 litres per minute.

The distinction between stocks and flows is important. Failure to keep them straight is a common source of confusion and even error. Note, for example, that a stock variable and a flow variable cannot be added together without specifying some time period for which the flow persists. We cannot add the stock of 100 litres of water in the tub to the flow of 10 litres per minute to get 110 litres. The new stock of water will depend on how long the flow persists; if it lasts for 20 minutes, the new stock will be 300 litres; if the flow persists for 60 minutes, the new stock will be 700 litres (or the tub will overflow!).

The amount of income earned is a flow; it is so much per year or per month or per hour. The amount of a consumer's expenditure is also a flow—so much spent per week or per month or per year. The amount of money in a bank account (earned, perhaps, in the past but unspent) is a stock—just so many thousands of dollars. The key test is always whether a time dimension is required to give the variable meaning.

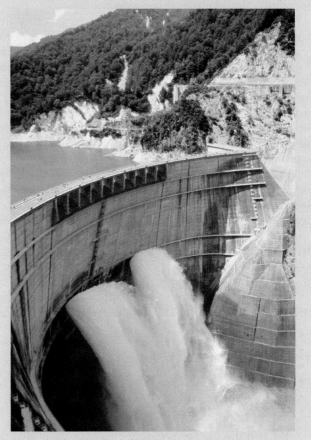

The amount of water behind the dam at any time is the stock of water; the amount moving through the gate is the flow, which is measured per unit of time.

Holding all other variables constant is often described by the expressions "other things being equal," "other things given," or the equivalent Latin phrase, *ceteris paribus*. When economists speak of the influence of the price of eggs on the quantity of eggs demanded, *ceteris paribus*, they refer to what a change in the price of eggs would do to the quantity of eggs demanded *if all other variables that influence the demand for eggs did not change.*

Quantity Demanded and Price[1]

We are interested in studying the relationship between the quantity demanded of a product and that product's price. This requires that we hold all other influences constant and ask, "How will the quantity demanded of a product change as its price changes?"

> A basic economic hypothesis is that the price of a product and the quantity demanded are related *negatively,* other things being equal. That is, the lower the price, the higher the quantity demanded; the higher the price, the lower the quantity demanded.

The great British economist Alfred Marshall (1842–1924) called this fundamental relation the "law of demand." In Chapter 6, we will derive the law of demand as a prediction that follows from more basic assumptions about the behaviour of individual consumers. For now, let's simply explore why this relationship seems reasonable. Products are used to satisfy desires and needs, and there is almost always more than one product that will satisfy any desire or need. Hunger may be alleviated by meat or vegetables; a desire for green vegetables can be satisfied by broccoli or spinach. The desire for a vacation may be satisfied by a trip to the ocean or to the mountains; the need to get there may be satisfied by different airlines, a bus, a car, or a train. For any general desire or need, there are almost always many different products that will satisfy it.

Now consider what happens if income, tastes, population, and the prices of all other products remain constant and the price of only one product changes. As the price goes up, that product becomes an increasingly expensive means of satisfying a desire. Many consumers will decide to switch wholly or partly to other products. Some consumers will stop buying it altogether; others will buy smaller amounts; still others may continue to buy the same quantity. But the net effect is that less will be demanded of the product whose price has risen. As meat becomes more expensive, for example, some consumers will switch to meat substitutes; others may forgo meat at some meals and eat less meat at others. Taken together as a group, consumers will want to buy less meat when its price rises.

Changes in prices lead most consumers to alter their choices. For example, as airfares rise, vacationers may switch to other types of trips, or perhaps to other ways altogether of spending their money.

---

[1] In this chapter we explore the demand curve for some product for the market as a whole—what we often call the *market demand curve*. In Chapter 6 we discuss how this market demand curve is derived by adding up, or *aggregating*, the demands of different individuals.

FIGURE 3-1   The Demand for Carrots

A Demand Schedule for Carrots

Reference Point	Price ($ per tonne)	Quantity Demanded (tonnes per year when average annual income is $50 000)
U	20	110
V	40	85
W	60	65
X	80	50
Y	100	40

A Demand Curve for Carrots

Both the table and the graph show the total quantity of carrots that would be demanded at various prices, *ceteris paribus.* For example, row *W* indicates that if the price of carrots were $60 per tonne, consumers would desire to purchase 65 tonnes of carrots per year, holding constant the values of the other variables that affect quantity demanded. The demand curve, labelled *D*, relates quantity of carrots demanded to the price of carrots; its negative slope indicates that quantity demanded increases as price falls.

Conversely, as the price goes down, the product becomes a cheaper method of satisfying a desire. Households will demand more of it. At the same time they will buy less of similar products whose prices have not fallen and as a result have become expensive *relative* to the product in question. For example, when the price of tomatoes falls, many shoppers will switch to tomatoes and cut their purchases of other vegetables that now are relatively more expensive.

Demand Schedules and Demand Curves

demand schedule A table showing the relationship between quantity demanded and the price of a commodity, other things being equal.

A **demand schedule** is one way of showing the relationship between quantity demanded and the price of a product, other things being equal. It is a table showing the quantity demanded at various prices.

The table in Figure 3-1 shows a hypothetical demand schedule for carrots.[2] It lists the quantity of carrots that would be demanded at various prices, given the assumption that all other variables are held constant. We should note in particular that average household income is assumed to be $50 000 per year because later we will want to see

---

[2] We realize that carrots are not a very exciting product to discuss, and many students wonder why we do not instead use MP3 players, restaurant meals, or cars as our hypothetical example. The model of demand and supply, however, best applies to products that are demanded by many consumers and supplied by many producers, each of which offers for sale a virtually identical ("homogeneous") version of the product. For this reason, we have chosen a simple agricultural product, but we could have illustrated the same principles with beef, wheat, copper, newsprint, oil, and a whole host of what economists call "commodities."

what happens when income changes. The table gives the quantities demanded for five selected prices, but in fact a separate quantity would be demanded at every possible price.

A second method of showing the relationship between quantity demanded and price is to draw a graph. The five price–quantity combinations shown in the table are plotted in Figure 3-1. Price is plotted on the vertical axis, and the quantity demanded is plotted on the horizontal axis.

The curve drawn through these points is called a **demand curve**. It shows the quantity that consumers would like to buy at each price. The negative slope of the curve indicates that the quantity demanded increases as the price falls. Each point on the demand curve indicates a single price–quantity combination. The demand curve as a whole shows something more.

demand curve The graphical representation of the relationship between quantity demanded and the price of a commodity, other things being equal.

> The demand curve represents the relationship between quantity demanded and price, other things being equal.

When economists speak of demand in a particular market, they are referring not just to the particular quantity being demanded at the moment (i.e., not just to one point on the demand curve) but to the entire demand curve—to the relationship between desired purchases and all the possible prices of the product.

The term **demand** therefore refers to the entire relationship between the quantity demanded of a product and the price of that product. In contrast, a single point on a demand schedule or curve is the quantity demanded at that point. This distinction between "demand" and "quantity demanded" is an extremely important one and we will examine it more closely later in this chapter.

demand The entire relationship between the quantity of a commodity that buyers want to purchase and the price of that commodity, other things being equal.

Shifts in the Demand Curve
The demand curve is drawn with the assumption that everything except the product's own price is being held constant. But what if other things change, as they often do? For example, consider an increase in average household income while price remains constant. If consumers spend some of their extra income on that product, the new quantity demanded cannot be represented by a point on the original demand curve. It must be represented on a new demand curve that is to the right of the old curve. Thus, a rise in income that causes more to be demanded *at each price* shifts the demand curve to the right, as shown in Figure 3-2. This shift illustrates the operation of an important general rule.

> A demand curve is drawn with the assumption that everything except the product's own price is held constant. A change in any of the variables previously held constant will shift the demand curve to a new position.

A demand curve can shift in two important ways. In the first case, more is desired at each price—the demand curve shifts rightward so that each price corresponds to a higher quantity than it did before. In the second case, less is desired at each price—the demand curve shifts leftward so that each price corresponds to a lower quantity than it did before.

We can assess the influence of changes in variables other than price by determining how changes in each variable shift the demand curve. A change will shift the demand curve to the right if it increases the amount that households want to buy at each price, other things remaining equal. It will shift the demand curve to the left if it decreases the amount that households want to buy at each price, other things remaining equal.

FIGURE 3-2   An Increase in the Demand for Carrots

Demand Schedules

Price ($ per tonne) p	Quantity Demanded (tonnes per year when average annual income is $50 000) D_0	Quantity Demanded (tonnes per year when average annual income is $60 000) D_1
20	110 U	140 U'
40	85 V	115 V'
60	65 W	95 W'
80	50 X	80 X'
100	40 Y	70 Y'

An increase in annual household income increases the quantity demanded at each price (for all normal goods). This is shown by the rightward shift in the demand curve, from D_0 to D_1. When average income rises from $50 000 to $60 000 per year, quantity demanded at a price of $60 per tonne rises from 65 tonnes per year to 95 tonnes per year. A similar rise occurs at every other price.

1. CONSUMERS' INCOME. If *average* income rises, consumers as a group can be expected to desire more of most products, other things being equal. Goods for which the quantity demanded increases when income rises are called *normal goods;* goods for which the quantity demanded falls when income rises are called *inferior goods.* The term *normal goods* reflects economists' empirical finding that the demand for most goods rises when income rises. We therefore expect that a rise in average consumer income shifts the demand curve for most products to the right, indicating that more will be demanded at any given price. Such a shift is illustrated in Figure 3-2.

A change in the *distribution* of income can also lead to changes in demand. In particular, a change in the distribution of income will cause an increase in the demand for products bought most by consumers whose incomes increase and a decrease in the demand for products bought most by consumers whose incomes decrease. If, for example, the government increases the child tax credit and at the same time raises basic tax rates, income will be transferred from households without children to households with children. Demands for products more heavily bought by persons without children will decline, while demands for products more heavily bought by households with children will increase.

2. PRICES OF OTHER GOODS. We saw that the negative slope of a product's demand curve occurs because the lower its price, the cheaper the product becomes relative to other products that can satisfy the same needs or desires. These other products are called **substitutes in consumption.** Another way for the same change to come about is that the price of the substitute product rises. For example, carrots can become cheap relative to broccoli either because the price of carrots falls or because the price of broccoli rises. Either change will increase the amount of carrots that consumers want to buy

substitutes in consumption Goods that can be used in place of another good to satisfy similar needs or desires.

as some consumers substitute away from broccoli and toward carrots. Thus, a rise in the price of a substitute for a product shifts the demand curve for the product to the right. More will be demanded at each price. For example, Coke and Pepsi are substitutes. If the price of Pepsi increases, the demand curve for Coke will shift to the right.

Complements in consumption are products that tend to be used jointly. Cars and gasoline are complements; so are CD players and speakers, golf clubs and golf balls, electric stoves and electricity, and airplane flights to Calgary and ski-lift tickets in Banff. Because complements tend to be consumed together, a fall in the price of one will increase the quantity demanded of *both* products. Thus, a fall in the price of a complement for a product will shift that product's demand curve to the right. More will be demanded at each price. For example, a fall in the price of airplane trips to Calgary will lead to a rise in the demand for ski-lift tickets in Banff, even though the price of those lift tickets is unchanged. (So the demand curve for ski-lift tickets will shift to the right.)

complements in consumption Goods that tend to be consumed together.

3. TASTES. Tastes have a powerful effect on people's desired purchases. A change in tastes may be long-lasting, such as the shift from typewriters to computers or from VCRs to DVD players, or it may be a short-lived fad as is common with many electronic games, such as the latest versions of Super Mario or Need for Speed. In either case, a change in tastes in favour of a product shifts the demand curve to the right. More will be demanded at each price. Of course, a change in tastes against some product has the opposite effect and shifts the demand curve to the left. Note that we include in "tastes" any changes in consumers' perception of quality of the product that may result from published research. For example, medical studies suggesting that drinking moderate amounts of red wine can have positive health effects may have contributed to an increase in demand for this product.

4. POPULATION. If there is an increase in population with purchasing power, the demands for all the products purchased by the new people will rise. Thus, we expect that an increase in population will shift the demand curves for most products to the right, indicating that more will be demanded at each price.

5. EXPECTATIONS ABOUT THE FUTURE. Our discussion has so far focused on how changes in the current value of variables may change demand. But it is also true that changes in people's *expectations about future values* of variables may change demand. For example, suppose you are thinking about buying a vacation property in a small town in Nova Scotia, and you have learned that in the near future a large high-tech firm will be moving its head office and several hundred employees to this same small town. Since their future movement into your town will probably increase the demand for housing and drive up the *future* price of houses, this expectation will lead you (and others like you) to increase your demand *today* so as to make the purchase before the price rises. Thus, the demand curve for houses will shift to the right today in anticipation of a future event.

Figure 3-3 summarizes the reasons that demand curves shift.

Movements Along the Curve Versus Shifts of the Whole Curve

Suppose you read in today's newspaper that a sharp increase in the world price of coffee beans has been caused by an increased worldwide demand for coffee. Then tomorrow you read that the rising price of coffee is reducing the typical consumer's purchases of coffee, as shoppers switch to other beverages. The two stories appear to contradict each other. The first associates a rising price with rising demand; the second associates a rising price with declining demand. Can both statements be true?

FIGURE 3-3   Shifts in the Demand Curve

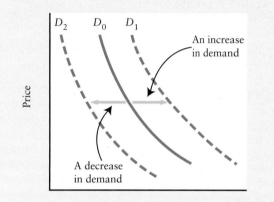

A rightward shift in the demand curve from D_0 to D_1 indicates an increase in demand; a leftward shift from D_0 to D_2 indicates a decrease in demand. An increase in demand means that more is demanded at each price. Such a rightward shift can be caused by a rise in income, a rise in the price of a substitute, a fall in the price of a complement, a change in tastes that favours that product, an increase in population, a redistribution of income toward groups that favour the product, or the anticipation of a future event that will increase the price.

A decrease in demand means that less is demanded at each price. Such a leftward shift can be caused by a fall in income, a fall in the price of a substitute, a rise in the price of a complement, a change in tastes that disfavours the product, a decrease in population, a redistribution of income away from groups that favour the product, or the anticipation of a future event that will decrease the price.

change in demand A change in the quantity demanded at each possible price of the commodity, represented by a shift in the whole demand curve.

change in quantity demanded A change in the specific quantity of the good demanded, represented by a change from one point on a demand curve to another point, either on the original demand curve or on a new one.

The answer is yes—because the two statements actually refer to different things. The first describes a shift in the demand curve; the second describes a movement along the demand curve in response to a change in price.

Consider first the statement that the increase in the price of coffee has been caused by an increased demand for coffee. This statement refers to a shift in the demand curve for coffee—in this case, a shift to the right, indicating more coffee demanded at each price. This shift, as we will see later in this chapter, will increase the price of coffee.

Now consider the second statement—that less coffee is being bought because of its rise in price. This refers to a movement along the *new* demand curve and reflects a change between two specific quantities demanded, one before the price increased and one afterward.

Possible explanations for the two stories are as follows:

1. A rise in population and income in coffee-drinking countries shifts the demand curve for coffee to the right. This, in turn, raises the price of coffee (for reasons we will soon study in detail). This was the first newspaper story.

2. The rising price of coffee is causing each individual household to cut back on its coffee purchases. The cutback is represented by an upward movement to the left along the new demand curve for coffee. This was the second newspaper story.

To prevent the type of confusion caused by our two newspaper stories, economists use a specialized vocabulary to distinguish between shifts of demand curves and movements along demand curves.

We have seen that "demand" refers to the *entire* demand curve, whereas "quantity demanded" refers to the quantity that is demanded at a specific price, as indicated by a particular *point* on the demand curve. Economists reserve the term **change in demand** to describe a change in the quantity demanded at *every* price. That is, a change in demand refers to a shift of the entire demand curve. The term **change in quantity demanded** refers to a movement from one point on a demand curve to another point, either on the same demand curve or on a new one.

> A change in quantity demanded can result from a shift in the demand curve with the price constant; from a movement along a given demand curve due to a change in the price; or from a combination of the two. [3]

We consider these three possibilities in turn.

An increase in demand means that the whole demand curve shifts to the right; a decrease in demand means that the whole demand curve shifts to the left. At any given price, an increase in demand causes an increase in quantity demanded, whereas a decrease in demand causes a decrease in quantity demanded. For example, in Figure 3-2 on page 54, the shift in the demand curve for carrots from D_0 to D_1 represents an increase in demand, and at a price of $40 per tonne, quantity demanded increases from 85 tonnes to 115 tonnes, as indicated by the move from V to V'.

A movement down and to the right along a demand curve represents an increase in quantity demanded; a movement up and to the left along a demand curve represents a decrease in quantity demanded. For example, in Figure 3-2, with the demand for carrots given by the curve D_1, an increase in price from $40 to $60 per tonne causes a movement along D_1 from V' to W', and quantity demanded decreases from 115 tonnes to 95 tonnes.

When there is a change in demand *and* a change in the price, the overall change in quantity demanded is the net effect of the shift in the demand curve and the movement along the new demand curve. Figure 3-4 shows the combined effect of an increase in demand, shown by a rightward shift in the whole demand curve, and an upward movement to the left along the new demand curve caused by an increase in price. The increase in demand causes an increase in quantity demanded at the initial price, whereas the movement along the new demand curve causes a decrease in the quantity demanded. Whether quantity demanded rises or falls overall depends on the relative magnitudes of these two changes.

FIGURE 3-4   Shifts of and Movements Along the Demand Curve

An increase in demand means that the demand curve shifts to the right, and hence quantity demanded will be higher at each price. A rise in price causes a movement upward and to the left along the demand curve, and hence quantity demanded will fall. The demand curve is originally D_0 and price is p_0, which means that quantity demanded is Q_0. Suppose demand increases to D_1, which means that at any particular price, there is a larger quantity demanded; for example, at p_0, quantity demanded is now Q_1. Now suppose the price rises above p_0. This causes a movement up and to the left along D_1, and quantity demanded falls below Q_1. As the figure is drawn, the quantity demanded at the new price p_2 is less than Q_1 but greater than Q_0. So in this case the combined effect of the increase in demand and the rise in price is an increase in quantity demanded from Q_0 to Q_2.

3.2 Supply

What determines the supply of any given product? Why do Canadian oil producers extract and sell more oil when the price of oil is high? Why do Canadian cattle ranchers raise and sell more beef when the price of cattle-feed falls? We start by developing a theory designed to explain the supply of some typical product.

Quantity Supplied

The amount of some good or service that producers want to sell in some time period is called the **quantity supplied** of that product. Quantity supplied is a flow; it is so much per unit of time. Note also that quantity supplied is the amount that producers

quantity supplied The amount of a commodity that producers want to sell during some time period.

A rise in the price of wheat, other things being equal, will lead farmers to plant less of other crops and plant more wheat.

are willing to offer for sale; it is not necessarily the amount that they succeed in selling, which is expressed by *quantity sold* or *quantity exchanged*.

As a general rule, any event that makes production of a specific product more profitable will lead firms to supply more of it. The quantity supplied of a product is influenced by the following key variables: [4]

- Product's own price
- Prices of inputs
- Technology
- Some government taxes or subsidies
- Prices of other products
- Number of suppliers

The situation with supply is the same as that with demand: There are several influencing variables, and we will not get far if we try to discover what happens when they all change at the same time. Again, we use the convenient *ceteris paribus* assumption to study the influence of the variables one at a time.

Quantity Supplied and Price

We begin by holding all other influences constant and ask, "How do we expect the total quantity of a product supplied to vary with its own price?"

> A basic hypothesis of economics is that the price of the product and the quantity supplied are related *positively*, other things being equal. That is, the higher the product's own price, the more its producers will supply; the lower the price, the less its producers will supply.

In later chapters we will derive this hypothesis as a prediction from more basic assumptions about the behaviour of individual profit-maximizing firms. For now we simply note that as the product's price rises, producing and selling this product becomes a more profitable activity. Firms interested in increasing their profit will therefore choose to increase their production.

Supply Schedules and Supply Curves

supply schedule A table showing the relationship between quantity supplied and the price of a commodity, other things being equal.

supply curve The graphical representation of the relationship between quantity supplied and the price of a commodity, other things being equal.

The general relationship just discussed can be illustrated by a **supply schedule**, which shows the relationship between quantity supplied of a product and the price of the product, other things being equal. The table in Figure 3-5 presents a hypothetical supply schedule for carrots.

A **supply curve**, the graphical representation of the supply schedule, is illustrated in Figure 3-5. Each point on the supply curve represents a specific price–quantity combination; however, the whole curve shows something more.

> The supply curve represents the relationship between quantity supplied and price, other things being equal; its positive slope indicates that quantity supplied increases when price increases.

FIGURE 3-5 The Supply of Carrots

A Supply Schedule for Carrots

Reference Point	Price ($ per tonne)	Quantity Supplied (tonnes per year)
u	20	20
v	40	45
w	60	65
x	80	80
y	100	95

A Supply Curve for Carrots

Both the table and the graph show the quantities that producers want to sell at various prices, *ceteris paribus*. For example, row *w* indicates that if the price of carrots were $60 per tonne, producers would want to sell 65 tonnes per year. The supply curve, labelled *S*, relates quantity of carrots supplied to the price of carrots; its positive slope indicates that quantity supplied increases as price increases.

When economists make statements about the conditions of supply, they are not referring just to the particular quantity being supplied at the moment—that is, not to just one point on the supply curve. Instead, they are referring to the entire supply curve, to the complete relationship between desired sales and all possible prices of the product.

Supply refers to the entire relationship between the quantity supplied of a product and the price of that product, other things being equal. A single point on the supply curve refers to the *quantity supplied* at that price.

Shifts in the Supply Curve
A shift in the supply curve means that at each price there is a change in the quantity supplied. An increase in the quantity supplied at each price is shown in Figure 3-6. This change appears as a rightward shift in the supply curve. In contrast, a decrease in the quantity supplied at each price would appear as a leftward shift. For supply, as for demand, there is an important general rule:

A change in any of the variables (other than the product's own price) that affects the quantity supplied will shift the supply curve to a new position.

Let's now consider the possible causes of shifts in supply curves.

1. PRICES OF INPUTS. All things that a firm uses to produce its outputs, such as materials, labour, and machines, are called the firm's *inputs*. Other things being equal, the higher the price of any input used to make a product, the less will be the profit from making that product. We expect, therefore, that the higher the price of any input used by a firm, the less the firm will produce and offer for sale at any given price of the

supply The entire relationship between the quantity of some commodity that producers wish to sell and the price of that commodity, other things being equal.

FIGURE 3-6   An Increase in the Supply of Carrots

Supply Schedules   Supply Curves

Price ($ per tonne) p	Quantity Supplied (tonnes per year before innovation) S_0	Quantity Supplied (tonnes per year after innovation) S_1
20	20 u	50 u'
40	45 v	75 v'
60	65 w	95 w'
80	80 x	110 x'
100	95 y	125 y'

A cost-saving innovation increases the quantity supplied at each price. This is shown by the rightward shift in the supply curve, from S_0 to S_1. As a result of a cost-saving innovation, the quantity that is supplied at a price of $100 per tonne rises from 95 to 125 tonnes per year. A similar rise occurs at every price.

product. A rise in the price of inputs therefore shifts the supply curve to the left, indicating that less will be supplied at any given price; a fall in the price of inputs makes production more profitable and therefore shifts the supply curve to the right.

2. TECHNOLOGY. At any time, what is produced and how it is produced depend on what is known. Over time, knowledge changes. The enormous increase in production per worker that has been going on in industrial societies for about 200 years is due largely to improved methods of production. The Industrial Revolution is more than a historical event; it is a present reality. Discoveries in chemistry have led to lower costs of production for well-established products, such as paints, and to a large variety of new products made of plastics and synthetic fibres. Such inventions as silicon chips have radically changed products, such as cell phones, computers, and televisions, and the consequent development of smaller computers has revolutionized the production and lowered the costs of countless other non-electronic products.

Any technological innovation that decreases the amount of inputs needed per unit of output reduces production costs and hence will increase the profits that can be earned at any given price of the product. Because increased profitability leads to increased willingness to produce, this change shifts the supply curve to the right.

For producers of agricultural products, extreme weather events are similar to a deterioration in technology because they reduce the amount of output that can be produced with a given amount of land, labour, and other inputs. Agricultural production generally depends on specific weather conditions, and extreme deviations from normal can lead to dramatic reductions in output. Droughts, floods, hurricanes, tornados, and early frosts are a few examples of extreme weather events that usually reduce the supply of agricultural products.

3. GOVERNMENT TAXES OR SUBSIDIES. We have just seen that anything increasing firms' costs will shift the supply curve to the left, and anything decreasing firms' costs will shift the supply curve to the right. As we will see in later chapters, governments often levy special taxes on the production of specific goods, such as gasoline, cigarettes, and alcohol. These taxes make the production and sale of these goods less profitable. The result is that the supply curve shifts to the left.

For other goods, governments often subsidize producers—that is, they pay producers a specific amount for each unit of the good produced. This often occurs for agricultural products, especially in the United States and the European Union. In such situations, the subsidy increases the profitability of production and shifts the supply curve to the right. For example, environmental concerns have led the U.S. and Canadian governments in recent years to provide subsidies for the production of biofuels. These subsidies have caused the supply curve for biofuels to shift to the right.

4. PRICES OF OTHER PRODUCTS. Changes in the price of one product may lead to changes in the supply of some other product because the two products are either *substitutes* or *complements* in the production process.

A prairie farmer, for example, can plant his field in wheat or oats. If the market price of oats falls, thus making oat production less profitable, the farmer will be more inclined to plant wheat. In this case, wheat and oats are said to be *substitutes* in production—for every extra hectare planted in one crop, one fewer hectare can be planted in the other. In this example, a reduction in the price of oats leads to an increase in the supply of wheat.

An excellent example in which two products are *complements* in production is oil and natural gas, which are often found together below Earth's surface. If the market price of natural gas rises, producers will do more drilling and increase their production of natural gas. But as more wells are drilled, the usual outcome is that more of *both* natural gas and oil are discovered and then produced. Thus, the rise in the price of natural gas leads to an increase in the supply of the complementary product—oil.

5. NUMBER OF SUPPLIERS. For given prices and technology, the total amount of any product supplied depends on the number of firms producing that product and offering it for sale. If profits are being earned by current firms, then more firms will choose to enter this industry and begin producing. The effect of this increase in the number of suppliers is to shift the supply curve to the right. Similarly, if the existing firms are losing money, they will eventually leave the industry; such a reduction in the number of suppliers shifts the supply curve to the left.

Movements Along the Curve Versus Shifts of the Whole Curve

As with demand, it is important to distinguish movements along supply curves from shifts of the whole curve. Economists reserve the term **change in supply** to describe a shift of the whole supply curve—that is, a change in the quantity that will be supplied at every price. The term **change in quantity supplied** refers to a movement from one point on a supply curve to another point, either on the same supply curve or on a new one. In other words, an increase in supply means that the whole supply curve has shifted to the right, so that the quantity supplied at any given price has increased; a movement up and to the right along a supply curve indicates an increase in the quantity supplied in response to an increase in the price of the product.

> A change in quantity supplied can result from a change in supply, with the price constant; a movement along a given supply curve because of a change in the price; or a combination of the two.

change in supply A change in the quantity supplied at each possible price of the commodity, represented by a shift in the whole supply curve.

change in quantity supplied A change in the specific quantity supplied, represented by a change from one point on a supply curve to another point, either on the original supply curve or on a new one.

Practise with Study Guide
Chapter 3, Exercise 4.

An exercise you might find useful is to construct a diagram similar to Figure 3-4 (see page 57), emphasizing the difference between a shift of the supply curve and a movement along the supply curve.

3.3 The Determination of Price

So far we have considered demand and supply separately. We now come to a key question: How do the two forces of demand and supply interact to determine price?

The Concept of a Market

Originally the term *market* designated a physical place where products were bought and sold. We still use the term this way to describe such places as Granville Island Market in Vancouver, Kensington Market in Toronto, or Jean Talon Market in Montreal. Once developed, however, theories of market behaviour were easily extended to cover products, such as wheat or oil, which can be purchased anywhere in the world at a price that tends to be uniform the world over. Today we can also buy and sell items in markets that exist in cyberspace—consider the online auction services provided by eBay—thus extending our viewpoint well beyond the idea of a single place to which consumers go to buy something.

For present purposes, a **market** may be defined as existing in any situation (such as a physical place or an electronic medium) in which buyers and sellers negotiate the exchange of some product or related group of products.

Individual markets differ in the degree of *competition* among the various buyers and sellers. In the next few chapters we will examine markets in which the number of buyers and sellers is sufficiently large that no one of them has any appreciable influence on the market price. This is a rough definition of what economists call *perfectly competitive markets*. Starting in Chapter 10, we will consider the behaviour of markets in which there are small numbers of either sellers or buyers. But our initial theory of markets, based on the interaction of demand and supply, will be a very good description of the markets for such things as wheat, pork, newsprint, coffee, copper, oil, and many other commodities.

market Any situation in which buyers and sellers can negotiate the exchange of goods or services.

excess demand

A situation in which, at the given price, quantity demanded exceeds quantity supplied.

eBay brings together buyers and sellers of thousands of different goods and services. It thus creates markets that exist only on the Internet.

Graphical Analysis of a Market

The table in Figure 3-7 brings together the demand and supply schedules from Figures 3-1 and 3-5. The quantities of carrots demanded and supplied at each price can now be compared.

There is only one price, $60 per tonne, at which the quantity of carrots demanded equals the quantity supplied. At prices less than $60 per tonne, there is a shortage of carrots because the quantity demanded exceeds the quantity supplied. This is a situation of **excess demand**. At prices greater than $60 per tonne, there is a surplus of carrots because the quantity supplied exceeds the quantity demanded. This is a situation of

FIGURE 3-7   Determination of the Equilibrium Price of Carrots

Demand and Supply Schedules

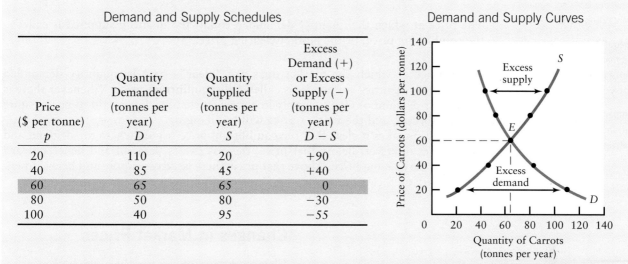

Price ($ per tonne) p	Quantity Demanded (tonnes per year) D	Quantity Supplied (tonnes per year) S	Excess Demand (+) or Excess Supply (−) (tonnes per year) D − S
20	110	20	+90
40	85	45	+40
60	65	65	0
80	50	80	−30
100	40	95	−55

The equilibrium price corresponds to the intersection of the demand and supply curves. At any price above $60, there is excess supply and thus downward pressure on price. At any price below $60, there is excess demand and thus upward pressure on price. Only at a price of $60 is there no pressure for price to change. Equilibrium occurs at point *E*, at a price of $60.

excess supply. This same story can also be told in graphical terms. The quantities demanded and supplied at any price can be read off the two curves; the excess supply or excess demand is shown by the horizontal distance between the curves at each price.

To examine the determination of market price, let's suppose first that the price is $100 per tonne. At this price, 95 tonnes are offered for sale, but only 40 tonnes are demanded. There is an excess supply of 55 tonnes per year. Sellers are then likely to cut their prices to get rid of this surplus. And purchasers, observing the stock of unsold carrots, will begin to offer less money for the product. In other words, *excess supply causes downward pressure on price.*

Now consider the price of $20 per tonne. At this price, there is excess demand. The 20 tonnes produced each year are snapped up quickly, and 90 tonnes of desired purchases cannot be made. Rivalry between would-be purchasers may lead them to offer more than the prevailing price to outbid other purchasers. Also, sellers may begin to ask a higher price for the quantities that they do have to sell. In other words, *excess demand causes upward pressure on price.*

Finally, consider the price of $60. At this price, producers want to sell 65 tonnes per year, and purchasers want to buy that same quantity. There is neither a shortage nor a surplus of carrots. There are no unsatisfied buyers to bid the price up, nor are there unsatisfied sellers to force the price down. Once the price of $60 has been reached, therefore, there will be no tendency for it to change.

Equilibrium implies a state of rest, or balance, between opposing forces. The **equilibrium price** is the one toward which the actual market price will tend. Once

excess supply A situation in which, at the given price, quantity supplied exceeds quantity demanded.

equilibrium price The price at which quantity demanded equals quantity supplied. Also called the market-clearing price.

disequilibrium price
A price at which quantity demanded does not equal quantity supplied.

disequilibrium A situation in a market in which there is excess demand or excess supply.

comparative statics The derivation of predictions by analyzing the effect of a change in some exogenous variable on the equilibrium.

established, it will persist until it is disturbed by some change in market conditions that shifts the demand curve, the supply curve, or both.

> The price at which the quantity demanded equals the quantity supplied is called the equilibrium price, or the market-clearing price. [5]

Any price at which the market does not "clear"—that is, quantity demanded does not equal quantity supplied—is called a **disequilibrium price**. Whenever there is either excess demand or excess supply in a market, that market is said to be in a state of **disequilibrium**, and the market price will be changing.

Figure 3-7 makes it clear that the equilibrium price occurs where the demand and supply curves intersect. Below that price, there is excess demand and hence upward pressure on the existing price. Above that price, there is excess supply and hence downward pressure on the existing price.[3]

CLOSING PRICES (SPOT)					
	Price	**Chg**		**Price**	**Chg**
Oil Texas US$/bbl	66.94	−2.62	**Pulp** NBSK US$/metric ton	654.88	0.00
Nat. Gas Henry Hub US$ mmbtu	4.02	−0.03	**Wheat** DK N. Spr US$ bshl	7.78	−0.14
Nat. Gas AECO C C$/gigajoule	3.13	−0.23	**Lumber** KD W. S-P-F, Mill US$	200.00	5.00
Gold US$/troy ounce	922.30	−12.90	**Framing Lumber** Composite	229.00	7.00
Silver US$/troy ounce	13.76	−0.45	**Corn** Ont. C$ tonne	161.51	−5.51
Zinc US$/lb	0.67	−0.03	**Feed Barley** Lthbrdge C$ tonne	187.00	0.00
Aluminum US$/lb	0.70	−0.05	**Feed Wheat** Thndr Bay C$ tonne	214.00	0.00
Copper US$/lb	2.14	−0.12	**Soybeans** Ont. #2 C$ tonne	467.01	−9.19
Lead US$/lb	0.72	−0.04	**Canola** InStore Van C$ tonne	498.10	−5.70

Many commodities are bought and sold every day on world markets, with prices that fluctuate frequently because of changes in the conditions of demand and supply.

Changes in Market Prices

Changes in any of the variables, other than price, that influence quantity demanded or supplied will cause a shift in the demand curve, the supply curve, or both. There are four possible shifts: an increase in demand (a rightward shift in the demand curve), a decrease in demand (a leftward shift in the demand curve), an increase in supply (a rightward shift in the supply curve), and a decrease in supply (a leftward shift in the supply curve).

To discover the effects of each of the possible curve shifts, we use the method known as **comparative statics**.[4] With this method, we derive predictions about how the *endogenous* variables (equilibrium price and quantity) will change following a change in some *exogenous* variable (the variables whose changes cause shifts in the demand and supply curves). We start from a position of equilibrium and then introduce the change to be studied. We then determine the new equilibrium position and compare it with the original one. The difference between the two positions of equilibrium must result from the change that was introduced, because everything else has been held constant.

---

[3] When economists graph a demand (or supply) curve, they put the variable to be explained (the dependent variable) on the horizontal axis and the explanatory variable (the independent variable) on the vertical axis. This is "backward" to what is usually done in mathematics. The rational explanation of what is now economists' odd practice is buried in the history of economics and dates back to Alfred Marshall's *Principles of Economics* (1890) [6]. For better or worse, Marshall's scheme is now used by all economists, although mathematicians never fail to wonder at this example of the odd ways of economists.

[4] The term *static* is used because we are not concerned with the actual path by which the market goes from the first equilibrium position to the second or with the time taken to reach the second equilibrium. Analysis of these movements would be described as *dynamic analysis*.

FIGURE 3-8   Shifts in Demand and Supply Curves

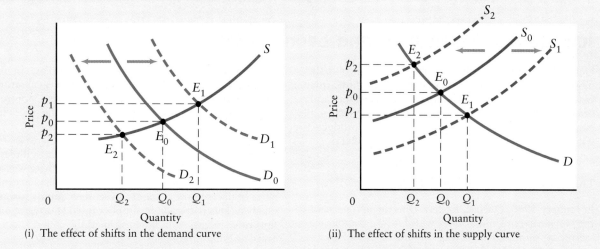

(i) The effect of shifts in the demand curve

(ii) The effect of shifts in the supply curve

Shifts in either demand or supply curves will generally lead to changes in equilibrium price and quantity. In part (i), suppose the original demand and supply curves are D_0 and S, which intersect to produce equilibrium at E_0, with a price of p_0 and a quantity of Q_0. An increase in demand shifts the demand curve to D_1, taking the new equilibrium to E_1. Price rises to p_1 and quantity rises to Q_1. Starting at E_0, a decrease in demand shifts the demand curve to D_2, taking the new equilibrium to E_2. Price falls to p_2 and quantity falls to Q_2.

In part (ii), the original demand and supply curves are D and S_0, which intersect to produce equilibrium at E_0, with a price of p_0 and a quantity of Q_0. An increase in supply shifts the supply curve to S_1, taking the new equilibrium to E_1. Price falls to p_1 and quantity rises to Q_1. Starting at E_0, a decrease in supply shifts the supply curve from S_0 to S_2, taking the new equilibrium to E_2. Price rises to p_2 and quantity falls to Q_2.

The changes caused by each of the four possible curve shifts are shown in Figure 3-8. Study the figure carefully. Previously, we had given the axes specific labels, but because it is now intended to apply to any product, the horizontal axis is simply labelled "Quantity." This means quantity per period in whatever units output is measured. "Price," the vertical axis, means the price measured as dollars per unit of quantity for the same product.

The effects of the four possible curve shifts are as follows:

1. An increase in demand causes an increase in both the equilibrium price and the equilibrium quantity exchanged.

2. A decrease in demand causes a decrease in both the equilibrium price and the equilibrium quantity exchanged.

3. An increase in supply causes a decrease in the equilibrium price and an increase in the equilibrium quantity exchanged.

4. A decrease in supply causes an increase in the equilibrium price and a decrease in the equilibrium quantity exchanged.

LESSONS FROM HISTORY 3-1

Ice Storms, Hurricanes, and Economics

Here are two simple examples of the demand and supply model in action. Both examples show how the weather—something that changes in unpredictable and often dramatic ways—can have significant effects on either the demand or the supply of various products, with obvious implications for the observed market price.

The Weather and a Demand Shock

In January 1998, Quebec, Eastern Ontario, and parts of the Northeastern United States were hit by a massive ice storm. So unprecedented was this storm in its magnitude that many electric power systems were devastated. Homes and businesses in the Montreal area went without power for as long as four weeks.

This electric power shortage had many economic effects, including lost factory production, damage to many businesses, the death of farm livestock, and the displacement of thousands of people into shelters. Another effect of the power shortage, as soon as it became clear that it would last for more than just a few

hours, was a sudden and substantial increase in the demand for portable gas-powered electric generators. Within just a few days, all stores in the greater Montreal area were sold out of such generators, and the prices for newly ordered units increased sharply.

Furthermore, the shortages and price increases for electric generators were not confined to the area directly hit by the ice storm. As it became clear that there was an excess demand for generators in Quebec, sellers in other parts of the country began to divert their supply toward Quebec. This reduction in supply caused shortages, and thus price increases, in other parts of the country, as far away as Edmonton.

The Weather and a Supply Shock

In late August 2005, Hurricane Katrina emerged from the Caribbean, gathered strength as it crossed the Gulf of Mexico, and unleashed its fury on New Orleans, Louisiana. The damage to New Orleans was massive, especially after the levee holding back Lake Pontchartrain

Practise with Study Guide
Chapter 3, Exercise 3 and
Short-Answer Question 4.

Demonstrations of these effects are given in the caption to Figure 3-8. The intuitive reasoning behind each is as follows:

1. **An increase in demand (the demand curve shifts to the right).** An increase in demand creates a shortage at the initial equilibrium price, and the unsatisfied buyers bid up the price. This rise in price causes a larger quantity to be supplied, with the result that at the new equilibrium more is exchanged at a higher price.

2. **A decrease in demand (the demand curve shifts to the left).** A decrease in demand creates a surplus at the initial equilibrium price, and the unsuccessful sellers bid the price down. As a result, less of the product is supplied and offered for sale. At the new equilibrium, both price and quantity exchanged are lower than they were originally.

3. **An increase in supply (the supply curve shifts to the right).** An increase in supply creates a surplus at the initial equilibrium price, and the unsuccessful suppliers force the price down. This drop in price increases the quantity demanded, and the new equilibrium is at a lower price and a higher quantity exchanged.

4. **A decrease in supply (the supply curve shifts to the left).** A decrease in supply creates a shortage at the initial equilibrium price that causes the price to be bid up. This rise in price reduces the quantity demanded, and the new equilibrium is at a higher price and a lower quantity exchanged.

broke, and much of the city was flooded. Katrina was the worst natural disaster in U.S. history; the cost of the damage to buildings, bridges, houses, and other infrastructure was estimated to be close to U.S.$125 billion.

Hurricane Katrina had an instant effect on the world market for oil. Over short periods of time, the world demand curve for oil is relatively steep, reflecting the fact that users of oil initially reduce their purchases only slightly when the price rises.

Hurricane Katrina interrupted the local production and distribution of oil, thereby causing a temporary reduction in world supply. Several large oilrigs in the Gulf of Mexico were damaged and were shut down or operating well below their capacity for several weeks. In addition, the major pipelines that transport this oil from the Gulf ports to the inland refineries were also seriously damaged. For both reasons, the supply curve for oil shifted to the left. And given the relatively steep demand curve, this reduction in supply caused a sharp increase in the equilibrium price. The price per barrel of oil, which had averaged roughly U.S.$40 earlier that year, reached U.S.$70 on August 29, and stayed above U.S.$65 for about a month. As the rigs and pipelines were repaired, and Gulf-area oil production began to

Hurricane Katrina in August 2005 damaged several oil platforms operating in the Gulf of Mexico and thus caused a temporary reduction in the supply of oil.

approach its pre-Katrina levels, the supply curve shifted back to the right and the price returned to levels between U.S.$55 and U.S.$60 per barrel.

✗ myeconlab   ADDITIONAL TOPICS

Economists often use data from market transactions to estimate demand and supply relationships. This is a difficult exercise, however, because the demand and supply curves in any given market are often shifting at the same time. To learn more about what is needed to identify a demand or supply curve by using real-world data, look for **Economic Data and the Identification Problem** in the *Additional Topics* section of this book's MyEconLab.

www.myeconlab.com

By using the tools we have learned in this chapter, we can link many real-world events that cause demand or supply curves to shift with changes in market prices and quantities. *Lessons from History 3-1* shows how we can use demand-and-supply analysis to examine the effects of two real-world weather shocks: Quebec's 1998 ice storm and Hurricane Katrina in 2005.

Our discussion of demand, supply, and equilibrium has explained why equilibrium price and quantity are found at the intersection of the demand and supply curves. And we have shown diagrams (Figures 3-7 and 3-8) illustrating this in the general case. But we have not presented a specific example of demand and supply and "solved" precisely for the equilibrium price and quantity. This is a useful exercise but requires some algebra. See *Extensions in Theory 3-2* for an algebraic solution to a specific model of demand and supply.

Practise with Study Guide Chapter 3, Exercise 5 and Extension Exercise E1.

EXTENSIONS IN THEORY 3-2

The Algebra of Market Equilibrium

This box presents an algebraic model of demand and supply and the method for determining the equilibrium price and quantity. For simplicity, we assume that the demand and supply curves are linear relationships between price and quantity.

Consider the following demand and supply curves:

Demand: $Q^D = a - bp$
Supply: $Q^S = c + dp$

where p is the price, Q^D is quantity demanded, Q^S is quantity supplied, and a, b, c, and d are positive constants. Both relationships are plotted in the accompanying figure.

What is the interpretation of the demand curve and how do we plot it? First, at a price of zero, consumers will buy a units—this is the horizontal intercept of the demand curve. Second, at a price of a/b, consumers will buy zero units, so a/b is the vertical intercept of the demand curve. Finally, the slope of the demand curve is $-1/b$; the quantity demanded increases by b units for every \$1 that price falls.

What is the interpretation of the supply curve, and how do we plot it? First, if the price is zero, suppliers will sell c units—this is the horizontal intercept of the supply curve. Second, for every \$1 increase in price, the quantity supplied increases by d units. Thus, the slope of the supply curve is $1/d$.

Given these demand and supply curves, the market equilibrium can be determined in two ways. The first is to construct a scale diagram and plot the two curves accurately. If you do this carefully, you will be able to read the equilibrium price and quantity off the diagram.

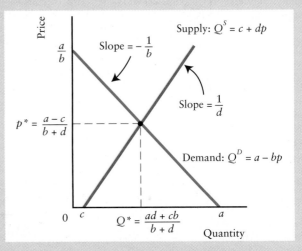

But your diagram will have to be very accurate for this to work!

A more precise method is to use algebra to solve for the equilibrium price and quantity. Here is how we do it. We know that in equilibrium quantity demanded equals quantity supplied, or $Q^D = Q^S$. We call the equilibrium quantity Q^*. But we also know that in equilibrium the price paid by the consumers will equal the price received by the producers—that is, there is only one equilibrium price, which we call p^*. Putting these two facts together we know that in equilibrium

Demand: $Q^* = a - bp^*$
Supply: $Q^* = c + dp^*$

Relative Prices and Inflation

The theory we have developed explains how individual prices are determined by the forces of demand and supply. To facilitate matters, we have made *ceteris paribus* assumptions. Specifically, we have assumed the constancy of all prices except the one we are studying. Does this mean that our theory is inapplicable to an inflationary world in which all prices are rising at the same time? Fortunately, the answer is no.

The price of a product is the amount of money that must be spent to acquire one unit of that product. This is called the **absolute price** or *money price*. A **relative price** is the ratio of two absolute prices; it expresses the price of one good in terms of (relative to) another.

We now have two equations and two unknown variables (p^* and Q^*) and can proceed to solve the system of equations. Since Q^* from the demand curve equals Q^* from the supply curve, it follows that

$$a - bp^* = c + dp^*$$

This implies

$$a - c = (b + d)p^*$$

which can be solved for p^* to get

$$p^* = \frac{a - c}{b + d}$$

This is the solution for the equilibrium market price. By substituting this value of p^* back into *either* the demand curve or the supply curve (it doesn't matter which), we get the solution for Q^*:

$$Q^* = a - bp^* = a - \frac{b(a - c)}{(b + d)}$$

which can be simplified to be

$$Q^* = \frac{a(b + d)}{(b + d)} - \frac{b(a - c)}{(b + d)}$$

which can be further simplified to be

$$Q^* = \frac{(ad + bc)}{b + d}$$

We now have the precise solutions for the equilibrium price and quantity in this market. Notice that the solutions for p^* and Q^* naturally depend on those (exogenous) variables that shift the demand and supply curves. For example, an increase in demand for the product would be reflected by an increase in a. This would shift the demand curve to the right, increasing both p^* and Q^*. A decrease in supply would have a different effect. It would be reflected by a decrease in c that would shift the supply curve to the left, leading to an increase in p^* and a reduction in Q^*.

Now let's do the same thing but with even more specific demand and supply curves. Suppose we have the following relationships:

$$Q^D = 18 - 3p$$
$$Q^S = 2 + 5p$$

The equilibrium condition is that $Q^D = Q^S = Q^*$. And when quantity is equal to Q^*, price will be equal to p^*. Thus, in equilibrium we will have

$$Q^* = 18 - 3p^*$$
$$Q^* = 2 + 5p^*$$

Since Q^* from the demand curve obviously equals Q^* from the supply curve, we have

$$18 - 3p^* = 2 + 5p^*$$

which can be solved for p^* to get

$$8p^* = 16$$
$$p^* = 2$$

Putting this value of p^* back into the demand curve we get

$$Q^* = 18 - 3(2)$$
$$Q^* = 12$$

We have therefore solved for the equilibrium price and quantity in this specific numerical model of demand and supply.

Mastering the algebra of demand and supply takes a little practice, but is worth the effort. If you would like to practise, try the Study Exercises at the end of the chapter (and Chapters 4 and 5) that deal with the algebra of demand and supply.

We have been reminded several times that what matters for demand and supply is the price of the product in question *relative to the prices of other products;* that is, what matters is the relative price. For example, if the price of carrots rises while the prices of other vegetables are constant, we expect consumers to reduce their quantity demanded of carrots as they substitute toward the consumption of other vegetables. In this case, the *relative* price of carrots has increased. But if the prices of carrots and all other vegetables are rising at the same rate, the relative price of carrots is constant. In this case we expect no substitution to take place between carrots and other vegetables.

In an inflationary world, we are often interested in the price of a given product as it relates to the average price of all other products. If, during a period when all prices were increasing by an average of 5 percent, the price of coffee increased by 30 percent, then the price of coffee increased relative to the prices of other goods as a whole. Coffee became *relatively* expensive. However, if coffee had increased in price by 30 percent when other prices increased by 40 percent, then the relative price of coffee would have fallen. Although the money price of coffee increased substantially, coffee became *relatively* cheap.

In this chapter we have been assuming that changes in a particular price occur when all other prices are constant. We can easily extend the analysis to an inflationary setting by remembering that any force that raises the price of one product when other prices remain constant will, given general inflation, raise the price of that product faster than the price level is rising. For example, consider a change in tastes in favour of carrots that raises their price by 5 percent when other prices are constant. The same change would raise their price by 8 percent if, at the same time, the general price level were rising by 3 percent. In each case, the price of carrots rises 5 percent *relative to the average of all prices*.

> In microeconomics, whenever we refer to a change in the price of one product, we mean a change in that product's relative price; that is, a change in the price of that product relative to the prices of all other goods.

myeconlab ADDITIONAL TOPICS

The world price of oil increased from about U.S.$15 per barrel in 1998 to more than U.S.$100 in 2008. For more details on the many recent developments in the world oil market, including the role of various geopolitical tensions, look for **A Primer on the Market for Crude Oil** in the *Additional Topics* section of this book's MyEconLab.

www.myeconlab.com

Summary

3.1 Demand

- The amount of a product that consumers want to purchase is called *quantity demanded*. It is a flow expressed as so much per period of time. It is determined by tastes, income, the product's own price, the prices of other products, the size of the population, and expectations about the future.
- The relationship between quantity demanded and price is represented graphically by a demand curve that shows how much will be demanded at each market price. Quantity demanded is assumed to increase as the price of the product falls, other things held constant. Thus, demand curves are negatively sloped.

- A shift in a demand curve represents a change in the quantity demanded at each price and is referred to as a *change in demand*.
- An increase in demand means the demand curve shifts to the right; a decrease in demand means the demand curve shifts to the left.
- It is important to make the distinction between a movement along a demand curve (caused by a change in the product's price) and a shift of a demand curve (caused by a change in any of the other determinants of demand).

3.2 Supply

LO ③ ④

- The amount of a good that producers wish to sell is called *quantity supplied*. It is a flow expressed as so much per period of time. It depends on the product's own price, the costs of inputs, the number of suppliers, government taxes or subsidies, the state of technology, and prices of other products.
- The relationship between quantity supplied and price is represented graphically by a supply curve that shows how much will be supplied at each market price. Quantity supplied is assumed to increase as the price of the product increases, other things held constant. Thus, supply curves are positively sloped.

- A shift in the supply curve indicates a change in the quantity supplied at each price and is referred to as a *change in supply*.
- An increase in supply means the supply curve shifts to the right; a decrease in supply means the supply curve shifts to the left.
- It is important to make the distinction between a movement along a supply curve (caused by a change in the product's price) and a shift of a supply curve (caused by a change in any of the other determinants of supply).

3.3 The Determination of Price

LO ⑤

- The *equilibrium price* is the price at which the quantity demanded equals the quantity supplied. At any price below equilibrium, there will be excess demand; at any price above equilibrium, there will be excess supply. Graphically, equilibrium occurs where the demand and supply curves intersect.
- Price rises when there is excess demand and falls when there is excess supply. Thus, the actual market price will be pushed toward the equilibrium price. When it is reached, there will be neither excess demand nor excess supply, and the price will not change until either the supply curve or the demand curve shifts.
- By using the method of *comparative statics*, we can determine the effects of a shift in either demand or

supply. An increase in demand raises both equilibrium price and equilibrium quantity; a decrease in demand lowers both. An increase in supply raises equilibrium quantity but lowers equilibrium price; a decrease in supply lowers equilibrium quantity but raises equilibrium price.
- The absolute price of a product is its price in terms of money; its relative price is its price in relation to other products. In an inflationary period, a rise in the *relative price* of one product means that its absolute price rises by more than the average of all prices; a fall in its relative price means that its absolute price rises by less than the average of all prices.

Key Concepts

Stock and flow variables
Ceteris paribus or "other things being equal"
Quantity demanded
Demand schedule and demand curve

Change in quantity demanded versus change in demand
Quantity supplied
Supply schedule and supply curve
Change in quantity supplied versus change in supply

Equilibrium, equilibrium price, and disequilibrium
Comparative statics
Relative price

Study Exercises

SAVE TIME. IMPROVE RESULTS.

Visit MyEconLab to practise Study Exercises and prepare for tests and exams. MyEconLab also offers a variety of other study tools to help you succeed.

www.myeconlab.com

1. Fill in the blanks to complete the statements about a supply-and-demand model, as applied in the following situations.

   a. Consider the market for cement in Toronto. If, *ceteris paribus*, half the producers in this market shut down, the _____ curve for cement will shift to the _____, indicating a(n) _____ in _____.

   b. Consider the market for Canadian softwood lumber (a normal good). If, *ceteris paribus*, average incomes in both Canada and the United States rise over several years, the _____ curve for lumber will shift to the _____, indicating a(n) _____ in _____.

   c. Consider the market for Quebec artisanal cheeses. If, *ceteris paribus*, the price of imported cheeses from France rises significantly, the _____ curve for Quebec cheeses will shift to the _____, indicating a(n) _____ in _____.

   d. Consider the market for milk in the United States. If *ceteris paribus*, the U.S. government decreases subsidies to dairy farmers, the _____ curve for milk will shift to the _____, indicating a(n) _____ in _____.

   e. Consider the world market for shipping containers. If, *ceteris paribus*, the price of steel (a major input) rises, the _____ curve for shipping containers will shift to the _____, indicating a(n) _____ in _____.

   f. Consider the market for hot dog buns. If, *ceteris paribus*, the price of wieners doubles, the _____ curve for hot dog buns will shift to the _____, indicating a(n) _____ in _____.

2. The following table shows hypothetical demand schedules for sugar for three separate months. To help make the distinction between changes in demand and changes in quantity demanded, choose the wording to make each of the following statements correct.

Quantity Demanded for Sugar (in kilograms)			
Price/kg	October	November	December
$1.50	11 000	10 500	13 000
1.75	10 000	9 500	12 000
2.00	9 000	8 500	11 000
2.25	8 000	7 500	10 000
2.50	7 000	6 500	9 000
2.75	6 000	5 500	8 000
3.00	5 000	4 500	7 000
3.25	4 000	3 500	6 000
3.50	3 000	2 500	5 000

   a. When the price of sugar rises from $2.50 to $3.00 in the month of October there is a(n) (*increase/ decrease*) in (*demand for/quantity demanded of*) sugar of 2000 kg.

   b. We can say that the demand curve for sugar in December shifted (*to the right/to the left*) of November's demand curve. This represents a(n) (*increase/decrease*) in demand for sugar.

   c. An increase in the demand for sugar means that quantity demanded at each price has (*increased/ decreased*), while a decrease in demand for sugar means that quantity demanded at each price has (*increased/decreased*).

   d. In the month of December, a price change for sugar from $3.50 to $2.75 per kilogram would mean a change in (*demand for/quantity demanded of*) sugar of 3000 kg.

   e. Plot the three demand schedules on a graph and label each demand curve to indicate whether it is the demand for October, November, or December.

3. For each of the following statements, determine whether there has been a change in supply or a change in quantity supplied. Draw a demand and supply diagram for each situation to show either a movement along the supply curve or a shift of the supply curve.

   a. The price of Canadian-grown peaches skyrockets during an unusually cold summer that reduces the size of the peach harvest.

   b. An increase in income leads to an increase in the price of beef and also to an increase in beef sales.

   c. Technological improvements in the microchip lead to price reductions for laptop computers and an increase in computer sales.

   d. Greater awareness of the health risks from smoking lead to a reduction in the price of cigarettes and to fewer cigarettes being sold.

4. The following diagram describes the hypothetical demand and supply for tuna in Canada in 2010.

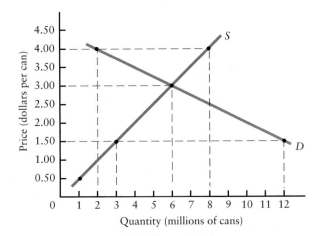

   a. Suppose the price of a can of tuna is $4.00. What is the quantity demanded? What is the quantity supplied? At this price, is there a shortage or a surplus? By what amount?

b. Suppose the price of a can of tuna is $1.50. What is the quantity demanded? What is the quantity supplied? At this price, is there a shortage or a surplus? By what amount?

c. What is the equilibrium price and quantity in this market?

5. Consider households' demand for chicken meat. For each of the events listed below, state and explain the likely effect on the demand for chicken. How would each event be illustrated in a diagram?

a. A medical study reports that eating chicken reduces the likelihood of suffering from particular types of heart problems.

b. A widespread bovine disease leads to an increase in the price of beef.

c. An increase in average household income.

6. Consider the world market for a particular quality of coffee beans. The following table shows the demand and supply schedules for this market.

Price (per kilogram)	Quantity Demanded (millions of kilograms per year)	Quantity Supplied
$2.00	28	10
$2.40	26	12
$3.10	22	13.5
$3.50	19.5	19.5
$3.90	17	22
$4.30	14.5	23.5

a. Plot the demand and supply schedules on a diagram.

b. Identify the amount of excess demand or supply associated with each price.

c. Identify the equilibrium price in this market.

d. Suppose that a collection of national governments were somehow able to set a minimum price for coffee equal to $3.90 per kilogram. Explain the outcome in the world coffee market.

7. Consider the supply for Grade A beef. As the price of beef rises, ranchers will tend to sell more cattle to the slaughterhouses. Yet a central prediction from the supply-and-demand model of this chapter is that an increase in the supply of beef reduces the equilibrium price. Reconcile the apparent contradiction. Use a diagram to do so.

8. Consider the world market for wheat. Suppose there is a major failure in Russia's wheat crop because of a severe drought. Explain the likely effect on the equilibrium price and quantity in the world wheat market. Also explain why Canadian wheat farmers certainly benefit from Russia's drought. The diagrams below provide a starting point for your analysis.

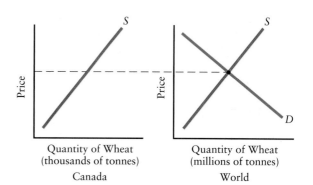

Quantity of Wheat
(thousands of tonnes)
Canada

Quantity of Wheat
(millions of tonnes)
World

9. The *New York Times* recently stated:

While the world's appetite for chocolate grows more voracious each year, cocoa farms around the globe are failing, under siege from fungal and viral diseases and insects. . . . Researchers predict a shortfall in beans from the cacao tree, the raw material from which chocolate is made, in as little as five to ten years.

Describe in terms of the supply-and-demand apparatus what is described in the quote. What is the implied prediction for the equilibrium price of chocolate? What is the implied prediction for the equilibrium quantity of chocolate?

10. This is a challenging question and is similar to the example shown in *Extensions in Theory 3-2* on page 68. It requires you to solve a supply-and-demand model as a system of *simultaneous equations* (meaning simply that both equations apply at the same time). Letting p be the price of the product, suppose the demand and supply functions for some product are given by

$$Q^D = 100 - 3p$$
$$Q^S = 10 + 2p$$

a. Plot both the demand curve and the supply curve.

b. What is the condition for equilibrium in this market?

c. By imposing the condition for equilibrium, solve for the equilibrium price.

d. Substitute the equilibrium price into either the demand or the supply function to solve for the equilibrium quantity. Check to make sure you get the same answer whether you use the demand function or the supply function.

e. Now suppose there is an increase in demand so that the new demand function is given by

$$Q^D = 180 - 3p$$

Compute the new equilibrium price and quantity. Is your result consistent with the "law" of demand?

f. Now suppose that, with the new demand curve in place, there is an increase in supply so that the new supply function is given by $Q^S = 90 + 2p$. Compute the new equilibrium price and quantity. Is your result consistent with the "law" of supply?

Discussion Questions

1. Suppose a government economist predicts that this spring's excellent weather will result in larger crops of wheat and canola than farmers had expected. But the economist warns consumers not to expect prices to decrease because the cost of production is rising and foreign demand for Canadian crops is increasing. "The classic pattern of supply and demand won't work this time," the economist says. Discuss his observation.

2. What do you think would be the effect on the equilibrium price and quantity of marijuana if its sale and consumption were legalized?

3. Classify the effect of each of the following as (i) a decrease in the demand for fish or (ii) a decrease in the quantity of fish demanded. Illustrate each diagrammatically.

   a. The government of Canada closes the Atlantic cod fishery.
   b. People buy less fish because of a rise in fish prices.
   c. The Catholic Church relaxes its ban on eating meat on Fridays.
   d. The price of beef falls and, as a result, consumers buy more beef and less fish.
   e. Fears of mercury poisoning lead locals to shun fish caught in nearby lakes.
   f. It is generally alleged that eating fish is better for one's health than eating meat.

4. Predict the effect on the price of at least one related product of each of the following events:

   a. Winter snowfall is at a record high in the interior of British Columbia, but drought continues in Quebec ski areas.
   b. A recession decreases employment in Oshawa automobile factories.
   c. The French grape harvest is the smallest in 20 years.
   d. The province of Ontario cancels permission for campers to cut firewood in provincial campgrounds.

5. Are the following two observations inconsistent?

   a. Rising demand for housing causes prices of new homes to soar.
   b. Many families refuse to buy homes as prices become prohibitive for them.

6. Look back at the supply-and-demand figure inside Extensions in Theory 3-2 on page 68. Notice that the supply curve has a positive horizontal intercept, suggesting that producers will wish to produce and sell a positive amount of this product even when the price is zero. Is this reasonable? Under what conditions might this occur?

What Macroeconomics Is All About

LO LEARNING OBJECTIVES

In this chapter you will learn

1 the meaning and importance of the key macroeconomic variables, including national income, unemployment, inflation, interest rates, exchange rates, and trade flows.

2 that most macroeconomic issues are about either long-run trends or short-run fluctuations, and that government policy is relevant for both.

Wherever you get your news—from newspapers, television, Internet blogs, radio, or discussions with friends—it is difficult to avoid news about the economy. Nearly every day there is some news story about changes in unemployment, swings in the stock market, or a government official expressing concerns about recent movements in inflation, the Canadian exchange rate, or the level of Canadian exports to other countries. This is true during recessions, like the one that began in late 2008, but it is also true when the economy is growing rapidly, as it was between 2002 and 2007.

Almost everyone cares about economic issues. Workers are anxious to avoid the unemployment that comes with recessions and to share in the rising income that is brought about by productivity growth. Firms are concerned about how interest rates, changes in exchange rates, and foreign competition affect their profits. Consumers want to know how changes in interest rates affect mortgage payments and how changes in exchange rates affect the prices of the goods they purchase. Pensioners worry that inflation may erode the purchasing power of their fixed dollar incomes.

Macroeconomics is the study of how the economy behaves in broad outline without dwelling on much of the detail that occurs in markets for individual products. Macroeconomics is concerned with the behaviour of economic *aggregates*, such as total output, total investment, total exports, and the price level, and with how government policy may influence these aggregates. These aggregates result from activities in many different markets and from the combined behaviour of millions of different decision makers.

An economy producing a lot of wheat and few computers is clearly different from one producing many computers but little wheat. An economy with cheap wheat and expensive computers is also different from one with cheap computers and expensive wheat. Studying aggregates may cause us to miss these important differences, but it focuses our attention on some important issues for the economy as a whole.

In return for suppressing some valuable detail, studying economic aggregates allows us to view the big picture. When aggregate output rises, the output of many commodities and the incomes of many people rise with it. When the price level rises, many people in the economy are forced to make adjustments. When the unemployment rate rises, many workers suffer reductions in their incomes. When significant disruptions occur in the credit markets, interest rates rise and borrowers find it more difficult to finance their desired purchases. Such movements in economic aggregates matter for most individuals because they influence the health of the industries in which they work and the prices of the goods that they purchase. This is why macroeconomic issues get airtime on the evening news, and it is one of the important reasons that we study macroeconomics.

It will become clear as we proceed through this chapter (and later ones) that macroeconomists consider two different aspects of the economy. They think about the *short-run* behaviour of macroeconomic variables, such as output, employment, and inflation, and about how government policy can influence these variables. This concerns, among other things, the study of *business cycles*. They also examine the long-run behaviour of the same variables, especially the long-run path of aggregate output. This is the study of *economic growth* and is concerned with explaining how investment and technological change affect our material living standards over long periods of time.

> **A full understanding of macroeconomics requires understanding the nature of short-run fluctuations as well as the nature of long-run economic growth.**

Before we examine some key macroeconomic variables, it is worth pointing out that there are two different streams of research in macroeconomics, even though the researchers in the two groups are generally interested in understanding the same macroeconomic phenomena. The first group of researchers takes an approach to macroeconomics that is based explicitly on *microeconomic foundations*. These economists build models of the economy that are populated by workers, consumers, and firms, all of whom are assumed to be *optimizers*. Having explicitly modelled these agents' optimization problems, and their resulting choices for work effort, consumption, and investment, the economists proceed to *aggregate* the choices of these agents to arrive at the model's values for aggregate employment, consumption, output, and so on.

The second group of researchers builds macroeconomic models based only implicitly on these same micro foundations. They do not explicitly model the choices of optimizing agents. Instead, these economists construct their models by using aggregate relationships for consumption, investment, and employment, each of which has been subjected to extensive empirical testing and is assumed to represent the behaviour of the many firms and consumers in the economy.

macroeconomics The study of the determination of economic aggregates, such as total output, total employment, the price level, and the rate of economic growth.

A second difference between these two approaches relates to the assumptions regarding the flexibility of wages and prices. Economists using the first approach usually assume that wages and prices are perfectly flexible and thus adjust quickly to clear their respective markets. In contrast, economists using the second approach usually assume that because of the nature of well-established institutions in both labour and product markets, such as labour unions, long-term employment contracts, or costs associated with changing prices, wages and prices are slow to adjust, and thus markets can be in disequilibrium for longer periods of time.

This textbook follows the second approach to macroeconomic analysis. The macro model we begin building in Chapter 21 is not explicitly derived from the behaviour of optimizing firms and consumers, although the macro relationships we introduce are well motivated by microeconomic behaviour. Moreover, the model begins in its simplest version by assuming *no* wage and price flexibility. But as we gradually make the model more complicated and also more realistic, we introduce more wage and price flexibility. In later chapters we will see that the degree of wage and price flexibility is crucial in determining how the economy responds to shocks of various kinds, including changes in government policy. We will also see that our macroeconomic model is sufficiently versatile that we can use it to illustrate the case of perfect wage/price flexibility as a special case.

19.1 Key Macroeconomic Variables

In this chapter, we discuss several important macroeconomic variables, with an emphasis on what they mean and why they matter for our well-being. Here and in Chapter 20 we also explain how the key macroeconomic variables are measured. The remainder of this book is about the causes and consequences of changes in each of these variables, the many ways in which they interact, and the effects they have on our well-being.

Output and Income

The most comprehensive measure of a nation's overall level of economic activity is the value of its total production of goods and services, called *national product*.

> One of the most important ideas in economics is that the production of output generates income.

As a matter of convention, economists define their terms so that, for the nation as a whole, all of the economic value that is produced ultimately belongs to someone in the form of an income claim on that value. For example, if a firm produces $100 worth of ice cream, that $100 ultimately represents income for the firm's workers, the firm's suppliers of material inputs, and the firm's owners. Thus, national product is *by definition* equal to national income.

There are several related measures of a nation's total output and total income. Their various definitions, and the relationships among them, are discussed in detail in the next chapter. In this chapter, we use the generic term *national income* to refer to both the value of total output and the value of the income claims generated by the production of that output.

Aggregating Total Output To measure total output, quantities of many different goods are *aggregated*. To construct such totals, we add up the *values* of the different products. We cannot add tonnes of steel to loaves of bread, but we can add the dollar value of steel production to the dollar value of bread production. We begin by multiplying the number of units of each good produced by the price at which each unit is sold. This yields a dollar value of production for each good. We then sum these values across all the different goods produced in the economy to give us the quantity of total output *measured in dollars*.

This value of total output gives the dollar value of national output, usually called **nominal national income**. A change in this measure can be caused by a change in either the physical quantities or the prices on which it is based. To determine the extent to which any change is due to quantities or to prices, economists calculate **real national income**. This measures the value of individual outputs, not at current prices, but at a set of prices that prevailed in some base period.

Nominal national income is often referred to as *current-dollar national income*. Real national income is often called *constant-dollar national income*. Denoted by the symbol Y, real national income tells us the value of current output measured at constant prices—the sum of the quantities valued at prices that prevailed in the base period. Since prices are held constant when computing real national income, changes in real national income from one year to another reflect *only* changes in quantities. Comparing real national incomes of different years therefore provides a measure of the change in real output that has occurred during the intervening period.

National Income: Recent History One of the most commonly used measures of national income is called *gross domestic product* (*GDP*). GDP can be measured in either real or nominal terms; we focus here on real GDP. The details of its calculation will be discussed in Chapter 20.

Part (i) of Figure 19-1 shows real national income produced by the Canadian economy since 1965; part (ii) shows its annual percentage change for the same period. The GDP series in part (i) shows two kinds of movement. The major movement is a positive trend that increased real output by approximately four times since 1965. This is what economists refer to as *long-term economic growth*.

A second feature of the real GDP series is *short-term fluctuations* around the trend. Overall growth so dominates the real GDP series that the fluctuations are hardly visible in part (i) of Figure 19-1. However, as can be seen in part (ii), the growth of GDP has never been smooth. In most years, GDP increases, but in 1982 and 1991 GDP actually decreased, as shown by the negative rate of growth in the figure. The significant reduction in growth for 2008 to almost zero marked the beginning of a significant recession. (The data for 2009, not displayed, will show negative GDP growth.)

The **business cycle** refers to this continual ebb and flow of business activity that occurs around the long-term trend. For example, a single cycle will usually include an interval of quickly growing output, followed by an interval of slowly growing or even falling output. The entire cycle may last for several years. No two business cycles are exactly the same—variations occur in duration and magnitude. Some expansions are long and drawn out. Others come to an end before high employment and industrial capacity are reached. Nonetheless, fluctuations are systematic enough that it is useful to identify common factors, as is done in *Applying Economic Concepts 19-1*.

Potential Output and the Output Gap National output represents what the economy *actually* produces. An important related concept is *potential* output, which measures what the economy would produce if all resources—land, labour, and productive capacity—were employed at their normal levels of utilization. This concept

---

nominal national income
Total national income measured in current dollars. Also called *current-dollar national income*.

real national income
National income measured in constant (base-period) dollars. It changes only when quantities change.

To see the most recent values for most of the macroeconomic variables discussed in this chapter, go to Statistics Canada's website: ***www.statcan.gc.ca*** *and search for "Latest Indicators."*

business cycle Fluctuations of national income around its trend value that follow a more or less wavelike pattern.

FIGURE 19-1   Growth and Fluctuations in Real GDP, 1965–2008

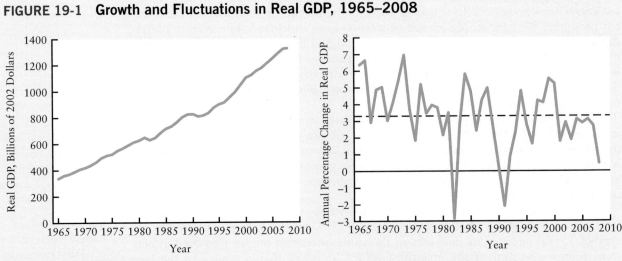

(i) The level of real GDP

(ii) Annual growth rate of real GDP

Real GDP measures the quantity of total output produced by the nation's economy over the period of a year. Real GDP is plotted in part (i). With only a few interruptions, it has risen steadily since 1965, demonstrating the long-term growth of the Canadian economy. Short-term fluctuations are obscured by the long-term trend in part (i) but are highlighted in part (ii). The growth rate fluctuates considerably from year to year. The long-term upward trend in part (i) reflects the positive average growth rate in part (ii), shown by the dashed line.

(*Source:* Adapted from Statistics Canada, CANSIM database, Series V3862685-380-0017, Gross Domestic Product. Search www.statcan.gc.ca for "GDP.")

potential output (Y*) The real GDP that the economy would produce if its productive resources were employed at their normal levels of utilization. Also called *potential GDP.*

output gap Actual national income minus potential national income, Y − Y*.

recessionary gap A situation in which actual output is less than potential output, Y < Y*.

inflationary gap A situation in which actual output exceeds potential output, Y > Y*.

Practise with Study Guide Chapter 19, Exercise 2.

is usually referred to as **potential output** (but is sometimes called *full-employment output*).[1] Its symbol, Y*, distinguishes it from actual output, indicated by Y. The value of potential output cannot be measured as precisely as real GDP; economists estimate potential output by using advanced statistical techniques.

The **output gap** measures the difference between potential output and actual output, and is computed as Y − Y*. When actual output is less than potential output (Y < Y*), the gap measures the market value of goods and services that are not produced because the economy's resources are not fully employed. When Y is less than Y*, the output gap is called a **recessionary gap**. When actual output exceeds potential output (Y > Y*), the gap measures the market value of production in excess of what the economy can produce on a sustained basis. Y can exceed Y* because the latter is defined for a *normal* rate of utilization of factors of production, and there are many ways in which these normal rates can be exceeded temporarily. Labour may work longer hours than normal or factories may operate an extra shift. When Y exceeds Y* there is often upward pressure on prices, and thus we say the output gap is an **inflationary gap.**

Figure 19-2 shows the path of potential GDP since 1985. The upward trend reflects the growth in the productive capacity of the Canadian economy over this period, caused by increases in the labour force, capital stock, and the level of technological knowledge. The figure also shows actual GDP (reproduced from Figure 19-1), which has kept approximately in step with potential GDP. The distance between the

---

[1] The words *real* and *actual* have similar meanings in everyday usage. When national income is measured, however, their meanings are different. *Real* national income is distinguished from *nominal* national income; and *actual* national income is distinguished from *potential* national income. The latter both refer to *real* measures of national income.

APPLYING ECONOMIC CONCEPTS 19-1

The Terminology of Business Cycles

The accompanying figure shows a stylized business cycle, with real GDP fluctuating around a steadily rising level of potential GDP—the economy's normal capacity to produce output. We begin our discussion of terminology with a trough.

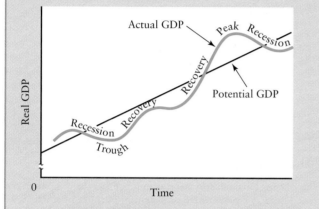

A *trough* is characterized by unemployed resources and a level of output that is low in relation to the economy's capacity to produce. There is thus a substantial amount of unused productive capacity. Business profits are low; for some individual companies, they are negative. Confidence about economic prospects in the immediate future is lacking, and, as a result, many firms are unwilling to risk making new investments.

The process of *recovery* moves the economy out of a trough. The characteristics of a recovery are many: run-down or obsolete equipment is replaced; employment, income, and consumer spending all begin to rise;

and expectations become more favourable. Investments that once seemed risky may be undertaken as firms become more optimistic about future business prospects. Production can be increased with relative ease merely by re-employing the existing unused capacity and unemployed labour.

Eventually the recovery comes to a *peak* at the top of the cycle. At the peak, existing capacity is used to a high degree; labour shortages may develop, particularly in categories of key skills, and shortages of essential raw materials are likely. As shortages develop, costs begin to rise, but because prices rise also, business remains profitable.

Peaks are eventually followed by slowdowns in economic activity. Sometimes this is just a slowing of the rate of increase in income, while at other times the slowdown turns into a *recession*. A **recession**, or contraction, is a downturn in economic activity. Common usage defines a recession as a fall in real GDP for two successive quarters. As output falls, so do employment and households' incomes. Profits drop, and some firms encounter financial difficulties. Investments that looked profitable with the expectation of continually rising income now appear unprofitable. It may not even be worth replacing capital goods as they wear out because unused capacity is increasing steadily. In historical discussions, a recession that is deep and long lasting is often called a *depression*, such as the Great Depression in the early 1930s during which the level of economic activity fell so much that output fell by 30 percent and the unemployment rate increased to 20 percent!

These terms are non-technical but descriptive. The entire falling half of the cycle is often called a *slump*, and the entire rising half is often called a *boom*.

two, which is the output gap, is plotted in part (ii) of Figure 19-2. Fluctuations in economic activity are apparent from fluctuations in the size of the output gap.

Why National Income Matters National income is an important measure of economic performance. Short-run movements in the business cycle receive the most attention in politics and in the press, but most economists agree that long-term growth—as reflected by the growth of *potential GDP*—is in many ways the more important of the two.

Recessions are associated with unemployment and lost output. When actual GDP is below potential GDP, economic waste and human suffering result from the failure to use the economy's resources at their normal intensity of use. Booms, although associated with high employment and high output, can bring problems of their own. When actual GDP exceeds potential GDP, inflationary pressure usually ensues, causing concern for any government that is committed to keeping the inflation rate low.

recession A downturn in the level of economic activity. Often defined precisely as two consecutive quarters in which real GDP falls.

FIGURE 19-2   Potential GDP and the Output Gap, 1985–2008

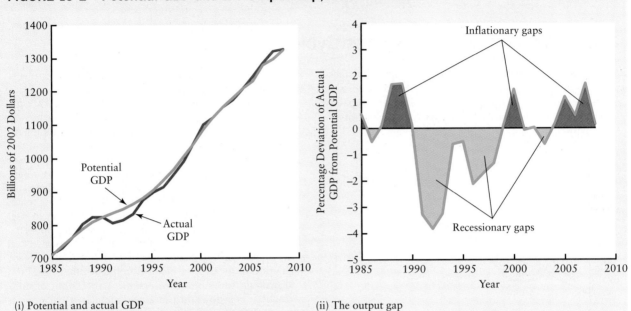

(i) Potential and actual GDP   (ii) The output gap

Potential and actual GDP both display an upward trend. The output gap measures the difference between an economy's potential output and its actual output; the gap is expressed here as a percentage of potential output. Since 1985, potential and actual GDP have almost doubled. The output gap in part (ii) shows clear fluctuations. Shaded areas show inflationary and recessionary gaps.

(*Source:* Actual GDP: Statistics Canada, CANSIM database, Series V3862685–380-0017 Gross Domestic Product. Output gap: www.bankofcanada.ca. Potential output is based on authors' calculations.)

The long-run trend in real per capita national income is an important determinant of improvements in a society's overall standard of living. When income per person grows, each generation can expect, on average, to be better off than preceding ones. For example, if real per capita income grows even at the relatively modest rate of 1.5 percent per year, the average person's lifetime income will be about *twice* that of his or her grandparents.

Although economic growth makes people materially better off *on average,* it does not necessarily make *every* individual better off—the benefits of growth are not usually shared equally by all members of the population. For example, if growth involves significant changes in the structure of the economy, such as a shift away from agriculture and toward manufacturing (as happened in the first part of the twentieth century), or away from manufacturing toward some natural resources (as has been happening in recent years), then these changes will reduce some people's material living standards for extended periods of time.

Employment, Unemployment, and the Labour Force

Practise with Study Guide
Chapter 19, Exercise 3.

National income and employment are closely related. If more is to be produced, either more workers must be used in production, or existing workers must produce more. The first change means a rise in employment; the second means a rise in output per person employed, which is a rise in *productivity*. In the short run, changes in productivity tend to be very small; most short-run changes in output are accomplished by changes in employment. Over the long run, however, changes in both productivity and employment are significant.

Employment denotes the number of adult workers (defined in Canada as workers aged 15 and over) who have jobs. **Unemployment** denotes the number of adult workers who are not employed but who are actively searching for a job. The **labour force** is the total number of people who are either employed or unemployed. The **unemployment rate** is the number of unemployed people expressed as a fraction of the labour force:

$$\text{Unemployment rate} = \frac{\text{Number of people unemployed}}{\text{Number of people in the labour force}} \times 100 \text{ percent}$$

The level of unemployment in Canada is estimated from the Labour Force Survey conducted each month by Statistics Canada. Persons who are currently without a job but who say they have searched actively for one during the sample period are recorded as unemployed.

Frictional, Structural, and Cyclical Unemployment When the economy is at potential GDP, economists say there is *full employment*. But for two reasons there will still be some unemployment even when the economy is at potential GDP.

First, there is a constant turnover of individuals in given jobs and a constant change in job opportunities. New people enter the workforce; some people quit their jobs; others are fired. It may take some time for these people to find jobs. So at any point in time, there is unemployment caused by the normal turnover of labour. Such unemployment is called *frictional unemployment*.

Second, because the economy is constantly adapting to shocks of various kinds, at any moment there will always be some mismatch between the characteristics of the labour force and the characteristics of the available jobs. The mismatch may occur, for example, because labour does not currently have the skills that are in demand or because labour is not in the part of the country where the demand is located. This is a mismatch between the *structure* of the supplies of labour and the *structure* of the demands for labour. Such unemployment is therefore called *structural unemployment*.

> **Even when the economy is at "full employment," some unemployment exists because of natural turnover in the labour market and mismatch between jobs and workers.**

Full employment is said to occur when the *only* unemployment is frictional and structural. At full employment, factors of production are being used at their normal intensity, and the economy is at potential GDP. When GDP is below potential GDP, unemployment rises above its full-employment level; when GDP is above potential GDP, unemployment falls below its full-employment level. Unemployment that is neither structural nor frictional is called *cyclical unemployment* because it changes with the ebb and flow of the business cycle.

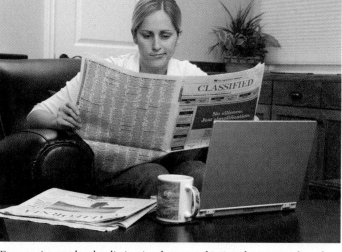

Economists make the distinction between frictional, structural, and cyclical unemployment. This distinction is important for analyzing the economy but it matters little to the individual who has difficulty finding an appropriate job.

employment The number of persons 15 years of age or older who have jobs.

unemployment The number of persons 15 years of age or older who are not employed and are actively searching for a job.

labour force The number of persons employed plus the number of persons unemployed.

unemployment rate Unemployment expressed as a percentage of the labour force, denoted *U*.

Unemployment also has *seasonal* fluctuations. For example, workers employed in the fishing industry often are unemployed during the winter, and ski instructors may be unemployed in the summer. Because these seasonal fluctuations are relatively regular and therefore easy to predict, Statistics Canada *seasonally adjusts* the unemployment statistics to remove these fluctuations, thus revealing more clearly the cyclical and trend movements in the data. For example, suppose that, on average, the Canadian unemployment rate increases by 0.3 percentage points in December. Statistics Canada would then adjust the December unemployment rate so that it shows an increase only if the increase in the *unadjusted* rate exceeds 0.3 percentage points. In this way, the (seasonally adjusted) December unemployment rate is reported to increase only if unemployment rises by more than its normal seasonal increase. All the unemployment (and other macroeconomic) data shown in this book are seasonally adjusted.

Employment and Unemployment: Recent History Figure 19-3 shows the trends in the labour force, employment, and unemployment since 1960. Despite booms and slumps, employment has grown roughly in line with the growth in the labour force. Although the long-term trend dominates the employment data, the figure also shows that the short-term fluctuations in the unemployment rate have been substantial. The unemployment rate has been as low as 3.4 percent in 1966 and as high as 12 percent in 1982. By early in 2008, after the economy had been growing steadily for several years, the unemployment rate was 5.8 percent, the lowest it had been in 30 years. With the onset of the recession that began late in 2008, however, the unemployment rate increased sharply. Part (ii) of Figure 19-3 also shows that there has been a slight upward trend in the unemployment rate over the past 50 years. In Chapter 31 we discuss how some structural changes in the economy can help explain this trend.

FIGURE 19-3   Labour Force, Employment, and Unemployment, 1960–2009

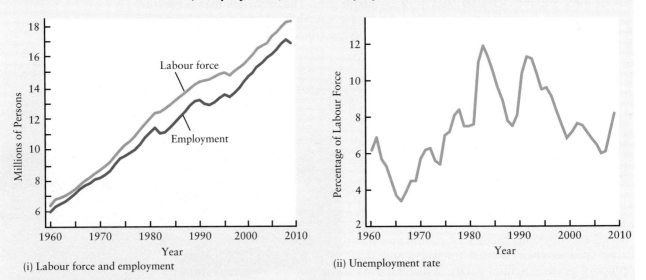

(i) Labour force and employment

(ii) Unemployment rate

The labour force and employment have grown since 1960 with only a few interruptions. The unemployment rate responds to the cyclical behaviour of the economy. The labour force and the level of employment in Canada have both almost tripled since 1960. Booms are associated with a low unemployment rate and slumps with a high unemployment rate.

(*Source:* These data are from Statistics Canada's CANSIM database. Labour force: Series V2062810. Employment: Series V2062811. Unemployment rate is based on authors' calculations. Current labour-force statistics are available on Statistics Canada's website at www.statcan.gc.ca by searching for "unemployment.")

Why Unemployment Matters The social significance of unemployment is enormous because it involves economic waste and human suffering. Human effort is the least durable of economic commodities. If a fully employed economy has 18 million people who are willing to work, their services must either be used this year or wasted. When only 16 million people are actually employed, one year's potential output of 2 million workers is lost forever. In an economy in which there is not enough output to meet everyone's needs, such a waste of potential output is cause for concern.

The loss of income associated with unemployment is clearly harmful to individuals. In some cases, the loss of income pushes people into poverty. But this lost income does not capture the full cost of unemployment. A person's spirit can be broken by a long period of desiring work but being unable to find it. Research has shown that crime, mental illness, and general social unrest tend to be associated with long-term unemployment.

In the not-so-distant past, only personal savings, private charity, or help from friends and relatives stood between the unemployed and starvation. Today, employment insurance and social assistance ("welfare") have created a safety net, particularly when unemployment is for short periods, as is most often the case in Canada. However, when an economic slump lasts long enough, as in the early 1980s and the early 1990s, some unfortunate people exhaust their employment insurance and lose part of that safety net. Short-term unemployment can be a feasible though difficult adjustment for many; long-term unemployment can be a disaster.

Productivity

Figure 19-1 on page 478 shows that Canadian real GDP has increased relatively steadily for many years, reflecting steady growth in the country's productive capacity. This long-run growth has had three general sources. First, as shown in Figure 19-3, the level of employment has increased significantly. Rising employment generally results from a rising population, but at times is also explained by an increase in the proportion of the population that chooses to participate in the labour force. Second, Canada's stock of physical capital—the buildings, factories, and machines used to produce output—has increased more or less steadily over time. Third, productivity in Canada has increased in almost every year since 1960.

Productivity is a measure of the amount of output that the economy produces per unit of input. Since there are many inputs to production—land, labour, and capital—we can have several different measures of productivity. One commonly used measure is **labour productivity**, which is the amount of real GDP produced per unit of labour employed. (The amount of labour employed can be measured either as the total number of employed workers or by the total number of hours worked.)

Productivity: Recent History Figure 19-4 shows two measures of Canadian labour productivity since 1976. The first is the amount of real GDP per employed worker (expressed in thousands of 2002 dollars). In 2008, real GDP per employed worker was $77 420. The second measure shows the amount of real GDP per *hour worked* (expressed in 2002 dollars). In 2008, real GDP per hour worked was $45.70.

The second measure is more accurate because the average number of hours worked per employed worker changes over time. In addition to fluctuating over the business cycle, it has shown a long-term decline, from just over 1850 hours per year in 1976 to just under 1700 hours per year in 2008. The second measure of productivity takes account of these changes in hours worked, whereas the first measure does not.

Practise with Study Guide
Chapter 19, Short-Answer
Question 3 and Exercise 4.

labour productivity The level of real GDP divided by the level of employment (or total hours worked).

FIGURE 19-4   Canadian Labour Productivity, 1976–2008

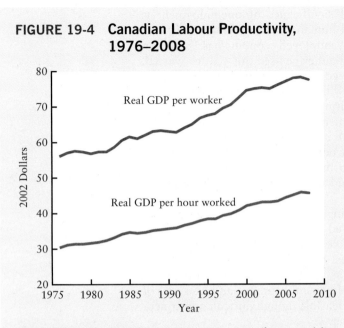

Rising labour productivity is an important contributor to rising material living standards. The figure shows two measures of labour productivity: real GDP per employed worker and real GDP per hour worked. The first is expressed in thousands of 2002 dollars per worker and has increased at an average annual rate of 1.1 percent. The second is expressed in 2002 dollars per hour and has grown at the annual rate of 1.3 percent.

(*Source:* All data are based on authors' calculations using Statistics Canada's CANSIM database. Real GDP: Series V3862685. Average hours worked per worker: Series V716596. Employment: annual averages of Series V2091072.)

One pattern is immediately apparent for both measures of productivity. There has been a significant increase in labour productivity over the past three decades. Real GDP per employed worker increased by 37.7 percent from 1976 to 2008, an annual average growth rate of 1.1 percent. Real GDP per hour worked increased by 50.2 percent over the same period, an annual average growth rate of 1.3 percent.

Why Productivity Matters Productivity growth is the single largest cause of rising material living standards over long periods of time. Over periods of a few years, changes in average real incomes have more to do with the ebb and flow of the business cycle than with changes in productivity; increases in employment during an economic recovery and reductions in employment during recessions explain much of the short-run movements in average real incomes. As is clear from Figure 19-1, however, these short-run fluctuations are dwarfed over many years by the steady upward trend in real GDP—an upward trend that comes in large part from rising productivity.

Why is the real income for an average Canadian this year so much greater than it was for the average Canadian 50 or 100 years ago? Most of the answer lies in the fact that the Canadian worker today is vastly more productive than was his or her counterpart in the distant past. This greater productivity comes partly from the better physical capital with which Canadians now work and partly from their greater skills. The higher productivity for today's workers explains why their *real wages* (the purchasing power of their earnings) are so much higher than for workers in the past.

The close connection between productivity growth and rising material living standards explains the importance that is now placed on understanding the determinants of productivity growth. It is a very active area of economic research, but there are still many unanswered questions. In Chapter 26 we address the process of long-run growth in real GDP and explore the determinants of productivity growth.

Inflation and the Price Level

Practise with Study Guide
Chapter 19, Exercise 5.

price level The average level of all prices in the economy, expressed as an index number.

Inflation means that prices of goods and services are going up, *on average*. If you are a typical reader of this book, inflation has not been very noticeable during your lifetime. When your parents were your age, however, high inflation was a major economic problem. (Some countries have had their economies almost ruined by very high inflation, called *hyperinflation*. We will say more about this in Chapter 27.)

For studying inflation, there are two related but different concepts that are sometimes confused, and it is important to get them straight. The first is the **price level**, which refers to the average level of all prices in the economy and is given by the symbol *P*. The second is the rate of **inflation**, which is the rate at which the price level is rising.

To measure the price level, the economic statisticians at Statistics Canada construct a *price index*, which averages the prices of various commodities according to how important they are. The best-known price index in Canada is the **Consumer Price Index (CPI)**, which measures the average price of the goods and services that are bought by the typical Canadian household. *Applying Economic Concepts 19-2* shows how a price index such as the CPI is constructed.

inflation A rise in the average level of all prices (the price level).

Consumer Price Index (CPI) An index of the average prices of goods and services commonly bought by households.

APPLYING ECONOMIC CONCEPTS 19-2

How the CPI Is Constructed

Although the details are somewhat more complicated, the basic idea behind the Consumer Price Index is straightforward, as is illustrated by the following hypothetical example.

Suppose we want to discover what has happened to the overall cost of living for typical university students. A survey of student behaviour in 2000 shows that the average university student consumed only three goods—pizza, coffee, and photocopying—and spent a total of $200 a month on these items, as shown in Table 1.

TABLE 1   Expenditure Behaviour in 2000

Product	Price	Quantity per Month	Expenditure per Month
Photocopies	$0.10 per sheet	140 sheets	$14.00
Pizza	8.00 per pizza	15 pizzas	120.00
Coffee	0.75 per cup	88 cups	66.00
Total expenditure			$200.00

By 2010, the price of photocopying has fallen to 5 cents per copy, the price of pizza has increased to $9.00, and the price of coffee has increased to $1.00. What has happened to the cost of living over this 10-year period? In order to find out, we calculate the cost of purchasing the 2000 bundle of goods at the prices that prevailed in 2010, as shown in Table 2.

The total expenditure required to purchase the bundle of goods that cost $200.00 in 2000 has risen to $230.00. The increase in required expenditure is $30.00, which is a 15-percent increase over the original $200.00.

If we define 2000 as the base year for the "student price index" and assign an index value of 100 to the cost of the average student's expenditure in that year, the value of the index in 2010 is 115. Thus, goods and services that cost $100.00 in the base year cost $115.00 in 2010, exactly what is implied by Table 2.

TABLE 2   2000 Expenditure Behaviour at 2010 Prices

Product	Price	Quantity per Month	Expenditure per Month
Photocopies	$0.05 per sheet	140 sheets	$7.00
Pizza	9.00 per pizza	15 pizzas	135.00
Coffee	1.00 per cup	88 cups	88.00
Total expenditure			$230.00

The Consumer Price Index, as constructed by Statistics Canada, is built on exactly the same principles as the preceding example. In the case of the CPI, many thousands of consumers are surveyed, and the prices of thousands of products are monitored, but the basic method is the same:

1. Survey the consumption behaviour of consumers.
2. Calculate the cost of the goods and services purchased by the average consumer in the year in which the original survey was done. Define this as the base period of the index.
3. Calculate the cost of purchasing the same bundle of goods and services in other years.
4. Divide the result of Step 3 (in each year) by the result of Step 2, and multiply by 100. The result is the value of the CPI for each year.

The CPI is not a perfect measure of the cost of living because it does not automatically account for ongoing quality improvements or for changes in consumers' expenditure patterns. Changes of this type require the underlying survey of consumer expenditure to be updated from time to time to make sure that the expenditure patterns in the survey approximately match consumers' actual expenditure patterns.

As we saw in Chapter 2, a price index is a pure number—it does not have any units. Yet as we all know, prices in Canada are expressed in dollars. When we construct a price index, the units (dollars) are eliminated because the price index shows the price of a basket of goods at some specific time *relative to the price of the same basket of goods in some base period*. Currently, the base year for Statistics Canada's calculation of the CPI is 2002, which means that the price of the basket of goods is set to be 100 in 2002. If the CPI in 2009 is computed to be 114, the meaning is that the price of the basket of goods is 14 percent higher in 2009 than in 2002.

> Since the price level is measured with an index number, its value at any specific time has meaning only when it is compared with its value at some other time.

By allowing us to compare the general price level at different times, a price index, such as the CPI, also allows us to measure the rate of inflation. For example, the value of the CPI in April 2009 was 113.9 and in April 2008 it was 113.5. The *rate of inflation* during that one-year period, expressed in percentage terms, is equal to the change in the price level divided by the initial price level, times 100:

$$\text{Rate of inflation}$$
$$= \frac{113.9 - 113.5}{113.5} \times 100 \text{ percent}$$
$$= 0.4 \text{ percent}$$

Inflation: Recent History The rate of inflation in Canada is currently around 2 percent per year and has been near that level since the early 1990s. But during the 1970s and 1980s inflation in Canada was both high and unpredictable from year to year. It was a serious macroeconomic problem.

Figure 19-5 shows the CPI and the inflation rate (measured by the annual rate of change in the CPI) from 1960 to 2009. What can we learn from this figure? First, we learn that the price level has not fallen at all since 1960 (in fact, the last time it fell was in 1953, and even then it fell only briefly). The cumulative effect of this sequence of repeated increases in the price level is quite dramatic: By 2009, the price level was more than six times as high as it was in 1960. In other words, you now pay more than $6 for what cost $1 in 1960. The second thing we learn is that, although the price level appears in the figure to be smoothly increasing, the rate of inflation is actually quite volatile. The increases in the inflation rate into double-digit levels in 1974 and 1979 were associated with major increases in the world prices of oil and foodstuffs and with loose monetary policy. The declines in inflation in the early 1980s and 1990s were delayed responses to major recessions.

Why Inflation Matters Money is the universal yardstick in our economy. This does not mean that we care only about money—it means simply that we measure *economic values* in terms of money, and we use money to conduct our economic affairs. Things as diverse as wages, share values in the stock market, the value of a house, and a university's endowment are all stated in terms of money. We value money, however, not for itself but for what we can purchase with it. The terms **purchasing power of money** and *real value of money* refer to the amount of goods and services that can be purchased with a given amount of money. The purchasing power of money is negatively related to the price level. For example, if the price level doubles, a dollar will buy only half as much, whereas if the price level halves, a dollar will buy twice as much. Inflation reduces the real value of anything whose price is *fixed* in dollar terms. Thus, the real value of a $20 bill, a savings account, or the balance that is owed on a student loan is reduced by inflation.

*To compute the rate of inflation from any point in your lifetime to today, check out the "inflation calculator" at the Bank of Canada's website: **www.bankofcanada.ca/en/rates/inflation_calc.htm**.*

purchasing power of money The amount of goods and services that can be purchased with a unit of money.

Inflation reduces the purchasing power of money. It also reduces the real value of any sum fixed in nominal (dollar) terms.

When analyzing the effects of inflation, economists usually make the distinction between *anticipated* and *unanticipated* inflation. If households and firms fully anticipate inflation over the coming year, they will be able to adjust many nominal prices and wages so as to maintain their real values. In this case, inflation will have fewer real effects on the economy than if it comes unexpectedly. For example, if workers and firms expect 2-percent inflation over the coming year, they can agree to increase nominal wages by 2 percent, thus leaving wages constant in real terms.

Unanticipated inflation, on the other hand, generally leads to more changes in the real value of prices and wages. Suppose workers and firms expect 2-percent inflation and they increase nominal wages accordingly. If actual inflation ends up being 5 percent, real wages will be reduced and the quantities of labour demanded by firms and supplied by workers will therefore be altered. As a result, the economy's allocation of resources will be affected more than when the inflation is anticipated.

Anticipated inflation has a smaller effect on the economy than unanticipated inflation.

In reality, inflation is rarely fully anticipated or fully unanticipated. Usually there is some inflation that is expected but also some that comes as a surprise. As a result, some adjustments in wages and prices are made by firms and workers and consumers but not all the adjustments that would be required to leave the economy's allocation of resources unaffected. We will see later, in our discussions of monetary policy and inflation in Chapters 29 and 30, how the distinction between anticipated and unanticipated inflation helps us to understand the cost of *reducing* inflation.

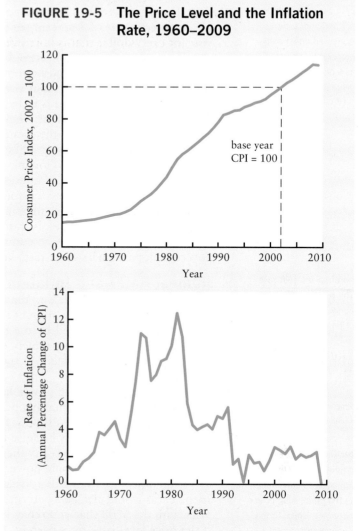

FIGURE 19-5   The Price Level and the Inflation Rate, 1960–2009

The rate of inflation measures the annual rate of increase in the price level. The trend in the price level has been upward over the past half-century. The rate of inflation has varied from almost 0 to more than 12 percent since 1960.

(*Source:* Based on authors' calculations using data from Statistics Canada's CANSIM database: Series V41690973, monthly seasonally adjusted consumer price index. The figures shown are annual averages of the monthly data.)

Interest Rates

If a bank lends you money, it will charge you *interest* for the privilege of borrowing the money. If, for example, you borrow $1000 today, repayable in one year's time, you may also be asked to pay $6.67 per month in interest. This makes $80 in interest over the year, which can be expressed as an interest rate of 8 percent per annum.

interest rate The price paid per dollar borrowed per period of time, expressed either as a proportion (e.g., 0.06) or as a percentage (e.g., 6 percent).

The **interest rate** is the price that is paid to borrow money for a stated period of time. It is expressed as a percentage amount per year per dollar borrowed. For example, an interest rate of 8 percent per year means that the borrower must pay 8 cents per year for every dollar that is borrowed.

There are many interest rates. A bank will lend money to an industrial customer at a lower rate than it will lend money to you—there is a lower risk of not being repaid. The rate charged on a loan that is not to be repaid for a long time will usually differ from the rate on a loan that is to be repaid quickly.

When economists speak of "the" interest rate, they mean a rate that is typical of all the various interest rates in the economy. Dealing with only one interest rate suppresses much interesting detail. However, because interest rates usually rise and fall together, at least for major changes, following the movement of one rate allows us to consider changes in the general level of interest rates. The *prime interest rate*, the rate that banks charge to their best business customers, is noteworthy because when the prime rate changes, most other rates change in the same direction. Another high-profile interest rate is the *bank rate*, the interest rate that the Bank of Canada (Canada's central bank) charges on short-term loans to commercial banks. The interest rate that the Canadian government pays on its short-term borrowing is also a rate that garners some attention.

Interest Rates and Inflation

How does inflation affect interest rates? To begin developing an answer, imagine that your friend lends you $100 and that the loan is repayable in one year. The amount that you pay her for making this loan, measured in dollar terms, is determined by the **nominal interest rate**. If you pay her $108 in one year's time, $100 will be repayment of the amount of the loan (which is called the *principal*) and $8 will be payment of the interest. In this case, the nominal interest rate is 8 percent per year.

nominal interest rate The price paid per dollar borrowed per period of time.

Practise with Study Guide Chapter 19, Exercise 6.

real interest rate The nominal rate of interest adjusted for the change in the purchasing power of money. Equal to the nominal interest rate minus the rate of inflation.

How much purchasing power has your friend gained or lost by making this loan? The answer depends on what happens to the price level during the year. The more the price level rises, the worse off your friend will be and the better the transaction will be for you. This result occurs because the more the price level rises, the less valuable are the dollars that you use to repay the loan. The **real interest rate** measures the return on a loan in terms of purchasing power.

If the price level remains constant over the year, the real rate of interest that your friend earns would also be 8 percent, because she can buy 8 percent more goods and services with the $108 that you repay her than with the $100 that she lent you. However, if the price level rises by 8 percent, the real rate of interest would be zero because the $108 that you repay her buys the same quantity of goods as the $100 that she originally gave up. If she is unlucky enough to lend money at 8 percent in a year in which prices rise by 10 percent, the real rate of interest that she earns is −2 percent. The repayment of $108 will purchase 2 percent fewer goods and services than the original loan of $100.

> **The burden of borrowing depends on the real, not the nominal, rate of interest.**

For example, a nominal interest rate of 8 percent combined with a 2-percent rate of inflation is a much greater real burden on borrowers than a nominal rate of 16 percent combined with a 14-percent rate of inflation. Figure 19-6 shows the nominal and real interest rates paid on short-term government borrowing since 1960.

Interest Rates and "Credit Flows"

A loan represents a flow of credit between lenders and borrowers, with the interest rate representing the price of this credit. Credit is essential to the healthy functioning of a modern economy. Most firms require credit at some point—to finance the construction of a factory, to purchase inventories of intermediate inputs, or to continue paying their workers in a regular fashion even though their revenues may arrive at irregular intervals. Most households also require credit at various times—to finance the purchase of a home or car or to finance a child's university education.

Banks play a crucial role in the economy by *intermediating* between those households and firms that have available funds and those households and firms who require funds. In other words, banks play a key role in "making the credit market"—in channelling the funds from those who have them to those who need them.

During normal times, these credit markets function very smoothly and most of us notice little about them. While there are fluctuations in the price of credit (the interest rate), they tend to be relatively modest. In the fall of 2008, however, credit markets in the United States, Canada, and most other countries were thrown into turmoil by the sudden collapse of several large financial institutions, mainly in the United States and the European Union. As a result, many banks became reluctant to lend to any but the safest borrowers, mostly out of fear that the borrowers would go bankrupt before they could repay the loan. The flows of credit slowed sharply and market interest rates spiked upward, reflecting the greater risk premium required by lenders. The reduction in the flow of credit was soon felt by firms who needed credit in order to finance material or labour inputs, and the effect was a reduction in production and employment. This *financial crisis*, by interrupting the vital flows of credit, was an important cause of the recession

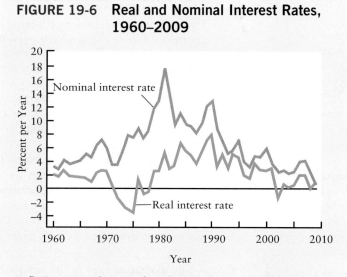

FIGURE 19-6   Real and Nominal Interest Rates, 1960–2009

Inflation over the past five decades has meant that the real interest rate has always been less than the nominal interest rate. The data for the nominal interest rate show the average rate on three-month Treasury bills in each year since 1960. The real interest rate is calculated as the nominal interest rate minus the actual rate of inflation over the same period. Through the early 1970s, the real interest rate was negative, indicating that the inflation rate exceeded the nominal interest rate. The 1980s saw real interest rates rise as high as 8 percent. Since then, real rates have declined again to levels that are closer to the long-term historical average.

(*Source:* Nominal interest rate: 3-month Treasury bill rate, Statistics Canada, CANSIM database, Series V122541. Real interest rate is based on authors' calculation of CPI inflation, using Series PCPISA from the Bank of Canada, www.bankofcanada.ca.)

that enveloped the global economy in late 2008 and through 2009. We will discuss banking and the flow of credit in more detail in Chapters 27, 28, and 29.

Why Interest Rates Matter   Changes in real interest rates affect the standard of living of savers and borrowers. Many retirees, for example, rely on interest earnings from their stock of accumulated assets to provide much of their household income, and thus benefit when real interest rates rise. In contrast, borrowers are made better off with low real interest rates. This point was dramatically illustrated during the 1970s when homeowners who had long-term fixed-rate mortgages benefited tremendously from several years of high and largely unanticipated inflation, which resulted in *negative* real interest rates (see Figure 19-6).

Interest rates also matter for the economy as a whole. As we will see in Chapter 21, real interest rates are an important determinant of the level of investment by firms. Changes in real interest rates lead to changes in the cost of borrowing and thus to changes in firms' investment plans. Such changes in the level of desired investment have important consequences for the level of economic activity. We will see in Chapters 28 and 29 how the Bank of Canada influences interest rates as part of its objective of controlling inflation.

The International Economy

Two important variables reflecting the importance of the global economy to Canada are the *exchange rate* and *net exports*.

Practise with Study Guide
Chapter 19, Exercise 7.

exchange rate The number of units of domestic currency required to purchase one unit of foreign currency.

The Exchange Rate If you are going on a holiday to France, you will need euros to pay for your purchases. Many of the larger banks, as well as any foreign-exchange office, will make the necessary exchange of currencies for you; they will sell you euros in return for your Canadian dollars. If you get 0.7 euros for each dollar that you give up, the two currencies are trading at a rate of 1 dollar = 0.7 euros or, expressed another way, 1 euro = 1.43 dollars.

As our example shows, the exchange rate can be defined either as dollars per euro or euros per dollar. In this book we adopt the convention of defining the **exchange rate** between the Canadian dollar and any foreign currency as the number of Canadian dollars required to purchase one unit of foreign currency. For example, in June 2009, 1 Canadian dollar was worth 61 euro cents; expressed the other way, 1 euro was worth 1.64 Canadian dollars. The exchange rate was therefore equal to 1.64, telling us that it took \$1.64 (Canadian) to purchase 1 euro.

> The exchange rate is the number of Canadian dollars required to purchase one unit of foreign currency.[2]

foreign exchange Foreign currencies that are traded on the foreign-exchange market.

The term **foreign exchange** refers to foreign currencies or claims on foreign currencies, such as bank deposits, cheques, and promissory notes, that are payable in foreign money. The **foreign-exchange market** is the market in which foreign exchange is traded—at a price expressed by the exchange rate.

foreign-exchange market The market in which different national currencies are traded.

Depreciation and Appreciation A rise in the exchange rate means that it takes *more* Canadian dollars to purchase one unit of foreign currency—this is a **depreciation** of the Canadian dollar. Conversely, a fall in the exchange rate means that it takes *fewer* Canadian dollars to purchase one unit of foreign currency—this is an **appreciation** of the dollar.

depreciation A rise in the exchange rate—it takes more units of domestic currency to purchase one unit of foreign currency.

Figure 19-7 shows the path of the Canadian–U.S. exchange rate since 1970. Since more than 80 percent of Canada's trade is with the United States, this is the exchange rate most often discussed and analyzed in Canada. In countries with trade more evenly spread across several trading partners, more attention is paid to what is called a *trade-weighted exchange rate*—this is a weighted-average exchange rate between the home country and its trading partners, where the weights reflect each partner's share in the home country's total trade. In Canada, the path of such a trade-weighted exchange rate is virtually identical to the Canadian–U.S. exchange rate shown in Figure 19-7, reflecting the very large proportion of total Canadian trade with the United States.

appreciation A fall in the exchange rate—it takes fewer units of domestic currency to purchase one unit of foreign currency.

As we will see in later chapters, both domestic policy and external events have important effects on the Canadian exchange rate. For example, most economists believe that the appreciation of the Canadian dollar between 1986 and 1992 was caused in part by the Bank of Canada's efforts to reduce the rate of inflation. The Bank's policy was controversial at the time, not least because of the effect it had on the exchange rate and the many

---

[2] Some economists use a reverse definition of the exchange rate—the number of units of foreign currency that can be purchased with one Canadian dollar. It is up to the student, then, to examine carefully the definition that is being used by a particular writer or speaker. In this book the exchange rate is defined as the number of Canadian dollars required to purchase one unit of foreign currency because this measure emphasizes that foreign currency, like any other good or service, has a price in terms of Canadian dollars. In this case, the price has a special name—the exchange rate.

export-oriented firms that were harmed by Canada's strong dollar. We examine the link between monetary policy and exchange rates in detail in Chapters 28 and 29.

The depreciation of the Canadian dollar in the late 1990s is thought by most economists to have resulted from a nearly 30-percent decline in the world prices of commodities, many of which are important Canadian exports. The appreciation of the Canadian dollar during the 2002–2007 period was associated with sharp increases in commodity prices. In both cases, the commodity prices were being driven by changes in global economic growth, illustrating the important point that events in faraway lands can have dramatic effects on the Canadian exchange rate. We examine the link between world commodity prices and the Canadian exchange rate in Chapter 35.

Exports and Imports
Canada has long been a trading nation, buying many goods and services from other countries—Canada's *imports*—and also selling many goods and services to other countries—Canada's *exports*.

FIGURE 19-7 Canadian–U.S. Dollar Exchange Rate, 1970–2009

The Canadian–U.S. exchange rate has been quite volatile over the past 40 years. The Canadian-dollar price of one U.S. dollar increased from just over $1 in the early 1970s to over $1.55 in 2003. By 2009 the exchange rate was about 1.20.

(*Source*: Annual average of monthly data, Statistics Canada, CANSIM database, Series V37432, foreign exchange rates in Canadian dollars.)

Figure 19-8 shows the dollar value of Canada's exports, imports, and *net exports* since 1970. Net exports is the difference between exports and imports and is often called the *trade balance*.

Canadian exports and imports have increased fairly closely in step with each other over the past 40 years. The trade balance has therefore fluctuated mildly over the years, but it has stayed relatively small, especially when viewed as a proportion of total GDP.

Also apparent in Figure 19-8 is that Canadian trade flows (both imports and exports) began to grow more quickly after 1990. The increased importance of international trade is largely due to the Canada–U.S. Free Trade Agreement, which began in 1989, and to the North American Free Trade Agreement (which added Mexico), which began in 1994.

19.2 Growth Versus Fluctuations

This chapter has provided a quick tour through macroeconomics and has introduced you to many important macroeconomic issues. If you take a few moments to flip again through the figures in this chapter, you will notice that most of the macroeconomic variables that we discussed are characterized by *long-run trends* and *short-run fluctuations*.

Figure 19-1 on page 478, which shows the path of real GDP, provides an excellent example of both characteristics. The figure shows that real GDP has increased by over four times since 1965—this is substantial *economic growth*. The figure also shows considerable, and sometimes dramatic, year-to-year *fluctuations* in the growth rate of GDP.

An important theme in this book is that a full understanding of macroeconomics requires an understanding of both long-run growth and short-run fluctuations. As we

FIGURE 19-8   Canadian Imports, Exports, and Net Exports, 1970–2008

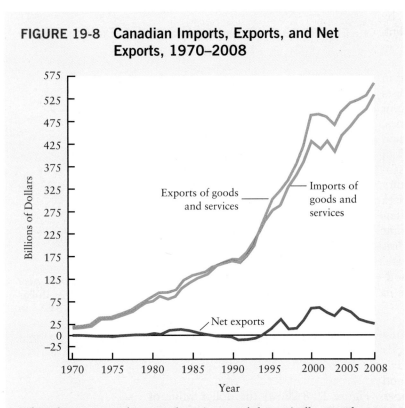

Though imports and exports have increased dramatically over the past 40 years, the trade balance has remained roughly in balance. The nominal values of imports and exports rose steadily over the past few decades because of both price increases and quantity increases. The growth of trade increased sharply after the early 1990s. The trade balance—net exports—is usually close to zero.

(*Source:* Statistics Canada, CANSIM database. Exports: Series V498103. Imports: Series V498106.)

International trade is very important to the Canadian economy. Exports and imports of goods and services each represent roughly 35 percent of Canada's GDP.

proceed through this book, we will see that these two characteristics of modern economies have different sources and explanations. And the government's macroeconomic policies have roles to play in both.

Long-Term Economic Growth

Both total output and output per person have risen for many decades in most industrial countries. These long-term trends have meant rising average living standards. Although long-term growth gets less play on the evening news than current economic developments, it has considerably more importance for a society's living standards from decade to decade and from generation to generation.

There is considerable debate regarding the ability of government policy to influence the economy's long-run rate of growth. Some economists believe that a policy designed to keep inflation low and stable will contribute to the economy's growth. Some, however, believe there are dangers from having inflation too low—that a moderate inflation rate is more conducive to growth than a very low inflation rate.

Many economists also believe that when governments spend less than they raise in tax revenue—and thus have a budget surplus—the reduced need for borrowing drives down interest rates and stimulates investment by the private sector. Such increases in investment imply a higher stock of physical capital available for future production and thus an increase in economic growth. Do government budget surpluses increase future growth? Or do budget surpluses have no effect at all on the economy's future ability to produce? We address this important debate in Chapter 32.

Finally, there is active debate regarding the appropriate role of the government in developing new technologies. Some economists believe that the private sector, left on its own, can produce a volume of inventions and innovation that will guarantee a satisfactory rate of long-term growth. Others point out that almost all of the major new technologies of the last 75 years were initially supported by public funds: The electronic computer was the creation of governments in the Second World War, miniaturized equipment came from the race to the moon, the Internet came from military communications research, the U.S. software industry was created by the U.S. Department of Defense, much of the early work on biotechnology came out of publicly funded research laboratories in universities and government institutions, and so on. The debate about the place of government in helping to foster inventions and innovations of truly fundamental technologies is an ongoing and highly important one.

Short-Term Fluctuations

Short-run fluctuations in economic activity, like the ones shown in part (ii) of Figure 19-1 (page 478), lead economists to wonder about the causes of *business cycles*. What caused the Great Depression in the 1930s, when almost one-fifth of the Canadian labour force was out of work and massive unemployment plagued all major industrial countries? Why did the Canadian economy begin a significant recession in 1990–1991, from which recovery was initially very gradual? What explains why, by 2007, the Canadian unemployment rate was lower than it had been in more than 30 years? What caused the worldwide recession that began in 2008?

Understanding business cycles requires an understanding of monetary policy. Most economists agree that the increase in inflation in the 1970s and early 1980s was related to monetary policy, though they also agree that other events were partly responsible. When the Bank of Canada implemented a policy in the early 1990s designed to reduce inflation, was it merely a coincidence that a significant recession followed? Most economists think not, though they also think that the slowdown in the U.S. economy was an important contributor to Canada's recession. Chapters 28 and 29 focus on how the Bank of Canada uses its policy to influence the level of economic activity.

Government budget deficits and surpluses also enter the discussion of business cycles. Some economists think that, in recessionary years, the government ought to increase spending (and reduce taxes) in an effort to stimulate economic activity. Similarly, they believe that taxes should be raised to slow down a booming economy. Indeed, several government policies, from income taxation to employment insurance, are designed to mitigate the short-term fluctuations in national income. Other economists believe that the government cannot successfully "fine-tune" the economy by making frequent changes in spending and taxing because our knowledge of how the economy works is imperfect and because such policies tend to be imprecise. We address these issues in Chapters 22 to 24.

What Lies Ahead?

There is much work to be done before any of these interesting policy debates can be discussed in more detail. Like firms that invest now to increase their production in the future, the next few chapters of this book will be an investment for you—an investment in understanding basic macro theory. The payoff will come when you are able to use a coherent model of the economy to analyze and debate some of the key macro issues of the day.

We begin in Chapter 20 by discussing the measurement of GDP. National income accounting is not exciting but is essential to a complete understanding of the chapters that follow. We then proceed to build a simple model of the economy to highlight some key macroeconomic relationships. As we proceed through the book, we modify the model, step by step, making it ever more realistic. With each step we take, more of today's controversial policy issues come within the grasp of our understanding. We hope that by the time you get to the end of the book, you will have developed some of the thrill for analyzing macroeconomic issues that we feel. Good luck, and enjoy the journey!

Summary

19.1 Key Macroeconomic Variables

- The value of the total production of goods and services in a country is called its national product. Because production of output generates income in the form of claims on that output, the total is also referred to as national income. One of the most commonly used measures of national income is gross domestic product (GDP).
- Potential output is the level of output produced when factors of production are employed at their normal intensity of use. The output gap is the difference between actual and potential output.
- The unemployment rate is the percentage of the labour force not employed and actively searching for a job. The labour force and employment have both grown steadily for the past half-century. The unemployment rate fluctuates considerably from year to year. Unemployment imposes serious costs in the form of economic waste and human suffering.
- Labour productivity is measured as real GDP per employed worker. It is an important determinant of material living standards.
- The price level is measured by a price index, which measures the price of a set of goods in one year relative to

their price in a base year. The inflation rate measures the rate of change of the price level. For almost 20 years, the annual inflation rate in Canada has been relatively close to 2 percent.
- The interest rate is the price that is paid to borrow money for a stated period and is expressed as a percentage amount per dollar borrowed. The nominal interest rate is this price expressed in money terms; the real interest rate is this price expressed in terms of goods or purchasing power.
- The flow of credit—borrowing and lending—is very important in a modern economy. Firms require credit to finance their operations and households require credit in order to make large purchases. Disruptions in the flow of credit can lead to increases in interest rates and reductions in economic activity.
- The exchange rate is the number of Canadian dollars needed to purchase one unit of foreign currency. A rise in the exchange rate is a depreciation of the Canadian dollar; a fall in the exchange rate is an appreciation of the Canadian dollar.

19.2 Growth Versus Fluctuations

- Most macroeconomic variables have both long-run trends and short-run fluctuations. The sources of the two types of movements are different.
- Important questions for macroeconomics involve the role of policy in influencing long-run growth as well as short-run fluctuations.

Key Concepts

National product and national income
Real and nominal national income
Potential and actual output
The output gap
Employment, unemployment, and the labour force

Full employment
Frictional, structural, and cyclical unemployment
Labour productivity
The price level and the rate of inflation

Real and nominal interest rates
The exchange rate
Depreciation and appreciation of the Canadian dollar
Exports, imports, and net exports

Study Exercises

SAVE TIME. IMPROVE RESULTS.

Visit MyEconLab to practise Study Exercises and prepare for tests and exams. MyEconLab also offers a variety of other study tools to help you succeed.
www.myeconlab.com

1. Fill in the blanks to make the following statements correct.

   a. The value of total production of goods and services in Canada is called its _____. National _____ and national _____ are equal because all production generates a claim on its value in the form of income.
   b. In measuring Canada's total output, it would be meaningless to add together all goods and services produced during one year (i.e., 50 000 trucks plus 14 million dozen eggs plus 100 million haircuts, etc.). Instead, total output is measured in _____.
   c. The difference between nominal national income and real national income is that with the latter, _____ are held constant to enable us to see changes in _____.
   d. If all of Canada's resources—its land, labour, and capital—are being employed at normal levels of utilization, then we say that Canada is producing its _____.
   e. The output gap measures the difference between _____ and _____. During booms, _____ is greater than _____ and during recessions _____ is less than _____.

2. Fill in the blanks to make the following statements correct.

   a. The labour force includes people who are _____ and people who are _____. The unemployment rate is expressed as the number of people who are _____ as a percentage of people in the _____.
   b. At any point in time, some people are unemployed because of the normal turnover of labour (new entrants to the labour force, job leavers, and job seekers). This unemployment is referred to as _____. Some people are said to be _____ unemployed because their skills do not match the skills necessary for the available jobs.
   c. Suppose 2001 is the base year in which the price of a basket of goods is set to be 100. If the price of the same basket of goods in 2011 is 137, then we can say that the price level is _____ and that the price of the basket of goods has increased by _____ percent between 2001 and 2011.
   d. Suppose Canada's CPI in May 2009 was 112.7 and in May 2010 was 113.4. The rate of inflation during that one-year period was _____ percent.
   e. The price that is paid to borrow money for a stated period of time is known as the _____.
   f. The real interest rate is equal to the nominal interest rate _____ the rate of inflation.
   g. The number of Canadian dollars required to purchase one unit of foreign currency is the _____ between the Canadian dollar and that foreign currency.
   h. A _____ in the exchange rate reflects a depreciation of the Canadian dollar; a _____ in the exchange rate reflects an appreciation of the Canadian dollar.

3. Consider the macroeconomic data shown below for a hypothetical country's economy.

Year	Real GDP Actual (billions of $)	Real GDP Potential (billions of $)	Output Gap (% of potential)	Unemployment Rate (% of labour force)
2003	1168	1188	—	11.1
2004	1184	1196	—	10.2
2005	1197	1205	—	9.1
2006	1211	1215	—	8.3
2007	1225	1225	—	7.6
2008	1240	1236	—	7.3
2009	1253	1247	—	7.1
2010	1262	1258	—	7.3
2011	1270	1270	—	7.6

   a. Compute the output gap for each year.
   b. Explain how GDP can exceed potential GDP.
   c. Does real GDP ever fall in the time period shown? What do economists call such periods?
   d. What is the unemployment rate when this economy is at "full employment"? What kind of unemployment exists at this time?

4. Consider the data shown below for the Canadian Consumer Price Index (CPI), drawn from the *Bank of Canada Review.*

Year	CPI (1992 = 100)	CPI Inflation (% change from previous year)
1990	93.3	4.83
1991	98.5	5.57
1992	100.0	—
1993	101.8	—
1994	102.0	0.20
1995	104.2	2.16
1996	105.9	—
1997	107.6	—
1998	108.9	1.21
1999	111.5	2.39
2000	115.1	—
2001	115.9	—
2002	120.4	—
2003	122.8	1.99
2004	125.4	—
2005	128.1	—

a. Compute the missing data in the table.
b. Do average prices ever fall in the time period shown? In which year do prices come closest to being stable?
c. Across which two consecutive years is the rate of inflation closest to being stable?
d. In a diagram with the price level on the vertical axis and time on the horizontal axis, illustrate the difference between a situation in which the price level is stable and a situation in which the rate of inflation is stable.

5. The data below show the nominal interest rate and the inflation rate for several developed economies as reported in *The Economist* on June 27, 2009.

Country	Nominal Interest Rate (on 10-year government bonds)	Inflation Rate (% change in CPI from previous year)	Real Interest Rate
Australia	5.62	2.5	—
Canada	3.56	0.1	—
Euro area	3.45	0.0	—
Japan	1.38	−0.1	—
Switzerland	2.36	−1.0	—
U.K.	3.70	2.2	—
U.S.A.	3.68	−1.3	—

a. Compute the real interest rate for each country, assuming that people expected the inflation rate at the time to persist.
b. If you were a lender, in which country would you have wanted to lend in June 2009? Explain.
c. If you were a borrower, in which country would you have wanted to borrow in June 2009? Explain.

6. Consider the following data drawn from *The Economist*. Recall that the Canadian exchange rate is the number of Canadian dollars needed to purchase one unit of some foreign currency.

Currency	Cdn Dollar Exchange Rate	
	June 2009	June 2008
U.S. dollar	1.15	1.01
Japanese yen	0.012	0.009
British pound	1.89	1.98
Swedish krona	0.147	0.167
Euro	1.62	1.58

a. Which currencies appreciated relative to the Canadian dollar from June 2008 to June 2009?
b. Which currencies depreciated relative to the Canadian dollar from June 2008 to June 2009?
c. Using the information provided in the table, can you tell whether the Japanese yen depreciated or appreciated *against the U.S. dollar* from June 2008 to June 2009? Explain.

Discussion Questions

1. Explain carefully what has happened to the CPI to justify each of the following newspaper headlines.

   a. "Prices on the rise again after a year of stability"
   b. "Inflation increases for three successive months"
   c. "Finance minister pleased at moderation in inflation rate"
   d. "Cost-of-living increases devastating pensioners"

2. Explain why during booms it is possible for the unemployment rate to increase even while total employment is rising.

3. Evaluate the following statements about unemployment.

   a. "Unemployment is a personal tragedy and a national waste."

   b. "No one needs to be unemployed these days; just look at the Help Wanted ads in the newspapers and the signs in the stores."
   c. "Employment insurance is a boondoggle for the lazy and unnecessary for the industrious."

4. Consider a 10-year period over which output per worker falls, but GDP increases. How can this happen? Do you think this is likely to be good for the economy?

5. When the Canadian dollar depreciates in foreign-exchange markets, many people view this as "good" for the Canadian economy. Who is likely to be harmed by and who is likely to benefit from a depreciation of the Canadian dollar?

The Measurement of National Income

This chapter provides a detailed look at the measurement of national income. Once we know more precisely what is being measured and how it is measured, we will be ready to build a macroeconomic model to explain the determination of national income. Understanding how national income is measured is an important part of understanding how and why it changes. Indeed, this is a general rule of all economics and all science: Before using any data, it is essential to understand how those data are developed and what they measure.

LEARNING OBJECTIVES

In this chapter you will learn

1 how the concept of value added solves the problem of "double counting" when measuring national income.

2 the income approach and the expenditure approach to measuring national income.

3 the difference between real and nominal GDP and the meaning of the GDP deflator.

4 about the many important omissions from official measures of GDP.

5 why real per capita GDP is a good measure of average material living standards but an incomplete measure of overall well-being.

20.1 National Output and Value Added

The central topic of macroeconomics is the overall level of economic activity—aggregate output and the income that is generated by its production. We start by asking: What do we mean by output?

This question may seem odd. Surely your local bakery knows what it produces. And if Air Canada or Imperial Oil or Bombardier does not know its own output, what does it know? If each firm knows the value of its total output, the national income statisticians simply have to add up each separate output value to get the nation's output—or is it really that simple?

The reason that obtaining a total for the nation's output is not that simple is that one firm's output is often another firm's input. The local baker uses flour that is the output of the flour milling company; the flour milling company, in turn, uses wheat that is the farmer's output. What is true for bread is true for most goods and services.

> **Production occurs in stages: Some firms produce outputs that are used as inputs by other firms, and these other firms, in turn, produce outputs that are used as inputs by yet other firms.**

If we merely added up the market values of all outputs of all firms, we would obtain a total greatly in excess of the value of the economy's actual output. Consider the example of wheat, flour, and bread. If we added the total value of the output of the wheat farmer, the flour mill, and the baker, we would be counting the value of the wheat three times, the value of the milled flour twice, and the value of the bread once.

The error that would arise in estimating the nation's output by adding all sales of all firms is called *double counting*. "Multiple counting" would actually be a better term because if we added up the values of all sales, the same output would be counted every time that it was sold by one firm to another. The problem of double counting could in principle be solved by distinguishing between two types of output. **Intermediate goods** are outputs of some firms that are used as inputs by other firms. **Final goods** are products that are not used as inputs by other firms, at least not in the period of time under consideration.

If the sales of firms could be easily disaggregated into sales of final goods and sales of intermediate goods, then measuring total output would be straightforward. It would simply equal the value of all *final* goods produced by firms. However, when Stelco sells steel to the Ford Motor Company, it does not care, and usually does not know, whether the steel is for final use (say, construction of a warehouse that will not be sold by Ford) or for use as part of an automobile that will be sold again. Even in our earlier example of bread, a bakery cannot be sure that its sales are for final use, for the bread may be further "processed" by a restaurant prior to its final sale to a customer. In general, it is extremely difficult if not impossible to successfully distinguish final from intermediate goods. The problem of double counting must therefore be resolved in some other manner.

To avoid double counting, economists use the concept of **value added**, which is the amount of value that firms and workers add to their products over and above the costs of intermediate goods. An individual firm's value added is

$$\text{Value added} = \text{Revenue} - \text{Cost of intermediate goods}$$

Consider an example of a steel mill. A steel mill's value added is the revenue it earns from selling the steel it produces minus the cost of the ore that it buys from the

intermediate goods All outputs that are used as inputs by other producers in a further stage of production.

final goods Goods that are not used as inputs by other firms but are produced to be sold for consumption, investment, government, or exports during the period under consideration.

value added The value of a firm's output minus the value of the inputs that it purchases from other firms.

Practise with Study Guide Chapter 20, Short-Answer Question 4, Exercises 1 and 2.

mining company, the cost of the electricity and fuel oil that it uses, and the costs of all other inputs that it buys from other firms.

We have said that a firm's value added equals its revenue minus the cost of intermediate goods *purchased from other firms*. Payments made to factors of production, such as the wages paid to workers or the profits paid to owners, are not purchases from other firms and hence are not subtracted from the firm's revenue when computing value added. But since the firm's revenue must be equal to the cost of intermediate goods *plus* these payments to factors of production, it follows that value added is exactly equal to the sum of these factor payments.[1]

Value added = Payments to factors of production

Value added is the correct measure of each firm's contribution to total output—the amount of market value that is produced by that firm.

The firm's value added is the *net value* of its output. It is this net value that is the firm's contribution to the nation's total output, representing the firm's own efforts that add to the value of what it takes in as inputs. The concept of value added is further illustrated in *Applying Economic Concepts 20-1*. In this simple example, as in all more complex cases, the value of the nation's total output is obtained by summing all the individual values added.

The sum of all values added in an economy is a measure of the economy's total output.

APPLYING ECONOMIC CONCEPTS 20-1

Value Added Through Stages of Production

Because the output of one firm often becomes the input of other firms, the total value of goods sold by all firms greatly exceeds the value of the output of final products. This general principle is illustrated by a simple example in which a mining company starts from scratch and produces iron ore valued at $1000; this firm's value added is $1000. The mining company then sells the iron ore to a different firm that produces steel valued at $1500. The steel producer's value added is $500 because the value of the goods is increased by $500 as a result of the firm's activities. Finally, the steel producer sells the steel to a metal fabricator who transforms the steel into folding chairs valued at $1800; the metal fabricator's value added is $300.

We find the value of the final goods, $1800, either by counting only the sales of the last firm or by taking the sum of the values added by each firm. This value is much smaller than the $4300 that we would obtain if we merely added up the market value of the output sold by each firm.

	Transactions at Three Different Stages of Production				
	Mining Company	Steel Producer	Metal Fabricator	All Firms	
A. Purchases from other firms	$ 0	$1000	$1500	$2500	Total interfirm sales
B. Payments to factors of production	1000	500	300	1800	Total value added
A + B = value of product	$1000	$1500	$1800	$4300	Total value of all sales

---

[1] We are ignoring here the role of indirect taxes, such as provincial sales taxes or the Goods and Services Tax (GST). Such taxes are included in the market value of a firm's output, but these taxes are remitted to the government and do not represent a payment to factors of production.

20.2 National Income Accounting: The Basics

The measures of national income and national product that are used in Canada derive from an accounting system called the National Income and Expenditure Accounts (NIEA), which are produced by Statistics Canada. These accounts are not simply collections of economic data. They have a logical structure, based on the simple yet important idea of the circular flow of income, which you first saw in Chapter 1 and which is shown again in Figure 20-1. The figure shows the overall flows of national income and expenditure and also how government, the financial system, and foreign countries enter the flows. The key point from the circular flow is as follows:

> The value of domestic output is equal to the value of the expenditure on that output and is also equal to the total income claims generated by producing that output.

FIGURE 20-1   The Circular Flow of Expenditure and Income

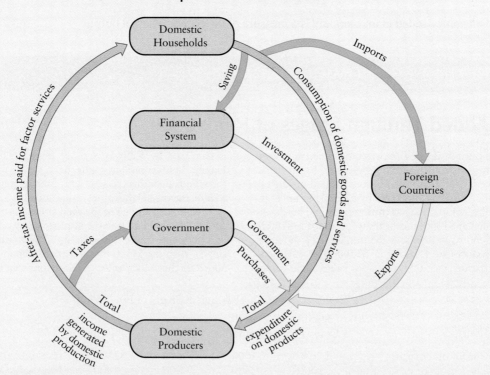

National income is equal to national product. Their flows are shown by the circular flow of income and expenditure. Consider first only the red lines. In this case, the flow would be a simple circle from households to producers and back to households. Now add the blue and green lines. The blue lines represent *injections* to the circular flow (exports, investment, and government purchases), while the green lines represent *withdrawals* from the circular flow (imports, saving, and taxes). Injections and withdrawals complicate the picture but do not change the basic relationship: Domestic production creates a claim on the value of that production. When all the claims are correctly added up, they must equal the total value of production.

The circular flow of income suggests three different ways of measuring national income. The first is simply to add up the value of all goods and services produced in the economy. This requires the concept of value added, which we discussed in the previous section. The remaining two approaches correspond to the two "halves" of the circular flow of income. One approach is to add up the total flow of *expenditure* on final domestic output; the other is to add up the total flow of *income* generated by the flow of domestic production. All three measures yield the same total, which is called **gross domestic product (GDP)**. When it is calculated by adding up the total value added in the economy, it is called *GDP by value added*. When it is calculated by adding up total expenditure for each of the main components of final output, the result is called *GDP on the expenditure side*. When it is calculated by adding up all the income claims generated by the act of production, it is called *GDP on the income side*.

The conventions of double-entry bookkeeping require that all value produced must be accounted for by a claim that someone has to that value. Thus, the two values calculated from the income and the expenditure sides are identical conceptually and differ in practical measurements only because of errors of measurement. Any discrepancy arising from such errors is then reconciled so that one common total is given as *the* measure of GDP. Both calculations are of interest, however, because each gives a different and useful breakdown. Also, having two independent ways of measuring the same quantity provides a useful check on statistical procedures and on errors in measurement.

GDP from the Expenditure Side

GDP for a given year is calculated from the expenditure side by adding up the expenditures needed to purchase the final output produced in that year. Total expenditure on final output is the sum of four broad categories of expenditure: consumption, investment, government purchases, and net exports. In the following chapters, we will discuss in considerable detail the causes and consequences of movements in each of these four expenditure categories. Here we define what they are and how they are measured. Throughout, it is important to remember that these four categories of expenditure are exhaustive—they are *defined* in such a way that all expenditure on final output falls into one of the four categories. Canadian GDP from the expenditure side for 2008 is shown in Table 20-1.

1. Consumption Expenditure Consumption **expenditure** includes expenditure on all goods and services sold to their final users during the year. It includes services, such as haircuts, dental care, and legal advice; non-durable goods, such as fresh vegetables, clothing, cut flowers, and fresh meat; and durable goods, such as cars, TVs, and air conditioners. *Actual* measured consumption expenditure is denoted by the symbol C_a.

gross domestic product (GDP) The total value of goods and services produced in the economy during a given period.

consumption expenditure Household expenditure on all goods and services. Represented by the symbol *C*.

TABLE 20-1   GDP from the Expenditure Side, 2008

Category	Billions of Dollars	Percent of GDP
Consumption		
Durable goods	112.4	
Semi-durable goods	70.5	
Non-durable goods	216.5	
Services	491.8	
	891.2	55.7
Investment		
Plant and equipment	201.0	
Residential structures	108.2	
Inventories	8.7	
	317.9	19.9
Government Purchases		
Current expenditure	313.7	
Investment	53.3	
	367.0	22.9
Net Exports		
Exports of goods and services	562.2	
Imports of goods and services	−536.8	
	25.4	1.6
Statistical Discrepancy	−1.4	0.0
Total GDP	1600.1	100.0

GDP measured from the expenditure side of the national accounts gives the size of the major components of aggregate expenditure.

(*Source:* Statistics Canada, "Gross Domestic Product, Expenditure-based, 2008," CANSIM database, table 380-0017 and cat. no. 13-001-XIB, www40.statcan.gc.ca/l01/cst01/econ04-eng.24p624p624p6htm.)

Practise with Study Guide Chapter 20, Short-Answer Question 1 and Exercise 6 (part a).

investment expenditure
Expenditure on the production of goods not for present consumption. Represented by the symbol I.

inventories Stocks of raw materials, goods in process, and finished goods held by firms to mitigate the effect of short-term fluctuations in production or sales.

capital stock The aggregate quantity of capital goods.

fixed investment The creation of new plant and equipment.

depreciation The amount by which the capital stock is depleted through the production process.

2. Investment Expenditure

Investment expenditure is expenditure on goods not for present consumption, including inventories; capital goods, such as factories, machines, and warehouses; and residential housing. Such goods are called *investment goods*. Let's examine these three categories in a little more detail.

CHANGES IN INVENTORIES. Almost all firms hold stocks of their inputs and their own outputs. These stocks are called **inventories**. Inventories of inputs and unfinished materials allow firms to maintain a steady stream of production despite interruptions in the deliveries of inputs bought from other firms. Inventories of outputs allow firms to meet orders despite fluctuations in the rate of production.

The accumulation of inventories during any given year counts as positive investment for that year because it represents goods produced but not used for current consumption. These goods are included in the national income accounts at market value, which includes the wages and other costs that the firm incurred in producing them as well as the profit that the firm will make when they are sold in the future. The drawing down of inventories, often called *decumulation*, counts as disinvestment (negative investment) because it represents a reduction in the stock of finished goods that are available to be sold.

NEW PLANT AND EQUIPMENT. All production uses capital goods, which are manufactured aids to production, such as tools, machines, and factory buildings. The economy's total quantity of capital goods is called the **capital stock**. Creating new capital goods is an act of investment and is called *business fixed investment*, often shortened to **fixed investment**.

NEW RESIDENTIAL HOUSING. A house or an apartment building is a durable asset that yields its utility over a long period of time. Because such an asset meets the definition of investment that we gave earlier, housing construction—the building of a *new* house—is counted as investment expenditure rather than as consumption expenditure. However, when an individual purchases a house from a builder or from another individual, an existing asset is simply transferred, and the transaction is not part of national income. Only when a new house is built does it appear as residential investment in the national accounts.

GROSS AND NET INVESTMENT. The total investment that occurs in the economy is called gross investment. Gross investment is divided into two parts: replacement investment and net investment. Replacement investment is the amount of investment required to replace that part of the capital stock lost through the process of **depreciation**. Net investment is equal to gross investment minus depreciation.

$$\text{Net investment} = \text{Gross investment} - \text{Depreciation}$$

When net investment is positive, the economy's capital stock is growing. If net investment is negative—which rarely happens—the economy's capital stock is shrinking.

All investment goods are part of the nation's total current output, and their production creates income whether the goods produced are a part of net investment or are merely replacement investment. Thus, all of gross investment is included in the calculation of national income. *Actual* total investment expenditure is denoted by the symbol I_a.

3. Government Purchases

When governments provide goods and services that households want, such as street-cleaning and firefighting, they are adding to the sum total of valuable output in the economy. With other government activities, the case may not seem so clear. Should expenditures by the federal government to send soldiers overseas, or to pay a civil servant to refile papers from a now-defunct department, be regarded as contributions to national income?

National income statisticians do not speculate about such matters. Instead they include all **government purchases** of goods and services as part of national income (some of which is government expenditure on investment goods). *Actual* government purchases of goods and services are denoted G_a.

COST VERSUS MARKET VALUE. Government output is typically valued at cost rather than at market value. In many cases, there is really no choice. What, for example, is the market value of the law courts? No one knows. But since we do know what it costs the government to provide these services, we value them at their cost of production.

Although valuing at cost is the only possible way to measure many government activities, it does have one curious consequence. If, because of an increase in productivity, one civil servant now does what two used to do, and the displaced worker shifts to the private sector, the government's measured contribution to national income will fall (but the private sector's contribution will rise). Conversely, if two workers now do what one worker used to do, the government's contribution will rise. Both changes could occur even though what the government actually produces has not changed. This is an inevitable but curious consequence of measuring the value of the government's output by the cost of producing it.

GOVERNMENT PURCHASES VERSUS GOVERNMENT EXPENDITURE. Only government *purchases* of currently produced goods and services are included as part of GDP. As a result, a great deal of government expenditure does *not* count as part of GDP. For example, when the government makes payments to a retired person through the Canada Pension Plan, there is no market transaction involved as the government is not purchasing any currently produced goods or services from the retiree. The payment itself does not add to total output. The same is true of payments for employment insurance and welfare, and interest on the national debt (which transfers income from taxpayers to holders of government bonds). These are examples of **transfer payments,** which are government expenditures that are not made in return for currently produced goods and services. They are not a part of expenditure on the nation's total output and are therefore not included in GDP. (Of course, the recipients of transfer payments often choose to spend their money on consumption goods. Such expenditure then counts in the same way as any other consumption expenditure.)

4. Net Exports

The fourth category of aggregate expenditure arises from foreign trade. How do imports and exports influence national income? **Imports** are domestic expenditure on foreign-produced goods and services, whereas **exports** are foreign expenditure on domestically produced goods and services.

IMPORTS. A country's national income is the total value of final goods produced in that country. If you buy a car that was made in Japan, only a small part of that value will represent expenditure on Canadian production. Some of it represents payment for the services of the Canadian dealers and for transportation; the rest is expenditure on Japanese products. If you take your next vacation in Italy, much of your expenditure will be on goods and services produced in Italy and thus will contribute to Italian GDP rather than to Canadian GDP.

Unsold merchandise becomes part of firms' inventories. In national-income accounting, firms' expenditures on inventories are considered one part of investment expenditure.

government purchases All government expenditure on currently produced goods and services, exclusive of government transfer payments. Represented by the symbol *G*.

transfer payment A payment to an individual or institution not made in exchange for a good or service.

imports The value of all domestically produced goods and services purchased from firms, households, or governments in other countries.

exports The value of all goods and services sold to firms, households, and governments in other countries.

Similarly, when a Canadian firm makes an investment expenditure on a machine that was made partly with imported raw materials, only part of the expenditure is on Canadian production; the rest is expenditure on foreign production. The same is true for government expenditure on such things as roads and dams; some of the expenditure is for imported materials, and only part of it is for domestically produced goods and services.

Consumption, investment, and government expenditures all have an import content. To arrive at total expenditure *on Canadian products,* we need to subtract from total Canadian expenditure any expenditure on imports. The value of actual imports is given the symbol IM_a.

EXPORTS. If Canadian firms sell goods to German households, the goods are part of German consumption expenditure but also constitute expenditure *on Canadian output.* Indeed, all goods and services that are produced in Canada and sold to foreigners must be counted as part of Canadian production and income; they are produced in Canada, and they create incomes for the Canadian residents who produce them. They are not purchased by Canadian residents, however, so they are not included as part of C_a, I_a, or G_a. Therefore, to arrive at the total value of expenditure *on Canadian output,* it is necessary to add in the value of Canadian exports of goods and services. The value of actual exports is denoted X_a.

net exports The value of total exports minus the value of total imports. Represented by the symbol *NX*.

It is customary to group actual imports and actual exports together as **net exports**. Net exports are defined as total exports minus total imports ($X_a - IM_a$), which is also denoted NX_a. When the value of Canadian exports exceeds the value of Canadian imports, net exports are positive. When the value of imports exceeds the value of exports, net exports are negative.

Total Expenditures Gross domestic product measured from the expenditure side is equal to the sum of the four major expenditure categories that we have just discussed. In terms of a simple equation, we have

$$GDP = C_a + I_a + G_a + (X_a - IM_a)$$

These data are shown in Table 20-1 for Canada in 2008, including some data on the expenditure in the various subcategories.

GDP from the Income Side

Practise with Study Guide
Chapter 20, Exercises 3 and 6
(part b).

As we said earlier, the conventions of national income accounting ensure that the production of a nation's output generates income *exactly* equal to the value of that production. Labour must be employed, land must be rented, and capital must be used. The calculation of GDP from the income side involves adding up factor incomes and other claims on the value of output until all of that value is accounted for.

1. Factor Incomes National income accountants distinguish three main components of factor incomes: wages and salaries, interest, and business profits.

WAGES AND SALARIES. Wages and salaries are the payment for the services of labour and they include all pre-tax labour earnings: take-home pay, income taxes withheld, employment-insurance contributions, pension-fund contributions, and other fringe benefits. In total, wages and salaries represent the part of the value of production that is paid to labour.

INTEREST. Interest includes interest that is earned on bank deposits, interest that is earned on loans to firms, and miscellaneous other investment income (but excludes interest income earned from loans to Canadian governments).[2]

BUSINESS PROFITS. Some profits are paid out as *dividends* to owners of firms; the rest are held by firms and are called *retained earnings*. Both dividends and retained earnings are included in the calculation of GDP. For accounting purposes, total profits include corporate profits, incomes of unincorporated businesses (mainly small businesses, farmers, partnerships, and professionals), and profits of government business enterprises and Crown corporations (such as Canada Post and Export Development Canada).

Profits and interest together represent the payment for the use of capital—interest for borrowed capital and profits for capital contributed by the owners of firms.

NET DOMESTIC INCOME. The sum of wages and salaries, interest, and profits is called *net domestic income at factor cost*. It is "net" because it excludes the value of output that is used as replacement investment. It is "domestic income" because it is the income accruing to domestic factors of production. It is "at factor cost" because it represents only that part of the value of final output that accrues to factors in the form of payments due to them for their services. As we will see next, some part of the value of final output does not accrue to the factors at all.

2. Non-factor Payments
Every time a consumer spends $10 on some item, less than $10 is generated as income for factors of production. This shortfall is due to the presence of indirect taxes and depreciation.

INDIRECT TAXES AND SUBSIDIES. An important claim on the market value of output arises out of indirect taxes, which are taxes on the production and sale of goods and services. In Canada, the most important indirect taxes are provincial sales taxes, excise taxes on specific products, and the federal Goods and Services Tax (GST).

For example, if a good's market price of $10.00 includes 60 cents in provincial sales taxes and 50 cents in federal GST, only $8.90 is available as income to factors of production. Governments are claiming $1.10 of the $10.00 initial value of the good. Adding up income claims to determine GDP therefore necessitates including the portion of the total market value of output that is the governments' claims exercised through their taxes on goods and services.

Sometimes the government gives subsidies to firms, which act like negative taxes. When these occur, it is necessary to *subtract* their value, since they allow factor incomes to *exceed* the market value of output. Suppose a municipal bus company spends $150 000 producing bus rides and covers its costs by selling $140 000 in fares and obtaining a $10 000 subsidy from the local government. The total income that the company will generate from its production is $150 000, but the total market value of its output is only $140 000, with the difference made up by the subsidy. To get from total income to the market value of its total output, we must subtract the amount of the subsidy.

DEPRECIATION. Another claim on the value of final output is depreciation. Depreciation is the value of capital that has been used up in the process of producing final output. It is part of gross profits, but because it is needed to compensate for capital used

---

[2] The treatment of interest in the national accounts is a little odd. Interest paid by the government is considered a transfer payment, whereas interest paid by private households or firms is treated as expenditure (and its receipt is counted as a factor payment). This is only one example of arbitrary decisions in national income accounting. Others are discussed in *Extensions in Theory 20-1* on page 507.

TABLE 20-2   GDP from the Income Side, 2008

Category	Billions of Dollars	Percent of GDP
Factor Incomes		
Wages, salaries, and supplementary income	$ 823.1	51.4
Interest and miscellaneous investment income	81.5	5.1
Business profits (including net income of farmers and unincorporated businesses)	327.6	20.5
Net domestic income at factor cost	1232.2	77.0
Non-factor Payments		
Depreciation	201.5	12.6
Indirect taxes less subsidies	165.0	10.3
Statistical discrepancy	1.4	0.0
Total	$1600.1	100.0

GDP measured from the income side of the national accounts gives the sizes of the major components of the income generated by producing the nation's output.

(*Source:* Statistics Canada, "Gross Domestic Product, Income-based, 2008," CANSIM database, table 380-0001 and cat. no. 13-001-X, www40.statcan.gc.ca/l01/cst01/econ03-eng.htm.)

up in the process of production, it is not part of net profits. Hence, depreciation is not income earned by any factor of production.

3. Total National Income

> **From the income side, GDP is the sum of factor incomes *plus* indirect taxes (net of subsidies) *plus* depreciation.**

The various components of the income side of the GDP in the Canadian economy in 2008 are shown in Table 20-2. Note that one of the terms in the table is called *statistical discrepancy.* This is a "fudge factor" to make sure that the independent measures of income and expenditure come to the same total. Statistical discrepancy is a clear indication that national income accounting is not error-free. Although national income and national expenditure are conceptually identical, in practice both are measured with slight error.

We have now seen the two methods for computing a country's national income. Both are correct and give us the same measure of GDP, but each gives us some different additional information. For some questions, such as what the likely future path of the nation's capital stock will be, it is useful to know the relative importance of consumption and investment. In this case, the expenditure approach for computing GDP provides some of the necessary information (Table 20-1 on page 501). For other questions, such as what is happening to the distribution of income between labour and capital, we need information about the composition of factor incomes. In this case, a useful starting point would be to examine GDP on the income side (Table 20-2).

Measuring national income is not problem-free. As in any accounting exercise, many arbitrary rules are used. Some of them seem odd, but the important thing is to use these rules consistently over time. Comparisons of GDP over time will then reflect genuine changes in economic activity, which is what we desire for the measure. *Extensions in Theory 20-1* discusses the issue of arbitrariness in national income accounting.

myeconlab   ADDITIONAL TOPICS

Canada and six other countries together form what is called the "G7" group of advanced industrialized nations. For a comparison of GDP growth in the G7 countries over the past decade, look for **Growth in Canada and Other G7 Countries** in the *Additional Topics* section of this book's MyEconLab.

EXTENSIONS IN THEORY 20-1

Arbitrary Decisions in National Income Accounting

National income accounting practices contain many arbitrary decisions. For example, goods that are finished and held in inventories are valued at market value, thereby anticipating their sale, even though the actual selling price may not be known. In the case of a Ford in a dealer's showroom, this practice may be justified because the *value* of this Ford is perhaps virtually the same as that of an identical Ford that has just been sold to a customer. However, what is the correct market value of a half-finished house or an unfinished novel? Accountants arbitrarily treat goods in process at cost (rather than at market value) if the goods are being made by firms. They ignore completely the value of the unfinished novel. The arbitrary nature of these decisions is inevitable: Because people must arrive at some practical compromise between consistent definitions and measurable magnitudes, any decision will be somewhat arbitrary.

Such arbitrary decisions surely affect the size of measured GDP. But does it matter? The surprising answer,

for many purposes, is no. It is wrong to think that just because a statistical measure is imperfect (as all statistical measures are), it is useless. Simple measures often give estimates that are quite accurate, and substantial improvements in sophistication may make only trivial improvements in these estimates.

In 2008, for example, Canadian GDP was measured as $1600.1 billion. It is certain that the market value of all production in Canada in that year was neither $500 billion nor $2500 billion, but it might well have been $1500 billion or $1700 billion had different measures been defined with different arbitrary decisions built in. Similarly, Canadian per capita GDP is about three times the Mexican per capita GDP and is about 20 percent less than U.S. per capita GDP. Other measures might differ, but it is unlikely that any measure would reveal the Mexican per capita GDP to be higher than Canada's, or Canada's to be significantly above that of the United States.

20.3 National Income Accounting: Some Further Issues

Now that we have examined the basics of national income accounting, we are ready to explore some more detailed issues. We discuss the distinction between GDP and the related concept of gross national product (GNP), the difference between real and nominal GDP, the major omissions from measured GDP, and the connection between GDP and "living standards."

GDP and GNP

A measure of national output closely related to GDP is **gross national product (GNP)**. The difference between GDP and GNP is the difference between *income produced* and *income received*. GDP measures the value of total output *produced in Canada* and the total income generated as a result of that production. GNP measures the total amount of income *received by Canadian residents,* no matter where that income was generated. How can GDP differ from GNP? Let's consider two examples.

For the first example, consider a Toyota factory located in Cambridge, Ontario. Suppose in 2010 that the value added generated by that factory is $100 million. Canadian

Toyota cars produced in Canada contribute to Canada's GDP. But the portion of profits that returns to foreign shareholders is not part of Canada's GNP.

gross national product (GNP) The value of total incomes earned by domestic residents.

GDP is therefore higher by $100 million as a result of that production. But suppose $5 million of the profits (part of the value added) generated at that factory is remitted to foreign owners. Since only $95 million of the value added generates income *for Canadian residents*, Canadian GNP is higher by only $95 million.

The second example involves any Canadian-owned business located outside of Canada. The value added produced by that business contributes to the GDP in a foreign country but not in Canada. But if there are profits remitted to the Canadian owners, those profits will be part of the income of Canadian residents and thus part of Canadian GNP.

> GDP measures the value of all production located in Canada, no matter who receives the income from that production. GNP measures the income received by Canadian residents, no matter where the production occurred to generate that income.

The relative sizes of GDP and GNP depend on the balance between income earned by Canadian residents from Canadian investments located abroad, and income paid to foreign residents from foreign-owned investments located in Canada. For most of Canada's history, Canada has been a *net debtor* country. Thus, the value of foreign-located assets owned by Canadian residents has been less than the value of Canadian-located assets owned by foreigners. As a result, the foreign-generated income received by Canadian residents is less than the Canadian-generated income going to foreigners. This makes Canadian GNP less than Canadian GDP. But the difference is small. In most years, GNP is only 3 or 4 percent lower than GDP.

Which Measure Is Better? Given the difference between GDP and GNP, we are naturally led to ask if one measure is better than the other. The answer depends on what we want to measure.

> GDP is superior to GNP as a measure of domestic economic activity. GNP is superior to GDP as a measure of the income of domestic residents.

If you want to know how easy it will be to find a job or whether factories are working double shifts or whether new buildings are going up, look to changes in the GDP. By its definition, it is the GDP that tells us how much is being produced within a nation's borders. To know how much income is available to the residents of a country, however, one should look at the GNP, which counts income earned abroad and subtracts income generated at home that accrues to residents of other nations. Thus, the GNP is a better measure of the income of a country's residents.

Disposable Personal Income Both GDP and GNP are important measures of overall economic activity and of national income. Most important to individual households, however, is **disposable personal income**, the part of national income that is available to households to spend or to save. The easiest way to calculate disposable personal income is to subtract from GNP the parts of the GNP that are not available to households. Hence, we must subtract all taxes (both income and sales taxes), depreciation, retained earnings, and interest paid to institutions. We then need to add in the transfer payments made to households. In recent years, disposable income has represented about 60 percent of GDP.

disposable personal income The part of national income that accrues to households and is available to spend or save.

Real and Nominal GDP

In Chapter 19, we distinguished between real and nominal measures of aggregate output. When we add up dollar values of outputs, expenditures, or incomes, we end up with what are called *nominal values*. Nominal GDP increased by 135.3 percent between 1990 and 2008. If we want to compare *real* GDP in 2008 to that in 1990, we need to determine how much of that nominal increase was due to increases in prices and how much was due to increases in quantities produced. Although there are many possible ways of doing this, the underlying principle is always the same: The value of output in each period is computed by using a common set of *base-period prices*. When this is done, economists say that real output is measured in *constant dollars*.

> Total GDP valued at current prices is called *nominal* GDP. GDP valued at base-period prices is called *real* GDP.

Any change in nominal GDP reflects the combined effects of changes in quantities and changes in prices. However, when real income is measured over different periods by using a common set of base-period prices, changes in real income reflect only changes in quantities. Table 20-3 shows real and nominal GDP for selected years in Canada since 1985.

Year	Nominal GDP (current prices)	Real GDP (2002 prices)	GDP Deflator
1985	485.7	716.1	67.8
1990	679.9	825.3	82.4
1995	810.4	898.8	90.2
2000	1076.6	1100.5	97.8
2002	1152.9	1152.9	100.0
2005	1373.8	1247.8	110.1
2008	1600.1	1321.4	121.1

TABLE 20-3 Nominal and Real GDP in Canada: Selected Years (billions of dollars)

Nominal GDP tells us about the money value of output; real GDP tells us about the quantity of physical output. Nominal GDP gives the total value of output in any year, valued at the prices of that year. Real GDP gives the total value of output in any year, *valued at prices from some base year*, in this case 2002. The comparison of real and nominal GDP implicitly defines a price index, changes in which reveal changes in the (average) prices of goods produced domestically. Note that in 2002, nominal GDP equals real GDP (measured in 2002 prices), and thus the GDP deflator equals 100.

(*Source:* Statistics Canada, CANSIM database. Real GDP: Series V1992067. Nominal GDP: Series V1997757.)

The GDP Deflator If nominal and real GDP change by different amounts over a given time period, then prices must have changed over that period. For example, if nominal GDP has increased by 6 percent and real GDP has increased by only 4 percent over the same period, we know that average prices must have increased by 2 percent. Comparing what has happened to nominal and real GDP over the same period implies the existence of a price index measuring the change in prices over that period— "implies" because no explicit price index is used in calculating either real or nominal GDP. However, an index can be inferred by comparing these two values. The *GDP deflator* is defined as follows:

Practise with Study Guide Chapter 20, Exercise 4 and Extension Exercise E1.

$$\text{GDP deflator} = \frac{\text{GDP at current prices}}{\text{GDP at base-period prices}} \times 100 = \frac{\text{Nominal GDP}}{\text{Real GDP}} \times 100$$

The **GDP deflator** is the most comprehensive available index of the price level because it includes all the goods and services that are produced by the entire economy. It uses the current year's basket of production to compare the current year's prices with those prevailing in the base period. (Because it uses the current basket of goods and services, it does not run into the CPI's problem of sometimes being based on an out-of-date basket.) The GDP deflator was 21.1 percent higher in 2008 than in the base year 2002 (see Table 20-3). Thus, for those goods and services produced in

GDP deflator An index number derived by dividing nominal GDP by real GDP. Its change measures the average change in price of all the items in the GDP.

2008, their average price increased by 21.1 percent over the previous six years. *Applying Economic Concepts 20-2* illustrates the calculation of real and nominal GDP and the GDP deflator for a simple hypothetical economy that produces only wheat and steel.

As we have said, a change in nominal GDP can be split into a change caused by prices and a change caused by quantities. For example, from the data in Table 20-3 we see that in 2008, Canadian nominal GDP was 135.3 percent higher than in 1990. This increase was due to a 47.0-percent increase in prices and a 60.1-percent increase in real GDP.[3]

GDP Deflator Versus the CPI   An important point about the GDP deflator is that it does not necessarily change in line with changes in the CPI. The two price indices are measuring different things. Movements in the CPI measure the change in the average price of consumer goods whereas movements in the GDP deflator reflect the change in the average price of goods produced in Canada. So changes in the world price of coffee, for example, would have a larger effect on the CPI than on the GDP deflator, since Canadians drink a lot of coffee but no coffee is produced here. Conversely, a change in the world price of wheat is likely to have a bigger effect on the GDP deflator than on the CPI since most of Canada's considerable production of wheat is exported to other countries, thus leaving a relatively small fraction to appear in the Canadian basket of consumer products.

> Changes in the GDP deflator and Consumer Price Index (CPI) similarly reflect overall inflationary trends. But changes in relative prices may lead the two price indices to move in different ways.

Prostitution and other illegal activities involve genuine market transactions, but they are not included in official measures of national income.

Omissions from GDP

National income as measured in the National Income and Expenditure Accounts provides an excellent measure of the flow of economic activity in organized markets in a given year. But much economic activity takes place outside the markets that the national income accountants survey. Although these activities are not typically included in the measure of GDP, they nevertheless use real resources and satisfy real wants and needs.

Illegal Activities   GDP does not measure illegal activities, even though many of them are ordinary business activities that produce goods and services sold in markets and that generate factor incomes. Many forms of illegal gambling, prostitution, and drug trade come into this category. To gain an accurate measure of the total demand for factors of production, of total marketable output, or of total incomes generated, we should include these activities, whether or not they are legal. The omission of illegal activities is no trivial matter: The drug trade alone is a multibillion-dollar business.

---

[3] For large percentage changes in price and quantity, the nominal percentage change is not exactly equal to the sum of the price and the quantity changes; generally, the relationship is multiplicative. In this case, prices and quantities are respectively 1.470 and 1.601 times their original values. Thus, nominal GDP is (1.470) × (1.601) = 2.353 times its original value, which is an increase of 135.3 percent. For small percentage changes, the sum is a very good approximation of the multiplicative change. For example, if prices grow by 2 percent and quantities by 3 percent, the nominal change is (1.02) × (1.03) = 1.0506, which is very close to 1.05.

APPLYING ECONOMIC CONCEPTS 20-2

Calculating Nominal and Real GDP

To see what is involved in calculating nominal GDP, real GDP, and the GDP deflator, an example may be helpful. Consider a simple hypothetical economy that produces only two commodities, wheat and steel.

Table 1 gives the basic data for output and prices in the economy for two years.

TABLE 1   Data for a Hypothetical Economy

	Quantity Produced		Prices	
	Wheat (bushels)	Steel (tonnes)	Wheat ($/bushel)	Steel ($/tonne)
Year 1	100	20	10	50
Year 2	110	16	12	55

Table 2 shows nominal GDP, calculated by adding the dollar values of wheat output and of steel output for each year. In year 1, the values of both wheat and steel production were $1000, so nominal GDP was $2000. In year 2, wheat output rose to $1320, and steel output fell to $880. Since the rise in the value of wheat was greater than the fall in the value of steel, nominal GDP rose by $200.

TABLE 2   Calculation of Nominal GDP

Year 1: $(100 \times \$10) + (20 \times \$50) = \$2000$
Year 2: $(110 \times \$12) + (16 \times \$55) = \$2200$

Table 3 shows real GDP, calculated by valuing output in each year *at year-2 prices;* that is, year 2 is used as the base year. In year 2, wheat output rose, but steel output fell. If we use year-2 prices, the fall in the value of steel output between years 1 and 2 exceeded the rise in the value of wheat output, and so real GDP fell.

TABLE 3   Calculation of Real GDP Using Year-2 Prices

Year 1: $(100 \times \$12) + (20 \times \$55) = \$2300$
Year 2: $(110 \times \$12) + (16 \times \$55) = \$2200$

In table 4, the ratio of nominal to real GDP is calculated for each year and multiplied by 100. This ratio implicitly measures the change in prices over the period in question and is called the *GDP deflator*. The deflator shows that average prices increased by 15 percent between year 1 and year 2.

TABLE 4   Calculation of the GDP Deflator

Year 1: $(2000/2300) \times 100 = 86.96$
Year 2: $(2200/2200) \times 100 = 100.00$

Throughout this box we have used year 2 as the base year. But we could just as easily have used year 1. The changes we would have computed in real GDP and the deflator would have been very similar— but not identical—to the ones we did compute using year 2 as the base year. The choice of base year matters because of different *relative* prices in the different years (note that the price of steel relative to the price of wheat is lower in year 2 than in year 1). Put simply, with different relative prices in different years, the various output changes are weighted differently depending on which prices we use, and thus the *aggregate* measure of real GDP changes by different amounts. (If you want to understand this point in more detail, try doing Study Exercise #8 on page 516.)

How do we choose the "right" base year? As with many other elements of national income accounting, there is some arbitrariness in the choice. There is no "right" year. The important thing is not which year to use—the important thing is to be clear about which year you are using and then, for a given set of comparisons, to be sure that you are consistent in your choice. In recent years, Statistics Canada has avoided this problem by using "chain weighting," a technique that essentially uses an average over several measures, each one corresponding to a different base year.

Note that some illegal activities do get included in national income measures, although they are generally misclassified by industry. The income is included because people sometimes report their illegally earned income as part of their earnings from legal activities. They do this to avoid the fate of Al Capone, the famous Chicago gangster in the 1920s and 1930s, who, having avoided conviction on many more serious charges, was finally caught and imprisoned for income-tax evasion.

The Underground Economy   A significant omission from GDP is the so-called underground economy. The transactions that occur in the underground economy are perfectly legal in themselves; the only illegality involved is that such transactions are not reported for tax purposes. One example of this is the carpenter who repairs a leak in your roof and takes payment in cash (and does not report it as income) to avoid taxation. Because such transactions go unreported, they are omitted from GDP.

The growth of the underground economy is facilitated by the rising importance of services in the nation's total output. It is much easier for a carpenter to pass unnoticed by government authorities than it is for a manufacturing establishment. Estimates of the value of income earned in the underground economy run from 2 percent to 15 percent of GDP. In some countries, the figures are even higher. The Italian underground economy, for example, has been estimated at close to 25 percent of that country's GDP.

"Home Production" and Other Non-market Activities   If a homeowner hires a firm to do some landscaping, the value of the landscaping enters into GDP (as long as the landscaper records the transaction and thus declares the income); if the homeowner does the landscaping herself, the value of the landscaping is omitted from GDP because there is no recorded market transaction. Such production of goods and services in the home is called *home production* and includes all of the "ordinary" work that is required to keep a household functioning. Other non-market activities include voluntary work, such as canvassing for a political party or coaching a local hockey team. Both home production and volunteer activities clearly add to economic well-being, and both use economic resources. Yet neither is included in official measures of national income since they are non-market activities.

Another extremely important non-market activity is *leisure*. If a lawyer voluntarily chooses to reduce her time at work from 2400 hours to 2200 hours per year, measured national income will fall by the lawyer's wage rate times 200 hours. Yet the value to the lawyer of the 200 hours of new leisure enjoyed outside of the marketplace must exceed the lost wages (otherwise she would not have chosen to reduce her work effort by 200 hours), so total economic well-being has increased even though measured GDP has fallen. Over the years, one of the most important ways in which economic growth has benefited people is by permitting increased amounts of leisure. Because the leisure time is not marketed, its value does not show up in measures of national income.

Economic "Bads"   When a coal-burning electric power plant sends sulphur dioxide into the atmosphere, leading to acid rain and environmental damage, the value of the electricity sold is included as part of GDP, but the value of the damage done by the acid rain is not deducted. Similarly, the gasoline that we use in our cars is part of national income when it is produced, but the environmental damage done by burning that gasoline is not deducted. To the extent that economic growth brings with it increases in pollution, congestion, and other disamenities of modern living, measurements of national income will overstate the

The extraction, refining, and transportation of oil are all included as goods and services in measures of GDP. But the environmental damage inflicted by an oil spill—an economic "bad"—is not included in any measure of GDP.

improvement in living standards. Such measures capture the increased output of goods and services, but they fail to account for the increased output of "bads" that generally accompany economic growth.

Do the Omissions Matter?   GDP does a good job of measuring the flow of goods and services through the market sector of the economy. Usually, an increase in GDP implies greater opportunities for employment for households that sell their labour services in the market.

> Unless the importance of unmeasured market activity changes rapidly, *changes* in GDP will probably do a satisfactory job of measuring *changes* in economic opportunities.

However, when the task at hand is measurement of the overall flow of goods and services available to satisfy people's wants, regardless of the source of the goods and services, then the omissions that we have discussed become undesirable and potentially serious. Still, in the relatively short term, changes in GDP will usually be a good measure of the direction, if not the exact magnitude, of changes in material living standards.

GDP and Living Standards

We have said that GDP does a good job of measuring the flow of economic activity during a given time period. But we have also said that many things are omitted from this measure, some of which represent beneficial economic activity and some of which represent economic "bads." These observations lead to the obvious question: To what extent does GDP provide even a rough measure of our living standards?

The answer depends on what we mean by "living standards." For many people, this term refers to our *purchasing power* or *real income*. When GDP rises, do we experience a rise in our average real incomes? The answer is not necessarily. As we will see in detail in Chapters 25 and 26, real GDP can rise for two general reasons. First, there may be an increase in the amounts of land, labour, and capital used as inputs to production. Second, these inputs may become more productive in the sense that there is an increase in the amount of output *per unit of input*. The *average* level of real income in the economy is best measured by real GDP *per person* but this does not necessarily rise whenever real GDP rises. If real GDP rises because more people become employed, real GDP per person may not rise. However, if real GDP rises because the existing labour force becomes more productive, then average real incomes will also rise. This explains why most economists believe that productivity growth is such an important determinant of living standards.

To many people, however, the term "living standards" is much broader than simply real per capita income—it includes such important but intangible things as religious and political freedom, the quality of local community life, environmental sustainability, the distribution of income, and our ability to prevent and treat illness and disease. And since measures of real GDP omit many of these intangible things that contribute positively to our overall well-being, it is not even clear that changes in real per capita GDP accurately reflect changes in this broader concept of living standards. For example, greater productivity may lead to an increase in real per capita income and thus to a rise in our average material living standards, but if this change also leads to greater environmental damage or greater inequality in the distribution of income, some people may argue that while our material living standards have increased, our overall well-being has declined.

> Changes in real per capita income are a good measure of average material living standards. But material living standards are only part of what most people consider their overall well-being.

---

myeconlab ADDITIONAL TOPICS

Some recent economic research attempts to uncover the determinants of individual well-being, or "happiness." One of the interesting findings is that income appears to be less important than several other aspects of life. See **What Makes People Happy?** in the *Additional Topics* section of this book's MyEconLab.

www.myeconlab.com

Summary

20.1 National Output and Value Added

- Each firm's contribution to total output is equal to its value added, which is the value of the firm's output minus the values of all intermediate goods and services—that is, the outputs of other firms—that it uses. The sum of all the values added produced in an economy is the economy's total output, which is called gross domestic product (GDP).

20.2 National Income Accounting: The Basics

- From the circular flow of income, there are three ways to compute national income. One is to add up each firm's value added. The second is to add up total expenditure on domestic output. The third is to add up the total income generated by domestic production. By standard accounting conventions, these three aggregations define the same total.
- From the expenditure side of the national accounts,

  $$\text{GDP} = C_a + I_a + G_a + (X_a - IM_a)$$

- C_a comprises consumption expenditures of households. I_a is investment in plant and equipment, residential construction, and inventory accumulation. G_a is government purchases of goods and services. $(X_a - IM_a)$ represents net exports of goods and services.
- GDP measured from the income side adds up all claims to the market value of production. Wages, interest, profits, depreciation, and indirect taxes net of subsidies are the major categories.

20.3 National Income Accounting: Some Further Issues

- GDP measures the value of all production located in Canada, no matter who receives the income from that production. GNP measures the income received by Canadian residents, no matter where the production occurred to generate that income. Because Canada is a net debtor, its GNP is usually 3 to 4 percent less than its GDP.
- Real measures of national income reflect changes in real quantities. Nominal measures of national income reflect changes in both prices and quantities. Any change in nominal income can be split into a change in quantities and a change in prices.
- The comparison of nominal and real GDP yields the implicit GDP price deflator, an index of the average price of all goods and services produced in the economy.

- GDP and related measures of national income must be interpreted with their limitations in mind. GDP excludes production resulting from activities that are illegal, that take place in the underground economy, or that do not pass through markets.
- Notwithstanding its limitations, GDP remains a useful measure of the total economic activity that passes through the nation's markets. Recorded *changes* in GDP will generally do an accurate job of measuring *changes* in economic activity.
- Real per capita GDP is a good measure of average material living standards. But because GDP omits many intangible things that contribute positively to our quality of life, GDP-based measures miss important parts of our overall well-being.

Key Concepts

Intermediate and final goods
Value added
GDP as the sum of all values added
GDP from the expenditure side

GDP from the income side
GNP versus GDP
Disposable personal income
GDP deflator

Omissions from GDP
Per capita GDP and productivity
Living standards and GDP

Study Exercises

1. Fill in the blanks to make the following statements complete.

   a. If, when measuring Canada's national output, we add the market values of all firms' outputs in Canada, then we are committing the error of _____. Such an amount would greatly _____ the economy's actual output.

   b. Statisticians use the concept of _____ to avoid double counting in measuring national income. Each firm's _____ is the value of its output minus the costs of _____ that it purchases from other firms.

   c. If we measure GDP from the expenditure side, we are adding four broad categories of expenditure: _____, _____, _____, and _____. As an equation it is written as GDP = _____.

   d. If we measure GDP from the income side, we are adding three main components of factor incomes: _____, _____ and _____. To these items we must add non-factor payments of _____ and _____.

2. Fill in the blanks to make the following statements correct.

   a. Comparing GDP and GNP, if we want the best measure of Canada's domestic economic activity, we should look at _____; if we want the best measure of the income of Canada's residents, then we should look at _____.

   b. If nominal GDP increases by 35 percent over a 10-year period, then it is unclear how much of this increase is due to increases in _____ and how much is due to increases in _____. To overcome this problem, we look at GDP valued at _____ prices and we refer to this measure as _____ national income.

   c. GDP divided by total population gives us a measure of _____.

   d. GDP divided by the number of employed persons in Canada gives us a measure of labour _____.

3. In measuring GDP from the expenditure side (GDP = $C_a + I_a + G_a + NX_a$), which of the following expenditures are included and within which of the four categories?

a. expenditures on automobiles by consumers
b. expenditures on automobiles by firms
c. expenditures on new machinery by Canadian-owned forest companies in Canada
d. expenditures on new machinery by Canadian-owned forest companies in the United States
e. expenditures on new machinery by U.S.-owned forest companies in Canada
f. reductions in business inventories
g. purchases of second-hand cars and trucks
h. the hiring of economic consultants by the Manitoba government
i. the purchase of Canadian-produced software by a firm in Japan

4. The list below provides some national income figures for the country of Econoland. All figures are in millions of dollars.

Wages and salaries	5000
Interest income	200
Personal consumption	3900
Personal saving	1100
Personal income taxes	200
Business profits	465
Indirect taxes	175
Subsidies	30
Government purchases	1000
Exports	350
Imports	390
Net private investment	950
Depreciation	150

a. Using the expenditure approach, what is the value of GDP for Econoland?
b. Using the income approach, what is the value of GDP?
c. What is the value of net domestic income at factor cost?

5. The table below shows data for real and nominal GDP for a hypothetical economy over several years.

Year	Nominal GDP (billions of $)	Real GDP (billions of 2008 $)	GDP Deflator
2006	775.3	798.4	—
2007	814.1	838.6	—
2008	862.9	862.9	—
2009	901.5	882.5	—
2010	951.3	920.6	—
2011	998.8	950.5	—

a. Compute the GDP deflator for each year.
b. Compute the total percentage change in nominal GDP from 2006 to 2011. How much of this change

was due to increases in prices and how much was due to changes in quantities?

6. Would inflation, as measured by the rate of change in the GDP deflator, ever be different from inflation as measured by the rate of change in the Consumer Price Index? Would it ever be the same? Explain.

7. For each of the following events, describe the likely effect on real GDP.

a. The Quebec ice storm of 1998 increases the demand for building materials to repair damage to homes.
b. The Quebec ice storm of 1998 damages many factories.
c. In a near-perfect growing season in 2006, Manitoba's wheat crop increases by 20 percent above normal levels.
d. A 30-percent fall in the world price of oil in 2008 causes Alberta-based oil producers to reduce their oil production (measured in barrels) by 5 percent.
e. Several new sports facilities are built in Vancouver in anticipation of the 2010 Winter Olympics.
f. The building of a larger arena in Toronto increases the demand for Maple Leafs tickets by Torontonians.
g. The building of a larger arena in Toronto increases the demand for Maple Leafs tickets by residents of Buffalo, New York.

8. Consider the following data for a hypothetical economy that produces two goods, milk and honey.

	Quantity Produced		Prices	
	Milk (litres)	Honey (kg)	Milk ($/litre)	Honey ($/kg)
Year 1	100	40	2	6
Year 2	120	25	3	6

a. Compute nominal GDP for each year in this economy.
b. Using year 1 as the base year, compute real GDP for each year. What is the percentage change in real GDP from year 1 to year 2?
c. Using year 1 as the base year, compute the price deflator for each year. What is the percentage change in real GDP from year 1 to year 2?
d. Now compute the GDP deflator for each year, using year 1 as the base year.
e. Now compute the GDP deflator for each year, using year 2 as the base year.
f. Explain why the measures of real GDP growth (and growth in the deflator) depend on the choice of base year.

Discussion Questions

1. Residents of some Canadian cities have recently become concerned about the growing proportion of their local real estate that is being bought up by foreign residents. What is the effect of this transfer of ownership on Canadian GDP and GNP?

2. What would be the effects of the following events on the measured value of Canada's real GDP? Speculate on the effects of each event on the true well-being of Canadians.

    a. destruction of thousands of homes by flood water
    b. destruction of hundreds of businesses by an ice storm
    c. complete cessation of all imports from Europe
    d. an increase in the amount of acid rain that falls
    e. an increase in the amount of spending on devices that reduce pollution at a major hydroelectricity plant
    f. reduction in the standard workweek from 37 hours to 30 hours
    g. hiring of all welfare recipients as government employees
    h. outbreak of hostilities in the Middle East in which Canadian troops became involved

3. In 2008, the United Nations ranked Canada fourth on the Human Development Index—a ranking of the "quality of life" in many countries. Yet in that year Canada ranked only tenth in terms of real per capita GDP. Explain how the two rankings can be different.

4. One way of estimating the size of the underground economy is to see the amount of cash Canadians are carrying relative to the total value of GDP. Why would a rapid rise in the ratio of cash held by the public to GDP indicate a rise in the underground economy?

5. A company's wages and salaries are part of its value added. Suppose, however, that the cleaning and machinery maintenance that its own employees used to do are now contracted out to specialist firms who come in to do the same work more cheaply. What happens to the company's value added when a company follows this recent trend of "contracting out"? What happens to value added in the economy as a whole?

The Simplest Short-Run Macro Model

ⓛ LEARNING OBJECTIVES

In this chapter you will learn

❶ the difference between desired expenditure and actual expenditure.

❷ the determinants of desired consumption and desired investment expenditures.

❸ the meaning of equilibrium national income.

❹ how a change in desired expenditure affects equilibrium income through the "simple multiplier."

In Chapters 19 and 20, we encountered a number of important macroeconomic variables. We considered how they are measured and how they have behaved over the past several decades. We now turn to a more detailed study of what *causes* these variables to behave as they do. In particular, we study the forces that determine real national income and the price level over short periods of time, say, up to a few years. In particular, in this chapter and the next two, we examine how the level of real GDP is determined and how it fluctuates around the level of potential GDP. For simplicity, we assume that potential GDP is constant; in later chapters we explore the long-run forces that explain the growth of potential GDP.

Real GDP and the price level are determined simultaneously. It is, however, easier to study them one at a time. So, in this chapter and the next, we simplify matters by seeing how real national income is determined *under the assumption that the price level is constant*. The simplified analysis is an important first step toward understanding how prices and GDP are determined together, which is the subject of Chapter 23.

Our ability to explain the behaviour of real GDP depends on our understanding of what determines the amount that households and firms desire to spend. So, we begin with an examination of their expenditure decisions.

21.1 Desired Aggregate Expenditure

In Chapter 20, we discussed how national income statisticians divide *actual* GDP into its expenditure components: consumption, investment, government purchases, and net exports. In this chapter and the next, we are concerned with a different concept. It is variously called *desired* or *planned* expenditure. Of course, most people would like to spend virtually unlimited amounts, if only they had the resources. Desired expenditure does not refer, however, to what people would like to do under imaginary circumstances; it refers to what people desire to spend out of the resources that they actually have. Recall from Chapter 20 that the *actual* values of the various categories of expenditure are indicated by C_a, I_a, G_a, and $(X_a - IM_a)$. Economists use the same letters without the subscript "*a*" to indicate the *desired* expenditure in the same categories: C, I, G, and $(X - IM)$.

Everyone makes expenditure decisions. Fortunately, it is unnecessary for our purposes to look at each of the millions of such individual decisions. Instead, it is sufficient to consider four main groups of decision makers: domestic households, firms, governments, and foreign purchasers of domestically produced commodities. The sum of their *desired* expenditures on domestically produced output is called **desired aggregate expenditure** (*AE*):

$$AE = C + I + G + (X - IM)$$

Desired expenditure need not equal actual expenditure, either in total or in any individual category. For example, firms might not plan to invest in inventory accumulation this year but might do so unintentionally if sales are unexpectedly low—the unsold goods that pile up on their shelves are undesired inventory accumulation. In this case, actual investment expenditure, I_a, will exceed desired investment expenditure, I.

> National income accounts measure *actual* expenditures in each of the four expenditure categories. National income theory deals with *desired* expenditures in each of these four categories.

You may be wondering why the distinction between desired and actual expenditure is so important. The answer will become clear in the next section where we discuss the concept of *equilibrium* national income, which involves the relationship between desired and actual expenditure. For now, however, the remainder of this section examines more fully the various components of desired expenditure.

AUTONOMOUS VERSUS INDUCED EXPENDITURE. In what follows, it will be useful to distinguish between *autonomous* and *induced* expenditure. Components of aggregate expenditure that do *not* depend on national income are called **autonomous expenditures**. Autonomous expenditures can and do change, but such changes do not occur systematically in response to changes in national income. Components of aggregate expenditure that *do* change systematically in response to changes in national income are called **induced expenditures**. As we will see, the induced response of desired aggregate expenditure to a change in national income plays a key role in the determination of equilibrium national income.

IMPORTANT SIMPLIFICATIONS. Our goal in this chapter is to develop the simplest possible model of national-income determination. To do so, we focus on only two of the four components of desired aggregate expenditure—consumption and investment.

desired aggregate expenditure (*AE*) The sum of desired or planned spending on domestic output by households, firms, governments, and foreigners.

autonomous expenditure Elements of expenditure that do not change systematically with national income.

induced expenditure Any component of expenditure that is systematically related to national income.

Consumption, which is typically between 55 and 60 percent of GDP, is by far the largest component of aggregate expenditure; it also provides the most important link between desired aggregate expenditure and real national income. Investment includes the accumulation of inventories plus expenditure on new machines or factories, which add to the stock of physical capital. Investment is smaller than consumption, typically only about 20 percent of GDP, but it is also more volatile; understanding investment is therefore important for understanding fluctuations in real national income.

We begin by considering a **closed economy**—that is, one that does not trade with other countries. We also suppose there is no government and that the price level is constant. These extreme assumptions serve a vital purpose. As we will soon see, the presence of government and foreign trade is *not* essential to understanding the basic principles of national-income determination. By simplifying the model as much as possible, we are better able to understand its structure and therefore how more complex versions of the model work. In following chapters we will complicate our simple macro model by adding a government and international trade and then by removing the assumption of a fixed price level. The result will be a much more complete model of the macro economy.

Desired Consumption Expenditure

Recall from Chapter 20 that *disposable income* is the amount of income households receive after deducting what they pay in taxes and adding what they receive in transfers. In our simple model with no government and no taxation, disposable income, Y_D, is equal to national income, Y. We define **saving** as all disposable income that is not spent on consumption.

> By definition, there are only two possible uses of disposable income—consumption and saving. When the household decides how much to put to one use, it has automatically decided how much to put to the other use.

Figure 21-1 shows the time series for real per capita consumption and disposable income in Canada since 1981. It is clear that the two variables tend to move together over time, although the relationship is not exact. The vertical distance between the two lines is the amount of saving done by households, and the figure shows that household saving as a share of disposable income has been declining over this period. In the early 1980s, household saving was roughly 25 percent of disposable income, whereas by 2008 it was less than 5 percent. What determines the amount of their disposable income that households decide to consume and the amount they decide to save? The factors that influence this decision are summarized in the *consumption function* and the *saving function*.

The Consumption Function The **consumption function** relates the total desired consumption expenditures of all households to the several factors that determine it. The key factors influencing desired consumption are assumed to be

- disposable income
- wealth
- interest rates
- expectations about the future

In building our simple macro model, we emphasize the role of disposable income in influencing desired consumption; but as we will see, changes in the other variables are also important.

closed economy An economy that has no foreign trade in goods, services, or assets.

saving All disposable income that is not spent on consumption.

consumption function The relationship between desired consumption expenditure and all the variables that determine it; in the simplest case, the relationship between desired consumption expenditure and disposable income.

Practise with Study Guide Chapter 21, Exercise 1.

FIGURE 21-1   Consumption and Disposable Income in Canada, 1981–2008

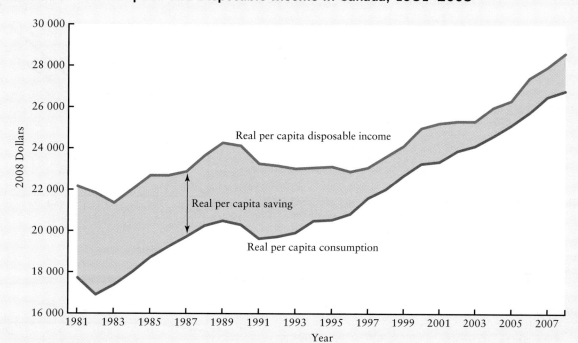

Per capita consumption and disposable income move broadly together over time. The relationship between consumption and disposable income is not exact, but they clearly move broadly together. The vertical distance between the lines is household saving, which as a share of income has been declining since 1981.

(*Source:* Based on authors' calculations using data from Statistics Canada, CANSIM database. Disposable income: Series V691566. Consumption expenditure: Series V691578. Population: Series V466668. Conversion from nominal to real values based on CPI: Series V737344.)

The assumption that desired consumption is related to disposable income is not surprising. As income rises, households naturally want to spend more, both now and in the future. For example, if a household's monthly disposable income permanently increases from $3000 to $3500, its monthly consumption will also increase, but probably by less than the full $500 increase. The remainder will be added to its monthly saving—money that will accumulate and help finance future vacations, education, home purchases, or even retirement.

Holding constant other determinants of desired consumption, an increase in disposable income is assumed to lead to an increase in desired consumption.

The consumption function has an interesting history in economics. *Extensions in Theory 21-1* discusses consumption behaviour in two hypothetical households and illustrates a debate regarding the importance of *current* disposable income in determining consumption. As the discussion shows, however, our simple assumption that desired consumption is positively related to current disposable income is a good approximation of the behaviour of the *average* household and therefore is suitable for explaining aggregate behaviour.

FIGURE 21-2 The Consumption and Saving Functions

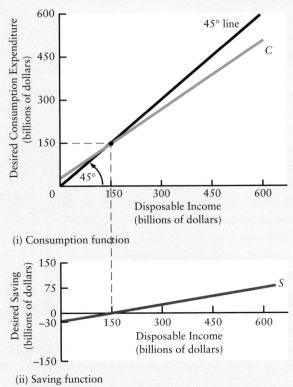

Disposable Income (Y_D)	Desired Consumption (C)	Desired Saving (S)	$APC = C/Y_D$	ΔY_D	ΔC	$MPC = \Delta C/\Delta Y_D$
0	30	−30	—			
30	54	−24	1.80	30	24	0.8
150	150	0	1.00	120	96	0.8
300	270	30	0.90	150	120	0.8
450	390	60	0.87	150	120	0.8
525	450	75	0.86	75	60	0.8
600	510	90	0.85	75	60	0.8

(i) Consumption function

(ii) Saving function

Both desired consumption and desired saving are assumed to rise as disposable income rises. Line C in part (i) of the figure relates desired consumption expenditure to disposable income by plotting the data from the second column of the accompanying table. The consumption function cuts the 45° line at the break-even level of disposable income. Note that the level of autonomous consumption is $30 billion. The slope of the consumption function is equal to the marginal propensity to consume, which is shown in the table to be 0.8.

The relationship between desired saving and disposable income is shown in part (ii) by line S, which plots the data from the third column of the table. The vertical distance between C and the 45° line in part (i) is by definition the height of S in part (ii); that is, any given level of disposable income must be either consumed or saved. Note that the level of autonomous saving is –$30 billion.

Practise with Study Guide
Chapter 21, Short-Answer
Question 1.

Part (i) of Figure 21-2 illustrates a hypothetical consumption function. The first two columns of the table show the value of desired consumption (C) associated with each value of disposable income (Y_D). There is clearly a positive relationship. The figure plots these points and connects them with a smooth line. In this hypothetical economy, the equation of the consumption function is

$$C = 30 + 0.8Y_D$$

In words, this equation says that if disposable income is zero, desired aggregate consumption will be $30 billion, and that for every one-dollar increase in Y_D, desired consumption rises by 80 cents.

The $30 billion is said to be *autonomous* consumption because it is autonomous (or independent) of the level of income. The $0.8Y_D$ is called *induced* consumption because it is induced (or brought about) by a change in income. In part (i) of Figure 21-2, the autonomous part of desired consumption is the vertical intercept of the consumption function. The induced part of consumption occurs as disposable income changes and we move along the consumption function.

EXTENSIONS IN THEORY 21-1

The Theory of the Consumption Function

Though it may seem natural to assume that a household's current consumption depends largely on its current disposable income, much debate and research has surrounded the issue of how to model consumption behaviour. To see what is involved, consider two quite different households.

The first household is short-sighted and spends everything it receives and puts nothing aside for a rainy day. When some overtime work results in a large paycheque, the members of the household go out and spend it. When it is hard to find work, the household's paycheque is small and its members reduce their expenditures. This household's monthly expenditure is therefore exactly equal to its current monthly disposable income.

The second household is forward-looking. Its members think about the future as much as the present and make plans that stretch over their lifetimes. They put money aside for retirement and for the occasional rainy day when disposable income may fall temporarily. An unexpected windfall of income will be saved. An unexpected shortfall of income will be cushioned by spending some of the accumulated savings that were put aside for just such a rainy day. In short, this household's monthly expenditure will be closely related to its *permanent* monthly disposable income—the average monthly income it expects over its lifetime. Fluctuations in its current monthly income will have little effect on its current consumption expenditure. Economists refer to this behaviour as *consumption smoothing.*

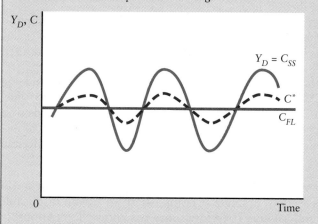

The figure shows the difference between our two sample households, short-sighted and forward-looking, and how their respective consumption expenditure is related to their current disposable income. We assume that disposable income, Y_D, fluctuates over time, as shown by the solid blue line. C_{SS} is the consumption path of the short-sighted household and is the same as

the path of disposable income. C_{FL} is the consumption path for the forward-looking household and is flat.

John Maynard Keynes (1883–1946), the famous English economist who developed much of the basic theory of macroeconomics, populated his theory with households whose current consumption expenditure depended mostly on their current income. But these households are not as extreme as the short-sighted households we just discussed. Keynes did not assume that households *never* saved. He simply assumed that their current level of expenditure and saving depended on their current level of income. To this day, a consumption function based on this assumption is called a *Keynesian consumption function.*

In the 1950s, two U.S. economists, Franco Modigliani and Milton Friedman, both of whom were subsequently awarded Nobel Prizes in economics, analyzed the behaviour of forward-looking households. Their theories, which Modigliani called the *life-cycle theory* and Friedman called the *permanent-income theory,* explain some observed consumer behaviour that cannot be explained by the Keynesian consumption function.

The differences between the theories of Keynes, on the one hand, and Friedman and Modigliani, on the other, are not as great as they might seem at first. To see why this is so, let us return to our two imaginary households.

Even the extremely short-sighted household may be able to do some consumption smoothing in the face of income fluctuations. Most households have some money in the bank and some ability to borrow, even if it is just from friends and relatives. As a result, every change in income need not be matched by an equal change in consumption expenditures.

In contrast, although the forward-looking household wants to smooth its pattern of consumption, it may not have the borrowing capacity to do so. Its bank may not be willing to lend money for consumption when the security consists of nothing more than the *expectation* that the household's income will be higher in later years. As a result, the household's consumption expenditure might fluctuate with its current income more than it would want.

The foregoing discussion suggests that the consumption expenditure of both types of households will fluctuate to some extent with their current disposable incomes and to some extent with their expectations of future disposable income. Moreover, in any economy there will be households of both types, and aggregate consumption will be determined by a mix of the two types. The consumption behaviour for the *average* household in such an economy is shown in the figure as the path C^*. Consumption fluctuates in response to changes in disposable income, rising when income rises and falling when income falls.

We now go on to examine the properties of the consumption function in more detail.

AVERAGE AND MARGINAL PROPENSITIES TO CONSUME. To discuss the consumption function concisely, economists use two technical expressions.

The **average propensity to consume (APC)** is desired consumption expenditure divided by disposable income:

$$APC = C/Y_D$$

The fourth column of the table in Figure 21-2 shows the APC calculated from the data in the table. Note that APC falls as disposable income rises.

The **marginal propensity to consume (MPC)** relates the *change* in desired consumption to the *change* in disposable income that brought it about. MPC is the change in desired consumption divided by the change in disposable income:

$$MPC = \Delta C/\Delta Y_D$$

where the Greek letter Δ, delta, means "a change in." The last column of the table in Figure 21-2 shows the MPC that corresponds to the data in the table. Note that in this simple example, the MPC is constant and equal to 0.8. [28]

THE SLOPE OF THE CONSUMPTION FUNCTION. The consumption function shown in Figure 21-2 has a slope of $\Delta C/\Delta Y_D$, which is, by definition, the marginal propensity to consume. The positive slope of the consumption function shows that the MPC is positive; increases in income lead to increases in desired consumption expenditure. The *constant* slope of the consumption function shows that the MPC is the same at any level of disposable income.

THE 45° LINE. Figure 21-2(i) contains a line that is constructed by connecting all points where desired consumption (measured on the vertical axis) equals disposable income (measured on the horizontal axis). Because both axes are given in the same units, this line has a positive slope equal to 1; that is, it forms an angle of 45° with the axes. The line is therefore called the *45° line*.

The 45° line is a useful reference line. In part (i) of Figure 21-2, the consumption function cuts the 45° line at what is called the "break-even" level of income—in this example, at $150 billion. When the consumption function is above the 45° line, desired consumption exceeds disposable income. In this case, desired saving must be negative; households are financing their consumption either by spending out of their accumulated saving or by borrowing funds. When the consumption function is below the 45° line, desired consumption is less than disposable income and so desired saving is positive; households are paying back debt or accumulating assets. At the break-even level of disposable income, desired consumption exactly equals disposable income and so desired saving is zero.

The Saving Function
Households decide how much to consume and how much to save. As we have said, this is only a single decision—how to divide disposable income between consumption and saving. Therefore, once we know the relationship between desired consumption and disposable income, we automatically know the relationship between desired saving and disposable income.

There are two saving concepts that are exactly parallel to the consumption concepts of APC and MPC. The **average propensity to save (APS)** is the proportion of

---

average propensity to consume (APC) Desired consumption divided by the level of disposable income.

marginal propensity to consume (MPC) The change in desired consumption divided by the change in disposable income that brought it about.

average propensity to save (APS) Desired saving divided by disposable income.

disposable income that households want to save, computed by dividing desired saving by disposable income:

$$APC = S/Y_D$$

The **marginal propensity to save (MPS)** relates the change in desired saving to the change in disposable income that brought it about:

$$MPS = \Delta S/\Delta Y_D$$

There is a simple relationship between the saving and the consumption propensities. *APC* and *APS* must sum to 1; and *MPC* and *MPS* must also sum to 1. Because all disposable income is either spent or saved, it follows that the fractions of income consumed and saved must account for all income (*APC* + *APS* = 1). It also follows that the fractions of any *increment* to income consumed and saved must account for all of that increment (*MPC* + *MPS* = 1). [29]

Look back at the table in Figure 21-2 and calculate *APC* and *APS* for yourself by computing C/Y_D and S/Y_D for each row in the table. You will notice that the sum of *APC* and *APS* is *always* 1. Similarly, calculate *MPC* and *MPS* by computing $\Delta C/\Delta Y_D$ and $\Delta S/\Delta Y_D$ for each row in the table. You will also notice that *MPC* and *MPS always* add to 1.

Part (ii) of Figure 21-2 shows the saving function in our simple model. Notice that it is positively sloped, indicating that increases in disposable income are assumed to lead to an increase in desired saving. Note also that the amount of desired saving is always equal to the vertical distance between the consumption function and the 45° line. When desired consumption exceeds income, desired saving is negative; when desired consumption is less than income, desired saving is positive.

Shifts of the Consumption Function
Earlier we said that desired consumption is assumed to depend on four things—disposable income, wealth, interest rates, and households' expectations about the future. In Figure 21-2, we illustrate the most important relationship—between desired consumption and disposable income. In this diagram, changes in disposable income lead to *movements along* the consumption function. Changes in the other three factors will lead to *shifts of* the consumption function. Let's see why.

A CHANGE IN HOUSEHOLD WEALTH. Household wealth is the value of all accumulated assets minus accumulated debts. The most common types of household assets are savings accounts, mutual funds (portfolios of stocks or bonds), Registered Retirement Savings Plans (RRSPs), and the ownership of homes and cars. The most common household debts are home mortgages, car loans, and outstanding lines of credit from banks.

What happens to desired consumption if household wealth increases? Suppose, for example, that a rising stock market (often called a "bull" market) leads to an increase in aggregate household wealth. To the extent that this increase in wealth is expected to persist, less current income needs to be saved for the future, and households will therefore tend to spend a larger fraction of their current income. The consumption function will shift up, and the saving function down, as shown in Figure 21-3. Current estimates suggest that an increase in aggregate wealth of $1 billion leads to an increase in desired aggregate consumption of approximately $50 million.

> **An increase in household wealth shifts the consumption function up; a decrease in wealth shifts the consumption function down.**

marginal propensity to save (MPS) The change in desired saving divided by the change in disposable income that brought it about.

Practise with Study Guide
Chapter 21, Extension
Exercise E2.

FIGURE 21-3 Shifts in the Consumption Function

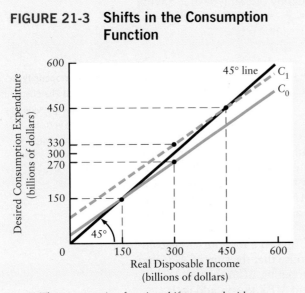

(i) The consumption function shifts upward with an increase in wealth, a decrease in interest rates, or an increase in optimism about the future

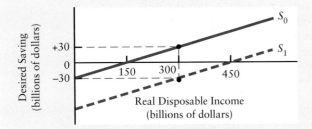

(ii) The saving function shifts downward with an increase in wealth, a decrease in interest rates, or an increase in optimism about the future

Changes in wealth, interest rates, or expectations about the future shift the consumption function. In part (i), line C_0 reproduces the consumption function from Figure 21-2(i). The consumption function then shifts up by $60 billion, so with disposable income of $300 billion, for example, desired consumption rises from $270 billion to $330 billion.

The saving function in part (ii) shifts down by $60 billion, from S_0 to S_1. At a disposable income of $300 billion, for example, desired saving falls from $30 billion to –$30 billion.

A CHANGE IN INTEREST RATES. Household consumption can be divided into consumption of *durable* and *non-durable* goods. Durable goods are goods that deliver benefits for several years, such as cars and household appliances. Non-durable goods are consumption goods that deliver benefits to households for only short periods of time, such as groceries, restaurant meals, and clothing. Since many durable goods are also expensive, many of them are purchased on credit—that is, households borrow in order to finance their purchases.

The cost of borrowing, as we discussed in Chapter 19, is the interest rate. A fall in the interest rate reduces the cost of borrowing and generally leads to an increase in desired consumption expenditure, especially of durable goods. That is, for any given level of disposable income, a fall in the interest rate leads to an increase in desired consumption; the consumption function shifts up and the saving function shifts down, as shown in Figure 21-3.

> A fall in interest rates usually leads to an increase in desired consumption at any level of disposable income; the consumption function shifts up. A rise in interest rates shifts the consumption function down.

A CHANGE IN EXPECTATIONS. Households' expectations about the future are important in determining their desired consumption. Suppose, for example, that large numbers of households become pessimistic about the future state of the economy and about their own employment prospects. In many cases, these fears will lead households to increase their current saving in anticipation of rough economic times (possibly unemployment) ahead. But increasing their current saving implies a reduction in current consumption (at the given level of disposable income). The result will be a downward shift in the consumption function.

The reverse also tends to be true. Favourable expectations about the future state of the economy will lead many households to increase their current desired consumption and reduce their current desired saving. The result will be an upward shift in the consumption function and a downward shift in the saving function.

> Expectations about the future state of the economy influence desired consumption. Optimism leads to an upward shift in the consumption function; pessimism leads to a downward shift in the consumption function.

Summary It is useful to summarize what we have learned so far about the consumption function. As you will soon see, it will play a crucial role in our simple model of national income determination. The main points are as follows:

1. Desired consumption is assumed to be positively related to disposable income. In a graph, this relationship is shown by the positive slope of the consumption function, which is equal to the marginal propensity to consume (*MPC*).

2. There are both *autonomous* and *induced* components of desired consumption. A movement along the consumption function shows changes in consumption induced by changes in disposable income. A shift of the consumption function shows autonomous changes in consumption.

3. An increase in household wealth, a fall in interest rates, or greater optimism about the future are all assumed to lead to an increase in desired consumption and thus an upward shift of the consumption function.

4. By definition, all disposable income is either consumed or saved. Therefore, there is a saving function associated with the consumption function. Any event that causes the consumption function to shift must also cause the saving function to shift by an equal amount in the opposite direction.

---

myeconlab ADDITIONAL TOPICS

Is our simple theory of the consumption function supported by empirical evidence? For some Canadian data on aggregate consumption and disposable income, look for **The Consumption Function in Canada** in the *Additional Topics* section of this book's MyEconLab.

www.myeconlab.com

Desired Investment Expenditure

Our simple macroeconomic model has only consumption and investment. Having spent considerable time discussing desired consumption expenditure, we are now ready to examine the determinants of desired investment. Recall from Chapter 20 the three categories of investment:

- inventory investment
- residential investment
- new plant and equipment

Investment expenditure is the most volatile component of GDP, and changes in investment are strongly associated with aggregate economic fluctuations. As shown in Figure 21-4, total investment in Canada fluctuates around an average of about 20 percent of GDP. In each of the last two recessions (1982 and 1991), investment as a share of GDP fell by approximately five percentage points. In contrast, consumption, government purchases, and net exports are much smoother over the business cycle, each typically changing by less than one percentage point. An important part of our understanding of business cycles will therefore rely on our understanding of the fluctuations in investment.

FIGURE 21-4   The Volatility of Investment, 1981–2008

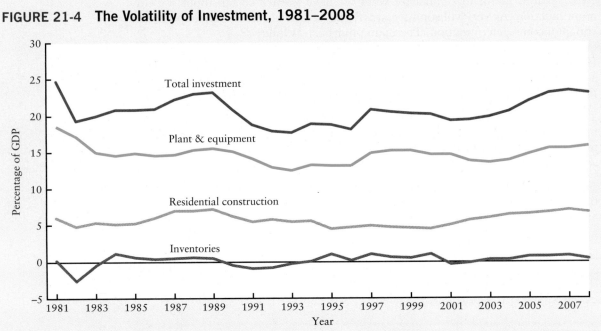

The major components of investment fluctuate considerably as a share of GDP. The recessions of the early 1980s and early 1990s are evident from the reductions in all components of investment.
(*Source:* Based on authors' calculations using data from Statistics Canada's CANSIM database. Series V498662, V49863, and V498804 are the three components of investment. They are shown here as a fraction of current dollar GDP, series V498086.)

What explains such fluctuations in investment? Here we examine three important determinants of aggregate investment expenditure:

- the real interest rate
- changes in the level of sales
- business confidence

Let's now examine these in turn.

Desired Investment and the Real Interest Rate
The real interest rate represents the real opportunity cost of using money (either borrowed money or retained earnings) for investment purposes. A rise in the real interest rate therefore reduces the amount of desired investment expenditure. This relationship is most easily seen if we separate investment into three components: inventories, residential construction, and new plant and equipment.

INVENTORIES. Changes in inventories represent only a small percentage of private investment in a typical year. As shown by the bottom line in Figure 21-4, inventory investment has been between –2 percent and 2 percent of GDP over the past 30 years. (Inventory investment of –2 percent in a year means that inventories *fall* by 2 percent of GDP.) But the average amount of inventory investment is not an adequate measure of its importance. Since inventory investment is one of the more volatile elements of total investment, it has an important influence on fluctuations in investment expenditure.

When a firm ties up funds in inventories, those same funds cannot be used elsewhere to earn income. As an alternative to holding inventories, the firm could lend the money out at the going rate of interest. Hence, the higher the real rate of interest, the higher the opportunity cost of holding an inventory of a given size; the higher the opportunity cost, the smaller the inventories that will be desired.

RESIDENTIAL CONSTRUCTION. Expenditure on residential housing is also volatile. Most houses are purchased with money that is borrowed by means of mortgages. Interest on the borrowed money typically accounts for more than one-half of the purchaser's annual mortgage payments; the remainder is repayment of the original loan, called the *principal*. Because interest payments are such a large part of mortgage payments, variations in interest rates exert a substantial effect on the demand for housing.

NEW PLANT AND EQUIPMENT. The real interest rate is also a major determinant of investment in new plant and equipment. When interest rates are high, it is expensive for

The largest part of investment by firms is in new plants and equipment, such as this expansion of a pulp mill in British Columbia.

firms to borrow funds that can be used to build new plants or purchase new equipment. Similarly, firms with cash on hand can earn high returns on interest-earning assets, again making investment in plant and equipment a less attractive alternative. Thus, high real interest rates lead to a reduction in desired investment in plant and equipment, whereas low real interest rates increase desired investment.

> The real interest rate reflects the opportunity cost associated with investment, whether it is investment in inventories, residential construction, or plant and equipment. The higher the real interest rate, the higher the opportunity cost of investment and thus the lower the amount of desired investment.

Figure 21-4 shows these three components of investment since 1981. Inventory investment is clearly the smallest of the three but in relative terms is actually the most volatile. Note that the three components move broadly together. They all fell in the 1981–1982 recession and again in the 1990–1991 recession.

Desired Investment and Changes in Sales

Firms hold inventories to meet unexpected changes in sales and production, and they usually have a target level of inventories that depends on their normal level of sales. Because the size of inventories is related to the level of sales, the *change* in inventories (which is part of current investment) is related to the *change* in the level of sales.

For example, suppose a firm wants to hold inventories equal to 10 percent of its monthly sales. If normal monthly sales are $100 000, it will want to hold inventories valued at $10 000. If monthly sales increase to $110 000, it will want to increase its inventories to $11 000. Over the period during which its stock of inventories is being increased, there will be a total of $1000 of new inventory investment.

> The higher the level of sales, the larger the desired stock of inventories. Changes in the rate of sales therefore cause temporary bouts of investment (or disinvestment) in inventories.

Changes in sales have similar effects on investment in plant and equipment. For example, if there is a general increase in consumers' demand for products that is expected to persist and that cannot be met by existing capacity, investment in new

FIGURE 21-5 **Desired Investment as Autonomous Expenditure**

In this simple macro model, desired investment is assumed to be autonomous with respect to current national income. In this example, the level of desired investment is $75 billion. However, changes in interest rates or business confidence will lead to upward or downward shifts in the investment function.

plant and equipment will be needed. Once the new plants have been built and put into operation, however, the rate of new investment will fall.

Desired Investment and Business Confidence Investment takes time. When a firm invests, it increases its future capacity to produce output. If it can sell the new output profitably, the investment will prove to be a good one. If the new output does not generate profits, the investment will have been a bad one. When it undertakes an investment, the firm does not know if it will turn out well or badly—it is betting on a favourable future that cannot be known with certainty.

When firms expect good times ahead, they will want to invest now so that they have a larger productive capacity in the future ready to satisfy the greater demand. When they expect bad times ahead, they will not invest because they expect no payoff from doing so.

> Investment depends on firms' expectations about the future state of the economy. Optimism about the future leads to more desired investment; pessimism leads to less desired investment.

Desired Investment as Autonomous Expenditure We have seen that desired investment is influenced by many things, and a complete discussion of the determination of national income is not possible without including all of these factors.

For the moment, however, our goal is to build the *simplest* model of the aggregate economy in which we can examine the interaction of actual national income and desired aggregate expenditure. To build this simple model, we begin by treating desired investment as *autonomous*—that is, we assume it to be unaffected by changes in national income. Figure 21-5 shows the investment function as a horizontal line.

It is important not to confuse the assumption that desired investment is *autonomous* with respect to national income (which we are making) with the assumption that it is *constant* (which we are not making). As we have said, investment is the most volatile component of aggregate expenditure, and it will therefore be important in our model that investment be able to change; shocks to firms' investment behaviour will end up being an important explanation for fluctuations in national income. Our assumption that investment is autonomous with respect to national income (and hence the *I* function in Figure 21-5 is horizontal) is mainly a simplifying one. But the assumption does reflect the fact that investment is an act undertaken by firms for *future* benefit, and thus the *current* level of GDP is unlikely to have a significant effect on desired investment.

The Conference Board of Canada publishes regular surveys of business and consumer confidence. Visit its website:
www.conferenceboard.ca.

aggregate expenditure (AE) function The function that relates desired aggregate expenditure to actual national income.

The Aggregate Expenditure Function

The **aggregate expenditure (AE) function** relates the level of desired aggregate expenditure to the level of actual income. (In both cases we mean *real* as opposed to *nominal* variables.) In the simplified economy of this chapter, in which there is no government

FIGURE 21-6   The Aggregate Expenditure Function

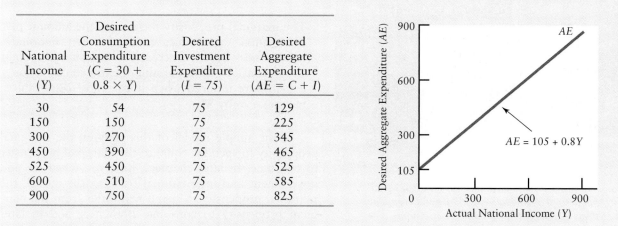

National Income (Y)	Desired Consumption Expenditure (C = 30 + 0.8 × Y)	Desired Investment Expenditure (I = 75)	Desired Aggregate Expenditure (AE = C + I)
30	54	75	129
150	150	75	225
300	270	75	345
450	390	75	465
525	450	75	525
600	510	75	585
900	750	75	825

The aggregate expenditure function relates desired aggregate expenditure to actual national income. The curve *AE* in the figure plots the data from the first and last columns of the accompanying table. Its intercept, which in this case is $105 billion, shows the sum of autonomous consumption and autonomous investment. The slope of *AE* is equal to the marginal propensity to spend, which in this simple economy is just the marginal propensity to consume.

and no international trade, desired aggregate expenditure is just equal to desired consumption plus desired investment, $C + I$.

$$AE = C + I$$

The table in Figure 21-6 shows how the *AE* function can be calculated, given the consumption function from Figure 21-2 on page 522 and the investment function from Figure 21-4 on page 528. In this specific case, all of desired investment expenditure is autonomous, as is the $30 billion of consumption that would be desired if national income were equal to zero. Total autonomous expenditure is therefore $105 billion—induced expenditure is just equal to induced consumption, which is equal to the *MPC* times disposable income $(0.8 \times Y_D)$. Furthermore, since our simple model has no government and no taxes, disposable income, Y_D, is equal to national income, *Y*. Hence, desired aggregate expenditure can be written as:

$$AE = \$105 \text{ billion} + (0.8)Y$$

The Marginal Propensity to Spend   The fraction of any increment to national income that people spend on purchasing domestic output is called the economy's **marginal propensity to spend**. The marginal propensity to spend is measured by the change in desired aggregate expenditure divided by the change in national income that brings it about, or $\Delta AE/\Delta Y$. This is the slope of the aggregate expenditure function. In this book, the marginal propensity to spend is denoted by the symbol *z*, which is a number greater than zero and less than 1. For the example given in Figure 21-6, the marginal propensity to spend is 0.8. If national income increases by a dollar, 80 cents will go into increased desired (consumption) expenditure; 20 cents will go into increased desired

marginal propensity to spend The change in desired aggregate expenditure on domestic output divided by the change in national income that brought it about.

Changes in firms' accumulated inventories often signal changes in desired aggregate expenditure and eventually induce firms to change their production decisions.

Practise with Study Guide
Chapter 21, Exercise 3.

saving. The marginal propensity to spend should not be confused with the marginal propensity to consume.

> **The marginal propensity to spend is the amount of extra total expenditure induced when national income rises by $1, whereas the marginal propensity to consume is the amount of extra consumption expenditure induced when households' disposable income rises by $1.**

In the simple model of this chapter, the marginal propensity to spend is equal to the marginal propensity to consume. In later chapters, however, when we add government and international trade to the model, the marginal propensity to spend will differ from the marginal propensity to consume. Both here and in later chapters, it is the more general measure—the marginal propensity to spend—that is important for determining equilibrium national income.

21.2 Equilibrium National Income

We have constructed an *AE* function that combines the spending plans of households and firms. The function shows, for any given level of *actual* national income, the level of *desired* aggregate spending. We are now ready to see what determines the *equilibrium* level of national income. When something is in equilibrium, there is no tendency for it to change. Any conditions that are required for something to be in equilibrium are called *equilibrium conditions*. We will see that the distinction between desired and actual expenditure is central to understanding the equilibrium conditions for national income.

In this chapter and the next, we make an important assumption that influences the nature of equilibrium. In particular, we assume that firms are able and willing to produce any amount of output that is demanded of them and that changes in their production levels do not require a change in their product prices. In this setting, we say that output is *demand determined*. This is an extreme assumption, and we will relax it in Chapter 23 when we discuss the determination of the price level. Until then, however, it is a very useful assumption that allows us to more easily understand how our macro model works.

Table 21-1 illustrates the determination of equilibrium national income for our simple model economy. Suppose firms are producing a final output of $300 billion, and thus *actual* national income is $300 billion. According to the table, at this level of actual national income, *desired* aggregate expenditure is $345 billion. If firms persist in producing a current output of only $300 billion in the face of desired aggregate expenditure of $345 billion, one of two things will happen.

One possibility is that households and firms will be unable to spend the extra $45 billion that they would like to spend, so lines or waiting lists of unsatisfied customers will appear. These shortages will send a signal to firms that they could increase their sales if they increased their production. When the firms do increase their production, actual national income rises. Of course, the individual firms are interested only in their own sales and profits, but their individual actions have as their inevitable consequence an increase in GDP.

A more realistic possibility is that all spenders will spend everything that they wanted to spend. But since desired expenditure exceeds the actual amount of output, this is possible only if some sales come from the producers' accumulated inventories. In our example, the fulfillment of plans to purchase $345 billion worth of goods in the face of a current output of only $300 billion will reduce inventories by $45 billion. As long as inventories last, more goods can be sold than are currently being produced. But since firms want to maintain a certain level of inventories, they will eventually increase their production. Once again, the consequence of each individual firm's decision to increase production is an increase in actual national income. Thus, the final response to an excess of desired aggregate expenditure over actual output is a rise in national income.

For any level of national income at which desired aggregate expenditure exceeds actual income, there will be pressure for actual national income to rise.

TABLE 21-1 Equilibrium National Income

Actual National Income (Y)	Desired Aggregate Expenditure (AE = C + I)	Effect
30	129	
150	225	Inventories are falling; firms increase output
300	345	
450	465	
525	525	Equilibrium income
600	585	Inventories are rising; firms reduce output
900	825	

National income is in equilibrium when desired aggregate expenditure equals actual national income. The data are from Figure 21-6.

Next consider the $900 billion level of actual national income in Table 21-1. At this level of output, desired expenditure on domestically produced goods is only $825 billion. If firms persist in producing $900 billion worth of goods, $75 billion worth must remain unsold. Therefore, inventories must rise. However, firms will not allow inventories of unsold goods to rise indefinitely; sooner or later, they will reduce the level of output to the level of sales. When they reduce their level of output, national income will fall.

For any level of income at which desired aggregate expenditure is less than actual income, there will be pressure for national income to fall.

Finally, look at the national income level of $525 billion in Table 21-1. At this level, and only at this level, desired aggregate expenditure is equal to actual national income. Purchasers can fulfill their spending plans without causing inventories to change. There is no incentive for firms to alter output. Because everyone wants to purchase an amount equal to what is actually being produced, output and income will remain steady; they are in equilibrium.

The equilibrium level of national income occurs where desired aggregate expenditure equals actual national income.

In other words, the *equilibrium condition* for our simple model of national income determination is

$$AE = Y$$

As we will now see, the combination of our AE function and this condition will determine the equilibrium level of national income.

FIGURE 21-7   Equilibrium National Income

Equilibrium national income is that level of national income where desired aggregate expenditure equals actual national income. If actual national income is below Y_0, desired aggregate expenditure will exceed national income, and output will rise. If national income is above Y_0, desired aggregate expenditure will be less than national income, and production will fall. Only when national income is equal to Y_0 will the economy be in equilibrium, as shown at E_0.

Practise with Study Guide
Chapter 21, Exercise 2.

Consider Figure 21-7. The line labelled *AE* graphs the specific aggregate expenditure function that we have been working with throughout this chapter. The 45° line ($AE = Y$) graphs the equilibrium condition that desired aggregate expenditure equals actual national income. Anywhere along the 45° line, the value of desired aggregate expenditure, which is measured on the vertical axis, is equal to the value of actual national income, which is measured on the horizontal axis.

Graphically, equilibrium occurs at the level of income at which the *AE* line intersects the 45° line. This is the level of income at which desired aggregate expenditure is just equal to actual national income. In Figure 21-7, the equilibrium level of national income (real GDP) is Y_0.

To understand how Figure 21-7 illustrates economic behaviour, consider some level of real GDP below Y_0. At this level of income, the *AE* curve lies above the 45° line, indicating that desired spending exceeds actual output. The vertical distance between *AE* and the 45° line reflects the size of this excess demand. As we said earlier, this excess demand may lead to a *reduction* in inventories and eventually lead firms to increase their production. Conversely, at any level of GDP above Y_0, the *AE* curve is below the 45° line, indicating that desired spending is less than actual output. The vertical distance between the curves in this case shows the size of the excess supply, which may lead to an *accumulation* of inventories and an eventual decrease in firms' production. Only when real GDP equals Y_0 is desired spending equal to actual output, thus providing firms with no incentive to change their production.

Now that we have explained the meaning of equilibrium national income, we will go on to examine the various forces that can *change* this equilibrium. We will then be well on our way to understanding some of the sources of short-run fluctuations in real GDP.

✗ myeconlab ADDITIONAL TOPICS

A different, but equivalent, way of thinking about the equilibrium level of national income involves comparing desired saving with desired investment. For more details, look for **Investment, Saving, and Equilibrium GDP** in the *Additional Topics* section of this book's MyEconLab.

www.myeconlab.com

21.3 Changes in Equilibrium National Income

Figure 21-7 shows that the equilibrium level of national income occurs where the *AE* function intersects the 45° line. Through the adjustment in firms' inventories and production levels, the level of actual national income will adjust until this equilibrium level is achieved. Because the *AE* function plays a central role in determining equilibrium national income, you should not be surprised to hear that *shifts* in the *AE* function are central to explaining why the equilibrium level of national income changes.

Practise with Study Guide
Chapter 21, Short-Answer
Question 2.

Shifts of the *AE* Function

The *AE* function shifts when one of its components shifts—that is, when there is a shift in the consumption function or in the investment function. As we have already mentioned, both the consumption function and the investment function will shift if there is a change in interest rates or expectations of the future state of the economy. A change in household wealth is an additional reason for the consumption function to shift. Let's now consider what happens when there is an upward shift in the *AE* function.

Upward Shifts in the *AE* Function Suppose households experience an increase in wealth and thus increase their desired levels of consumption spending at each level of disposable income. Or suppose firms' expectations of higher future sales lead them to increase their planned investment. What is the effect of such events on national income?

Because any increase in autonomous expenditure shifts the entire *AE* function upward, the same analysis applies to each of the changes mentioned. Two types of shifts in *AE* can occur. First, if the same addition to expenditure occurs at all levels of income, the *AE* function shifts parallel to itself, as shown in part (i) of Figure 21-8. Second, if there is a change in the marginal propensity to spend, the slope of the *AE* function changes, as shown in part (ii) of Figure 21-8.

Figure 21-8 shows that an upward shift in the *AE* function increases equilibrium national income. After the shift in the *AE* curve, income is no longer in equilibrium at its original level because at that level desired aggregate expenditure exceeds actual national income. Given this excess demand, firms' inventories are being depleted and firms respond by increasing production. Equilibrium national income rises to the higher level indicated by the intersection of the *new AE* curve with the 45° line.

Downward Shifts in the *AE* Function What happens to national income if there is a decrease in the amount of consumption or investment expenditure desired at each level of income? These changes shift the *AE* function downward, as shown in Figure 21-8 by the movement from the dashed *AE* curve to the solid *AE* curve. An equal reduction in desired expenditure at all levels of income shifts *AE* parallel to itself. A fall in the marginal propensity to spend out of national income reduces the slope of the *AE* function. In both cases, the equilibrium level of national income decreases; the new equilibrium is found at the intersection of the 45° line and the *new AE* curve.

FIGURE 21-8   Shifts in the Aggregate Expenditure Function

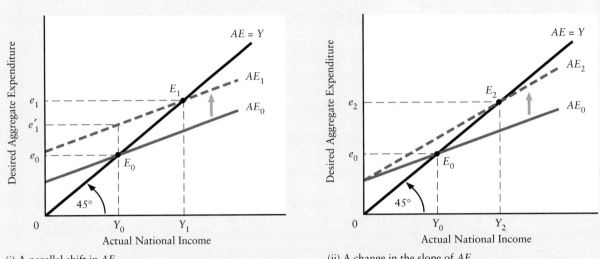

(i) A parallel shift in *AE*

(ii) A change in the slope of *AE*

Upward shifts in the *AE* function increase equilibrium income; downward shifts decrease equilibrium income. In parts (i) and (ii), the *AE* function is initially AE_0 with equilibrium national income equal to Y_0.

In part (i), a parallel upward shift in the *AE* curve from AE_0 to AE_1 reflects an increase in desired expenditure at each level of national income. For example, at Y_0, desired expenditure rises from e_0 to e_1' and therefore exceeds actual national income. Equilibrium is reached at E_1, where income is Y_1. The increase in desired expenditure from e_1' to e_1, represented by a movement along AE_1, is an induced response to the increase in income from Y_0 to Y_1.

In part (ii), a non-parallel upward shift in the *AE* curve from AE_0 to AE_2 reflects an increase in the marginal propensity to spend. This leads to an increase in equilibrium national income. Equilibrium is reached at E_2, where national income is equal to Y_2.

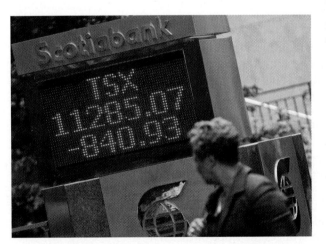

Changes in household wealth, such as those created by large swings in stock-market values, are predicted to lead to changes in households' desired consumption expenditure, thus changing the equilibrium level of national income.

The Results Restated We have derived two important general propositions from our simple model of national income determination:

1. A rise in the amount of desired aggregate expenditure at each level of national income will shift the *AE* curve upward and increase equilibrium national income.

2. A fall in the amount of desired aggregate expenditure at each level of national income will shift the *AE* curve downward and reduce equilibrium national income.

In addition, part (ii) of Figure 21-8 suggests a third general proposition regarding the effect of a change in the *slope* of the *AE* function:

3. An increase in the marginal propensity to spend, z, steepens the *AE* curve and increases equilibrium national income. Conversely, a decrease in the marginal propensity to spend flattens the *AE* curve and decreases equilibrium national income.

The Multiplier

We have learned how specific changes in the *AE* function cause equilibrium national income to rise or fall. We would now like to understand what determines the *size* of these changes. A measure of the magnitude of such changes is provided by the *multiplier*. A change in autonomous expenditure increases equilibrium national income by a *multiple* of the initial change in autonomous expenditure. That is, the change in national income is *larger than* the initial change in desired expenditure.

> The multiplier is the change in equilibrium national income divided by the change in autonomous expenditure that brought it about. In the simple macro model, the multiplier is greater than 1.[1]

To see why the multiplier is greater than 1 in this model, consider a simple example. Imagine what would happen to national income if Kimberley-Clark decided to spend an additional $500 million per year on the construction of new paper mills. Initially, the construction of the paper mills would create $500 million worth of new national income and a corresponding amount of income for households and firms on which the initial $500 million is spent. But this is not the end of the story. The increase in national income of $500 million would cause an induced increase in desired consumption.

Electricians, masons, and carpenters—who would gain new income directly from the building of the paper mills—would spend some of it on food, clothing, entertainment, cars, TVs, and other commodities. When output expanded to meet this demand, new incomes would be created for workers and firms in these industries. When they, in turn, spent their newly earned incomes, output would rise further. More income would be created, and more expenditure would be induced. Indeed, at this stage, we might wonder whether the increases in income would ever come to an end. To deal with this concern, we need to consider the multiplier in somewhat more precise terms.

Let autonomous expenditure be denoted by *A*. Now consider an increase in autonomous expenditure of ΔA, which in our example was $500 million per year. Remember that ΔA stands for *any* increase in autonomous expenditure; this could be an increase in investment or in the autonomous component of consumption. The *AE* function shifts upward by ΔA. National income is no longer in equilibrium because desired aggregate expenditure now exceeds actual national income. Equilibrium is restored by a *movement along* the new *AE* curve.

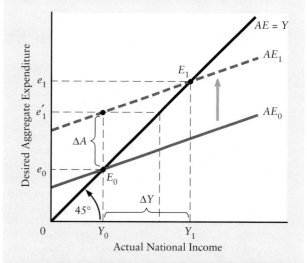

FIGURE 21-9   The Simple Multiplier

An increase in autonomous aggregate expenditure increases equilibrium national income by a multiple of the initial increase. The initial equilibrium is at E_0, where AE_0 intersects the 45° line. At this point, desired aggregate expenditure, e_0, is equal to actual national income, Y_0. An increase in autonomous expenditure of ΔA then shifts the *AE* function upward to AE_1.

Equilibrium occurs when income rises to Y_1. Here desired expenditure, e_1, equals national income, Y_1. The increase in desired expenditure from e'_1 to e_1 represents the induced increase in expenditure that occurs as national income rises. Because ΔY is greater than ΔA, the simple multiplier is greater than 1 ($\Delta Y/\Delta A > 1$).

---

[1] In this chapter and the next, we assume that firms can readily change their output in response to changes in demand (perhaps because there is some unemployed labour and capital). This assumption of *demand-determined output* is central to the result of a multiplier greater than one. We relax this assumption in later chapters.

APPLYING ECONOMIC CONCEPTS 21-1

The Multiplier: A Numerical Example

Consider an economy that has a marginal propensity to spend out of national income of 0.80. Suppose an increase in business confidence leads many firms to increase their investment in new buildings and factories. Specifically, suppose desired investment increases by $1 billion per year. National income initially rises by $1 billion, but that is not the end of it. The factors of production that received the first $1 billion spend $800 million. This second round of spending generates $800 million of new income. This new income, in turn, induces $640 million of third-round spending, and so it continues, with each successive round of new income generating 80 percent as much in new expenditure. Each additional round of expenditure creates new income and yet another round of expenditure.

The table carries the process through 10 rounds. Students with sufficient patience (and no faith in mathematics) may compute as many rounds in the process as they want; they will find that the sum of the rounds of expenditures approaches a limit of $5 billion, which is five times the initial increase in expenditure. [30]

Notice that most of the total change in national income occurs in the first few rounds. Of the total change of $5 billion, 68 percent ($3.4 billion) occurs after only five rounds of activity. By the end of the tenth round, 89 percent ($4.5 billion) of the total change has taken place.

Round of Spending	Increase in Expenditure (millions of dollars)	Cumulative Total (millions of dollars)
1 (initial increase)	1000.0	1000.0
2	800.0	1800.0
3	640.0	2440.0
4	512.0	2952.0
5	409.6	3361.6
6	327.7	3689.3
7	262.1	3951.4
8	209.7	4161.1
9	167.8	4328.9
10	134.2	4463.1
11 to 20 combined	479.3	4942.4
All others	57.6	5000.0

simple multiplier The ratio of the change in equilibrium national income to the change in autonomous expenditure that brought it about, calculated for a constant price level.

Practise with Study Guide Chapter 21, Short-Answer Question 4.

The **simple multiplier** measures the change in equilibrium national income that occurs in response to a change in autonomous expenditure when the price level is constant (reflecting the assumption that output is demand determined). We refer to it as "simple" because we have simplified the situation by assuming that the price level is fixed (an assumption we will remove in Chapter 23). Figure 21-9 illustrates the simple multiplier and makes clear that it is greater than 1. *Applying Economic Concepts 21-1* provides a numerical example.

The Size of the Simple Multiplier The size of the simple multiplier depends on the slope of the *AE* function—that is, on the marginal propensity to spend, *z*.

As shown in Figure 21-10, a high marginal propensity to spend means a steep *AE* curve. The expenditure induced by any initial increase in income is large, with the result that the final rise in income is correspondingly large. By contrast, a low marginal propensity to spend means a relatively flat *AE* curve. The expenditure induced by the initial increase in income is small, and the final rise in income is not much larger than the initial rise in autonomous expenditure that brought it about.

> The larger the marginal propensity to spend, the steeper the *AE* function and thus the larger the simple multiplier.

FIGURE 21-10   The Size of the Simple Multiplier

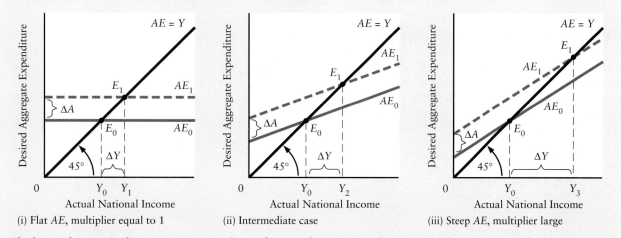

(i) Flat *AE*, multiplier equal to 1   (ii) Intermediate case   (iii) Steep *AE*, multiplier large

The larger the marginal propensity to spend out of national income (z), the steeper is the *AE* curve and the larger is the simple multiplier. In each part of the figure, the initial *AE* function is AE_0, equilibrium is at E_0, with income Y_0. The *AE* curve then shifts upward to AE_1 as a result of an increase in autonomous expenditure of ΔA. ΔA is the same in each part. The new equilibrium in each case is at E_1.

In part (i), the *AE* function is horizontal, indicating a marginal propensity to spend of zero ($z = 0$). The change in equilibrium income ΔY is only the increase in autonomous expenditure because there is no induced expenditure by the people who receive the initial increase in income. The simple multiplier is then equal to 1, its minimum possible value.

In part (ii), the *AE* curve slopes upward but is still relatively flat (z is low). The increase in equilibrium national income to Y_2 is only slightly greater than the increase in autonomous expenditure that brought it about. The simple multiplier is slightly greater than 1.

In part (iii), the *AE* function is quite steep (z is high). Now the increase in equilibrium income to Y_3 is much larger than the increase in autonomous expenditure that brought it about. The simple multiplier is much larger than 1.

We can derive the precise value of the simple multiplier by using elementary algebra. (The formal derivation is given in *Extensions in Theory 21-2*.) The result is

$$\text{Simple Multiplier} = \frac{\Delta Y}{\Delta A} = \frac{1}{1 - z}$$

For the simple model we have developed in this chapter, $z = 0.8$ and so the simple multiplier $= 1/(1 - 0.8) = 1/0.2 = 5$. In this model, therefore, a \$1 billion increase in autonomous expenditure leads to a \$5 billion increase in equilibrium national income.

Recall that z is the marginal propensity to spend out of national income and is between zero and 1. The smallest simple multiplier occurs when z equals zero. In this case, $(1 - z)$ equals 1 and so the multiplier equals 1. On the other hand, if z is very close to 1, $(1 - z)$ is close to zero and so the multiplier becomes very large. The relationship between the slope of the *AE* function (z) and the size of the multiplier is shown in Figure 21-10.

A Realistic Estimate for the Simple Multiplier   To estimate the size of the simple multiplier in an actual economy, we need to estimate the value of the marginal propensity to spend out of national income in that economy. Evidence suggests that the Canadian value is much smaller than the 0.8 that we used in our example, in large part

EXTENSIONS IN THEORY 21-2

The Algebra of the Simple Multiplier

Basic algebra is all that is needed to derive the exact expression for the simple multiplier. Readers who feel at home with algebra may want to follow this derivation. Others can skip it and rely on the graphical and numerical arguments that have been given in the text.

First, we derive the equation for the *AE* curve. Desired aggregate expenditure comprises autonomous expenditure and induced expenditure. In the simple model of this chapter, autonomous expenditure is equal to investment plus autonomous consumption. Induced expenditure is equal to induced consumption. Hence, we can write

$$AE = zY + A \qquad [1]$$

where *A* is autonomous expenditure and zY is induced expenditure, *z* being the marginal propensity to spend out of national income. In the simple model of this chapter, with no government and no international trade, *z* is equal to the marginal propensity to consume.

Now we write the equation of the 45° line,

$$AE = Y \qquad [2]$$

which states the equilibrium condition that desired aggregate expenditure equals actual national income. Equations 1 and 2 are two equations with two unknowns, *AE*

and *Y*. To solve them, we substitute Equation 1 into Equation 2 to obtain

$$Y = zY + A \qquad [3]$$

Equation 3 can be easily solved to get *Y* expressed in terms of *A* and *z*. The solution is

$$Y = \frac{A}{1 - z} \qquad [4]$$

Equation 4 tells us the equilibrium value of *Y* in terms of autonomous expenditures and the marginal propensity to spend out of national income. Now consider a $1 increase in *A*. The expression $Y = A/(1 - z)$ tells us that if *A* changes by one dollar, the resulting change in *Y* will be $1/(1 - z)$ dollars. Generally, for a change in autonomous spending of ΔA, the resulting change in *Y* will be

$$\Delta Y = \frac{\Delta A}{1 - z} \qquad [5]$$

Dividing through by ΔA gives the value of the multiplier:

$$\text{Simple Multiplier} = \frac{\Delta Y}{\Delta A} = \frac{1}{1 - z} \qquad [6]$$

because our simple model currently has no taxation by government or spending on foreign goods and services. Both of these important elements (which we discuss in the next chapter) reduce the amount of each new dollar of income that is spent on domestic output—that is, they reduce the value of *z*. For the current Canadian economy, a realistic estimate of *z* is about 0.20. Hence, a realistic estimate of the simple multiplier in Canada is approximately $1/(1 - 0.20) = 1/0.80 = 1.25$.

Economic Fluctuations as Self-Fulfilling Prophecies

Expectations about the future play an important role in macroeconomics. We said earlier that households' and firms' expectations about the future state of the economy influence desired consumption and desired investment. But as we have just seen, changes in desired aggregate expenditure will, through the multiplier process, lead to changes in national income. This link between expectations and national income suggests that expectations about a healthy economy can actually produce a healthy economy—what economists call a *self-fulfilling prophecy*.

Imagine a situation in which many firms begin to feel optimistic about future economic prospects. This optimism may lead them to increase their desired investment, thus shifting up the economy's *AE* function. As we have seen, however, any upward shift in the *AE* function will lead to an increase in national income. Such "good" economic times will then be seen by firms to have justified their initial optimism. Many firms in such a situation may take pride in their ability to predict the future—but this would be misplaced pride. The truth of the matter is that if enough firms are optimistic and take actions based on that optimism, their actions will *create* the economic situation that they expected.

Now imagine the opposite situation in which many firms begin to feel pessimistic about future economic conditions. This pessimism may lead them to scale down or cancel planned investment projects. Such a decline in planned investment would shift the *AE* function down and lead to a decrease in national income. The "bad" economic times will then be seen by the firms as justification for their initial pessimism, and many will take pride in their predictive powers. But again their pride would be misplaced; the truth is that sufficient pessimism on the part of firms will tend to *create* the conditions that they expected.

The aggregate consequences of pessimism on the part of both firms and consumers were an important contributing factor to the global recession that started in late 2008. In many countries, including Canada, the events surrounding the financial crisis of 2007–2008 led to a shattering of economic optimism. Measures of business and consumer confidence fell by more than had been observed in decades, and this decline in confidence partly explained the large declines in investment and household consumption that occurred at the time and lasted for more than a year. As we will see in later chapters, governments took actions to replace this drop in private-sector demand with increases in government spending.

Summary

21.1 Desired Aggregate Expenditure   LO ❶ ❷

- Desired aggregate expenditure (*AE*) is equal to desired consumption plus desired investment plus desired government purchases plus desired net exports. It is the amount that economic agents want to spend on purchasing the national product.

$$AE = C + I + G + (X - IM)$$

- The relationship between disposable income and consumption is called the consumption function. The constant term in the consumption function is autonomous expenditure. The part of consumption that responds to income is called induced expenditure.
- A change in disposable income leads to a change in desired consumption and desired saving. The respon-

siveness of these changes is measured by the marginal propensity to consume (*MPC*) and the marginal propensity to save (*MPS*), both of which are positive and sum to 1, indicating that all disposable income is either consumed or saved.

- Changes in wealth, interest rates, or expectations about the future lead to a change in autonomous consumption. As a result, the consumption function shifts.
- Firms' desired investment depends, among other things, on real interest rates, changes in sales, and business confidence. In our simplest model of the economy, investment is treated as autonomous with respect to changes in national income.

21.2 Equilibrium National Income   LO ❸

- Equilibrium national income is defined as that level of national income at which desired aggregate expenditure equals actual national income. At incomes above

equilibrium, desired expenditure is less than national income. In this case, inventories accumulate and firms will eventually reduce output. At incomes below equilibrium, desired expenditure exceeds national income. In this case, inventories are depleted and firms will eventually increase output.

- Equilibrium national income is represented graphically by the point at which the aggregate expenditure (*AE*) curve cuts the 45° line—that is, where desired aggregate expenditure equals actual national income.

21.3 Changes in Equilibrium National Income   LO 4

- Equilibrium national income is increased by a rise in either autonomous consumption or autonomous investment expenditure. Equilibrium national income is reduced by a fall in these desired expenditures.
- The magnitude of the effect on national income of shifts in autonomous expenditure is given by the multiplier. It is defined as $\Delta Y/\Delta A$, where ΔA is the change in autonomous expenditure.
- The simple multiplier is the multiplier when the price level is constant. The simple multiplier $= \Delta Y/\Delta A = 1/(1 - z)$, where z is the marginal propensity to spend

out of national income. The larger is z, the larger is the simple multiplier.
- It is a basic prediction of our simple macro model that the simple multiplier is greater than 1.
- Expectations play an important role in the determination of national income. Optimism can lead households and firms to increase desired expenditure, which, through the multiplier process, leads to increases in national income. Pessimism can similarly lead to decreases in desired expenditure and national income.

Key Concepts

Desired versus actual expenditure
The consumption function
Average and marginal propensities to consume
Average and marginal propensities to save

The aggregate expenditure (*AE*) function
Marginal propensity to spend
Equilibrium national income

Effect on national income of shifts in the *AE* curve
The simple multiplier
The size of the multiplier and slope of the *AE* curve

Study Exercises

1. Fill in the blanks to make the following statements correct.

    a. The equation for *actual* national income from the expenditure side is written as: GDP = _____.
    b. The equation for *desired* aggregate expenditure is written as: *AE* = _____.
    c. National income accounts measure _____ expenditures in four broad categories. National income theory deals with _____ expenditure in the same four categories.

    d. The equation for a simple consumption function is written as $C = a + bY$. The letter a represents the _____ part of consumption. The letters bY represent the _____ part of consumption. When graphing a consumption function, the vertical intercept is given by the letter _____, and the slope of the function is given by the letter _____.

    e. In the simple macro model of this chapter, all investment is treated as _____ expenditure, meaning that it is unaffected by changes in national income.

f. The aggregate expenditure function in the simple macro model of this chapter is written as $AE =$ _____ and is graphed with _____ on the vertical axis and _____ on the horizontal axis.

g. An example of an aggregate expenditure function is $AE = \$47$ billion $+ 0.92Y$. Autonomous expenditure is _____ and the marginal propensity to spend out of national income is _____. In the simple model in this chapter, the marginal propensity to spend is the same as the marginal propensity to consume because _____.

2. Fill in the blanks to make the following statements correct.

a. If actual national income is $200 billion and desired aggregate expenditure is $180 billion, inventories may begin to _____, firms will _____ the level of output, and national income will _____.

b. If actual national income is $200 billion and desired aggregate expenditure is $214 billion, inventories may begin to _____, firms will _____ the level of output, and national income will _____.

c. If households experience an increase in wealth that leads to an increase in desired consumption, the AE curve will shift _____. Equilibrium national income will _____ to the level indicated by the intersection of the AE curve with the _____ line.

d. When autonomous desired expenditure increases by $10 billion, national income will increase by _____ than $10 billion. The magnitude of the change in national income is measured by the _____.

e. The larger is the marginal propensity to spend, the _____ is the multiplier. Where z is the marginal propensity to spend, the multiplier is equal to _____.

3. Consider the following table showing aggregate consumption expenditures and disposable income. All values are expressed in billions of constant dollars.

Disposable Income (Y_D)	Desired Consumption (C)	$APC = C/Y_D$	$MPC = \Delta C/\Delta Y_D$
0	150	—	
100	225	—	—
200	300	—	—
300	375	—	—
400	450	—	—
500	525	—	—
600	600	—	—
700	675	—	—
800	750	—	—

a. Compute the average propensity to consume for each level of income and fill in the table.

b. Compute the marginal propensity to consume for each successive change in income and fill in the table.

c. Plot the consumption function on a scale diagram. What is its slope?

4. This question relates to desired saving, and is based on the table from Question 3.

a. Compute desired saving at each level of disposable income. Plot the saving function on a scale diagram. What is its slope?

b. Show that the average propensity to save plus the average propensity to consume must equal 1.

5. In the chapter we explained at length the difference between *desired* expenditures and *actual* expenditures.

a. Is national income accounting based on desired or actual expenditures? Explain.

b. Suppose there were a sudden decrease in desired consumption expenditure. Explain why this would lead to an equally sudden increase in *actual* investment expenditure. Which type of investment would rise?

c. Illustrate the event from part (b) in a 45°-line diagram. Illustrate the increase in actual investment.

6. Consider the following diagram of the AE function and the 45° line.

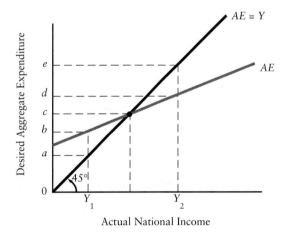

a. Suppose the level of actual national income is Y_1. What is the level of desired aggregate expenditure? Is it greater or less than actual output? Are inventories being depleted or accumulated?

b. If actual income is Y_1, explain the process by which national income changes toward equilibrium.

c. Suppose the level of actual national income is Y_2. What is the level of desired aggregate expenditure? Is it greater or less than actual output? Are inventories being depleted or accumulated?

d. If actual income is Y_2, explain the process by which national income changes toward equilibrium.

7. Consider a simple model like the one developed in this chapter. The following equations show the levels of desired consumption and investment:

$$C = 500 + 0.9Y$$

$$I = 100$$

Y	C	I	AE
0	—	—	—
2 000	—	—	—
4 000	—	—	—
6 000	—	—	—
8 000	—	—	—
10 000	—	—	—

a. Complete the table above.
b. What is the equilibrium level of national income in this model? Why?

8. Suppose you are given the following information for an economy without government spending, exports, or imports. C is desired consumption, I is desired investment, and Y is income. C and I are given by:

$$C = 1400 + 0.8Y$$

$$I = 400$$

a. What is the equation for the aggregate expenditure (AE) function?
b. Applying the equilibrium condition that $Y = AE$, determine the level of equilibrium national income.

c. Using your answer from part (b), determine the values of consumption, saving, and investment when the economy is in equilibrium.

9. Consider an economy characterized by the following equations:

$$C = 500 + 0.75Y + 0.05W$$

$$I = 150$$

where C is desired consumption, I is desired investment, W is household wealth, and Y is national income.

a. Suppose wealth is constant at $W = 10\,000$. Draw the aggregate expenditure function on a scale diagram along with the 45° line. What is the equilibrium level of national income?
b. The marginal propensity to spend in this economy is 0.75. What is the value of the simple multiplier?
c. Using your answer from part (b), what would be the change in equilibrium national income if desired investment increased to 250? Can you show this in your diagram?
d. Now suppose household wealth increases from 10 000 to 15 000. What happens to the AE function and by how much does national income change?

10. The "Paradox of Thrift" is a famous idea in macroeconomics—one that we will discuss in later chapters. The basic idea is that if every household in the economy tries to increase its level of desired saving, the level of national income will fall and they will end up saving no more than they were initially. Use the model and diagrams of this chapter to show how an (autonomous) increase in desired saving would reduce equilibrium income and lead to no change in aggregate saving. (Though it is not essential, you may find it useful to see **Investment, Saving, and Equilibrium GDP** in the *Additional Topics* section of MyEconLab.)

Discussion Questions

1. Relate the following newspaper headlines to shifts in the *C*, *S*, *I*, and *AE* functions and to changes in equilibrium national income.

a. "Revival of consumer confidence leads to increased spending."
b. "High mortgage rates discourage new house purchases."
c. "Concern over future leads to a reduction in inventories."

d. "Accelerated depreciation allowances in the new federal budget set off boom on equipment purchases."
e. "Consumers spend as stock market soars."

2. Why might an individual's marginal propensity to consume be higher in the long run than in the short run? Why might it be lower? Is it possible for an individual's average propensity to consume to be greater than 1 in the short run? In the long run? Can a country's average

propensity to consume be greater than 1 in the short run? In the long run?

3. Explain why a sudden, unexpected fall in consumer expenditure would initially cause an increase in actual investment expenditure by firms.

4. In the simple model of this chapter, aggregate investment was assumed to be autonomous. The simple multiplier was $1/(1 - z)$, where z was the marginal propensity to spend. With autonomous investment, the marginal propensity to spend is simply the marginal propensity to consume. Now suppose that investment is *not* completely autonomous. That is, suppose that $I = \bar{I} + mY$, where $\bar{I}$ is autonomous investment and m is the "marginal propensity to invest" ($m > 0$). Explain how this modification to the simple model changes the simple multiplier.

22

Adding Government and Trade to the Simple Macro Model

LEARNING OBJECTIVES

In this chapter you will learn

1 how government purchases and tax revenues are related to national income.

2 how exports and imports are related to national income.

3 how to distinguish between the marginal propensity to consume and the marginal propensity to spend.

4 why the presence of government and foreign trade reduces the value of the simple multiplier.

5 how government can use fiscal policy to influence the level of national income.

In Chapter 21, we developed a simple short-run model of national income determination in a closed economy with fixed prices. In this chapter, we add a government and a foreign sector to that model. In Chapter 23, we will expand the model further to explain the determination of the price level.

Adding government to the model allows us to study *fiscal policy*, the government's use of its taxing and spending powers to affect the level of national income. Adding foreign trade allows us to examine some ways in which external events affect the Canadian economy. Fortunately, the key elements of the previous chapter's theory of income determination are unchanged even after government and the foreign sector are incorporated.

22.1 Introducing Government

A government's **fiscal policy** is defined by its plans for taxes and spending. Government spending and taxation influence national income in both the short and the long run. Our discussion of fiscal policy begins in this chapter; we go into more detail in Chapter 24 and again in Chapter 32.

fiscal policy The use of the government's tax and spending policies to achieve government objectives.

Government Purchases

In Chapter 20, we distinguished between government *purchases of goods and services* and government *transfer payments*. The distinction bears repeating here. When the government hires a bureaucrat, buys office supplies, or purchases fuel for the Canadian Forces, it is adding directly to the demands for the economy's current output of goods and services. Hence, desired government purchases, G, are part of aggregate desired expenditure.

The other part of government spending, transfer payments, also affects desired aggregate expenditure but only indirectly. Consider welfare or employment-insurance benefits, for example. These government expenditures place no direct demand on the nation's production of goods and services since they merely transfer funds from taxpayers to the recipients. However, when recipients spend some of these payments on consumption, their spending is part of aggregate expenditure. Thus, government transfer payments do affect aggregate expenditure but only through the effect these transfers have on households' *disposable* income.

In this chapter we make the simple assumption that the level of government purchases, G, is autonomous with respect to the level of national income. As GDP rises or falls, the level of the government's transfer payments will generally change, but we assume that G does not automatically change just because GDP changes. We then view any change in G as a result of a government policy decision.

Net Tax Revenues

Taxes reduce households' disposable income relative to national income. In contrast, transfer payments raise disposable income relative to national income. For the purpose of calculating the effect of government policy on desired consumption expenditure, it is the net effect of the two that matters.

Net taxes are defined as total tax revenue received by the government minus total transfer payments made by the government, and it is denoted T. (For the remainder of this chapter, the term "taxes" means "net taxes" unless stated otherwise.) Because transfer payments are smaller than total tax revenues, net tax revenues are positive. Disposable income is therefore substantially less than national income. (It was about two-thirds of Canadian GDP in 2010.)

net taxes Total tax revenue minus transfer payments, denoted T.

In the model in this chapter, we assume that net tax revenues vary directly with the level of national income, but that the *tax rate* is an autonomous policy variable. As national income rises, a tax system with given tax rates will yield more revenue (net of transfers). For example, when income rises, people will pay more income tax in total even though the tax *rates* are unchanged. In addition, when income rises, the government generally reduces its transfers to households. We will use the following simple form for government net tax revenues, T:

$$T = tY$$

net tax rate The increase in net tax revenue generated when national income rises by one dollar. Also called the *marginal propensity to tax*.

where t is the **net tax rate** or the *marginal propensity to tax*—the increase in net tax revenue generated when national income increases by $1.

It may be tempting to think of t as the income-tax rate, but note that we are trying to represent in a simple way what in reality is a complex tax and transfer structure that includes, in addition to several different types of financial transfers to households, the taxation of personal income, corporate income, overall expenditures, the value of property, and expenditure on specific products. For that reason, we avoid associating t with any specific type of tax or transfer. Instead, in what follows we simply refer to t as the *net tax rate*.

The Budget Balance

budget surplus Any excess of current revenue over current expenditure.

budget deficit Any shortfall of current revenue below current expenditure.

The *budget balance* is the difference between total government revenue and total government expenditure; equivalently, it equals net tax revenue minus government purchases, $T - G$. When net revenues exceed purchases, the government has a **budget surplus**. When purchases exceed net revenues, the government has a **budget deficit**. When the two amounts are equal, the government has a *balanced budget*.

When the government runs a budget deficit, it must borrow the excess of spending over revenues. It does this by issuing additional *government debt* (bonds or treasury bills). When the government runs a surplus, it uses the excess revenue to buy back outstanding government debt. Budget deficits and government debt are the principal topics of Chapter 32.

Practise with Study Guide Chapter 22, Exercise 1.

Provincial and Municipal Governments

Many people are surprised to learn that the combined activities of the many Canadian provincial and municipal governments account for *more* purchases of goods and services than does the federal government. The federal government raises about the same amount of tax revenue as do the provincial and municipal governments combined but transfers a considerable amount of its revenue to the provinces.

> When measuring the overall contribution of government to desired aggregate expenditure, all levels of government must be included.

The federal Department of Finance designs and implements Canada's fiscal policy. See its website: **www.fin.gc.ca**.

As we proceed through this chapter discussing the role of government in the determination of national income, think of "the government" as the combination of all levels of government—federal, provincial, territorial, and municipal.

Summary

Before introducing foreign trade, let's summarize how the presence of government affects our simple model.

1. All levels of government add directly to desired aggregate expenditure through their purchases of goods and services, G. Later in this chapter when we are constructing the aggregate expenditure (AE) function for our model, we will include G and we will treat it as autonomous expenditure.

2. Governments also collect tax revenue and make transfer payments. Net tax revenues are denoted T and are positively related to national income. Since T does not represent any expenditure on goods and services, it is not included directly in the AE function. T will enter the AE function *indirectly*, however, through its effect on disposable income (Y_D) and consumption. Recall that $Y_D = Y - T$ and that desired consumption depends on Y_D.

22.2 Introducing Foreign Trade

Of all the goods and services produced in Canada in a given year, roughly 35 percent are exported. A similar value of goods and services is imported into Canada every year. Thus, although *net* exports may contribute only a few percent to Canada's GDP in a typical year, foreign trade is tremendously important to Canada's economy.

Canada imports all kinds of goods and services, from French wine and Peruvian anchovies to Swiss financial and American architectural services. Canada also exports a variety of goods and services, including timber, nickel, automobiles, engineering services, computer software, flight simulators, and commuter jets. U.S.–Canadian trade is the largest two-way flow of trade between any two countries in the world today.

Practise with Study Guide Chapter 22, Short-Answer Question 1 and Exercise 3.

Net Exports

Exports depend on spending decisions made by foreign households and firms that purchase Canadian products. Typically, exports will not change as a result of changes in Canadian national income. We therefore treat exports as autonomous expenditure.

Imports, however, depend on the spending decisions of Canadian households and firms. Almost all consumption goods have an import content. Canadian-made cars, for example, use large quantities of imported components in their manufacture. Canadian-made clothes most often use imported cotton or wool. And most restaurant meals contain some imported fruits, vegetables, or meats. Hence, as consumption rises, imports will also increase. Because consumption rises with national income, we also get a positive relationship between imports and national income. In this chapter, we use the following simple form for imports:

marginal propensity to import The increase in import expenditures induced by a $1 increase in national income. Denoted by m.

$$IM = mY$$

where m is the **marginal propensity to import**, the amount that desired imports rise when national income rises by $1.

In our simple model, net exports can be described by the following simple equation:

$$NX = X - mY$$

International trade is very important for the Canadian economy. More than $2.5 billion worth of goods and services flows across the Canada–U.S. border every day, much of it in trucks like these.

FIGURE 22-1   The Net Export Function

Actual National Income (Y)	Exports (X)	Imports (IM = 0.1 Y)	Net Exports (NX = X − IM)
0	72	0	72
300	72	30	42
600	72	60	12
720	72	72	0
900	72	90	−18

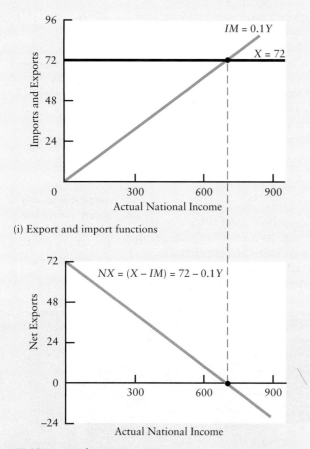

(i) Export and import functions

(ii) Net export function

Net exports fall as national income rises. The data are hypothetical. In part (i), exports are constant at $72 billion while imports rise with national income; the marginal propensity to import is assumed to be 0.10. Therefore, net exports, shown in part (ii), decline with national income. The slope of the import function in part (i) is equal to the marginal propensity to import. The slope of the net export function in part (ii) is the negative of the marginal propensity to import.

Since exports are autonomous with respect to Y but imports are positively related to Y, we see that *net exports* are negatively related to national income. This negative relationship is called the *net export function*. Data for a hypothetical economy with autonomous exports and with imports that are 10 percent of national income ($m = 0.1$) are illustrated in Figure 22-1. In this example, exports form the autonomous component and imports the induced component of desired net exports.

Shifts in the Net Export Function

The net export function is drawn under the assumption that everything affecting net exports, except domestic national income, remains constant. The two major factors that must be held constant are foreign national income and international relative prices. A change in either factor will shift the net export function. Notice that anything affecting Canadian exports will shift the net export function parallel to itself, upward if exports increase and downward if exports decrease. Also notice that anything affecting the *proportion of income* that Canadian consumers want to spend on imports will change the *slope* of the net export function. Let's now explore some of these changes in detail.

Changes in Foreign Income
An increase in foreign income, other things being equal, will lead to an increase in the quantity of Canadian goods demanded by foreign countries—that is, to an increase in Canadian exports. This change causes the X curve to shift upward and therefore the NX function also to shift upward, parallel to its original position. A fall in foreign income leads to a reduction in Canadian exports and thus to a parallel downward shift in the net export function.

Changes in International Relative Prices
Any change in the prices of Canadian goods *relative* to those of foreign goods will cause both imports and exports to change. These changes will shift the net export function.

Consider what happens with a rise in Canadian prices relative to those in foreign countries. The increase in Canadian prices means that foreigners now see Canadian goods as more expensive relative both to goods produced in their own country and to goods imported from countries other than Canada. As a result, the value of Canadian exports will fall.[1] The *X* curve shifts down in Figure 22-2. Similarly, Canadians will see imports from foreign countries become cheaper relative to the prices of Canadian-made goods. As a result, they will shift their expenditures toward foreign goods and away from Canadian goods. That is, Canadians will spend a higher fraction of national income on imports—the *IM* curve in Figure 22-2 will rotate up. The combination of these two effects is that the net export function shifts downward and becomes steeper. A fall in Canadian prices relative to foreign prices would have the opposite effect, shifting the *X* function up and the *IM* function down, and thus shifting the *NX* function up.

> A rise in Canadian prices relative to those in other countries reduces Canadian net exports at any level of national income. A fall in Canadian prices increases net exports at any level of national income.

The most important cause of a change in international relative prices is a change in the exchange rate. A *depreciation* of the Canadian dollar means that foreigners must pay less of their money to buy one Canadian dollar, and Canadian residents must pay more Canadian dollars to buy a unit of any foreign currency. As a result, the price of foreign goods in terms of Canadian dollars rises, and the price of Canadian goods in terms of foreign currency falls. This reduction in the relative price of Canadian goods will cause a shift in expenditure away from foreign goods and toward Canadian goods. Canadian residents will import less at each level of Canadian national income, and foreigners will buy more Canadian exports. The net export function thus shifts upward.

An example may help to clarify the argument. Suppose something causes the Canadian dollar to depreciate relative to the euro (the common currency in the European Union). The depreciation of the Canadian dollar leads Canadians to switch away from French wines and German cars, purchasing instead more B.C. wine and Ontario-made cars. This reduction in imports is reflected by the downward rotation of the *IM* curve. The depreciation of the Canadian dollar relative to the euro also stimulates Canadian exports. Quebec furniture and Maritime vacations now appear cheaper to Europeans than previously, and so their expenditure on such Canadian goods increases. This increase in Canadian exports is reflected by an upward shift in the *X* curve. The overall effect is that the net export function shifts up and becomes flatter.

FIGURE 22-2   Shifts in the Net Export Function

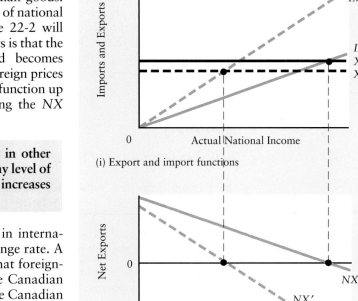

(i) Export and import functions

(ii) Net export function

Changes in international relative prices shift the *NX* function. A rise in Canadian prices relative to foreign prices lowers exports from *X* to *X'* and raises the import function from *IM* to *IM'*. This shifts the net export function downward from *NX* to *NX'*. A fall in Canadian prices has the opposite effect.

For lots of interesting information on Canada's international trade, go to the website for the Department of Foreign Affairs and International Trade: www.dfait.gc.ca.

---

[1] The rise in Canadian prices leads to a reduction in the quantity of Canadian goods demanded by foreigners. But in order for the *value* of Canadian exports to fall, the price elasticity of demand for Canadian exports must exceed 1 (so that the quantity reduction dominates the price increase). Throughout this book, we make this realistic assumption.

One final word of caution regarding prices, exchange rates, and net exports. It is important to keep in mind that the simple model in this chapter treats prices and exchange rates as *exogenous* variables. That is, though we can discuss what happens if they change, we do not yet *explain* where these changes come from. Of course, in the actual economy the price level and the exchange rate are key macroeconomic variables that we want to understand. In the next chapter, the price level becomes *endogenous* in our model and we therefore consider why it changes. In Chapter 35, we explain in detail what causes the exchange rate to change. For now, however, keep in mind that the price level and the exchange rate are exogenous variables—we can explain what happens in our model *if* they change but we cannot use the current simple version of our model to explain *why* they change.

Summary

How does the presence of foreign trade modify our basic model? Let's summarize.

1. Foreign firms and households purchase Canadian-made goods. Changes in foreign income and international relative prices (including exchange rates) will affect Canadian exports (X), but we assume that X is autonomous with respect to Canadian national income. When we construct the economy's aggregate expenditure (AE) function, we will include X since it represents expenditure on domestic goods.

2. All components of domestic expenditure (C, I, and G) include some import content. Since C is positively related to national income, imports (IM) are also related positively to national income. When we construct the economy's AE function, which shows the desired aggregate expenditure on *domestic* products, we will *subtract IM* because these expenditures are on foreign goods.

22.3 Equilibrium National Income

As in Chapter 21, equilibrium national income is the level of income at which desired aggregate expenditure equals actual national income. The addition of government and net exports changes the calculations that we must make but does not alter the meaning of equilibrium or the basic workings of the model.

Desired Consumption and National Income

When net taxes (taxes net of transfers) are positive, disposable income (Y_D) is less than national income (Y). We take several steps to determine the relationship between consumption and national income in the presence of taxes.

1. First, assume that the net tax rate, t, is 10 percent, so that net tax revenues are 10 percent of national income:

$$T = (0.1)Y$$

2. Disposable income must therefore be 90 percent of national income:

$$Y_D = Y - T = (0.9)Y$$

3. The consumption function we used last chapter is given as

$$C = 30 + (0.8)Y_D$$

which tells us that the *MPC* out of disposable income is 0.8.

4. We can now substitute $(0.9)Y$ for Y_D in the consumption function. By doing so, we get

$$C = 30 + (0.8)(0.9)Y$$
$$\Rightarrow C = 30 + (0.72)Y$$

We can therefore express desired consumption as a function of Y_D or as a *different* function of Y. In this example, 0.72 is equal to the *MPC* times $(1 - t)$, where t is the net tax rate. So, whereas 0.8 is the marginal propensity to consume out of *disposable* income, 0.72 is the marginal propensity to consume out of *national* income.

Practise with Study Guide
Chapter 22, Exercise 2.

In the presence of taxes, the marginal propensity to consume out of national income is less than the marginal propensity to consume out of disposable income.

The *AE* Function

In Chapter 21, the only components of desired aggregate expenditure were consumption and investment. We now add government purchases and net exports. The separate components in their general form are

$C = a + bY_D$ consumption
I autonomous investment
G autonomous government purchases
$T = tY$ net tax revenues
X autonomous exports
$IM = mY$ imports

Our first step in constructing the *AE* function is to express desired consumption in terms of national income. By using the four steps from above, we write desired consumption as

$$C = a + b(1 - t)Y$$

Now we sum the four components of desired aggregate expenditure:

$$AE = C + I + G + (X - IM)$$
$$= a + b(1 - t)Y + I + G + (X - mY)$$
$$AE = \underbrace{[a + I + G + X]}_{\substack{\text{Autonomous} \\ \text{expenditure}}} + \underbrace{[b(1 - t) - m]Y}_{\substack{\text{Induced} \\ \text{expenditure}}}$$

In this last equation, we can see the distinction between autonomous aggregate expenditure and induced aggregate expenditure. The first set of square brackets brings together all the autonomous parts of expenditure. The second set of square brackets brings together all the parts of expenditure that change when national income changes—the induced part of consumption and imports. This second term in square brackets shows how much total desired spending changes when national income changes by one dollar—the marginal propensity to spend out of national income.

Figure 22-3 graphs the *AE* function for our hypothetical economy in which we assume that desired investment is $75 billion and the level of government purchases is $51 billion. Notice that the slope of the *AE* function measures the change in desired aggregate expenditure (*AE*) that comes about from a $1 increase in national income (*Y*). This is the marginal propensity to spend out of national income and is equal to $b(1 - t) - m$.

Note that, unlike in Chapter 21, the marginal propensity to spend out of national income is not simply equal to the marginal propensity to consume. To understand why, suppose the economy produces $1 of extra national income and that the response to this is governed by the relationships in Figure 22-3. Because 10 cents is collected by the government as net taxes, 90 cents becomes disposable income, and 80 percent of this

Practise with Study Guide Chapter 22, Exercises 4, 6, and 7.

FIGURE 22-3   The Aggregate Expenditure Function

The aggregate expenditure function is the sum of desired consumption, investment, government purchases, and net export expenditures. The autonomous components of desired aggregate expenditure are desired investment, desired government purchases, desired export expenditures, and the constant term in desired consumption expenditure. These sum to $228 billion in the given example and this sum is the vertical intercept of the *AE* curve. The induced component is $(b(1 - t) - m)Y$, which in our example is equal to $(0.8(0.9) - 0.1)Y = 0.62Y$.

The equation for the *AE* function is $AE = 228 + 0.62Y$. The slope of the *AE* function, $\Delta AE/\Delta Y$, is 0.62, indicating that a $1 increase in *Y* leads to a 62-cent increase in desired expenditure. This is the marginal propensity to spend on domestic output. The equilibrium level of national income is $600 billion, the level of *Y* where the *AE* function intersects the 45° line.

Point	Actual National Income (*Y*)	Desired Consumption Expenditure (*C* = 30 + 0.72*Y*)	Desired Investment Expenditure (*I* = 75)	Desired Government Expenditure (*G* = 51)	Desired Net Export Expenditure (*X* − *IM* = 72 − 0.1*Y*)	Desired Aggregate Expenditure (*AE* = *C* + *I* + *G* + *X* − *IM*)
A	0	30	75	51	72	228
B	150	138	75	51	57	321
C	300	246	75	51	42	414
D	600	462	75	51	12	600
E	900	678	75	51	−18	786

amount (72 cents) is spent on consumption. However, 10 cents of all expenditure goes to imports, so expenditure on *domestic* goods rises by only 62 cents (72 − 10). Hence, z, the marginal propensity to spend, is 0.62. In algebraic terms,

$$
\begin{aligned}
z &= b(1 - t) - m \\
&= (0.8)(1 - 0.1) - 0.1 \\
&= 0.72 - 0.1 \\
&= 0.62
\end{aligned}
$$

Equilibrium National Income

As in Chapter 21, we are assuming (for now) that firms are able and willing to produce whatever level of output is demanded of them at a constant price level. When output is *demand determined* in this way, the equilibrium level of national income is that level of national income where desired aggregate expenditure (along the *AE* function) equals the actual level of national income. As also was true in Chapter 21, the 45° line shows the *equilibrium condition*—the collection of points where $Y = AE$. Thus, the equilibrium level of national income in Figure 22-3 is at point *D*, where the *AE* function intersects the 45° line.

Suppose national income is less than its equilibrium amount. The forces leading back to equilibrium are exactly the same as those described in Chapter 21. When households, firms, foreign demanders, and governments try to spend at their desired amounts, they will try to purchase more goods and services than the economy is currently producing. Hence, some of the desired expenditure must either be frustrated or take the form of purchases of inventories of goods that were produced in the past. As firms see their inventories being depleted, they will increase production, thereby increasing the level of national income.

The opposite sequence of events occurs when national income is greater than desired aggregate expenditure. Now the total of desired household consumption, business investment, government purchases, and net foreign demand on the economy's production is less than national output. Firms will notice that they are unable to sell all their output. Their inventories will be rising, and sooner or later they will seek to reduce the level of output until it equals the level of sales. When they do, national income will fall.

Finally, when national income is equal to desired aggregate expenditure ($600 billion in Figure 22-3), there is no pressure for output to change. Desired consumption, investment, government purchases, and net exports just add up to national output.

---

myeconlab   **ADDITIONAL TOPICS**

An alternative (but equivalent) approach to determining the equilibrium level of national income is based on the relationship between national saving and the accumulation of national assets. For more details, look for **The Saving–Investment Approach to Equilibrium in an Open Economy with Government** in the *Additional Topics* section of this book's MyEconLab.

22.4 Changes in Equilibrium National Income

Changes in any of the components of desired aggregate expenditure will cause changes in equilibrium national income. In Chapter 21, we investigated the consequences of shifts in the consumption function and in the investment function. Here we take a first look at fiscal policy—the effects of changes in government spending and taxation. We also consider shifts in the net export function. First, we explain why the simple multiplier is reduced by the presence of taxes and imports.

The Multiplier with Taxes and Imports

In Chapter 21, we saw that the *simple multiplier*, the amount by which equilibrium real GDP changes when autonomous expenditure changes by one dollar, was equal to $1/(1 - z)$, where z is the marginal propensity to spend out of national income. In the simple model of Chapter 21, with no government and no international trade, z was simply the marginal propensity to consume out of disposable income. But in the more complex model of this chapter, which contains both government and foreign trade, we have seen that the marginal propensity to spend out of national income is slightly more complicated.

> The presence of imports and taxes reduces the marginal propensity to spend out of national income and thus reduces the value of the simple multiplier.

Let's be more specific. In Chapter 21, the marginal propensity to spend, z, was just equal to the marginal propensity to consume. Let ΔY be the change in equilibrium real GDP brought about by a change in autonomous spending, ΔA. We then have the following relationships:

Without Government and Foreign Trade:

$$z = MPC$$

$$\text{Simple multiplier} = \frac{\Delta Y}{\Delta A} = \frac{1}{1 - z}$$

$$= \frac{1}{1 - MPC}$$

In our example, the MPC was 0.8 and so the simple multiplier was equal to 5.

$$\text{Simple multiplier} = 1/(1 - 0.8) = 1/0.2 = 5$$

In our expanded model with government and foreign trade, the marginal propensity to spend out of national income must take account of the presence of net taxes and imports, both of which reduce the value of z.

With Government and Foreign Trade:

$$z = MPC(1 - t) - m$$

$$\text{Simple multiplier} = \frac{\Delta Y}{\Delta A} = \frac{1}{1 - z}$$

$$= \frac{1}{1 - [MPC(1 - t) - m]}$$

In our example, $t = 0.1$ and $m = 0.1$. This makes the simple multiplier equal to 2.63.

$$\text{Simple multiplier} = 1/\{1 - [0.8(1 - 0.1) - 0.1]\} = 1/[1 - (0.72 - 0.1)]$$
$$= 1/(1 - 0.62) = 2.63$$

What is the central point here? Because net taxes and imports both increase in response to an increase in national income, every increase in GDP induces a smaller increase in desired expenditure *on domestically produced goods* than would be the case in the simpler world with no taxes or imports. The result is that the overall change in equilibrium GDP is lower.

> The higher is the marginal propensity to import, the lower is the simple multiplier. The higher is the net tax rate, the lower is the simple multiplier.

Applying Economic Concepts 22-1 examines what the size of the simple multiplier is likely to be in the Canadian economy. You may be surprised at the result!

Net Exports

Earlier in this chapter, we discussed the determinants of net exports and of shifts in the net export function. As with the other elements of desired aggregate expenditure, if the net export function shifts upward, equilibrium national income will rise; if the net export function shifts downward, equilibrium national income will fall.

Generally, exports themselves are autonomous with respect to domestic national income. Foreign demand for Canadian products depends on foreign income, on foreign and Canadian prices, and on the exchange rate, but it does not depend on Canadian income. Export demand could also change because of a change in tastes. Suppose foreign consumers develop a taste for Canadian-made furniture and desire to consume $1 billion more per year of these goods than they had in the past. The net export function (and the aggregate expenditure function) will shift up by $1 billion, and equilibrium national income will increase by $1 billion times the simple multiplier.

Fiscal Policy

In Chapter 19 we introduced the concept of potential GDP, the level of GDP that would exist if all factors of production were fully employed. Deviations of actual GDP (Y) from potential GDP (Y^*) usually create problems. When $Y < Y^*$, factor incomes are low and unemployment of factors is high; when $Y > Y^*$, rising costs create inflationary pressures. To reduce these problems, governments often try to *stabilize* the level of real GDP close to Y^*. Any attempt to use government policy in this manner is called **stabilization policy**, and here we focus on stabilization through fiscal policy. In

stabilization policy Any policy designed to reduce the economy's cyclical fluctuations and thereby stabilize national income.

APPLYING ECONOMIC CONCEPTS 22-1

How Large Is Canada's Simple Multiplier?

In our macro model, the "simple multiplier" expresses the overall change in equilibrium national income resulting from an increase in desired autonomous spending. But to the extent that increases in output are only possible in the short run by increasing the level of employment, the multiplier can also tell us something about the total change in employment that will result from an initial increase in spending. And this is the way we usually hear about the effects of the multiplier in the popular press.

Imagine you are listening to a news story on the radio or TV about a recent announcement by the government to increase its annual spending by $5 billion on the repairs of highways and bridges. Rather than claiming that the $5 billion increase in spending will lead to an overall increase in national income by several times this amount, the official making the announcement is likely to speak in terms of the number of jobs "created" in the economy as a result of the new government spending. For example, the official might claim that this new spending will *directly* create 5000 new jobs and that an additional 10 000 new jobs will be created *indirectly*. With such a claim, the government official appears to believe that the simple multiplier is equal to 3—the total increase in employment (and output) will be three times the direct increase. Is a simple multiplier of 3 a realistic estimate for Canada?

In the simple model we have developed in this chapter, we have used values for key parameters that are simple to work with but not necessarily realistic. In particular, we assumed values of t and m that are well below their actual values. To find a realistic estimate for the multiplier in Canada, we need to use more realistic values for the net tax rate (t) and the marginal propensity to import (m). In Canada a reasonable value for t is 0.3, the approximate

share of combined government net taxation in GDP. Imports into Canada are close to 35 percent of GDP and so $m = 0.35$ is a reasonable value. If we use these more realistic values for t and m, and continue the reasonable assumption that the marginal propensity to consume out of disposable income is 0.8, the implied value of z is

$$z = MPC(1 - t) - m$$
$$= 0.8(1 - 0.3) - 0.35 = 0.21$$

and so the implied value of the simple multiplier is

$$\text{Simple multiplier} = 1/(1 - z) = 1/0.79 = 1.27$$

Two main lessons emerge from this analysis:

1. Net taxes and imports reduce the size of the simple multiplier.

2. Realistic values of t and m in Canada suggest a simple multiplier that is much closer to 1 than to 2 and certainly far below the value of 5 that we used in the very simple model of Chapter 21.

So the next time you hear a government official make claims about how new spending plans are likely to have large effects on the level of employment and economic activity, think about what the implied value of the simple multiplier must be in order for the claims to be reasonable. The analysis here suggests that the simple multiplier in Canada is probably only moderately greater than 1.*

---

* In the next two chapters we will see that once we allow for a price level that can adjust to changes in demand, the multiplier gets even smaller.

Chapters 24 and 32, we examine various issues of fiscal policy in more detail, including why the real-world practice of fiscal policy is more complicated than our simple model suggests.

Fiscal policy involves the use of government spending and taxation, often motivated by the desire to alter national income and hence employment. Because government purchases increase desired aggregate expenditure and taxation decreases it, the *directions* of the required changes in spending and taxation are generally easy to determine once we know the direction in which the government wants to change national income. But the *timing* and *magnitude* of the changes are more difficult issues. The issue of timing is difficult because it takes an uncertain amount of time before fiscal policies have an effect on real GDP. The issue of magnitude is difficult because the level of potential output is not measured directly and can only be estimated imperfectly.

The basic idea of fiscal stabilization policy follows from what we have already learned. A reduction in net tax rates or an increase in government purchases shifts the

AE curve upward, setting in motion the multiplier process that tends to increase equilibrium national income. An increase in tax rates or a decrease in government purchases shifts the *AE* curve downward and tends to decrease equilibrium income.

   If the government targets Y^* as its desired level of real GDP, it can alter net taxes or purchases, or both, in an attempt to push the economy toward that target. First, suppose real GDP is well below Y^*. In this case, the government would like to increase real GDP. The available fiscal tools are to raise government purchases, or to increase disposable income by lowering tax rates or increasing transfer payments. Second, suppose the economy is "overheated," meaning that real GDP is above Y^*. What can the government do? The fiscal tools at its command are to reduce government purchases or to reduce disposable income by raising tax rates or reducing transfer payments. Each of these measures has a depressing effect on real GDP.

Changes in government purchases and tax rates can have significant effects on desired aggregate expenditure and thus on equilibrium national income.

   Figure 22-4 illustrates the two situations: one in which the government's objective is to increase the level of real GDP, and the other in which the government's objective is

FIGURE 22-4   The Use of Fiscal Stabilization Policy

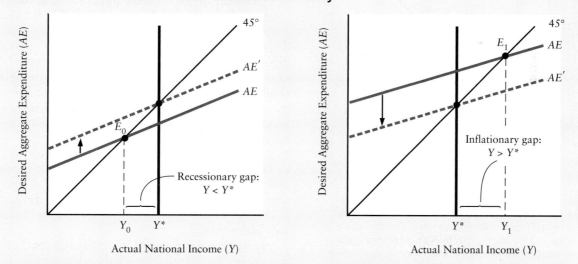

(i) Equilibrium $Y < Y^*$ (ii) Equilibrium $Y > Y^*$

Stabilization policy can be used to bring national income closer to the level of potential GDP, Y^*. In parts (i) and (ii), Y^* is the level of potential GDP, where all factors of production are fully employed. In part (i), the initial equilibrium is at E_0 where national income is Y_0, which is less than Y^*; this is a recessionary gap. The government could increase purchases, reduce taxes, or raise transfer payments to shift the *AE* function upward to *AE'* and thus increase equilibrium national income. In part (ii), the initial equilibrium is at E_1 where national income is Y_1, which is greater than Y^*; this is an inflationary gap. The government could reduce purchases, increase taxes, or reduce transfer payments to shift the *AE* function downward to *AE'* and thus reduce equilibrium national income.

Practise with Study Guide
Chapter 22, Exercise 5 and
Extension Exercise E1.

to reduce the level of real GDP. In both cases, the target level of real GDP is the level of potential GDP, Y^*, at which there is full employment. Let's now examine these two fiscal tools—government purchases and taxation—in a little more detail.[2]

Changes in Government Purchases Suppose the government decides to reduce its purchases of all economic consulting services, thus eliminating $100 million per year in spending. Planned government purchases (G) would fall by $100 million, shifting AE downward by the same amount. How much would equilibrium income change? This amount can be calculated by using the simple multiplier. Government purchases are part of autonomous expenditure, so a *change* in government purchases of ΔG will lead to a *change* in equilibrium national income equal to the simple multiplier times ΔG. In this example, equilibrium income will fall by $100 million times the simple multiplier. Earlier we argued that a realistic value for the simple multiplier in Canada is about 1.25. Using this value in our example, the effect of the $100 million reduction in G is to reduce equilibrium national income by $125 million.

Increases in government purchases would have the opposite effect. If the government increases its spending by $1 billion on new highways, equilibrium national income will rise by $1 billion times the simple multiplier.

FIGURE 22-5   The Effect of Changing the Tax Rate

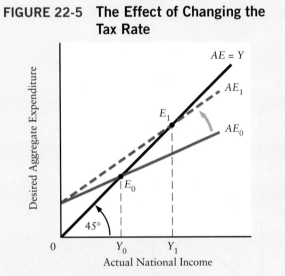

Changing taxes changes equilibrium income by rotating the *AE* curve. A reduction in the net tax rate rotates the *AE* curve from AE_0 to AE_1. The new curve has a steeper slope because the lower net tax rate withdraws a smaller amount of national income from the desired consumption flow. Equilibrium income rises from Y_0 to Y_1. An increase in the net tax rate has the opposite effect.

Changes in Tax Rates If tax rates change, the relationship between disposable income and national income changes. As a result, the relationship between desired consumption and national income also changes. Consequently, a change in tax rates will cause a change in z, the marginal propensity to spend out of national income.

Consider first a decrease in tax rates. If the government decreases its net tax rate so that it collects 5 cents less out of every dollar of national income, disposable income rises in relation to national income. Hence, consumption also rises at every level of national income. This increase in consumption results in an upward *rotation* of the *AE* curve—that is, an increase in the slope of the curve, as shown in Figure 22-5. The result of this shift will be an increase in equilibrium national income.

A rise in tax rates has the opposite effect. A rise in tax rates causes a decrease in disposable income, and hence consumption expenditure, at each level of national income. This results in a downward *rotation* of the *AE* curve and decreases the level of equilibrium national income.

Note that when the *AE* function rotates, as happens if anything causes z to change, the simple multiplier is *not* used to tell us about the resulting change in equilibrium national income. The simple multiplier is only useful to tell us how much equilibrium

---

[2] The government would rarely attempt to *reduce* the level of GDP. But in a situation where real GDP is above potential output and also growing more quickly, it may try to reduce the growth rate of GDP, thus closing the gap between real GDP and potential output.

national income changes in response to a change in *autonomous* desired spending—that is, in response to a *parallel shift* in the *AE* function.

---

myeconlab ADDITIONAL TOPICS

Governments can also combine an increase in government purchases with an increase in tax revenues in such a way that the budget is left unchanged. How do such balanced budget changes affect the level of national income? To see more details on this type of fiscal policy, look for **What Is the Balanced Budget Multiplier?** in the *Additional Topics* section of this book's MyEconLab.

www.myeconlab.com

22.5 Demand-Determined Output

In this and the preceding chapter, we have discussed the determination of the four categories of aggregate expenditure and have seen how they simultaneously determine equilibrium national income in the short run. An algebraic exposition of the complete model is presented in the appendix to this chapter.

Our macro model is based on three central concepts, and it is worth reviewing them.

Equilibrium National Income The equilibrium level of national income is that level at which *desired* aggregate expenditure equals *actual* national income. If actual national income exceeds desired expenditure, firms will eventually reduce production, causing national income to fall. If actual national income is less than desired expenditure, firms will eventually increase production, causing national income to rise.

The Simple Multiplier The simple multiplier measures the change in equilibrium national income that results from a change in the *autonomous* part of desired aggregate expenditure. The simple multiplier is equal to $1/(1 - z)$, where z is the marginal propensity to spend out of national income. In the model of Chapter 21, in which there is no government and no international trade, z is simply the marginal propensity to consume out of disposable income. In our expanded model that contains both government and foreign trade, z is reduced by the presence of net taxes and imports. To review:

$$\text{Simple multiplier} = 1/(1 - z)$$

Closed economy with no government:	$z = MPC$
Open economy with government:	$z = MPC(1 - t) - m$

Demand-Determined Output The model that we have examined is constructed *for a given price level*—that is, the price level is assumed to be constant. This assumption of a given price level is related to another assumption that we have been making. We have been assuming that firms are able and willing to produce any amount of output that is demanded without requiring any change in prices. When this is true, national income depends only on how much is demanded—that is, national income is *demand determined*. Things get more complicated if firms are either unable or unwilling to produce enough to meet all demands without requiring a change in prices. We deal with this possibility in Chapter 23 when we consider *supply-side* influences on national income.

There are two situations in which we might expect national income to be demand determined. First, when there are unemployed resources and firms have excess capacity, firms will often be prepared to provide whatever is demanded from them at unchanged prices. In contrast, if the economy's resources are fully employed and firms have no excess capacity, increases in output may be possible only with higher unit costs, and these cost increases may lead to price increases.

The second situation occurs when firms are *price setters*. Readers who have studied some microeconomics will recognize this term. It means that the firm has the ability to influence the price of its product, either because it is large relative to the market or, more usually, because it sells a product that is *differentiated* to some extent from the products of its competitors. Firms that are price setters often respond to changes in demand by altering their production and sales, at least initially, rather than by adjusting their prices. Only after some time has passed, and the change in demand has persisted, do such firms adjust their prices. This type of behaviour corresponds well to our short-run macro model in which changes in demand lead to changes in output (for a given price level).

> Our simple model of national income determination assumes a constant price level. In this model, national income is demand determined.

In the following chapters, we expand the model by making the price level an *endogenous* variable. In other words, movements in the price level are explained within the model. We do this by considering the *supply side* of the economy—that is, those things that influence firms' abilities to produce output, such as technology and factor prices. When we consider the demand side and the supply side of the economy simultaneously, we will see that changes in desired aggregate expenditure usually cause both prices and real GDP to change.

Summary

22.1 Introducing Government

- Government desired purchases, G, are assumed to be part of autonomous aggregate expenditure. Taxes minus transfer payments are called net taxes and affect aggregate expenditure indirectly through households' disposable income. Taxes reduce disposable income, whereas transfers increase disposable income.

- The budget balance is defined as net tax revenues minus government purchases, $(T - G)$. When $(T - G)$ is positive, there is a budget surplus; when $(T - G)$ is negative, there is a budget deficit.

22.2 Introducing Foreign Trade

- Exports are foreign purchases of Canadian goods, and do not depend on Canadian national income. Desired imports are assumed to increase as national income increases. Hence, net exports decrease as national income increases.
- Changes in international relative prices lead to shifts in the net export function. A depreciation of the Canadian dollar implies that Canadian goods are now cheaper relative to foreign goods. This leads to a rise in exports and a fall in imports, shifting the net export function up. An appreciation of the Canadian dollar has the opposite effect.

22.3 Equilibrium National Income

- As in Chapter 21, national income is in equilibrium when desired aggregate expenditure equals actual national income. The equilibrium condition is

  $Y = AE$, where $AE = C + I + G + (X - IM)$

- The slope of the AE function in the model with government and foreign trade is $z = MPC (1 - t) - m$, where MPC is the marginal propensity to consume out of disposable income, t is the net tax rate, and m is the marginal propensity to import.

22.4 Changes in Equilibrium National Income

- The presence of taxes and net exports reduces the value of the simple multiplier. With taxes and imports, every increase in national income induces less new spending than in a model with no taxes or imports.
- An increase in government purchases shifts up the AE function and thus increases the equilibrium level of national income. A decrease in the net tax rate makes the AE function rotate upward and increases the equilibrium level of national income.
- An increase in exports can be caused by an increase in foreign demand for Canadian goods, a fall in the Canadian price level, or a depreciation of the Canadian dollar. An increase in exports shifts the AE function up and increases the equilibrium level of national income.

22.5 Demand-Determined Output

- Our simple model of national income determination is constructed for a given price level. That prices are assumed not to change in response to an increase in desired expenditure reflects a related assumption that output is demand determined.
- Output may be demand determined in two situations: if there are unemployed resources, or if firms are price setters.

Key Concepts

Taxes, transfers, and net taxes
The budget balance
The net export function

Calculation of the simple multiplier in
   an open economy with government
Stabilization policy

Fiscal policy and equilibrium income
Demand-determined output

Study Exercises

1. Consider the following table showing national income and government net tax revenues in billions of dollars. Assume that the level of government purchases is $155 billion.

Actual National Income (Y)	Net Tax Revenues (T)	Budget Balance ($T - G$)
100	45	—
200	70	—
300	95	—
400	120	—
500	145	—
600	170	—
700	195	—
800	220	—

   a. Compute the government's budget balance for each level of national income and fill in the table.
   b. What is the value of the net tax rate? Explain what this rate represents.
   c. Suppose the government decides to increase the level of its purchases of goods and services by $15 billion. What happens to the budget balance for any level of national income?

2. Consider the following table showing national income and imports in billions of dollars. Assume that the level of exports is $300 billion.

Actual National Income (Y)	Imports (IM)	Net Exports ($X - IM$)
100	85	—
200	120	—
300	155	—
400	190	—
500	225	—
600	260	—
700	295	—
800	330	—

   a. Compute the level of net exports for each level of national income and fill in the table.
   b. Plot the net export function on a scale diagram. Explain why it is downward sloping.
   c. What is the value of the marginal propensity to import? Explain what it represents.

   d. Suppose one of Canada's major trading partners experiences a significant recession. Explain how this affects the net export function in your diagram.

3. Each of the following headlines describes an event that will have an effect on desired aggregate expenditure. What will be the effect on equilibrium national income? In each case, describe how the event would be illustrated in the 45° line diagram.

   a. "Minister takes an axe to the armed forces."
   b. "Russia agrees to buy more Canadian wheat."
   c. "High-tech firms to cut capital outlays."
   d. "Finance minister pledges to cut income-tax rates."
   e. "U.S. imposes import restrictions on Canadian lumber."
   f. "U.S. housing collapse means smaller market for B.C. lumber."
   g. "Weak dollar spurs exports from Ontario manufacturers."
   h. "Prime minister promises burst of infrastructure spending."

4. The following diagram shows desired aggregate expenditure for the economy of Sunset Island. The AE curve assumes a net tax rate (t) of 10 percent, autonomous exports of $25 billion, and a marginal propensity to import (m) of 15 percent.

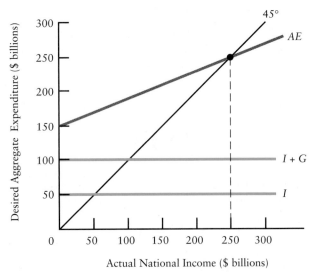

a. What is the level of desired investment expenditure (I)?
b. What is the level of government purchases (G)?
c. What is the autonomous portion of consumption?
d. What is total autonomous expenditure?
e. Starting from equilibrium national income of $250 billion, suppose government purchases decreased by $25 billion. Describe the effect on the AE curve and on equilibrium national income.
f. Starting from equilibrium national income of $250 billion, suppose the net tax rate increased from 10 percent to 30 percent of national income. Describe the effect on the AE curve and on equilibrium national income.
g. Starting from equilibrium national income of $250 billion, suppose investment increased by $50 billion. Describe the effect on the AE curve and on equilibrium national income.
h. Starting from equilibrium national income of $250 billion, suppose the marginal propensity to import fell from 15 percent to 5 percent of national income. Describe the effect on the AE curve and on equilibrium national income.

5. The economy of Sunrise Island has the following features:

   - fixed price level
   - no foreign trade
   - autonomous desired investment (I) of $20 billion
   - autonomous government purchases (G) of $30 billion
   - autonomous desired consumption (C) of $15 billion
   - marginal propensity to consume out of disposable income of 0.75
   - net tax rate of 0.20 of national income

   a. Write an equation expressing consumption as a function of disposable income.
   b. Write an equation expressing net tax revenues as a function of national income.
   c. Write an equation expressing disposable income as a function of national income.
   d. Write an equation expressing consumption as a function of national income.
   e. What is the marginal propensity to spend out of national income?
   f. Calculate the simple multiplier for Sunrise Island.

6. The following table shows alternative hypothetical economies and the relevant values for the marginal propensity to consume out of disposable income (MPC), the net tax rate (t), and the marginal propensity to import, m.

Economy	MPC	t	m	z	Simple Multiplier $1/(1 - z)$
A	0.75	0.2	0.15	—	—
B	0.75	0.2	0.30	—	—
C	0.75	0.4	0.30	—	—
D	0.90	0.4	0.30	—	—

a. Recall that z, the marginal propensity to spend out of national income, is given by the simple expression $z = MPC(1 - t) - m$. By using this expression, compute z for each of the economies and fill in the table.
b. Compare Economies A and B (they differ only by the value of m). Which one has the larger multiplier? Explain why the size of the multiplier depends on m.
c. Compare Economies B and C (they differ only by the value of t). Which one has the larger multiplier? Explain why the size of the multiplier depends on t.
d. Compare Economies C and D (they differ only by the value of MPC). Which one has the larger multiplier? Explain why the size of the multiplier depends on MPC.

7. This question is based on the *Additional Topic* **The Saving-Investment Approach to Equilibrium in an Open Economy with Government,** which is found on this book's MyEconLab. Consider the diagram below that shows the national saving function and the national asset formation function.

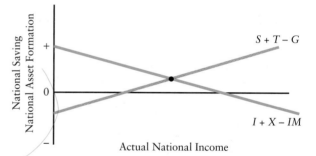

a. Explain why the national asset formation function is downward sloping. What determines its slope?
b. Explain why the national saving function is upward sloping. What determines its slope?
c. Suppose the government decided to increase its level of purchases. How would this policy change be illustrated in the diagram? What would happen to national income?
d. Suppose domestic firms decided to increase their desired investment. How would this change be illustrated in the diagram? What would happen to national income?
e. Suppose the Canadian government reduced net-tax rates. How would this change be illustrated in the diagram? What would happen to national income?

8. This question requires you to solve a macro model algebraically. Reading the appendix to this chapter will help you to answer this question. But, just in case, we lead you through it step by step. The equations for the model are as follows:

   i) $C = a + bY_D$ Consumption
   ii) $I = I_0$ Investment (autonomous)
   iii) $G = G_0$ Government purchases (autonomous)

iv) $T = tY$ Net tax revenue
v) $X = X_0$ Exports (autonomous)
vi) $IM = mY$ Imports

a. Step 1: Recall that $Y_D = Y - T$. By using this fact, substitute the tax function into the consumption function and derive the relationship between desired consumption and national income.

b. Step 2: Sum the four components of desired aggregate expenditure (C, I, G, NX). This is the aggregate expenditure (AE) function. Collect the autonomous terms separately from the induced terms.

c. Step 3: Recall the equilibrium condition, $Y = AE$. Form the equation $Y = AE$, where AE is your expression for the AE function from part (b).

d. Step 4: Now collect terms and solve for Y. This is the equilibrium value of national income.

e. Step 5: Suppose the level of autonomous expenditure, which we could call A, rises by ΔA. What is the effect on the level of equilibrium national income?

9. This question repeats the exercise of Question 8, but for specific numerical values. The equations of the model are

$C = 50 + 0.7Y_D$ $T = (0.2)Y$
$I = 75$ $X = 50$
$G = 100$ $IM = (0.15)Y$

a. Compute the AE function and plot it in a diagram. What is total autonomous expenditure?

b. What is the slope of the AE function?

c. Compute the equilibrium level of national income.

d. Suppose X rises from 50 to 100. How does this affect the level of national income?

e. What is the simple multiplier in this model?

Discussion Questions

1. The Canadian federal government embarked on a significant path of deficit reduction in the mid-1990s. What fiscal measures were at its disposal? Why might a reduction of 10 percent in government expenditure accomplish much less than a 10-percent decrease in the deficit, at least in the first instance?

2. In the 2009 federal budget, the minister of finance presented a plan to stimulate a slowing economy. What fiscal tools were at his disposal? Would $5 billion of new spending have the same effect as $5 billion in reduced personal income taxes?

3. For many years in Canada it was typical for the federal government's forecasts of its own budget surplus to be less than the forecasts made by private-sector economists. Much of the discrepancy seemed to be accounted for by assumptions about the state of the economy over the coming year. How do assumptions about the economy affect estimates of the budget deficit or surplus?

4. Classify each of the following government activities as either government purchases or transfers.

   a. Welfare payments for the poor
   b. Payments to teachers in public schools
   c. Payments to teachers at a military college
   d. Payments on account of hospital and medical care
   e. Public Health Service vaccination programs

5. The trade deficit that the United States has with China has received much attention in recent years. Given an economy in equilibrium, what is the relationship between saving and investment if the government budget remains balanced but there exists a trade deficit? What additional role must foreigners play in this situation? Can you explain why this situation is viewed by many Americans as troublesome? Do you agree with them?

6. In Chapter 20 we examined how national income was *measured*. By using the expenditure approach, we showed that GDP is always equal to the sum of consumption, investment, government purchases, and net exports. In Chapters 21 and 22 we examined the *determination* of national income. We showed that equilibrium national income occurs when actual national income equals the sum of desired consumption, investment, government purchases, and net exports. Does this mean that national income is always at its equilibrium level? Explain the important difference between "actual" and "desired" expenditures.

An Algebraic Exposition of the Simple Macro Model

We start with the definition of desired aggregate expenditure:

$$AE = C + I + G + (X - IM) \qquad [1]$$

For each component of AE, we write down a behavioural function.

$$C = a + bY_D \text{ (consumption function)} \qquad [2]$$

$$I = I_0 \text{ (autonomous investment)} \qquad [3]$$

$$G = G_0 \text{ (autonomous government purchases)} \qquad [4]$$

$$X = X_0 \text{ (autonomous exports)} \qquad [5]$$

$$IM = mY \text{ (imports)} \qquad [6]$$

where a is autonomous consumption spending, b is the marginal propensity to consume, and m is the marginal propensity to import. Obviously, the "behavioural" functions for investment, government purchases, and exports are very simple: These are all assumed to be independent of the level of national income.

Before deriving aggregate expenditure, we need to determine the relationship between national income (Y) and disposable income (Y_D), because it is Y_D that determines desired consumption expenditure. Y_D is defined as income after net taxes. In Chapter 22 we examined a very simple linear tax of the form

$$T = tY \qquad [7]$$

Taxes must be subtracted from national income to obtain disposable income:

$$Y_D = Y - tY = Y(1 - t) \qquad [8]$$

Substituting Equation 8 into the consumption function allows us to write consumption as a function of national income.

$$C = a + b(1 - t)Y \qquad [9]$$

Now we can add up all the components of desired aggregate expenditure, substituting Equations 3, 4, 5, 6, and 9 into Equation 1:

$$AE = a + b(1 - t)Y + I_0 + G_0 + X_0 - mY \qquad [10]$$

Equation 10 is the AE function, which shows desired aggregate expenditure as a function of actual national income.

In equilibrium, desired aggregate expenditure must equal actual national income:

$$AE = Y \qquad [11]$$

Equation 11 is the equilibrium condition for our model. It is the equation of the 45° line in the figures in this chapter.

To solve for the equilibrium level of national income, we want to solve for the level of Y that satisfies both Equations 10 and 11. That is, solve for the level of Y that is determined by the intersection of the AE curve and the 45° line. Substitute Equation 11 into Equation 10:

$$Y = a + b(1 - t)Y + I_0 + G_0 + X_0 - mY \qquad [12]$$

Group all the terms in Y on the right-hand side, and subtract them from both sides:

$$Y = Y[b(1 - t) - m] + a + I_0 + G_0 + X_0 \qquad [13]$$

$$Y - Y[b(1 - t) - m] = a + I_0 + G_0 + X_0 \qquad [14]$$

Notice that $[b(1 - t) - m]$ is exactly the marginal propensity to spend out of national income, defined earlier as z. When national income goes up by one dollar, only $1 - t$ dollars go into disposable income, and only b of that is spent on consumption. Additionally, m is spent on imports, which are not expenditures on domestic national income. Hence $[b(1 - t) - m]$ is spent on domestic output.

Substituting z for $[b(1 - t) - m]$ and solving Equation 14 for equilibrium Y yields

$$Y = \frac{a + I_0 + G_0 + X_0}{1 - z} \qquad [15]$$

Notice that the numerator of Equation 15 is total autonomous expenditure, which we call A. Hence, Equation 15 can be rewritten as

$$Y = \frac{A}{1 - z} \qquad [16]$$

Notice also that if autonomous expenditure rises by some amount $\Delta A, Y$ will rise by $\Delta A/(1 - z)$. So, the simple multiplier is $1/(1 - z)$.

The Algebra Illustrated

The numerical example that was carried through Chapters 21 and 22 can be used to illustrate the preceding exposition. In that example, the behavioural equations are:

$$C = 30 + 0.8Y_D \qquad [17]$$

$$I = 75 \qquad [18]$$

$$G = 51 \qquad [19]$$

$$X - IM = 72 - 0.1Y \qquad [20]$$

$$T = 0.1Y \qquad [21]$$

From Equation 8, disposable income is given by $Y(1 - t) = 0.9Y$. Substituting this into Equation 17 yields

$$C = 30 + 0.72Y$$

as in Equation 9.

Now, recalling that in equilibrium $AE = Y$, we add up all the components of AE and set the sum equal to Y, as in Equation 12:

$$Y = 30 + 0.72Y + 75 + 51 + 72 - 0.1Y \qquad [22]$$

Collecting terms yields

$$Y = 228 + 0.62Y$$

Subtracting $0.62Y$ from both sides gives

$$0.38Y = 228$$

and dividing through by 0.38, we have

$$Y = \frac{228}{0.38} = 600$$

This can also be derived by using Equation 16. Autonomous expenditure is 228, and z, the marginal propensity to spend out of national income, is 0.62. Thus, from Equation 16, equilibrium income is $228/(1 - 0.62) = 600$, which is exactly the equilibrium we obtained in Figure 22-3 on page 554.

Output and Prices in the Short Run

In Chapters 21 and 22, we developed a simple model of national income determination. We saw that changes in wealth, interest rates, the government's fiscal policies, or expectations about the future lead to changes in desired aggregate expenditure. Through the multiplier process, such changes in desired expenditure caused equilibrium national income to change.

The simple model in Chapters 21 and 22 had a constant price level. We assumed that firms were prepared to provide more output when it was demanded without requiring an increase in prices. In this sense, we said that output was *demand determined*.

The actual economy, however, does not have a constant price level. Rather than assuming it is constant, we would like to understand what causes it to change. We therefore expand our model to make the price level an *endogenous* variable—one that is explained within the model.

We make the transition to a variable price level in three steps. First, we study the consequences for national income of *exogenous* changes in the price level—changes that happen for reasons that are not explained by our model of the economy. We ask how changes in the price level affect desired aggregate expenditure. That is, we examine the *demand side* of the economy. Second, we examine the *supply side* by exploring the relationship among the price level, the prices of factor inputs, and the level of output producers would like to supply. Finally, we examine the concept of *macroeconomic equilibrium* that combines both the demand and the supply sides to determine the price level and real GDP simultaneously.

LEARNING OBJECTIVES

In this chapter you will learn

1 why an exogenous change in the price level shifts the *AE* curve and changes the equilibrium level of real GDP.

2 how to derive the aggregate demand (*AD*) curve and what causes it to shift.

3 the meaning of the aggregate supply (*AS*) curve and why it shifts when technology or factor prices change.

4 how to define *macroeconomic equilibrium*.

5 how aggregate demand and aggregate supply shocks affect equilibrium real GDP and the price level.

23.1 The Demand Side of the Economy

Consider the macro model in Chapter 22. What happens to equilibrium GDP in that model when the price level changes for some exogenous reason? To find out, we need to understand how a change in the price level affects desired aggregate expenditure.

Exogenous Changes in the Price Level

The *AE* curve shifts in response to a change in the price level. This shift occurs because a change in the price level affects desired consumption expenditures and desired net exports. These are the changes on which we will focus in this chapter. (In later chapters, we will see that changes in the price level will also change interest rates and thus shift the *AE* curve for an additional reason.)

Changes in Consumption   You might think it is obvious that a fall in the price level leads to an increase in desired consumption for the simple reason that the demand curves for most individual products are negatively sloped. As we will see in a few pages, however, this logic is incorrect in the context of an aggregate model—our focus here is on the aggregate price level rather than on the prices of individual products. The relationship between the price level and desired consumption has to do with how changes in the price level lead to changes in household *wealth* and thus to changes in desired spending.

Much of the private sector's total wealth is held in the form of assets with a fixed nominal value. The most obvious example is money itself. We will discuss money in considerable detail in Chapters 27 and 28, but for now just note that most individuals and businesses hold money in their wallets, in their cash registers, or in their bank accounts. What this money can buy—its real value—depends on the price level. The higher the price level, the less a given amount of money can purchase. For this reason, a rise in the domestic price level lowers the real value of money holdings. Similarly, a reduction in the price level raises the real value of money holdings.

Changes in the price level cause changes in the real value of cash held by households and firms. This change in wealth leads to changes in the amount of desired consumption expenditure.

> A rise in the price level lowers the real value of money held by the private sector. A fall in the price level raises the real value of money held by the private sector.

Other examples of assets that have fixed nominal values include government and corporate bonds. The bondholder has lent money to the issuer of the bond and receives a repayment from the issuer when the bond matures. What happens when there is a change in the price level in the intervening period? A rise in the price level means that the repayment to the bondholder is lower in real value than it otherwise would be. This is a decline in wealth for the bondholder. However, the issuer of the bond, having made a repayment of lower real value because of the increase in the price level, has experienced an increase in wealth. In dollar terms, the bondholder's reduction in wealth is exactly offset by the issuer's increase in wealth.

> **Changes in the price level change the wealth of bondholders and bond issuers, but because the changes offset each other, there is no change in aggregate wealth.[1]**

In summary, a rise in the price level leads to a reduction in the real value of the private sector's wealth. And as we saw in Chapter 21, a reduction in wealth leads to a decrease in autonomous desired consumption and thus to a downward shift in the AE function. A fall in the domestic price level leads to a rise in wealth and desired consumption and thus to an upward shift in the AE curve.

Changes in Net Exports When the domestic price level rises (and the exchange rate remains unchanged), Canadian goods become more expensive relative to foreign goods. As we saw in Chapter 22, this change in international relative prices causes Canadian consumers to reduce their purchases of Canadian-made goods, which have now become relatively more expensive, and to increase their purchases of foreign goods, which have now become relatively less expensive. At the same time, consumers in other countries reduce their purchases of the now relatively more expensive Canadian-made goods. We saw in Chapter 22 that these changes cause a downward shift in the net export function.

> **A rise in the domestic price level (with a constant exchange rate) shifts the net export function downward, which causes a downward shift in the AE curve. A fall in the domestic price level shifts the net export function upward and hence the AE curve upward.**

Changes in Equilibrium GDP

Because it causes downward shifts in both the net export function and the consumption function, an exogenous rise in the price level causes a downward shift in the AE curve, as shown in Figure 23-1. When the AE curve shifts downward, the equilibrium level of real GDP falls.

Conversely, with a fall in the price level, Canadian goods become relatively cheaper internationally, so net exports rise. Also, the purchasing power of nominal assets increases, so households spend more. The resulting increase in desired expenditure on Canadian

FIGURE 23-1   Desired Aggregate Expenditure and the Price Level

An exogenous change in the price level causes the AE curve to shift and equilibrium GDP to change. At the initial price level, the AE curve is given by the solid line AE_0, and hence equilibrium is at E_0 with real GDP equal to Y_0. An increase in the price level causes the AE curve to shift downward to the dashed line, AE_1. As a result, equilibrium changes to E_1 and equilibrium GDP falls to Y_1.

---

[1] Some economists argue that in the case of *government* bonds, there *will* be a change in aggregate wealth when the price level changes. The argument relies on changes in the wealth of the bond issuers (governments) not being recognized by taxpayers, the individuals who are ultimately responsible for repaying government debt. We discuss government debt in Chapter 32.

goods causes the *AE* curve to shift upward. The equilibrium level of real GDP therefore rises.

A CHANGE OF LABELS. In Chapters 21 and 22 the horizontal axis was labelled "Actual National Income" because we wanted to emphasize the important difference between *actual* income and *desired* expenditure. Notice in Figure 23-1, however, that we have labelled the horizontal axis "Real GDP." We use GDP rather than *national income* but these two words have the same meaning. It is still *actual,* as opposed to *desired,* but we leave that off, also for simplicity. Finally, we add *real* because from this chapter onward the price level will be changing and thus it is necessary to distinguish changes in nominal GDP from changes in real GDP.

The Aggregate Demand Curve

We have just seen, in the simple model from Chapters 21 and 22, that the price level and real equilibrium GDP are negatively related to each other. This negative relationship can be shown in an important new concept, the *aggregate demand curve.*

Recall that the *AE* curve is drawn with real GDP on the horizontal axis and desired aggregate expenditure on the vertical axis, and that it is plotted for a *given* price level. We are now going to let the price level vary and keep track of the various equilibrium points that occur as the *AE* function shifts. By doing so we can construct an **aggregate demand (*AD*) curve** that shows the relationship between the price level and the equilibrium level of real GDP. It will be plotted with the price level on the vertical axis and real GDP on the horizontal axis. Because the horizontal axes of both the *AE* and the *AD* curves measure real GDP, the two curves can be placed one above the other so that the levels of GDP on both can be compared directly. This is shown in Figure 23-2.

Now let us see how the *AD* curve is derived. Given a value of the price level, P_0, equilibrium GDP is determined in part (i) of Figure 23-2 at the point where the AE_0 curve crosses the 45° line. The equilibrium level of real GDP is Y_0. Part (ii) of the figure shows the same equilibrium level of GDP, Y_0, plotted against the price level P_0. The equilibrium point in part (i), E_0, corresponds to point E_0 on the *AD* curve in part (ii).

As the price level rises to P_1, the *AE* curve shifts down to AE_1 and the equilibrium level of real GDP falls to Y_1. This determines a second point on the *AD* curve, E_1. By joining these points, we trace out the *AD* curve.

> For any given price level, the *AD* curve shows the level of real GDP for which desired aggregate expenditure equals actual GDP.

Note that because the *AD* curve relates equilibrium GDP to the price level, changes in the price level that cause *shifts in* the *AE* curve are simply *movements along* the *AD* curve. A movement along the *AD* curve thus traces out the response of equilibrium GDP to a change in the price level.[2]

The *AD* Curve Is Not a Micro Demand Curve!
Figure 23-2 provides us with sufficient information to establish that the *AD* curve is negatively sloped.

aggregate demand (*AD*) curve A curve showing combinations of real GDP and the price level that make desired aggregate expenditure equal to actual national income.

Practise with Study Guide Chapter 23, Exercise 1.

---

[2] Our discussion of Figure 23-2 is for an economy open to international trade, and we emphasized the reduction of consumption and net exports that occurs in response to a rise in the price level. In a *closed* economy, however, the second effect is absent, resulting in a steeper *AD* curve than what is shown in Figure 23-2.

1. A rise in the price level causes the *AE* curve to shift downward and hence leads to a movement upward and to the left along the *AD* curve, reflecting a fall in the equilibrium level of GDP.

2. A fall in the price level causes the *AE* curve to shift upward and hence leads to a movement downward and to the right along the *AD* curve, reflecting a rise in the equilibrium level of GDP.

In Chapter 3, we saw that demand curves for individual goods, such as coffee, MP3 players, and automobiles, are negatively sloped. However, the reasons for the negative slope of the *AD* curve are different from the reasons for the negative slope of individual demand curves used in microeconomics. Why is this the case?

A "micro" demand curve describes a situation in which the price of one commodity changes *while the prices of all other commodities and consumers' dollar incomes are constant.* Such an individual demand curve is negatively sloped for two reasons. First, as the price of the commodity falls, the purchasing power of each consumer's income will rise, and this rise in real income will lead to more units of the good being purchased. Second, as the price of the commodity falls, consumers buy more of that commodity and fewer of the now relatively more expensive substitutes.

The first reason does not apply to the *AD* curve because the dollar value of national income is not being held constant as the price level changes and we move along the *AD* curve. The second reason applies to the *AD* curve but only in a limited way. A change in the price level does not change the *relative* prices of domestic goods and thus does not cause consumers to substitute between them. However, a change in the domestic price level (for a given exchange rate) *does* lead to a change in *international* relative prices and thus to some substitution between domestic and foreign products; this is the link between the price level and net exports that we discussed earlier.

To summarize, the *AD* curve is negatively sloped for two reasons:

1. A fall in the price level leads to a rise in private-sector wealth, which increases desired consumption and thus leads to an increase in equilibrium GDP.

2. A fall in the price level (for a given exchange rate) leads to a rise in net exports and thus leads to an increase in equilibrium GDP.

FIGURE 23-2   Derivation of the *AD* Curve

(i) Aggregate expenditure

(ii) Aggregate demand

As the price level rises, the *AE* curve shifts down and the economy moves upward along the *AD* curve

Equilibrium GDP is determined by the *AE* curve for each given price level; the level of equilibrium GDP and its associated price level are then plotted to yield a point on the *AD* curve. When the price level is P_0, the *AE* curve is AE_0, and hence equilibrium GDP is Y_0, as shown in part (i). Plotting Y_0 against P_0 yields the point E_0 on the *AD* curve in part (ii).

An increase in the price level to P_1 causes the *AE* curve to shift downward to AE_1 and causes equilibrium GDP to fall to Y_1. Plotting this new level of GDP against the higher price level yields a second point, E_1, on the *AD* curve. A further increase in the price level to P_2 causes the *AE* curve to shift downward to AE_2, and thus causes equilibrium GDP to fall to Y_2. Plotting P_2 and Y_2 yields a third point, E_2, on the *AD* curve.

A change in the price level causes a shift of the *AE* curve but a movement along the *AD* curve.

aggregate demand shock

Any shift in the aggregate demand curve.

In later chapters, after we have discussed interest rates in detail, we will introduce a third reason for the negative slope of the *AD* curve.

Shifts in the *AD* Curve What can cause the *AD* curve to shift? For a given price level, any event that leads to a change in equilibrium GDP will cause the *AD* curve to shift. The event could be a change in government policy, such as the level of government purchases or taxation (or, as we will see later, a policy-induced change in interest rates). Or the event could be something beyond the government's control, such as a change in households' consumption expenditure, firms' investment behaviour, or foreigners' demand for Canadian exports.

Figure 23-3 shows a shift in the *AD* curve. Because the *AD* curve plots equilibrium GDP as a function of the price level, anything that alters equilibrium GDP *at a given price level* must shift the *AD* curve. In other words, any change—other than a change in the price level—that causes the *AE* curve to shift will also cause the *AD* curve to shift. Such a shift is called an **aggregate demand shock**.

For example, in the 2002–2007 period, strong economic growth in the United States and elsewhere led to an increase in demand for Canadian-produced raw materials. This increase in demand caused an upward shift in Canada's net export function. This event, taken by itself, would shift Canada's *AE* function upward and thus would shift Canada's *AD* curve to the right.

Beginning in 2008, however, a dramatic slowdown in world economic growth, caused in large part by the collapse of the U.S. housing market and the resulting worldwide financial crisis, led to a reduction in foreign demand for Canadian products. There was also an associated reduction in both investment and consumption expenditure in Canada, driven partly by the pessimism that accompanied the crisis. The overall effect was a downward shift in the *AE* curve and thus a leftward shift of the *AD* curve.

FIGURE 23-3   The Simple Multiplier and Shifts in the *AD* Curve

(i) Aggregate expenditure

(ii) Aggregate demand

A change in autonomous expenditure changes equilibrium GDP for any given price level. The simple multiplier measures the resulting horizontal shift in the *AD* curve. The original *AE* curve is AE_0 in part (i). Equilibrium is at E_0, with GDP of Y_0 at price level P_0. This yields point E_0 on the curve AD_0 in part (ii).

The *AE* curve in part (i) then shifts upward from AE_0 to AE_1 because of an increase in autonomous desired expenditure of ΔA. Equilibrium GDP now rises to Y_1, with the price level still constant at P_0. Thus, the *AD* curve in part (ii) shifts to the right to point E_1, indicating the higher equilibrium GDP of Y_1 associated with the same price level P_0. The size of the horizontal shift, ΔY, is equal to the simple multiplier times ΔA.

> For a given price level, an increase in autonomous aggregate expenditure shifts the *AE* curve upward and the *AD* curve to the right. A fall in autonomous aggregate expenditure shifts the *AE* curve downward and the *AD* curve to the left.

Remember the following important point. In order to shift the *AD* curve, the change in autonomous expenditure must be caused by something *other than* a change in the domestic price level. As we saw earlier in this chapter, a change in aggregate expenditure caused by a change in the domestic price level leads to a movement along (not a shift of) the *AD* curve.

The Simple Multiplier and the *AD* Curve We saw in Chapters 21 and 22 that the simple multiplier measures the size of the change in equilibrium national income in response to a change in autonomous expenditure *when the price level is held constant*. It follows that this multiplier gives the size of the *horizontal* shift in the *AD* curve in response to a change in autonomous expenditure, as illustrated in Figure 23-3.

> The simple multiplier measures the horizontal shift in the *AD* curve in response to a change in autonomous desired expenditure.

If the price level remains constant and producers are willing to supply everything that is demanded at that price level, the simple multiplier will also show the change in equilibrium income that will occur in response to a change in autonomous expenditure. This mention of producers' willingness to supply output brings us to a discussion of the *supply side* of the economy.

23.2 The Supply Side of the Economy

So far, we have explained how the equilibrium level of GDP is determined *when the price level is taken as given* and how that equilibrium changes as the price level is changed exogenously. We are now ready to take the important next step: adding an *explanation* for changes in the price level. To do this, we need to take account of the supply decisions of firms.

The Aggregate Supply Curve

Aggregate supply refers to the total output of goods and services that firms would like to produce. The **aggregate supply (*AS*) curve** relates the price level to the quantity of output that firms would like to produce and sell *on the assumption that technology and the prices of all factors of production remain constant*. What does the *AS* curve look like?

The Positive Slope of the *AS* Curve To study the slope of the *AS* curve, we need to see how costs are related to output and then how prices are related to output.

COSTS AND OUTPUT. Suppose firms want to increase their output above current levels. What will this do to their costs per unit of output—usually called their **unit costs**? The aggregate supply curve is drawn on the assumption that technology and the prices of all factors of production remain constant. This does not, however, mean that unit costs will be constant. As output increases, less efficient standby plants may have to be used, and less efficient workers may have to be hired, while existing workers may have to be paid overtime rates for additional work. For these and other similar reasons, unit costs will tend to rise as output rises, even when technology and input prices are constant. (Readers

aggregate supply (*AS*) curve A curve showing the relation between the price level and the quantity of aggregate output supplied, for given technology and factor prices.

unit cost Cost per unit of output, equal to total cost divided by total output.

For many firms, increases in output will drive up their unit costs. As a result, they will be prepared to supply more output only at a higher price. This behaviour gives rise to an upward-sloping AS curve.

who have studied microeconomics will recognize the *law of diminishing returns* as one reason that costs rise in the short run as firms squeeze more output out of a fixed quantity of capital equipment.)

PRICES AND OUTPUT. To consider the relationship between price and output, we need to consider firms that sell in two distinct types of markets: those in which firms are *price takers* and those in which firms are *price setters*.

Some industries, especially those that produce raw materials, contain many individual firms. In these cases, each firm is too small to influence the market price, which is set by the overall forces of demand and supply. Each firm must accept whatever price is set by the market. Such firms are said to be *price takers*. When the market price changes, these firms will react by altering their level of production.

> **If their unit costs rise with output, price-taking firms will produce more only if price increases. They will produce less if the price falls.**

Many other industries, including most of those that produce manufactured products, contain few enough firms that each can influence the market price of its product. Most firms in these industries sell products that differ from one another, although all are similar enough to be thought of as a single product produced by one industry. For example, no two kinds of automobiles are exactly the same, but all are sufficiently alike that we have no trouble talking about the automobile industry and its product, automobiles. In such cases, each firm must quote a price at which it is prepared to sell each of its products; that is, the firm is a *price setter*. If the demand for the output of price-setting firms increases sufficiently to take their outputs into the range in which their unit costs rise, these firms will not increase their outputs unless they can pass at least some of these extra costs on through higher prices. When demand falls, they will reduce output, and competition among them will tend to cause a reduction in prices whenever their unit costs fall.

> **Price-setting firms will increase their prices when they expand their output into the range where unit costs are rising. They will eventually decrease their prices if a reduction in their output leads to a reduction in unit costs.**

This is the basic behaviour of firms in response to the changes in demand and prices when technology and factor prices are constant, and it explains the slope of the *AS* curve, such as the one shown in Figure 23-4.

> **The actions of both price-taking and price-setting firms cause the price level and the supply of output to be positively related—the aggregate supply (*AS*) curve is positively sloped.**

The Increasing Slope of the *AS* Curve

In Figure 23-4 we see that at low levels of GDP the *AS* curve is relatively flat, but as GDP rises the *AS* curve gets progressively steeper. What explains this shape?

When output is low (below potential output), firms typically have excess capacity—some plant and equipment are idle. When firms have excess capacity, only a small increase in the price of their output may be needed to induce them to expand production. Indeed, if firms have enough excess capacity, they may be willing to sell more at their existing prices when the demand for their product increases. In this case, output is truly demand determined up to the level at which costs begin to rise. Once output is pushed above normal capacity, however, unit costs tend to rise quite rapidly. Many higher-cost production methods may have to be adopted—such as standby capacity, overtime, and extra shifts. These higher-cost production methods will not be used unless the selling price of the output has risen enough to cover them. The more output is expanded beyond normal capacity, the more that unit costs rise and hence the larger is the rise in price that is necessary to induce firms to increase output. This increasing slope of the *AS* curve is sometimes called the *first asymmetry* in the behaviour of aggregate supply. (The second will be discussed in the next chapter.)

As we will see later in this chapter, the shape of the *AS* curve is crucial for determining how the effect of an aggregate demand shock is divided between a change in the price level and a change in real GDP.

Shifts in the Aggregate Supply Curve

For a given level of output, anything that changes firms' production costs will cause the *AS* curve to shift. Two sources of such changes are of particular importance: changes in the prices of inputs and changes in productivity. Input prices can, however, change for two different reasons. First, input prices may change because of things that are internal to our model. For example, if a rise in production increases the demand for inputs and thus bids up their prices, this will shift the *AS* curve upward and to the left. This shift is *endogenous* to our macro model, and we will discuss shifts of this type in Chapter 24. Second, input prices may change because of forces unconnected to our model—*exogenous* forces. For example, the world price of oil may rise and since this will raise the input prices of virtually all firms, it will also shift the *AS* curve upward and to the left. Shifts in the *AS* curve caused by such exogenous forces are called **aggregate supply shocks**. Let's now examine these shocks in more detail.

Changes in Input Prices When factor prices change, the *AS* curve shifts. If factor prices rise, firms will find the profitability of their current production reduced. For any given level of output to be produced, an increase in the price level will be required. If prices do not rise, firms will react by decreasing production. For the economy as a

FIGURE 23-4 The Aggregate Supply Curve

The *AS* curve is positively sloped, indicating that firms will provide more aggregate output only at a higher price level. The *AS* curve is drawn for a given level of technology and factor prices. At price level P_0, firms are prepared to produce and supply output equal to Y_0. An expansion of their output to Y_1 leads to an increase in unit costs, and thus firms are prepared to supply Y_1 only at a higher price level, P_1.

The higher is the level of output, the faster unit costs tend to rise with each extra increment to output. This explains why the *AS* curve becomes steeper as output rises.

aggregate supply shock
Any shift in the aggregate supply (*AS*) curve caused by an exogenous force.

Changes in the prices of raw materials—such as the lumber shown here—lead to changes in firms' production costs. Such changes cause shifts in the AS curve.

FIGURE 23-5   Shifts in the *AS* Curve

For any given level of output, anything that increases firms' costs will shift the *AS* curve upward (and to the left). Starting from (P_0, Y_0), a rise in input prices or a reduction in productivity would increase firms' unit costs. Firms would be prepared to continue supplying output of Y_0 only at the higher price level P_1. Or, at the initial price level P_0, firms would now be prepared to supply output of only Y_1. In either case, the *AS* curve has shifted up (or to the left) from AS_0 to AS_1. This is called a reduction in aggregate supply.

A fall in input prices or an increase in productivity would cause the *AS* curve to shift down (and to the right). This is an increase in aggregate supply.

whole, there will be less output supplied at each price level than before the increase in factor prices. Or, to put it another way, there will be a higher price level for each level of output than before the increase in factor prices. Thus, if factor prices rise, the *AS* curve shifts upward (and to the left). This is a decrease in aggregate supply and is shown in Figure 23-5.

Similarly, a fall in factor prices causes the *AS* curve to shift downward (and to the right). There will be more output supplied at each price level. Or, to put the same point differently, the same amount of output will be supplied at a lower price level. This is an increase in aggregate supply. A dramatic example of such a reduction in factor prices occurred in 1997 and 1998 when the world prices of raw materials fell by an average of 30 percent. In the many countries that use raw materials as inputs in manufacturing, the *AS* curves shifted to the right. The opposite happened in 2002–2008 when energy and other commodity prices increased dramatically, thus shifting the *AS* curves to the left.

Changes in Productivity If labour productivity rises—that is, each worker can produce more with a given amount of effort and other resources—the unit costs of production will fall. Lower costs typically lead to lower prices, as competing firms cut prices in attempts to raise their market shares. That the same output can now be sold at a lower price causes a shift in the *AS* curve downward and to the right. This shift is an increase in aggregate supply. A reduction in productivity leads to an increase in firms' costs and shifts the aggregate supply curve to the left, as illustrated in Figure 23-5.

> A change in either factor prices or productivity will shift the *AS* curve because any given output will be supplied at a different price level than previously. An increase in factor prices or a decrease in productivity shifts the *AS* curve to the left; an increase in productivity or a decrease in factor prices shifts the *AS* curve to the right.

23.3 Macroeconomic Equilibrium

We are now ready to see how both real GDP and the price level are simultaneously determined by the interaction of aggregate demand and aggregate supply. To begin, we assume that input prices and technology are constant.

The equilibrium values of real GDP and the price level occur at the intersection of the *AD* and *AS* curves, as shown by the pair Y_0 and P_0 that arises at point E_0 in Figure 23-6. The combination of real GDP and price level that is on both the *AD* and the *AS* curves is called a *macroeconomic equilibrium*.

Practise with Study Guide
Chapter 23, Exercise 2.

To see why the point (Y_0, P_0) is the only macroeconomic equilibrium, first consider what Figure 23-6 shows would happen if the price level were below P_0. At this lower price level, the desired output of firms, as given by the AS curve, is less than desired aggregate expenditure—there is an excess demand for goods. Conversely, at a price level above P_0, the desired output by firms exceeds desired aggregate expenditure—there is an excess supply of goods.

> Only at the combination of real GDP and price level given by the intersection of the AS and AD curves are demand behaviour and supply behaviour consistent.

Macroeconomic equilibrium thus requires that two conditions be satisfied. The first is familiar to us because it comes from Chapters 21 and 22. At the prevailing price level, desired aggregate expenditure must be equal to actual GDP—that is, households are just willing to buy all that is produced. The AD curve is constructed in such a way that this condition holds everywhere along it. The second requirement for macroeconomic equilibrium is introduced by consideration of aggregate supply. At the prevailing price level, firms must want to produce the prevailing level of GDP, no more and no less. This condition is fulfilled everywhere along the AS curve. Only where the two curves intersect are both conditions fulfilled simultaneously.

Changes in the Macroeconomic Equilibrium

The aggregate demand and aggregate supply curves can now be used to understand how various shocks to the economy change both real GDP and the price level.

FIGURE 23-6 Macroeconomic Equilibrium

Macroeconomic equilibrium occurs at the intersection of the AD and AS curves and determines the equilibrium values for real GDP and the price level. Given the AD and AS curves in the figure, macroeconomic equilibrium occurs at E_0.

If the price level were equal to P_1, the desired output of firms would be Y_1. However, at P_1, the level of output that is consistent with expenditure decisions would be Y_2. Hence, when the price level is less than P_0, the desired output of firms will be less than the level of real GDP that is consistent with expenditure decisions. Conversely, for any price level above P_0, the desired output of firms exceeds the level of output that is consistent with expenditure decisions.

The only price level at which the supply decisions of firms are consistent with desired expenditure is P_0. At P_0, firms want to produce Y_0. When they do so, they generate a real GDP of Y_0; when real GDP is Y_0, decision makers want to spend exactly Y_0, thereby purchasing the nation's output. Hence, all decisions are consistent with each other.

As indicated earlier, a shift in the AD curve is called an aggregate demand shock. A rightward shift in the AD curve is an increase in aggregate demand; it means that at all price levels, expenditure decisions will now be consistent with a higher level of real GDP. This is called a *positive* shock. Similarly, a leftward shift in the AD curve is a decrease in aggregate demand—that is, at all price levels, expenditure decisions will now be consistent with a lower level of real GDP. This is called a *negative* shock.

Also as indicated earlier, a shift in the AS curve caused by an exogenous force is called an aggregate supply shock. A rightward shift in the AS curve is an increase in aggregate supply; at any given price level, more real GDP will be supplied. This is a *positive* shock. A leftward shift in the AS curve is a decrease in aggregate supply; at any given price level, less real GDP will be supplied. This is a *negative* shock.

Practise with Study Guide
Chapter 23, Exercise 3.

> Aggregate demand and supply shocks are labelled according to their effect on real GDP. Positive shocks increase equilibrium GDP; negative shocks reduce equilibrium GDP.

Let's now examine aggregate demand and supply shocks in detail.

Aggregate Demand Shocks

Practise with Study Guide
Chapter 23, Extension
Exercise E1.

Figure 23-7 shows the effects of an increase in aggregate demand—a positive AD shock. This increase could have occurred because of, say, increased investment or government purchases, an increase in foreigners' demand for Canadian goods, or an increase in household consumption resulting from a reduction in personal income taxes or an increase in transfer payments. (Remember that each of these events causes the AE curve to shift up, and therefore the AD curve to shift to the right.) Whatever the cause, the increase in aggregate demand means that more domestic output is demanded at any given price level. As is shown in the figure, the increase in aggregate demand causes both the price level and real GDP to rise in the new macroeconomic equilibrium. Conversely, a decrease in demand causes both the price level and real GDP to fall.

> Aggregate demand shocks cause the price level and real GDP to change in the same direction; both rise with an increase in aggregate demand, and both fall with a decrease in aggregate demand.

The Multiplier When the Price Level Varies We saw earlier in this chapter that the simple multiplier gives the size of the horizontal shift in the AD curve in response to a change in autonomous expenditure. If the price level remains constant and firms supply all that is demanded at the existing price level (as would be the case with a horizontal AS curve), the simple multiplier gives the increase in equilibrium national income.

But what happens in the more usual case in which the AS curve slopes upward? As can be seen in Figure 23-7, when the AS curve is positively sloped, the change in real GDP caused by a change in autonomous expenditure is no longer equal to the size of the horizontal shift in the AD curve. Part of the expansionary impact of an increase in demand is dissipated by a rise in the price level, and only part is transmitted to a rise in real GDP. Of course, an increase in output does occur; thus, a multiplier may still be calculated, but its value is not the same as that of the *simple* multiplier.

> When the AS curve is upward sloping, an aggregate demand shock leads to a change in the price level. As a result, the multiplier is smaller than the simple multiplier.

Why is the multiplier smaller when the AS curve is positively sloped? The answer lies in the behaviour

FIGURE 23-7   Aggregate Demand Shocks

Shifts in aggregate demand cause the price level and real GDP to move in the same direction. An increase in aggregate demand shifts the AD curve to the right, from AD_0 to AD_1. Macroeconomic equilibrium moves from E_0 to E_1. The price level rises from P_0 to P_1, and real GDP rises from Y_0 to Y_1, reflecting a movement along the AS curve.

that is summarized by the *AE* curve. To understand this, it is useful to think of the final change in real GDP as occurring in two stages, as shown in Figure 23-8.

First, with a constant price level, an increase in autonomous expenditure shifts the *AE* curve upward (from AE_0 to AE'_1). This increase in autonomous expenditure is shown in part (ii) by a shift to the right of the *AD* curve. The movement marked ① is the end of the first stage, but is not the end of the whole story.

In the second stage we must take account of the rise in the price level that occurs because of the positive slope of the *AS* curve. As we saw earlier in this chapter, a rise in the price level, via its effect on net exports and desired consumption, leads to a downward shift in the *AE* curve (from AE'_1 to AE_1). This second shift of the *AE* curve partly counteracts the initial rise in real GDP and so reduces the size of the multiplier. The second stage shows up as a downward shift of the *AE* curve in part (i) of Figure 23-8 and a movement upward and to the left along the new *AD* curve, as shown by arrow ② in part (ii).

The Importance of the Shape of the *AS* Curve

We have now seen that the shape of the *AS* curve has important implications for how the effects of an aggregate demand shock are divided between changes in real GDP and changes in the price level. Figure 23-9 highlights the price level and GDP effects of aggregate demand shocks by considering these shocks in the presence of an *AS* curve with three distinct ranges.

Over the *flat* range, any change in aggregate demand leads to no change in prices and, as seen earlier, a response of output equal to that predicted by the simple multiplier.

Over the *intermediate* range, along which the *AS* curve is positively sloped, a shift in the *AD* curve gives rise to appreciable changes in both real GDP and the price level. Because of the increase in the price level, the multiplier in this case is positive, but smaller than the simple multiplier.

Over the *steep* range, very little more can be produced, no matter how large the increase in demand. This range deals with an economy near its capacity constraints. Any change in aggregate demand leads to a sharp change in the price level and to little or no change in real GDP. The multiplier in this case is nearly zero.

> The effect of any given shift in aggregate demand will be divided between a change in real output and a change in the price level, depending on the conditions of aggregate supply. The steeper the *AS* curve, the greater the price effect and the smaller the output effect.

FIGURE 23-8   The Multiplier When the Price Level Varies

(i) Aggregate expenditure

(ii) Aggregate demand and supply

An increase in autonomous expenditure causes the *AE* curve to shift upward, but the rise in the price level causes it to shift part of the way down again. Hence, the multiplier is smaller than when the price level is constant. Originally, equilibrium is at point E_0 in both part (i) and part (ii). Desired aggregate expenditure then shifts by ΔA to AE'_1, shifting the *AD* curve to AD_1. These shifts are shown by arrow ① in both parts. But the adjustment is not yet complete.

The shift in the *AD* curve raises the price level to P_1 because the *AS* curve is positively sloped. The rise in the price level shifts the *AE* curve down to AE_1, as shown by arrow ② in part (i). This is shown as a movement along the new *AD* curve, as indicated by arrow ② in part (ii). The new equilibrium is thus at E_1. The amount Y_0Y_1 is ΔY, the actual increase in real GDP. The multiplier, adjusted for the effect of the price increase, is the ratio $\Delta Y / \Delta A$ in part (i).

FIGURE 23-9   The Effects of Increases in Aggregate Demand

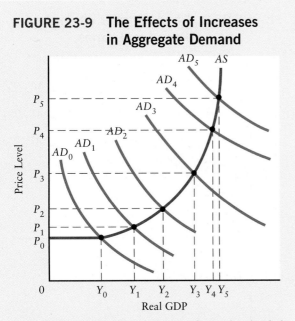

The effect of increases in aggregate demand is divided between increases in real GDP and increases in the price level, depending on the slope of the AS curve. Because of the increasing slope of the AS curve, increases in aggregate demand up to AD_0 have virtually no impact on the price level. Successive further increases bring larger price increases and relatively smaller output increases. By the time aggregate demand is at AD_4 or AD_5, virtually all of the effect is on the price level.

Extensions in Theory 23-1 deals with the special case of a horizontal *AS* curve—sometimes called a *Keynesian AS* curve. In that case, the aggregate supply curve determines the price level, and the *AD* curve determines real GDP.

Reconciliation with Previous Analysis

One of the central points of this chapter is that aggregate demand shocks typically lead to changes in *both* the price level and the level of real GDP. Furthermore, with a vertical *AS* curve, such aggregate demand shocks will result in no change in real GDP, but only a change in the price level. How do we reconcile this possibility with the analysis of Chapters 21 and 22, where shifts in *AE always* change real GDP? The answer is that each *AE* curve is drawn on the assumption that there is a constant price level. An upward shift in the *AE* curve shifts the *AD* curve to the right. However, a positively sloped *AS* curve means that the price level rises, and this rise shifts the *AE* curve back down, offsetting some of its initial rise. This process was explained in Figure 23-8.

It is instructive to consider an extreme version of Figure 23-8, one with a vertical *AS* curve. If you draw this diagram for yourself, you will note that an increase in autonomous expenditure shifts the *AE* curve upward, thus raising the amount demanded. However, a vertical *AS* curve means that output cannot be expanded to satisfy the increased demand. Instead, the extra demand merely forces prices up, and as prices rise, the *AE* curve shifts down again. The rise in prices continues until the *AE* curve is back to where it started. Thus, the rise in prices offsets the expansionary effect of the original shift and consequently leaves both real aggregate expenditure and equilibrium real GDP unchanged.

A vertical *AS* curve, however, is quite unrealistic. Most economists agree that the *AS* curve is shaped something like the one shown in Figure 23-9—that is, relatively flat for low levels of GDP and becoming steeper as GDP rises.

We now complete our discussion of changes in the macroeconomic equilibrium by discussing supply shocks.

Aggregate Supply Shocks

A negative aggregate supply shock, shown by a shift to the left in the *AS* curve, means that less real output will be supplied at any given price level. A positive aggregate supply shock, shown by a shift to the right in the *AS* curve, means that more real output will be supplied at any given price level.

Figure 23-10 illustrates the effects on the price level and real GDP of a negative aggregate supply shock. This could have occurred because of, say, an increase in the world price of important inputs, such as oil, copper, or iron ore. As can be seen from the figure, following the decrease in aggregate supply, the price level rises and real GDP

Practise with Study Guide
Chapter 23, Exercises 4 and 5.

EXTENSIONS IN THEORY 23-1

The Keynesian *AS* Curve

In this box, we consider an extreme version of the *AS* curve that is horizontal over some range of real GDP. It is called the *Keynesian aggregate supply curve*, after John Maynard Keynes (1883–1946), who in his famous book *The General Theory of Employment, Interest and Money* (1936) pioneered the study of the behaviour of economies under conditions of high unemployment. Despite its name, this curve does not describe Keynes's own views on the behaviour of the price level. It is instead the version of aggregate supply used by many of Keynes's followers in their early attempts to express Keynes's work in a formal model—something Keynes himself did not do.

The behaviour that gives rise to the Keynesian *AS* curve can be described as follows. When real GDP is below potential GDP, individual firms are operating with excess capacity. They then respond to changes in demand by altering output while keeping prices constant. In other words, they will supply whatever they can sell at their existing prices as long as they are producing below their normal capacity.*

Under these circumstances, the economy has a horizontal *AS* curve, indicating that any output up to potential output will be supplied at the going price level. The amount that is actually produced is then determined by the position of the *AD* curve, as shown in the figure. Thus, real GDP is said to be *demand determined*. If demand rises enough so that firms are trying to squeeze more than normal output out of their plants, their costs will rise and so will their prices. Hence, the horizontal Keynesian *AS* curve applies only to levels of GDP below potential GDP.

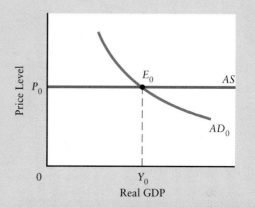

This special case of a horizontal *AS* curve corresponds to the macro model that we developed in Chapters 21 and 22. Recall that in that simple model we assumed a constant price level. In other words, if the *AS* curve is horizontal, our macro model in this chapter is *exactly the same* as the simple version in Chapters 21 and 22. In this case, a change in autonomous expenditure, ΔA, will lead to increases in equilibrium GDP equal to ΔA times the simple multiplier. (In Figure 23-3 on page 574 this is exactly the distance of the horizontal shift in the *AD* curve in response to any given ΔA.)

---

* There is considerable evidence that many firms do behave like this for short periods of time. One possible explanation for this behaviour is that changing prices frequently is too costly, so firms set the best possible (profit-maximizing) prices when output is at normal capacity and then do not change prices in the face of short-term fluctuations in demand.

---

falls. Conversely, a positive aggregate supply shock leads to an increase in real GDP and a decrease in the price level.

> **Aggregate supply shocks cause the price level and real GDP to change in opposite directions. With an increase in supply, the price level falls and GDP rises; with a decrease in supply, the price level rises and GDP falls.**

Oil-price increases provided three major examples of negative aggregate supply shocks, the first two during the 1970s and the third between 2002 and 2008. The economy is especially responsive to changes in the price for oil because, in addition to being used to produce energy, oil is an input into plastics and many other materials that are widely used in manufacturing. Massive increases in oil prices occurred during

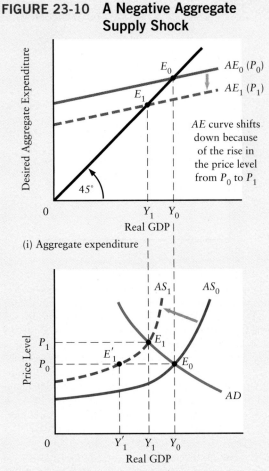

FIGURE 23-10   A Negative Aggregate Supply Shock

(i) Aggregate expenditure

(ii) Aggregate demand and supply

Aggregate supply shocks cause the price level and real GDP to move in opposite directions. The original equilibrium is at E_0, with GDP of Y_0 appearing in both parts of the figure. The price level is P_0 in part (ii), and at that price level, the desired aggregate expenditure curve is AE_0 in part (i).

A negative aggregate supply shock now shifts the AS curve in part (ii) to AS_1. At the original price level of P_0, firms are now only willing to supply Y'_1. The fall in supply causes a rise in the price level. The new equilibrium is reached at E_1, where the AD curve intersects AS_1. At the new and higher equilibrium price level of P_1, the AE curve has shifted down to AE_1, as shown in part (i).

1973–1974 and 1979–1980, caused by the successful efforts of the OPEC countries to form a cartel and restrict the output of oil. These increases in the price of oil caused leftward shifts in the AS curve in most countries. Real GDP fell while the price level rose. (We will discuss shortly the more recent oil-price increases that occurred in the 2002–2008 period.)

Commodity prices have provided an important recent example of a positive aggregate supply shock. The Southeast Asian countries of Indonesia, Malaysia, Thailand, and South Korea are all significant users of raw materials. When their economies plunged into a major recession in 1997 and 1998, the world demand for raw materials fell, and the prices of such goods fell as a result. From 1997 to 1998, the average price of raw materials fell by approximately 30 percent.

Though these were clearly bad economic times for much of Southeast Asia, the reduction in raw materials prices was a *positive* aggregate supply shock for countries that used raw materials as inputs for production. In countries like Canada, the United States, and most of Western Europe, the AS curves shifted to the right. The effect was to increase real GDP and reduce the price level.[3]

A Word of Warning

We have discussed the effects of aggregate demand and aggregate supply shocks on the economy's price level and real GDP. Students are sometimes puzzled, however, because some events would appear to be *both* demand and supply shocks. How do we analyze such complicated shocks? For example, when the world price of oil rises, as it did significantly between 2002 and 2008, this is a *negative supply shock* because oil is an important input to production for many firms. But for Canada, which produces and exports oil, doesn't the increase in the world price of oil also imply an increase in export revenue? And doesn't this imply a *positive demand shock*?

The answer to both questions is yes. An increase in world oil prices is indeed a negative aggregate supply shock to any country that uses oil as an input (which means most countries). But for those countries

---

[3] Actually, it is more accurate to say that this shock reduced the price level *compared with what it otherwise would have been*. Because of ongoing inflation, the causes of which we will discuss in Chapters 29 and 30, the price level in Canada rarely falls. But we have been assuming throughout this chapter that there is no ongoing inflation, and in that setting a positive AS shock like the one described in the text would indeed cause the price level to fall.

LESSONS FROM HISTORY 23-1

The Asian Crisis and the Canadian Economy

In the summer of 1997, the currencies of several countries in Southeast Asia plummeted (relative to the U.S. and Canadian dollars) as their central banks were no longer able to "peg" their exchange rates. In Chapter 35 we will discuss how such pegged exchange rates operate. For now, the important point is that, for various reasons, banks, firms, and households in these countries had accumulated a large stock of debt denominated in foreign currencies, especially U.S. dollars. The sudden depreciations of their currencies—in some cases by 70 percent in just a few days—led to dramatic increases in the amount of domestic income required to pay the interest on this debt. Financial institutions went bankrupt, manufacturing firms were unable to access credit, workers were laid off, and economic output fell sharply. By late in 1997, the economies of Malaysia, Indonesia, Thailand, South Korea, and the Philippines were suffering major recessions.

How did this Asian crisis affect Canada? It had offsetting positive and negative effects on the level of economic activity in Canada. The events in Asia generated both a *negative* aggregate demand shock and a *positive* aggregate supply shock for Canada.

To understand the demand side of the story, we must recognize that these Asian economies are impor-

tant users of raw materials. When their level of economic activity declined sharply, so too did their demand for raw materials. Indeed, average raw materials prices fell by roughly 30 percent between 1997 and 1998. But raw materials are an important export for Canada. The decline in the world's demand for raw materials implied a reduction in demand for Canadian goods. As a result, Canadian producers of copper, pork, newsprint, lumber, iron ore, and many other raw materials suffered significantly. In terms of our macroeconomic model, the demand part of the Asian crisis is represented as a leftward shift of the Canadian AD curve.

But the story does not end there. Also important to Canada is the fact that many Canadian manufacturing firms use raw materials as inputs for their production of car parts, pre-fabricated houses and trailers, electrical equipment, and so on. A dramatic reduction in the prices of raw materials implies a reduction in costs for manufacturing firms. This is a positive aggregate supply shock, and is illustrated by a rightward shift of the Canadian AS curve.

What is the overall effect on the Canadian economy? The effect of each shock taken separately is to reduce the price level—so the overall effect is unambiguously a lower price level.* In contrast, the effect on real GDP would appear to be ambiguous since the AD shock reduces GDP whereas the AS shock increases it. But this is not quite right. Since Canada is a net exporter of raw materials (it exports more raw materials than it imports), it must experience a decrease in national income when these prices fall. In other words, the net effect of the negative demand shock and the positive supply shock is to reduce Canadian GDP. The figure is therefore drawn with the AD shock being larger than the AS shock and so the new equilibrium level of GDP, Y_1, is lower than in the initial equilibrium, Y_0.

Negative demand shock as demand for Canada's exports (raw materials) falls

AS_0

AS_1

Positive supply shock as price of inputs (raw materials) falls

AD_0

AD_1

Canada's Price Level

P_0

P_1

0

Y_1 Y_0

Canada's Real GDP

*Recall footnote 3 on page 584. We are assuming in this analysis that there is no ongoing inflation, so a positive AS shock or a negative AD shock reduces the price level. A more accurate description for the Canadian economy in 1998, with some ongoing inflation, is that the price level fell below what it otherwise would have been. This appears as a reduction in the rate of inflation.

For information on OPEC,
see its website:
www.opec.org.

that also produce and export oil—like Canada—a rise in the price of oil generates an increase in income to domestic oil producers and is thus a positive aggregate demand shock. It is no surprise that the economies of the oil-producing regions of Canada, especially Alberta, Saskatchewan, and Newfoundland and Labrador, were booming during the 2002–2008 period, when the price of oil increased from about U.S.$30 per barrel to more than U.S.$75 per barrel (and was very briefly at almost $U.S.150 per barrel).

A complete analysis of the macroeconomic effect of a rise in world oil prices must consider both a leftward shift of the *AS* curve and, for those countries that produce oil, a rightward shift of the *AD* curve. The equilibrium price level will certainly increase, but the overall effect on real GDP will depend on the relative importance of the demand-side and supply-side effects.

Our discussion here has been about the macroeconomic effects of oil-price increases, but the central message is more general:

> **Many economic events—especially changes in the world prices of raw materials—cause both aggregate demand and aggregate supply shocks in the same economy. The overall effect on real GDP in that economy depends on the relative importance of the two separate effects.**

This general principle should be kept in mind whenever our *AD/AS* macro model is used to analyze the macroeconomy. *Lessons from History 23-1* uses our model to interpret the effects of the 1997–1998 Asian economic crisis on the Canadian economy. As you will see in that discussion, the Asian crisis generated both *AD* and *AS* shocks for Canada.

Ⓧ myeconlab   ADDITIONAL TOPICS

The increase in the world price of oil from 2002 to 2008 was dramatic, but many observers were surprised at its modest impact on the Canadian economy. For more information on how changes in oil prices affect Canada and why the negative *AS* effect is smaller now than in the 1970s, look for **Oil Prices and the Canadian Economy** in the *Additional Topics* section of this book's MyEconLab.

www.myeconlab.com

Summary

23.1 The Demand Side of the Economy

- The *AE* curve shows desired aggregate expenditure for each level of GDP at a particular price level. Its intersection with the 45° line determines equilibrium GDP for that price level. Equilibrium GDP thus occurs where desired aggregate expenditure equals actual GDP. A change in the price level causes a shift in the *AE* curve: upward when the price level falls and downward when the price level rises. This leads to a new equilibrium level of real GDP.

- The *AD* curve plots the equilibrium level of GDP that corresponds to each possible price level. A change in equilibrium GDP following a change in the price level is shown by a movement along the *AD* curve.

- A rise in the price level lowers exports and lowers autonomous consumption expenditure. Both of these changes reduce equilibrium GDP and cause the *AD* curve to have a negative slope.

- The *AD* curve shifts horizontally when any element of autonomous expenditure changes, and the simple multiplier measures the size of the shift.

23.2 The Supply Side of the Economy   ⓛ ❸

- Firms' unit costs usually rise when their output rises, and thus they are willing to supply more output only at higher prices. As a result, the *AS* curve is upward sloping.
- Each *AS* curve is drawn for given levels of factor (input) prices and productivity.

- An increase in productivity or a decrease in factor prices shifts the *AS* curve to the right. This is an increase in aggregate supply. A decrease in productivity or an increase in factor prices shifts the *AS* curve to the left. This is a decrease in aggregate supply.

23.3 Macroeconomic Equilibrium   ⓛ ❹ ❺

- Macroeconomic equilibrium refers to equilibrium values of real GDP and the price level, as determined by the intersection of the *AD* and *AS* curves. Shifts in the *AD* and *AS* curves, called aggregate demand and aggregate supply shocks, change the equilibrium values of real GDP and the price level.
- When the *AS* curve is positively sloped, an aggregate demand shock causes the price level and real GDP to move in the same direction. When the *AS* curve is flat, shifts in the *AD* curve primarily affect real GDP. When the *AS* curve is steep, shifts in the *AD* curve primarily affect the price level.
- In the usual case with a positively sloped *AS* curve, a demand shock leads to a change in the price level. As a

result, the multiplier is smaller than the simple multiplier in Chapter 22.
- An aggregate supply shock moves equilibrium GDP along the *AD* curve, causing the price level and real GDP to move in opposite directions. A leftward shift in the *AS* curve causes a reduction in real GDP and an increase in the price level. A rightward shift causes an increase in real GDP and a fall in the price level.
- Some events are both aggregate supply and aggregate demand shocks. Changes in the world prices of raw materials, for example, shift the *AS* curve. If the country (like Canada) is also a producer of such raw materials, there will also be a shift in the *AD* curve. The overall effect then depends on the relative sizes of the separate effects.

Key Concepts

Effects of an exogenous change in the price level
Relationship between the *AE* and *AD* curves

Negative slope of the *AD* curve
Positive slope of the *AS* curve
Macroeconomic equilibrium
Aggregate demand shocks

The multiplier when the price level varies
Aggregate supply shocks

Study Exercises

1. Fill in the blanks to make the following statements correct.

   a. In the simple macro model of the previous two chapters, the price level was _____. In the macro model of this chapter, the price level is _____.

   b. A change in the price level shifts the *AE* curve because the price level change affects desired _____ and desired _____.

   c. A rise in the price level causes a(n) _____ in households' wealth, which leads to a _____ in desired consumption, which causes the *AE* curve to shift _____. A fall in the price level causes a(n) _____ in households' wealth, which leads to a _____ in desired consumption, which causes the *AE* curve to shift _____.

   d. A rise in the domestic price level causes net exports to _____, which causes the *AE* curve to shift _____. A fall in the domestic price level causes net exports to _____, which causes the *AE* curve to shift _____.

   e. Equilibrium GDP is determined by the position of the *AE* function for each given price level. An equilibrium point for a particular price level corresponds to one point on the _____ curve.

   f. A rise in the price level causes a downward shift of the _____ curve and a movement upward along the _____ curve.

   g. An increase in autonomous expenditure, with no change in the price level, causes the *AE* curve to _____ and causes the *AD* curve to _____.

2. Fill in the blanks to make the following statements correct.

   a. The _____ curve relates the price level to the quantity of output that firms would like to produce and sell.

   b. Each aggregate supply curve is drawn under the assumption that _____ and _____ remain constant.

   c. The aggregate supply curve is upward sloping because firms will produce more output only if price _____ to offset higher unit costs.

   d. The aggregate supply curve is relatively flat when GDP is below potential output because firms typically have _____ and are able to expand production without much increase in unit costs.

   e. The aggregate supply curve is relatively steep when GDP is above potential output because firms are operating above _____ and _____ are rising rapidly.

   f. The aggregate supply curve shifts in response to changes in _____ and changes in _____. These are known as supply _____.

3. Fill in the blanks to make the following statements correct.

   a. Macroeconomic equilibrium occurs at the intersection of _____ and _____, and determines equilibrium levels of _____ and _____.

   b. A positive *AD* shock will cause the price level to _____ and real GDP to _____. A negative *AD* shock will cause the price level to _____ and real GDP to _____.

   c. A positive *AS* shock will cause the price level to _____ and real GDP to _____. A negative *AS* shock will cause the price level to _____ and real GDP to _____.

   d. In previous chapters, the simple multiplier measured the change in real GDP in response to a change in autonomous expenditure when the price level was constant. When the price level varies, the multiplier is _____ than the simple multiplier.

   e. An increase in autonomous government spending is a _____ *AD* shock, which will initially cause a(n) _____ shift of the *AE* curve and a(n) _____ shift of the AD curve. Given an upward-sloping aggregate supply curve, there will be a _____ in the price level, which leads to a partial _____ shift of the *AE* curve.

4. Consider the effects of an exogenous increase in the domestic price level. For each of the assets listed, explain how the change in the price level would affect the wealth of the asset holder. Then explain the effect on *aggregate* (private sector) wealth.

   a. Cash holdings
   b. Deposits in a bank account
   c. A household mortgage
   d. A corporate bond that promises to pay the bondholder $10 000 on January 1, 2011
   e. A government bond that promises to pay the holder $10 000 on January 1, 2011

5. Consider the following simplified *AE* function:

$$AE = 350 + 0.8Y + 0.1 \ (M/P)$$

where *AE* is desired aggregate expenditure, *Y* is real GDP, *M* is the private sector's *nominal wealth,* and *P* is the price level. Suppose that *M* is constant and equal to 6000.

   a. Explain why the expression for *AE* above makes sense. Why do *M* and *P* enter the *AE* function?

   b. Fill in the table below:

P	M/P	AE
1	6000	950 + 0.8Y
2	—	—
3	—	—
4	—	—
5	—	—
6	—	—

c. Plot each of the *AE* functions—one for each price level—on the same scale 45°-line diagram.

d. Compute the level of equilibrium national income (*Y*) for each of the values of *P*. For example, when *P* = 1, *AE* = 950 + 0.8*Y*. Thus the equilibrium level of *Y* is such that *Y* = 950 + 0.8*Y*, which implies *Y* = 4750.

e. Plot the pairs of price level and equilibrium national income on a scale diagram with *P* on the vertical axis and *Y* on the horizontal axis.

6. Consider the following diagram showing the *AD* curves in two different economies. One economy is Autarkland—it does not trade with the rest of the world (*autarky* is a situation in which a country does not trade with other countries). The other economy is Openland—it exports to and imports from the rest of the world.

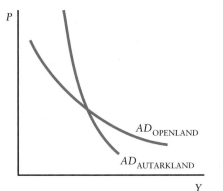

a. Explain why an increase in the domestic price level (for a given exchange rate) reduces net exports in Openland. How would you illustrate this with the *AE* curve in the 45°-line diagram?

b. Explain why the *AD* curve is steeper in Autarkland than in Openland.

c. If there are never any net exports in Autarkland, why isn't the *AD* curve vertical? Explain what other aspect of the economy generates a downward-sloping *AD* curve.

7. The economy of Neverland has the following *AD* and *AS* schedules. Denote Y_{AD} as the level of real GDP along the *AD* curve; let Y_{AS} be the level of real GDP along the *AS* curve. GDP is shown in billions of 2002 dollars.

Price Level	Y_{AD}	Y_{AS}
90	1100	750
100	1000	825
110	900	900
120	800	975
130	700	1050
140	600	1125

a. Plot the *AD* and *AS* curves on a scale diagram.

b. What is the price level and level of real GDP in Neverland's macroeconomic equilibrium?

c. Suppose the level of potential output in Neverland is $950 billion. Is the current equilibrium level of real GDP greater than or less than potential? How does one refer to this particular output gap?

8. Each of the following events is either a *cause* or a *consequence* of a shift in the *AD* or *AS* curve in Canada. Identify which it is and, if it is a cause, describe the effect on equilibrium real GDP and the price level.

a. OPEC's actions significantly increased the world price of oil in 1979–1980.

b. During 1996–2001, Canadian real GDP was growing at a healthy pace but inflation showed no signs of rising.

c. World commodity prices increased sharply from 2002 to 2008. Many of these commodities are both produced in Canada and used as important inputs for Canadian firms.

d. The end of the Cold War led to large declines in defence spending in many countries (including Canada).

e. Several provinces lowered their personal income tax rates in the late 1990s.

f. The federal government increased its level of government purchases (*G*) in the early 2000s.

g. The beginning of a recession in the United States in 2008 led to a large reduction in the demand for many Canadian exports.

9. The following diagrams show the *AD* and *AS* curves in two different economies.

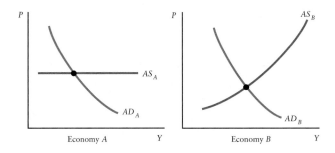

a. Explain what aspect of firms' behaviour might give rise to the horizontal *AS* curve in Economy A.

b. Explain what aspect of firms' behaviour gives rise to the upward-sloping *AS* curve in Economy B.

c. In which economy is output demand determined? Explain.

d. Consider the effects of an increase in autonomous expenditure. Which economy has the larger multiplier? Explain your reasoning.

10. This question involves algebraically solving the system of two equations given by the AD and AS curves. The equations for the curves are given by:

$$AD: \quad Y_{AD} = 710 - 30P + 5G$$

$$AS: \quad Y_{AS} = 10 + 5P - 2P_{OIL}$$

where Y is real GDP, P is the price level, G is the level of government purchases, and P_{OIL} is the world price of oil.

a. Explain the various terms in the AD curve. What is the value of the simple multiplier? (Hint: the simple multiplier is the change in equilibrium real GDP when some autonomous component of expenditure, like G, changes by $1 if the price level is held constant.)

b. Explain the various terms in the AS curve. Explain why the price of oil enters negatively.

c. Solve for the equilibrium value of real GDP and the price level.

d. Using your solution to part (c), what is the effect of a change in G on equilibrium Y and P?

e. Using your solution to part (c), what is the effect of a change in P_{OIL} on equilibrium Y and P?

Discussion Questions

1. This chapter discussed the meaning of aggregate demand and aggregate supply shocks, and several examples were given of each. But some shocks can be both demand-side shocks and supply-side shocks. Consider the prices of many commodities, such as lumber, newsprint, oil, copper, grains, and iron ore. The prices of such commodities are determined in world markets and are subject to significant fluctuations from year to year. For example, in 2002–2008, there was a significant increase in the prices of many such commodities. Explain how such a rise in commodity prices can lead to both an increase in Canadian aggregate demand and a fall in Canadian aggregate supply. How would you determine the net effect on real GDP and the price level?

2. Show the effects on the price level and real GDP of a major union wage settlement that significantly increases wages. Is this a supply shock, a demand shock, or both?

3. In the following table are the combinations of output and price level given by real GDP and the CPI, respectively, for some recent years. Treat each pair as if it is the intersection of an AD and an AS curve. Plot these data. Then think about the possible shifts in the AD or AS curves that could have caused them. Is it possible to know what the underlying shifts are? Why or why not?

Year	CPI (2002 = 100)	Real GDP (billions of 2002 dollars)
1998	91.3	991.0
1999	92.9	1045.8
2000	95.4	1100.5
2001	97.8	1120.1
2002	100.0	1152.9
2003	102.8	1174.6
2004	104.7	1211.2
2005	107.0	1247.8
2006	109.1	1283.4
2007	111.5	1315.9
2008	114.1	1321.4

4. Beginning in 2006, the Canadian government reduced both personal and corporate income taxes. Explain the effects of such a policy on the macroeconomic equilibrium. Is this a demand-side or a supply-side policy? Explain.

From the Short Run to the Long Run: The Adjustment of Factor Prices

In the previous three chapters, we developed a model of the *short-run* determination of the equilibrium levels of real GDP and the price level. In this chapter, we discuss how this short-run macroeconomic equilibrium evolves, through an adjustment process in which wages and other factor prices change, into a *long-run* equilibrium, in which real GDP is equal to potential output, Y^*. In the next two chapters we examine theories explaining why Y^* increases over many years—what we call *long-run economic growth.* Before we proceed, however, we will define carefully our assumptions regarding the short run, the adjustment process, and the long run.

LO LEARNING OBJECTIVES

In this chapter you will learn

1. why output gaps cause wages and other factor prices to change.

2. how induced changes in factor prices affect firms' costs and shift the *AS* curve.

3. why real GDP gradually returns to potential output following an *AD* or *AS* shock.

4. why lags and uncertainty place limitations on the use of fiscal stabilization policy.

The Short Run

These are the defining characteristics of the *short run* in our macroeconomic model:

- Factor prices are assumed to be exogenous; they may change, but any change is not explained within the model.
- Technology and factor supplies are assumed to be constant (and therefore Y^* is constant).

With these assumptions, the short-run macroeconomic equilibrium is determined by the intersection of the AD and AS curves, both of which are subject to shocks of various kinds. The level of real GDP fluctuates around a *constant* level of potential output, Y^*. This version of our macroeconomic model is convenient to use when analyzing the economy over short periods. Even though factor prices, technology, and factor supplies are rarely constant, even over short periods of time, the simplifying assumption that they are constant in our short-run model allows us to focus on the most important changes over this time span: the fluctuations of real GDP relative to the level of potential output—what economists call *business cycles*.

The Adjustment of Factor Prices

As we will see in detail in this chapter, our theory of the *adjustment process* that takes the economy from the short run to the long run is based on the following assumptions:

- Factor prices are assumed to adjust in response to output gaps.
- Technology and factor supplies are assumed to be constant (and therefore Y^* is constant).

This chapter will explain our model's prediction that deviations of real GDP from potential output cause wages and other factor prices to adjust. It will also explain how this adjustment is central to the economy's evolution from its short-run equilibrium to its long-run equilibrium. Note that, as in the short-run version of the model, the adjustment process is assumed to take place with a constant level of potential output.

Our theory of the macroeconomic adjustment process is useful for examining how the effects of shocks or policies differ in the short and long runs. As we will see, the assumption that potential output is constant leads to the prediction that AD or AS shocks have no long-run effect on real GDP; output eventually returns to Y^*.

In reality, neither technology nor factor supplies are constant over time; the level of potential output is continually changing. Our assumption throughout much of this chapter of a constant value for Y^* is a simplifying one, allowing us to focus on the *adjustment process* that brings the level of real GDP back to potential output.

The Long Run

As we will see in Chapters 25 and 26, these are defining characteristics of the *long run* in our macro model:

- Factor prices are assumed to have fully adjusted to any output gap.
- Technology and factor supplies are assumed to be changing.

A central prediction of our model is that, after factor prices have fully adjusted, real GDP will return to the level of potential output. The second assumption above implies that the level of potential output is changing (and typically growing). Thus, in the long-run version of our macroeconomic model, our focus is not on the nature of business cycles but rather on the nature of *economic growth*—where technological change and the growth of factor supplies play key roles.

The economy is probably never "in" the long run in the sense that factor prices have fully adjusted to all AD and AS shocks. This is because such shocks are not isolated events but instead events that occur more-or-less continually. So, before the full adjustment to one shock is complete, another shock occurs and sets the adjustment process in motion again. Nonetheless, the long-run version of our model is very useful for examining some issues. For example, if we want to understand why our children's material standard of living will be significantly greater than our grandparents', we should not focus on short-run issues of AD or AS shocks and stabilization policies; the effects of particular shocks will disappear after a few years. Instead, we will gain more understanding if we abstract from short-run issues and focus on why Y^* increases dramatically over periods of several decades.

Summary

The three states of the economy central to macroeconomic analysis are summarized in Table 24-1. Note for each state the assumptions made regarding factor prices and the level of potential output and the implied causes of output changes. As we proceed through this chapter and the next two, you may find it useful to refer back to this table.

You already know from Chapter 23 how the short-run version of our macro model works. And now that you have a sketch of what is meant by the adjustment process

TABLE 24-1   Three Macroeconomic States

	The Short Run	The Adjustment Process	The Long Run
Assumptions	Factor prices are exogenous	Factor prices are flexible/endogenous	Factor prices are fully adjusted/endogenous
	Technology and factor supplies (and therefore Y^*) are constant/exogenous	Technology and factor supplies (and therefore Y^*) are constant/exogenous	Technology and factor supplies (and therefore Y^*) are changing/endogenous
Changes in Real GDP	AD/AS shocks cause Y to fluctuate around a constant Y^*	Following AD or AS shocks, Y eventually returns to Y^*	Changes in Y^* determine changes in Y
Why We Study This State	Allows for analysis of the fluctuations of Y around Y^*	Allows for analysis of the adjustment process from the short-run equilibrium to the long-run equilibrium	Allows for analysis of the nature of economic growth; why Y^* increases over long periods of time

and the long run, we are ready to fill in the details. In this chapter we will see how this adjustment process takes the economy from its short-run equilibrium to its long-run equilibrium. To repeat, we make the following important assumptions for our theory of the macroeconomic adjustment process:

- Factor prices are assumed to adjust in response to output gaps.
- Technology and factor supplies are assumed to be constant (and therefore Y^* is constant).

24.1 The Adjustment Process

We develop our theory of the adjustment process by examining the relationship among output gaps, factor markets, and factor prices. We begin by understanding the broad outline of how this process works. We then go on to discuss *how well* it works in greater detail.

Potential Output and the Output Gap

Recall that *potential output* is the total output that can be produced when all productive resources—land, labour, and capital—are being used at their *normal rates of utilization*. When a nation's actual output diverges from its potential output, the difference is called the output gap.

Although growth in potential output has powerful effects from one decade to the next, its change from one *year* to the next is small enough that we ignore it when studying the year-to-year behaviour of real GDP and the price level. In this chapter, therefore, we view variations in the output gap as determined solely by variations in *actual* GDP around a constant level of *potential* GDP. (In Chapter 26 we will examine why potential output changes over periods of several years.)

Figure 24-1 shows real GDP being determined in the short run by the intersection of the *AD* and *AS* curves. Potential output is assumed to be constant, and it is shown by identical vertical lines in the two parts of the figure. In part (i), the *AD* and *AS* curves intersect to produce an equilibrium real GDP less than potential output. The result, as we saw in Chapter 19, is called a *recessionary gap* because recessions are often characterized as having GDP below potential output. In part (ii), the *AD* and *AS* curves intersect to produce an equilibrium real GDP above potential output, resulting in what is called an *inflationary gap*. The way in which an inflationary output gap puts upward pressure on prices will become clear in the ensuing discussion.

Factor Prices and the Output Gap

We make two key assumptions in our macro model regarding factor prices and the output gap. First, when real GDP is above potential output, there will be pressure on factor prices to rise because of a higher than normal demand for factor inputs. Second, when real GDP is below potential output, there will be pressure on factor prices to fall because of a lower than normal demand for factor inputs. These relationships are assumed to hold for the prices of all factors of production, including labour, land, and capital equipment.

FIGURE 24-1   Output Gaps in the Short Run

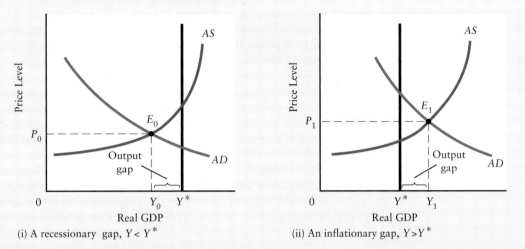

(i) A recessionary gap, $Y < Y^*$ (ii) An inflationary gap, $Y > Y^*$

The output gap is the difference between actual GDP and potential GDP, $Y - Y^*$. Potential output is shown by the vertical line at Y^*. A recessionary gap, shown in panel (i), occurs when actual output is less than potential GDP. An inflationary gap, shown in panel (ii), occurs when actual output is greater than potential output.

Before we examine the detailed relationship between factor prices and output gaps, it is worth noting that even in the absence of an output gap, the presence of ongoing inflation influences factor prices, especially wages. Wage contracts often allow for changes in the price level that are expected to occur during the life of the contract. For the discussion in this chapter, however, we make the simplifying assumption that the price level is expected to be constant (and therefore inflation is expected to be zero); hence changes in money wages are also expected to be changes in real wages. We will discuss inflation in considerable detail in Chapters 29 and 30.

Output Above Potential, $Y > Y^*$ Here is the reasoning behind our first assumption. Sometimes the AD and AS curves intersect where real GDP exceeds potential, as illustrated in part (ii) of Figure 24-1. Because firms are producing beyond their normal capacity output, there is an unusually large demand for all factor inputs, including labour. Labour shortages will emerge in some industries and among many groups of workers. Firms will try to bid workers away from other firms in order to maintain the high levels of output and sales made possible by the boom conditions.

As a result of these tight labour-market conditions, workers will find that they have considerable bargaining power with their employers, and they will

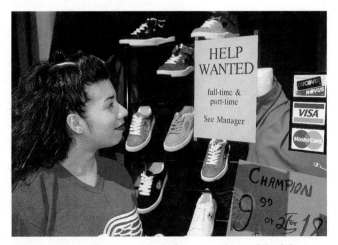

When output is above potential, the excess demand for labour tends to push up wages.

put upward pressure on wages. Firms, recognizing that demand for their goods is strong, will be anxious to maintain a high level of output. To prevent their workers from either striking or quitting and moving to other employers, firms will be willing to accede to some of these upward pressures.

> The boom that is associated with an inflationary gap generates a set of conditions—high profits for firms and unusually large demand for labour—that tends to cause wages (and other factor prices) to rise.

This increase in factor prices will increase firms' unit costs. As unit costs increase, firms will require higher prices in order to supply any given level of output, and the *AS* curve will therefore shift up. This shift has the effect of reducing equilibrium real GDP and raising the price level. Real GDP moves back toward potential and the inflationary gap begins to close.

In our model, factor prices are assumed to continue rising as long as some inflationary gap remains. In other words, they will continue rising until the *AS* curve shifts up to the point where the equilibrium level of GDP is equal to potential GDP. At this point, there is no more pressure for factor prices to rise, firms' costs are stable, and the *AS* curve stops shifting.

Output Below Potential, $Y < Y^*$

Here is the reasoning behind our second assumption regarding factor prices. Sometimes the *AD* and *AS* curves intersect where real GDP is less than potential, as illustrated in part (i) of Figure 24-1. Because firms are producing below their normal-capacity output, there is an unusually low demand for all factor inputs, including labour. There will be labour surpluses in some industries and among some groups of workers. Firms will have below-normal sales and not only will resist upward pressures on wages but also may seek reductions in wages.

> The slump that is associated with a recessionary gap generates a set of conditions—low profits for firms and low demand for labour—that tends to cause wages (and other factor prices) to fall.[1]

When it occurs, this reduction in factor prices will reduce firms' unit costs. As unit costs fall, firms require a lower price in order to supply any given level of output, and the *AS* curve therefore shifts down. This shift has the effect of increasing equilibrium real GDP and reducing the price level. Real GDP moves back toward potential and the recessionary gap begins to close.

In our model, wages and other factor prices are assumed to fall as long as some recessionary gap remains. As factor prices fall, the *AS* curve shifts down, and this process continues until the equilibrium level of GDP is equal to potential output. At this point, there is no longer pressure for factor prices to fall, firms' unit costs are stable, and the *AS* curve stops shifting.

Downward Wage Stickiness

At this stage, we encounter an important asymmetry in the economy's aggregate supply behaviour. Boom conditions (an inflationary gap), along with labour shortages, cause wages and unit costs to rise. The experience of

---

[1] Because of ongoing inflation and productivity growth, nominal wages rarely fall, even when there is a low demand for labour. But remember that in this chapter, to allow us to focus on the adjustment process, we are assuming that technology is constant and expected inflation is zero. Thus nominal (and real) wages and other factor prices are assumed to fall when real GDP is below potential output. With some ongoing inflation in our model, the assumption would be modified so that nominal wages rise less than prices, thus implying a reduction in real wages.

many developed economies, however, suggests that the downward pressures on wages during slumps (recessionary gaps) often do not operate as strongly or as quickly as the upward pressures during booms. Even when wages do fall, they tend to fall more slowly than they would rise in an equally sized inflationary gap. This *downward wage stickiness* implies that the downward shift in the *AS* curve and the downward pressure on the price level are correspondingly slight.[2]

> Both upward and downward adjustments to wages and unit costs do occur, but there are differences in the speed at which they typically operate. Booms can cause wages to rise rapidly; recessions usually cause wages to fall only slowly.

The Phillips Curve The factor-price adjustment process that we have been discussing was explored many years ago in a famous study of wages and unemployment in the United Kingdom. A. W. Phillips observed that wages tend to fall in periods of high unemployment and rise in periods of low unemployment. The resulting negative relationship between unemployment and the rate of change in wages has been called the *Phillips* curve ever since. *Extensions in Theory 24-1* discusses the Phillips curve and its relationship to the aggregate supply (*AS*) curve.

Inflationary and Recessionary Gaps Now it should be clear why the output gaps are named as they are. When real GDP exceeds potential GDP, there will normally be rising unit costs, and the *AS* curve will be shifting upward. This will in turn push the price level up and create temporary inflation. The larger the excess of real GDP over potential GDP, the greater the inflationary pressure. The term *inflationary gap* emphasizes this salient feature of the economy when $Y > Y^*$.

When actual output is less than potential output, as we have seen, there will be unemployment of labour and other productive resources. Unit costs will tend to fall slowly, leading to a slow downward shift in the *AS* curve. Hence, the price level will be falling only slowly so that *unemployment* will be the output gap's most obvious result. The term *recessionary gap* emphasizes this salient feature that high rates of unemployment occur when $Y < Y^*$.

Potential Output as an "Anchor"

We have just argued that there is pressure on wages and other factor prices to change when output is above or below potential. When they occur, these changes in factor prices lead to changes in firms' unit costs that shift the *AS* curve and change the equilibrium level of GDP. Moreover, we assumed that this process of factor-price adjustment will continue as long as some output gap remains, coming to a halt only when the equilibrium level of GDP is equal to potential GDP, Y^*. This leads to an important prediction from our macroeconomic model regarding the distinction between the short-run and long-run effects of aggregate demand and supply shocks.

Potential output acts like an anchor for the level of real GDP. Following aggregate demand or supply shocks that push real GDP below or above potential, the adjustment of factor prices brings real GDP back to potential output.

---

[2] This is the second asymmetry in aggregate supply that we have encountered. The first involves the changing slope of the *AS* curve, discussed in Chapter 23.

EXTENSIONS IN THEORY 24-1

The Phillips Curve and the Adjustment Process

In the 1950s, Professor A. W. Phillips of the London School of Economics was conducting pioneering research on macroeconomic policy. In his early models, he related the rate of inflation to the difference between actual and potential output. Later he investigated the empirical underpinnings of this equation by studying the relationship between the rate of increase of wages and the level of unemployment. He studied these variables because unemployment data were available as far back as the mid-nineteenth century, whereas very few data on output gaps were available when he did his empirical work. In 1958, he reported that a stable relationship had existed between these two variables for 100 years in the United Kingdom. This relationship came to be known as the Phillips curve. The **Phillips curve** provided an explanation, rooted in empirical observation, of the speed with which wage changes shifted the *AS* curve by changing firms' unit costs.

In the form in which it became famous, the Phillips curve related wage changes to the level of unemployment. But we can express the same information in a slightly different way. Note that unemployment and output gaps are negatively related—a recessionary gap is associated with high unemployment, and an inflationary gap is associated with low unemployment. We can therefore create another Phillips curve that plots wage changes against output (rather than against unemployment). Both figures show the same information.

When output equals Y^* the corresponding unemployment rate is sometimes called the natural rate of unemployment, and is denoted U^*. Inflationary gaps (when $Y > Y^*$ and $U < U^*$) are associated with increases in wages. Recessionary gaps (when $Y < Y^*$ and $U > U^*$) are associated with *decreases* in wages.* Thus, a Phillips curve that plots wage changes against real GDP is upward sloping, whereas a Phillips curve that plots wage changes against the unemployment rate is downward sloping. Both versions of the Phillips curve are shown in the accompanying figure.

When output is at potential, all factors are being used at their normal rates of utilization. There is neither upward nor downward pressure on wages (or other factor prices) because there is neither an excess demand nor an excess supply of labour. Hence, the Phillips curve cuts the horizontal axis at Y^* (and at U^*). This is how Phillips drew his original curve.

The Phillips curve is *not* the same as the *AS* curve. The *AS* curve has the *price level* on the vertical axis whereas the Phillips curve has the *rate of change of wages* on the vertical axis. How are the two curves related? The economy's location on the Phillips curve indicates how the *AS* curve is shifting as a result of the existing output gap.

For example, consider an economy that begins at point A in all three diagrams; there is no output gap and wages are therefore stable. Now, suppose a positive aggregate demand shock causes real GDP to increase to Y_1 (and unemployment to fall to U_1) and thus produces an inflationary gap. The excess demand for labour puts

---

* Recall that we are assuming productivity to be constant so that changes in wages imply changes in unit labour costs. When productivity is growing, however, recessionary output gaps cause unit labour costs to fall. This requires only that wages are growing more slowly than productivity, not actually falling.

Phillips curve Originally, a relationship between the unemployment rate and the rate of change of money wages. Now often drawn as a relationship between GDP and the rate of change of money wages.

> Following an aggregate demand or supply shock, the short-run equilibrium level of output may be different from potential output. Any output gap is assumed to cause wages and other factor prices to adjust, eventually bringing the equilibrium level of output back to potential. In this model, therefore, the level of potential output acts like an "anchor" for the economy.

We now go on to examine our theory of the factor-price adjustment process in greater detail, illustrating it for the cases of positive and negative shocks to aggregate demand and supply. We will also examine this factor-price adjustment process following changes in fiscal policy. The idea that Y^* acts as an "anchor" for the economy will become clear: Shocks of various kinds may cause output to rise above or fall below Y^* in the short run, but the adjustment of factor prices to output gaps ensures that output eventually returns to Y^*.

upward pressure on wages and the economy moves along the Phillips curve to point *B*, where wages begin rising. The increase in wages increases unit costs and causes the *AS* curve to shift up. Thus, each point on the Phillips curve determines the rate at which the *AS* curve is shifting. To complete the example, note that as the *AS* curve shifts up, the level of GDP will fall back toward Y^* and the inflationary gap will begin to close. The economy moves back along the Phillips curve toward point *A*. When all adjustment is complete, the new equilibrium will be at point *C* in part (iii) of the figure, with output equal to Y^* and the price level and nominal wages higher than initially. On the Phillips curve, the economy will be back at point *A*, where real GDP equals Y^* and wages are constant (but at a higher level than before the demand shock occurred).

Note that the convex shape of the Phillips curve is not accidental—it reflects the adjustment asymmetry we

mentioned in the text. The convexity of the Phillips curve implies that an inflationary gap of a given amount will lead to faster wage increases than an equally sized recessionary gap will lead to wage reductions. In other words, an inflationary gap will cause the *AS* curve to shift up more quickly than a recessionary gap will cause the *AS* curve to shift down.

Finally, you might be wondering what would happen if the Phillips curve were to shift. And what would cause such a shift? As we will see in Chapter 30 when we discuss the phenomenon of sustained inflation, an important cause of shifts of the Phillips curve is changes in firms' and households' *expectations* of future inflation. In this chapter, however, we have assumed that expected inflation is zero. But whether there is expected inflation or not, the Phillips curve embodies the factor-price adjustment process that is the focus of this chapter.

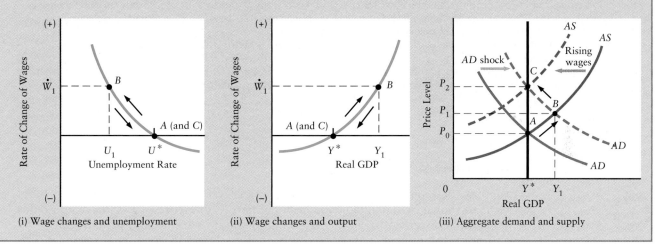

(i) Wage changes and unemployment   (ii) Wage changes and output   (iii) Aggregate demand and supply

24.2 Aggregate Demand and Supply Shocks

We can now study the consequences of aggregate demand and aggregate supply shocks in our model, distinguishing between the immediate effects of *AD* and *AS* shocks and the longer-term effects, after factor prices have adjusted fully. It is necessary to examine expansionary and contractionary shocks separately because the adjustment of factor prices is not symmetrical for the two cases. Let's begin with demand shocks.

FIGURE 24-2   The Adjustment Process Following a Positive Aggregate Demand Shock

(i) Positive AD shock

(ii) Wage adjustment shifts AS

A positive AD shock first raises prices and output along the AS curve. It then induces a shift of the AS curve that further raises prices but lowers output along the new AD curve. In part (i), the economy is in equilibrium at E_0, at its level of potential output, Y^*, and price level P_0. The AD curve then shifts from AD_0 to AD_1. This moves equilibrium to E_1, with income Y_1 and price level P_1, and opens up an inflationary gap.

In part (ii), the inflationary gap results in an increase in wages and other factor prices, shifting the AS curve upward. As this happens, output falls and the price level rises along AD_1. Eventually, when the AS curve has shifted to AS_1, output is back to Y^* and the inflationary gap has been eliminated. However, the price level has risen to P_2. The long-run result of the aggregate demand shock is therefore a higher price level with no change in real GDP.

Expansionary *AD* Shocks

Practise with Study Guide
Chapter 24, Exercises 1 and 2.

Suppose the economy starts with a stable price level and real GDP equal to potential GDP, as shown by the initial equilibrium in part (i) of Figure 24-2. Now suppose this situation is disturbed by an increase in autonomous expenditure, perhaps caused by an upturn in business confidence and a resulting boom in investment spending. Figure 24-2(i) shows the effects of this aggregate demand shock in raising both the price level and real GDP. The AD curve shifts from AD_0 to AD_1, the economy moves along the AS curve, and real GDP rises above Y^*. An inflationary gap opens up.

We have assumed that an inflationary gap leads to increases in wages, which cause unit costs to rise. The AS curve begins to shift up as firms respond to the higher input costs by increasing their output prices. As seen in part (ii) of the figure, the upward shift of the AS curve causes a further rise in the price level, but this time the price rise is associated with a *fall* in output (along the AD_1 curve).

The cost increases (and the consequent upward shifts of the AS curve) continue until the inflationary gap has been removed—that is, until in part (ii) real GDP returns to Y^*. Only then is there no excess demand for labour, and only then do wages and unit costs, and hence the AS curve, stabilize.

> **The adjustment in wages and other factor prices eventually eliminates any boom caused by a demand shock; real GDP returns to its potential level.**

FIGURE 24-3   The Adjustment Process Following a Negative Aggregate Demand Shock

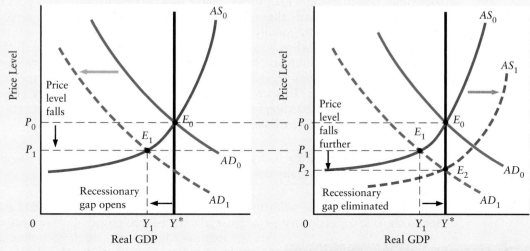

(i) Negative *AD* shock   (ii) Wage adjustment shifts *AS*

A negative *AD* shock first lowers the price level and GDP along the *AS* curve and then induces a (possibly slow) shift of the *AS* curve that further lowers prices but raises output along the new *AD* curve. In part (i), the economy is in equilibrium at E_0, at its level of potential output, Y^*, and price level P_0. The *AD* curve then shifts to AD_1, moving equilibrium to E_1, with income Y_1 and price level P_1, and opens up a recessionary gap.

Part (ii) shows the adjustment back to potential output that occurs from the supply side of the economy. The fall in wages shifts the *AS* curve downward. Real GDP rises, and the price level falls further along the new *AD* curve. Unless wages are completely rigid, the *AS* curve eventually reaches AS_1, with equilibrium at E_2. The price level stabilizes at P_2 when real GDP returns to Y^*, closing the recessionary gap.

Contractionary *AD* Shocks

Suppose again that the economy starts with stable prices and real GDP equal to potential, as shown in part (i) of Figure 24-3. Now assume there is a *decline* in aggregate demand. This negative aggregate demand shock might be a reduction in investment expenditure, or perhaps a decline in the world demand for Canadian lumber or automobiles.

The first effects of the decline are a fall in output and some downward adjustment of prices, as shown in part (i) of the figure. As real GDP falls below potential, a recessionary gap is created, and unemployment rises. At this point we must analyze two separate cases. The first occurs when wages fall quickly in response to the excess supply of labour. The second occurs when wages fall only slowly.

Practise with Study Guide
Chapter 24, Exercise 6.

Flexible Wages Suppose wages (and other factor prices) fell quickly in response to the recessionary gap. The *AS* curve would therefore shift quickly downward as the lower wages led to reduced unit costs.

As shown in part (ii) of Figure 24-3, the economy would move along the new *AD* curve, with falling prices and rising output, until real GDP was quickly restored to potential, Y^*. We conclude that if wages were to fall rapidly whenever there was unemployment, the resulting shift in the *AS* curve would quickly eliminate recessionary gaps.

> Flexible wages that fall rapidly in the presence of a recessionary gap provide an automatic adjustment process that pushes the economy back quickly toward potential output.

Sticky Wages As we noted earlier, the experience of most economies suggests that wages typically do not fall rapidly in response to even large recessionary gaps. It is sometimes said that wages are "sticky" in the downward direction. This does not mean that wages never fall, only that they tend to fall much more slowly in a recessionary gap than they rise in an equally sized inflationary gap. When wages are sticky, the analysis is the same as when wages are flexible, and thus Figure 24-3 tells the correct story. The significant difference, however, is that the *AS* curve shifts more slowly when wages are sticky and thus recessionary gaps may not be removed by the adjustment process for a long time. In such cases, the recessionary gap is usually closed as the result of an eventual expansion in aggregate demand that occurs for reasons discussed later in this chapter in *Extensions in Theory 24-2* on page 604.

> If wages are downwardly sticky, the economy's adjustment process is sluggish and thus recessionary gaps may not be eliminated quickly.[3]

The weakness of the adjustment process following a negative demand shock does not mean that recessionary gaps must always be prolonged. Rather, this weakness

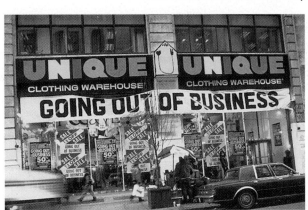

means that speedy recovery back to potential output must be generated mainly from the demand side. If wages are downwardly sticky and the economy is to avoid a persistent recessionary gap, a quick recovery requires a rightward shift of the *AD* curve. This often happens when private-sector demand revives. But it also raises the possibility that government *stabilization policy* can be used to accomplish such a rightward shift in the *AD* curve. This is an important and contentious issue in macroeconomics, one to which we will return often throughout the remainder of this book.

The slow downward adjustment of wages and prices when output is below potential means that the recessionary effects of negative shocks sometimes persist for long periods.

The difference in the speed of adjustment of wages (and other factor prices) is the important asymmetry in the behaviour of aggregate supply that we noted earlier in this chapter. This asymmetry helps to explain two key facts about the Canadian economy. First, high unemployment can persist for quite long periods without causing decreases in wages and prices of sufficient magnitude to remove the unemployment. An example is the 1991–1995 period when unemployment was high and output was considerably below potential. Second, booms, along with labour shortages and production beyond normal capacity, do not persist for long periods without causing increases in wages and the price level. The periods 1987–1990, 1999–2001, and 2004–2007 all displayed output above potential and pressure on wages and prices to rise.

Aggregate Supply Shocks

We have discussed the economy's adjustment process that returns real GDP to Y^* following an aggregate demand shock. The same adjustment process operates following an aggregate supply shock.

---

[3] The causes of downward wage stickiness have been hotly debated among macroeconomists for years. We discuss several possible reasons in Chapter 31 when examining the causes of cyclical unemployment.

Consider an economy that has a stable price level and real GDP at its potential level, as illustrated by point E_0 in part (i) of Figure 24-4. Suppose there is an increase in the world price of an important input, such as oil. An increase in the price of oil increases unit costs for firms and causes the AS curve to shift upward. Real GDP falls and the price level increases—a combination often called *stagflation*. The short-run equilibrium is at point E_1 in Figure 24-4. With the opening of a recessionary gap, the economy's adjustment process comes into play, though sticky wages reduce the speed of this adjustment.

In our macro model, the recessionary gap caused by the negative supply shock causes firms to shut down and workers to be laid off. The excess supply of labour (and other factors) eventually pushes wages down and begins to reverse the initial increase in unit costs caused by the increase in the price of oil. This adjustment is shown in part (ii) of the figure. As wages fall, the AS curve shifts back toward its starting point, and real GDP rises back toward its potential level, Y^*. Eventually, the economy returns to its initial point, E_0. Note, however, that *relative* prices will have changed when the economy returns to E_0. The price level is back to P_0, its starting point, but real wages are lower while the relative price of oil is higher.

We leave it to the reader to analyze the adjustment process following a positive aggregate supply shock. The logic of the analysis is exactly the same as illustrated in Figure 24-4, except that the initial shift in the AS curve is to the right, creating an inflationary gap.

Exogenous changes in input prices cause the AS curve to shift, creating an output gap. The adjustment process then reverses the initial AS shift and brings the economy back to potential output and the initial price level.

FIGURE 24-4   The Adjustment Process Following a Negative Aggregate Supply Shock

(i) Negative AS shock

(ii) Wage adjustment returns AS to initial position

A negative AS shock caused by an increase in input prices causes real GDP to fall and the price level to rise. The economy's adjustment process then reverses the AS shift and returns the economy to its starting point. The economy begins at point E_0 in part (i). The increase in the price of oil increases unit costs and causes the AS curve to shift up to AS_1. Real GDP falls to Y_1 and the price level rises to P_1. A recessionary gap is created. In part (ii), the excess supply of labour associated with the recessionary gap causes wages to fall, possibly slowly. As wages fall, unit costs fall and so the AS curve shifts back down to AS_0. The economy is finally in long-run equilibrium at Y^* and P_0, its starting point.

In this chapter we have emphasized the adjustment of wages to output gaps, and how this adjustment process returns real GDP to Y^* following AD or AS shocks. However, there are *additional* forces in the economy that also help to explain how real GDP changes over the business cycle. *Extensions in Theory 24-2* examines the dynamics of the business cycle in more detail.

Long-Run Equilibrium

Following any AD or AS shocks, we have assumed that the adjustment process continues until real GDP returns to Y^*. The economy is said to be in a state of *long-run*

EXTENSIONS IN THEORY 24-2

The Business Cycle: Additional Pressures for Adjustment

In earlier chapters we described the *business cycle* as the ebb and flow of economic activity that alternately tends to create recessionary and inflationary output gaps. In this chapter, we have seen that the factor-price adjustment process tends to eliminate such output gaps whenever they appear. The business cycle itself provides an *additional* set of pressures that reinforces the adjustment of factor prices and helps to return real GDP to Y^*.

During the expansionary phase of the business cycle, real GDP is growing; as the peak of the cycle is reached, real GDP is typically well above Y^* and unemployment is low. Expectations of rising sales and profits created during the economic expansion often lead to gains in stock-market prices that are not justified by current earnings; in addition, firms may undertake capital investments based on the assumption that the economic expansion will continue. As real GDP rises further above Y^*, however, bottlenecks and shortages eventually arise and restrict further expansion, thus slowing the growth rate of real GDP. When growth slows in this way, there is often a drastic revision in firms' expectations. A sell-off of stocks may cause their prices to tumble, thereby reducing consumers' wealth and confidence and hence causing them to curtail their consumption expenditures. The slowdown in growth, combined with the collapse of confidence, can lead firms to reduce their desired investment. These reductions in household consumption and business investment work, through the economy's multiplier process, to reduce real GDP. Thus, even in the absence of wage increases, an economic expansion usually contains the seeds of its own demise; real GDP tends to move back toward Y^*.

Once underway, the economic downturn tends to feed on itself as confidence wanes even further, leading to more cuts in investment and consumer spending. The downturn often overshoots Y^*, creating a recessionary gap. A trough is eventually reached, in which real GDP is well below Y^* and unemployment is high. At this point, the pace of economic activity begins to rise. Stocks of durable consumer goods, such as automobiles and home appliances, that were not replaced during the downturn eventually become depleted or obsolete enough that normal replacement expenditures recover, leading to an increase in the demand for such goods. Similarly, much of firms' replacement investment that has been put off during the economic downturn can be postponed no longer and investment expenditure recovers. The resulting recovery in both household and business spending can cause a revival of favourable expectations concerning the future, leading to further increases in spending. The increases in household consumption and business investment work, through the economy's multiplier process, to increase real GDP. Thus, even in the absence of falling wages, an economic downturn is usually followed by a recovery with real GDP rising back toward Y^*.

In summary, we should note two distinct forces that tend to return real GDP to Y^*. During an inflationary gap, both rising wages (which shift the AS curve to the left) and the intrinsic dynamics of the business cycle (which shift the AD curve to the right) are powerful forces. However, since wages are quite slow to adjust in the downward direction, the business cycle dynamics typically play a much larger role than the wage-adjustment process in bringing about a recovery from a recession. In this chapter, we have concentrated on understanding how the wage-adjustment process works. It must be remembered, however, that its strength is asymmetric, strong in removing an inflationary gap but much weaker in removing a recessionary one.

equilibrium when factor prices are no longer adjusting to output gaps. As we have seen, wages and other factor prices are assumed to be stable only when the level of real GDP is equal to potential output, Y^*. Thus, in our model, the economy is in its long-run equilibrium when the intersection of the AD and AS curves occurs at Y^*.

The value of Y^* depends on real variables, such as the labour force, capital stock, and the level of technology, but is independent of nominal variables, such as the price level. In other words, the level of output that firms will produce in the long run is independent of the price level. The vertical line at Y^* that we have seen in our diagrams is therefore sometimes called a *long-run aggregate supply curve*—the relationship between the price level and the amount of output supplied by firms *after all factor prices have adjusted to output gaps*. This vertical line is also sometimes called a *Classical aggregate supply curve* because the Classical economists were mainly concerned with the behaviour of the economy in long-run equilibrium.[4]

Figure 24-5 shows an *AD/AS* diagram without the usual upward-sloping *AS* curve. It is useful to omit this curve if our focus is on the state of the economy *after* all factor prices have fully adjusted and output has returned to Y^*. We can use this diagram to examine how shocks affect the economy's long-run equilibrium.

As shown in part (i) of Figure 24-5, any shift in the *AD* curve will cause a change in the price level in the long run but will not affect the level of potential output, Y^*. In our model, the only way that real GDP can change in the long run (*after* factor prices have fully adjusted) is for the level of Y^* to change, as in part (ii) of the figure.

> In the long run, real GDP is determined solely by Y^*; the role of aggregate demand is only to determine the price level.

We will discuss the long-run behaviour of the economy in detail in Chapters 25 and 26. There we develop theories explaining why Y^* grows over extended periods of time and why this growth is important for determining our material living standards.

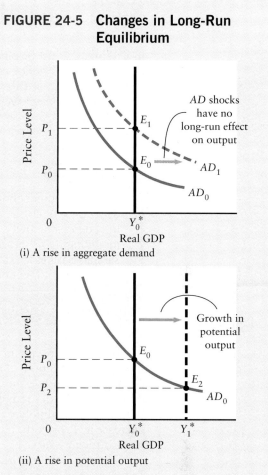

FIGURE 24-5 Changes in Long-Run Equilibrium

(i) A rise in aggregate demand

(ii) A rise in potential output

Potential output determines the long-run equilibrium value of real GDP. Given Y^*, aggregate demand determines the long-run equilibrium value of the price level. In both parts of the figure, the initial long-run equilibrium is at E_0, so the price level is P_0 and real GDP is Y_0^*.

In part (i), a shift in the AD curve from AD_0 to AD_1 moves the long-run equilibrium from E_0 to E_1. This raises the price level from P_0 to P_1 but leaves real GDP unchanged at Y_0^* in the long run.

In part (ii), an increase in potential output from Y_0^* to Y_1^* moves the long-run equilibrium from E_0 to E_2. This raises real GDP from Y_0^* to Y_1^* and lowers the price level from P_0 to P_2.

---

[4] The Classical school of economic thought began with Adam Smith (1723–1790) and was developed through the work of David Ricardo (1772–1823), Thomas Malthus (1766–1834), and John Stuart Mill (1806–1873). These economists emphasized the long-run behaviour of the economy. Beginning in the middle of the nineteenth century, Neoclassical economists devoted much time and effort to studying short-term fluctuations. *The General Theory of Employment, Interest and Money* (1936), written by John Maynard Keynes (1883–1946), was in a long tradition of the study of short-term fluctuations. Where Keynes differed from the Neoclassical economists was in approaching the issues from a macroeconomic perspective that emphasized fluctuations in expenditure. Each of the economists mentioned in this footnote, along with several others, is discussed in more detail in the timeline at the back of the book.

24.3 Fiscal Stabilization Policy

In Chapter 22, we briefly considered the basic concepts of fiscal stabilization policy. In principle, this policy can be used to stabilize real GDP at or near potential output. In the remainder of this chapter, we look into taxing and spending as tools of fiscal stabilization policy. We will return to more advanced issues of fiscal policy in Chapter 32.

---

myeconlab **ADDITIONAL TOPICS**

Though macroeconomists tend to focus on fluctuations in real GDP when describing business cycles, there is no single "best" measure of the changes in economic activity. For a detailed description of several popular measures— including GDP growth, housing starts, and capacity utilization—look for **Several Measures of Economic Fluctuations in Canada** in the *Additional Topics* section of this book's MyEconLab.

www.myeconlab.com

Because increases in government purchases (G) increase aggregate demand and increases in taxation (T) decrease aggregate demand, the *direction* of the required changes in spending and taxation is generally easy to determine once we know the direction of the desired change in real GDP. For example, if output is currently below potential, a fiscal policy designed to increase real GDP will include an increase in G, a decrease in T, or both. However, the *timing, magnitude,* and *mixture* of the changes are more difficult issues.

There is no doubt that the government can exert a major influence on real GDP. Prime examples are the massive increases in military spending during major wars. Canadian federal expenditure during the Second World War rose from 12.2 percent of GDP in 1939 to 41.8 percent in 1944. At the same time, the unemployment rate fell from 11.4 percent to 1.4 percent. Economists agree that the increase in government spending helped to bring about the rise in output and the associated fall in unemployment. More recently, the Canadian government dramatically increased spending in an effort to dampen the effects of the major global recession that began in late 2008. Most economists agree that this "fiscal stimulus" contributed significantly to real GDP growth in the 2009–2010 period.

In the heyday of "activist" fiscal policy, from about 1945 to about 1970, many economists were convinced that the economy could be stabilized adequately just by varying the size of the government's taxes and expenditures. That day is past. Today, economists are more aware of the many limitations of fiscal policy.

For information on the federal Department of Finance, the ministry in charge of fiscal policy, see **www.fin.gc.ca**.

The Basic Theory of Fiscal Stabilization

In our macroeconomic model, a reduction in tax rates or an increase in government purchases will shift the *AD* curve to the right, causing an increase in real GDP. An increase in tax rates or a cut in government expenditure will shift the *AD* curve to the left, causing a decrease in real GDP.

FIGURE 24-6   The Closing of a Recessionary Gap

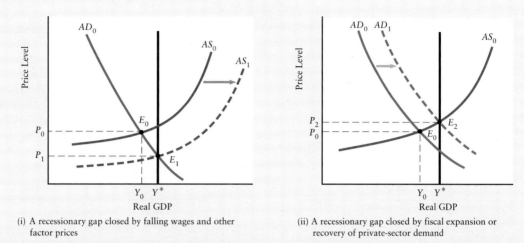

(i) A recessionary gap closed by falling wages and other factor prices

(ii) A recessionary gap closed by fiscal expansion or recovery of private-sector demand

A recessionary gap may be closed by a (slow) downward shift of the AS curve or an increase in aggregate demand. Initially, equilibrium is at E_0, with real GDP at Y_0 and the price level at P_0. There is a recessionary gap.

As shown in part (i), the gap might be removed by a shift in the AS curve to AS_1, as will eventually happen when wages and other factor prices fall in response to excess supply. The shift in the AS curve causes a movement down and to the right along AD_0 to a new equilibrium at E_1, achieving potential output Y^* and lowering the price level to P_1.

As shown in part (ii), the gap might also be removed by a shift of the AD curve to AD_1, caused by an expansionary fiscal policy or a recovery of private-sector spending. The shift in the AD curve causes a movement up and to the right along AS_0. This movement shifts the equilibrium to E_2, raising output to Y^* and the price level to P_2.

How Fiscal Stabilization Works   A more detailed look at how fiscal stabilization works will help to show some of the complications that arise when implementing fiscal policy.

Practise with Study Guide
Chapter 24, Exercises 3 and 5, and Extension Exercise E1.

CLOSING A RECESSIONARY GAP. A recessionary gap is shown in Figure 24-6; the economy's short-run equilibrium is at point E_0 with real GDP below Y^*. Such a recessionary gap can be closed in three ways, returning real GDP to Y^*. First, as often happens in practice, private-sector demand recovers and the AD curve shifts to the right, as shown in part (ii) of the figure. If such a recovery does not occur rapidly, the economy's adjustment process will come into play. The excess supply of factors at E_0 will eventually cause wages and other factor prices to fall, shifting the AS curve downward and restoring output to Y^*, as shown in part (i) of the figure. However, as we also discussed, because of the stickiness of wages, this process may take a long time. Policymakers may not be prepared to wait the time necessary for the recessionary gap to correct itself. The government can instead use expansionary fiscal policy to shift the AD curve to the right and close the recessionary gap. It would do this by reducing tax rates, increasing transfers, or increasing the level of government purchases.

The advantage of using fiscal policy rather than allowing the economy's adjustment process to operate is that it may substantially shorten what might otherwise be a long recession. One disadvantage is that the use of fiscal policy may stimulate the economy just before private-sector spending recovers on its own. As a result, the economy may overshoot its potential output, and an inflationary gap may open up. In this case, fiscal policy that is intended to promote economic stability can actually cause instability.

FIGURE 24-7   The Closing of an Inflationary Gap

 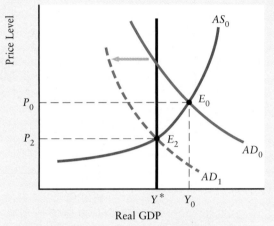

(i) An inflationary gap closed by rising wages and other factor prices

(ii) An inflationary gap closed by contractionary fiscal policy or a reduction in private-sector demand

An inflationary gap may be removed by an upward shift of the *AS* curve or by a leftward shift of the *AD* curve. Initially, equilibrium is at E_0, with real GDP at Y_0 and the price level at P_0. There is an inflationary gap.

As shown in part (i), the gap might be removed by a shift in the *AS* curve to AS_1, as will happen when wages and other factor prices rise in response to the excess demand. The shift in the *AS* curve causes a movement up and to the left along AD_0. This movement establishes a new equilibrium at E_1, reducing output to its potential level Y^* and raising the price level to P_1.

As shown in part (ii), the gap might also be removed by a shift in the *AD* curve to AD_1 caused by, for example, a contractionary fiscal policy. The shift in the *AD* curve causes a movement down and to the left along AS_0. This movement shifts the equilibrium to E_2, lowering income to Y^* and the price level to P_2.

CLOSING AN INFLATIONARY GAP. An inflationary gap is illustrated in Figure 24-7; the economy's short-run equilibrium is at point E_0, with real GDP above Y^*. There are three ways such an inflationary gap may be closed, returning real GDP to Y^*. First, private-sector demand may fall, thus shifting the *AD* curve to the left. If this does not occur rapidly, the economy's adjustment process will come into play; excess demand for factors will cause wages and other factor prices to rise, shifting the *AS* curve upward and gradually restoring output to Y^*. Alternatively, the government can use a contractionary fiscal policy to shift the *AD* curve to the left and close the inflationary gap. The government would do this by increasing tax rates or reducing its level of purchases.

The advantage of using a contractionary fiscal policy to close the inflationary gap is that it avoids the inflationary increase in prices that would otherwise occur. One disadvantage is that if private-sector expenditures fall because of natural causes, real GDP may be pushed below potential, thus opening up a recessionary gap.

This discussion leads to a key proposition:

> **When the economy's adjustment process is slow to operate, or produces undesirable side effects, such as rising prices, there is a potential stabilization role for fiscal policy.**

The Paradox of Thrift Suppose you have a good job but you are sufficiently unsure about your economic future that you decide to increase the fraction of disposable income that you save. Your increased saving today would not influence your current income but these funds would accumulate and be useful in the future if your economic situation changed for the worse. Most people would agree that a decision to increase your saving in these circumstances would be prudent.

But what would happen if *many people* did the same thing at the same time? In our macroeconomic model, an increase in the country's total desired saving would shift the *AD* curve to the left and *reduce* the equilibrium level of real GDP in the short run. Thus, frugality on the part of individuals, which may seem to be prudent behaviour for each individual taken separately, ends up reducing short-run real GDP. This phenomenon is known as the *paradox of thrift*—the paradox being that what may be good for any individual when viewed in isolation ends up being undesirable for the economy as a whole.

The policy implication of this phenomenon is that a major and persistent recession can be battled by encouraging

When the Canadian economy entered a significant recession in the fall of 2008, Canadian households and firms responded by decreasing their level of spending. Governments generally understood that such frugality on the part of the private sector generated a need for greater public spending, thus stimulating aggregate demand and dampening the overall effects of the recession.

governments, firms, and households to reduce their saving and therefore increase their spending. In times of unemployment and recession, a greater desire to save will only make things worse. This result goes directly against the idea that we should "tighten our belts" when times are tough. The notion that it is not only possible but even *desirable* to spend one's way out of a recession touches a sensitive point with people raised on the belief that success is based on hard work and frugality; as a result, the idea often arouses great hostility.

As is discussed in *Lessons from History 24-1,* the implications of the paradox of thrift were not generally understood during the Great Depression of the 1930s. Most governments, faced with depression-induced reductions in tax revenues, reduced their expenditures to balance their budgets. As a result, many economists argue that the fiscal policies at the time actually made things worse. When Nobel Prize–winning economist Milton Friedman (many years later) said, "We are all Keynesians now," he was referring to the general acceptance of the view that the government's budget is much more than just the revenue and expenditure statement of a very large organization. Whether we like it or not, the sheer size of the government's budget inevitably makes it a powerful tool for influencing the economy.

The paradox of thrift applies to shifts in aggregate demand that have been caused by changes in saving (and hence spending) behaviour. That is why it applies only in the short run, when the *AD* curve plays an important role in the determination of real GDP.

The paradox of thrift does not apply after factor prices have fully adjusted and the economy has achieved its new long-run equilibrium. Remember that in the long run, aggregate demand does not influence the level of real GDP—output is determined only by the level of potential output, Y^*. In the long run, the more people and government save, the larger is the supply of funds available for investment. As we will see in Chapter 26, this increase in the pool of available funds will reduce interest rates and encourage more investment by firms. The greater rate of investment leads to a higher rate of growth of potential output.

LESSONS FROM HISTORY 24-1

Fiscal Policy in the Great Depression

The Great Depression, which is usually dated as beginning with the massive stock-market crash on October 29, 1929, was one of the most dramatic economic events of the twentieth century. As the accompanying figure shows, Canadian real GDP plummeted by almost 30 percent from its peak in 1929 to its low point in 1933. The price level actually *fell* beginning in 1930 and declined by about 20 percent over the next five years. The unemployment rate increased from 3 percent of the labour force in 1929 to an unparalleled 19.3 percent four years later. To put these numbers in perspective, by today's standards a very serious recession (like the most recent one that began in late 2008) sees real GDP fall by 2–3 percent, the unemployment rate rise to 9–10 percent, and prices continue rising but perhaps at a slower rate. The economic events of the 1930s certainly deserve to be called the Great Depression!

The Great Depression was not just a catastrophic event that happened exogenously—its depth and duration were made worse by some fundamental mistakes in policy. Failure to understand the implication of the paradox of thrift led many countries to adopt disastrous fiscal policies during the Great Depression. In addition, failure to understand the role of automatic stabilizers has led many observers to conclude, erroneously, that fiscal expansion was tried in the Great Depression but failed. Let us see how these two misperceptions are related.

The Paradox of Thrift in Action

In 1932, Canadian Prime Minister R. B. Bennett said, "We are now faced with the real crisis in the history of Canada. To maintain our credit we must practise the most rigid economy and not spend a single cent." His government that year—at the deepest point in the recession—brought down a budget based on the principle of trying to balance revenues and expenditures, and it included *increases* in tax rates.

In the same year, Franklin Roosevelt was elected U.S. president on a platform of fighting the Great Depression with government policies. In his inaugural address he urged, "Our great primary task is to put people to work. . . . [This task] can be helped by insistence that the federal, state, and local governments act forthwith on the demand that their costs be drastically reduced. . . ."

Across the Atlantic, King George V told the British House of Commons in 1931, "The present condition of the national finances, in the opinion of His Majesty's ministers, calls for the imposition of additional taxation and for the effecting of economies in public expenditure."

As the paradox of thrift predicts, these policies tended to worsen, rather than cure, the Depression.

Interpreting the Deficits in the 1930s

In general, governments can have a budget deficit for two different reasons. First, a government might increase its level of purchases without increasing its tax revenues. Such a *deficit-financed* increase in government spending represents an expansion in aggregate demand. Second, a government might leave its purchases unchanged but have lower tax revenues. If

---

The paradox of thrift—the idea that an increase in saving reduces the level of real GDP—is only true in the short run. In the long run, the path of real GDP is determined by the path of potential output. The increase in saving has the long-run effect of increasing investment and therefore increasing potential output.

Automatic Fiscal Stabilizers The fiscal policies that we have been discussing are referred to as *discretionary* because the government uses its discretion in changing its taxation or its purchases in an attempt to change the level of real GDP. However, even if the government makes no active decisions regarding changes in its purchases or taxation, the mere existence of the government's tax-and-transfer system will act as an *automatic stabilizer* for the economy. Let's see how this works.

the lower tax revenues are caused by a policy decision to reduce *tax rates*, then this policy also represents an expansion in aggregate demand. But if the decline in tax revenues is caused by a fall in real GDP with unchanged tax rates, the existing budget deficit *does not* represent an expansion in aggregate demand. These distinctions are central to interpreting the budget deficits of the 1930s.

Government budget deficits did increase in the 1930s, but they were not the result of a program of deficit-financed public expenditure. Rather, they were the result of the fall in tax revenues, brought about by the fall in real GDP as the economy sank into depression. The various governments did not advocate programs of massive deficit-financed spending to shift the *AD* curve to the right. Instead, they hoped that a small amount of government spending in addition to numerous policies designed to stabilize prices and to restore confidence would lead to a recovery of private investment expenditure that would substantially shift the *AD* curve. To have expected a massive revival of private investment expenditure as a result of the puny increase in aggregate demand that was instituted by the federal government now seems hopelessly naïve.

When we judge these policies from the viewpoint of modern theory, their failure is no mystery. Indeed, Professor E. Cary Brown of MIT, after a careful study for the United States, concluded, "Fiscal policy seems to have been an unsuccessful recovery device in the thirties—not because it did not work, but because it was not tried." Once the massive, war-geared expenditure of the 1940s began, output responded sharply and unemployment all but evaporated. A similar pattern occurred in Canada, as seen clearly in the figure.

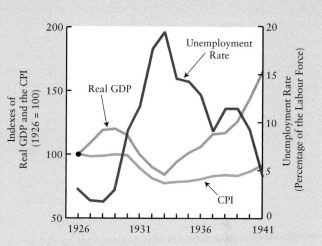

The performance of the Canadian and U.S. economies from 1930 to 1945 is well explained by the macroeconomic theory that we have developed in the last few chapters. It is clear that the governments did not effectively use fiscal policy to stabilize their economies. War brought the Depression to an end because war demands made acceptable a level of government expenditure sufficient to remove the recessionary gap. Had the Canadian and American administrations been able to do the same in the early 1930s, it might have ended the waste of the Great Depression many years sooner.

(*Source:* Urquhart, M.C., and K.A.H. Buckley, ed. 1965. *Historical Statistics of Canada.* Toronto: Macmillan.)

When we first introduced government to our macro model in Chapter 22, we made the assumptions that government purchases (*G*) were autonomous with respect to national income but that government net tax revenues (*T*) were positively related to national income. Specifically, we assumed that

$$T = tY$$

where *t* is the net tax rate. This positive relationship between *T* and *Y* has an important implication for the stability of the economy in response to shocks to autonomous expenditure.

For example, consider a shock that shifts the *AD* curve to the right and thus increases the short-run level of real GDP. As real GDP increases, tax revenues rise and, as there are fewer low-income households and unemployed persons requiring assistance, transfer payments fall. The rise in net tax revenues (taxes minus transfers) dampens the extent to which the rise in national income leads to induced increases in spending (and then, through the multiplier process, to further increases in real GDP). In other words, the tax-and-transfer system reduces the value of the multiplier and thus acts as an **automatic stabilizer** for the economy. In the absence of the tax-and-transfer system, the multiplier would be larger and thus any given positive shock would lead to a larger shift in the *AD* curve and thus to a larger increase in real GDP.

The same is true in the presence of a negative *AD* shock. As real GDP declines in response to the shock, government's net tax revenues fall, thus dampening the extent to which the fall in *Y* leads to induced reductions in spending and thus further reductions in output.

automatic stabilizers
Elements of the tax-and-transfer system that reduce the responsiveness of real GDP to changes in autonomous expenditure.

Even in the absence of discretionary fiscal stabilization policy, the presence of net taxes that vary with national income provides the economy with an automatic stabilizer.

At the end of Chapter 22 we argued that realistic Canadian values for our model's key parameters are as follows:

- marginal propensity to consume (*MPC*) = 0.8
- net tax rate (*t*) = 0.3
- marginal propensity to import (*m*) = 0.35

The implied value of *z*, the marginal propensity to spend on national income, is therefore

$$z = MPC(1 - t) - m$$
$$= (0.8)(0.7) - 0.35 = 0.21$$

As a result, a realistic value for the simple multiplier in Canada is

$$\text{Simple multiplier} = 1/(1 - z) = 1/0.79 = 1.27$$

The lower is the net tax rate, the larger is the simple multiplier and thus the less stable is real GDP in response to shocks to autonomous spending. For example, if the net tax rate were reduced to 20 percent (*t* = 0.20), the value of *z* would rise to 0.29 and the simple multiplier would rise to $1/(1 - 0.29) = 1/0.71 = 1.41$. The larger multiplier implies that a shock to autonomous expenditure would result in a larger shift in the *AD* curve and thus a larger total change in GDP—that is, the economy would be less stable. Therefore, whatever benefits might arise from a reduction in the net tax rate (and we will see later that lower tax rates may tend to increase the economy's long-run growth rate), one drawback is that the tax reduction would lead to the economy being less stable following shocks to autonomous expenditure.[5]

The great advantage of automatic fiscal stabilizers is that they are "automatic." As long as the tax-and-transfer system is in place (and there is no sign of its imminent disappearance!) some stability is provided without anyone having to make active decisions about fiscal policy. As we see next, the sorts of decisions required for successful *discretionary* fiscal policy are not simple, and some attempts to provide stability through discretionary fiscal policy may actually reduce the stability of the economy.

[5] We have said that automatic stabilizers reduce the multiplier so that a given change in autonomous expenditures leads to a smaller shift in the *AD* curve than would otherwise be the case. It is also true that the same automatic stabilizers lead to a *steeper AD* curve; the result is that real GDP is more stable in the presence of *AS* shocks.

Practical Limitations of Discretionary Fiscal Policy

According to our earlier discussion of fiscal stabilization policy, returning the economy to potential output would appear to be a simple matter of changing taxes and government spending, in some combination. Why do so many economists believe that such policies would be "as likely to harm as help"? Part of the answer is that the practical use of discretionary fiscal policy is anything but simple.

Decision and Execution Lags To change fiscal policy requires making changes in taxes and government expenditures. The changes must be agreed on by the Cabinet and passed by Parliament. The political stakes in such changes are generally very large; taxes and spending are called "bread-and-butter issues" precisely because they affect the economic well-being of almost everyone. Even if economists agreed that the economy would be helped by, say, a tax cut, politicians would likely spend a good deal of time debating *whose* taxes should be cut and by *how much*. If the assessment by economists was that an increase in government spending was desirable, the lengthy political debate would then be about what *type* of spending should increase and whether it should focus on particular industries or regions. The delay between the initial recognition of a recessionary or inflationary gap and the enactment of legislation to change fiscal policy, which may be several months long, is called a **decision lag.**

Once policy changes are agreed on, there is still an **execution lag**, adding time between the enactment of the legislation and the implementation of the policy action. Furthermore, once the new policies are in place, it will usually take still more time for their economic consequences to be felt. Because of these lags, it is quite possible that by the time a given policy decision has any impact on the economy, circumstances will have changed such that the policy is no longer appropriate.

Both decision lags and execution lags were apparent in the fiscal response to the major recession that began in late 2008. The economies of many countries, including Canada's, experienced a very rapid slowdown in late 2008, driven largely by the global financial crisis that began a year earlier. However, the slowdown was so rapid that it created a great deal of confusion among economists and politicians. And in many countries it was not clear which fiscal actions would be necessary, or when. In Canada, the situation was even more complicated because of a federal election campaign, which understandably distracted many politicians from focusing on the economy.

When the Conservatives were re-elected and passed an early budget in January 2009, the execution lags soon became apparent. The budget contained a combination of increased spending on infrastructure and selected tax reductions. This infrastructure spending, however, was to be shared between the federal and provincial governments. It soon became apparent that the negotiations between the different levels of government—often driven by political concerns—slowed the process, and the spending occurred later than initially intended.

Temporary Versus Permanent Tax Changes To make matters even more frustrating, changes in taxation that are known to be temporary are generally less effective than measures that are expected to be permanent. For example, if households know that an announced tax cut will last only a year, they may recognize that the effect on their long-run consumption possibilities is small and may choose to save their tax-cut-induced increase in disposable income rather than spend it. If so, the effect of the tax cut on aggregate demand will be nil. Thus, the more closely household consumption expenditure is related to *lifetime* income rather than to *current* income, the smaller will be the effects on current consumption of tax changes that are known to be of short duration. Or, to use the language that we used when introducing the consumption

decision lag The period of time between perceiving some problem and reaching a decision on what to do about it.

execution lag The time that it takes to put policies in place after a decision has been made.

function in Chapter 21, the more forward-looking are households, the smaller will be the effects of what are perceived to be temporary changes in taxes.

The Role of Discretionary Fiscal Policy

fine tuning The attempt to maintain output at its potential level by means of frequent changes in fiscal or monetary policy.

Attempts to use discretionary fiscal policy to "fine tune" the economy are thus fraught with difficulties. **Fine tuning** refers to the use of fiscal (and monetary) policy to offset virtually all fluctuations in private-sector spending so as to keep real GDP at or near its potential level. However, neither economic nor political science has yet advanced far enough to allow policymakers to undo the consequences of every aggregate demand or supply shock. Nevertheless, many economists still argue that when a recessionary gap is large enough and persists for long enough, *gross tuning* may be appropriate. **Gross tuning** refers to the use of fiscal and monetary policy to remove large and persistent output gaps. Other economists believe that fiscal policy should not be used for economic stabilization under any circumstances. Rather, they would argue, tax and spending behaviour should be the outcome of public choices regarding the long-term size and financing of the public sector and should not be altered for short-term considerations. We return to these debates in Chapter 32.

gross tuning The use of macroeconomic policy to stabilize the economy such that large deviations from potential output do not persist for extended periods of time.

The global economic slowdown that began in 2008 led Canada and many other countries to significantly increase government spending in an effort to stimulate their slumping economies. See *Applying Economic Concepts 24-1* for a discussion of the Canadian federal budget of 2009.

Fiscal Policy and Growth

Practise with Study Guide
Chapter 24, Exercise 4.

Fiscal policy has both short-run and long-run effects on the economy. Its short-run effects, which we have discussed in this chapter, are reflected by shifts in the *AD* curve and changes in the level of GDP. However, the theory presented here predicts that the adjustment of factor prices will eventually bring real GDP back to Y^* so that the long-run effects of any given fiscal policy will depend on the policy's effects on Y^*. In both of the following examples, to highlight the difference between the short-run and long-run effects of the policies, we imagine starting in a macroeconomic equilibrium with real GDP equal to Y^*.

Increases in Government Purchases

A fiscal expansion created by an increase in government purchases (G) will shift the *AD* curve to the right and increase real GDP in the short run. As factor prices rise in response to the inflationary output gap, output will return back to Y^* but at a higher price level. As we will see in detail in later chapters, even though real GDP may return to Y^*, the *composition* of output will be altered. From the national-income accounting we saw in Chapter 20, we know that $Y = C_a + I_a + G_a + NX_a$, where the "$a$" subscripts denote the actual components of aggregate expenditure. If real GDP returns to Y^* after factor prices have fully adjusted, then the *rise* in G_a must be equal to the *fall* in $C_a + I_a + NX_a$. In this case we say that the increase in government purchases has "crowded out" private expenditures. Of particular concern is the possibility that private investment in plant and equipment will be reduced. If investment is crowded out, there will be a slower rate of accumulation of physical capital, and this will likely lead to a reduction in the future growth rate of potential output.[6]

---

[6] Since some of the rise in G_a may be government investment in such things as roads or power plants or other productivity-enhancing infrastructure, the overall effect on the path of Y^* depends on the productivity of the new public investment compared with that of the private investment that was crowded out.

APPLYING ECONOMIC CONCEPTS 24-1

Canada's Fiscal Response to the 2008–2009 Recession

A major global recession began in the closing months of 2008, with a large number of developed economies experiencing reductions in real GDP. The proximate cause of the recession was the collapse in U.S. housing prices, which started in 2006 and continued for three years. This collapse led to massive declines in the values of home mortgages and related financial securities that had been purchased by banks and other financial institutions around the world. What began as a U.S. housing problem therefore soon became a global financial crisis. The financial crisis and associated bank failures led to a sharp decline in the flow of credit, which is an essential input to most firms who need credit to finance their operations and capital purchases. It was only a matter of time before production and employment were affected in most countries.

The sharp decline in U.S. and global economic activity soon affected the Canadian economy. Canadian exports declined sharply in 2008 and 2009 across many industries but especially in the forestry and auto sectors, which are closely connected with the housing and auto sectors in the United States. Real GDP declined at an annual rate of more than 5 percent during the first half of 2009. Over this same short period, more than 300 000 Canadian jobs were lost and the unemployment rate increased by over three percentage points.

The remarkable synchronized nature of the global recession was testimony to the importance of financial markets, and especially the flow of credit, in the operation of modern economies. It also led to an unprecedented coordination among the leaders of the world's major economies. In late 2008 in Washington, D.C., the leaders of the G20 countries (the largest developed and developing countries) met and agreed to implement a package of measures designed to restore financial and economic stability. Central to their discussion was the stated need to take fiscal actions (increased government spending and/or reduced taxes) to provide economic stimulus of approximately 1–2 percent of GDP.

In January 2009, the Canadian government responded to these economic events with a budget aimed at stimulating the economy, both to dampen the pace of economic decline (by shifting the *AD* curve to the right) and to offer some protection to those Canadians who would most likely bear the burden of the recession—unemployed workers and low-income households.

The government accepted the majority view among economists (and discussed in Chapter 22) that direct government spending on goods and services provides more stimulus to the economy than does an equal dollar amount of tax reductions. The primary focus of the budget was therefore on infrastructure spending—for public projects at all levels of government, social housing, universities and colleges, and First Nations. The desire to protect the unemployed and low-income households led to the adoption of some targeted income-tax reductions and expansions of the employment-insurance program. The infrastructure and income-tax measures involved "partnering" with the provincial and territorial governments, thus increasing the scale of the fiscal stimulus.

Overall, the federal government's 2009 budget proposed approximately $23 billion of stimulus measures for the 2009–2010 fiscal year and $17 billion for the following year. Including the proposed partnering measures taken by lower levels of government, the total stimulus values were approximately $30 billion and $22 billion in the two fiscal years, an average across the two years of about 1.7 percent of annual GDP.

Even though an increase in government purchases may have no effect on the *current level* of potential output, the crowding out of private investment may reduce the *future growth rate* of potential output.

In this situation, the short-run stimulative benefits of the fiscal expansion need to be weighed against the possible long-run costs of lower growth. If the economy is currently in a deep recession and the economy's adjustment process is slow, the gain in short-run economic activity may well outweigh the costs of slower growth. After all, part of Keynes's central message was that the state of the world at potential output is not very interesting to members of a society who are a long way from it.

The analysis is slightly different, however, if the fiscal expansion is undertaken when real GDP is initially well below Y^*. In an ideal situation, the increase in government purchases is just enough to increase real GDP back to Y^* and is then reduced as private consumption and investment expenditure recover. In this case, the fiscal policy has put to work resources that would otherwise have been idle and it has no crowding out effect because it is reduced as private expenditure recovers. There is then a short-term gain from raising real GDP above what it would otherwise have been. There may even be some long-term gain to growth if the increased government expenditure was on productive assets, such as infrastructure. Of course, this is an ideal situation. If the government expenditure does not fall as private expenditure recovers, the situation becomes the first case with an expansionary fiscal policy combined with an economy already at Y^*. In this case, the short-run simulative benefits of the fiscal expansion need to be weighed against the long-run costs.

Reductions in Taxes A fiscal expansion created by a reduction in taxes is a little more complicated to analyze because there are likely to be longer-term, supply-side effects. The short-run demand-side effects are straightforward. Reductions in the GST rate or in the corporate or personal income-tax rates that are thought to be long-lasting will increase both investment and consumption spending and shift the AD curve to the right. The level of real GDP will rise in the short run. As wages and other factor prices increase, however, the level of output will gradually return to Y^*.

What is the long-run effect of lower taxes on the level of potential output? Lower corporate income-tax rates make investment more profitable to firms, and any increase in investment will tend to increase the future growth rate of potential output. Lower GST rates and personal income-tax rates may have a similar effect. To the extent that high tax rates discourage work effort, reductions in tax rates will lead to increases in the labour force and consequent increases in the level of potential output.

> **Reductions in tax rates generate a short-run demand stimulus and may also generate a longer-run increase in the level and growth rate of potential output.**

If reduced tax rates *do* lead to a higher growth rate of potential output, there would appear to be no clear tradeoff between the short-run and long-run effects of the fiscal expansion. The economy benefits in the short run from the increase in economic activity and in the long run from the increase in the growth rate. The absence of a tradeoff may, however, be illusory. Even though the growth rate of potential output is higher, the reduced tax revenues lead to fewer resources under the command of government. This means less public spending on many of the things that citizens value, such as national parks, public education, health care, roads, bridges, airports, other infrastructure, and research and development.

Another extreme possibility, however, is that the reduction in tax rates leads to such a significant increase in potential output that the government's tax revenues actually increase. (We saw this possibility in Chapter 18 with the Laffer curve, the relationship between tax rates and total tax revenues.) In this case, the tax reduction unleashes such a flood of investment and work effort that the increase in national income is sufficient to more than offset the reduction in tax rates, thus leaving the government able to fund more worthwhile public spending than before. This idea is central to what is often called "supply side" economics, as popularized during the early 1980s by advisors to U.S. President Ronald Reagan and British Prime Minister Margaret Thatcher. More recently, the central idea that tax reductions may significantly stimulate economic activity and growth played an important role in the policies of former premiers Ralph Klein of Alberta and Mike Harris of Ontario, as well as in the tax cuts implemented in 2004 by former U.S. President George W. Bush. In these cases, there is ample evidence that the tax cuts helped to generate significant increases in economic activity; there is little or no evidence, however, that they led to *increases* in government tax revenue.

Summary

24.1 The Adjustment Process

- Potential output, Y^*, is the level of real GDP at which all factors of production are being used at their normal rates of utilization.
- The output gap is the difference between potential output and the actual level of real GDP, the latter determined by the intersection of the AD and AS curves.
- An inflationary gap means that Y is greater than Y^*, and hence there is excess demand in factor markets. As a result, wages and other factor prices rise, causing firms' unit costs to rise. The AS curve shifts upward, and the price level rises.

- A recessionary gap means that Y is less than Y^*, and hence there is excess supply in factor markets. Wages and other factor prices fall but perhaps very slowly. As firms' unit costs fall, the AS curve gradually shifts downward, eventually returning output to potential.
- In our macro model, the level of potential output, Y^*, acts as an "anchor" for the economy. Given the short-run equilibrium as determined by the AD and AS curves, wages and other factor prices will adjust, shifting the AS curve, until output returns to Y^*.

24.2 Aggregate Demand and Supply Shocks

- Beginning from a position of potential output, an expansionary demand shock creates an inflationary gap, causing wages and other factor prices to rise. Firms' unit costs rise, shifting the AS curve upward and bringing output back toward Y^*.
- Beginning from a position of potential output, a contractionary demand shock creates a recessionary gap. Because factor prices tend to be sticky downward, the adjustment process tends to be slow, and a recessionary gap tends to persist for some time.
- Aggregate supply shocks, such as those caused by changes in the prices of inputs, lead the AS curve to shift, changing real GDP and the price level. But the

economy's adjustment process reverses the shift in AS, tending eventually to bring the economy back to its initial level of output and prices.
- In the short run, macroeconomic equilibrium is determined by the intersection of the AD and AS curves. In the long run, the economy is in equilibrium only when real GDP is equal to potential output. In the long run, the price level is determined by the intersection of the AD curve and the vertical Y^* curve.
- Shocks to the AD or AS curves can change real GDP in the short run. Only changes in the level of potential output can change output in the long run.

24.3 Fiscal Stabilization Policy

- In principle, fiscal policy can be used to stabilize output at Y^*. To remove a recessionary gap, governments can shift AD to the right by cutting taxes or increasing spending. To remove an inflationary gap, governments can pursue the opposite policies.
- In the short run, increases in desired saving on the part of firms, households, and governments lead to reductions in real GDP. This phenomenon is called the paradox of thrift. In the long run, the paradox of thrift does not apply, and increased saving will lead to increased investment and economic growth.
- Because government tax and transfer programs tend to reduce the size of the multiplier, they act as automatic stabilizers. When real GDP changes, disposable income changes by less because of taxes and transfers.
- Discretionary fiscal policy is subject to decision lags and execution lags that limit its ability to take effect quickly.

Some economists argue that these limitations are so severe that discretionary fiscal policy should never be used for stabilization because it will end up increasing instability. Others argue that the economy's adjustment process works so slowly that discretionary fiscal policy can play a useful role in stabilizing the economy.
- Fiscal policy has different effects in the short and long run. In the short run, a fiscal expansion created by an increase in government purchases (G) will increase real GDP. In the long run, the rise in G will "crowd out" private spending. If private investment is crowded out, the growth rate of potential output may be reduced.
- In the short run, a fiscal expansion created by a reduction in income taxes has a similar effect on real GDP. In the long run, if the tax reduction leads to more investment and work effort, there will be a positive effect on the level and growth rate of potential output.

Key Concepts

The output gap and factor prices
Inflationary and recessionary gaps
Asymmetry of wage adjustment:
  flexible and sticky wages
The Phillips curve

Potential output as an "anchor" for
  the economy
Short-run versus long-run effects of
  AD and *AS* shocks
Fiscal stabilization policy

The paradox of thrift
Decision lags and execution lags
Automatic stabilizers
Fine tuning and gross tuning

Study Exercises

1. Fill in the blanks to make the following statements
correct.

   a. In our short-run macro model, it is assumed that
   factor prices are _____ and the level of
   potential output is _____. Changes in real
   GDP are caused by fluctuations in _____
   and _____.

   b. During the adjustment process highlighted in this
   chapter, the central assumption is that factor prices
   are _____ and responding to _____.
   Potential output is assumed to be _____, and
   acts as a(n) _____ for real GDP following
   AD or *AS* shocks.

2. Fill in the blanks to make the following statements
correct.

   a. When actual GDP is higher than potential GDP, we
   say that there is a(n) _____ gap. When
   actual GDP is less than potential GDP we say there
   is a(n) _____ gap.

   b. An inflationary gap leads to excess demand for
   labour, which causes wages and thus _____
   costs to rise. Firms require higher _____ in
   order to supply any level of output, and so the *AS*
   curve shifts _____.

   c. A recessionary gap leads to excess supply of labour,
   which causes wages and thus _____ costs to
   fall. Firms reduce _____ for any level of
   output supplied, and so the *AS* curve shifts
   _____.

   d. The downward adjustment of wages in response to
   a recessionary gap is much _____ than the
   upward adjustment of wages in response to
   a(n) _____ gap. Economists refer to this
   phenomenon as _____.

3. Fill in the blanks to make the following statements
correct.

   a. Beginning with output equal to potential, suppose
   there is a sudden increase in demand for Canadian
   exports. This is a(n) _____ shock to the
   Canadian economy, which will result in the
   _____ curve shifting to the _____ and
   the opening of a(n) _____ gap. Firms' unit
   costs will start to _____ and the
   _____ curve will shift _____. Long-
   run equilibrium will be restored at _____
   output and _____ price level.

   b. Beginning with output equal to potential, suppose
   there is a drop in business confidence and investment falls. This is a(n) _____ shock to the
   Canadian economy, which shifts the _____
   curve to the left and creates a(n) _____ gap.
   Unit costs will start to _____ and the
   _____ curve will shift _____. Long-
   run equilibrium will (slowly) be restored at
   _____ output and _____ price level.

   c. Beginning with output equal to potential, suppose
   there is a large and sudden increase in the price of
   electricity. This is a(n) _____ shock to

the Canadian economy, which will result in the _____ curve shifting _____ and the opening of a(n) _____ gap. If wages are downwardly sticky the economy's _____ process could be very slow and the _____ will persist for a long time.

d. Beginning with output equal to potential, suppose there is a large and sudden decrease in the price of electricity. This is a(n) _____ shock to the Canadian economy, which will result in the _____ curve shifting _____ and the opening of a(n) _____ gap. Unit costs will start to _____ and the _____ curve will shift _____, restoring equilibrium at _____ output and _____ price level.

4. Fill in the blanks to make the following statements correct.

   a. In the long run, total output is determined only by _____. In the long run, aggregate demand determines the _____.

   b. Permanent increases in real GDP are possible only if _____ is increasing.

   c. Suppose illiteracy in Canada were eliminated, and the school dropout rate were reduced to zero. The effect would be a permanent _____ in productivity and a(n) _____ in potential output.

   d. A reduction in corporate income tax is likely to make _____ more attractive and thus shift the _____ curve to the right. The result is a(n) _____ in the short-run level of real GDP. In the long run, the greater rate of _____ by firms will lead to a greater rate of growth of _____.

5. The following diagram shows two economies, A and B. Each are in short-run equilibrium at point E, where the AD and AS curves intersect.

   a. Explain why in Economy A wages and other factor prices will begin to rise, and why this will increase firms' unit costs.

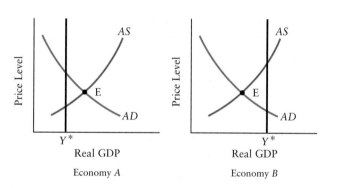

   b. Following your answer in part (a), show the effect on the AS curve. Explain what happens to real GDP and the price level.

   c. Explain why in Economy B wages and other factor prices will begin to fall, and why this will decrease firms' unit costs.

   d. Following your answer in part (c), show the effect on the AS curve. Explain what happens to real GDP and the price level.

6. The table shows several possible situations for the economy in terms of output gaps and the rate of change of wages. Real GDP is measured in billions of dollars. Assume that potential output is $800 billion.

Situation	Real GDP	Output Gap	Rate of Wage Change	Shift of AS Curve (+/0/−)
A	775	—	−2.0%	—
B	785	—	−1.2%	—
C	795	—	−0.2%	—
D	800	—	0.0%	—
E	805	—	1.0%	—
F	815	—	2.4%	—
G	825	—	4.0%	—
H	835	—	5.8%	—

   a. Compute the output gap $(Y - Y^*)$ for each situation and fill in the table.

   b. Explain why wages rise when output is greater than potential but fall when output is less than potential.

   c. For each situation, explain whether the economy's AS curve is shifting up, shifting down, or stationary. Fill in the table.

   d. Plot the Phillips curve on a scale diagram for this economy. (See Extensions in Theory 24-1 on pages 598–599 for a review of the Phillips curve.)

7. Consider an economy that is in equilibrium with output equal to Y^*. There is then a significant reduction in the world's demand for this country's goods.

   a. Illustrate the initial equilibrium in a diagram.

   b. What kind of shock occurred—aggregate demand or aggregate supply? Show the effects of the shock in your diagram.

   c. Explain the process by which the economy will adjust back toward Y^* in the long run. Show this in your diagram.

   d. Explain why policymakers may want to use a fiscal expansion to restore output back to Y^* rather than wait for the process you described in part (c). What role does downward wage stickiness play in the policymakers' thinking?

8. Consider an economy that is in equilibrium with output equal to Y^*. There is then a significant reduction

in the world price of an important raw material, such as iron ore.

a. Illustrate the initial equilibrium in a diagram.
b. What kind of shock occurred—aggregate demand or aggregate supply? Show the effects of the shock in your diagram.
c. Explain the process by which the economy will adjust back toward Y^* in the long run. Show this in your diagram.
d. Is there a strong case for using a fiscal contraction to return output to Y^*? Explain why or why not.

9. In our discussion of automatic fiscal stabilizers, we argued that income taxes and transfers increased the stability of real GDP in the face of AD and AS shocks. Recall from Chapter 22 that the simple multiplier is given by $1/[1 - MPC(1 - t) - m]$.

a. Explain how the size of the simple multiplier is related to the *slope* of the AD curve. (You may want to review the relationship between the AE curve and the AD curve, as discussed in Chapter 23.)
b. Explain how the slope of the AD curve affects the stability of real GDP in the presence of AS shocks.
c. Now explain how the size of the simple multiplier is related to the size of the *shift* in the AD curve for any given change in autonomous expenditure.
d. For any given AS curve, show how the size of the AD shift affects the stability of real GDP.
e. Finally, explain how the economy's automatic stabilizers depend on the sizes of MPC, t, and m.

10. The following diagram shows the AD, AS, and Y^* curves for an economy. Suppose the economy begins at point A. Then the government increases its level of purchases (G).

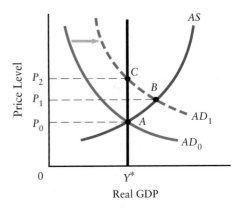

a. Describe the short-run effects of this fiscal expansion.
b. Describe the adjustment process, and the new long-run equilibrium for the economy.
c. Explain how the *composition* of real GDP has changed from the initial to the new long-run equilibrium.
d. Repeat (a), (b), and (c) for a fiscal expansion generated by a reduction in the net tax rate.

Discussion Questions

1. Discuss the following two statements in terms of short-run versus long-run outcomes.

a. "Starting from potential output, an increase in government spending can produce more output and employment at the cost of a once-and-for-all rise in the price level."
b. "Increased government spending can never lead to a permanent increase in output."

2. Politicians are sometimes accused of adopting policies that bring "short-term gain at the cost of long-term pain," whereas statesmen offer "short-term pain to buy long-term gain." What policies that shift aggregate demand or aggregate supply curves might come under one or the other of these descriptions?

3. If downward flexibility of money wages would allow the economy's adjustment process to eliminate recessionary gaps quickly, why do workers usually resist wage cuts during times of economic slump?

4. Which of the following would be automatic stabilizers?

a. Employment-insurance payments
b. Cost-of-living escalators in government contracts and pensions
c. Income taxes
d. Free university tuition for unemployed workers after six months of unemployment, provided that they are under 30 years old and have had five or more years of full-time work experience since high school

5. During 1998 and 1999, the Canadian economy was experiencing a sufficiently high rate of growth of real GDP that many economists predicted an increase in inflation. Yet inflation declined slightly. At the same time, world commodity prices continued their decline that had begun in mid-1997. Explain the behaviour of the Canadian economy—high growth and falling inflation—in terms of aggregate demand and

aggregate supply curves. What role, if any, is played by the falling commodity prices? What role is played by the U.S. economy, which at this point was experiencing very strong growth?

6. In 2007–2008 Prime Minister Stephen Harper announced cuts to personal and corporate income-tax rates. He argued that these policies would provide necessary stimulus for an economy that then appeared to be entering a recession.

a. Does a reduction in personal income taxes produce a demand-side or a supply-side stimulus to the economy? Explain.
b. Discuss the likely time frame for each possible effect on the Canadian economy.
c. By late 2008, the economy was slowing dramatically. Why might many commentators at that time have argued that the tax cuts did not address the *immediate* needs of the Canadian economy?

25

The Difference Between Short-Run and Long-Run Macroeconomics

LEARNING OBJECTIVES

In this chapter you will learn

1. why economists think differently about short-run and long-run changes in macroeconomic variables.

2. that any change in real GDP can be decomposed into changes in factor supply, the utilization rate of factors, and productivity.

3. why short-run changes in GDP are mostly caused by changes in factor utilization, whereas long-run changes in GDP are mostly caused by changes in factor supplies and productivity.

4. that macroeconomic policies will only have a long-run effect on output if they influence factor supplies or productivity.

In Chapters 21, 22, and 23, we developed a model of the economy in the short run. In Chapter 24, we extended this model to show how the economy evolves, through a process of factor-price adjustment, from its short-run equilibrium to its long-run equilibrium. There we saw how the level of potential output, Y^*, acts as an "anchor" for the economy. Aggregate demand or supply shocks can lead to short-run deviations of real GDP from Y^*, but the economy's adjustment process ensures that real GDP returns to Y^* in the long run. We are now set to examine why Y^* grows over periods of many years—a process that we call *long-run economic growth*.

In this chapter, we focus on the distinction between the short run and the long run in macroeconomics. This distinction becomes especially important when policymakers try to evaluate the effects of various policies. Different economists will sometimes use different time frames for the evaluation of any given policy. For example, one economist may say that a fiscal expansion is desirable because it will provide stimulus to an economy with high unemployment; another economist may claim that it will have negative effects on the economy's long-run growth. These two views may be entirely consistent with each other (as we saw at the end of the previous chapter), but the observer is left confused because it is not clear in the debate whether the discussion is about the short-run or the long-run effects of the policy.

In this chapter, we seek to clarify the distinction between short-run GDP fluctuations and long-run GDP growth. With this distinction firmly in place, we will be ready for the detailed discussion of long-run economic growth in the next chapter.

25.1 Two Examples from Recent History

We begin with two examples of the difference between short-run and long-run macroeconomic relationships. Though the specific examples date from the 1990s, the principles involved apply more generally.

Inflation and Interest Rates in Canada

In the early 1990s, Canada's central bank (the Bank of Canada) embarked on a policy designed to reduce the rate of inflation. For reasons that we will see in detail in Chapters 29 and 30, the Bank's policy was controversial. When his term expired in 1994, the Bank's governor, John Crow, was replaced by his senior deputy governor, Gordon Thiessen. Though Thiessen was committed to following Crow's policy of reducing inflation, he was equally committed to explaining the policy to an often-skeptical public. As we will see, the explanation relies crucially on making the distinction between short-run and long-run macroeconomic relationships.

In April 1995, Governor Thiessen was interviewed on CBC Radio. Thiessen was asked about the Bank's policy of reducing inflation, from about 6 percent a few years earlier, and maintaining it since then between 1 percent and 3 percent annually. Thiessen argued that the high nominal interest rates of the past were caused mostly by high inflation. The main reason for this connection between inflation and nominal interest rates is that inflation erodes the value of money. Lenders need to be compensated for the inflation-induced fall in the real value of their money between the time they lend it and the time that they are repaid. This requires charging a nominal interest rate high enough to cover the effects of inflation. Thus, higher inflation pushes up interest rates; lower inflation pushes them down.

At this point, the interviewer had no problem with Thiessen's line of argument, as he easily recalled the time back in 1981 when inflation was at an all-time high of 12 percent and mortgage rates at Canada's banks were an astounding 20 percent! In contrast, by 1995, the rate of inflation was down to just over 2 percent and mortgage rates were only 8 percent. So periods of high inflation did indeed appear to coincide with periods of high interest rates.

Thiessen then started the next part of his argument. He stated that in order to reduce the rate of inflation the Bank of Canada had to reduce the growth rate of the money supply. This action, he admitted, would tighten up credit-market conditions and push up interest rates. Understandably confused at this point, the interviewer asked the inevitable question: How can a policy that raises interest rates be a necessary part of a policy designed to *reduce* both inflation and interest rates?

Thiessen understood the apparent contradiction and was ready with his answer. He stressed that the key to answering the question is to understand the different short-run and long-run effects of monetary policy. Thiessen argued that, in the short run, a policy by the Bank of Canada to reduce the growth rate of money will make credit scarcer (as we will see in detail in Chapter 28). This greater scarcity of credit causes both nominal and real interest rates to rise. Firms will reduce their investment in new factories, machines, and warehouses, and households will purchase fewer big-ticket items, such as cars, ski vacations, and furniture. Such reductions in expenditure will lead, through the multiplier process that we have already seen, to a reduction in real

GDP. But as firms scale back their production and real GDP falls, workers get laid off and the unemployment rate increases—the economy enters a recession. In short, the Bank of Canada's contractionary monetary policy shifts the *AD* curve to the left and generates a reduction in GDP. When we examine the detailed workings of monetary policy in later chapters, we will see that a monetary policy designed to reduce inflation is usually effective precisely because *it creates a temporary recession.*

So much for the short-run effects of the Bank's policy. What happens as wages and other factor prices adjust and the economy therefore starts to approach its new long-run equilibrium? As we saw in Chapter 24, the excess supply of labour that is a key part of the unemployment and recession puts downward pressure on wages. In other words, wages start to increase at a slower rate than before and maybe even begin to fall. As wage growth declines, the pressure on prices to rise also declines. That is, the rate of inflation falls. As inflation falls, and the rate of erosion of money's value falls with it, nominal interest rates will also fall. In the new long-run equilibrium, both inflation and nominal interest rates will be lower than before the policy was initiated. As Gordon Thiessen said in the interview, "The best way to get low interest rates is to get low inflation."

The details of monetary policy will be discussed in Chapters 28 and 29, and this argument will be repeated in considerable detail. At that time, we will more clearly see the difference between the short-run and long-run effects of monetary policy. Economists have a special term to reflect this difference. In the long run, economists say that *money is neutral*—meaning that changes in the money supply have no long-run effect on *real* variables, such as GDP, employment, and investment, but do have an effect on *nominal* variables, such as the price level or the rate of inflation. This long-run neutrality of money is another way of stating that changes in the money supply do not change the level of potential output, Y^*. In the short run, however, economists say that *money is not neutral* because changes in the money supply affect real variables. In other words, monetary policy shifts the *AD* curve and generates short-run changes in real GDP. Understanding this difference is crucial to understanding most debates about monetary policy.

Saving and Growth in Japan

For the entire decade of the 1990s, the Japanese economy showed very little growth. Many economists argued that an important part of the solution to Japan's economic malaise was for its firms and consumers to spend more. One problem with Japan, they argued, was that its firms and consumers saved "too much." On the other hand, many of these same economists acknowledged that Japan's remarkable economic success in the 40 years following the Second World War—high growth rates of real GDP and low unemployment—was to a significant extent due to its high saving rate. But if "too much" saving was an important reason for Japan's economic slump during the 1990s, how could high saving also have been a primary reason for its remarkable economic success over four decades? How can both of these views be correct?

Once again, the key to understanding this apparent contradiction is to recognize that the short-run effect of saving is different from its long-run effect. We saw this distinction in Chapter 24 when we discussed the "paradox of thrift," but it is worth repeating. In the short run, with factor prices and technology more or less

The high private saving rate in Japan is one reason that the Japanese economic recovery in the late 1990s was so slow.

constant, an increase in households' desire to save, perhaps caused by some uncertainty about future economic events, implies a reduction in expenditure. Uncertainty leads firms to spend less on investment goods; households spend less on all sorts of consumer goods. This reduction in expenditure leads, through the usual multiplier process, to a reduction in output. In terms of our macro model, the *AD* curve shifts to the left and real GDP falls. Increased saving in the short run, therefore, can be one reason why an economy, such as Japan's, enters or remains in an economic slump.

But if an increase in firms' and households' saving can cause a recession, how can a high saving rate also help to explain Japan's many years of healthy economic growth? The answer is that in the long run, after wages and factor prices adjust to the recessionary gap, greater saving leads to a larger pool of financial capital. This larger pool of available funds drives down the price of credit—the interest rate—and makes firms' investment projects more profitable. More investment in factories, machines, and warehouses leads to a higher level of potential output, and it is to this higher level of potential output that the economy converges in the long run. This long-run relationship among saving, investment, and growth explains the striking correlation that we will see in the next chapter—countries with high long-run investment rates tend to be countries with high rates of long-run per capita GDP growth.

Economists have special terminology to describe this difference between the short run and the long run. Economists say that national income in the short run is largely *demand determined,* meaning that changes in demand will lead to changes in output in the same direction. Thus, an increase in the desire to save, which is a reduction in the desire to spend, leads to less total spending and a reduction in national income. Even though aggregate supply (*AS*) shocks also affect output in the short run (as we saw in Chapters 23 and 24), the term *demand determined* reflects the fact that the position of the aggregate demand (*AD*) curve is important for determining the level of real GDP. In the long run, however, economists say that national income is *supply determined,* meaning that sustained increases in output will be possible only if the level of potential output increases; the position of the *AD* curve has no effect on real GDP in the long run. Increases in potential output require either more factors of production (such as labour and capital) or technological change that improves productivity.

A Need to Think Differently

These two examples from recent history suggest that a complete understanding of macroeconomics requires an understanding of both the short run and the long run. Such an understanding, in turn, requires us to think differently about short-run and long-run behaviour. It is one thing to say that macroeconomic variables behave differently over the short run than over the long run; it is quite another to understand *why* this is the case.

In this chapter, we emphasize the distinction between viewing short-run changes in GDP as deviations of output from potential, and long-run changes in GDP as changes in the level of potential output. We introduce a simple method of GDP accounting that clarifies this distinction and also shows us the various sources of short-run and long-run changes in GDP.[1]

---

[1] It is worth emphasizing the different use of the terms "short run" and "long run" in macroeconomics and in microeconomics. In microeconomics, the short run for a firm or industry is the span of time during which the amount of physical capital is constant; the long run is the period of time during which firms are able to adjust their capital stock. In macroeconomics, however, the key distinction relates to whether wages and other factor prices have fully adjusted to excess demand or supply (the output gap) in the aggregate economy. Economists take wages and other factor prices to be given in the short run, but fully adjusted to the output gap in the long run.

25.2 Accounting for Changes in GDP

The simplest illustration of the distinction between short-run and long-run changes in economic activity is the behaviour of real GDP over time, as shown in Figure 25-1. The figure shows the path of Canadian real GDP and potential GDP, beginning from 1985. Actual GDP is measured by Statistics Canada. Potential GDP is the level of output that the economy produces when all factors of production are being utilized at their "normal" rates. But Statistics Canada can't tell us the value of potential GDP because it is not an observed variable—it must be estimated. The value of potential GDP is estimated by combining three pieces of information: the amounts of available factors of production (such as the labour force and the capital stock); an estimate of these factors' "normal" rates of utilization; and an estimate of each factor's productivity.

Figure 25-1 shows two different types of changes in GDP. First, some changes involve departures of actual GDP from potential GDP. For example, notice that actual GDP is equal to potential GDP at point A in 1990. As the Canadian economy then entered a major recession, actual GDP dropped below potential GDP to point B in 1992. An economic recovery then took place, eventually taking actual GDP back to potential GDP at point C in 1999. Such changes in GDP are what economists call short-run changes in GDP—they involve primarily the opening and then closing of an output gap.

The second type of change in GDP involves changes in potential GDP, with little or no change in the output gap. For example, the change in actual GDP from point A in 1990 to point D in 2008 represents entirely a change in potential GDP. We know this because the output gap in both years was zero (that is, in both 1990 and 2008 GDP was equal to potential GDP). Such changes in GDP are what economists call long-run changes in GDP—they involve a change in potential GDP, with little or no change in the output gap.

> When studying long-run trends in GDP, economists focus on the change in potential output. When studying short-run fluctuations, economists focus on the change in the output gap.

Figure 25-1 may make us wonder whether short-run changes in GDP have a different cause than long-run changes. In our macro model this is certainly the case; output is determined in the short run by the AD and AS curves but in the long run only by the level of Y^*. To explore the different causes of changes in GDP, we turn to a very simple accounting framework that applies to *all* changes in GDP.

Practise with Study Guide
Chapter 25, Exercise 1.

FIGURE 25-1 Actual and Potential GDP in Canada, 1985–2008

Long-run changes in GDP are reflected by changes in the level of potential GDP. Short-run changes in GDP are shown mostly by changes in the output gap.

(*Source:* Actual GDP: Statistics Canada CANSIM database, Series V1992067. Potential GDP: based on authors' calculations using data on the output gap from www.bankofcanada.ca.)

GDP Accounting: The Basic Principle

Suppose we could break down any change in GDP into its component parts. By understanding how each component changes, we can then gain some insights into how short-run changes differ from long-run changes. To break up GDP into the parts we want to study, we do the following obvious but useful things. First, we write

$$GDP = GDP$$

This is obviously true! Next, we multiply the right-hand side of the equation by F/F, where F is the economy's total available stock of factors, such as land, labour, and capital. This gives

$$GDP = F \times (GDP/F)$$

Next, we multiply the right-hand side by F_E/F_E, where F_E is the number of the economy's factors that are employed. After re-ordering the terms, we have

$$GDP = F \times (F_E/F) \times (GDP/F_E) \qquad (25\text{-}1)$$

It may seem like we have done nothing useful since we have simply twice multiplied the right-hand side of an obviously true equation by one. But, in fact, Equation 25-1 is very useful when thinking about the different sources of GDP changes.

First, however, note that Equation 25-1 implies that we have added together units of labour and land and capital to get a meaningful number for the economy's "available factors," F. This is not actually possible since different factors are measured in different units. For example, we can't add together six workers and five machines and two hectares of land to get a total of 13 factors. In the next section, we will focus on a single factor to avoid this problem. For now, however, our point is simplified by thinking about the economy's total available factors, F, and the number of those factors that are employed, F_E.

To make the discussion less cumbersome, let's name the three components of Equation 25-1.

1. F is the economy's *factor supply;* it is the total amount of all factors of production that the economy currently possesses.

2. F_E/F is the *factor utilization rate;* it is the fraction of the total supply of factors that is actually used or employed at any time.

3. GDP/F_E is a simple measure of *productivity* because it shows the amount of output (GDP) per unit of input employed (F_E).

Note that Equation 25-1 does nothing more than separate any change in GDP into a change in one or more of the three components, F, F_E/F, or GDP/F_E. For example, Canadian GDP increased dramatically in the 50 years between 1950 and 2000. Also, Canadian GDP increased by only a few percentage points from 2007 to 2010. In both cases, the increase in GDP can be attributed to changes in one or more of the three components—either the factor supply (F) increased, the factor utilization rate (F_E/F) increased, or the level of productivity (GDP/F_E) increased.

> **Any change in GDP can be decomposed into a change in factor supply, a change in factor utilization, and a change in productivity.**

The usefulness of this accounting exercise becomes clear when we recognize that two of these components, factor supply and productivity, change mostly over long periods of time, whereas the third component, factor utilization, changes mostly over shorter periods. This points us toward a better understanding of the difference between short-run and long-run changes in GDP. We discuss each component in turn.

The Long Run: Factor Supply

Two main factors of production—labour and capital—account for most of the change in the economy's factor supply, F.

Practise with Study Guide
Chapter 25, Short-Answer
Question 2.

LABOUR. The economy's supply of labour can increase for two main reasons. First, population can increase. An increase in population can be caused, in turn, either by greater immigration, an increase in birth rates, or a decrease in the mortality rate. The second way to increase the economy's supply of labour is to increase the fraction of the population that chooses to seek employment. This fraction is called the *labour-force participation rate*. In Canada, the labour-force participation rate is currently about 66 percent. It has increased steadily from the 1960s, mostly because of the increase in the participation rate of married women and the coming-of-age of the baby-boom generation.

No matter how the economy's supply of labour increases, the important point for our purposes is that such changes are mostly *long-run changes*. Population growth, through whatever means, is a very gradual process. Changes in labour-force participation also tend to be gradual. As a result, the economy's supply of labour does not usually change significantly from year to year. Over a period of many years, however, the increase in the supply of labour can be very substantial.

CAPITAL. The economy's supply of physical capital—machines, factories, and warehouses—increases for one reason. Firms that choose to purchase or build such investment goods today are accumulating physical capital that will be used to produce output in the future. Thus, today's flow of investment expenditure adds to the economy's stock of physical capital.[2]

As is the case for labour, the economy's stock of physical capital changes only very gradually. This is not to be confused with the very dramatic swings in investment that are often observed over the course of the business cycle. The difference is that investment is the *flow* that contributes to the *stock* of capital. But the economy's capital stock is so large compared with the annual flow of investment expenditure that even dramatic swings in the annual flow of investment generate almost imperceptible changes in the stock of capital.

> Changes in the economy's supply of labour and capital occur gradually, but over periods of many years their growth is considerable. As a result, changes in factor supply are important for explaining long-run changes in output but relatively unimportant for explaining short-run changes.

The Long Run: Productivity

Practise with Study Guide
Chapter 25, Short-Answer
Question 3.

The economy's level of productivity (GDP/F_E) is a measure of the average amount of output that is produced per unit of input. In practice, there are several possible measures of productivity, each one measuring something slightly different. Although there is more than one measure of productivity, Equation 25-1 uses the concept of output per employed factor, GDP/F_E. An increase in productivity is called *productivity growth*. Productivity growth is an important source

---

[2] The part of investment that represents a change in inventories does not add to the economy's capital stock, but this component of investment is typically quite small (though volatile).

of long-term increases in per capita income and thus in rising living standards, and we will say much more about it in Chapter 26.

The economy's level of productivity changes only slowly over time. For example, the average rate of productivity growth in Canada over the past few decades has been about 1.5 percent per year. Such low growth rates do not lead to significant changes in GDP or living standards over short periods of time but can generate huge improvements in living conditions over many years. For example, you may barely notice a 2 percent increase in your income from one year to the next, but you would surely notice the doubling that this annual growth rate would produce if it were sustained over 35 years. [31]

> **The economy's level of productivity changes only gradually from year to year but grows substantially over periods of many years. As a result, productivity growth is very important for explaining long-run changes in output but less important for explaining short-run changes.**

The Short Run: Factor Utilization

In Chapters 21 to 23 we examined in detail the behaviour of the economy in the short run. Here we review some of these now-familiar concepts but express them in a way that helps us to understand our central equation decomposing the changes in real GDP.

The factor utilization rate (F_E/F) is the last remaining component from our equation. Recall that it is simply the fraction of the total supply of factors that is employed. An immediate question comes to mind: Why would firms ever use fewer factors than are available to them? The answer has to do with how firms respond to changes in the demand for their product. When a firm's sales start dropping off, it must make a choice. It can continue producing at the current rate and let its inventories build up. Or it can reduce its rate of production. For a firm that is interested in maximizing profits, there is a limit to the amount of costly inventories it will be prepared to accumulate. Eventually, a reduction in demand for its product leads the firm to reduce its output and, in turn, reduce its employment of factors. Workers are laid off and equipment and other physical capital are used less intensively, thus lowering the value of F_E/F for the economy.

Similarly, a firm that is faced with a sudden increase in demand for its product has two alternatives. It can continue with its previous rate of production and satisfy the increased demand by letting its inventories run down. Or it can increase its rate of production by hiring more available workers and machines. Since profit-maximizing firms do not want to miss an opportunity to make a profitable sale, as would happen if the stockpile of inventories gets fully depleted, eventually the increase in demand leads them to increase production and hire more factors. Extra workers are hired, existing workers work overtime, and machines and other physical capital are used more intensively, thus increasing F_E/F for the economy.

These responses by firms to changes in demand are only the firms' short-run responses. A low factor utilization rate describes *excess supply* in the factor markets. As we saw in Chapter 24, such a situation of excess supply typically causes some downward pressure on wages and other factor prices. This reduction of factor prices, in turn, reduces firms' costs, shifts the *AS* curve downward, and puts downward pressure on product prices. Similarly, in the case of the increase in demand, the situation of a high factor utilization rate describes *excess demand* in factor markets. Such excess demand causes upward pressure on wages and other factor prices. As factor prices rise, firms' costs increase, the *AS* curve shifts upward, and there is upward pressure on the price level. As we saw in Chapter 24, this process of factor-price adjustment in response to output gaps continues in our model until output returns to potential, at which point all factors of production are being used at their "normal" rates of utilization.[3]

> The factor utilization rate fluctuates in response to short-run changes in output caused by aggregate demand or aggregate supply shocks. Over time, however, excess supply or excess demand for factors causes an adjustment in factor prices that brings the factor utilization rate back to its "normal" level.

What do we mean by a "normal" factor utilization rate? In Chapter 19 we briefly discussed the fact that even when the economy is at potential output, some unemployment still exists. The rate of unemployment when real GDP is equal to potential output is often called the *natural rate of unemployment*. This "natural" or "normal" rate of unemployment is the rate of unemployment against which we compare the actual unemployment rate to judge whether the labour market has excess supply or excess demand. That is, if unemployment is above the natural rate, there is an excess supply of labour; if unemployment is below the natural rate, there is an excess demand for labour. For physical capital, the utilization rate is called the *capacity utilization rate* because the amount of physical capital largely determines the productive *capacity* of a given plant or factory. As with labour, so too is there a "natural" or "normal" capacity utilization rate for capital.

> Changes in the factor utilization rate are important for explaining short-run changes in GDP. But after factor prices have fully adjusted, GDP returns to Y^* and the factor utilization rate returns to its "normal" level. As a result, changes in the factor utilization rate are not important for explaining long-run changes in GDP.

GDP Accounting: An Application

We made some strong statements in the previous section regarding the relative importance of short-run versus long-run changes in productivity, factor supplies, and factor utilization. Are these statements supported by the evidence? In this section, we apply the accounting exercise from Equation 25-1 to Canadian GDP data to illustrate the basic arguments. Unfortunately, we cannot use *exactly* the same equation because, as we noted then, it is not possible to add units of labour together with units of physical capital and units of land. By using exactly the same intuition as earlier, however, we can express the GDP accounting equation in terms of a single factor of production—labour. Letting L be the labour force and E be the number of individuals employed, the new equation is[4]

$$GDP = L \times (E/L) \times (GDP/E) \qquad (25\text{-}2)$$

The basic interpretation of Equation 25-2 is the same as for Equation 25-1, except now the discussion relates only to labour. The labour force (L) is the supply of labour.

---

[3] The "normal" rates of factor utilization are not constant over time. Changes in taxes, individuals' preferences for work, and technology may all affect the long-run "normal" rate of factor utilization. In Chapter 31 we address this issue for labour when we discuss changes in the NAIRU (non-accelerating inflation rate of employment).

[4] We get this equation by beginning with GDP = GDP. We then multiply the right-hand side by E/E and then by L/L.

FIGURE 25-2   Three Sources of Changes in GDP

(i) Labour force

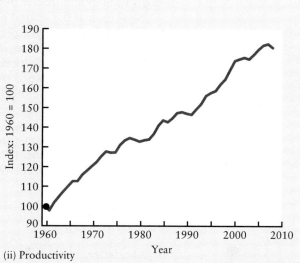

(ii) Productivity

(iii) Employment rate

The sources of long-run changes in GDP differ from the sources of short-run changes in GDP. Panel (i) shows the upward trend in the Canadian labour force. Panel (ii) shows the upward trend in productivity, measured as GDP per worker. Both show substantial growth over the long run, but relatively small short-run fluctuations. Panel (iii) shows the employment rate, the fraction of the labour force that is employed. It shows almost no long-run trend but considerable short-run fluctuations.

(*Source:* All data for figures are authors' calculations using data from Statistics Canada CANSIM database. Labour force: Series V2091051. Employment: Series V2091072. Real GDP: Series V1992067.)

The employment rate (E/L) is the fraction of the labour force actually employed (which is equal to one minus the unemployment rate). And the measure of productivity—in this case, labour productivity—is GDP/E.

Figure 25-2 shows the behaviour of these three components for Canada beginning in 1960. Each variable is expressed as an index number, with the value in 1960 set equal to 100. Expressing each variable in this way makes it easy to see each variable's percentage change over the five decades. Note that the vertical scale is different for each of the three variables. We do this intentionally so that we can see whatever trend and volatility exist for each variable separately. If we used the same vertical scale for graphing productivity and employment that we use for graphing the labour force, we would barely notice the fluctuations that do exist in these two variables.

The first panel in the figure shows the growth of the Canadian labour force. From 1960 to 2008, the index number increased from 100 to 287, an increase of 187 percent.

It is clear from the graph that any short-run fluctuations in the Canadian labour force are dwarfed in importance by the long-run upward trend.

Now look at the second panel, showing the growth of Canadian labour productivity. The level of GDP per person employed, expressed as an index number, increases from 100 in 1960 to 180 in 2008, an increase of 80 percent. Like the labour force, the level of labour productivity has its short-run fluctuations, but it is clear that the overriding change—the upward trend—takes place over many years.

Finally, consider the third panel, showing the Canadian employment rate—the utilization rate of labour. Compared with the other two variables graphed in Figure 25-2, the employment rate shows much more short-run volatility and much less long-run change. The employment rate (expressed as an index number) is almost exactly the same in 2008 as it was in 1960. There is very little change over the long run, but considerable changes are occurring over shorter periods of time.

Summing Up

To summarize, we can decompose *any* change in GDP into changes in factor supply, the factor utilization rate, and productivity. But these three components typically contribute to GDP changes over different spans of time. In particular, factor supply and productivity typically change only gradually and hence are important for explaining long-run changes in GDP but are not usually helpful in explaining short-run changes in GDP. In contrast, the factor utilization rate is quite volatile over short periods of time but returns to its normal level over several years. Thus, changes in the factor utilization rate are important for explaining short-run changes in GDP but are not of much importance for explaining long-run changes.

> ### myeconlab   ADDITIONAL TOPICS
>
> Canada and many other developed economies experienced a "productivity slowdown" in the early 1970s. And in recent years, many economists have expressed concern about Canada's slow rate of productivity growth compared with that of its major trading partners, especially the United States. For more information on Canada's recent productivity performance, and what can be done about it, look for **Understanding and Addressing Canada's Productivity Challenges** in the *Additional Topics* section of this book's MyEconLab.
>
> **www.myeconlab.com**

25.3 Policy Implications

Practise with Study Guide
Chapter 25, Exercises 2 and 3.

Economists think differently about short-run and long-run macroeconomic relationships. When thinking about short-run fluctuations, economists focus on understanding why actual GDP deviates from potential GDP. As we have seen in previous chapters, such changes in real GDP are caused by aggregate demand and aggregate supply shocks. When thinking about long-run growth, however, economists focus on understanding why potential GDP changes over time. As we have said, such long-run growth has its source in the growth of factor supplies and productivity. Thus, in understanding long-run growth, economists focus on what causes factor supplies and productivity to change.

> **When studying short-run fluctuations, economists focus on the deviations of actual output from potential output. When studying long-run growth, economists focus on changes in potential output.**

Through the development of our macro model in the previous four chapters, we have a better understanding of what causes the *AD* and *AS* curves to shift, and thus a better understanding of the causes of short-run fluctuations in real GDP. Our picture of the short run will be more fully developed after we discuss monetary policy and interest rates in Chapters 27 and 28, and exchange rates and international trade in Chapter 35.

What we have not yet done, however, is discuss in detail why potential output grows substantially over long periods of time, thereby improving average living standards from one generation to the next. In the next chapter we explore the issue of long-run economic growth, focusing on the importance of capital accumulation and technological change.

Before we do that, however, it is worth returning to a point that we raised at the beginning of this chapter—that the distinction between the short run and the long run has an important implication for the role and effectiveness of various macroeconomic policies.

We have discussed in this chapter how changes in demand may cause actual GDP to depart from potential GDP. For example, firms may feel optimistic about the future and increase their investment expenditure, thereby increasing the overall level of demand. Or the government may increase its purchases of goods and services, thus adding to demand. Or foreigners may decide to increase their demand for Canadian goods, thus adding to the overall demand for goods produced by Canadian firms. All of these changes would increase the overall level of demand in the economy and, in the short run, would lead actual GDP to rise above potential GDP. Conversely, any decrease in the demand for goods would, in the short run, cause actual GDP to fall below potential GDP.

In the long run, however, the economy has an adjustment process that tends to return the factor utilization rate to its "normal" level. As we saw in Chapter 24, when actual GDP is above potential GDP, there is an excess demand for factors. This causes factor prices to rise and thus the *AS* curve to shift upward, bringing actual GDP back to potential. Conversely, when actual GDP is less than potential GDP, there is an excess supply of factors. This tends to cause factor prices to fall (though perhaps slowly) and thus the *AS* curve to shift downward, thereby bringing actual GDP back to potential.

This adjustment process that brings the economy back to the level of potential output in the long run implies a stark result regarding the effects of macroeconomic policy:

> **Fiscal and monetary policies affect the short-run level of GDP because they alter the level of demand and thus the position of the *AD* curve. But unless they are able to affect the level of *potential* output, Y^*, they will have no long-run effect on GDP.**

As we saw in the previous chapter, fiscal policy can have important effects on the level of potential output—both through changes in government purchases and investment and through changes in personal and corporate taxes. In Chapters 28 and 29 we will explore monetary policy in detail and will see that it has few if any effects on the level of potential output.

Looking Ahead

The discussion in this chapter has focused on one topic—the difference between the short run and the long run in macroeconomics. We have shown that short-run movements in GDP are mostly accounted for by changes in the factor utilization rate. For example, as economic events cause the *AD* or *AS* curves to shift, output will deviate from *Y** and the factor utilization rate will change. In contrast, long-run changes in GDP are mostly accounted for by growth in factor supplies and productivity, which lead to increases in *Y**. This difference forces economists to think differently about macroeconomic relationships that exist over a few months as compared to those that exist over several years.

In the previous four chapters we examined in detail the behaviour of the economy in the short run, and the adjustment process that brings the economy from a short-run equilibrium to a long-run equilibrium. We are now ready to take the next step and examine the causes of long-run economic growth.

Summary

25.1 Two Examples from Recent History

- Macroeconomic variables behave differently over the short run and over the long run. One example: A monetary policy designed to reduce inflation and nominal interest rates in the long run requires an *increase* in interest rates in the short run. Another example: An increase in households' or firms' saving rates will reduce the level of output in the short run, but it will increase output in the long run.
- In the short run, there is some adjustment of output and employment but little adjustment of wages and prices. In the long run, full adjustment of wages and prices is assumed to take place.

25.2 Accounting for Changes in GDP

- All changes in GDP can be accounted for by changes in one or more of the following three variables:
  1. Supply of factors
  2. Factor utilization rates
  3. Factor productivity
- Long-run changes in GDP are caused mostly by changes in factor supplies and factor productivity; the utilization rate of factors does not change significantly over the long run.
- Short-run changes in GDP are caused mostly by changes in the factor utilization rate; factor supplies and productivity have relatively minor short-run fluctuations.

25.3 Policy Implications

- When studying short-run fluctuations, economists focus on changes in the output gap and tend to ignore changes in potential output. When studying long-run fluctuations, economists focus on changes in potential output and ignore changes in the output gap.
- Fiscal and monetary policies affect GDP in the short run because they affect the level of demand, and thus the position of the *AD* curve. Any long-run effect on real GDP comes through their effect on *potential GDP*.

Key Concepts

Short-run fluctuations
Long-run trends

Changes in the output gap versus
    changes in potential output
Accounting for changes in GDP

Factor supplies
Factor utilization rates
Productivity

Study Exercises

myeconlab   SAVE TIME. IMPROVE RESULTS.

Visit MyEconLab to practise Study Exercises and prepare for tests and exams.
MyEconLab also offers a variety of other study tools to help you succeed.
www.myeconlab.com

1. Fill in the blanks to make the following statements correct.

   a. Short-run changes in real GDP are caused by _____ and _____ shocks, with little or no change in _____. In the short run, _____ prices and the level of _____ are assumed to be constant.

   b. Long-run trends in GDP involve changes in _____ output. Short-run fluctuations in GDP involve changes in the _____ with little or no change in _____.

   c. Any change in GDP is caused by changes in at least one of the following three component parts: _____, _____, and _____.

   d. Long-run changes in GDP are caused mainly by changes in _____ and _____. Short-run changes in GDP are caused mainly by changes in _____.

   e. The economy's adjustment process returns the _____ rate to its "normal" level in the long run.

   f. Fiscal and monetary policies alter the level of output in the short run by causing the _____ curve to shift. There will be a long-run effect on output only if _____ changes.

2. Consider Economies A, B, and C for which you are given data for the factor supply (F), the numbers of factors employed (F_E), and the GDP, for two different time periods.

Economy	Time Period	F	F_E	GDP	F_E/F	GDP/F_E
A	Period 1	1000	800	$100 000	____	____
	Period 2	1300	1040	$155 000	____	____
B	Period 1	2000	1800	$225 000	____	____
	Period 2	2000	1500	$187 500	____	____
C	Period 1	6500	6175	$399 000	____	____
	Period 2	6500	6175	$665 000	____	____

   a. For each economy, and for each period, calculate the factor utilization rate (F_E/F) and a measure of productivity (GDP/F_E). Fill in the table.

   b. For each economy, and for each period, use the numbers from the table to substitute into Equation 25-1 (GDP = $F \times F_E/F \times$ GDP/F_E).

   c. For each economy, describe whether you think the economy has experienced a short-run or a long-run change in GDP from Period 1 to Period 2. Explain.

   d. Do you detect an important difference between Economies A and C? Explain.

3. Using the basic equation of GDP accounting that we developed in this chapter (GDP = $F \times F_E/F \times$ GDP/F_E), calculate the economy's GDP in each of the following cases.

   a. Factor supply is 4 million units, the factor utilization rate is 0.85, and the GDP per unit of input employed is $150.

b. Factor supply is 1.25 million units, the factor utilization rate is 0.9, and the GDP per unit of input employed is $110.

c. Factor supply is 250 million units, the factor utilization rate is 0.92, and the GDP per unit of input employed is $185.

4. Consider the data below for a hypothetical country.

Year	Real GDP (billions of constant dollars)	Labour Force (millions of people)	Employment (millions of people)
1960	100	1.5	1.4
1965	130	1.6	1.45
1970	175	1.75	1.55
1975	250	1.95	1.65
1980	230	2.15	1.85
1985	265	2.40	2.0
1990	300	2.70	2.2
1995	340	3.0	2.8
2000	375	3.3	3.05
2005	410	3.6	3.4
2010	450	3.95	3.7

a. Using the definitions in the chapter, compute the employment rate and the level of productivity (measured as GDP per worker) for each year.

b. For each five-year period, compute the percentage change in the labour force, the employment rate, and the level of productivity. Compute the same three things over the entire 50-year period.

c. Compute the percentage change in real GDP over each five-year period. Do it also for the entire 50-year period.

d. Based on Equation 25-2 (page 630), it can be shown that the percentage change in real GDP is approximately equal to the percentage change in the labour force *plus* the percentage change in the employment rate *plus* the percentage change in the level of productivity. Compare the sum of your answers from part (b) with your answers from part (c). Are they close?

e. For each five-year period, what fraction of the percentage change in GDP is accounted for by the change in the employment rate?

f. Over the entire 50-year period, what fraction of the percentage change in GDP is accounted for by the change in the employment rate?

5. Go to Statistics Canada's website (**www.statcan.gc.ca**) and look for data on capacity utilization rates in Canadian industries. The capacity utilization rate is the fraction of the capital stock that is utilized or employed. How has this variable changed over the past several decades? Contrast the short-run versus the long-run movements.

6. At the beginning of the chapter we discussed the short-run and long-run effects of an increase in desired saving (as applied to Japan's economy). Based on what you learned in Chapter 24 regarding the economy's adjustment process, use the *AD/AS* model to do the following:

a. Show the short-run effects of an increase in desired saving (assuming that the economy is initially in a long-run equilibrium with $Y = Y^*$).

b. Describe the adjustment process that brings the economy to its new long-run equilibrium.

c. Compare the initial and the new long-run equilibrium. What is the long-run effect of the increase in desired saving?

Discussion Questions

1. Figure 25-1 on page 626 shows the path of actual GDP and the path of potential GDP. The chapter mentioned that the economy has an adjustment mechanism that brings actual GDP back to potential.

a. Describe this adjustment process, and how it relates to the concept of market-clearing.

b. If, following the implementation of some policy, actual GDP eventually returns to potential GDP, does this mean that policy can have no long-run effect on GDP?

Long-Run Economic Growth

Most economists agree that economic growth is the single most powerful engine for generating long-term increases in material living standards. What happens to our living standards over time depends largely on the growth in real GDP in relation to the growth in population—that is, it depends on the growth of real per capita GDP. Growth in real per capita GDP does not necessarily make *everybody* in Canada materially better off in the short term. But it does increase the *average* standard of living over the long term.

What determines the long-run growth rate of per capita GDP in Canada? Is this something that is beyond our control, or are there some government policies that can stimulate economic growth? If there are, what are the costs of such policies, and are the benefits worth the costs?

In this chapter we examine this important issue of economic growth, beginning with some basic concepts and then moving on to explore the costs and benefits of growth. In the remainder of the chapter we consider various theories of economic growth and then go on to examine the idea that there may be *limits to growth* imposed by resource exhaustion and environmental degradation.

LEARNING OBJECTIVES

In this chapter you will learn

1. about the costs and benefits of economic growth.

2. the four fundamental determinants of growth in real GDP.

3. the main elements of Neoclassical growth theory.

4. about new growth theories based on endogenous technical change and increasing returns.

5. why resource exhaustion and environmental degradation create serious challenges for public policy directed at sustaining economic growth.

26.1 The Nature of Economic Growth

*The Centre for the Study of Living Standards is an Ottawa-based research institute that studies the determinants of economic growth. Visit its website at **www.csls.ca**.*

Figure 26-1 shows the paths of three variables in the Canadian economy since 1960, each of which relates to long-run economic growth. Each variable is expressed as an index number, which takes a value of 100 in 1960. The first is real GDP, which shows an overall growth from 1960 to 2008 of 417 percent, an average annual growth rate of 3.7 percent. Though real GDP is an accepted measure of the amount of annual economic activity, it is not a good measure of average material living standards because it does not take into account the growth in the population—more income is not necessarily better if more people have to share it. The second variable shown is the index of real *per capita* GDP. It shows an overall growth of 178 percent between 1960 and 2008, an annual average growth rate of 2.3 percent.

As we will see in this chapter, one of the most important reasons that both GDP and per capita GDP increase over many years is growth in *productivity*. The third variable provides one measure of productivity; it is an index of real GDP *per employed worker*. Its overall growth for 1960 to 2008 is 80 percent, an average annual growth rate of 1.4 percent. Therefore, the average Canadian worker produced 80 percent more in 2008 than in 1960.

economic growth

Sustained, long-run increases in the level of real GDP.

The three variables in Figure 26-1 show different aspects of **economic growth**, a term that economists usually reserve for describing sustained or long-run increases in real GDP. This chapter will discuss each of these three aspects of economic growth—real GDP, real per capita GDP, and productivity.

FIGURE 26-1   Three Aspects of Economic Growth

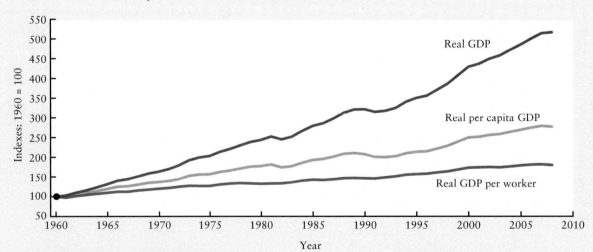

Real GDP, real per capita GDP, and productivity have all grown substantially over the past half-century. Each variable shown is an index number with 1960 = 100. Real GDP has grown faster than real per capita GDP because the population has grown. Real per capita GDP has grown faster than real GDP per worker because the level of employment has grown faster than the population.

(*Source:* All variables are based on authors' calculations, using data from Statistics Canada, CANSIM database. Real GDP: Series V1992067. Employment: Series V2091072. Population: Series V2062809.)

The average annual growth rates shown in Figure 26-1 may seem small, especially those for the measure of productivity. It is important to realize, however, that because these growth rates are sustained for many years, they have a profound influence on material living standards from one generation to the next. Table 26-1 illustrates the cumulative effect of what appear to be very small differences in growth rates. Notice that if one country grows faster than another, the gap in their respective living standards will widen progressively. If, for example, Canada and France start from the same level of income but Canada grows at 3 percent per year while France grows at 2 percent per year, Canada's income will be twice France's in 72 years. [31] You may not care much whether the economy grows at 2 percent or 3 percent per year, but your children and grandchildren certainly will.

We now examine in more detail the benefits and costs of economic growth.

Practise with Study Guide
Chapter 26, Exercise 1.

Benefits of Economic Growth

The benefits of economic growth—in particular, increases in income—may appear obvious. It certainly appears that way to the pro-growth author of the open letter in *Applying Economic Concepts 26-1*. But it is important to distinguish between the increases in average living standards that economic growth brings more or less automatically, and the reduction in poverty that economic growth makes possible but that may still require active policy to make a reality.

Rising Average Material Living Standards

Economic growth is a powerful means of improving average material living standards. A family that is earning $48 000 today can expect an income of about $58 500 within 10 years (in constant dollars) if it experiences a 2 percent annual growth rate in its income. If it has a 4 percent growth rate, its income in 10 years will be $71 050.

TABLE 26-1   The Cumulative Effect of Economic Growth

| | Annual Growth Rate | | | | |
Year	1%	2%	3%	5%	7%
0	100	100	100	100	100
10	111	122	135	165	201
30	135	182	246	448	817
50	165	272	448	1 218	3 312
70	201	406	817	3 312	13 429
100	272	739	2 009	14 841	109 660

Small differences in income growth rates make enormous differences in levels of income over a few decades. Let income be 100 in year 0. At a growth rate of 3 percent per year, it will be 135 in 10 years, 448 after 50 years, and more than 2000 in a century. Notice the difference between 2 percent and 3 percent growth—even small differences in growth rates make big differences in future income levels.

A family often finds that an increase in its income can lead to changes in the pattern of its consumption—extra money buys important amenities of life and also allows more saving for the future. Similarly, economic growth that raises average income tends to change the whole society's consumption patterns, shifting away from tangible goods and toward services. In Canada and other rich, developed countries services account for roughly 70 percent of aggregate consumption, whereas this ratio is significantly lower in poorer, developing countries.

Another example of how economic growth can improve living standards involves environmental protection. In developing countries, most resources are devoted to providing basic requirements of life, such as food, shelter, and clothing. These countries typically do not have the "luxury" of being concerned about environmental degradation. Some people in richer societies may consider this a short-sighted view, but the fact is that the concerns associated with hunger *today* are much more urgent than the concerns associated with *future* environmental problems. In contrast, richer countries are wealthy enough that they can more easily afford to provide the basic requirements of life *and* devote significant resources to environmental protection. Economic growth

APPLYING ECONOMIC CONCEPTS 26-1

An Open Letter from a Supporter of the "Growth Is Good" School

Dear Citizen:

You live in the world's first civilization that is devoted principally to satisfying *your* needs rather than those of a privileged minority. Past civilizations have always been based on leisure and high consumption for a tiny upper class, a reasonable living standard for a small middle class, and hard work with little more than subsistence consumption for the great mass of people.

The continuing Industrial Revolution that began about 250 years ago is based on mass-produced goods for you, the ordinary citizen. It ushered in a period of sustained economic growth that has dramatically raised consumption standards of ordinary citizens. Consider a few examples that were not available to your eighteenth century ancestors: travel, live and recorded music, art, good food, universal literacy, inexpensive books, and a genuine chance to be educated. In addition, modern medical practices have eliminated a host of health scourges that killed and maimed vast numbers of your predecessors, resulting in a great increase in your life expectancy over that of your grandparents and great-grandparents. Finally, there is leisure to provide time and energy to enjoy the thousands of goods and services of the modern developed economy.

Would any ordinary family seriously prefer to go back to the world of 150 or 500 years ago in its same *relative* social and economic position? Surely the answer is no. However, for those with incomes in the top 1 or 2 percent of the income distribution, economic growth has destroyed much of their privileged consumption position. They must now vie with the masses when they visit the world's beauty spots and be annoyed, while lounging on the terrace of a palatial mansion, by the sound of charter flights carrying ordinary people to inexpensive holidays in faraway places. Many of the rich lament the loss of exclusive rights to luxury consumption, and it is not surprising that they find their intellectual apologists.

Whether they know it or not, the anti-growth economists are not the social revolutionaries they think they are. They say that growth has produced wasteful consumption of all kinds of frivolous products that add nothing to human happiness. They also argue that growth has led to pollution and is placing the world's scarce natural resources under extreme stress. However, the democratic solution to pollution is not to go back to the time when so few people consumed that pollution was trivial but rather to learn to control the pollution that mass consumption tends to create. And the solution must involve better management of the world's resources, not a decision to leave them unused altogether.

It is only through further growth that the average citizen will be able to enjoy consumption standards (of travel, culture, medical and health care, and so on) now available only to people in the top 25 percent of the income distribution—which includes the intellectuals who earn large royalties from the books they write in which they denounce growth. If you think that extra income confers little real benefit, just ask those in the top 25 percent to trade incomes with average citizens.

Ordinary citizens, do not be deceived by disguised elitist doctrines. Remember that the very rich and the elite have much to gain by stopping growth and even more by rolling it back, but you have everything to gain by letting it go forward.

Onward!

A. N. Optimist

provides the higher incomes that often lead to a demand for a cleaner environment, thus leading to higher average living standards that are not directly captured by measures of per capita GDP.

Alleviation of Poverty Not everyone benefits equally from growth. Many of the poorest members of the population are not even in the labour force and hence are unlikely to share in the higher wages that, along with profits, are the primary means by which the gains from growth are distributed. For this reason, even in a growing economy, redistribution policies will be needed if poverty is to be reduced.

A rapid growth rate makes the alleviation of poverty easier politically. If existing income is to be redistributed, someone's standard of living will actually have to be lowered. However, when there is economic growth and when some of the *increment* in income is redistributed (through active government policy), it is possible to reduce income inequalities while simultaneously allowing all incomes to rise. It is much easier for a rapidly growing economy to be generous toward its less fortunate citizens—or neighbours—than it is for a static economy.

Costs of Economic Growth

Applying Economic Concepts 26-2 contains an open letter from an anti-growth advocate who argues that we are caught up in a never-ending search for "more" and as a result are losing sight of the real values that guided our ancestors. You may or may not accept this particular line of argument, but it is important to recognize that economic growth does have some real costs. Let's see what they are.

APPLYING ECONOMIC CONCEPTS 26-2

An Open Letter from a Supporter of the "Growth Is Bad" School

Dear Citizen:

You live in a world that is being despoiled by a mindless search for ever-higher levels of material consumption at the cost of all other values. Once upon a time, men and women knew how to enjoy creative work and to derive satisfaction from simple activities. Today, many workers are just a mindless cog in assembly lines that turn out more and more goods that the advertisers must work overtime to persuade the worker to consume.

Statisticians count the increasing flow of material output as a triumph of modern civilization. You wake to the hum of your air conditioner, watch the shopping channel while you dress for work, brew your chemically treated decaffeinated coffee, and eat your bread baked from super-refined flour; you climb into your car to sit in vast traffic jams on exhaust-polluted highways.

Television commercials tell you that by consuming more, you are happier, but happiness lies not in increasing consumption but in increasing the ratio of *satisfaction of wants* to *total wants*. Because the more you consume, the more the advertisers persuade you that you want to consume, you are almost certainly less happy than the average citizen in a small town in 1900, whom we can visualize sitting on the family porch, sipping lemonade, and enjoying the antics of the children as they jump rope by using pieces of old clothesline.

Today, the landscape is dotted with endless factories that produce the plastic trivia of modern society. They drown you in a cloud of noise, air, and water pollution. The countryside is despoiled by strip mines, petroleum refineries, acid rain, and polluting power plants, producing energy that is devoured insatiably by modern factories and motor vehicles. And global warming, caused by our excessive consumption of fossil fuels, threatens to raise the sea level by so much over the next 50 years that anarchy will prevail as hundreds of millions of people are dispossessed of their coastal dwellings.

Now is the time to stop this madness. We must end this crazy rush to produce more and more output, reduce pollution, reverse global warming, and seek justice through a more equitable distribution of existing total income.

Many years ago, Thomas Malthus taught us that if we do not limit population voluntarily, nature will do it for us in a cruel and savage manner. Today, the same is true of output: If we do not halt its growth voluntarily, the halt will be imposed on us by a disastrous increase in pollution and a rapid exhaustion of natural resources.

Citizens, awake! Shake off the worship of growth, learn to enjoy the bounty that is yours already, and reject the endless, self-defeating search for increased happiness through ever-increasing consumption.

Upward!

B. E. Warned

Practise with Study Guide
Chapter 26, Exercise 3.

The Opportunity Cost of Economic Growth In a world of scarcity, almost nothing is free. Growth requires heavy investment of resources in capital goods, as well as in such activities as education. Often these investments yield no immediate return in terms of goods and services for consumption; thus, they imply that sacrifices are being made by the current generation of consumers.

> Economic growth, which promises more goods and services tomorrow, is achieved by consuming fewer goods today. For the economy as a whole, this sacrifice of current consumption is the primary cost of growth.

An example will suggest the importance of this cost. Suppose a hypothetical economy is operating at potential output and is experiencing growth in real GDP at the rate of 2 percent per year. Its citizens consume 85 percent of the GDP and invest 15 percent. But suppose that if they immediately decrease their consumption to 77 percent of GDP (and increase investment to 23 percent), they will produce more capital and thus shift at once to a 3 percent growth rate. The new growth rate can be maintained as long as they keep saving and investing 23 percent of real GDP. Should they do it?

Figure 26-2 illustrates the choice in terms of time paths of consumption. With the assumed figures, it takes 10 years for the actual amount of consumption to catch up to what it would have been had no reallocation been made. In the intervening 10 years, a good deal of consumption is lost, and the cumulative losses in consumption must be made up before society can really be said to have broken even. It takes an *additional* nine years before total consumption over the whole period is as large as it would have been if the economy had remained on the 2 percent path. [32] Over a longer period, however, the payoff from the growth policy becomes enormous. After 30 years,

FIGURE 26-2 The Opportunity Cost of Economic Growth

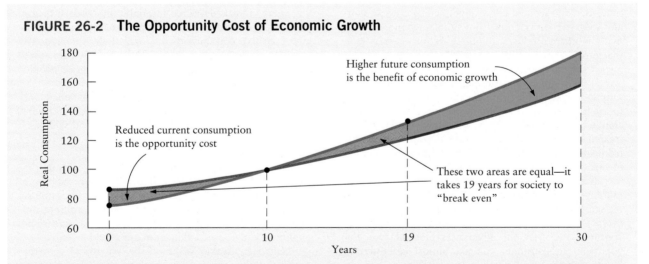

Transferring resources from consumption to investment lowers current consumption but raises growth and therefore future consumption. The example assumes that GDP in year 0 is 100 and that growth of 2 percent per year is possible when consumption equals 85 percent of GDP. The consumption path in this case is shown by the red line, starting at 85 and growing by 2 percent per year. It is further assumed that to achieve a 3 percent growth rate, consumption must fall to 77 percent of GDP. A shift from the red path to the blue path in year 0 decreases consumption for 10 years but increases it thereafter. By year 19 the gains in consumption have made up for the losses from the first 10 years. After 30 years, consumption is 21 percent higher than it would be on the original (red) path.

consumption in the more rapidly growing economy is 21 percent higher than in the slower-growing economy. After 50 years, it is 48 percent higher.

Social Costs of Economic Growth A growing economy is also a changing economy. Part of growth is accounted for by existing firms expanding and producing more output, hiring more workers, and using more equipment and intermediate goods. But another aspect of growth is that existing firms are overtaken and made obsolete by new firms, old products are made obsolete by new products, and existing skills are made obsolete by new skills.

> The process of economic growth renders some machines obsolete and also leaves the skills of some workers partly obsolete.

Economic growth is often associated with the demise of some firms and industries and the expansion of others. Some workers will find it necessary to retrain in order to gain employment in the expanding firms and industries.

No matter how well trained workers are at age 25, in another 25 years many will find that their skills are at least partly obsolete. A high growth rate usually requires rapid adjustments in the labour force, which can cause much upset and misery to some of the people affected by it.

It is often argued that costs of this kind are a small price to pay for the great benefits that growth can bring. Even if this is true in the aggregate, these personal costs are borne very unevenly. Indeed, many of the people for whom growth is most costly (in terms of lost jobs or lowered incomes) share least in the fruits that growth brings.

ⓧ myeconlab **ADDITIONAL TOPICS**

We have been discussing the benefits of economic growth—sustained increases in per capita incomes. Some modern research, however, suggests that rising income is less important for people's happiness than traditionally thought. For more information, go to **What Makes People Happy?** in the *Additional Topics* section of this book's MyEconLab.

w w w . m y e c o n l a b . c o m

Sources of Economic Growth

Economic growth has four fundamental determinants:

1. *Growth in the labour force.* This may be caused by growth in population or by increases in the fraction of the population that chooses to participate in the labour force.

2. *Growth in human capital.* **Human capital** is the term economists use to refer to the set of skills that workers have. Human capital can increase through either formal education or on-the-job training. Human capital can be thought of as the *quality* of the labour force, but because of its importance we will treat it as a separate factor of production from labour.

human capital The set of skills workers acquire through formal education and on-the-job training.

3. *Growth in physical capital.* The stock of physical capital (such as factories, machines, electronic equipment, and transportation and communications facilities) increases only through the process of investment. We include here improvements in the *quality* of the physical capital.

4. *Technological improvement.* This is brought about by innovation that introduces new products, new ways of producing existing products, and new forms of organizing economic activity.

The various theories of economic growth that we explore in the remainder of this chapter can be viewed as theories of these different sources of growth. For example, some theories emphasize the role of increases in physical capital in explaining growth; others emphasize the role of increases in human capital; still others emphasize the importance of technological improvements.

26.2 Established Theories of Economic Growth

In this section we discuss some of the theories of economic growth that have been used by economists for many years. Despite the appearance of some quite different theories in recent years (which we will see later), these established theories remain relevant and contain important insights about the growth process. Learning these provides a solid basis for examining the newer theories in the next section. We begin with a detailed study of the relationship among saving, investment, and economic growth. We then examine the precise predictions of what economists call the Neoclassical growth theory. For simplicity, we assume that the economy is closed—there is no trade in goods or assets with the rest of the world.

Focus on the Long Run

In previous chapters we saw how shifts in the *AD* or *AS* curves led to changes in the short-run equilibrium level of real GDP. The discussion in this chapter focuses instead on the behaviour of the economy in the long run and thus on the growth rate of potential output. We assume that all factor-price adjustment has occurred, and thus real GDP equals Y^*.

> The theory of economic growth is a long-run theory. It concentrates on the growth of potential output over long periods of time, not on short-run fluctuations of output around potential.

Though we will focus on the long-run behaviour of the economy, we can use some of the insights we developed in the short-run version of our macro model. Remember back to Chapter 21 when we were building the simplest short-run macro model (with no government or foreign trade). The equilibrium level of real GDP in that model was such that real GDP was equal to desired aggregate expenditure, which in turn was equal to desired consumption plus desired investment:

$$Y = C + I$$

We can rearrange this equilibrium condition (as we did in the *Additional Topic* cited in Chapter 21) to get

$$Y - C = I$$

or

$$S = I$$

which says that, in equilibrium, desired saving equals desired investment. This is just an alternative way to think about exactly the same equilibrium.

Recall also that in Chapter 21 we took the real interest rate as given, or *exogenous*. Thus, taking the real interest rate as given in our short-run model, the condition that desired saving equals desired investment determined the equilibrium level of real GDP.

We will now extend our model in a way that helps us to consider the long-run behaviour of the economy. In particular, we will allow the interest rate to be an *endogenous* variable—that is, a variable whose value is explained within the model. As you will soon see, when the interest rate is endogenous to the model, the sources of economic growth can be clearly studied.

Fortunately, the equilibrium condition from the simple short-run model also applies in the long run. In the long run, with real GDP equal to Y^*, we can use the saving/investment equilibrium condition by turning it "on its head." That is, we can take the level of output as given (at Y^*) and use the condition that desired saving equals desired investment to determine the equilibrium real interest rate. This long-run perspective of our model will tell us a great deal about the relationship among saving, investment, and economic growth—and the interest rate will play an important role.

Investment, Saving, and Growth

We now complicate our model slightly by adding a government sector that purchases goods and services (G) and collects taxes (T). National saving is the sum of private saving and public (government) saving. Desired private saving is the difference between disposable income and desired consumption. With real GDP equal to Y^* in the long run, desired private saving is equal to

$$\text{Private saving} = Y^* - T - C$$

Public saving is equal to the combined budget surpluses of the federal, provincial, and municipal governments:

$$\text{Public saving} = T - G$$

National saving is therefore equal to

$$\text{National saving} = NS = Y^* - T - C + (T - G) \Rightarrow NS = Y^* - C - G$$

For a given level of output in the long run, an increase in household consumption or government purchases must imply a reduction in national saving.[1]

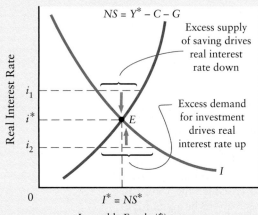

FIGURE 26-3   **The Long-Run Connection Between Saving and Investment**

$NS = Y^* - C - G$

Excess supply of saving drives real interest rate down

Excess demand for investment drives real interest rate up

Real Interest Rate

i_1

i^* E

i_2

I

0 $I^* = NS^*$

Loanable Funds ($)

In the long run, the condition that desired national saving equals desired investment determines the equilibrium real interest rate. Investment demand by firms is negatively related to the real interest rate. The supply of national (private plus public) saving is positively related to the real interest rate, since increases in the interest rate lead to a decline in desired consumption (C). Notice that real GDP in this figure is held constant at Y^* since the analysis applies to the long run.

At point E the market for loanable funds clears and the real interest rate is i^*. At this real interest rate, the amount of investment is I^*, which equals the amount of national saving, NS^*.

Figure 26-3 shows the supply of national saving as a function of the real interest rate. We label the horizontal axis "Loanable Funds," which is measured in dollars. The real interest rate is shown on the vertical axis. The national saving (NS) curve is upward sloping because, as we first saw in Chapter 21, an increase in the interest rate is assumed to lead households to reduce their current consumption, especially on big-ticket items and durable goods, such as cars, furniture, and appliances, that are often purchased on credit. Note also that the NS curve is quite steep, in keeping with empirical evidence suggesting that household consumption responds only modestly to changes in the real interest rate.

Figure 26-3 also shows a downward-sloping investment demand curve, I. As we first saw in Chapter 21, all components of desired investment (plant and equipment, inventories, and residential investment) are negatively related to the real interest rate because, whether the investment is financed by borrowing or by using the firm's retained earnings, the real interest rate reflects the opportunity cost of using these funds.

Our long-run model of saving and investment is now complete. In the short-run model in Chapter 21, the economy is in equilibrium when desired saving equals desired investment. We have now modified that setting in only two ways. First, we have added government. Second, and more important, since we are examining the economy in the long run, we are holding real GDP constant at Y^* and letting the equilibrium condition that desired saving equal desired investment determine the real interest rate in the market for loanable funds.

In the long-run version of our macro model, with real GDP equal to Y^*, the equilibrium interest rate is determined where desired national saving equals desired investment.

In Figure 26-3, equilibrium in the market for loanable funds occurs at interest rate i^* where $NS = I$. Imagine what would happen if the real interest rate were above i^* at i_1. At this high interest rate, the amount of desired saving exceeds the amount of desired investment, and this excess supply of loanable funds pushes down the price of

---

[1] It appears in our NS equation that changes in taxes have no effect on the level of national saving, but this is misleading. Changes in T may affect national saving through an *indirect* effect on C. For example, as we saw at the end of Chapter 24, a reduction in taxes is likely to lead to an increase in consumption spending and therefore to a reduction in national saving (for given values of Y^* and G).

FIGURE 26-4   Increases in Investment Demand and the Supply of National Saving

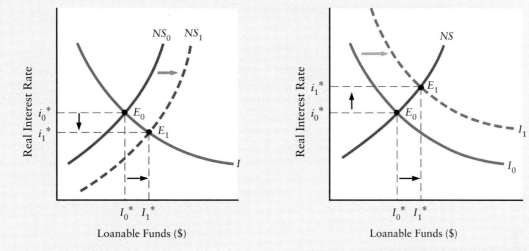

(i) Increase in the supply of saving   (ii) Increase in the demand for investment

Changes in the supply of national saving or the demand for investment will change the equilibrium real interest rate and the rate of growth of potential output. In part (i), the increase in the supply of national saving pushes down the real interest rate and encourages more investment. In part (ii), the increase in the demand for investment pushes up the real interest rate and encourages more saving. In both cases, there is an increase in the equilibrium amount of investment (and saving) and the economy moves from E_0 to E_1; this higher rate of capital accumulation leads to an increase in the economy's long-run rate of growth.

credit—the real interest rate. Conversely, if the interest rate is below i^* at i_2, the quantity of desired investment exceeds the quantity of desired saving, and this excess demand for loanable funds pushes up the real interest rate. Only at point E is the economy in equilibrium, with the real interest rate equal to i^* and desired investment equal to desired saving.

Let's now see how changes in the supply of saving or investment demand lead to changes in the real interest rate and what these changes imply for the economy's long-run economic growth.

An Increase in the Supply of National Saving Suppose the supply of national saving increases, so that the NS curve shifts to the right, as shown in part (i) of Figure 26-4. This increase in the supply of national saving could happen either because household consumption (C) falls or because government purchases (G) fall (or because T rises, which reduces C). A decline in either C or G means that national saving rises at any real interest rate and so the NS curve shifts to the right.

The increase in the supply of national saving leads to an excess supply of loanable funds and thus to a decline in the real interest rate. As the interest rate falls, firms decide to undertake more investment projects and the economy moves from the initial equilibrium E_0 to the new equilibrium E_1. At the new equilibrium, more of the economy's resources are devoted to investment than before, and thus the country's capital stock is rising at a faster rate. The higher rate of investment therefore leads to a higher future growth rate of potential output.

> In the long run, an increase in the supply of national saving reduces the real interest rate and encourages more investment. The higher rate of investment leads to a higher future growth rate of potential output.

An Increase in Investment Demand Now suppose firms' demand for investment increases so that the *I* curve shifts to the right, as shown in part (ii) of Figure 26-4. The increase in desired investment might be caused by technological improvements that increase the productivity of investment goods or by a government tax incentive aimed at encouraging investment. Whatever its cause, the increase in investment demand creates an excess demand for loanable funds and therefore leads to a rise in the real interest rate. The rise in the interest rate encourages households to reduce their current consumption and increase their desired saving. At the new equilibrium, E_1, both the real interest rate and the amount of investment are higher than at the initial equilibrium. The greater investment means faster growth in the economy's capital stock and therefore a higher future rate of growth of potential output.

> In the long run, an increase in the demand for investment pushes up the real interest rate and encourages more saving by households. The higher rate of saving (and investment) leads to a higher future growth rate of potential output.

Summary In our macro model, which we have now extended to enable us to determine the real interest rate in long-run equilibrium, there is a close relationship among saving, investment, and the rate of economic growth. We can see this relationship most clearly when studying the market for loanable funds. Let's summarize our results.

1. In long-run equilibrium, with $Y = Y^*$, the condition that desired national saving equals desired investment determines the equilibrium interest rate in the market for loanable funds. This equilibrium also determines the flows of investment and saving.

2. An increase in the supply of national saving will lead to a fall in the real interest rate and thus to an increase in the amount of investment. This is a shift of the *NS* curve and a movement along the *I* curve.

3. An increase in the demand for investment will lead to a rise in the real interest rate and thus to an increase in the amount of national saving. This is a shift of the *I* curve and a movement along the *NS* curve.

4. A shift in either the *NS* or the *I* curve will lead to a change in the equilibrium real interest rate and to a change in the amount of the economy's resources devoted to investment. An increase in the equilibrium amount of investment implies a greater growth rate of the capital stock and thus a higher future growth rate of potential output.

Investment and Growth in Industrialized Countries Our model predicts that countries with high rates of investment are also countries with high rates of real GDP growth. To provide evidence in support of this prediction, Figure 26-5 shows data from the most industrialized countries between 1950 and 2004. Each point in the figure corresponds to a single country and shows that country's annual average investment rate (as a percentage of GDP) plotted against the annual average growth rate in real per capita GDP. What is clear from the figure is a positive relationship between investment rates and growth rates, as suggested by our model.

FIGURE 26-5   Cross-Country Investment and Growth Rates, 1950–2004

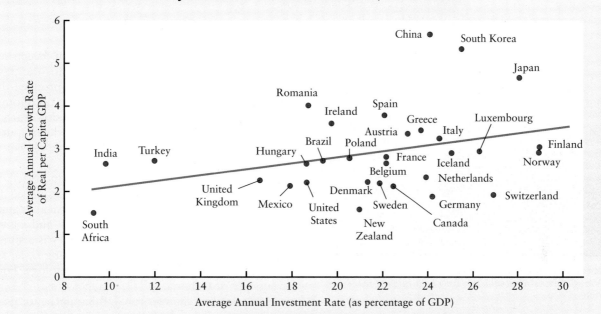

There is a positive relationship between a country's investment rate (as a percentage of GDP) and its growth rate of real per capita GDP. For each of the countries, the annual averages for investment rates and per capita GDP growth rates are computed between 1950 and 2004. Each point represents the average values of these variables for a single country over this 54-year period. The straight line is the "line of best fit" between the growth rates and the investment rates. Countries with high investment rates tend to be countries with high rates of economic growth.

(*Source:* Based on authors' calculations by using data from the Penn World Tables 6.2. The data for South Korea starts in 1953, Romania in 1960, and Germany, Hungary, and Poland in 1970. Alan Heston, Robert Summers, and Bettina Aten, Penn World Table Version 6.2, Center for International Comparisons of Production, Income and Prices at the University of Pennsylvania, September 2006.)

ⵊ **myeconlab**   **ADDITIONAL TOPICS**

We have been discussing the relationship between investment and saving in a model of a *closed* economy. In the reality of today's globalized financial markets, however, billions of dollars of financial capital flow across international boundaries every day. For more details about how our model can be modified for an open economy, look for **Investment and Saving in Globalized Financial Markets** in the *Additional Topics* section of this book's MyEconLab.

www.myeconlab.com

Neoclassical Growth Theory

Recall the four fundamental sources of economic growth that we discussed at the beginning of this section. Much of what is referred to as *Neoclassical growth theory* is based on the idea that these four forces of economic growth can be connected by what is called the **aggregate production function**. This is an expression for the relationship between the total amounts of labour (*L*) and physical capital (*K*) employed, the quality

aggregate production function The relationship between the total amount of each factor of production employed in the nation and the nation's total GDP.

of labour's human capital (*H*), the state of technology (*T*), and the nation's total level of output (GDP). The aggregate production function can be expressed as

$$GDP = F_T (L, K, H)$$

Hong Kong is an example of an economy that has had very high rates of investment and also very high rates of real GDP growth.

It is an *aggregate* production function because it relates the economy's *total* output to the *total* amount of the factors that are used to produce that output.[2] (Those who have studied microeconomics will recall that a micro production function, such as is discussed in Chapters 7 and 8, relates the output of *one firm* to the factors of production employed by *that firm*.)

The production function above—indicated by F_T—tells us how much GDP will be produced for given amounts of labour and physical capital employed, given levels of human capital, and a given state of technology. Using the notation F_T is a simple way of indicating that the function relating *L*, *K*, and *H* to GDP depends on the state of technology. For a given state of technology (*T*), changes in either *L*, *K*, or *H* will lead to changes in GDP. Similarly, for given values of *L*, *K*, and *H*, changes in *T* will lead to changes in GDP. [33]

> When discussing long-run economic growth, we focus on the changes in potential output. We therefore interpret GDP in the aggregate production function as potential output.

Practise with Study Guide Chapter 26, Exercise 2.

law of diminishing marginal returns The hypothesis that if increasing quantities of a variable factor are applied to a given quantity of fixed factors, the marginal product of the variable factor will eventually decrease.

Properties of the Aggregate Production Function

The key aspects of the Neoclassical theory are that the aggregate production function displays diminishing marginal returns when any one of the factors is increased on its own and constant returns to scale when all factors are increased together (and in the same proportion). To explain the meaning of these concepts more clearly, we will assume for simplicity that human capital and physical capital can be combined into a single variable called capital and that technology is held constant; we therefore focus on the effects of changes in *K* or *L*. This is an appropriate simplification when dealing with the Neoclassical theory since early versions of the theory focused on the importance of *K* and *L*; changes in technology and human capital played very minor roles.

1. DIMINISHING MARGINAL RETURNS. To begin, suppose that the labour force grows while the stock of capital remains constant. More and more people go to work using a fixed quantity of capital. The amount that each new worker adds to total output is called labour's *marginal product*. The operation of the **law of diminishing marginal returns** tells us that the employment of additional workers (or hours of work) will eventually add less to total output than the previous worker did. In other words, each

---

[2] Natural resources (including land, forests, mineral deposits, etc.) are also important inputs to the production process. We leave them out of this discussion only for simplicity.

additional worker will sooner or later produce a diminishing marginal product. A simple production function is shown in Figure 26-6 and the law of diminishing marginal returns is illustrated.

The law of diminishing returns applies to any factor that is varied while the other factors are held constant. Hence, successive amounts of capital added to a fixed supply of labour will also eventually add less and less to GDP.

> **According to the law of diminishing marginal returns, whenever equal increases of one factor of production are combined with a fixed amount of another factor, the increment to total production will eventually decline.**

FIGURE 26-6   The Aggregate Production Function and Diminishing Marginal Returns

Units of Labour (1)	Units of Output (GDP) (2)	Average Product of Labour (GDP/L) (3)	Marginal Product of Labour (ΔGDP/ΔL) (4)
1	12.0	12.0	
			5.0
2	17.0	8.5	
			3.8
3	20.8	6.9	
			3.2
4	24.0	6.0	
			2.8
5	26.8	5.4	
			2.6
6	29.4	4.9	
			2.5
7	31.9	4.6	
			2.1
8	34.0	4.2	
			2.0
9	36.0	4.0	
			1.9
10	37.9	3.8	

(i) Total output

(ii) Marginal and average product of labour

With one input held constant, the other input has a declining average and marginal product. We have assumed a hypothetical aggregate production function given by: GDP = $4\sqrt{KL}$; we have also assumed that K is constant and equal to 9. Column 2 shows total output as more of the variable factor, labour, is used with a fixed amount of capital. Total output is plotted in part (i) of the figure. Both the average product of labour and the marginal product of labour decline continuously. They are plotted in part (ii) of the figure.

constant returns to scale
A situation in which output increases in proportion to the change in all inputs as the scale of production is increased.

Practise with Study Guide Chapter 26, Exercise 4 and Extension Exercise E1.

2. CONSTANT RETURNS TO SCALE. The other main property of the Neoclassical aggregate production function is that it displays **constant returns to scale**. Remember that we are assuming for simplicity that labour and capital are the only two inputs. In that setting, the amounts of labour and capital are both changed in equal proportion; with constant returns to scale, total output will also change by that proportion. For example, if L and K both increase by 10 percent, then GDP will also increase by 10 percent. [34]

Economic Growth in the Neoclassical Model Now that we understand the properties of the aggregate production function, we can examine the predictions of the Neoclassical growth theory. Recall the four fundamental sources of growth:

1. Growth in labour force

2. Growth in human capital

3. Growth in physical capital

4. Technological improvement

What does the Neoclassical theory predict will happen when each of these elements changes? In this section, we focus on the effects of labour-force growth and the accumulation of physical and human capital (combined), holding constant the level of technology. In the next section, we focus on technological change.

1. LABOUR-FORCE GROWTH. Over the long term, we can associate labour-force growth with population growth (although in the short term, the labour force can grow if participation rates rise even though the population remains constant). As more labour is used, more output will be produced. For a given stock of capital, however, the law of diminishing marginal returns tells us that sooner or later, each additional unit of labour employed will cause smaller and smaller additions to GDP. Once both the marginal product and average product of labour are falling (with each additional increment to labour), we get an interesting result. Although economic growth continues in the sense that total output is growing, material living standards are actually *falling* because average GDP *per person* is falling (real GDP is growing more slowly than the population). If we are interested in growth in living standards, we are concerned with increasing real GDP per person.

> In the Neoclassical growth model with diminishing marginal returns, increases in population (with a fixed stock of capital) lead to increases in GDP but an eventual decline in material living standards.

2. PHYSICAL AND HUMAN CAPITAL ACCUMULATION. Consider the accumulation of both physical and human capital. Growth in physical capital occurs whenever there is positive (net) investment in the economy. For example, if Canadian firms produce $100 billion of capital goods this year, and only $20 billion is for the replacement of old, worn-out equipment, then Canada's capital stock increases by $80 billion.

How does human capital accumulate? Human capital has several aspects. One involves improvements in the health and longevity of the population. Of course, these are desired as ends in themselves, but they also have consequences for both the size and the productivity of the labour force. There is no doubt that improvements in the health of workers tend to increase productivity per worker-hour by cutting down on illness, accidents, and absenteeism. A second aspect of human capital concerns technical training—from learning to operate a machine or software program to learning how to be a scientist. This training depends on the current state of knowledge, and advances in knowledge allow us not only to build more productive physical capital but also to create more effective human capital. Also, the longer a person has been educated, the more adaptable and, hence, the more productive in the long run that person is in the face of new and changing challenges.

The accumulation of capital—either physical or human—affects GDP in a manner similar to population growth. The law of diminishing marginal returns implies that, eventually, each successive unit of capital will add less to total output than each previous unit of capital.

There is, however, a major contrast with the case of labour-force growth because it is output *per person* that

Increases in the amount and quality of physical capital lead to improvements in the productivity of labour. These productivity improvements raise material living standards, as measured by real per capita GDP.

determines living standards, not output per unit of capital. Thus, for a constant population, increases in the stock of physical or human capital *always* lead to increases in living standards because output *per person* increases. However, because the increases in capital are subject to diminishing marginal returns, successive additions to the economy's capital stock bring smaller and smaller increases in per capita output.

> **In the Neoclassical model, capital accumulation leads to improvements in living standards, but because of the law of diminishing marginal returns, these improvements become smaller with each additional increment of capital.**

3. BALANCED GROWTH WITH CONSTANT TECHNOLOGY. Now consider what happens if labour and capital (both human and physical capital) grow at the same rate. This is what economists call "balanced" growth. In this case, the Neoclassical assumption of constant returns to scale means that GDP grows in proportion to the increases in inputs. For example, if capital and labour both increase by 2 percent per year, then GDP also increases by 2 percent per year. As a result, per capita output (GDP/L) remains constant. Thus, balanced growth in labour and capital leads to growth in total GDP but unchanged per capita GDP.

This balanced growth is not, however, the kind of growth that concerns people interested in explaining rising living standards. Since increases in living standards are determined largely by increases in *per capita* output, it is clear that balanced growth is unable to explain *rising* living standards.

> **If capital and labour grow at the same rate, GDP will increase. But in the Neoclassical growth model with constant returns to scale, such balanced growth will not lead to increases in per capita output and therefore will not generate improvements in living standards.**

The Neoclassical growth theory predicts that growth in the labour force leads to declining per capita income, and capital accumulation leads to ever-diminishing growth rates of per capita income. Even increases in labour and capital together cannot explain increases in per capita income. What we observe in many countries around the world, however, is sustained growth in real per capita incomes. How does the Neoclassical theory explain this observation, if not through growth in labour or capital? The answer is technological change, to which we now turn.

The Importance of Technological Change

In Neoclassical growth theory, technological change is assumed to be exogenous—that is, it is not explained by the theory itself. This is an important weakness of the theory because it means that the theory is unable to explain perhaps the most important determinant of long-run improvements in living standards. For now we focus on the importance of technological change itself and on how it might be measured. In the next section we move beyond Neoclassical growth theory and see some more modern theories designed to explain the sources of technological change.

embodied technical change Technical change that is intrinsic to the particular capital goods in use.

New knowledge and inventions can contribute markedly to the growth of potential output, even without capital accumulation or labour-force growth. To illustrate this point, suppose the proportion of a society's resources devoted to the production of capital goods is just sufficient to replace capital as it wears out. If the old capital is merely replaced in the same form, the capital stock will be constant, and there will be no increase in the capacity to produce. However, if there is a growth of knowledge so that as old equipment wears out it is replaced by different and more productive equipment, then productive capacity will be growing.

The increase in productive capacity created by installing new and better capital goods is called **embodied technical change**. This term reflects the idea that technological improvements are contained in the new capital goods. Thus, even if the *quantity* of capital may be unchanged, improvements in its *quality* lead to increases in the economy's productive capacity. Embodied technical change has been enormously important through history and continues to be important today. Consider how improvements in the quality of airplanes have revolutionized transportation over the past 50 years, or how improvements in the quality of electronics have revolutionized communications over the same period. Indeed, once you start thinking about embodied technical change, you see many examples of it around you on a daily basis.

Many improvements in technology are embodied in the capital stock, making it difficult to estimate the change in technology independently from the change in the capital stock. Each computer above is a single machine, yet the new laptop has far more capabilities than the 25-year old desktop because of its embodied technological advances.

Less obvious but nonetheless important are technical changes that are embodied in *human* capital. These are changes that result from a better-educated, more experienced labour force; better management practices and techniques; improved design, marketing, and organization of business activities; and feedback from user experience leading to product improvement.

> **Many innovations are embodied in either physical or human capital. These innovations cause continual changes in the techniques of production and in the nature of what is produced. Embodied technical change leads to increases in potential output even if the amounts of labour and capital are held constant.**

Not all technological change is embodied in capital. Examples of *disembodied* technical change include the development of new materials and production processes; both are examples in which technological improvement allows for more output to be produced from the same capital and labour. However, such disembodied technological changes often get quickly embodied in capital as machines or skills are modified to incorporate the latest developments. Thus, distinguishing precisely between embodied and disembodied technological change is often difficult.

We have been discussing the benefits of technological change in terms of raising overall living standards. Ever since the Industrial Revolution, however, some workers have feared the effects of technological change. Technological change, after all, is often responsible for workers losing their jobs as employers replace less efficient labour with more efficient equipment. *Lessons from History 26-1* examines the relationship between technological progress and changes in employment. The main lesson we learn is that technological change over the years has created far more jobs than it has destroyed.

Can We Measure Technological Change? Technological change is obviously important. You need only look around you at the current products and production methods that did not exist a generation ago, or even a few years ago, to realize how the advance of technology changes our lives. But *how much* does technology change? Unfortunately, technology is not something that is easily measured and so it is very difficult to know just how important it is to the process of economic growth.

In 1957, Robert Solow, an economist at MIT who was awarded the Nobel Prize 30 years later for his research on economic growth, attempted to measure the amount of technical change in the United States. He devised a way to infer from the data (under some assumptions about the aggregate production function) how much of the observed growth in real GDP was due to the growth in labour and capital and how much was due to technical change. His method led to the creation of what is now called the "Solow residual." The Solow residual is the amount of growth in GDP that cannot be accounted for by growth in the labour force or by growth in the capital stock. Since Solow was thinking about changes in GDP as having only three possible sources— changes in capital, changes in labour, and changes in technology—the "residual" was naturally interpreted as a measure of technical change.

Today, economists do not view the Solow residual as a precise estimate of the amount of technical change. One reason is that much technical change is known to be embodied in new physical and human capital. Thus, capital accumulation and technological change are inherently connected. For example, imagine a firm that adds to its stock of capital by purchasing two new computers. These new computers embody the latest technology and are more productive than the firm's existing computers. In this case, there has been an increase in the capital stock but there has also been an increase—though not easily measured—in the level of technology. Solow's method would attribute all the change in (embodied) technology to the change in the capital stock, even though we know that a technological change has taken place. Thus, in the

LESSONS FROM HISTORY 26-1

Should Workers Be Afraid of Technological Change?

From time immemorial people have observed that technological change destroys particular jobs and have worried that it will destroy jobs in general. Should they worry?

Technological change *does* destroy particular jobs. When water wheels were used to automate the production of cloth in twelfth-century Europe, there were riots and protests among the workers who lost their jobs. A century ago, 50 percent of the labour force in North America and Europe was required to produce the required food. Today, less than 5 percent of the labour force is needed in the high-income countries to feed all their citizens. In other words, out of every 100 jobs that existed in 1900, 50 were in agriculture and 45 of those were destroyed by technological progress over the course of the twentieth century.

Just as technological change destroys some jobs, it also creates many new jobs. The displaced agricultural workers did not join the ranks of the permanently unemployed—although some of the older ones may have, their children did not. Instead they, and their children, took jobs in manufacturing and service industries and helped to produce the mass of new goods and services—such as automobiles, refrigerators, computers, and foreign travel—that have raised living standards over the century.

Worries that technological change will cause general unemployment have been recorded for centuries, but, so far at least, there is no sign that those displaced by technological change (or their children) are being forced into the ranks of the permanently unemployed. Over all of recorded history, technological change has created more jobs than it has destroyed.

But how about today? Aren't there good reasons to be more afraid of technological change now than in the past? Modern technologies have two aspects that worry some observers. First, they tend to be *knowledge intensive*. A fairly high degree of literacy and numeracy, as well as familiarity with computers, is needed to work with many of these new technologies. Second, through the process of globalization, unskilled workers in advanced countries have come into competition with unskilled workers everywhere in the world. Both of these forces are decreasing the relative demand for unskilled workers in developed countries and have led to falling relative wages for unskilled workers in countries like Canada. If labour markets are insufficiently flexible, this change in relative demand may also lead to some structural unemployment.

For these reasons, some people blame the high unemployment rates in Europe (and to a lesser extent, in Canada) on the new technologies. This is hard to reconcile, however, with the fact that the lowest unemployment rates in the industrialized countries have (until very recently) been recorded in the United States, the most technologically dynamic of all countries. This suggests that the cause of high European unemployment rates may be not enough technological change and too much inflexibility in labour markets rather than too much technological change.

presence of embodied technical change that gets measured as increases in capital, the Solow residual is, at best, an underestimate of the true amount of technological change.

Despite these problems, Solow's method of "growth accounting" and the Solow residual are still widely used by economists in universities and government. The Solow residual often goes by another name—the rate of growth of *total factor productivity* (*TFP*).

myeconlab   ADDITIONAL TOPICS

The aging of Canada's baby-boom generation over the next three decades will lead to a reduction in Canadian economic growth and will produce challenges for Canadian governments. For more details, see **The Economic and Fiscal Challenges of Population Aging** in the *Additional Topics* section of this book's MyEconLab.

26.3 New Growth Theories

In recent years, economists have developed new theories of economic growth that go beyond the established Neoclassical theory based on diminishing marginal returns and exogenous technical change. Economic growth is an active area of research in which there is considerable debate over whether new theories are necessary, or whether the established theories do an adequate job of explaining the process of long-term economic growth.

In this section, we give a brief discussion of two strands of this new research—models that emphasize *endogenous technological change* and models based on *increasing marginal returns*.

Endogenous Technological Change

In Neoclassical growth theory, innovation increases the amount of output producible from a given level of factor inputs. But this innovation is itself unexplained. The Neoclassical model thus views technological change as *exogenous*. It has profound effects on economic variables but it is not itself influenced by economic causes. It just happens.

Yet research by many scholars has established that technological change is responsive to such economic signals as prices and profits; in other words, it is *endogenous* to the economic system. Though much of the earliest work on this issue was done in Europe, the most influential overall single study was by an American, Nathan Rosenberg, whose trailblazing 1982 book *Inside the Black Box: Technology and Economics* argued this case in great detail.

Technological change stems from research and development and from innovating activities that put the results of R&D into practice. These are costly and highly risky activities, undertaken largely by firms and usually in pursuit of profit. It is not surprising, therefore, that these activities respond to economic incentives. If the price of some particular input, such as petroleum or skilled labour, goes up, R&D and innovating activities may be directed to altering the production function to economize on these expensive inputs. This process is not simply a substitution of less expensive inputs for more expensive ones within the confines of known technologies; rather, it is the *development of new technologies* in response to changes in relative prices.

There are several important implications of this new understanding that, to a great extent, growth is achieved through costly, risky, innovative activity that often occurs in response to economic signals.

Learning by Doing The pioneering theorist of innovation, Joseph Schumpeter (1883–1950), developed a model in which innovation flowed in one direction from a pure discovery "upstream," to more applied R&D, then to working machines, and finally to output "downstream."

In contrast, modern research shows that innovation involves a large amount of "learning by doing" at all of its stages. (We discuss this kind of learning in more detail in Chapter 33.) What is

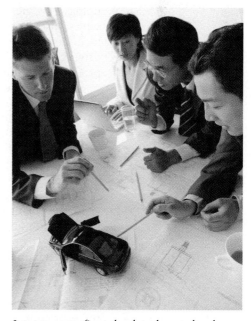

Japanese auto firms developed an early advantage over their North American competitors by involving their production departments in all stages of the design process.

learned downstream then modifies what must be done upstream. The best innovation-managing systems encourage such "feedback" from the more applied steps to the purer researchers and from users to designers.

This interaction is illustrated, for example, by the differences that existed for many years between the Japanese automobile manufacturers and their North American competitors in the handling of new models. North American design was traditionally centralized: Design production teams developed the overall design and then instructed their production sections and asked for bids from parts manufacturers to produce according to specified blueprints. As a result, defects in the original design were often not discovered until production was underway, causing many costly delays and rejection of parts already supplied. In contrast, Japanese firms involved their design and production departments and their parts manufacturers in all stages of the design process. Parts manufacturers were not given specific blueprints for production; instead, they were given general specifications and asked to develop their own detailed designs. As they did so, they learned. They then fed information about the problems they were encountering back to the main designers while the general outlines of the new model were not yet finalized. As a result, the Japanese were able to design a new product faster, at less cost, and with far fewer problems than were the North American firms. In recent years, however, the North American automotive firms have adopted many of these Japanese design and production methods.

Knowledge Transfer The diffusion of technological knowledge from those who have it to those who want it is not costless (as it was assumed to be in Schumpeter's model). We often tend to think that once a production process is developed, it can easily be copied by others. In practice, however, the diffusion of new technological knowledge is not so simple. Firms need research capacity just to adopt the technologies developed by others. Some of the knowledge needed to use a new technology can be learned only through experience by plant managers, technicians, and operators.

For example, research has shown that most industrial technologies require technology-specific organizational skills that cannot be "embodied" in the machines themselves, instruction books, or blueprints. The needed knowledge is *tacit* in the sense that it cannot be taught through books and can be acquired only by experience—much like driving a car or playing a video game. Acquiring tacit knowledge requires a deliberate process of building up new skills, work practices, knowledge, and experience.

The fact that diffusion is a costly and time-consuming process explains why new technologies take considerable time to diffuse, first through the economy of the originating country and then through the rest of the world. If diffusion were simple and virtually costless, the puzzle would be why technological knowledge and best industrial practices did not diffuse very quickly. As it is, decades can pass before a new technological process is diffused everywhere that it could be employed.

Market Structure and Innovation Because it is highly risky, innovation is encouraged by strong rivalry among firms and discouraged by monopoly practices. Competition among three or four large firms often produces much innovation, but a single firm, especially if it serves a secure home market protected by trade barriers, often seems much less inclined to innovate. The reduction in trade barriers over the past several decades and the increasing globalization of markets as a result of falling transportation and communication costs have increased international competition. Whereas one firm in a national market might have had substantial monopoly power three or four decades ago, today it is more likely to be in intense competition with firms based in other countries. This greater international competition may lead to more innovation.

An important implication of this general idea is that policies that make firms more competitive—either by lowering protective tariffs or by reducing domestic regulations that hamper competition—are likely to have a positive effect on the amount of innovation and thus on an economy's rate of growth of productivity. This is a central conclusion in *The Power of Productivity,* an influential book published in 2004 by William Lewis.

Shocks and Innovation One interesting consequence of endogenous technical change is that shocks that would be unambiguously adverse to an economy operating with fixed technology can sometimes provide a spur to innovation that proves a blessing in disguise. A sharp rise in the price of one input can raise costs and lower the value of output per person for some time. But it may lead to a wave of innovations that reduce the need for this expensive input and, as a side effect, greatly raise productivity. One example is the development of fuel-efficient automobiles following large increases in the world price of oil in the 1970s.

Sometimes individual firms will respond differently to the same economic signal. Sometimes those that respond by altering technology will do better than those that concentrate their efforts on substituting within the confines of known technology. For example, in *The Competitive Advantage of Nations,* Harvard economist Michael Porter tells the story of the consumer electronics industry, in which some U.S. firms moved their operations abroad to avoid high, rigid labour costs. They continued to use their existing technology and went where labour costs were low enough to make that technology pay. Their Japanese competitors, however, stayed at home. They innovated away most of their labour costs and then built factories in the United States to replace the factories of U.S. firms that had gone abroad!

Increasing Marginal Returns

We saw earlier that Neoclassical theories of economic growth assume that investment in capital is subject to diminishing marginal returns. New growth theories emphasize the possibility of *increasing returns* that remain for considerable periods of time: As investment in some new area, product, or production technology proceeds through time, new increments of investment are *more* productive than previous increments. Economists have noted a number of sources of increasing marginal returns. These fall under the two general categories of *market-development costs* and *knowledge.*

Market-Development Costs For three reasons, there may be important costs associated with the initial development of the market. These costs result in increasing marginal returns to investment.

1. Investment in the early stages of development of a country, province, or town may create new skills and attitudes in the workforce that are then available to all subsequent firms, whose costs are therefore lower than those encountered by the initial firms. (For those who have studied microeconomics, the early firms are conferring a positive *externality* on those who follow them, as described in Chapter 16.)

The development of the electric car has been expensive for those companies involved at early stages. As a result, there may be significant advantages to other firms who follow the pioneers.

2. Each new firm may find the environment more and more favourable to its investment because of the physical infrastructure that has been created by those who came before.

3. The first investment in a new product will encounter countless production problems that, once overcome, cause fewer problems to subsequent investors.

In each of these examples, the returns to later investment are greater than the returns to the same investment made earlier for the simple reason that the economic environment becomes more fully developed over time. Early firms must incur costs in order to develop various aspects of the market, but some benefits of this development are then reaped by later firms that need not incur these costs. As a result, the investment returns for "followers" can be substantially greater than the investment returns for "pioneers." In short, doing something really new is difficult, whereas making further variations on an accepted and developed new idea becomes progressively easier over time.

Another important issue concerns the behaviour of customers. When a new product is developed, customers will often resist adopting it, both because they may be conservative and because they know that new products often experience "growing pains." Customers also need time to learn how best to use the new product—they need to do what is called "learning by using." And it may take time and "using experience" before producers get all the bugs out of the design of new products.

Slow acceptance of new products by customers is not necessarily irrational. When a sophisticated new product comes on the market, no one is sure if it will be a success, and the first customers to buy it take the risk that the product may subsequently turn out to be a failure. They also incur the costs of learning how to use it effectively. Many potential users take the not unreasonable attitude of letting others try a new product, following only after the product's success has been demonstrated. This makes the early stages of innovation especially costly and risky.

> Successive increments of investment associated with an innovation often yield a range of increasing marginal returns as costs that are incurred in earlier investment expenditure provide publicly available knowledge and experience and as customer attitudes and abilities become more receptive to new products.

A computer is a private good because if I own it then you cannot also own it. But the knowledge required to build the computer is a public good. And knowledge, unlike traditional factors of production, is not necessarily subject to the law of diminishing returns.

Knowledge An even more fundamental aspect of the new growth theories is the shift from the economics of goods to the economics of *ideas*. Physical goods, such as factories and machines, exist in one place at one time. This has two consequences. First, when physical goods are used by someone, they cannot be used by someone else. Second, if a given labour force is provided with more and more physical objects to use in production, sooner or later diminishing marginal returns will be encountered.

Ideas have different characteristics. Once someone develops an idea, it is available for use by everyone simultaneously. Ideas can be used by one person without reducing their use by others. For example, if one firm uses a truck, another firm cannot use it at the same time; but one firm's use of a revolutionary design for a new suspension system on a truck does not prevent other firms from using that design as well. Ideas are often not subject to the same use restrictions as goods. (For those who have studied microeconomics, some knowledge has aspects that make it a *public good,* as we discussed in Chapter 16.) Ideas are also not necessarily subject to diminishing marginal returns. As our knowledge increases, each increment of new knowledge does not inevitably add less to our productive ability than each previous increment.

New growth theories stress the importance of ideas in producing what is called *knowledge-driven growth.* New knowledge provides the input that allows investment to produce increasing rather than diminishing marginal returns. Because there are no practical limits to human knowledge, there need be no immediate boundaries to finding new ways to produce more output by using less of all inputs.

> **Neoclassical growth theories gave economics the name "the dismal science" by emphasizing diminishing marginal returns under conditions of given technology. The new growth theories are more optimistic because they emphasize the unlimited potential of knowledge-driven technological change.**

Probably the most important contrast between these new theories and the Neoclassical theory concerns investment and income. In the Neoclassical model, diminishing marginal returns to investment imply a limit to the possible increase of per capita GDP. In the new models, investment alone can hold an economy on a "sustained growth path" in which per capita GDP increases without limit, provided that the investment embodies the results of continual advances in technological knowledge.

26.4 Are There Limits to Growth?

See the United Nations' website for international data on economic development: *www.un.org.* Click on "Economic and Social Development" and then go to "Statistics."

Many opponents of growth argue that sustained world growth is undesirable; some argue that it is impossible. The idea that economic growth is limited by nature is not new. In the early 1970s, a group called the "Club of Rome" published a book entitled *The Limits to Growth,* which focused on the limits to growth arising from the finite supply of natural resources. Extrapolating from the oil shortages caused by the OPEC cartel, the Club of Rome concluded that industrialized countries faced an imminent absolute limit to growth. Do such limits really exist? We now discuss the two issues of resource exhaustion and environmental degradation.

Resource Exhaustion

The years since the Second World War have seen a rapid acceleration in the consumption of the world's resources, particularly fossil fuels and basic minerals. World population has increased from fewer than 2.5 billion to more than 6 billion in that period;

The development of the Alberta oil sands has significantly increased Canada's oil-production capacity. At the same time, it has raised concerns regarding environmental degradation, including substantial emissions of greenhouse gases.

this increase alone has intensified the demand for the world's resources. Furthermore, as people attain higher incomes, they consume more resources. Thus, not only are there more people in the world, but many of those people are consuming increasing quantities of resources.

The resources available today could not possibly support all of the world's population at a standard of living equal to that of the average Canadian family—at least, not at the current level of technological development. Our current resources and our present capacity to cope with pollution and environmental degradation are insufficient to accomplish this rise in global living standards with present technology.

Most economists, however, agree that absolute limits to growth, based on the assumptions of constant technology and fixed resources, are not relevant. As emphasized by the new growth theories we discussed in the previous section, technology changes continually, as do the available stocks of resources. For example, 75 years ago, few would have thought that the world could produce enough food to feed its present population of 6 billion people, let alone the 10 billion at which the population is projected to stabilize sometime later this century. Yet significant advances in agricultural methods make this task now seem feasible. Further, while existing resources are being depleted, new ones are constantly being discovered or developed. One example is the development of the Alberta oil sands. In the early 1970s, this resource appeared to be far too expensive to develop and therefore an unlikely source of economical oil. Almost four decades later, after considerable technological improvement, the oil sands now rank among the world's largest reserves of economical petroleum.

Another consideration relates to both resource use and technological progress. Along with advances in technological knowledge typically comes an increase in the economy's *resource efficiency*—a reduction in the amount of resources needed to produce one unit of output. In Canada, for example, an average dollar of real GDP is currently produced with nearly 40 percent less energy than was the case in 1978, and if we focus just on petroleum use, the improvement in efficiency is almost 50 percent. More generally, every dollar's worth of real GDP produced in the world has used steadily fewer and fewer resources over the past century, in a process often called the "de-materialization" of production. Such improvements in resource efficiency do not eliminate the concerns about resource exhaustion, but they do underline the importance of recognizing the role of technological change when considering limits to economic growth.

> **Technology is constantly advancing, and many things that seemed impossible a generation ago will be commonplace a generation from now. Such technological advance makes any absolute limits to economic growth less likely.**

Yet there is surely cause for some concern. Although many barriers can be overcome by technological advances, such achievements are not instantaneous and are certainly not automatic. There is a critical problem of timing: How soon can we discover and put into practice the knowledge required to solve the problems that are made ever more imminent by the growth in the population, the affluence of the rich nations, and the aspirations of the billions who now live in poverty? There is no guarantee that a whole generation will not be caught in transition between technologies, with enormous social and political consequences.

A final point worth noting is that the extent of resource depletion is not something that "just happens." Since natural resources are typically owned by the public, government policy can be used to influence the rate of resource extraction if that objective is deemed to be appropriate. If we fail to protect some key natural resources, it will not be because we lacked the ability or the technology to do so, only that we lacked the political will to make contentious and difficult decisions— decisions that may nonetheless be in our long-run interests.

Environmental Degradation

A much more important problem associated with economic growth is the generation of pollution and the degradation of our natural environment. Air, water, and soil are polluted by a variety of natural activities, and, for billions of years, the environment has coped with them. The Earth's natural processes had little trouble coping with the pollution generated by its 1 billion inhabitants in 1800. But the 6 billion people who now exist put such extreme demands on the Earth's ecosystems that there are now legitimate concerns about "environmental sustainability." Smoke, sewage, chemical waste, hydrocarbon and greenhouse-gas emissions, spent nuclear fuel, and a host of other pollutants threaten to overwhelm the Earth's natural regenerative processes.

> **Conscious management of pollution was unnecessary when the world's population was 1 billion people, but such management has now become a pressing matter.**

Reducing the extent of environmental degradation, however, is different from advocating an "anti-growth" position. To put it differently, there is nothing inconsistent about an economy displaying *both* high rates of economic growth and active environmental protection. As students of microeconomics will recognize, an important part of a policy designed to reduce the extent of environmental degradation is to get polluters (firms or households) to face the full cost of their polluting activities—especially the external costs that their activities impose on society. This often involves levying some form of tax on polluters for every unit of pollution emitted. Although such policies, if stringently enforced, will lead to output reductions in specific industries, they need not lead to reductions in the *overall* level of economic activity. And long-run economic growth is related to growth in the overall level of economic activity, not to the growth of specific industries.

Furthermore, many technological advances reduce the amount of pollution per unit of output and also reduce the costs of dealing with whatever pollution remains. Rich, advanced economies, such as Canada, the United States, and the European Union, create less pollution per dollar of GDP and find it easier to bear the cost of pollution clean-up than do poorer, less technologically advanced economies.

APPLYING ECONOMIC CONCEPTS 26-3

Climate Change and Economic Growth

Though the underlying cause of the rising global temperatures observed over the past century is still debated, the bulk of the scientific evidence points to a clear causal link. The burning of fossil fuels leads to the emission of carbon dioxide and other "greenhouse gases," which accumulate in the atmosphere and remain there for many years. This rising atmospheric concentration of gases acts like a greenhouse to lock in the sun's warmth, thus increasing average global temperature.

As a result of this "global warming," the polar ice caps have been melting significantly, the world's deserts have been gradually increasing in size, and extreme weather events are becoming more frequent and severe. The melting of the Antarctic and Greenland ice caps is predicted to cause a significant increase in sea level, with potentially catastrophic effects for the many highly populated island and coastal regions of Asia and Africa. The creeping desertification and changing rainfall patterns are predicted to cause significant reductions in agricultural productivity, especially in the developing countries. The effects of climate change will be felt by people in many countries, but the most dramatic effects

are likely to be experienced in the lowest-income countries least prepared to shoulder the burden.

The world's annual emissions of greenhouse gases have been increasing steadily, broadly in line with the growth of the world economy. In the absence of policies aimed at reducing these emissions, they are predicted to increase by approximately 100 percent by 2050. Yet the weight of scientific evidence suggests that in order to stabilize the atmospheric concentration of greenhouse gases (at a level well above today's), and thus to stabilize the Earth's average temperature (at a level 1–2°C above today's average temperature), annual emissions will need to fall by 80–90 percent from *current* levels by 2050. Achieving such reductions will certainly affect the world's economic growth.

What is the connection between global warming and economic growth? First, modern economic growth is a central cause of global warming. Since energy is an important input to production for most goods and services, and since the burning of fossil fuels is one of the most efficient ways to produce energy, it is not surprising that a close relationship exists between the growth of real GDP and the growth of greenhouse-gas emissions. But reducing

None of this implies that environmental issues are not serious. It is possible that our management of these issues will be sufficiently inadequate that growth will be impaired and our living standards will suffer by significant amounts. If this happens, it will probably *not* be because we lacked the technology or know-how to solve these problems once they were recognized. If we do create environmental disasters, more likely it will be because we failed to respond quickly enough (if at all) to the growing dangers as they were occurring.

Some scientists believe, for example, that we may already be too late to reverse the forces leading to global warming and that dramatic changes in sea level are now a virtual certainty at some point in the not-too-distant future. Others argue that it is not too late to take significant actions that would reduce the extent of global warming. Concerted global actions and considerable political will in many countries must be part of the solution. *Applying Economic Concepts 26-3* explores in more detail the problem of climate change caused by greenhouse-gas emissions associated with the burning of fossil fuels.

Conclusion

The world faces many problems. Starvation and poverty are the common lot of citizens in many countries and are not unknown even in such countries as Canada and the United States, where average living standards are very high. Growth has raised the average citizens of advanced countries from poverty to plenty in the course of two centuries—a short time in terms of human history. Further growth is needed if people emissions by reducing world GDP is probably both unrealistic and undesirable. As the world's population continues to grow, and the people of the developing world strive to increase their per capita incomes to levels closer to ours, there will inevitably be a rise in global GDP.

The more realistic way to reduce greenhouse-gas emissions is to reduce our reliance on energy and, in particular, our reliance on those forms of energy that release greenhouse gases into the atmosphere. Most economists argue that any effective policy to reduce the world's emissions of greenhouse gases must involve placing a price on the emission of greenhouse gases, either through a direct tax (such as a "carbon tax") or by directly restricting the amount of total emissions and then allowing the distribution of emissions among firms to be determined through the trading of costly emissions permits (a "cap-and-trade" system). Either policy approach will increase the cost associated with emitting greenhouse gases and thus will create incentives for firms and households to use non-emitting forms of energy. Incentives will also be created for the further development of non-emitting energy sources such as solar, wind, nuclear, and hydro electricity.

Since these policies will be effective only by imposing costs on firms and households, their use will highlight a second connection between economic growth and global warming. These higher costs will lead to the adoption of cleaner energy systems and thus a reduction of greenhouse-gas emissions, but they will also lead to a reduction in the growth rate of real GDP. Current estimates suggest that reducing Canadian greenhouse-gas emissions by approximately 20 percent from current levels by 2020 would lead to a reduction in real GDP by between 4 and 8 percent from the level that would otherwise exist in 2020. This implies a reduction in the growth rate of real GDP over this period of approximately 0.5 percent per year.

Policymakers are thus faced with difficult choices. First, they must estimate the costs to the economy of taking the "business as usual" approach and thus experiencing the predicted changes in the world climate over the next several decades. Then they must estimate the costs associated with taking aggressive policy actions designed to dramatically reduce the emission of greenhouse gases. Finally, they need to choose a policy approach, appropriately weighing the costs of inaction against the costs of action. These will be very difficult decisions to make, partly because of the uncertainty surrounding the impact of any policies and partly because of the considerable political pressures generated by advocates on both sides of the debate.

myeconlab ADDITIONAL TOPICS

Many of the insights about the determinants of economic growth that we explored in this chapter apply also to economic growth in the developing countries. But the developing countries also have some unique economic and institutional challenges, some which have plagued them for many years. For a detailed discussion, look for **Challenges Facing the Developing Countries** in the *Additional Topics* section of this book's MyEconLab.

www.myeconlab.com

in developing countries are to escape material poverty, and further growth would help advanced countries to deal with many of their pressing economic problems.

Rising population and rising per capita consumption, however, put pressure on the world's natural ecosystems, especially through the many forms of pollution. Further growth must be *sustainable* growth, which must in turn be based on knowledge-driven technological change. Past experience suggests that new technologies will use less of all resources per unit of output. But if they are to dramatically reduce the demands placed on the Earth's ecosystems, price and policy incentives will be needed to direct technological change in more "environmentally friendly" ways. Just as present technologies are much less polluting than the technologies of a century ago, the technologies of the future must be made much less polluting than today's.

There is no guarantee that the world will solve the problems of sustainable growth, but there is nothing in modern growth theory and existing evidence to suggest that such an achievement is impossible.

Summary

26.1 The Nature of Economic Growth

- Sustained increases in real GDP are due mainly to economic growth, which continuously pushes the Y^* curve outward, thereby increasing potential output.
- Growth is frequently measured by the growth rate of potential real GDP per person. The cumulative effects of even small differences in growth rates become very large over periods of a decade or more.
- The most important benefit of growth lies in its contribution to the long-run struggle to raise average living standards and to escape poverty. Growth also facilitates the redistribution of income among people.

- Growth, though often beneficial, is never costless. The opportunity cost of growth is the diversion of resources from current consumption to capital formation. For individuals who are left behind in a rapidly changing world, the costs are higher and more personal.
- There are four fundamental determinants of growth: increases in the labour force; increases in physical capital; increases in human capital; and improvements in technology.

26.2 Established Theories of Economic Growth

- The long-run relationship among saving, investment, and economic growth is most easily observed in the market for loanable funds, in which the interest rate is determined by the equality of desired investment and desired national saving.
- Increases in the supply of national saving will reduce the interest rate and encourage more investment by firms, thus increasing the rate of growth of potential output.
- Increases in the demand for investment will increase the interest rate and encourage an increase in household saving. The higher saving (and investment) in equilibrium leads to a higher growth rate of potential output.
- Neoclassical growth theory assumes an aggregate production function that displays diminishing marginal returns (when one factor is changed in isolation) and constant returns to scale (when all factors are changed in equal proportions).

- In a balanced growth path, the quantity of labour, the quantity of capital, and real GDP all increase at a constant rate. But since per capita output is constant, living standards are not rising.
- Changes in output that cannot be accounted for by changes in the levels of physical and human capital and in the size of the labour force are defined to be growth in total factor productivity (TFP). Although it is sometimes associated with technological change, TFP does not measure all of such change because much of it is embodied in new physical and human capital.
- In the Neoclassical growth model, technological change is assumed to be exogenous—unaffected by the size of the labour force, the size of the capital stock, or the level of economic activity.

26.3 New Growth Theories

- Unlike the Neoclassical growth theory, new growth theories emphasize endogenous technological change that responds to market signals, such as prices and profits. In particular, shocks that would be adverse in a setting of fixed technology may provide a spur to innovation and result in technological improvements.
- New growth theories also suggest that investment embodying new technologies may be subject to *increasing* rather than diminishing marginal returns.

Investment that embodies a continuing flow of new technologies can explain ongoing growth in per capita incomes caused by capital accumulation—a phenomenon difficult to explain with the Neoclassical growth model.
- Knowledge is an important input to the production process and, because it is a public good that can be used simultaneously by many, may not be subject to diminishing marginal returns.

26.4 Are There Limits to Growth?

- The critical importance of increasing knowledge and new technology to the goal of sustaining growth is highlighted by the great drain on existing natural resources that has resulted from the explosive growth of population and output in recent decades. Without continuing technological change, the present needs and aspirations of the world's population cannot come anywhere close to being met.
- Rising population and rising real incomes place pressure on resources. Technological improvements, however, lead to less resource use per unit of output produced and also to the discovery and development of new resources.

- The increase in population has similar effects on pollution: The Earth's environment could cope naturally with much of human pollution 200 years ago, but the present population is so large that pollution has outstripped nature's coping mechanisms.
- Although problems associated with environmental degradation have been surmounted in the past, there is no guarantee that the ones now being encountered, such as the effects of global warming, will become objects of policy attention before the effects can be reversed.

Key Concepts

The cumulative nature of growth
Benefits and costs of growth
The market for loanable funds and the
  equilibrium interest rate
Saving, investment, and growth
Neoclassical growth theory

The aggregate production function
Diminishing marginal returns
Constant returns to scale
Balanced growth
Total factor productivity

Endogenous technical change
Increasing marginal returns to
  investment
The economics of goods and of ideas
Resource depletion and pollution

Study Exercises

1. Fill in the blanks to make the following statements correct.

   a. Long-run, sustained increases in real GDP are the result of increases in potential output, which we call _____.
   b. Increases in living standards are possible with increases in real _____.
   c. The primary cost of economic growth is the sacrifice of current _____ in exchange for investment that raises future _____.
   d. The four fundamental determinants of growth are
      - _____
      - _____
      - _____
      - _____

2. Fill in the blanks to make the following statements correct.

   a. An increase in the interest rate leads to a(n) _____ in the amount of national saving because households reduce their _____.
   b. An increase in the interest rate leads firms to _____ their amount of desired investment.
   c. In the long run, with output equal to potential, equilibrium in the market for loanable funds determines the interest rate as well as the amount of _____ and _____ in the economy.
   d. Following a shift in either the supply of national saving or the demand for investment, there will be a change in both the equilibrium _____ and the amount of _____ in the economy.

e. An increase in the amount of the economy's resources devoted to _____ leads to an increase in the growth rate of _____.

3. Fill in the blanks to make the following statements correct.

a. An important aspect of Neoclassical growth theory is that changes in the supply of one factor, all else held constant, imply eventually _____ marginal returns to that factor.

b. In Neoclassical growth theory, an increase in the labour force _____ total output and _____ the level of per capita output.

c. When a new harvesting machine replaces an old harvesting machine on a farm and is more productive than the old one, we say there has been _____ technical change.

d. Some new growth theories are based on the assumption that technological change is _____ to the economic system; others are based on the possibility that there are _____ marginal returns to investment.

e. Neoclassical growth theories are pessimistic because they emphasize _____ returns with a given state of _____. Modern growth theories are more optimistic because they emphasize the unlimited potential of _____.

4. In the text we said that, over many years, small differences in growth rates can have large effects on the level of income. This question will help you understand this important point. Consider an initial value of real GDP equal to Y_0. If real GDP grows at a rate of g percent annually, after N years real GDP will equal $Y_0(1 + g)^N$. Now consider the following table. Let the initial level of GDP in all cases be 100.

| | Real GDP With Alternative Growth Rates | | | | | |
Year	1% (1)	1.5% (2)	2% (3)	2.5% (4)	3% (5)	3.5% (6)
0	100	100	100	100	100	100
1	—	—	—	—	—	—
3	—	—	—	—	—	—
5	—	—	—	—	—	—
10	—	—	—	—	—	—
20	—	—	—	—	—	—
30	—	—	—	—	—	—
50	—	—	—	—	—	—

a. By using the formula provided above, compute the level of real GDP in column 1 for each year. For example, in Year 1, real GDP will equal $100(1.01)^1 = 101$.

b. Now do the same for the rest of the columns.

c. In Year 20, how much larger (in percentage terms) is real GDP in the 3-percent growth case compared with the 1.5-percent growth case?

d. In Year 50, how much larger (in percentage terms) is real GDP in the 3-percent growth case compared with the 1.5-percent growth case?

5. The diagram below shows two paths for aggregate consumption. One grows at a rate of 3 percent per year; the other grows at 4 percent per year but begins at a lower level.

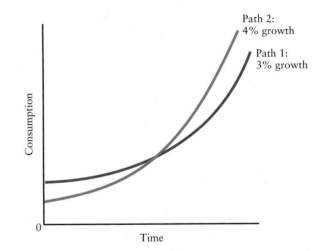

a. Suppose the economy jumps from Path 1 to Path 2 in Year 0 because its rate of capital accumulation increases. What is the opportunity cost in this economy for this increase in capital accumulation?

b. Suppose the economy jumps from Path 1 to Path 2 in Year 0 because its rate of R&D expenditures increases. The greater R&D leads to technological improvements that generate the higher growth rate. What is the opportunity cost to this economy for the increase in R&D expenditures?

c. Show in the figure the "break-even" point for the economy after both of the changes described above. Explain.

6. Consider an economy in the long run with real GDP equal to the level of potential output, Y^*.

a. Draw the diagram of the market for loanable funds. Explain the slopes of the investment demand curve and the national saving curve.

b. Suppose the government pursued a fiscal contraction by reducing the level of government purchases. Explain what would happen to the equilibrium interest rate, the amount of investment in the economy, and the long-run growth rate.

c. Now suppose the fiscal contraction occurs by increasing taxes. Explain what effect this would have on the interest rate, investment, and long-run growth rate.

7. The Neoclassical growth theory is based on the existence of an aggregate production function—showing the relationship between labour (L), capital (K), technology (T), and real GDP (Y). The table below shows various values for L, K, and T. In all cases, the aggregate production function is assumed to take the following form:

$$Y = T \times \sqrt{KL}$$

Labour (L)	Capital (K)	Technology (T)	Real GDP (Y)
10	20	1	—
15	20	1	—
20	20	1	—
25	20	1	—
10	20	1	—
15	30	1	—
20	40	1	—
25	50	1	—
20	20	1	—
20	20	3	—
20	20	4	—
20	20	5	—

a. Compute real GDP for each case and complete the table.

b. In the first part of the table, capital is constant but labour is increasing. What property of the production function is displayed? Explain.

c. In the second part of the table, capital and labour are increasing by the same proportion. What property of the production function is displayed? Explain.

d. What type of growth is being shown in the third part of the table?

8. In the early 1970s the Club of Rome, extrapolating from the rates of resource use at the time, predicted that the supply of natural resources (especially oil) would be used up within a few decades. Subsequent events appear to have proven them wrong.

a. What is predicted to happen to the price of oil (and other natural resources) as population and per capita incomes rise?

b. Given your answer to part (a), what is the likely response by firms and consumers who use such resources?

c. Explain why resource exhaustion should, through the workings of the price system, lead to technological developments that reduce the use of the resource.

9. Consider the market for loanable funds and the relationship among saving, investment, and the interest rate. In what follows, assume that the economy is in a long-run equilibrium with $Y = Y^*$.

a. Suppose the government wants to encourage national saving. How could it do this, and what would be the effects of such a policy? Illustrate in a diagram.

b. Suppose instead that the government wants to encourage investment. How might this be accomplished, and what would be the effects? Illustrate in a diagram.

c. It is often heard in public debate that "high interest rates are bad for investment and growth." Is this true? Can you come up with a simple rule of thumb to describe the relationship between interest rates, investment, and growth?

Discussion Questions

1. Economic growth is often studied in macroeconomic terms, but in a market economy, who makes the decisions that lead to growth? What kinds of decisions and what kinds of actions cause growth to occur? How might a detailed study of individual markets be relevant to understanding economic growth?

2. Discuss the following quote from a recent newspaper article: "Economics and the environment are not strange bedfellows. Environment-oriented tourism is one creative way to resolve the conflict between our desire for a higher standard of living and the realization that nature cannot absorb everything we throw at it. The growing demand for ecotourism has placed a premium on the remaining rain forests, undisturbed flora and fauna, and endangered species of the world."

3. "The case for economic growth is that it gives man greater control over his environment, and consequently increases his freedom." Explain why you agree or disagree with this statement by Nobel laureate W. Arthur Lewis.

4. Dr. David Suzuki, an opponent of further economic growth, has argued that despite the fact that "in the twentieth century the list of scientific and technological achievements has been absolutely dazzling, the costs of such progress are so large that negative economic growth may be right for the future." Policies to achieve this include "rigorous reduction of waste, a questioning and distrustful attitude toward technological progress, and braking demands on the globe's resources." Identify some of the benefits and costs of economic growth, and evaluate Suzuki's position. What government policies would be needed to achieve his ends?

5. In this chapter we discussed four fundamental determinants of growth in real output: increases in the labour force; increases in the stock of physical capital; increases in human capital; and improvements in technology. For each of the four, give an example of a government policy that is likely to increase growth. Discuss also the likely cost associated with each policy. Does one of your proposed policies appear better (in a cost–benefit sense) than the others?

6. The Solow residual has been called a "measure of our ignorance" of the causes of growth. Explain this viewpoint. Is the Solow residual a good measure of technical change?

7. This question is based on the MyEconLab *Additional Topic* **Investment and Saving in Globalized Financial Markets.** Consider the market for loanable funds and the long-run relationship among saving, investment, and economic growth.

   a. For a closed economy, if the government wants a higher long-run growth rate, explain why it can directly promote saving *or* investment.

   b. For an open economy, explain why the amount of investment (and growth rate of output) is unlikely to be affected by a policy that encourages national saving.

   c. If desired saving need not be equal to desired investment in an open economy, what accounts for the difference?

27

Money and Banking

In the next three chapters, we look at the role of money and monetary policy. The role of money may seem obvious—money is what people use to buy things. Yet as we will see, increasing the amount of money circulating in Canada would not make the average Canadian better off in the long run. Although money allows those who have it to buy someone else's output, the total amount of goods and services available for everyone to buy depends on the total output produced, not on the total amount of money that people possess. In other words, an increase in the quantity of money is unlikely to increase the level of potential real GDP, Y^*, and thus unlikely to affect our long-run living standards. However, most economists agree that changes in the amount of money have important short-run effects on national income. A complete understanding of money's role in the economy requires that we recognize the distinction between the short run and the long run.

We begin by talking in detail about what money is and how it evolved over the centuries to its current form. We then examine the Canadian banking system, which includes a central bank (the Bank of Canada) and many commercial banks. Finally, we explain the process whereby commercial banks "create" money, seemingly out of thin air. This money creation process will play a central role in our discussion of how money influences the level of economic activity, a topic we begin in the next chapter.

LO LEARNING OBJECTIVES

In this chapter you will learn

❶ about the various functions of money, and how money has evolved over time.

❷ that modern banking systems include both privately owned commercial banks and government-owned central banks.

❸ how commercial banks create money through the process of taking deposits and making loans.

❹ the various measures of the money supply.

27.1 The Nature of Money

What exactly is money? In this section, we describe the functions of money and briefly outline its history.

What Is Money?

medium of exchange
Anything that is generally acceptable in return for goods and services sold.

In economics, *money* is defined as any generally accepted medium of exchange. A **medium of exchange** is anything that will be widely accepted in a society in exchange for goods and services. Although its medium-of-exchange role is perhaps its most important one, money also acts as a *store of value* and as a *unit of account*. Different kinds of money vary in the degree of efficiency with which they fulfill these functions. As we will see, the *money supply* is measured by using different definitions for different purposes.

Money as a Medium of Exchange

barter A system in which goods and services are traded directly for other goods and services.

Practise with Study Guide Chapter 27, Exercise 1.

If there were no money, goods would have to be exchanged by barter. **Barter** is the system whereby goods and services are exchanged directly with each other. The major difficulty with barter is that each transaction requires a *double coincidence of wants:* Anyone who specialized in producing one commodity would have to spend a great deal of time searching for satisfactory transactions. For example, the barber who needs his sink repaired would have to find a plumber who wants a haircut. In a world of many different goods and many different people, the effort required to make transactions would be extreme. The use of money as a medium of exchange solves this problem. People can sell their output for money and then, in separate transactions, use the money to buy what they want from others.

> The double coincidence of wants is unnecessary when a medium of exchange is used.

By facilitating transactions, money makes possible the benefits of specialization and the division of labour, two concepts we first discussed in Chapter 1. As a result, money greatly contributes to the efficiency of the economic system. Not surprisingly, money has been called one of the great inventions contributing to human freedom and well-being.

To serve as an efficient medium of exchange, money must have a number of characteristics. It must be both easily recognizable and readily acceptable. It must have a high value relative to its weight (otherwise it would be a nuisance to carry around). It must be divisible, because money that comes only in large denominations is useless for transactions having only a small value. It must be reasonably durable (notice that Canadian paper money can easily survive several trips through a washing machine!). Finally, it must be difficult, if not impossible, to counterfeit.

Money as a Store of Value

Money is a convenient means of storing purchasing power; goods may be sold today for money and the money may then be stored until it is needed for some future purchase. To be a satisfactory store of value, however, money must have a relatively stable value. Recall from the beginning of Chapter 23 that a rise in the price level is also a decrease in the purchasing power of money. When the price level is stable, the purchasing power of a given sum of money is also stable; when the price level is highly variable, so is the purchasing power of money, and the usefulness of money as a store of value is undermined.

Between the early 1970s and the early 1990s, inflation in Canada was high enough and sufficiently variable to diminish money's usefulness as a store of value. Since 1992, however, inflation has been low and relatively stable, thus increasing money's effectiveness as a store of value. Even Canada's high-inflation experience, however, is very modest compared with that in some other countries, such as Chile in the mid-1970s, Bolivia in the mid-1980s, Argentina, Romania, and Brazil in the early 1990s, and Zimbabwe in the mid 2000s. One of the most infamous experiences of very high inflation—*hyperinflation*—comes from Germany in the early 1920s. This case is discussed in *Lessons from History 27-1.*

Money as a Unit of Account Money may also be used purely for accounting purposes without having a physical existence of its own. For instance, a government store in a truly communist society might say that everyone was allocated so many "dollars" to use each month. Goods could then be assigned prices and each consumer's purchases recorded, the consumer being allowed to buy until the allocated supply of dollars was exhausted. These dollars need have no existence other than as entries in the store's books, yet they would serve as a perfectly satisfactory unit of account.

Whether they could also serve as a medium of exchange between individuals depends on whether the store would agree to transfer dollar credits from one customer to another at the customer's request. Canadian banks transfer dollars credited to deposits in this way each time you make a purchase with your ATM or debit card. Thus, a bank deposit can serve as both a unit of account and a medium of exchange. Notice that the use of *dollars* in this context suggests a further sense in which money is a unit of account. People think about values in terms of the monetary unit with which they are familiar.

The Origins of Money

The origins of money go far back in antiquity. Most primitive societies are known to have made some use of it.

Metallic Money All sorts of commodities have been used as money at one time or another, but gold and silver proved to have great advantages. They were precious because their supplies were relatively limited, and they were in constant demand by the wealthy for ornament and decoration. Hence, these metals tended to have high and stable prices. Further, they were easily recognized, they were divisible into extremely small units, and they did not easily wear out. For these reasons, precious metals came to circulate as money and to be used in many transactions.

Before the invention of coins, it was necessary to carry the metals in bulk. When a purchase was made, the requisite quantity of the metal was carefully weighed on a scale. The invention of coinage eliminated the need to weigh the metal at each transaction, but it created an important role for an authority, usually a king or queen, who made the coins and affixed his or her seal, guaranteeing the amount of precious metal that the coin contained. This was clearly a great convenience, as long as traders knew that they could accept the coin at its "face value." The face value was nothing more than a statement that a certain weight of metal was contained therein.

However, coins often could not be taken at their face value. The practice of clipping a thin slice off the edge of the coin and keeping the valuable metal became common. This, of course, served to undermine the acceptability of coins, even if they were stamped. To get around this problem, the idea arose of minting the coins with a rough edge. The absence of the rough edge would immediately indicate that the coin had been

LESSONS FROM HISTORY 27-1

Hyperinflation and the Value of Money

Hyperinflation is generally defined as inflation that exceeds 50 percent per month. At this rate of inflation, a chocolate bar that costs $1 on January 1 would cost $129.74 by December 31 of the same year. When prices are rising at such rapid rates, is it possible for money to maintain its usefulness as a medium of exchange or as a store of value? Several examples from history have allowed economists to study the role of money during hyperinflation. This historical record is not very reassuring. In a number of instances, prices rose at an ever-accelerating rate until a nation's money ceased to be a satisfactory store of value, even for the short period between receipt and expenditure, and hence ceased also to be useful as a medium of exchange.

A spectacular example of hyperinflation is the experience of Germany in the period after the First World War. The price index in the accompanying table shows that a good purchased for one 100-mark note in July 1923 would cost *10 million* 100-mark notes only four months later! Although Germany had experienced substantial inflation during the First World War, averaging more than 30 percent per year, the immediate postwar years of 1920 and 1921 gave no sign of explosive inflation. Indeed, prices were relatively stable until 1922 and 1923 when they exploded. On November 15, 1923, the German mark was officially repudiated, its value wholly destroyed. How could such a dramatic increase in prices happen?

When inflation becomes so high that people lose confidence in the purchasing power of their currency, they rush to spend it. People who have goods become increasingly reluctant to accept the rapidly depreciating money in exchange. The rush to spend money accelerates the increase in prices until people finally become unwilling to accept money on any terms. What was once money ceases to be money. The price system can then be restored only by repudiation of the old monetary unit and its replacement by a new unit.

About a dozen hyperinflations in world history have been documented, among them the collapse of the continental during the American Revolution in 1776, the ruble during the Russian Revolution in 1917, the drachma during and after the German occupation of Greece in the Second World War, the pengö in Hungary in 1945 and 1946, the Chinese national currency from 1946 to 1948, the Bolivian peso in 1984–1985, and the Argentinian peso in the early 1990s. Between 2004 and 2008, there was a massive hyperinflation in Zimbabwe—the largest in recorded history—that increased average prices by more than 90 septillion percent (that is a 90 with 24 extra zeros!)

During hyperinflation money loses its value so quickly that people cease to accept it as a means of payment. At that point, money may as well be used for wallpaper.

Every one of these hyperinflations was accompanied by great increases in the money supply; new money was printed to give governments purchasing power that they could not or would not obtain by taxation. Further, every hyperinflation occurred in the midst of a major political upheaval in which grave doubts existed about the stability and the future of the government itself.

Is hyperinflation likely in the absence of civil war, revolution, or collapse of the government? Most economists think not. Further, it is clear that high inflation rates over a period of time do not mean the inevitable or even likely onset of hyperinflation, however serious the distributive and social effects of such rates may be.

Date	German Wholesale Price Index (1913 = 1)
January 1913	1
January 1920	13
January 1921	14
January 1922	37
July 1922	101
January 1923	2 785
July 1923	74 800
August 1923	944 000
September 1923	23 900 000
October 1923	7 096 000 000

clipped. This practice, called *milling,* survives on Canadian dimes, quarters, and two-dollar coins (but not pennies, nickels, or loonies!) as an interesting anachronism to remind us that there were days when the market value of the metal in the coin was equal to the face value of the coin.

Not to be outdone by the cunning of their subjects, some rulers were quick to seize the chance of getting something for nothing. The power to mint coins placed rulers in a position to work a very profitable fraud. They often used some suitable occasion—a marriage, an anniversary, an alliance—to remint the coinage. Subjects would be ordered to bring their coins in to the mint to be melted down and coined afresh with a new stamp. Between the melting down and the recoining, however, the rulers had only to toss some further inexpensive base metal in with the molten gold. This *debasing* of the coinage allowed the ruler to earn a handsome profit by minting more new coins than the number of old ones

Canadian quarters are intentionally produced with rough or bumpy edges. Such "milling" of coins is now unnecessary, but many decades ago when coins were made from precious metals, it was useful in preventing individuals from clipping the coins.

collected and putting the extras in the royal vault. Through debasement, the amount of money in the economy (but not the amount of gold) had increased.

The eventual result was inflation. The subjects had the same number of coins as before and hence could demand the same quantity of goods. When rulers paid their bills, however, the recipients of the extra coins could be expected to spend them. This caused a net increase in demand, which in turn bid up prices. Thus, increasing the money supply by debasing the coinage was a common cause of inflation.

GRESHAM'S LAW. The early experience of currency debasement led to the observation known as **Gresham's law,** after Sir Thomas Gresham (1519–1579), an advisor to the Elizabethan court, who coined the phrase "bad money drives out good."

When Queen Elizabeth I came to the throne of England in the middle of the sixteenth century, the coinage had been severely debased. Seeking to help trade, Elizabeth minted new coins that contained their full face value in gold. However, as fast as she fed these new coins into circulation, they disappeared. Why?

Suppose you possessed one of these new coins and one of the old ones, each with the same face value, and had to make a purchase. What would you do? You would use the debased coin to make the purchase and keep the undebased one; you part with less gold that way. Suppose you wanted to obtain a certain amount of gold bullion by melting down the gold coins (as was frequently done). Which coins would you use? You would use new, undebased coins because you would part with less face value that way (it would take more of the debased coins than the new coins to get a given amount of gold bullion). The debased coins (bad money) would thus remain in circulation, and the undebased coins (good money) would disappear into peoples' private hoards—the "bad" money would drive out the "good" money.

Gresham's law The theory that "bad," or debased, money drives "good," or undebased, money out of circulation.

> **Gresham's law predicts that when two types of money are used side by side, the one with the greater intrinsic value will be driven out of circulation.**

Gresham's insights have proven helpful in explaining the experience of a number of modern high-inflation economies. For example, in the 1970s, inflation in Chile raised

The development of paper money, such as this bank note issued by The Montreal Bank more than a century ago, was an important step in the evolution of modern, fractional-reserve banking systems. Paper money allowed individuals to avoid the cumbersome transportation of gold when making their daily transactions.

the value of the metallic content in coins above their face value. Coins quickly disappeared from circulation as private citizens sold them to entrepreneurs who melted them down for their metal. Only paper currency remained in circulation and was used even for tiny transactions, such as purchasing a pack of matches. Gresham's law is one reason that modern coins, unlike their historical counterparts, are merely tokens that contain a metallic value that is only a small fraction of their face value.

Paper Money   The next important step in the history of money was the evolution of paper currency. Artisans who worked with gold required secure safes, and the public began to deposit gold with these goldsmiths for safekeeping. Goldsmiths would give their depositors receipts promising to return the gold on demand. When a depositor wanted to make a large purchase, he could go to his goldsmith, reclaim some of his gold, and pay it to the seller of the goods. If the seller had no immediate need for the gold, he would carry it back to the goldsmith for safekeeping.

If people knew the goldsmith to be reliable, there was no need to go through the cumbersome and risky business of physically transferring the gold. The buyer needed only to transfer the goldsmith's receipt to the seller, who would accept it as long as he was confident that the goldsmith would pay over the gold whenever it was needed. If the seller wanted to buy a good from a third party, who also knew the goldsmith to be reliable, this transaction could also be effected by passing the goldsmith's receipt from the buyer to the seller. This transferring of paper receipts rather than gold was essentially the invention of paper money.

When it first came into being, paper money represented a promise to pay so much gold on demand. In this case, the promise was made first by goldsmiths and later by banks. Such paper money was *backed* by precious metal and was *convertible on demand* into this metal. In the nineteenth century, private banks commonly issued paper money, called **bank notes**, nominally convertible into gold. As with the goldsmiths, each bank issued its own notes, and these notes were convertible into gold at the issuing bank. Thus, in the nineteenth century, bank notes from many different banks circulated side by side, each of them being backed by gold at the bank that issued them.

bank notes Paper money issued by commercial banks.

FRACTIONALLY BACKED PAPER MONEY. Early on, many goldsmiths and banks discovered that it was not necessary to keep one ounce of gold in the vaults for every claim to one ounce circulating as paper money. At any one time, some of the bank's customers would be withdrawing gold, others would be depositing it, and most would be trading in the bank's paper notes without any need or desire to convert them into gold. As a result, the bank was able to issue more paper money redeemable in gold than the amount of gold that it held in its vaults. This was good business because the money could be invested profitably in interest-earning loans to households and firms. To this day, banks have many more claims outstanding against them than they actually have in reserves available to pay those claims. We say that the currency issued in such a situation is *fractionally backed* by the reserves.

The major problem with a fractionally backed convertible currency was maintaining its convertibility into the precious metal behind it. The imprudent bank that issued too much paper money would find itself unable to redeem its currency in gold when the demand for gold was even slightly higher than usual. It would then have to suspend payments, and all holders of its notes would suddenly find that the notes were worthless. The prudent bank that kept a reasonable relationship between its note issues and its gold reserves would find that it could meet a normal range of demand for gold without any trouble.

If, for whatever reason, the public lost confidence in the banks and demanded redemption of its currency *en masse,* the banks would be unable to honour their pledges. The history of nineteenth- and early-twentieth-century banking on both sides of the Atlantic is full of examples of banks that were ruined by "panics," or sudden runs on their gold reserves. When these happened, the banks' depositors and the holders of their notes would find themselves with worthless pieces of paper.

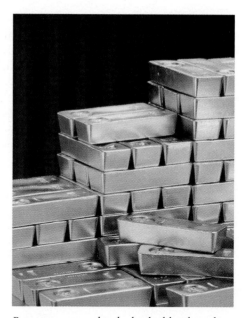

Paper money used to be backed by the value of gold—meaning that it was redeemable for gold. But now money is not redeemable for anything except itself—people hold it because they know that others will accept it as payment for goods and services.

Fiat Money As time went on, currency (notes and coins) issued by private banks became less common, and central banks took control of issuing currency. In time, *only* central banks were permitted by law to issue currency. Originally, the central banks issued currency that was fully convertible into gold. In those days, gold would be brought to the central bank, which would issue currency in the form of "gold certificates" that asserted that the gold was available on demand. The reserves of gold thus set an upper limit on the amount of currency that could circulate in the economy. This practice of backing the currency with gold is known as a **gold standard.**

However, central banks, like private banks before them, could issue more currency than they had in gold because in normal times only a small fraction of the outstanding currency was presented for payment at any one time. Thus, even though the need to maintain convertibility into gold put some upper limit on note issuance, central banks had substantial discretionary control over the quantity of currency outstanding. For example, if the central bank decided to hold gold reserves equal to at least 20 percent of its outstanding currency, the total amount of currency would be limited to five times the gold reserves. But the central bank would nonetheless have complete discretion in choosing this fraction; the smaller the fraction held in reserves, the larger the supply of paper currency that could be supported with a given stock of gold.

During the period between the World Wars (1919–1939), almost all the countries of the world abandoned the gold standard; their currencies were thus no longer convertible into gold. Money that is not convertible by law into anything valuable derives its value from its acceptability in exchange. Such **fiat money** is widely acceptable because it is declared by government order, or *fiat,* to be legal tender. *Legal tender* is anything that by law must be accepted when offered either for the purchase of goods or services or to repay a debt.

gold standard A currency standard whereby a country's currency is convertible into gold at a fixed rate of exchange.

fiat money Paper money or coinage that is neither backed by nor convertible into anything else but is decreed by the government to be accepted as legal tender.

Today, no country allows its currency to be converted into gold on demand. Gold backing for Canadian currency was eliminated in 1940, although note issues continued to carry the traditional statement "will pay to the bearer on demand" until 1954. Today's Bank of Canada notes *simply* say, "This note is legal tender." It is, in other words, fiat money pure and simple.[1]

> **If fiat money is generally acceptable, it is a medium of exchange. If its purchasing power remains stable, it is a satisfactory store of value. If both of these things are true, it serves as a satisfactory unit of account. Today, almost all currency is fiat money.**

Many people are disturbed to learn that present-day paper money is neither backed by nor convertible into anything more valuable—that it consists of nothing but pieces of paper whose value derives from common acceptance and from confidence that it will continue to be accepted in the future. Many people believe that their money should be more "substantial" than this. Yet money is, in fact, nothing more than generally acceptable pieces of paper.

Modern Money: Deposit Money

Early in the twentieth century, private banks lost the authority to issue bank notes, and this authority was reserved for central banks (which we discuss shortly). Yet, as we will see, they did not lose the power to create *deposit money*.

Today's bank customers frequently deposit coins and paper money with the banks for safekeeping, just as in former times they deposited gold. Such a deposit is recorded as a credit to the customer's account. A customer who wants to pay a debt may come to the bank and claim the money in dollars and then pay the money to other persons who may themselves redeposit the money in a bank.

deposit money Money held by the public in the form of deposits with commercial banks.

As with gold transfers, this is a tedious procedure. It is more convenient to have the bank transfer claims to their money that is deposited in the bank. As soon as cheques, which are written instructions to the bank to make a transfer, became widely accepted in payment for commodities and debts, bank deposits became a form of money called **deposit money**. Cheques, unlike bank notes, do not circulate freely from hand to hand; hence cheques themselves are not money. However, a balance in a bank account *is* money; the cheque transfers money from one person to another. Because cheques are easily drawn and deposited and are relatively safe from theft, they are widely used. In recent years, the development of automatic transfers and debit cards has taken the place of cheques for many transactions. Many employers, for example, pay their workers by transferring money directly into their bank accounts rather than by issuing them cheques. And the use of a debit card instantly (electronically) transfers funds from

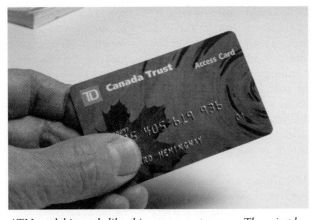

ATM or debit cards like this one are not money. They simply allow consumers to have convenient access to their bank deposits, which are money.

---

[1] See *A History of the Canadian Dollar* (written by James Powell and published by the Bank of Canada) for a detailed and very readable discussion of the evolution of Canadian money.

the bank account of the purchaser to the bank account of the seller. In both cases, the electronic transmission has the same effect as if a cheque were used—but it is faster, simpler, and more secure.

When commercial banks lost the right to issue notes of their own, the form of bank money changed, but the substance did not. Today, banks have money in their vaults (or on deposit with the central banks), just as they always have. Once it was gold; today it is the legal tender of the times, fiat money. It is true today, just as in the past, that most of the bank's customers are content to pay their bills by passing among themselves the bank's promises to pay money on demand. Only a small proportion of the transactions made by the bank's customers are made in cash.

> **Bank deposits are money. Today, just as in the past, banks create money by issuing more promises to pay (deposits) than they have cash reserves available to pay out.**

⋈ myeconlab   ADDITIONAL TOPICS

Any discussion of financial markets and banking systems includes many terms that you may find unfamiliar. For a brief guide to and description of various financial assets, look for **A Quick Introduction to Financial Assets** in the *Additional Topics* section of this book's MyEconLab.

w w w . m y e c o n l a b . c o m

27.2 The Canadian Banking System

Many types of institutions make up a modern banking system, such as exists in Canada today. The **central bank** is the government-owned and government-operated institution that is the sole money-issuing authority and serves to control the banking system. Through it, the government's monetary policy is conducted. In Canada, the central bank is the Bank of Canada, often called just the Bank.

Financial intermediaries are privately owned institutions that serve the general public. They are called *intermediaries* because they stand between savers, from whom they accept deposits, and investors, to whom they make loans. For many years, government regulations created sharp distinctions among the various types of financial intermediaries by limiting the types of transactions in which each could engage. The past two decades have seen a sweeping deregulation of the financial system so that many of these traditional distinctions no longer apply. In this book, we use the term *commercial banks* to extend to all financial intermediaries that accept deposits and create deposit money, including chartered banks, trust companies, credit unions, and caisses populaires.

central bank A bank that acts as banker to the commercial banking system and often to the government as well. Usually a government-owned institution that controls the banking system and is the sole money-issuing authority.

The Bank of Canada

All advanced free-market economies have, in addition to commercial banks, a central bank. Many of the world's early central banks were private, profit-making institutions that provided services to ordinary banks. Their importance, however, caused them to develop close ties with government. Central banks soon became instruments of the government, though not all of them were publicly owned. The Bank of England, one of the world's oldest and most famous central banks, began to operate as the central bank of England in the seventeenth century, but it was not formally taken over by the government until 1947.

The similarities in the functions performed and the tools used by the world's central banks are much more important than the differences in their organization. Although our attention is given to the operations of the Bank of Canada, its basic functions are similar to those of the Bank of England, the Federal Reserve System in the United States, or the European Central Bank (the sole issuer of the euro).

The European Central Bank's website is **www.ecb.int**.

Organization of the Bank of Canada The Bank of Canada commenced operations on March 11, 1935. It is a publicly owned corporation; all profits accruing from its operations are remitted to the Government of Canada. The responsibility for the Bank's affairs rests with a board of directors composed of the governor, the senior deputy governor, the deputy minister of finance, and 12 directors. The governor is appointed by the directors, with the approval of the federal cabinet, for a seven-year term. Since the Bank's inception, there have been eight governors:

- Graham Towers (1935–1954)
- James Coyne (1955–1961)
- Louis Rasminsky (1961–1973)
- Gerald Bouey (1973–1987)
- John Crow (1987–1994)
- Gordon Thiessen (1994–2001)
- David Dodge (2001– 2008)
- Mark Carney (2008–)

The Bank of Canada is located on Wellington Street in Ottawa, across the street from the Parliament Buildings.

The organization of the Bank of Canada is designed to keep the operation of monetary policy free from day-to-day political influence. The Bank is not responsible to Parliament for its day-to-day behaviour in the way that the department of finance is for the operation of fiscal policy. In this sense, the Bank of Canada has considerable autonomy in the way it carries out monetary policy. But the Bank is not completely independent. The *ultimate* responsibility for the Bank's actions rests with the government, since it is the government that must answer to Parliament. This system is known as "joint responsibility," and it dates back to 1967.

Under the system of joint responsibility, the governor of the Bank and the minister of finance consult regularly. In the case of fundamental disagreement over monetary policy, the minister of finance has the option of issuing an explicit *directive* to the governor. In such a case (which has not happened since the inception of joint responsibility), the governor would simply carry out the minister's directive (or resign), and the responsibility for monetary policy would rest with the government. In the absence of such a directive, however, responsibility for monetary policy rests with the governor of the Bank.

For information on the Bank of Canada, see its website: **www.bankofcanada.ca**.

The system of joint responsibility keeps the conduct of monetary policy free from day-to-day political influence while ensuring that the government retains ultimate responsibility for monetary policy.[2]

TABLE 27-1   **Assets and Liabilities of the Bank of Canada, December 2008 (millions of dollars)**

Assets		Liabilities	
Government of Canada securities	40 984.8	Notes in circulation	53 731.3
Advances to commercial banks	1 902.3	Government of Canada deposits	23 604.0
Net foreign-currency assets	119.5	Deposits of commercial banks (reserves)	25.9
Other assets	35 576.9	Other liabilities and capital	1 222.3
Total	78 583.5	Total	78 583.5

The balance sheet of the Bank of Canada shows that it serves as banker to the commercial banks and to the government of Canada, and as issuer of our currency; it also suggests the Bank's role as regulator of money markets and the money supply. The principal liabilities of the Bank are the basis of the money supply. Bank of Canada notes are currency, and the deposits of the commercial banks give them the reserves they need to create deposit money. The Bank's holdings of Government of Canada securities arise from its operations designed to regulate the money supply and financial markets.

(*Source:* Bank of Canada, *Annual Report 2008*, p. 46. © Bank of Canada 2009, www.bankofcanada.ca/en/annual/2008/annuel_report08.pdf.)

Basic Functions of the Bank of Canada

A central bank serves four main functions: as a banker for private banks, as a bank for the government, as the regulator of the nation's money supply, and as a regulator and supporter of financial markets. The first three functions are reflected in Table 27-1, which shows the balance sheet of the Bank of Canada.

BANKER TO THE COMMERCIAL BANKS. The central bank accepts deposits from commercial banks and will, on order, transfer them to the account of another bank. In this way, the central bank provides the commercial banks with the equivalent of a chequing account and with a means of settling debts to other banks. The deposits of the commercial banks with the Bank of Canada—also called *reserves*—appear in Table 27-1. In December 2008 the banks had just under $26 million on reserve at the Bank of Canada. Notice that the cash reserves of the commercial banks deposited with the central bank are liabilities of the central bank, because it promises to pay them on demand.

---

[2] This system was motivated by the "Coyne Affair" in 1961, during the Progressive Conservative government of John Diefenbaker. James Coyne, then governor of the Bank of Canada, disagreed with the minister of finance, Donald Fleming, over the conduct of monetary policy and was eventually forced to resign. Louis Rasminsky then accepted the position as governor of the Bank on the condition that the *Bank of Canada Act* be modified to incorporate the idea of joint responsibility. The *Bank of Canada Act* was so amended in 1967. For a discussion of the early history of the Bank of Canada, see George Watts, *The Bank of Canada: Origins and Early History* (Carleton University Press, 1993).

Historically, one of the earliest services provided by central banks was that of "lender of last resort" to the banking system. Central banks would lend money to private banks that had sound investments (such as government securities) but were in urgent need of cash. If such banks could not obtain ready cash, they might be forced into insolvency, because they could not meet the demands of their depositors, in spite of their being basically sound. Today's central banks continue to be lenders of last resort.

Table 27-1 shows that in December 2008, the Bank of Canada had $1.9 billion in outstanding loans to commercial banks. This is actually a large amount by the standards of recent history, and reflects the Bank of Canada's policy actions during the 2007–2008 financial crisis. At that time commercial banks were reluctant to lend to one another; and any lending occurred at high interest rates. To maintain the flow of credit and help reduce interest rates, the Bank of Canada provided liquidity to commercial banks by extending short-term loans.

Table 27-1 reveals a second unusual aspect of the Bank's balance sheet caused by the financial crisis. The asset category labelled "other assets" is usually very small, typically less than $3 billion, and includes assets of no great interest to our discussion. But during 2008, in an effort to provide liquidity to the commercial banks, the Bank of Canada purchased large amounts of government securities *on a temporary basis*. In this case, the Bank agreed to sell the securities back to the commercial banks after a short period of time, typically a month. During the intervening period, however, the commercial banks would benefit from having greater liquidity. These temporary purchases by the Bank of Canada account for most of these "other assets."

BANKER TO THE FEDERAL GOVERNMENT. Governments, too, need to hold their funds in an account into which they can make deposits and on which they can write cheques. The Government of Canada keeps some of its chequing deposits at the Bank of Canada. In December 2008, the federal government had $23.6 billion in deposits at the Bank of Canada.[3]

When the government requires more money than it collects in taxes, it needs to borrow, and it does so by issuing government securities (short-term Treasury bills or longer-term bonds). Most are sold directly to financial institutions and large institutional investors, but in most years the Bank of Canada buys some and credits the government's account with a deposit for the amount of the purchase. In December 2008, the Bank of Canada held $40.9 billion in Government of Canada securities. These securities are an asset for the Bank of Canada but a liability for the government. (It is largely by earning interest on these securities that the Bank of Canada earns a profit every year—a profit that is eventually remitted to the government.)

REGULATOR OF THE MONEY SUPPLY. One of the most important functions of a central bank is to regulate the *money supply*. Though we have not yet defined the money supply precisely—and there are several different definitions of the money supply that we will encounter—we will see that most measures of the money supply include currency in circulation plus deposits held at commercial banks. Table 27-1 shows that the majority of a central bank's liabilities (its promises to pay) are either currency held by the public or the reserves of the commercial banks.[4] These reserves, in turn, underlie the deposits of households and firms—in exactly the same way that the nineteenth-century goldsmith's holdings of gold underlay its issue of notes.

---

[3] This amount is far larger than is normal—usually there is less than $2 billion in the Government of Canada's account at the Bank of Canada. The large amount in 2008 reflected, again, the unusual (and temporary) actions of the Bank of Canada during the financial crisis.

[4] Currency is a liability for the central bank because holders of currency can take it back to the central bank and redeem it for . . . currency! In the days of the gold standard, currency was redeemable for gold. Today, it is just redeemable for itself.

By changing its liabilities (currency plus reserves), the Bank of Canada can change the money supply. The Bank can change the levels of its assets and liabilities in many ways and, as its liabilities rise and fall, so does the money supply. In Chapter 29, we will explore in detail how this happens and how it is related to the Bank's decisions regarding monetary policy. At that point we will see how the Bank's holdings of government securities (its largest asset) are closely related to the value of notes in circulation (its largest liability).

REGULATOR AND SUPPORTER OF FINANCIAL MARKETS. Central banks usually assume a major responsibility to support the country's financial system and to prevent serious disruption by wide-scale panic and resulting bank failures.

Various institutions—including commercial banks, credit unions, trust companies, and caisses populaires—are in the business of borrowing on a short-term basis and lending on a long-term basis. Large, unanticipated increases in interest rates tend to squeeze these institutions. The average rate they earn on their investments rises only slowly as old contracts mature and new ones are made, but they must either pay higher rates to hold on to their deposits or accept wide-scale withdrawals that could easily bring about insolvency. Such dramatic events are relatively rare in the Canadian banking sector, though Canadian banks have failed in the past and it is possible that more may fail in the future.

As we have already mentioned, during the financial crisis of 2007–2008 the Bank of Canada played a much more active role than usual in supporting financial markets. At that time, commercial banks around the world dramatically reduced their interbank lending after the failure and subsequent takeover of some large U.S. and U.K. financial institutions. The reduction in lending reflected heightened uncertainty regarding the credit-worthiness of *all* commercial banks. In response, the Bank of Canada took unprecedented actions designed to keep credit flowing as normally as possible in Canada, including the significant provision of short-term loans to Canadian financial institutions.

Commercial Banks in Canada

All Canadian banks owned in the private sector are referred to as **commercial banks.** The Canadian banking system is controlled by the provisions of the *Bank Act,* first passed in 1935 and revised several times since. Under the *Bank Act,* charters can be granted to financial institutions to operate as banks and, until 1980, there were only a few such *chartered banks,* most of which were very large and each of which operated under identical regulatory provisions. The 1980 revisions to the *Bank Act* allowed foreign banks to commence operations in Canada, although the Act severely limited the scale and scope of their activity. Subsequent revisions have removed some of these restrictions and made it easier to obtain new banking charters, but the revisions have maintained the distinction between these newer institutions and banks operating under what are essentially the pre-1980 provisions of the *Bank Act.*

Commercial banks have common attributes: they hold deposits for their customers; they permit certain deposits to be transferred by cheque from an individual account to other accounts held in any bank branch in the country; they invest in government securities (short-term Treasury bills and longer-term bonds); they make loans to households and firms; and they often divide these loans into small pieces and repackage them into securities, each of which contains a diversified collection of many pieces from the original loans—a process called *securitization.*

Banks are not the only financial institutions in the country. Many other privately owned, profit-seeking institutions, such as trust companies and credit unions, accept

commercial bank A privately owned, profit-seeking institution that provides a variety of financial services, such as accepting deposits from customers and making loans and other investments.

deposits and grant loans for specific purposes. Finance companies make loans to households for practically any purpose—sometimes at very high interest rates. Department stores and credit-card companies will extend credit so that purchases can be made on a buy-now, pay-later basis.

Commercial banks are subject to federal regulations and until 1994 were required to hold reserves with the Bank of Canada against their deposit liabilities. Other institutions are subject to various federal and provincial regulations concerning ownership and control and the types of financial activities in which they are allowed to engage. Thus, there are differences among all types of financial institutions, not just between banks and others.

The Provision of Credit From the perspective of the overall economy, the most important role played by commercial banks and other financial institutions is that of *financial intermediary*. Banks borrow (accept deposits) from households and firms that have money that they do not currently need, and they lend (provide credit) to those households and firms that need credit to achieve their objectives. They therefore act as essential *intermediaries* in the credit market.

Credit is often referred to as the "lifeblood" of a modern economy and for good reason. Households often require credit to make large purchases, such as home appliances and cars, and they almost always use credit (a mortgage) when they buy a house. Without easy access to credit, most of these household purchases would either be delayed by many years or impossible altogether. Firms also require credit to finance several aspects of their operations. For example, payments for workers and for material inputs often must be made well before revenue from the associated production is received. In addition, firms often finance their capital investments—purchases of equipment or the construction of facilities—with the use of borrowed money. Without easy access to credit, many firms would be unable to conduct their normal business operations and, as a result, the level of economic activity would decline.

This crucial function of banks and other financial institutions—the provision of credit—is easy to overlook when credit markets are functioning smoothly. Like the flow of electricity, we usually take it for granted in our daily activities, only to be reminded of its importance when the next power failure occurs. Similarly, when the credit markets cease to function well, as they did during the financial crisis of 2007 and 2008, their importance to the economy becomes clear to all. Indeed, the economic recession that began in the United States in 2008 and quickly spread around the world originated in the failure of some large U.S. and U.K. banks, which in turn led to a reduction in the flow of credit and a rise in interest rates (the price of credit) in most countries. The effect on economic activity was quick and significant. A central part of the policy response, in Canada and elsewhere, involved taking actions to ensure that banks and other financial institutions were in a position to extend credit in a normal manner. We will say more about the monetary policy response to this financial crisis in Chapter 29.

Interbank Activities Commercial banks have a number of interbank cooperative relationships. For example, banks often share loans. Even the biggest bank cannot meet all the credit needs of a giant corporation, and often a group of banks will offer a "pool loan," agreeing on common terms and dividing the loan up into manageable segments. Another form of interbank cooperation is the bank credit card. Visa and MasterCard are the two most widely used credit cards, and each is operated by a group of banks.

Probably the most important form of interbank cooperation is cheque clearing and collection, including the clearing of electronic transfers through debit cards. Bank deposits are an effective medium of exchange only because banks accept each other's

myeconlab ADDITIONAL TOPICS

The proximate cause of the global recession of 2009–2010 was the collapse of the U.S. housing market beginning in 2007, which, in turn, led to a global financial crisis. For a brief summary of the remarkable events and subsequent policy responses, look for **The U.S. Housing Collapse and the Financial Crisis of 2007–2008** in the *Additional Topics* section of this book's MyEconLab.

www.myeconlab.com

cheques and allow funds to be transferred electronically when purchases are made with debit cards. If a depositor in the Bank of Montreal writes a cheque to someone who deposits it in an account at CIBC, the Bank of Montreal now owes money to CIBC. This creates a need for the banks to present cheques to each other for payment. The same is true for transactions made with bank debit cards.

Millions of such transactions take place in the course of a day, and they result in an enormous sorting and bookkeeping job. Multibank systems make use of a **clearing house** where interbank debts are settled. At the end of the day, all the cheques drawn by the Bank of Montreal's customers and deposited in CIBC are totalled and set against the total of all the cheques drawn by CIBC's customers and deposited in the Bank of Montreal. It is necessary only to settle the difference between the two sums. The actual cheques are passed through the clearing house back to the bank on which they were drawn. Both banks are then able to adjust the individual accounts by a set of book entries. A flow of cash between banks is necessary only when there is a net transfer of cash from the customers of one bank to those of another. This flow of cash is accompanied by a daily transfer of deposits held by the commercial banks with the Bank of Canada.

clearing house An institution in which interbank indebtedness, arising from the transfer of cheques between banks, is computed and offset and net amounts owing are calculated.

Banks as Profit Seekers Banks are private firms that seek to make profits. A commercial bank provides a variety of services to its customers: the convenience of deposits that can be transferred by personal cheque or debit card, a safe and convenient place to earn a modest but guaranteed return on savings, and often financial advice and wealth-management services.

Table 27-2 is the combined balance sheet of the chartered banks in Canada. The bulk of any bank's liabilities are deposits owed to its depositors. The principal assets of a bank are the *securities* it owns (including government bonds), which pay interest or dividends, and the interest-earning *loans* it makes to individuals and to businesses, both in Canada and abroad (which may be denominated in foreign currencies). A bank loan is a liability to the borrower (who must pay it back) but an asset to the bank.

Commercial banks attract deposits by paying interest to depositors and by providing them with services, such as clearing cheques, automated teller machines, debit cards, and the provision of regular monthly statements. Banks earn profits by lending and investing money deposited with them for more than they pay their depositors in terms of interest and other services provided. They also earn profits through the wealth-management and investment services they provide to their customers.

Competition for deposits is active among commercial banks and between banks and other financial institutions. Interest paid on deposits, special high-interest certificates of deposit (CDs), advertising, personal solicitation of accounts, giveaway programs for new deposits to existing accounts, and improved services are all forms of competition for funds.

TABLE 27-2   Consolidated Balance Sheet of the Canadian Chartered Banks, December 2008 (millions of dollars)

Assets		Liabilities	
Reserves (including deposits with Bank of Canada)	5 980	Chequable deposits	257 436
Government of Canada securities	242 942	Savings deposits	509 000
Mortgage and non-mortgage loans	1 105 410	Time deposits	350 086
Canadian securities (corporate and provincial and municipal governments)	181 094	Government of Canada deposits	4 676
		Foreign-currency liabilities	1 334 998
Foreign-currency assets	1 341 636	Shareholders' equity	141 721
Other assets	305 165	Other liabilities	584 310
Total	3 182 227	Total	3 182 227

Reserves are only a tiny fraction of deposit liabilities. If all the chartered banks' customers who held chequable deposits tried to withdraw them in cash, the banks could not meet this demand without liquidating approximately $250 billion of other assets. This would be impossible without assistance from the Bank of Canada.

(*Source:* Adapted from Bank of Canada, *Banking and Financial Statistics,* June 2009, Tables C3 and C4. © Bank of Canada 2009, http://epe.lac-bac.gc.ca/100/201/301/bank_can_banking_fin_stats-ef/2009/2009-06.pdf.)

Reserves

Practise with Study Guide
Chapter 27, Short-Answer
Question 2.

Commercial banks keep sufficient cash on hand to be able to meet depositors' day-to-day requirements for cash. However, just as the goldsmiths of long ago discovered that only a fraction of the gold they held was ever withdrawn at any given time, and just as banks of long ago discovered that only a small fraction of convertible bank notes was actually converted, so too do modern bankers know that only a small fraction of their deposits will be withdrawn in cash at any one time.

> The reserves needed to ensure that depositors can withdraw their deposits on demand will normally be quite small.

In abnormal times, however, nothing short of 100 percent would do the job if the commercial banking system had to stand alone. If a major bank were to fail, it would probably cause a general loss of confidence in the ability of other banks to redeem their deposits. The results would then be devastating. Until relatively recently, such an event—or even the rumour of it—could lead to a **bank run** as depositors rushed to withdraw their money. Faced with such a panic, banks would have to close until either they had borrowed enough funds or sold enough assets to meet the demand, or the demand subsided. However, banks could not instantly turn their loans into cash because the borrowers would have the money tied up in such things as real estate or business enterprises. Neither could the banks obtain cash by selling their securities to the public because payments would be made by cheques, which would not provide cash to pay off depositors.

bank run A situation in which many depositors rush to withdraw their money, possibly leading to a bank's financial collapse.

The difficulty of providing sufficient reserves to meet abnormal situations is alleviated by the central bank, which can provide all the reserves that are needed to meet any abnormal situation. It can do this in two ways. First, it can lend reserves directly to commercial banks on the security of assets that are sound but not easy to liquidate quickly, such as interest-earning residential or commercial mortgages. Second, it can enter the open market and buy all the government securities that commercial banks need to sell. Once the public finds that deposits can be turned into cash, any panic would usually subside and any further drain of cash out of banks would cease.

The possibility of a bank run in Canada has been all but eliminated by the provision of deposit insurance by the Canada Deposit Insurance Corporation (CDIC), a federal Crown corporation. The CDIC guarantees that, in the unlikely event of a bank failure, depositors will get their money back, up to a limit of $100 000 per eligible deposit (there are seven different types of deposit that are eligible for CDIC insurance). Most depositors will not rush to withdraw all of their money as long as they are certain they can get it when they need it.

The late Jimmy Stewart plays George Bailey in It's a Wonderful Life. *In this scene, Bailey, the owner of a small commercial bank, explains to his panicking customers why they can't all take their money out at the same time. It is a great illustration of the workings of a fractional-reserve banking system.*

myeconlab ADDITIONAL TOPICS

Although deposit insurance provides benefits to depositors in the form of enhanced security, some economists argue that it encourages excessive risk-taking on the part of the banks themselves. For more details about the debate over deposit insurance, look for **The Costs and Benefits of Deposit Insurance** in the *Additional Topics* section of this book's MyEconLab.

w w w . m y e c o n l a b . c o m

Target and Excess Reserves Canada's banks hold cash reserves against their deposit liabilities for the simple reason that they want to avoid situations in which they cannot satisfy their depositors' demands for cash, and it is costly for them to borrow from other banks or from the Bank of Canada when they run short of reserves. Look again at Table 27-2. Notice that the chartered banks' cash reserves of just under $6 billion are less than 1 percent of their *deposit* liabilities of more than $1 trillion. Thus, if the holders of even 1 percent of deposits demanded cash, the banks would be unable to meet the demand without outside help. Reserves can be as low as they are because, first, banks know that it is very unlikely that even 1 percent of their total deposits will be withdrawn at any given time and, second, because the banks know that the Bank of Canada will help them out in time of temporary need. The Canadian banking system is thus a **fractional-reserve system**, with commercial banks holding reserves—either as cash or as deposits at the Bank of Canada—of just a small fraction of their total deposits.

A bank's **reserve ratio** is the fraction of its deposits that it *actually* holds as reserves at any point in time, either as cash or as deposits with the Bank of Canada. A bank's target reserve ratio is the fraction of its deposits it would *ideally* like to hold as

fractional-reserve system A banking system in which commercial banks keep only a fraction of their deposits in cash or on deposit with the central bank.

reserve ratio The fraction of its deposits that a commercial bank holds as reserves in the form of cash or deposits with the central bank.

target reserve ratio The fraction of its deposits that a commercial bank wants to hold as reserves.

reserves. This **target reserve ratio** will generally not be constant over time. During holiday seasons, for example, banks may choose to hold more reserves because they know, based on past experience, that there will be heavy demands for cash.

At any given time, any commercial bank will probably not be exactly at its target level of reserves. Reserves may be slightly above or slightly below the target, but the commercial bank will take actions to restore its actual reserves toward its target level. Any reserves in excess of the target level are called **excess reserves**. As we will see next, a bank can expand or contract its portfolio of loans to adjust its actual reserves toward its target level. Understanding this process is the key to understanding the "creation" of deposit money.

excess reserves Reserves held by a commercial bank in excess of its target reserves.

27.3 Money Creation by the Banking System

We noted before that the *money supply* refers to both currency and deposits at commercial banks. The fractional-reserve system provides the leverage that permits commercial banks to create new deposits and thus to create new money. The process is important, so it is worth examining in some detail.

Some Simplifying Assumptions

To focus on the essential aspects of how banks create money, suppose that banks can invest in only one kind of asset—loans—and that there is only one kind of deposit—a chequable deposit. Two other assumptions are provisional and will be relaxed after we have developed some basic ideas about the creation of money:

1. *Fixed target reserve ratio.* We assume that all banks have the same target reserve ratio, which does not change. In our numerical illustration, we will assume that the target reserve ratio is 20 percent (0.20); that is, for every $5 of deposits, the banks want to hold $1 in cash reserves, investing the rest in new loans.

2. *No cash drain from the banking system.* We also assume that the public holds a fixed amount of the currency in circulation. In particular, we assume that the amount of currency held by the public is *not* a constant ratio of their bank deposits. (Later on we will assume that the amount of currency held by the public grows as total bank deposits grow.)

The Creation of Deposit Money

Practise with Study Guide Chapter 27, Exercise 4.

A hypothetical balance sheet, with assets and liabilities, is shown for TD Canada Trust (TD) in Table 27-3. TD has assets of $200 of reserves, held partly as cash on hand and partly as deposits with the central bank, and $900 of loans outstanding to its customers. Its liabilities are $100 to investors (owners) who contributed capital to start the bank and $1000 to current depositors. The bank's ratio of reserves to deposits is 0.20 (200/1000), exactly equal to its target reserve ratio.

What Is a New Deposit?   In what follows, we are interested in knowing how the commercial banking system can "create money" when confronted with a new deposit. But what do we mean by a new deposit? By "new," we mean a deposit of cash that is new to the *commercial banking system*. There are three examples.

- First, an individual might immigrate to Canada and bring cash. When that cash is deposited into a commercial bank, it constitutes a new deposit to the (Canadian) banking system.
- Second, an individual who had some cash stashed under his bed (or in a safety deposit box) has now decided to deposit it into an account at a commercial bank.
- Third is the most interesting but also the most complicated example. If the Bank of Canada were to purchase a government security from an individual or from a firm, it would purchase that asset with a cheque drawn on the Bank of Canada. When the individual or firm deposits the cheque with a commercial bank, it would be a new deposit to the commercial banking system.

The important point to keep in mind here is that the *source* of the new deposit is irrelevant to the process of money creation by the commercial banks. In the discussion that follows, we use the example of the Bank of Canada buying government securities from firms or households as a way of generating a new deposit. But this is not crucial. We use this example because, as we will see in Chapter 29, this is how the Bank of Canada would directly alter the level of reserves in the banking system if it chose to do so. But the general process of money creation we are about to describe applies to *any* new deposit, whatever its source.

The Expansion of Money from a Single New Deposit

Suppose the Bank of Canada enters the open market and buys $100 worth of Government of Canada bonds from John Smith. The Bank issues a cheque to Smith, who then deposits the $100 cheque into his account at TD Canada Trust. This $100 is a wholly new deposit for the commercial bank, and it results in a revised balance sheet (Table 27-4). As a result of the new deposit, TD's cash assets and deposit liabilities have both increased by $100. More important, TD's ratio of reserves to deposits has increased from 0.20 to 0.27 (300/1100). The bank now has $80 in excess reserves; with $1100 in deposits, its target reserves are only $220.

TD can now lend the $80 in excess reserves that it is holding. As it lends the $80, it increases its loan portfolio by $80 but reduces its cash reserves by the same amount. Table 27-5 shows TD's balance sheet after this new loan is made. Notice that TD has restored its reserve ratio to 20 percent, its target reserve ratio.

So far, of the $100 initial deposit at TD, $20 is held by TD as reserves against the deposit and $80 has been lent out in the system. As a result, other banks have received new deposits of $80 stemming from the loans made by TD; persons receiving payment from those who borrowed the $80 from TD will have deposited those payments in their own banks.

The banks that receive deposits from the proceeds of TD's loan are called second-round banks, third-round banks, and so on. In this case, the second-round

TABLE 27-3 The Initial Balance Sheet of Canada Trust (TD)

Assets ($)		Liabilities ($)	
Reserves (cash and deposits with the central bank)	200	Deposits	1 000
Loans	900	Capital	100
	1 100		1 100

TD Canada Trust has reserves equal to 20 percent of its deposit liabilities. The commercial bank earns profits by finding profitable investments for much of the money deposited with it. In this balance sheet, loans are its income-earning assets.

TABLE 27-4 TD's Balance Sheet Immediately After a New Deposit of $100

Assets ($)		Liabilities ($)	
Reserves	300	Deposits	1 100
Loans	900	Capital	100
	1 200		1 200

The new deposit raises liabilities and assets by the same amount. Because both cash and deposits rise by $100, the bank's actual reserve ratio, formerly 0.20, increases to 0.27. The bank now has excess reserves of $80.

TABLE 27-5   TD's Balance Sheet After Making a New Loan of $80

Assets ($)		Liabilities ($)	
Reserves	220	Deposits	1 100
Loans	980	Capital	100
	1 200		1 200

TD converts its excess cash reserves into new loans. The bank keeps $20 as a reserve against the initial new deposit of $100. It lends $80 to a customer, who writes a cheque to someone who deals with another bank. Comparing Tables 27-3 and 27-5 shows that the bank has increased its deposit liabilities by the $100 initially deposited and has increased its assets by $20 of cash reserves and $80 of new loans. It has also restored its target reserve ratio of 0.20.

TABLE 27-6   Changes in the Balance Sheets of Second-Round Banks

Assets ($)		Liabilities ($)	
Reserves	+16	Deposits	+80
Loans	+64		
	+80		+80

Second-round banks receive cash deposits and expand loans. The second-round banks gain new deposits of $80 as a result of the loan granted by TD. These banks keep 20 percent of the cash that they acquire as their reserve against the new deposit, and they can make new loans using the other 80 percent.

banks receive new deposits of $80, and when the cheques clear, they have new reserves of $80. Because they desire to hold only $16 in additional reserves to support the new deposits, they have $64 of excess reserves. They now increase their loans by $64. After this money has been spent by the borrowers and has been deposited in other, third-round banks, the balance sheets of the second-round banks will have changed, as in Table 27-6.

The third-round banks now find themselves with $64 of new deposits. Against these they want to hold only $12.80 as reserves, so they have excess reserves of $51.20 that they can immediately lend out. Thus, there begins a long sequence of new deposits, new loans, new deposits, and new loans. These stages are shown in Table 27-7.

The new deposit of $100 to the banking system has led, through the banks' desire to lend their excess reserves, to the creation of new money. After the completion of the process depicted in Table 27-7, the total change in the combined balance sheets of the entire banking system is shown in Table 27-8.

If v is the target reserve ratio, a new deposit to the banking system will increase the total amount of deposits by $1/v$ times the new deposit.[35]

In our example, where $v = 0.2$ and the new deposit equals $100, total deposits in the banking system will eventually increase by (1/0.2) times $100—that is, by $500.

In our example in which there was an initial new deposit of $100, this $100 was also the amount by which reserves increased in the banking system as a whole. This is because the entire amount of new cash eventually ends up in reserves held against a much larger volume of new deposits. Identifying a new deposit as the change in reserves in the banking system permits us to state our central result slightly differently.

With no cash drain from the banking system, a banking system with a target reserve ratio of v can change its deposits by $1/v$ times any change in reserves.

Recalling that the Greek letter delta, Δ means "the change in," we can express this result in a simple equation:

$$\Delta \text{ Deposits} = \frac{\Delta \text{ Reserves}}{v}$$

The "multiple expansion of deposits" that we have just described applies in reverse to a withdrawal of funds. Deposits of the banking system will fall by $1/v$ times the amount withdrawn from the banking system creating a "multiple contraction of deposits."

Excess Reserves and Cash Drains

The two simplifying assumptions that were made earlier can now be relaxed.

Excess Reserves If banks do not choose to lend their excess reserves, the multiple expansion that we discussed will not occur. Go back to Table 27-4. If TD Canada Trust had been content to hold 27 percent of its deposits in reserves, it would have done nothing more. Other things being equal, banks will choose to lend their excess reserves because of the profit motive, but there may be times when they believe that the risk is too great. It is one thing to be offered a good rate of interest on a loan, but if the borrower defaults on the payment of interest and principal, the bank will be the loser. Similarly, if the bank expects interest rates to rise in the future, it may hold off making loans now so that it will have reserves available to make more profitable loans after the interest rate has risen.

> **Deposit creation does not happen automatically; it depends on the decisions of bankers. If commercial banks do not choose to lend their excess reserves, there will not be an expansion of deposits.**

Recall that we have said that the money supply includes both currency and bank deposits. What we have just seen is that the behaviour of commercial banks is crucial to the process of deposit creation. It follows that the money supply is thus at least partly determined by the commercial banks—in response, for example, to changes in national income, interest rates, and expectations of future business conditions.

Cash Drain Until now, we have been assuming that the public holds a fixed amount of cash, so that when deposits were multiplying in the economy, there was no change in the amount of cash held by the public. But now suppose that instead of holding a fixed *number* of dollars, people decide to hold an amount of cash equal to a fixed *fraction* of their bank deposits. An extra $100 that now gets injected into the banking system as a new cash deposit will not all stay in the banking system. As the amount of deposits multiplies, some fraction of that $100 will be added to the cash held by the public. In such a situation, any multiple expansion of bank deposits will be accompanied by what is called a *cash drain* to the public. This cash drain will reduce the maximum expansion of bank deposits in exactly the same way that taxes and imports reduced the value of the simple multiplier in Chapter 22.

TABLE 27-7 The Sequence of Loans and Deposits After a Single New Deposit of $100

Bank	New Deposits	New Loans	Addition to Reserves
TD	100.00	80.00	20.00
2nd-round bank	80.00	64.00	16.00
3rd-round bank	64.00	51.20	12.80
4th-round bank	51.20	40.96	10.24
5th-round bank	40.96	32.77	8.19
6th-round bank	32.77	26.22	6.55
7th-round bank	26.22	20.98	5.24
8th-round bank	20.98	16.78	4.20
9th-round bank	16.78	13.42	3.36
10th-round bank	13.42	10.74	2.68
Total for first 10 rounds	446.33	357.07	89.26
All remaining rounds	53.67	42.93	10.74
Total for banking system	500.00	400.00	100.00

The banking system as a whole can create deposit money whenever it receives new deposits. The table shows the process of the creation of deposit money on the assumptions that all the loans made by one set of banks end up as deposits in another set of banks (the next-round banks), that the target reserve ratio (v) is 0.20, and that banks always lend out any excess reserves. With no cash drain to the public, the banking system as a whole eventually increases deposit money by $1/v$, which, in this example, is five times the amount of any increase in reserves that it obtains.

TABLE 27-8 Change in the Combined Balance Sheets of All the Banks in the System Following the Multiple Expansion of Deposits

Assets ($)		Liabilities ($)	
Reserves	+100	Deposits	+500
Loans	+400		
	+500		+500

The reserve ratio is returned to 0.20. The entire initial deposit of $100 ends up as additional reserves of the banking system. Therefore, deposits rise by $(1/0.2)$ times the initial deposit—that is, by $500.

Practise with Study Guide
Chapter 27, Exercise 6.

In the case of a cash drain, the relationship between the eventual change in deposits and an injection of cash into the banking system is slightly more complicated. If new cash is injected into the system, it will ultimately show up either as reserves or as cash held by the public. If c is the ratio of cash to deposits that people want to maintain, the final change in deposits will be given by

$$\Delta \text{Deposits} = \frac{\Delta \text{New cash deposit}}{c + v}$$

For example, suppose the Bank of Canada were to purchase $100 of government securities from some current bondholders. As the bondholders deposit their $100 into their bank accounts, there is an injection of $100 into the banking system. If commercial banks' target reserve ratio is 20 percent and there is *no* cash drain, the eventual expansion of deposits will be $500 ($\Delta$ Deposits = $100/0.20$). But if there is a cash drain of 10 percent, the eventual expansion of deposits will only be $333.33 ($\Delta$ Deposits = $100/(0.10 + 0.20)$). [36]

> **The larger is the cash drain from the banking system, the smaller will be the total expansion of deposits created by a new cash deposit.**

Realistic Expansion of Deposits So far we have explained the expansion of deposits in the banking system by using reserve-deposit and cash-deposit ratios that are easy to work with but unrealistic for Canada. In particular, we have been assuming a reserve-deposit ratio (v) equal to 20 percent, whereas Table 27-2 on page 686 shows that Canadian commercial banks hold reserves equal to *approximately 1 percent* of their deposit liabilities. A realistic value for the cash-deposit ratio in Canada is roughly 5 percent—indicating that firms and households hold cash outside the banks equal to 5 percent of the value of their bank deposits. Putting these more realistic values for v and c into our equation, we see that a $100 cash injection (new deposit) to the banking system will eventually lead to a total change in deposits equal to $100/(c + v)$ = $100/(0.01 + 0.05)$ = $100/(0.06)$ = $1666.67. Therefore, small changes in the amount of cash can lead, through the commercial banks' process of deposit creation, to very large changes in the total level of deposits. Commercial banks really do create a lot of (deposit) money out of thin air!

27.4 The Money Supply

Several times in this chapter we have mentioned the *money supply* without ever defining it precisely. But now that you are familiar with the balance sheets of the Bank of Canada and the commercial banking system, and are comfortable with the idea of deposit creation by the commercial banks, we are ready to be more precise about what we mean by the money supply.

money supply The total quantity of money in an economy at a point in time. Also called the *supply of money*.

The total stock of money in the economy at any moment is called the **money supply** or the *supply of money*. Economists use several alternative definitions for the money supply, most of which are regularly reported in the *Bank of Canada Review*—a quarterly publication of the Bank of Canada. Each definition of the money supply includes the amount of currency in circulation *plus* some types of deposit liabilities of the financial institutions.

Money supply = Currency + Bank deposits

The different definitions vary only by which deposit liabilities are included. We begin by looking at the different kinds of deposits.

Kinds of Deposits

Over the past 30 years or so, banks have evolved a bewildering array of different types of deposits. From our point of view, the most important distinction is between deposits that can be readily transferred by cheque, internet banking, phone, or debit card, and those that cannot be so easily transferred. The first type of deposits are media of exchange; the second type are not.

For many years, the distinction lay between *demand deposits,* which earned little or no interest but were "chequable," and *savings deposits,* which earned a higher interest return but were "non-chequable." Today, however, it is so easy to transfer funds from accounts that are technically non-chequable to other accounts that are chequable that the distinction becomes quite blurred. The deposit that is genuinely tied up for a period of time now takes the form of a **term deposit**, which has a specified withdrawal date a minimum of 30 days into the future, and which pays a much reduced interest rate in the event of early withdrawal. Term and other non-chequable deposits pay significantly higher interest rates than do chequable deposits.

term deposit An interest-earning bank deposit, subject to notice before withdrawal.

Non-bank financial institutions, such as asset-management firms, now offer *money market mutual funds* and *money market deposit accounts*. These accounts earn higher interest and are chequable, although some are subject to minimum withdrawal restrictions and others to prior notice of withdrawal.

> The long-standing distinction between money and other highly liquid assets used to be that, narrowly defined, money was a medium of exchange that did not earn interest, whereas other liquid assets earned interest but were not media of exchange. Today, this distinction has almost completely disappeared.

Definitions of the Money Supply

Different definitions of the money supply include different types of deposits. Until recently, a common definition of the money supply used by the Bank of Canada was called M1, which included currency in circulation plus chequable deposits held at the chartered banks. But M1 did not include similar deposits at other financial institutions or any non-chequable deposits. With the changing nature of deposits, it is now more common to use broader measures of the money supply. Two commonly used measures in Canada today are M2 and M2+. **M2** includes currency in circulation plus chequable and non-chequable deposits at the chartered banks; **M2+** includes M2 plus similar deposits at other financial institutions (trust and mortgage-loan companies, credit unions and caisses populaires) and holdings of money-market mutual funds. Table 27-9 shows the composition of M2 and M2+ in Canada as of September 2009.

M2 Currency plus deposits at the chartered banks.

M2+ M2 plus deposits at other financial institutions.

The Bank of Canada computes other measures of the money supply even broader than M2+. These are referred to as M2++, M3, and so on, where each measure is broader than the previous one, meaning that it includes more types of financial assets. For example, M2++ includes M2+ plus holdings of Canada savings bonds and non-money-market funds. In general, the broader the measure of the money supply, the more the concept of money being measured includes assets that do not serve as a direct medium of exchange but do serve the store-of-value function and can be converted into a medium of exchange.

TABLE 27-9　M2 and M2+ in Canada, September 2009 (millions of dollars)

Currency	54 254
Demand Deposits	
Personal	177 761
Non-personal	231 286
Notice and Term Deposits	
Personal	463 604
Non-personal	27 075
Adjustment	−2 496
M2	**951 484**
Deposits at:	
Trust and mortgage-loan companies	21 777
Credit unions and caisses populaires	207 396
Money-market mutual funds	65 240
Other	51 322
M2+	**1 297 219**

M2 and M2+ are two commonly used measures of the money supply in Canada. M2 includes chequable (demand) and non-chequable deposits at the chartered banks; M2+ adds deposits at other financial institutions. These deposits all serve the medium-of-exchange function of money. Still broader measures (like M2++ and M3) include financial assets that best serve the store-of-value function but can readily be converted into a medium of exchange.

(*Source:* Adapted from Bank of Canada, *Weekly Financial Statistics*, November 27, 2009, http://epe.lac-bac.gc.ca/100/201/301/weekly_fin_stats/2009/091127.pdf.)

near money Liquid assets that are easily convertible into money without risk of significant loss of value and can be used as short-term stores of value but are not themselves media of exchange.

money substitute Something that serves as a medium of exchange but is not a store of value.

Practise with Study Guide Chapter 27, Short-Answer Question 2.

Near Money and Money Substitutes

Recall our early discussion of money as a medium of exchange and as a store of value. In arriving at empirical measures of money, we must consider some assets that do not perform one or both of these roles perfectly. This brings us to the concepts of *near money* and *money substitutes*.

Assets that adequately fulfill the store-of-value function and are readily converted into a medium of exchange but are not themselves a medium of exchange are sometimes called **near money**. Term deposits are a good example of near money. When you have a term deposit, you know exactly how much purchasing power you hold (at current prices), and, given modern banking practices, you can turn your deposit into a medium of exchange—cash or a chequing deposit—at a moment's notice (though you may pay a penalty in the form of reduced interest if you withdraw the funds before the end of the specified term).

Why then does everybody not keep his or her money in such deposits instead of in demand deposits or currency? The answer is that the inconvenience of continually shifting money back and forth may outweigh the interest that can be earned. One week's interest on $100 (at 5 percent per year) is only about 10 cents, not enough to cover bus fare to the bank, the time spent going to an ATM, or perhaps even the time spent making an online transfer. For money that will be needed soon, it would hardly pay to shift it to a term deposit.

Things that serve as media of exchange but are not a store of value are sometimes called **money substitutes**. Credit cards are a prime example. With a credit card, many transactions can be made without either cash or a cheque. The evidence of credit, the credit slip you sign and hand over to the store, is not money, because it cannot be used to make other transactions. The credit card serves the short-run function of a medium of exchange by allowing you to make purchases, even though you have no cash or bank deposit currently in your possession. But this is only temporary; money remains the final medium of exchange for these transactions when the credit-card bill is paid.

Choosing a Measure

Since the eighteenth century, economists have known that the amount of money in circulation is an important economic variable. As theories became more carefully specified in the nineteenth and early twentieth centuries, they included a variable called the "money supply." But for theories to be useful (and especially for the predictions to be testable), we must be able to identify real-world counterparts of these theoretical variables.

The specifics of the definition of money have changed and will continue to change over time. New monetary assets are continually being developed to serve some, if not all, of the functions of money, and they are more or less readily convertible into money. There is no single, timeless definition of money and what is only near money or a money substitute. Indeed, as we have seen, the Bank of Canada uses several definitions of money.

The Role of the Bank of Canada

In this chapter, we have seen that the commercial banking system, when confronted with a new deposit, can create a multiple expansion of bank deposits. This shows how the reserves of the banking system are systematically related to the money supply. In Chapter 29 we will see the details of how the Bank of Canada conducts its monetary policy and how its actions influence the total amount of reserves in the banking system. At that point we will have a more complete picture of the connection among the Bank's monetary policy, reserves in the banking system, and the overall money supply.

Recall that in the previous chapter we examined how in the long run, with real GDP equal to Y^*, the real interest rate was determined by saving and investment. In the next chapter, we return to the short-run version of our macro model (in which Y is no longer assumed to equal Y^*) but add money to that model explicitly. There we will see how the interaction of money demand and money supply determines the equilibrium interest rate in the short run. We will also see how changes in the money market lead to changes in desired aggregate expenditure and real GDP. In Chapter 29 we examine the details of the Bank of Canada's monetary policy, with an emphasis on its current policy regime of *inflation targeting*.

Summary

27.1 The Nature of Money

- Money is anything that serves as a medium of exchange, a store of value, and a unit of account.
- Money arose because of the inconvenience of barter, and it developed in stages: from precious metal to metal coinage, to paper money convertible to precious metals, to token coinage and paper money fractionally backed by precious metals, to fiat money, and to deposit money.

27.2 The Canadian Banking System

- The banking system in Canada consists of two main elements: the Bank of Canada (which is the central bank) and the commercial banks.
- The Bank of Canada is a government-owned corporation that is responsible for the day-to-day conduct of monetary policy. Though the Bank has considerable autonomy in its policy decisions, ultimate responsibility for monetary policy resides with the government.
- Commercial banks and other financial institutions play a key role as intermediaries in the credit market.

Significant interruptions in the flow of credit usually lead to increases in interest rates and reductions in the level of economic activity.

- Commercial banks are profit-seeking institutions that allow their customers to transfer deposits from one bank to another by means of cheques or debit cards. They create money as a by-product of their commercial operations by making or liquidating loans and various other investments.

27.3 Money Creation by the Banking System

- Because most customers are content to pay by cheque or debit card rather than with cash, banks need only small reserves to back their deposit liabilities. It is this *fractional-reserve aspect* of the banking system that enables commercial banks to create deposit money.
- When the banking system receives a new cash deposit, it can create new deposits equal to some multiple of this

amount. For a target reserve ratio of v and a cash–deposit ratio of c, the total change in deposits following a new cash deposit is

$$\Delta \text{ Deposits} = \frac{\text{New cash deposit}}{c + v}$$

27.4 The Money Supply

- The money supply—the stock of money in an economy at a specific moment—can be defined in various ways. M1, the narrowest definition, includes currency and chequable deposits. M2 includes M1 plus savings deposits and smaller term deposits. M2+ includes M2 plus deposits at non-bank financial institutions and money-market mutual funds.

- Near money includes interest-earning assets that are convertible into money on a dollar-for-dollar basis but that are not currently a medium of exchange. Money substitutes are things such as credit cards that serve as a medium of exchange but are not money.

Key Concepts

Medium of exchange, store of value, and unit of account
Fully backed, fractionally backed, and fiat money

The banking system and the Bank of Canada
Target reserve ratio and excess reserves
The creation of deposit money

Demand and term deposits
The money supply
Near money and money substitutes

Study Exercises

1. Fill in the blanks to make the following statements correct.

   a. Money serves three functions: _____, _____, and _____.

   b. Suppose children at a summer camp are each given a credit of $20.00 at the snack shop, where purchases are recorded but no cash is exchanged. This is an example of money as a _____ and a _____.

   c. Paper money and coins that are not convertible into anything with intrinsic value, but are declared by the government to be legal tender, are known as _____.

   d. The Bank of Canada has four main functions in the Canadian economy:
   - _____
   - _____
   - _____
   - _____

e. Canada has a _____-reserve banking system, in which commercial banks keep only a fraction of their total deposits in reserves. A commercial bank has a _____ ratio that governs what it attempts to keep as reserves.

2. Fill in the blanks to make the following statements correct. Answer these questions in the sequence given.

a. Suppose the Bank of Canada purchases a $1000 bond from Bob's Fishing Supplies, and Bob's deposits its cheque at the CIBC. This is a _____ deposit to the banking system and will allow the commercial banks to _____.

b. If the CIBC has a target reserve ratio of 5 percent, it will keep _____ dollars as reserves and will lend _____ dollars.

c. Assuming there is no cash drain from the banking system, the ultimate effect is a(n) _____ in deposits in the banking system of _____ × $1000 = _____.

d. Suppose the Bank of Canada sells a $1000 bond to Bob's Fishing Supplies, and Bob's pays for that bond with a cheque drawn on its account at the CIBC. This is a _____ of funds from the banking system and will cause the commercial banks to _____.

e. If the CIBC pays the $1000 from its reserves, its reserve ratio will then be _____ its target rate of 5 percent. If the CIBC keeps its reserves at the new level, its loans must fall by _____ to restore the 5-percent target reserve ratio.

3. Which of the following items can be considered money in the Canadian economy? Explain your answers by discussing the three functions of money—medium of exchange, store of value, and unit of account.

a. A Canadian $100 bill
b. A Visa credit card
c. A well-known painting by Robert Bateman
d. An interest-earning savings account
e. A U.S. Treasury bill payable in three months
f. A share of Tim Hortons stock
g. A $1 bill of Canadian Tire money

4. The table below shows the balance sheet for the Regal Bank, a hypothetical commercial bank. Assume that the Regal Bank has achieved its target reserve ratio.

Balance Sheet: Regal Bank

Assets		Liabilities	
Reserves	$ 200	Deposits	$4000
Loans	$4200	Capital	$ 400

a. What is the Regal Bank's target reserve ratio?
b. What is the value of the owners' investment in the bank?
c. Suppose someone makes a new deposit to the Regal Bank of $100. Draw a new balance sheet showing the *immediate* effect of the new deposit. What is the Regal Bank's new reserve ratio?
d. Suppose instead that someone *withdraws* $100 cash from the Regal Bank. Show the new balance sheet and the new reserve ratio.

5. Consider a new deposit to the Canadian banking system of $1000. Suppose that all commercial banks have a target reserve ratio of 10 percent and there is no cash drain. The following table shows how deposits, reserves, and loans change as the new deposit permits the banks to "create" money.

Round	Δ Deposits	Δ Reserves	Δ Loans
First	$1000	$100	$900
Second	—	—	—
Third	—	—	—
Fourth	—	—	—
Fifth	—	—	—

a. The first round has been completed in the table. Now, recalling that the new loans in the first round become the new deposits in the second round, complete the second round in the table.
b. By using the same approach, complete the entire table.
c. You have now completed the first five rounds of the deposit-creation process. What is the total change in deposits *so far* as a result of the single new deposit of $1000?
d. This deposit-creation process will go on forever, but it will have a *finite* sum. In the text, we showed that the eventual total change in deposits is equal to $1/v$ times the new deposit, where v is the target reserve ratio. What is the eventual total change in deposits in this case?
e. What is the eventual total change in reserves? What is the eventual change in loans?

6. Consider a withdrawal of $5000 from the Canadian banking system. Suppose all commercial banks have a target reserve ratio of 8 percent and there is no cash drain.

a. Using a table like that shown in the previous question, show the change in deposits, reserves, and loans for the first three "rounds" of activity.
b. Compute the eventual total change in deposits, reserves, and loans.

7. Consider an individual who immigrates to Canada and deposits $3000 in Canadian currency into the Canadian banking system. Suppose all commercial banks have a target reserve ratio of 10 percent and individuals choose to hold cash equal to 10 percent of their bank deposits.

   a. In the text, we showed that the eventual total change in deposits is equal to $1/(v + c)$ times the new deposit, where v is the target reserve ratio and c is the ratio of cash to deposits. What is the eventual total change in deposits in this case?
   b. What is the eventual total change in reserves?
   c. What is the eventual total change in loans?

8. Consider an individual who moves to Canada and brings with him $40 000 in Canadian currency, which he deposits in a Canadian bank. For each of the cases below, compute the overall change in deposits and reserves in the Canadian banking system as a result of this new deposit.

   a. 10 percent target reserve ratio; no cash drain; no excess reserves
   b. 10 percent target reserve ratio; 5 percent cash drain; no excess reserves
   c. 10 percent target reserve ratio; 5 percent cash drain; 5 percent excess reserves

9. This question is intended to illustrate the similarity between the simple multiplier from Chapters 21 and 22 and the deposit multiplier that we examined in this chapter.

   a. Recalling the macro model of Chapters 21 and 22, suppose the marginal propensity to spend out of GDP, z, is 0.6. If autonomous spending increases by $1000, fill in the table below.

Round	ΔAE	ΔY
First	$1000	$1000
Second	—	—
Third	—	—
Fourth	—	—
Fifth	—	—

   b. The sum of the values in the third column should be

   $$\Delta Y = \$1000 + z\,\$1000 + z^2\,\$1000 + z^3\,\$1000 + \ldots$$

   What is the total change in GDP?

   c. Now consider the process of deposit creation from this chapter. Consider a new deposit of $1000 and a target reserve ratio, v, of 0.25 (with no cash drain). Fill in the following table:

Round	Δ Deposits	Δ Reserves	Δ Loans
First	$1000	$250	$750
Second	—	—	—
Third	—	—	—
Fourth	—	—	—
Fifth	—	—	—

   d. The sum of the values in the first column should be

   $$\text{Deposits} = \$1000 + (1 - v)\$1000 + (1 - v)^2\,\$1000 + (1 - v)^3\,\$1000 + \ldots$$

   What is the total change in deposits?

   e. Explain why taxes and imports for the simple multiplier in Chapter 21 are similar to a reserve ratio for the deposit multiplier in this chapter.

Discussion Questions

1. A Canadian who receives a U.S. coin has the option of spending it at face value or taking it to the bank and converting it to Canadian money at the going rate of exchange. When the rate of exchange was near par (in the early 1970s), so that $1 Canadian was within 3 cents of U.S.$1, U.S. and Canadian coins circulated side by side, exchanged at face value. Use Gresham's law to predict which coinage disappeared from circulation in Canada when the Canadian dollar fell to U.S.$0.67 in the late 1990s. Why did a 3-cent differential not produce this result?

2. During hyperinflations in several foreign countries after the Second World War, American cigarettes were sometimes used in place of money. What made them suitable?

3. Suppose that on January 1, 2008, a household had $100 000, which it wanted to hold for use one year later. Calculate, by using resources available online or in your university library, which of the following would have been the best store of value over that period. Will the best store of value over that period necessarily be the best over the next 24 months?

   a. The (Canadian) dollar
   b. Stocks whose prices moved with the Toronto Stock Exchange (S&P/TSX) index
   c. A Government of Canada 5.75 percent bond coming due in 2029
   d. Gold
   e. A house whose value changed with the average house price in Canada

4. If all depositors tried to turn their deposits into cash at once, they would find that there are not sufficient reserves in the system to allow all of them to do this at the same time. Why then do we not still have panicky runs on the banks? Would it be better for the Bank of Canada to impose a 100-percent reserve requirement? What effect would such a reserve requirement have on the banking system's ability to create money? Would it preclude any possibility of a panic?

5. Compared with their use a few years ago, credit and bank cards are used extensively today to facilitate purchases of goods and services all over the world. Does this distort the true measure of money in the economy? Should credit and bank cards be incorporated in the definitions of M1 or M2?

6. During the financial crisis of 2007–2008, the governor of the Bank of Canada expressed concern that the commercial banks were "hoarding" cash rather than extending a more appropriate volume of loans. Why might the banks do this, and what is the implication for the money supply?

28

Money, Interest Rates, and Economic Activity

In Chapter 27, we learned how the commercial banking system multiplies a given amount of reserves into deposit money and thus influences the nation's money supply. We also learned that because the Bank of Canada can set the amount of commercial-bank reserves, it too has an influence on the money supply. What we have not yet discussed, however, is *how* the Bank influences the amount of reserves. We will leave that discussion until next chapter when we examine the details of Canadian monetary policy. For now, just think of the nation's money supply as being determined jointly by the actions of the Bank of Canada and the commercial banking system.

In this chapter, we focus on how money affects the economy. Understanding the role of money, however, requires an understanding of the interaction of money supply and money demand. To examine the nature of money demand, we begin by examining how households decide to divide their total holdings of assets between money and interest-earning assets (which here are called "bonds"). Once that is done, we put money supply and money demand together to examine *monetary equilibrium.* Only then can we ask how changes in the supply of money or in the demand for money affect the economy in the short term—interest rates, real GDP, and the price level. We begin with a discussion of the relationship between bond prices and interest rates.

28.1 Understanding Bonds

At any moment, households have a stock of financial wealth that they hold in several forms. Some of it is money in the bank or in the wallet. Some may be in *Treasury bills* and *bonds,* which are IOUs issued by the government or corporations. Some may be in *equity,* meaning ownership shares of a company.

To simplify our discussion, we will group financial wealth into just two categories, which we call "money" and "bonds." By money we mean all assets that serve as a medium of exchange—that is, paper money, coins, and deposits on which cheques can be drawn. By bonds we mean all other forms of financial wealth; this includes interest-earning financial assets and claims on real capital (equity). This simplification is useful because it emphasizes the important distinction between interest-earning and non-interest-earning assets. This distinction is central for understanding the demand for money.

Economists often simplify the analysis of financial assets by considering only two types of assets—non-interest-bearing "money" and interest-bearing "bonds."

Before discussing how individuals decide to divide their assets between money and bonds, we need to make sure we understand what bonds are and how they are priced. This requires an understanding of *present value.*

---

myeconlab   ADDITIONAL TOPICS

For readers interested in learning more about the stock market, the market in which equities are traded, look for **A Beginner's Guide to the Stock Market** in the *Additional Topics* section of this book's MyEconLab.

www.myeconlab.com

Present Value and the Interest Rate

A bond is a financial asset that promises to make one or more specified payments at specified dates in the future. The **present value (*PV*)** of any asset refers to the value now of the future payments that the asset offers. Present value depends on the interest rate because when we calculate present value, the interest rate is used to *discount* the value of the future payments into their *present* value. Let's consider two examples to illustrate the concept of present value.

present value (*PV*) The value now of one or more payments or receipts made in the future; often referred to as discounted present value.

A Single Payment One Year Hence   We start with the simplest case. What is the value *now* of a bond that will return a single payment of $100 in one year's time?

Suppose the interest rate is 5 percent. Now ask how much you would have to lend out at that interest rate today in order to have $100 a year from now. If we use *PV* to stand for this unknown amount, we can write $PV \times (1.05) = \$100$. Thus, $PV = \$100/1.05 = \$95.24$.[1] This tells us that the present value of \$100 receivable in one year's time is \$95.24; if you lend out \$95.24 for one year at 5 percent interest you will get back the \$95.24 plus \$4.76 in interest, which makes \$100.

We can generalize this relationship with a simple equation. If R_1 is the amount we receive one year from now and i is the annual interest rate, the present value of R_1 is:

$$PV = \frac{R_1}{1+i}$$

If the interest rate is 7 percent ($i = 0.07$) and the bond pays \$100 in one year ($R_1 = \$100$), the present value of that bond is $PV = \$100/1.07 = \$93.46$. Notice that, when compared with the previous numerical example, the higher interest rate leads to a lower present value. The future payment of \$100 gets discounted at a higher rate and so is worth less at the present time.

Practise with Study Guide
Chapter 28, Exercise 1.

A Sequence of Future Payments Now consider a more complicated case, but one that is actually more realistic. Many bonds promise to make "coupon" payments every year and then return the face value of the bond at the end of the term of the loan. For example, imagine a three-year bond that promises to repay the face value of \$1000 in three years, but will also pay a 10 percent coupon payment of \$100 at the end of each of the three years that the bond is held. How much is this bond worth now? We can compute the present value of this bond by adding together the present values of each of the payments. If the market interest rate is 7 percent, the present value of this bond is

$$PV = \frac{\$100}{1.07} + \frac{\$100}{(1.07)^2} + \frac{\$1100}{(1.07)^3}$$

The first term is the value today of receiving \$100 one year from now. The second term is the value today of receiving the second \$100 payment two years from now. Note that we discount this second payment twice—once from Year 2 to Year 1, and once again from Year 1 to now—and thus the denominator shows an interest rate of 7 percent *compounded* for two years. Finally, the third term shows the value today of the \$1100 repayment (\$1000 of face value plus \$100 of coupon payment) three years from now. The present value of this bond is

$$PV = \$93.46 + \$87.34 + \$897.93$$
$$= \$1078.73$$

In general, any asset that promises to make a sequence of payments into the future of $R_1, R_2, \ldots$, and so on, up to R_T has a present value given by

$$PV = \frac{R_1}{1+i} + \frac{R_2}{(1+i)^2} + \cdots + \frac{R_T}{(1+i)^T}$$

It is useful to try another example. Let's continue with the case in which the bond repays its face value of \$1000 three years from now and makes three \$100 coupon

---

[1] Notice that in this type of formula, the interest rate is expressed as a decimal fraction where, for example, 5 percent is expressed as 0.05, so $1 + i$ equals 1.05.

payments at the end of each year the bond is held. But this time we assume the market interest rate is 9 percent. In this case, the present value of the bond is

$$PV = \frac{\$100}{1.09} + \frac{\$100}{(1.09)^2} + \frac{\$1100}{(1.09)^3}$$

$$= \$91.74 + \$84.17 + \$849.40$$

$$= \$1025.31$$

Notice that when the market interest rate is 9 percent, the present value of the bond is lower than the present value of the same bond when the market interest rate is 7 percent. The higher interest rate implies that any future payments are discounted at a higher rate and thus have a lower present value.

A General Relationship   There are many types of bonds. Some make no coupon payments and only a single payment (the "face value") at some point in the future. This is the case for short-term government bonds called *Treasury bills*. Other bonds, typically longer-term government or corporate bonds, make regular coupon payments as well as a final payment of the bond's face value. Though there are many types of bonds, they all have one thing in common: They promise to make some payment or sequence of payments in the future. Because bonds make payments in the future, their present value is negatively related to the market interest rate.

> The present value of any bond that promises a future payment or sequence of future payments is negatively related to the market interest rate.

Present Value and Market Price

Most bonds are bought and sold in financial markets in which there are large numbers of both buyers and sellers. The present value of a bond is important because it establishes the price at which a bond will be exchanged in the financial markets.

> The present value of a bond is the most someone would be willing to pay now to own the bond's future stream of payments.

To understand this concept, let us return to our example of a bond that promises to pay $100 one year from now. When the interest rate is 5 percent, the present value of this bond is $95.24. To see why this is the maximum that anyone would pay for this bond, suppose that some sellers offer to sell the bond at some other price, say, $98. If, instead of paying this amount for the bond, a potential buyer lends $98 out at 5 percent interest, he or she would have at the end of one year more than the $100 that the bond will produce. (At 5 percent interest, $98 yields $4.90 in interest, which when added to the principal makes $102.90.) Clearly, no well-informed individual would pay $98—or, by the same reasoning, any sum in excess of $95.24—for the bond. Thus, at any price above the bond's present value, the lack of demand will cause the price to fall.

Now suppose the bond is offered for sale at a price less than $95.24, say, $90. A potential buyer could borrow $90 to buy the bond and would pay $4.50 in interest on the loan. At the end of the year, the bond yields $100. When this is used to repay the $90 loan and the $4.50 in interest, $5.50 is left as profit. Clearly, it would be worthwhile for someone to buy the bond at the price of $90 or, by the same argument, at any price less than $95.24. Thus, at any price below the bond's present value, the abundance of demand will cause the price to rise.

This discussion should make clear that the present value of an asset determines its equilibrium market price. If the market price of any asset is greater than the present value of its income stream, no one will want to buy it, and the resulting excess supply will push down the market price. If the market price is below its present value, there will be a rush to buy it, and the resulting excess demand will push up the market price. When the bond's market price is exactly equal to its present value, there is no pressure for the price to change.

> The equilibrium market price of any bond will be the present value of the income stream that it produces.

Interest Rates, Market Prices, and Bond Yields

We now have two relationships that can be put together to tell us about the link between the market interest rate and bond prices. Let's restate these two relationships.

1. The present value of a bond is negatively related to the market interest rate.

2. A bond's equilibrium market price will be equal to its present value.

Putting these two relationships together, we come to a key relationship:

> An increase in the market interest rate leads to a fall in the price of any given bond. A decrease in the market interest rate leads to an increase in the price of any given bond.

Remember that a bond is a financial investment for the purchaser. The cost of the investment is the price of the bond, and the return on the investment is the sequence of future payments. Thus, for a given sequence of future payments, a lower bond price implies a higher rate of return on the bond, or a higher *bond yield*.

To illustrate the yield on a bond, consider a simple example of a bond that promises to pay $1000 two years from now. If you purchase this bond for $857.34, your return on your investment will be 8 percent per year because $857.34 compounded for two years at 8 percent will yield $1000 in two years.

$$\$857.34 \times (1.08)^2 = \$1000$$

In other words, your yield on the bond will be 8 percent per year.

Notice that we are making a distinction between the concept of the *yield* on a bond and the *market interest rate*. The bond yield is a function of the sequence of payments and the bond price. The market interest rate is the rate at which you can borrow or lend money in the credit market.

Although they are logically distinct from each other, there is a close relationship between the market interest rate and bond yields. A rise in the market interest rate will lead to a decline in the present value of any bond and thus to a decline in its equilibrium price. As the bond price falls, its yield or rate of return rises. Thus, we see that market interest rates and bond yields tend to move in the same direction.

An increase in the market interest rate will reduce bond prices and increase bond yields. A reduction in the market interest rate will increase bond prices and reduce bond yields. Therefore, market interest rates and bond yields tend to move together.

Because of this close relationship between bond yields and market interest rates, economists discussing the role of money in the macroeconomy typically refer to "the" interest rate—or perhaps to "interest rates" in general—rather than to any specific interest rate among the many different rates corresponding to the many different financial assets. Since these rates all tend to rise or fall together, it is a very useful simplification to refer only to "the" interest rate, meaning the rate of return that can be earned by holding interest-earning assets rather than money.

Bond Riskiness

Sometimes the yields on specific bonds rise or fall even when there is no change in the market interest rate. This occurs when there is a change in the perceived *riskiness* of the bond. If the bond purchasers (lenders) perceive that bond issuers (borrowers) are unlikely to be able to fulfill their future repayment obligations, the expected present value of the bond declines. A lower expected present value leads fewer buyers to be interested in purchasing that bond and, as a result, its equilibrium market price declines. As the market price falls, the yield on that bond rises. Bonds with high yields reflect high-risk investments.

An increase in the riskiness of any bond leads to a decline in its expected present value and thus to a decline in the bond's price. The lower bond price implies a higher bond yield.

It is rare in Canada that government bonds are perceived as risky, but many corporations are sometimes believed to be in precarious financial situations and thus their bonds are perceived to be risky assets. As a result, there are often very high yields (low bond prices) on specific corporate bonds. *Applying Economic Concepts 28-1* discusses the relationship among bond prices, bond yields, riskiness, and *term to maturity* of government and corporate bonds.

28.2 The Demand for Money

The amount of money that everyone in the economy wants to hold is called the **demand for money**. At any given time, households and firms have a specific stock of financial assets, and they must decide in which form to hold these assets. Remember that we make the simplifying assumption that there are only two types of assets—money and bonds. Therefore, if households and firms are choosing how to divide their given stock of assets between money and bonds, it follows that if we know the demand for money, we also know the demand for bonds. If people want to hold $1 billion more of their assets in the form of money, they must also wish to hold $1 billion less of bonds.

demand for money The total amount of money balances that the public wants to hold for all purposes.

APPLYING ECONOMIC CONCEPTS 28-1

Understanding Bond Prices and Bond Yields

Various kinds of bonds are traded every day, and they differ in terms of the issuer, price, yield, riskiness, and term to maturity. We focus here on how to understand these bond characteristics.

How to Read the Bond Tables

The accompanying table shows seven bond listings just as they appeared on www.globeinvestor.com on June 29, 2009. The five columns are as follows:

1. **Issuer.** This is the issuer of the bond—that is, the borrower of the money. The first five bonds shown are issued by the Government of Canada. The last two are issued by firms whose names you surely recognize.

2. **Coupon.** This is the coupon rate—the annual rate of interest that the bond pays before it matures. For example, a 6 percent coupon rate means that the bondholder (the lender) will receive 6 percent of the face value of the bond every year until the bond matures.

3. **Maturity.** This is when the bond matures and the face value is repaid to the bondholder. All debt obligations are then fulfilled.

4. **Price.** This is the market price of the bond, expressed as the price per $100 of face value. For example, a price of $104.81 means that for every $100 of face value, the purchaser must pay $104.81. When the price is greater than $100, we say there is a *premium;* when the price is less than $100, we say the bond is selling at a *discount.*

5. **Yield.** This is the rate of return earned by the bondholder if the bond is bought at the *current* price and held to maturity, earning all regular coupon payments.

Issuer	Coupon (%)	Maturity	Price ($)	Yield (%)
1. Canada	5.50	June 1, 2010	104.59	0.50
2. Canada	9.50	June 1, 2010	108.25	0.50
3. Canada	4.00	June 1, 2016	106.62	2.94
4. Canada	8.00	June 1, 2023	144.78	3.82
5. Canada	8.00	June 1, 2027	150.68	4.01
6. Loblaws	7.10	June 1, 2016	111.31	5.14
7. Bell Canada	8.88	April 17, 2026	96.75	9.26

Three Reasons for Holding Money

Why do firms and households hold money? There are three reasons. First, households and firms hold money in order to carry out transactions. Economists call this the *transactions demand* for money. You carry money in your pocket or keep it in a chequing account in order to have it readily available for your upcoming transactions; it would be very inconvenient to have to sell bonds or withdraw money from your GIC (guaranteed investment certificate) every time you wanted to spend. Similarly, firms are continually making expenditures on intermediate inputs and payments to labour and they keep money available in their chequing accounts to pay these expenses.

A second and related reason firms and households hold money is that they are uncertain about when some expenditures will be necessary, and they hold money as a precaution to avoid the problems associated with missing a transaction. This is referred to as the *precautionary demand* for money. For example, you might hold some cash because of the possibility that you might need to take an unplanned taxi ride during a rainstorm; a small business may hold cash because of the possibility that it might need the emergency services of a tradesperson, such as a plumber or an electrician. In the days before the invention of ATMs, the precautionary demand for money was quite

Bond Prices and Yields

Three general patterns can be seen in the accompanying table. First, for a given issuer and maturity, there is a positive relationship between the bond price and the coupon rate. Rows 1 and 2, for example, show two bonds, both issued by the Government of Canada and both maturing on June 1, 2010. The common issuer suggests a common risk of non-repayment (in this case a very low risk). The first bond has a 5.50 percent coupon whereas the second has a 9.50 percent coupon. Not surprisingly, the higher coupon payments make the second bond a more attractive asset and thus its market price is higher—$108.25 as compared with $104.59. Note, however, that the implied yield on the two bonds is identical. If this weren't the case, demand would shift toward the high-yield (low-price) bond, driving down the yield (increasing the price) until the two yields were the same.

Second, for a given bond issuer, there is a positive relationship between the bond yield and the term to maturity. This is shown in the first five rows, as yields rise from 0.50 percent on bonds maturing in 11 months' time (from the date of the listing) to 4.01 percent on bonds maturing in 18 years' time. This positive relationship is often referred to as the *yield curve* or the *term structure of interest rates*. The higher yields on longer-term bonds reflect what is often called a *term premium*—the higher yield that bondholders must be paid in order to induce them to have their money tied up for longer periods of time.

Third, for a given term to maturity, there is a positive relationship between the bond yield and the perceived riskiness of the bond issuer. Compare rows 3 and 6, for example. Both bonds have identical maturity dates in 2016, but one is issued by the Government of Canada while the other is issued by Loblaws. Though it is almost impossible for the Government of Canada to go bankrupt and almost inconceivable that it would default on its debt, it is certainly possible for Loblaws to do so. This difference explains the more than two-percentage-point difference in yields. The same is true between rows 5 and 7 where the more than five-percentage-point yield difference is attributable to the higher likelihood of default by Bell Canada than by the Canadian government.

If you run your eyes down the bond tables, you will easily see those corporations viewed by the market as being risky borrowers because the yields on their bonds will be higher—often dramatically so—than the yields on similar-maturity government bonds. For example, in the summer of 2009 when the automobile companies were experiencing great difficulty, the bonds issued by Ford Credit Canada (and maturing only six months later) were selling at such a discount that the implied annual yield was more than 15 percent. Such high yields represent a great investment opportunity only if you are prepared to take the associated risk. Beware!

large since to be caught on a weekend or away from home without sufficient cash could be a serious matter. Today, this motive for holding money is less important.

The third reason for holding money applies more to large businesses and to professional money managers than to individuals because it involves *speculating* about how interest rates are likely to change in the future. Economists call this the *speculative demand* for money. To understand this reason for holding money, recall what we said earlier about the negative relationship between interest rates and bond prices. If interest rates are expected to rise in the future, bond prices will be expected to fall. Whenever bond prices fall, bondholders experience a decline in the value of their bond holdings. The expectation of increases in *future* interest rates will therefore lead to the holding of more money (and fewer bonds) *now* as financial managers adjust their portfolios in order to preserve their values.

The Determinants of Money Demand

We have just seen three general reasons that firms and households hold money. We now want to examine which key macroeconomic variables affect the *amount* of money

FIGURE 28-1   Money Demand as a Function of the Interest Rate, Real GDP, and the Price Level

The quantity of money demanded is assumed to be negatively related to the interest rate and positively related to real GDP and the price level. The negative slope of the M_D curve comes from the choice between holding money and holding bonds. A fall in the interest rate from i_1 to i_0 lowers the opportunity cost of holding money because the rate of return on bonds declines. Thus the decision to hold more money (the movement from A to B as the interest rate falls) is the "flip side" of the decision to hold fewer bonds.

We show the initial money demand curve as M_D (Y, P), indicating that the curve is drawn for given values of Y and P. Increases in Y or P shift the M_D curve to the right; decreases in Y or P shift the M_D curve to the left.

that is demanded in our macro model. We focus on three: the interest rate, the level of real GDP, and the price level.

The Interest Rate No matter what benefits households or firms receive from holding money, there is also a cost. The cost of holding money is the income that *could have been earned* if that wealth were instead held in the form of interest-earning bonds. This is the *opportunity cost* of holding money. In our macro model, we assume that an increase in the interest rate leads firms and households to reduce their desired money holdings. Conversely, a reduction in the interest rate means that holding money is less costly and so firms and households are assumed to increase their desired money holdings.

Other things being equal, the demand for money is assumed to be negatively related to the interest rate.[2]

This negative relationship between interest rates and desired money holdings is shown in Figure 28-1 and is drawn as the money demand (M_D) curve. Remember that the decision to hold money is also the decision *not* to hold bonds, and so movements along the M_D curve imply the substitution of assets between money and bonds. For example, as interest rates decline, bonds become a less attractive asset and money becomes more attractive, so firms and households substitute away from bonds and toward money.

Let's now see why changes in real GDP and the price level cause the M_D curve to shift.

Real GDP As we said earlier, an important reason for holding money is to make transactions. Not surprisingly, the amount of transactions that firms and households want to make is positively related to the level of income and production in the economy—that is, to the level of real GDP. This positive relationship between real GDP and desired money holdings is shown in Figure 28-1 by a rightward shift of the M_D curve to M_D'. At any given interest rate, an increase in Y is assumed to generate more transactions and thus greater desired money holdings.

An increase in real GDP increases the volume of transactions in the economy and is assumed to cause an increase in desired money holding.

[2] The opportunity cost of holding money is the interest that could have been earned on bonds—this is the *nominal* interest rate. In the presence of expected inflation, we must distinguish between the *nominal* and *real* interest rates. In this chapter we assume, however, that expected inflation is zero, and so we simply speak of "the" interest rate. We discuss inflation in detail in Chapter 30.

The Price Level An increase in the price level leads to an increase in the *dollar* value of transactions even if there is no change in the *real* value of transactions. That is, as P rises, households and firms will need to hold more money in order to carry out the same real value of transactions. This positive relationship between the price level and desired money holdings is also shown in Figure 28-1 as a rightward shift of the M_D curve to M_D'.

> An increase in the price level is assumed to cause an increase in desired money holdings.

We can be more precise than just saying that there is a positive relationship between P and desired money holdings. Suppose, for example, that Y and i are constant but that all prices in the economy increase by 10 percent. Since Y is unchanged, the *real* value of desired transactions should also be unchanged. Furthermore, since i is unchanged, the opportunity cost of holding money is constant. Therefore, in order to make the same transactions as before, households and firms must not just hold more money than before—they must hold precisely 10 percent more. In other words, we assume that if real GDP and the interest rate are constant, the demand for money is *proportional* to the price level.

Money Demand: Summing Up

We have discussed why firms and households hold money and we have examined the relationship in our macroeconomic model between desired money holding and three macroeconomic variables. Since the demand for money reflects firms' and households' preference to hold wealth in the form of a *liquid* asset (money) rather than a less liquid asset (bonds), economists often refer to the money demand function as a *liquidity preference* function. We can summarize our assumptions regarding money demand with the following algebraic statement:

$$M_D = M_D \overset{- + +}{(i, Y, P)}$$

This equation says that the amount of money firms and households want to hold at any given time depends on (is a function of) three variables; the sign above each variable indicates whether that variable positively or negatively affects desired money holding. Our central assumptions are as follows:

1. An increase in the interest rate increases the opportunity cost of holding money and leads to a reduction in the quantity of money demanded.

2. An increase in real GDP increases the volume of transactions and leads to an increase in the quantity of money demanded.

3. An increase in the price level increases the dollar value of a given volume of transactions and leads to an increase in the quantity of money demanded.

Remember that money demand is also related to bond demand. Firms and households must decide at any time how to divide their financial assets between money and bonds. So our statements here about money demand apply in reverse to the demand for bonds. For example, in Figure 28-1, if the economy moves down the M_D curve from point A to point B as the interest rate falls, firms and households are deciding to hold more money

People hold money in order to make transactions. As real GDP rises, the volume of transactions also rises, and so people typically decide to hold more money.

and fewer bonds. The lower interest rate means a lower opportunity cost for holding money, and so people choose to hold more; but the lower interest rate equally means that bonds are a less attractive asset, and so people choose to hold fewer bonds. In other words, the movement from *A* to *B* involves a substitution away from holding bonds and toward holding money.

28.3 Monetary Equilibrium and National Income

So far, this chapter has been devoted to understanding bonds and how they relate to the demand for money. In the previous chapter we examined the supply of money. We are now ready to put these two sides of the money market together to develop a theory of how interest rates are determined. You may recall, however, that we already saw in Chapter 26 a theory of how interest rates are determined. But remember that Chapter 26 was a discussion of long-run economic growth, and real GDP was assumed to be equal to Y^* throughout that discussion. What we do in this chapter and the next is to return to the short-run version of our macro model (in which Y is not assumed to equal Y^*) but make it more complete by adding money and interest rates explicitly. Here we will see how changes in the money market affect interest rates, aggregate expenditure, and the equilibrium level of real GDP in the short run.

We begin by examining the concept of *monetary equilibrium*—this shows how interest rates are determined in the short run by the interaction of money demand and money supply. We then explore what economists call the *monetary transmission mechanism*—the fairly involved chain of events that takes us from changes in the interest rate, through to changes in desired aggregate expenditure, to changes in the level of real GDP.[3]

Monetary Equilibrium

Practise with Study Guide Chapter 28, Short-Answer Questions 1, 2 and 6, and Exercise 2.

monetary equilibrium A situation in which the demand for money equals the supply of money.

Figure 28-2 illustrates the money market. The money supply (M_S) curve is vertical, indicating that it is assumed to be independent of the interest rate. The money supply increases (M_S shifts to the right) if the central bank increases reserves in the banking system or if the commercial banks decide to lend out a larger fraction of those reserves. The money supply decreases (M_S shifts to the left) if the central bank decreases reserves in the banking system or if the commercial banks decide to reduce lending. The money demand (M_D) curve is downward sloping, indicating that firms and households decide to hold more money and fewer bonds when the interest rate falls.

Monetary equilibrium occurs when the quantity of money demanded equals the quantity of money supplied. In Chapter 3, we saw that in a competitive market for some commodity the price will adjust to establish equilibrium. In the market for money, the interest rate is that "price" that adjusts to bring about equilibrium. Let's see how this equilibrium is achieved.

---

[3] In the long-run discussion in Chapter 26, people's wealth is changing (because of investment and saving) and the long-run equilibrium interest rate equates desired saving with desired investment. In the short-run theory in this chapter, we assume that people's wealth is constant and we emphasize how they divide that wealth between money and bonds. The resulting short-run equilibrium interest rate fluctuates around the long-run equilibrium interest rate, which evolves more gradually as wealth accumulates.

When a single household or firm finds that it is holding a smaller fraction of its wealth in money than it wants, it can sell some bonds and add the cash proceeds to its money holdings. Such behaviour by an individual firm or a household will have a negligible effect on the economy.

But what happens when *all* the firms and households try to add to their money balances? They all try to sell bonds to obtain the extra money they desire. But what one person can do, all persons cannot do simultaneously. At any moment, the economy's total supply of money and bonds is fixed. Thus, as everyone tries to sell bonds, an excess supply of bonds develops. But since people are simply trying to switch between a given amount of bonds and money, the excess supply of bonds implies an excess demand for money, as shown at interest rate i_1 in Figure 28-2.

What happens when there is an excess supply of bonds? Like any other good or service, an excess supply causes a fall in the market price. As we saw earlier in the chapter, a fall in the price of bonds implies an increase in the interest rate. As the interest rate rises, people economize on money balances because the opportunity cost of holding such balances is rising. Eventually, the interest rate will rise enough that people will no longer be trying to add to their money balances by selling bonds. At that point, there is no longer an excess supply of bonds (or an excess demand for money), and the interest rate will stop rising. The demand for money again equals the supply, as at point E in Figure 28-2.

Suppose now there is more money than firms and households want to hold. That is, there is an excess supply of money, as at interest rate i_2 in Figure 28-2. The excess supply of money implies an excess demand for bonds—people are trying to "get rid of" their excess money balances by acquiring bonds. But when all households try to buy bonds, they bid up the price of bonds, and the interest rate falls. As the interest rate

FIGURE 28-2 Monetary Equilibrium

The interest rate rises when there is an excess demand for money and falls when there is an excess supply of money. The fixed quantity of money M_0 is shown by the vertical supply curve M_S. The demand for money is given by M_D; its negative slope indicates that a fall in the rate of interest causes the quantity of money demanded to increase. Monetary equilibrium is at E, with a rate of interest of i_0.

If the interest rate is i_1, there will be an excess demand for money of M_0M_1. Bonds will be offered for sale in an attempt to increase money holdings. This will force the rate of interest up to i_0 (the price of bonds falls), at which point the quantity of money demanded is equal to the fixed available quantity of M_0. If the interest rate is i_2, there will be an excess supply of money M_2M_0. Bonds will be demanded in return for excess money balances. This will force the rate of interest down to i_0 (the price of bonds rises), at which point the quantity of money demanded is equal to the fixed supply of M_0.

falls, households and firms become willing to hold larger quantities of money. The interest rate falls until firms and households stop trying to convert bonds into money. In other words, it continues until everyone is content to hold the existing supply of money and bonds, as at point E in Figure 28-2.

> **Monetary equilibrium occurs when the interest rate is such that the quantity of money demanded equals the quantity of money supplied.**

The theory of interest-rate determination depicted in Figure 28-2 is often called the *liquidity preference theory of interest*. This name reflects the fact that a demand to hold money (rather than bonds) is a demand for the more liquid of the two assets—a preference for liquidity. The theory determines how the interest rate fluctuates in the short term as people seek to achieve *portfolio balance*, given fixed supplies of both money and bonds.

The Monetary Transmission Mechanism

monetary transmission mechanism The channels by which a change in the demand for or supply of money leads to a shift of the aggregate demand curve.

The connection between changes in the demand for and supply of money and the level of aggregate demand is called the **monetary transmission mechanism**. It operates in three stages:

1. Changes in the demand for money or the supply of money cause a change in the equilibrium interest rate.

2. The change in the interest rate leads to a change in desired investment and consumption expenditure (and net exports in an open economy).

3. The change in desired aggregate expenditure leads to a shift in the *AD* curve and thus to short-run changes in real GDP and the price level.

Let's examine these three stages in more detail.

1. Changes in the Interest Rate The interest rate will change if the equilibrium depicted in Figure 28-2 is disturbed by a change in either the supply of money or the demand for money. For example, as shown in part (i) of Figure 28-3, we see the following sequence of events when there is an increase in the supply of money but no change in the money demand curve:

↑ money supply ⇒ excess supply of money at initial interest rate ⇒ firms and households buy bonds ⇒ ↑ bond prices ⇒ ↓ equilibrium interest rate

FIGURE 28-3   Changes in the Equilibrium Interest Rate

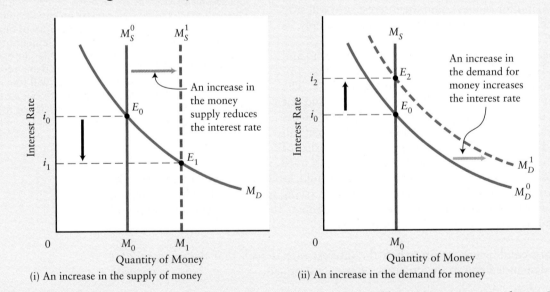

(i) An increase in the supply of money

(ii) An increase in the demand for money

Changes in the supply of money or in the demand for money cause the equilibrium interest rate to change. In both parts of the figure, the money supply is shown by the vertical curve M_S, and the demand for money is shown by the negatively sloped curve M_D. The initial monetary equilibrium is at E_0, with corresponding interest rate i_0. In part (i), an increase in the money supply causes M_S^0 to shift to M_S^1. The new equilibrium is at E_1, where the interest rate has fallen to i_1. In part (ii), an increase in the demand for money shifts M_D^0 to M_D^1. The new monetary equilibrium occurs at E_2, and the new equilibrium interest rate increases to i_2.

Note that the original increase in the supply of money could be caused either by the central bank increasing the reserves in the banking system or by the commercial banks lending out a higher fraction of their existing reserves.

As shown in part (ii) of Figure 28-3, an increase in the demand for money, with an unchanged supply of money, leads to the following sequence of events:

↑ money demand ⇒ excess demand for money at initial interest rate ⇒ firms and households sell bonds ⇒ ↓ bond prices ⇒ ↑ equilibrium interest rate

Note that the original increase in the demand for money could be caused by an increase in real GDP or by an increase in the price level. It could also be caused by an increased preference to hold money rather than bonds, as would happen if there were an increase in the perceived riskiness of bonds.

Changes in either the demand for or the supply of money cause changes in the equilibrium interest rate.

2. Changes in Desired Investment and Consumption The second link in the monetary transmission mechanism relates interest rates to desired investment and consumption expenditure. We saw in Chapter 21 that desired investment, which includes expenditure on inventory accumulation, residential construction, and business fixed investment, responds to changes in the interest rate. Other things being equal, a decrease in the interest rate reduces the opportunity cost of borrowing or using retained earnings for investment purposes. As a result, the lower interest rate leads to an increase in desired investment expenditure. We also saw that consumption expenditure, especially on big-ticket items, like cars and furniture, that are often purchased on credit, is negatively related to the interest rate. In Figure 28-4, this negative relationship

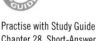

Practise with Study Guide Chapter 28, Short-Answer Question 3.

FIGURE 28-4   The Effects of Changes in the Money Supply on Desired Investment Expenditure

(i) Money demand and supply

(ii) Investment demand

Increases in the money supply reduce the interest rate and increase desired investment expenditure. In part (i), equilibrium in the money market is at E_0, with a quantity of money of M_0 and an interest rate of i_0. The corresponding level of desired investment is I_0 (point A) in part (ii). An increase in the money supply to M_1 reduces the interest rate to i_1 and increases investment expenditure by ΔI to I_1 (point B).

FIGURE 28-5   The Effects of Changes in the Money Supply on Aggregate Demand

(i) A shift in aggregate expenditure

(ii) A shift in aggregate demand

Changes in the money supply cause shifts in the *AE* and *AD* functions. In Figure 28-4, an increase in the money supply increased desired investment expenditure by ΔI. In part (i) of this figure, the *AE* function shifts up by ΔI. At the fixed price level P_0, equilibrium GDP rises from Y_0 to Y_1, as shown by the rightward shift in the *AD* curve in part (ii).

between desired expenditure and the interest rate is labelled I^D for investment demand, reflecting the fact that investment is the *most* interest-sensitive part of expenditure.

The first two links in the monetary transmission mechanism are shown in Figure 28-4.[4] Although the analysis in Figure 28-4 illustrates a change in the money supply, remember that the transmission mechanism can also be set in motion by a change in the demand for money. In part (i), we see that an increase in the money supply reduces the equilibrium interest rate. In part (ii), we see that a fall in the interest rate leads to an increase in desired investment expenditure.

3. Changes in Aggregate Demand The third link in the monetary transmission mechanism is from changes in desired expenditure to shifts in the *AE* function and in the *AD* curve. This is familiar ground. In Chapter 23, we saw that a shift in the aggregate expenditure curve (caused by something *other than* a change in the price level) leads to a shift in the *AD* curve. This situation is shown again in Figure 28-5.

> An increase in the money supply causes a reduction in the interest rate and an increase in desired investment and other interest-sensitive expenditure; it therefore causes a rightward shift of the *AD* curve. A decrease in the money supply causes an increase in the interest rate and a decrease in desired investment; it therefore causes a leftward shift of the *AD* curve.

The entire monetary transmission mechanism is summarized in Figure 28-6 for the case of an expansionary monetary shock. An increase in money supply or a decrease in money demand reduces the interest rate, increases desired investment expenditure, and increases aggregate demand.

An Open-Economy Modification

So far, the emphasis in our discussion of the monetary transmission mechanism has been on the effect that a change in the interest rate has on desired

---

[4] In part (i) of Figure 28-4, it is the *nominal* interest rate—the rate of return on bonds—that affects money demand. In part (ii), however, it is the *real* interest rate that influences desired investment expenditure. It is therefore worth emphasizing that we are continuing with the assumption that inflation is expected to be zero and so the nominal and real interest rates are the same. This assumption allows us to use the same vertical axis in the two parts of the figure.

investment. In an open economy, however, where financial capital flows easily across borders, the monetary transmission mechanism is a little more complex.

Financial capital is very mobile across international boundaries. Bondholders, either in Canada or abroad, are able to substitute among Canadian bonds, U.S. bonds, German bonds, or bonds from almost any country you can think of. Bonds from different countries are generally not *perfect* substitutes for each other because of varying amounts of political and economic instability, and thus different levels of *risk* are associated with the different bonds. But bonds from similar countries—Canada and the United States, for example—are often viewed as very close substitutes.

The ability of bondholders to substitute easily between bonds from different countries implies that monetary disturbances that cause changes in interest rates often lead to international flows of financial capital, which in turn cause changes in exchange rates and changes in exports and imports.

To understand how capital mobility adds a second channel to the monetary transmission mechanism, consider an example. Suppose the Bank of Canada decides to increase the money supply. As shown in Figure 28-4, the increase in money supply reduces the interest rate and increases desired investment expenditure. This is the first channel of the monetary transmission mechanism. But the story does not end there.

The reduction in Canadian interest rates also makes Canadian bonds less attractive relative to foreign bonds. Canadian and foreign investors alike will sell some of their Canadian bonds and buy more of the high-return foreign bonds. But to buy foreign bonds, it is necessary first to exchange Canadian dollars for foreign currency. The increase in the demand for foreign currency causes the Canadian dollar to depreciate relative to other currencies.

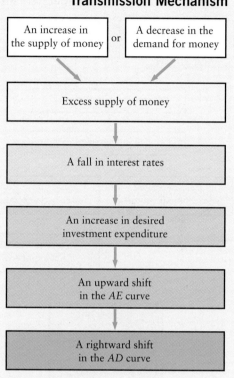

FIGURE 28-6   Summary of the Monetary Transmission Mechanism

| An increase in the supply of money | or | A decrease in the demand for money |

Excess supply of money

A fall in interest rates

An increase in desired investment expenditure

An upward shift in the *AE* curve

A rightward shift in the *AD* curve

An increase in the Canadian money supply reduces Canadian interest rates and leads to a capital outflow. This outflow of financial capital causes the Canadian dollar to depreciate.

As the Canadian dollar depreciates, however, Canadian goods and services become less expensive relative to those from other countries. As we first saw in Chapter 22, this change in international relative prices causes households and firms—both in Canada and abroad—to substitute away from foreign goods and toward Canadian goods. Imports fall and exports rise.

So the overall effect of the increase in the Canadian money supply is not just a fall in interest rates and an increase in investment. Because of the international mobility of financial capital, the low Canadian interest rates also lead to a capital outflow, a depreciation of the Canadian dollar, and an increase in Canadian net exports. This increase in net exports, of course, *strengthens* the positive effect on aggregate demand already coming from the increase in desired investment.

This complete open-economy monetary transmission mechanism is shown in Figure 28-7. This figure is based on Figure 28-6, but simply adds the second channel

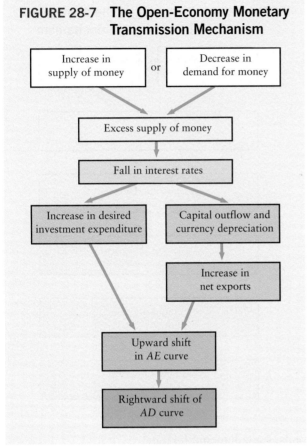

FIGURE 28-7   **The Open-Economy Monetary Transmission Mechanism**

Practise with Study Guide
Chapter 28, Extension
Exercise E1.

of the transmission mechanism that works through capital mobility, exchange rates, and net exports.

> **In an open economy with capital mobility, an increase in the money supply results in an increase in aggregate demand for two reasons. First, the reduction in interest rates causes an increase in investment. Second, the lower interest rate causes a capital outflow, a currency depreciation, and a rise in net exports.**

Our example has been that of a monetary expansion. A monetary contraction has the opposite effect, but the logic of the mechanism is the same. A reduction in the Canadian money supply raises Canadian interest rates and reduces desired investment expenditure. The higher Canadian interest rates attract foreign financial capital as bondholders sell low-return foreign bonds and purchase high-return Canadian bonds. This action increases the demand for Canadian dollars in the foreign-exchange market and thus causes the Canadian dollar to appreciate. Finally, the appreciation of the Canadian dollar increases Canadians' imports of foreign goods and reduces Canadian exports to other countries. Canadian net exports fall.

The Slope of the *AD* Curve

We can now use the monetary transmission mechanism to add to the explanation of the negative slope of the *AD* curve. In Chapter 23, we mentioned two reasons for its negative slope: the change in wealth and the substitution between domestic and foreign goods, both of which occur when the price level changes. A third effect operates through interest rates, and works as follows. A rise in the price level raises the money value of transactions and thus leads to an increase in the demand for money. For a given vertical M_S curve, the increase in money demand means that the M_D curve shifts to the right, raising the equilibrium interest rate. The higher interest rate then leads to a reduction in desired investment expenditure. We therefore have a third reason that the price level and the level of aggregate demand are negatively related. This third reason for the negative slope of the *AD* curve is important because, empirically, the interest rate is the most important link between monetary factors and real expenditure flows.

myeconlab   **ADDITIONAL TOPICS**

For more details about how changes in the price level influence money demand, interest rates, and investment, and help explain the negative slope of the *AD* curve, look for **Interest Rates and the Slope of the *AD* Curve** in the *Additional Topics* section of this book's MyEconLab.

www.myeconlab.com

28.4   The Strength of Monetary Forces

In the previous section we saw that a change in the money supply leads to a change in interest rates. The change in interest rates, in turn, leads to changes in investment and, through capital flows and changes in the exchange rate, to changes in net exports. Thus, a change in the money supply leads to a change in desired aggregate expenditure and therefore to a shift in the *AD* curve. From our analysis in Chapter 24, we know that a shift in the *AD* curve will lead to different effects in the short run and in the long run. It is in the long run that factor prices tend to fully adjust to excess demands or excess supplies, and output tends to return to the level of potential output, Y^*. Let's begin by examining the long-run effects of increases in the money supply, and then turn to a long-standing debate about the strength of monetary forces in the short run.

Long-Run Neutrality of Money

We saw in Chapter 24 that, starting from a long-run equilibrium with real GDP equal to Y^*, any shock—either to aggregate demand or to aggregate supply—that creates an output gap sets in place an adjustment process that will eventually close that gap and return real GDP to its potential level, Y^*. The operation of this adjustment process following an increase in the money supply is illustrated in Figure 28-8, where we assume that Y^* is unaffected by changes in the money supply.

In the figure, the only long-run effect of a shift in the *AD* curve following a change in the money supply is a change in the price level. This result is often referred to as the *neutrality of money*.

In the eighteenth and nineteenth centuries, economists focused most of their attention on understanding the economy's long-run equilibrium and were less concerned with short-run fluctuations. These Classical economists believed that the "money" side of the economy was independent from the "real" side of the economy in the long run. This belief was referred to as the *Classical Dichotomy* and

FIGURE 28-8   The Long-Run Neutrality of Money

(i) M_D and M_S

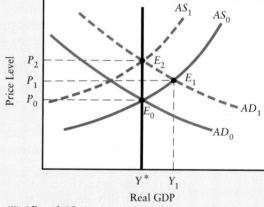

(ii) *AD* and *AS*

The long-run neutrality of money implies that the only long-run effect of an increase in the money supply is a higher price level. The economy begins in long-run equilibrium at E_0 in both diagrams, with real GDP equal to Y^* and the price level equal to P_0. An increase in the money supply from M_S^0 to M_S^1 reduces interest rates immediately to i_1' and stimulates aggregate demand, thus shifting the aggregate demand curve from AD_0 to AD_1. As real GDP and the price level increase, the demand for money increases to M_D^1, thus pushing i_1' up to i_1. The point E_1 in part (i) therefore corresponds to E_1 in part (ii). Since real GDP is now above Y^*, wages and other factor prices start to increase, thus shifting the *AS* curve upward. The adjustment process continues until Y is back to Y^* and the price level has increased to P_2. In the new long-run equilibrium, the higher price level (with unchanged Y^*) has increased money demand to M_D^2, thus restoring the interest rate to its initial level, i_0.

money neutrality The idea that a change in the supply of money has no effect on any real variables but only affects the price level.

embodied the idea of **money neutrality**. The Classical view was that in the long run, relative prices, real GDP, employment, investment, and all other real variables in the economy were determined by real factors, such as the demands and supplies for various goods, which were in turn determined by firms' technologies and consumers' preferences.

The long-run effects of an expansion in the money supply, in their view, would be an increase in the price level but no change in the level of real GDP or any other real economic variables. In terms of Figure 28-8, the Classical economists were concerned with the movement from E_0 to E_2, a change caused by an increase in the money supply; real GDP would be unaffected but the price level would increase.

> The Classical economists emphasized the economy's long-run equilibrium. In their view, changes in the supply of money had no effect on real GDP or other real variables; the only effect was to change the price level.

Economists now focus more on the short-run effects of changes in monetary policy. Nevertheless, most modern economists recognize that the Classical view provides a good description of the economy's long-run equilibrium, after wages and other factor prices have fully adjusted and real GDP has returned to the level of potential output, Y^*. Modern economists' view that the neutrality of money holds in the long run leads them to stress the strong link between changes in the money supply and changes in the price level, at least over long periods of time. Figure 28-9 shows a scatter plot of inflation and money growth for a large sample of countries over a 40-year period. Each point in the figure represents the rates of inflation and money supply growth for one country averaged over the 40-year period. The vertical axis measures each country's average annual inflation rate. The horizontal axis measures each country's average annual rate of growth of the money supply. As is clear in the figure, there is a close positive relationship between money supply growth and inflation, as reflected by the tight bunching of points around the upward-sloping line, the "line of best fit" between money supply growth and inflation. The slope of the line of best fit is 0.97, indicating that two countries that differ in their money growth rates by 10 percent will, on average, differ in their inflation rates by 9.7 percent.

> Many modern economists believe that money is neutral in the long run. Long-run neutrality implies that, in the absence of other shocks to the economy, changes in money and changes in the price level are closely linked over long periods of time.

Long-run money neutrality is debatable, however. Though most economists agree that the macroeconomic adjustment process tends to bring Y back to Y^* in the long run, some economists argue that the value of Y^* is itself influenced by the short-run path of real GDP. For example, a positive shock that raises Y above the current Y^* may lead to an increase in Y^*; or a negative shock that reduces Y may also cause a decline in Y^*. The hypothesis that the path of real GDP may influence the value of Y^* is known as *hysteresis*, and there is some empirical support for it, especially in some Western European countries.

One possible explanation for hysteresis is the depreciation of human capital that often accompanies prolonged unemployment. Consider a negative shock that reduces real GDP and increases unemployment. If wages and other factor prices are slow to adjust, the unemployment will persist, and some individuals may experience long spells of unemployment. If prolonged lack of work leads these individuals' skills to depreciate, they may eventually become "unemployable," even after the aggregate economy recovers. In this case, the fall in the level of real GDP, if prolonged, will lead to a fall in

FIGURE 28-9 Inflation and Money Growth Across Many Countries, 1978–2007

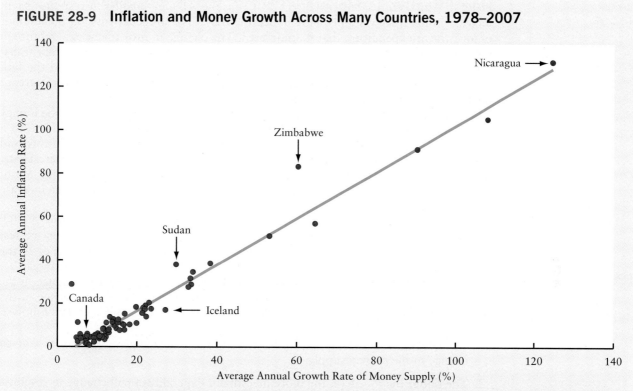

Countries with higher inflation rates tend to be countries with higher rates of growth of the money supply. This figure plots long-run data for many countries. Each point shows the average annual inflation rate and the average annual growth rate of the money supply for a specific country for the 1978–2007 period. For all countries, the inflation data refer to the rate of change of the Consumer Price Index; the money supply data refer to the growth rate of currency. The positive relationship between inflation and money supply growth (with a slope of the best-fit line very close to 1) is consistent with the proposition of long-run money neutrality.

(*Source:* Based on authors' calculations by using data from *International Financial Statistics*, International Monetary Fund, www.imf.org.)

the level of potential output. (Or equivalently, the rise in the unemployment rate will lead to a rise in the natural rate of unemployment.)

As we said earlier, there is some empirical support for hysteresis, but it is contentious. In Canada, the weight of the empirical evidence is against it and in favour of the hypothesis that the long-run path of Y^* is independent of the short-run path of real GDP. In the macro model developed and analyzed in this book, it is assumed that Y^* is unaffected by the path of Y, and thus the model generates the prediction of long-run money neutrality. But it should be kept in mind that this particular behaviour of Y^* remains a debatable hypothesis and should constantly be tested with data.

Short-Run Non-neutrality of Money

There is less debate regarding the short-run effects of money: A change in the money supply affects the short-run equilibrium level of real GDP. For a given *AS* curve, the short-run effect of a change in the money supply on real GDP and the price level is determined by the extent of the shift of the *AD* curve.

How Effective Is Monetary Policy? The AD curve shifts in response to an increase in the money supply. How much the AD curve shifts depends on the amount of investment expenditure that is stimulated. The change in investment expenditure in turn depends on the strength of two of the linkages that make up the monetary transmission mechanism: the link between money supply and interest rates, and the link between interest rates and investment. Let's look more closely at these separate parts of the monetary transmission mechanism.

First, consider how much interest rates fall in response to an increase in the money supply. If the M_D curve is steep, a given increase in the money supply will lead to a large reduction in the equilibrium interest rate. A steep M_D curve means that firms' and households' desired money holding is not very sensitive to changes in the interest rate, so interest rates have to fall a lot to get people to be content to hold a larger amount of money. The flatter is the M_D curve, the less interest rates will fall for any given increase in the supply of money.

Second, consider how much investment expenditure increases in response to a fall in interest rates. If the I^D curve is relatively flat, then any given reduction in interest rates will lead to a large increase in firms' desired investment. The steeper is the I^D curve, the less investment will increase for any given reduction in interest rates.

It follows that the size of the shift of the AD curve in response to a change in the money supply depends on the shapes of the M_D and I^D curves. The influence of the shapes of the two curves is shown in Figure 28-10 and can be summarized as follows:

1. The steeper the M_D curve, the more interest rates will change in response to a given change in the money supply.

2. The flatter the I^D curve, the more investment expenditure will change in response to a given change in the interest rate, and hence the larger will be the shift in the AD curve.

The combination that produces the largest shift in the AD curve for a given change in the money supply is a steep M_D curve and a flat I^D curve. This combination is illustrated in part (i) of Figure 28-10. It accords with the view that monetary policy is relatively effective as a means of influencing real GDP in the short run. The combination that produces the smallest shift in the AD curve is a flat M_D curve and a steep I^D curve. This combination is illustrated in part (ii) of Figure 28-10. It accords with the view that monetary policy is relatively ineffective in the short run.

> The effectiveness of monetary policy in inducing short-run changes in real GDP depends on the slopes of the M_D and I^D curves. The steeper is the M_D curve, and the flatter is the I^D curve, the more effective is monetary policy.

Practise with Study Guide
Chapter 28, Exercises 4 and 5.

Keynesians Versus Monetarists Figure 28-10 characterizes a famous debate among economists that occurred in the three decades following the Second World War. Some economists, following the ideas of John Maynard Keynes, argued that changes in the money supply led to relatively small changes in interest rates and that investment was relatively insensitive to changes in the interest rate. These economists, who called themselves *Keynesians*, concluded that monetary policy was not a very effective method of stimulating aggregate demand—they therefore emphasized the value of using fiscal policy (as Keynes himself had argued during the Great Depression). Another group of economists, led by Milton Friedman, argued that changes in the money supply caused

FIGURE 28-10   Two Views on the Strength of Monetary Changes

(i) Changes in the money supply are effective

(ii) Changes in the money supply are ineffective

The effect of a change in the money supply on aggregate demand depends on the slopes of the M_D and I^D curves. Initially, in parts (i) and (ii), the money supply is M_S^0, and the economy has an interest rate of i_0 and investment expenditure of I_0. The central bank then expands the money supply from M_S^0 to M_S^1. The rate of interest thus falls from i_0 to i_1, as shown in each of the left panels. This causes an increase in investment expenditure of ΔI, from I_0 to I_1, as shown in each of the right panels.

In part (i), the demand for money is insensitive to the interest rate, so the increase in the money supply leads to a large fall in the interest rate. Further, desired investment expenditure is highly interest sensitive, so the large fall in interest rates also leads to a large increase in investment expenditure. Hence, in this case, the change in the money supply will be very effective in stimulating aggregate demand.

In part (ii), the demand for money is more sensitive to the interest rate, so the increase in the money supply leads to only a small fall in the interest rate. Further, desired investment expenditure is much less sensitive to the interest rate, and so the small fall in interest rates leads to only a small increase in investment expenditure. Hence, in this case, the change in the money supply will be less effective in stimulating aggregate demand.

sharp changes in interest rates, which, in turn, led to significant changes in investment expenditure. These economists called themselves *Monetarists* and concluded that monetary policy was a very effective tool for stimulating aggregate demand.[5]

---

[5] Monetarists argued that monetary policy was very effective for stimulating aggregate demand but they *did not* advocate an "activist" monetary policy. One of their concerns was that monetary forces were so strong that an activist monetary policy would destabilize the economy. We address these issues in Chapter 29.

Today, this debate between Keynesians and Monetarists is all but over. A great deal of empirical research devoted to uncovering the relationship between interest rates and money demand suggests that money demand is relatively insensitive to changes in the interest rate. That is, the M_D curve is quite steep and, as a result, changes in the money supply cause relatively large changes in interest rates (as argued by the Monetarists). The evidence is much less clear, however, on the slope of the I^D curve. Though the evidence confirms that I^D is downward sloping, there is no consensus on whether the curve is steep or flat. Part of the problem facing researchers is that an important determinant of investment is not observable. Firms' expectations about the future—what Keynes famously called firms' "animal spirits"—have a significant effect on their investment decisions (thus shifting the I^D curve), but this variable is not easily measured by researchers. The unobservability of this variable makes it very difficult to estimate precisely the relationship between interest rates and investment. Another problem is that the I^D curve is an aggregation of a number of different investment demands (plant, equipment, inventories, new housing, and durable consumer goods), each subject to different influences. While each type of investment is responsive to changes in the interest rate, their individual differences make it difficult to estimate the responsiveness of *aggregate* desired investment (I^D) to changes in the interest rate.

Though empirical research over the years has, to a large extent, filled in the gaps in our knowledge and narrowed the differences between the Keynesian and Monetarist positions, there is still plenty of debate about the effectiveness and the appropriate objectives of monetary policy. Many economists argue that central bankers should be mindful of the long-run perspective of the Classical economists and expect a limited influence from monetary policy on the long-run level of real GDP. In this view, monetary policy should attempt to offset only the largest and most persistent of the shocks that hit the economy, while maintaining a long-run focus on the behaviour of the price level. Other economists argue that short-run fluctuations in income and employment are so important that monetary policy ought to be actively engaged in reducing the economy's fluctuations in the face of aggregate demand and supply shocks. Further, some of these economists argue that hysteresis is a real possibility and thus the central bank's actions in the short run may indeed have effects on long-run levels of real GDP and employment.

In the next chapter we examine the details of how monetary policy is conducted in Canada. For several reasons, the real-world practice of monetary policy is more complex than it appears in this chapter. But as we will see, the Bank of Canada's system of *inflation targeting* can be viewed as a means of providing both short-run stabilization and a long-run focus on the behaviour of the price level.

*For brief descriptions of the contributions to economics of the Nobel laureates, go to **www.nobel.se/economics/laureates/**.*

Summary

28.1 Understanding Bonds   🅛🅞 ❶

- The present value of any bond that promises to pay some sequence of payments in the future is negatively related to the market interest rate. A bond's present value determines its market price. Thus, there is a negative relationship between the market interest rate and the price of a bond.
- The yield on a bond is the rate of return the bondholder receives, having bought the bond at its purchase price

and then receiving the stream of future payments the bond offers. For a given stream of future payments, a lower purchase price implies a higher bond yield.
- An increase in the perceived riskiness of bonds will lead to a reduction in bond prices and thus an increase in bond yields. These changes are associated with investors' adjustment of their portfolios out of bonds and toward money.

28.2 The Demand for Money   (LO) ❷

- In our macro model, households and firms are assumed to divide their financial assets between interest-bearing "bonds" and non-interest-bearing "money." They hold money to facilitate both expected and unexpected transactions, and also to protect against the possibility of a decline in bond prices (a rise in interest rates).
- No matter why money is held, the cost of doing so is the interest that could have been earned if bonds were held instead. This is the opportunity cost of holding money.
- Households' and firms' desired money holdings are assumed to be influenced by three key macroeconomic variables:

1. Increases in the interest rate reduce desired money holdings.
2. Increases in real GDP increase desired money holdings.
3. Increases in the price level increase desired money holdings.

- These relationships are captured in the M_D curve, which is drawn as a negative relationship between interest rates (i) and desired money holding (M_D). Increases in real GDP (Y) or the price level (P) lead to a rightward shift of this M_D curve.

28.3 Monetary Equilibrium and National Income   (LO) ❸ ❹

- In the short run, the interest rate is determined in the money market by the interaction of money supply and money demand. Monetary equilibrium is established when the interest rate is such that the quantity of money supplied is exactly equal to the quantity of money demanded.
- The first stage in the monetary transmission mechanism occurs when the equilibrium interest rate changes. A change in the money supply (coming from the central bank or the commercial banking system) or in the demand for money (coming from a change in Y or P) will lead to a change in the equilibrium interest rate.

- The second stage of the monetary transmission mechanism is that any change in the interest rate leads to a change in desired investment and consumption expenditure. In an open economy with capital mobility, the change in the interest rate leads to capital flows, changes in the exchange rate, and changes in net exports.
- The third stage of the monetary transmission mechanism is that any change in desired investment, consumption, or net exports leads to a shift in the aggregate demand (AD) curve, and thus to a change in real GDP and the price level.

28.4 The Strength of Monetary Forces   (LO) ❺ ❻

- Changes in the money supply have different effects on the economy in the short run and in the long run.
- In the long run, after wages and other factor prices have fully adjusted to any output gaps, real GDP returns to potential output, Y^*. In our macro model it is assumed that the money supply does not influence Y^*, and so the only long-run effect of changes in the money supply is changes in the price level.
- Many modern economists believe that the neutrality of money is a property of the economy in the long run.

There is a strong positive correlation between the rate of money growth and the rate of inflation across countries when viewed over the long run.
- In the short run, the effects of a change in the money supply depend on the shape of the M_D and I^D curves. The steeper is the M_D curve and the flatter is the I^D curve, the more effective changes in the money supply will be in causing short-run changes in real GDP.

Key Concepts

The interest rate and present value
Interest rates, bond prices, and bond yields
Reasons for holding money

The money demand (M_D) function
Monetary equilibrium
The monetary transmission mechanism
The investment demand (I^D) function

Effects of changes in the money supply
Long-run money neutrality
Debate between Keynesians and Monetarists

Study Exercises

1. Fill in the blanks to make the following statements correct.

   a. Monetary equilibrium occurs when the quantity of _____ equals the quantity of _____. Monetary equilibrium determines the _____.

   b. When there is an excess supply of money, households and firms will attempt to _____ bonds. This action will cause the price of bonds to _____ and the interest rate to _____.

   c. When there is an excess demand for money, households and firms will attempt to _____ bonds. This action will cause the price of bonds to _____ and the interest rate to _____.

   d. The _____ _____ _____ refers to the three stages that link the money market to aggregate demand. The first link is between monetary equilibrium and the _____; the second link is between the _____ and desired _____; the third link is between desired _____ and _____.

   e. Suppose the economy is in equilibrium and then the Bank of Canada increases the money supply. The first effect will be an excess _____ of/for money, which will then lead to a _____ in the interest rate, which will in turn lead to a(n) _____ in desired investment.

   f. Suppose the economy is in equilibrium and the Bank of Canada decreases the money supply. The first effect will be an excess _____ of/for money, which will lead to a _____ in the interest rate, which will in turn lead to a(n) _____ in desired investment.

   g. Through the monetary transmission mechanism, a rightward shift of the AD curve can be caused by a(n) _____ in the money supply; a leftward shift of the AD curve can be caused by a(n) _____ in the money supply.

   h. In an open economy with capital mobility, an increase in the money supply causes interest rates to _____, which leads to a capital outflow. This causes a(n) _____ of the Canadian dollar and thus to a(n) _____ in net exports, which leads the AD curve to shift _____.

2. Fill in the blanks to make the following statements correct.

   a. The theory of long-run neutrality of money predicts that changes in the money supply have no effect on _____ in the long run.

   b. If the demand for money is not very sensitive to changes in the interest rate, then the M_D curve will be relatively _____. An increase in the money supply will lead to a _____ reduction in the interest rate.

   c. If the demand for money is very sensitive to changes in the interest rate, then the M_D curve will be relatively _____. An increase in the money supply will lead to a _____ reduction in the interest rate.

   d. A relatively flat investment demand curve means that a change in the interest rate will have a _____ effect on _____, which leads to a relatively large shift in the _____ curve.

   e. A relatively steep investment demand curve means that a change in the interest rate will have a _____ effect on _____, which leads to a relatively small shift in the _____ curve.

   f. Changes in the money supply will have the largest effect on the position of the AD curve when the M_D curve is _____ and the I^D curve is _____.

3. The following table shows the stream of income produced by several different assets. In each case, P_1, P_2, and P_3 are the payments made by the asset in Years 1, 2, and 3.

Asset	Market Interest Rate (i)	P_1	P_2	P_3	Present Value
Treasury Bill	4%	$1000	$0	$0	—
Bond	3%	$0	$0	$5000	—
Bond	5%	$200	$200	$200	—
Stock	6%	$50	$40	$60	—

a. For each asset, compute the asset's present value. (Note that the market interest rate, i, is not the same in each situation.)

b. Explain why the market price for each asset will be the asset's present value.

4. The table below provides information for six different bonds: current market price (P), the face value of the bond (FV), and the number of years before the bond matures (N).

Bond Number	Market Price (P)	Face Value (FV)	Years to Maturity (N)
1a	$926	$1000	1
1b	$850	$1000	1
2a	$1270	$2000	5
2b	$838	$2000	5
3a	$1760	$5000	10
3b	$684	$5000	10

a. In each case, compute the bond's yield, assuming that you buy the bond at its current market price and hold the bond until it matures. There are no coupons. If x is the bond's yield, then $P(1 + x)^N = FV$.

b. Suppose bonds 1a, 2a, and 3a are all issued by the same borrower. Can you offer an explanation for the relationship between the bond yields and the terms to maturity?

c. Suppose bonds 1b, 2b, and 3b are all issued by the same borrower. What can you conclude about the riskiness of the "a" borrower versus that of the "b" borrower? Explain.

d. Notice that the market interest rate is not shown in the table. Explain why knowledge of the market interest rate is unnecessary in order to compute a bond's yield, once you already know the bond's market price. What aspect of the bond does the market interest rate influence, if anything?

5. Imagine a bond that promises to make coupon payments of $100 one year from now and $100 two years from now, and to repay the principal of $1000 three years from now. Suppose also that the market interest rate is 8 percent per year, and that no perceived risk is associated with the bond.

a. Compute the present value of this bond.

b. Suppose the bond is being offered for $995. Would you buy the bond at that price? What do you expect to happen to the bond price in the very near future?

c. Suppose the bond is instead being offered at a price of $950. Would you buy the bond at that price? Do you expect the bond price to change in the near future?

d. If the price of the bond is equal to its computed present value from (a), what is the implied bond yield?

e. Explain why bond yields and the market interest rate tend to move together so that economists can then sensibly speak about "the" interest rate.

6. What motives for holding money—transactions, precautionary, or speculative—do you think explain the following holdings? Explain.

a. Currency in the cash register of the local grocery store at the start of each working day.

b. Money to meet Queen's University's bi-weekly payroll deposited in the local bank.

c. A household tries to keep a "buffer" of $1000 in its savings account.

d. An investor sells bonds for cash, which she then deposits in a low-return bank account.

e. You carry $20 in your pocket even though you have no planned expenditures.

7. The diagram below shows the demand for money and the supply of money.

a. Explain why the M_D function is downward sloping.

b. Suppose the interest rate is at i_A. Explain how firms and households attempt to satisfy their excess demand for money. What is the effect of their actions?

c. Suppose the interest rate is at i_B. Explain how firms and households attempt to dispose of their excess supply of money. What is the effect of their actions?

d. Now suppose there is an increase in the transactions demand for money (perhaps because of growth in real GDP). Beginning at i^*, explain what happens in the money market. How is this shown in the diagram?

8. The following diagrams show the determination of monetary equilibrium and the demand for investment. The economy begins with money supply M_S, money demand M_D, and investment demand I^D. The interest rate is i_0 and desired investment is I_0.

a. Beginning at the initial equilibrium, suppose the Bank of Canada increases the money supply. What happens in the money market and what happens to desired investment expenditure?

b. Beginning in the initial equilibrium, suppose there is a reduction in the demand for money (caused, perhaps, by bonds becoming more attractive to firms and households). What happens in the money market and what happens to desired investment expenditure?

c. Explain why an increase in money supply can have the same effects on desired investment expenditure as a reduction in money demand.

9. In the text we discussed why, in an open economy with international capital mobility, there is a second part to the monetary transmission mechanism. (It may be useful to review Figure 28-7 on page 716 when answering this question.)

a. Explain why an increase in Canada's money supply makes investors shift their portfolios away from Canadian bonds and toward foreign bonds.

b. Explain why this portfolio adjustment leads to a depreciation of the Canadian dollar.

c. Why would such a depreciation of the Canadian dollar lead to an increase in Canada's net exports?

d. Now suppose that the Bank of Canada does not change its policy at all, but the Federal Reserve (the U.S. central bank) increases the U.S. money supply. What is the likely effect on Canada? Explain.

10. In the text we discussed the historical debate between Keynesians and Monetarists regarding the effectiveness of monetary policy in changing real GDP (see Figure 28-10 on page 721 to review). Using the same sort of diagram, discuss two conditions in which a change in the money supply would have *no* short-run effect on real GDP.

Discussion Questions

1. Historically, construction of new houses has been one of the most interest-sensitive categories of aggregate expenditure. Recently, the financial press has carried a number of stories suggesting that because of financial deregulation and innovations in housing finance, this interest sensitivity has apparently decreased. If this is true, what are the implications for monetary policy?

2. Suppose you alone know that the Bank of Canada is going to engage in policies that will raise interest rates sharply, starting next month. How might you make profits by purchases or sales of bonds now, with the intention to sell in a few months' time?

3. In the late 1990s, central bankers in Canada and elsewhere (especially the United States) expressed concern about the dramatic increases in stock-market values. In December 1996, U.S. Federal Reserve Chairman Alan Greenspan alarmed the markets by referring to investors' "irrational exuberance."

a. Explain why central bankers might be concerned about "excessive" increases in stock-market values.

b. Explain how a policy-induced increase in interest rates would affect the stock market.

c. Suppose prices in the stock market fell sharply for reasons unrelated to domestic interest rates. What would be the likely effect on aggregate demand?

4. In 2008, stock markets in Canada and other developed countries experienced very large declines, largely in response to the failure of several large U.S. and European banks and the resulting disruption in global financial markets.

a. Explain how such stock-market declines affect wealth and thus are likely to affect the *AD* curve.

b. If the central banks attempt to keep output close to *Y**, what is their likely response? Explain.

c. Did the Bank of Canada act as predicted in part (b)? Explain how you know.

5. Explain the likely effects of a U.S. recession on the demand for Canadian exports. What would be the effect on Canadian aggregate demand? Suppose the Bank of Canada viewed its monetary policy as being appropriate (for keeping output close to potential) before any U.S. recession. What would you then predict to be the Bank's response to the foreign recession?

6. In the text we discussed how capital mobility in an open economy added a second part to the transmission mechanism. In this setting, discuss why changes in the Federal Reserve's policy in the United States are carefully watched—and often matched—by the Bank of Canada.

Monetary Policy in Canada

In the previous two chapters we encountered many details about money and why it is so important for the economy. In Chapter 27 we saw how commercial banks, through their activities of accepting deposits and extending loans, create deposit money. These bank deposits, together with the currency in circulation, make up the nation's money supply. In Chapter 28 we examined the variables that influence households' and firms' money demand. We then put money demand together with money supply to examine how interest rates are determined in the short run in monetary equilibrium. Finally, we examined the monetary transmission mechanism—the chain of cause-and-effect events describing how changes in money demand or supply lead to changes in interest rates, aggregate demand, real GDP, and the price level.

Chapters 27 and 28 presented a general view of the role of money in the economy. What is still missing is a detailed account of how the Bank of Canada conducts its monetary policy. We begin this chapter by describing some technical details about how the Bank influences the monetary equilibrium and thereby sets in motion the monetary transmission mechanism. We then discuss the Bank's current system of inflation targeting and how this system helps to stabilize the economy. Finally, we discuss some limitations for monetary policy and some of the Bank's major challenges over the past 30 years.

29.1 How the Bank of Canada Implements Monetary Policy

The monetary transmission mechanism describes how changes in the demand for or supply of money cause changes in the interest rate, which then lead to changes in aggregate demand, real GDP, and the price level. But how does the Bank of Canada influence the money market and thereby implement its monetary policy?

As we saw in Chapter 27, the money supply is the sum of currency in circulation and total bank deposits, and commercial banks play a key role in influencing the level of these deposits. As a result, the Bank of Canada cannot directly *set* the money supply. As we will soon see, the Bank of Canada is also unable to directly *set* interest rates. In what follows, therefore, we speak of the Bank "targeting" the money supply or interest rates rather than "setting" them directly.

Money Supply Versus the Interest Rate

In general, any central bank has two alternative approaches for implementing its monetary policy—it can choose to target the money supply or it can choose to target the interest rate. These two approaches are illustrated in Figure 29-1, which shows money demand, money supply, and the equilibrium interest rate. But for any given M_D curve, the central bank must choose one approach or the other; it cannot target *both* the money supply and the interest rate independently. If it chooses to target the money supply, monetary equilibrium will determine the interest rate. Alternatively, if the central bank targets the interest rate, the money supply must adjust to accommodate the movement along the M_D curve.

> In principle, monetary policy can be implemented either by targeting the money supply or by targeting the interest rate. But for a given M_D curve, both cannot be targeted independently.

Part (i) of Figure 29-1 shows how the Bank of Canada could attempt to shift the M_S curve directly, by changing the amount of currency in circulation in the economy. It could do this by buying or selling government securities in the financial markets—transactions called *open-market operations*. For example, by using currency to buy $100 000 of government bonds from a willing seller, the Bank of Canada would increase the amount of cash reserves in the banking system by $100 000. As we saw in Chapter 27, commercial banks would then be able to lend out these new reserves and would thereby increase the amount of deposit money in the economy. The combined effect of the new reserves and the new deposit money would be an increase in the money supply, a shift of the M_S curve to the right. For a given M_D curve, this increase in money supply would lead to a reduction in the equilibrium interest rate and, through the various parts of the transmission mechanism, to an eventual increase in aggregate demand.

The Bank of Canada does not implement its monetary policy in this way, for three reasons. First, while the Bank of Canada *can* control the amount of cash reserves in the banking system (through its open-market operations) it *cannot* control the process of deposit expansion carried out by the commercial banks. And since the money supply is the sum of currency and deposits, it follows that the Bank can influence the money

Practise with Study Guide
Chapter 29, Exercises 1 and 2.

FIGURE 29-1   Two Approaches to the Implementation of Monetary Policy

(i) Central bank targets the money supply

(ii) Central bank targets the interest rate

Monetary policy can be implemented either by targeting the money supply directly or by targeting the interest rate directly—but not both. In part (i), the Bank of Canada could attempt to shift the M_S curve directly and thereby change the equilibrium interest rate. But because the Bank cannot directly control the money supply, and because the slope and position of the M_D curve are uncertain, this is an ineffective way to conduct monetary policy. The Bank's chosen method is illustrated in part (ii), whereby it targets the interest rate directly. It then accommodates the resulting change in money demand through its open-market operations.

supply but cannot *control* it. For example, if the Bank increased the amount of cash reserves in the system, the commercial banks might choose not to expand their lending, and as a result the overall increase in the money supply would be far smaller than the Bank initially intended.

The second reason the Bank does not try to target the money supply directly is the uncertainty regarding the slope of the M_D curve. Even if the Bank had perfect control over the money supply (which it does not), it would be unsure about the change in the interest rate that would result from any given change in the supply of money. Since it is the change in the interest rate that ultimately determines the subsequent changes in aggregate demand, this uncertainty would make the conduct of monetary policy very difficult.

Finally, in addition to being uncertain about the *slope* of the M_D curve, the Bank is also unable to predict accurately the *position* of the M_D curve at any given time. Changes in both real GDP and the price level cause changes in money demand that the Bank can only approximate. Even more difficult to predict are the changes in money demand that occur as a result of innovations in the financial sector. During the late 1970s and early 1980s, for example, the creation of new types of bank deposits led to unprecedented and unpredicted changes in money demand, as people transferred funds between bank accounts of different types. Unpredictable changes in the demand for money make a monetary policy based on the direct control of the money supply difficult to implement.

In summary, the disadvantages of conducting monetary policy by targeting the money supply are as follows:

1. The Bank of Canada cannot control the process of deposit creation.

2. There is uncertainty regarding the slope of the M_D curve.

3. There is uncertainty regarding the position of the M_D curve.

If the Bank of Canada chose to target the money supply, it would have little control over the resulting interest rate. It therefore chooses *not* to implement its monetary policy in this way.

The alternative approach to implementing monetary policy is to target the interest rate directly. This is the approach used by most central banks, including the Bank of Canada. As part (ii) of Figure 29-1 shows, if the Bank can directly change the interest rate, the result will be a change in the quantity of money demanded. In order for this new interest rate to be consistent with monetary equilibrium, the Bank must *accommodate* the change in the amount of money demanded—that is, it must alter the supply of money in order to satisfy the change in desired money holdings by firms and households (we will see shortly how this occurs).

Why does the Bank of Canada choose to implement its monetary policy in this manner? Let's consider the advantages. First, while the Bank cannot control the money supply for the reasons we have just discussed, it *is* able to almost completely control a particular market interest rate. (We will see shortly which rate it targets and how it does so.) Second, the Bank's uncertainty about the slope and position of the M_D curve is not a problem when the Bank chooses instead to target the interest rate directly. If the Bank ascertains that a lower interest rate is necessary in order to achieve its policy objectives, it can act directly to reduce the interest rate. Any uncertainty about the M_D curve then implies uncertainty about the ultimate change in the quantity of money, but it is the interest rate that matters, through the transmission mechanism, for determining the level of aggregate demand.

Finally, the Bank can more easily *communicate* its policy actions to the public by targeting the interest rate than by targeting the level of reserves in the banking system. Changes in the interest rate are more meaningful to firms and households than changes in the level of reserves or the money supply. For example, if we hear that mortgage-lending rates at commercial banks have just decreased by one percentage point, most people can readily assess what this means for their plans to buy a new house financed by a mortgage. In contrast, if we were to hear that the level of reserves in the banking system had just increased by $1 billion, it would not be clear to most people what this means, or that it would have any effect on interest rates, or by how much. Even the Bank itself might be uncertain about the magnitude of these effects.

In summary, these are the advantages of conducting monetary policy by targeting the interest rate:

1. The Bank of Canada is able to control a particular market interest rate.

2. Uncertainty about the slope and position of the M_D curve does not prevent the Bank of Canada from establishing its desired interest rate.

3. The Bank of Canada can easily communicate an interest-rate change to the public.

The Bank of Canada and the Overnight Interest Rate

Practise with Study Guide
Chapter 29, Exercises 3 and 4.

We have just explained why the Bank of Canada chooses to implement its monetary policy by targeting the interest rate rather than by trying to influence the money supply directly. But *how* does the Bank do this, and *which* interest rate (among many) does it target?

As we discussed in Chapter 28, there are many interest rates in the Canadian economy. Commercial banks pay different rates to depositors on each of several different types of bank deposits. They also lend at different rates for different kinds of loans—home mortgages, small business loans, personal lines of credit, and car loans, to name just a few. In addition, government securities trade at different yields (interest rates) depending on the term to maturity. Economists refer to the overall pattern of interest rates corresponding to government securities of different maturities as the *term structure of interest rates*. Because bondholders generally require a higher rate of return in order to lend their funds for a longer period of time, yields on government securities generally increase as the term to maturity increases. At any given time, the yield on 90-day Treasury bills is usually less than that on 5-year government bonds, which in turn is less than the yield on 30-year bonds. Furthermore, because these various assets are viewed as close substitutes by bondholders, the different rates tend to rise and fall together.

overnight interest rate
The interest rate that commercial banks charge one another for overnight loans.

The interest rate corresponding to the shortest period of borrowing or lending is called the **overnight interest rate**, which is the interest rate that commercial banks charge one another for overnight loans. Banks that need cash because they have run short of reserves can borrow in the *overnight market* from banks that have excess reserves available. The overnight interest rate is a market-determined interest rate that fluctuates daily as the cash requirements of commercial banks change.

The Bank of Canada exercises considerable influence over the overnight interest rate. As this rate rises or falls, the other interest rates in the economy—from short-term lines of credit to longer-term home mortgages and government securities—tend to rise or fall as well. Thus, by influencing the overnight interest rate, the Bank of Canada also influences the longer-term interest rates that are more relevant for determining aggregate consumption and investment expenditure.

How does the Bank of Canada influence the overnight interest rate? The Bank's tool for conducting its monetary policy—what economists sometimes call the Bank's *policy instrument*—is a *target* that it sets for the overnight interest rate. This target is the midpoint of a 0.5 percentage point range within which the Bank would like to see the actual overnight interest rate. The Bank announces its target for the overnight interest rate eight times per year at pre-specified dates called *fixed announcement dates,* or FADs.

bank rate The interest rate the Bank of Canada charges commercial banks for loans.

When the Bank sets its target for the overnight rate, it also sets two other rates: one at the top and one at the bottom of the 0.5 percentage point range. At the upper rate, called the **bank rate**, the Bank of Canada stands ready to lend to commercial banks any amount of cash they desire. At the lower rate, the Bank stands ready to accept any deposits from commercial banks and to pay them this interest rate. By changing its target for the overnight rate, and by changing the other two rates in lock-step, the Bank of Canada can more or less control the actual overnight interest rate. The 0.5 percentage point range is often referred to as the Bank's *target range* for the overnight interest rate.[1]

---

[1] In the spring of 2009, the Bank of Canada reduced its target for the overnight rate to 0.25 percent (and reduced the bank rate to 0.5 percent). It also decided at that time to pay commercial banks 0.25 percent on any deposits they held at the Bank of Canada (rather than reducing this rate to zero). As a result, the Bank's target range temporarily narrowed from 0.5 to 0.25 percentage points.

Consider an example that illustrates the Bank's control over the overnight interest rate. We begin by assuming that the Bank's announced target for the overnight interest rate is 4 percent. The Bank is then willing to lend to commercial banks at the bank rate, 4.25 percent. The Bank is also willing to pay 3.75 percent on any deposits it receives from commercial banks. In this case, what will be the *actual* overnight interest rate? Without knowing more details about commercial banks' demands and supplies for overnight funds, we cannot know exactly what the rate will be, but we can be sure that it will be within the Bank's target range—that is, *between* 3.75 percent and 4.25 percent. It will not be above 4.25 percent because any borrower would rather borrow from the Bank of Canada at 4.25 percent than at a higher rate from any commercial lender. Similarly, it will not be below 3.75 percent because any lender would rather lend to the Bank of Canada at 3.75 percent than accept a lower rate from any commercial borrower. Thus, the Bank can ensure that the actual overnight interest rate remains within its target range.

The Bank's policy instrument is its target for the overnight interest rate. By raising or lowering its target rate, the Bank affects the actual overnight interest rate. Changes in the overnight rate then lead to changes in other, longer-term, interest rates.

Figure 29-2 shows the path of the actual overnight interest rate and the Bank's target rate since 2000. It is almost impossible to tell the difference between the two lines

FIGURE 29-2   The Overnight Interest Rate: Target and Actual

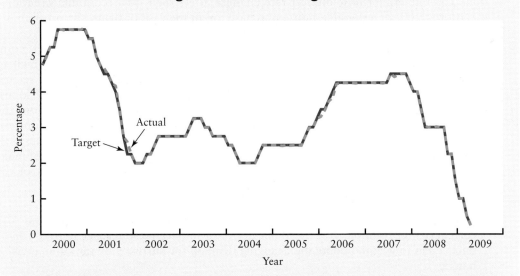

By setting a target for the overnight interest rate, the Bank of Canada exercises considerable influence over the actual overnight interest rate. By establishing an upper lending rate (the bank rate) and a lower borrowing rate, the Bank can ensure that the actual overnight interest rate remains within the Bank's target range. Since 2000, there have been only small differences between the actual overnight interest rate, the dashed green line, and the Bank's target for the overnight rate, the solid red line.

(*Source:* All data are from the Bank of Canada: www.bankofcanada.ca. Overnight interest rate: Series V122514. Bank rate: Series V122530. The Bank's target rate is the bank rate minus 0.25 percentage points.)

in the figure, which shows the considerable influence that the Bank of Canada's actions have on the actual overnight interest rate.

For the reasons just discussed, the Bank of Canada's approach to monetary policy involves setting the target for the overnight interest rate rather than trying to directly influence the money supply. At least, this is the Bank's approach during *normal* times. As explained in *Applying Economic Concepts 29-1*, however, the unusual events during the financial crisis of 2007–2008 led the Bank to implement "unconventional" policies in which at times the focus was more on changes in the money supply than on changes in interest rates. Once the crisis passed, the Bank returned to its normal procedures as described here.

The Money Supply Is Endogenous

When the Bank of Canada changes its target for the overnight rate, the change in the actual overnight rate happens almost instantly. Changes in other market interest rates, from home mortgage rates and the prime interest rate to the yields on short- and long-term government securities, also happen very quickly, usually within a day or two. As these rates adjust, firms and households begin to adjust their borrowing behaviour, but these changes take considerably longer to occur. For example, if the Bank of Canada lowered its target for the overnight rate by 25 basis points (0.25 percentage points), commercial banks might follow immediately by reducing the rate on home mortgages. But individuals will not respond to this rate reduction by immediately increasing their demand for home mortgages. Usually such changes take a while to occur, as borrowers think carefully about how interest-rate changes affect their own economic situations, the affordability of a possible house purchase, or, in the case of firms, the profitability of a potential investment.

As the demand for new loans gradually adjusts to changes in interest rates, commercial banks often find themselves in need of more cash reserves with which to make new loans. When this occurs, banks can sell some of their government securities to the Bank of Canada for cash and then use this cash to extend new loans. By buying government securities with cash in such an **open-market operation**, the Bank of Canada increases the amount of currency in circulation in the economy. This new currency arrives at the commercial banks as cash reserves, which can then be loaned out to firms or households. As we saw in Chapter 27, this process of making loans results in an expansion in deposit money and thus an expansion of the money supply.

open-market operation The purchase and sale of government securities on the open market by the central bank.

> Through its open-market operations, the Bank of Canada changes the amount of currency in circulation. But the Bank does not initiate these transactions; it conducts them to accommodate the changing demand for currency by the commercial banks.

Economists often say that the amount of currency in circulation (and also the money supply) is *endogenous*. It is not directly controlled by the Bank of Canada, but instead is determined by the economic decisions of households, firms, and commercial banks. The Bank of Canada is *passive* in its decisions regarding the money supply; it conducts its open-market operations to accommodate the changing demand for currency coming from the commercial banks. *Applying Economic Concepts 29-2* discusses in more detail how the Bank of Canada conducts open-market operations in response to this changing demand.

"Unconventional" Monetary Policy During the 2007–2008 Financial Crisis

The Bank of Canada normally conducts its monetary policy by setting its target for the overnight interest rate. By offering to lend to commercial banks at an interest rate 1/4 of a percentage point above this target, and to accept deposits and pay an interest rate 1/4 of a percentage point below the target, the Bank is able to keep the overnight interest rate within a narrow range. This control gives it significant influence on longer-term interest rates and thus on aggregate demand.

Note that the Bank is usually able to control the overnight interest rate in this manner without *actually* extending loans to or accepting deposits from commercial banks. The mere knowledge on the part of commercial banks that the Bank of Canada is *prepared* to take these actions is enough to keep the actual overnight interest rate close to the target. With the onset of the financial crisis of 2007–2008, however, the Bank needed to take some "unconventional" actions.

The financial crisis originated with the collapse of prices in the U.S. housing market and the associated increase in the number of homeowners who then "walked away" from their homes because the value of their property was less than the amount they owed on their mortgages. For the banks and other financial institutions that had purchased billions of dollars worth of mortgage-backed securities, the collapse in the value of homes and mortgages implied a collapse in the value of their assets; these losses were large enough in some cases to cause the failures of some large U.S. and U.K. commercial and investment banks in 2008. These failures, in turn, led to significant disruptions in global credit markets as commercial banks and other financial institutions came to fear "counterparty risk"—they were reluctant to extend even short-term loans to one another out of fear that the borrower (the counterparty) would go bankrupt before repaying the loan. But with the flow of credit interrupted in this manner, there was a genuine risk that the level of economic activity would soon be affected.

In this setting, the Bank of Canada significantly reduced its target for the overnight interest rate, as is evident in Figure 29-2. In addition, it took "unconventional" actions, designed to restore the flow of credit in the economy. The Bank eased the terms by which it extended loans to financial institutions, both by broadening the class of assets it was prepared to hold as collateral and by extending the length of the loans. By doing so, the Bank was able to increase liquidity in the financial sector and thus increase interbank lending. The Bank's actions appeared to be effective and well timed. As the financial crisis progressed, it became clearer that Canadian banks and financial institutions were less exposed to the mortgage-backed securities that had created such havoc in the U.S. and U.K. financial sectors. With this knowledge, the fear of counterparty risk in the Canadian financial sector gradually declined and the credit markets gradually returned to normal. But the Bank's actions, taken early and amid a time of great confusion, helped to keep financial markets operating relatively smoothly and thus helped to sustain the flow of credit.

Despite similar actions being taken in central banks in other countries, the scale of the global financial crisis led to a global recession. The decline in global economic activity led to a steep decline in demand for Canada's exports. By the spring of 2009, Canada was in a deep recession and the Bank of Canada was considering some further unconventional policy actions. This time, however, the situation was quite different from that in 2008. Having reduced its target for the overnight interest rate to 0.25 percent from 4.5 percent in mid-2007, the Bank could no longer reduce it further. What could the Bank then do if the depth of the recession suggested a need for even more expansionary monetary policy?

The Bank indicated that it was prepared, if necessary, to embark on policies of "quantitative easing" or "credit easing." Quantitative easing would involve the Bank directly purchasing longer-term government securities and doing so with newly created money, thereby directly increasing the money supply. This would be nothing more than an open-market purchase of bonds, as we describe in *Applying Economic Concepts 29-2* on page 736. Credit easing would involve the Bank directly purchasing private-sector securities and would be intended to help restore the flow of credit to selected segments of the financial markets.

As of early 2010, however, the Bank of Canada had not yet embarked on policies of either quantitative or credit easing. But both remain as possible "unconventional" policy actions when the Bank desires an expansionary monetary policy but when the target for the overnight rate cannot be lowered further.

APPLYING ECONOMIC CONCEPTS 29-2

What Determines the Amount of Currency in Circulation?

The Bank of Canada uses its *policy instrument*—its target for the overnight interest rate—to influence the money market and implement its monetary policy. A reduction in the Bank's target for the overnight rate will reduce market interest rates and lead to a greater demand for borrowing and hence spending by firms and households. In contrast, an increase in the Bank's target for the overnight rate will tend to raise market interest rates and reduce the demand for borrowing and spending by firms and households.

In response to these changes in the demand for loans, commercial banks may find themselves either with too few cash reserves with which to make new loans or with too many cash reserves for the amount of loans they want to make. What happens in each case?

If Banks Need More Cash

Suppose that at the current market interest rates and level of economic activity, commercial banks are facing a growing demand for loans. If banks have excess reserves, these loans can be made easily. But once banks reach their target reserve ratio, they will be unable to extend new loans without increasing their cash reserves. Banks can increase their cash reserves by selling some of their government bonds to the Bank of Canada. In this case, the Bank of Canada is *purchasing* government bonds from the commercial banks. This transaction is called an *open-market purchase.*

Suppose a commercial bank wants to sell a $10 000 bond to the Bank of Canada. As the accompanying balance sheets show, this transaction does not change the total assets or liabilities for the commercial bank, although it changes the *form* of its assets. With more cash reserves (and fewer bonds), the commercial bank can now make more loans. For the Bank of Canada, however, there *is* a change in the level of assets and liabilities. Its holdings of bonds (assets) have increased and the amount of currency in circulation (liabilities) has also increased. Open-market purchases by the Bank of Canada are the means by which the amount of currency in the economy increases.

If Banks Have Excess Reserves

Now suppose that at the current market interest rates and level of economic activity the commercial banks cannot find enough suitable borrowers to whom they can lend their excess cash reserves. The commercial banks can reduce their excess cash reserves by using the cash to purchase government bonds from the Bank of Canada. In this case, the Bank of Canada is *selling* government bonds to the commercial banks. This transaction is called an *open-market sale.*

The changes are the opposite of those shown in the accompanying balance sheets. The commercial bank now has less cash and more (interest-earning) bonds, but its total assets and liabilities are unchanged. The Bank of Canada now has fewer bonds and there is also less currency in circulation in the economy.

**An Open-Market Purchase of Bonds
from a Commercial Bank**

Commercial Bank Balance Sheet

Assets		Liabilities
Bonds	− $10 000	No change
Cash Reserves	+ $10 000	

Bank of Canada Balance Sheet

Assets		Liabilities	
Bonds	+ $10 000	Currency in Circulation	+ $10 000

Currency in a Growing Economy

If you look at the Bank of Canada's balance sheets (like the one we showed in Chapter 27) over several years, you will notice that the amount of currency in circulation rarely (if ever) falls. In an economy where real GDP is steadily growing, the demand for loans by firms and households is also usually growing, as is the demand for currency by commercial banks. In some years, the demand for currency is growing very quickly, in which case the Bank of Canada has many open-market purchases. In other years, the demand for currency grows only slowly, in which case the Bank has fewer (or smaller) open-market purchases. In a typical year, however, the amount of currency in circulation increases by about 5 percent, which in 2009 represented about $3 billion. Thus, in a typical week, the Bank of Canada purchases about $55 million of government bonds in the open market.

Expansionary and Contractionary Monetary Policies

We can now clarify the meaning of a *contractionary* or an *expansionary* monetary policy. As we saw earlier, unpredictable shifts in the money demand curve imply that there is no clear relationship between changes in the interest rate and changes in the quantity of money in circulation. And since what matters for the monetary transmission mechanism is the change in interest rates, economists label a monetary-policy action as being expansionary or contractionary depending on how the policy affects interest rates, rather than on how it affects the overall amount of money.

If the Bank of Canada wants to stimulate the level (or growth rate) of aggregate demand, it will reduce its target for the overnight interest rate, and the effect will soon be felt on longer-term market interest rates. Reducing the interest rate is an *expansionary* monetary policy because it leads to an expansion of aggregate demand. If the Bank instead wants to reduce aggregate demand (or its growth rate), it will increase its target for the overnight interest rate, and longer-term market interest rates will soon rise as a result. Increasing the interest rate is a *contractionary* monetary policy because it leads to a contraction (or slowing) of aggregate demand.

As the longer-term market interest rates change, the various steps in the monetary transmission mechanism come into play. As we saw in Chapter 28, in an open economy like Canada's there are two separate channels in this transmission mechanism. First, desired investment and consumption expenditure will begin to change. At the same time, international capital flows in response to changes in interest rates will cause the exchange rate to change, which, in turn, causes net exports to change. Taken together, the total changes in aggregate expenditure lead to shifts in the *AD* curve, which then lead to changes in real GDP and the price level. The monetary transmission mechanism is reviewed in Figure 29-3.

FIGURE 29-3 The Monetary Transmission Mechanism

Monetary policy influences aggregate demand through the monetary transmission mechanism. The Bank of Canada sets a target for the overnight interest rate, which influences other market interest rates as well. The change in interest rates leads, via the monetary transmission mechanism, to changes in desired aggregate expenditure. Aggregate demand and aggregate supply then determine the price level and the level of real GDP.

29.2 Inflation Targeting

In the previous section we examined the technical details of how the Bank of Canada implements its monetary policy. In this section we examine the Bank's policy objectives and how it conducts its monetary policy to achieve those objectives. Our emphasis is on the Bank's policy of *inflation targeting*.

Why Target Inflation?

During the last few decades of the twentieth century, central banks the world over came to accept two economic propositions. The first proposition is that high inflation is damaging to the economy and is costly for firms and individuals. Among other things, inflation reduces the real purchasing power of those people whose incomes are stated in nominal (dollar) terms and insufficiently *indexed* to adjust for changes in the price level. For example, seniors whose pension incomes are not indexed to inflation suffer a reduction in their real incomes whenever inflation occurs.

The *uncertainty* generated by inflation is also damaging to the economy. When inflation is high, it tends to be quite volatile, and this volatility makes it difficult to predict. As a result, periods of high inflation are often characterized as having much *unexpected* inflation. As we first discussed in Chapter 19, unexpected inflation leads to reallocations of real income between workers and firms and borrowers and lenders that may be viewed as undesirable. (Because many contracts are set in nominal terms over periods of several years, even *expected* inflation has this effect.)

Finally, high inflation undermines the ability of the price system to signal changes in relative scarcity through changes in relative prices. For example, if the prices of construction materials rise when inflation is high, consumers may be unable to discern whether the price is rising relative to other goods and services or whether it is rising only because of a widespread inflation. As a result, both producers and consumers will make mistakes regarding their own production and consumption decisions that they would not have made in the absence of high inflation.

> High and uncertain inflation leads to arbitrary income redistributions and also undermines the efficiency of the price system.

The second proposition that came to be accepted by most central banks is that the effects of monetary policy are different in the short run and in the long run. While in the short run monetary policy can have a profound influence on real economic variables, such as real GDP, employment, and investment, its long-run impact appears to fall mostly on nominal variables, such as the price level and the inflation rate. Because of the economy's adjustment process that we examined in detail in Chapter 24, real GDP tends to return in the long run to its potential level, Y^*. As a result, monetary policy is unlikely to have a systematic and *sustained* influence on real economic variables. However, monetary policy does have a systematic and sustained influence on the rate of inflation.

A related proposition also came to be accepted by central banks. Various demand and supply shocks that are unrelated to monetary policy cause shifts in the *AD* and *AS* curves and thus cause temporary changes in the rate of inflation as the economy responds to these shocks. But over time it became clear that *sustained* inflation was not caused by such shocks—instead, *sustained* inflation appeared to occur only in those situations in which monetary policy was allowing continual and rapid growth in the money supply. In other words, central banks came to recognize that *sustained* inflation was ultimately created by monetary policy.

Most economists and central bankers believe that monetary policy is the most important determinant of a country's long-run rate of inflation.

In summary, central banks have come to accept two propositions about inflation:

1. High inflation is costly for individuals and damaging to the economy.

2. Inflation is the only macroeconomic variable over which central banks have a systematic and sustained influence.

Given these two propositions, which over the years have been increasingly supported by both theoretical reasoning and empirical evidence, it is not surprising that central banks have come to focus their attentions on the reduction and control of inflation.

In the early 1990s, many central banks around the world—the Bank of Canada being among the first—adopted formal systems of *inflation targeting*. The Bank of Canada first adopted its formal inflation targets in 1991 when the annual rate of inflation was almost 6 percent. The targets were expressed as a 2-percentage-point band, in recognition of the fact that it is unrealistic to expect the Bank to keep the inflation rate at a single, precise value in the face of the many shocks that influence it in the short term. Beginning in 1992, the Bank of Canada's target range for inflation was 3–5 percent, with the range falling to 2–4 percent by 1993 and to 1–3 percent by the end of 1995. The Bank's formal inflation targets were renewed in 1996 and again in 2001 and 2006 (with the current targets in place until 2011). Today, the Bank of Canada conducts its monetary policy with the objective of keeping inflation at or near the 2-percent target. Figure 29-5 on page 742 shows the inflation rate and the 1–3 percent target range since 1992.

The overall success of inflation targeting, in Canada and elsewhere, has led many central banks to adopt formal inflation targets. New Zealand was the first adopter, in 1990, and Canada was second, in 1991. Formal inflation targets were adopted soon thereafter in Israel, the United Kingdom, Australia, Finland, Spain, and Sweden. Since the mid-1990s, the list has grown to include Chile, Brazil, Colombia, Mexico, the Czech Republic, Poland, South Africa, Thailand, and others. The U.S. Federal Reserve has *not* yet adopted a formal inflation target, although its current chairman, Ben Bernanke, has indicated that he would like the Federal Reserve to do so.

The Role of the Output Gap

The Bank of Canada recognizes that its monetary policy has real and important effects on the economy in the short run, even though its long-run influence is mainly limited to the price level and the inflation rate. The Bank also recognizes that the long-run effects of its policies follow only after the short-run effects on real GDP are experienced, after which the economy's adjustment process tends to return real GDP to the level of potential output. As a result, the Bank of Canada closely monitors the level of real GDP in the short run and also the gap between real GDP and Y^*—the output gap.

FIGURE 29-4   The Output Gap, Inflation, and Monetary Policy

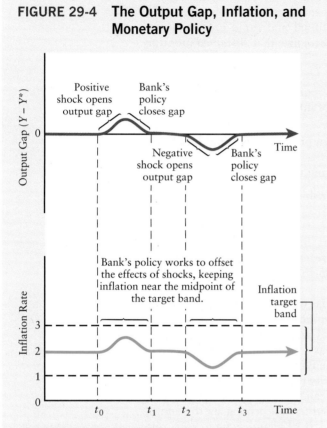

The Bank of Canada closely monitors the output gap to determine the necessary policy for maintaining inflation near its target. The economy begins with no output gap and the inflation rate at 2 percent. At time t_0 a positive shock pushes real GDP above Y^* and increases inflationary pressure. The Bank can then implement a contractionary monetary policy to close the output gap and reduce inflation back toward 2 percent. At time t_2 a negative shock reduces real GDP below Y^* and reduces inflationary pressure. The Bank can then implement an expansionary monetary policy to close the output gap and increase inflation back toward 2 percent.

To understand why the Bank closely monitors the output gap in the short run, consider Figure 29-4, which shows hypothetical time paths for the output gap $(Y - Y^*)$ in part (i), and for the rate of inflation with the 1–3 percent target band in part (ii). Until time t_0, the economy is growing with Y equal to Y^* and inflation is more or less constant at the midpoint of the target band. At t_0, a positive shock pushes real GDP above Y^* and opens up an inflationary output gap. Labour and other factors of production are used intensively in order to increase output, and this generates excess demand in factor markets. Wages and other factor prices begin to rise, pushing up firms' costs and adding to the inflationary pressure. The rate of inflation begins to rise above the midpoint of the target band.

At this point, the Bank of Canada must make a decision. It can choose to leave its policy unchanged and let the economy's adjustment process operate. The *AS* curve will shift upward and eventually return real GDP to Y^* but only through more inflation. The other choice for the Bank is to attempt to close the output gap by "pulling" real GDP back toward Y^* with a contractionary monetary policy, shifting the *AD* curve to the left and bringing the rate of inflation back to its starting point near the midpoint of the target band.

The opposite situation can also occur, as shown in the figure at time t_2, when a negative shock pushes real GDP below Y^* and pushes inflation toward the bottom end of the target band. The Bank is again faced with a choice. It can do nothing and let real GDP return (perhaps slowly) to Y^*, but allow inflation to fall even further as the *AS* curve shifts down during the adjustment process. Or it can try to close the output gap by creating a monetary expansion to shift the *AD* curve to the right and "pull" real GDP back toward Y^*, raising the rate of inflation back toward the midpoint of the target band.

> Output gaps create pressure for the rate of inflation to change. To keep the rate of inflation close to the 2-percent target, the Bank of Canada closely monitors real GDP in the short run and designs its policy to keep real GDP close to potential output.

Practise with Study Guide
Chapter 29, Exercise 5.

Inflation Targeting as a Stabilizing Policy

Figure 29-4 also shows why an inflation-targeting policy helps to stabilize the economy. If the Bank of Canada is committed to keeping the rate of inflation near 2 percent, positive shocks to the economy that create an inflationary gap and threaten to increase the rate of inflation will be met by a contractionary monetary policy. The Bank will increase interest rates and shift the *AD* curve to the left. This policy will reduce the size of the output gap and push the rate of inflation back down toward 2 percent. Similarly, if a negative shock to the economy creates a recessionary gap and threatens to reduce the rate of inflation, a central bank committed to its inflation targets will respond with an expansionary monetary policy. In this situation, the Bank of Canada will reduce interest rates and shift the *AD* curve to the right. This policy will reduce the size of the output gap and push the inflation rate back toward the 2-percent target.

> **Inflation targeting is a stabilizing policy. Positive shocks will be met with a contractionary monetary policy; negative shocks will be met with an expansionary monetary policy.**

Some economists go so far as to refer to a policy of inflation targeting as an "automatic" stabilizer. But this is an exaggeration, as we can see by recalling our discussion in Chapter 24 of automatic *fiscal* stabilizers, caused by taxes and transfers that vary with the level of national income. The automatic fiscal stabilizers we discussed in Chapter 24 were truly "automatic" in the sense that no group of policymakers had to actively adjust policy—the stabilizers were built right into the tax-and-transfer system. With inflation targeting, however, there must be an active policy decision to keep inflation close to its target rate, and only then will the Bank's policy adjustments work to stabilize the economy following either positive or negative shocks. But as long as the Bank wants to maintain its inflation target, and have it perceived as being *credible*, then it is committed to carrying out such policy adjustments.

> **Inflation targets are not as "automatic" a stabilizer as the fiscal stabilizers built into the tax-and-transfer system. But if the central bank is committed to maintaining the credibility of its inflation target, its policy adjustments will act to stabilize the economy.**

Complications in Inflation Targeting

So far, our discussion of inflation targeting makes the conduct of monetary policy seem straightforward. But there are several details that complicate the task considerably. In this section we discuss two complications for the conduct of monetary policy, and in the next section we address a more general difficulty.

Volatile Food and Energy Prices Sometimes the rate of inflation increases for reasons unrelated to a change in the output gap. For example, many commodities whose prices are included in the Consumer Price Index (CPI) are internationally traded goods and their prices are determined in world markets. Oil is an obvious example, as are many fruits and vegetables. When these prices rise suddenly, perhaps because of political instability in the Middle East (oil) or because of poor crop conditions in tropical countries (fruits and vegetables), the measured rate of inflation of the Canadian CPI also rises. Yet these price increases have little or nothing to do with the size of the output gap in Canada and thus have little implication for what policy should be followed by the Bank of Canada. By focusing exclusively on the rate of inflation of the CPI, the Bank would be misled about the extent of inflationary pressures coming from excess demand in Canada.

FIGURE 29-5   Canadian CPI and Core Inflation, 1992–2009

The CPI inflation rate is more volatile than the "core" inflation rate. The core rate of inflation in Canada is the rate of change of a special price index constructed by removing food, energy, and the effects of indirect taxes from the overall Consumer Price Index. For both series shown here, the inflation rate is computed monthly but is the rate of change in the price index from 12 months earlier.

(*Source:* Based on authors' calculations using data from Statistics Canada, CANSIM database, Series V36397 and V735319.)

For this reason, the Bank of Canada pays attention to what is called the "core" rate of inflation. This is the rate of growth of a special price index, one that is constructed by extracting food, energy, and the effects of indirect taxes (such as the GST or excise taxes) from the Consumer Price Index. Figure 29-5 shows the paths of core and CPI inflation since 1992. As is clear from the figure, even though the two measures of inflation move broadly together, core inflation is much less volatile than is CPI inflation.

> **Because of the volatility of food and energy prices that is often unrelated to the level of the output gap in Canada, the Bank of Canada closely monitors the rate of "core" inflation even though its formal target of 2 percent applies to the rate of CPI inflation. Changes in core inflation are a better indicator of Canadian excess demand than are changes in CPI inflation.**

Note the sharp divergence between the two inflation rates in 1994. At that time, there were substantial decreases in the excise taxes on cigarettes, and those tax reductions led to a sharp decline in the CPI inflation rate. But this decline in CPI inflation was tax-created rather than caused by the opening of a recessionary output gap, and thus it would have been inappropriate for the Bank of Canada to respond to this decline in inflation by implementing an expansionary monetary policy. Instead, the Bank focused on the core inflation rate that excludes the effect of changes in indirect taxes. The core inflation rate in 1994 was relatively stable and close to the midpoint of the 1–3 percent target band, indicating no need for a change in monetary policy.

Note also the volatility of the CPI inflation rate during 2008. Energy and commodity prices had been rising for the previous few years, but they increased especially rapidly in the early part of 2008. This helped to push the CPI inflation rate above 3 percent. But then the worst part of the financial crisis occurred in the autumn of that year, energy and commodity prices plunged, and the CPI inflation rate fell quickly to below 1 percent. Meanwhile, the core rate of inflation was much less volatile and remained close to 2 percent.

The Exchange Rate and Monetary Policy

Given the large amount of trade that Canadian firms and households do with the rest of the world, it is not surprising that the Bank of Canada pays close attention to movements in the exchange rate, the Canadian-dollar price of one unit of foreign currency. However, because changes in the exchange rate can have several different causes, care must be taken when drawing inferences about the desired change in monetary policy resulting from changes in the exchange rate. As we will see, there is no simple "rule of thumb" for how the Bank should react to a change in the exchange rate. Recall that the Bank's objective is to keep the inflation rate near the midpoint of the 1–3 percent target band, and it does this by responding to changes in the output gap so as to offset changes in emerging inflationary pressure. The Bank's appropriate policy response to a change in the exchange rate depends crucially on the *cause* of the change.

> **Many economic events can lead to changes in the exchange rate. The cause of any change must be known before the appropriate monetary policy response can be determined.**

We consider two different examples. In the first, an appreciation of the Canadian dollar leads the Bank to tighten its monetary policy by raising its target for the overnight interest rate. In the second example, an appreciation of the Canadian dollar leads the Bank to loosen its monetary policy by reducing its target for the overnight interest rate. In both cases, the Bank's actions are consistent with its objective of keeping the inflation rate near the midpoint of the 1–3 percent target band.

For the first example, suppose that the economies of Canada's trading partners are booming and thus demanding more Canadian exports. Foreigners' heightened demand for Canadian goods creates an increase in demand for the Canadian dollar in foreign-exchange markets. The Canadian dollar therefore appreciates. But the increase in demand for Canadian goods has added directly to Canadian aggregate demand. If this shock persists, it will eventually add to domestic inflationary pressures. In this case, if the Bank notes the appreciation of the dollar (and correctly determines its cause), it can take action to offset the positive demand shock by tightening monetary policy by raising its target for the overnight interest rate.

The second example involves an increase in demand for Canadian *assets* rather than Canadian goods and has quite different implications from the first example. Suppose that investors, because of events happening elsewhere in the world, decide to liquidate some of their foreign assets and purchase more Canadian assets instead. In this case, the increase in demand for Canadian assets leads to an increase in demand for the

Canadian dollar in foreign-exchange markets. This causes an appreciation of the Canadian dollar. As the dollar appreciates, however, Canadian exports become more expensive to foreigners. There will be a reduction in Canadian net exports and thus a reduction in Canadian aggregate demand. If this shock persists, it will eventually reduce inflationary pressure in Canada. In this case, if the Bank notes the appreciation of the dollar (and correctly determines its cause), it can take action to offset the negative demand shock by loosening monetary policy by reducing its target for the overnight interest rate.

Notice in both examples that the Canadian dollar appreciated as a result of the external shock, but the causes of the appreciation were different. In the first case, there was a positive demand shock to net exports, which then caused the appreciation, which in turn dampened the initial increase in net exports. But the overall effect on the demand for Canadian goods was positive. In the second case, there was a positive shock to the *asset* market, which then caused the appreciation, which in turn reduced the demand for net exports. The overall effect on the demand for Canadian goods was negative. Thus, in the first case, the appropriate response for monetary policy was contractionary, whereas in the second case the appropriate response for monetary policy was expansionary.

Changes in the exchange rate can signal the need for changes in the stance of monetary policy. Only once the cause of the exchange-rate change is determined, however, can the Bank of Canada design a policy response appropriate for keeping inflation close to its target.

(X) **myeconlab** **ADDITIONAL TOPICS**

For a more detailed discussion of how movements in the exchange rate complicate the implementation of monetary policy, look for **Monetary Policy and the Exchange Rate in Canada** in the *Additional Topics* section of this book's MyEconLab.

www.myeconlab.com

29.3 Long and Variable Lags

In Chapter 28 we encountered a debate that was prominent from the 1950s to the early 1980s. *Monetarists* argued that monetary policy was potentially very powerful in the sense that a given change in the money supply would lead to a substantial change in aggregate demand, whereas *Keynesians* were associated with the view that monetary policy was much less powerful.

This debate had some of its roots in differing interpretations of the causes of the Great Depression, especially as it occurred in the United States amid a large number of commercial-bank failures. One interesting part of the debate is why Canada and the United Kingdom had collapses in economic activity similar in magnitude to that in the United States even though they did not suffer the same banking crisis. *Lessons from History 29-1* provides a brief summary of this interesting debate and applies some of the lessons about monetary policy we have learned in the past two chapters.

The debate between the Monetarists and the Keynesians was about more than just the *effectiveness* of monetary policy. The debate sometimes also focused on the question of whether active use of monetary policy in an attempt to stabilize output and the price level was likely to be successful, or whether it would instead lead to an increase in fluctuations in those variables. This debate is as important today as it was then, and at its centre is the role of *lags*.

What Are the Lags in Monetary Policy?

Experience has shown that lags in the operation of policy can sometimes cause stabilization policy to be destabilizing. In Chapter 24, we discussed how decision and implementation lags might limit the extent to which active use of fiscal policy can be relied upon to stabilize the economy. Although both of these sources of lags are less relevant for monetary policy, the full effects of monetary policy nevertheless occur only after quite long time lags. There are two reasons that a change in monetary policy does not affect the economy instantly.

Changes in Expenditure Take Time   When the Bank of Canada changes its target for the overnight interest rate, the actual overnight rate changes almost instantly. Other, longer-term market interest rates also change quickly, usually within a day or two. However, it takes more time before households and firms adjust their spending and borrowing plans in response to the change in interest rates. Consumers may respond relatively quickly and alter their plans for purchasing durable goods like cars and appliances. But it takes longer for firms to modify their investment plans and then put them into effect. It may take a year or more before the full increase in investment expenditure occurs in response to a fall in interest rates.

In an open economy like Canada's, the change in the interest rate also leads to capital flows and a change in the exchange rate. These changes occur very quickly. But the effect on net exports takes more time while purchasers of internationally traded goods and services switch to lower-cost suppliers.

The Multiplier Process Takes Time   Changes in consumption, investment, and net export expenditures brought about by a change in monetary policy set off the multiplier process that increases national income. This process, too, takes some time to work out. Furthermore, although the end result is fairly predictable, the speed with which the entire expansionary or contractionary process works itself out can vary in ways that are hard to predict. Thus, though the overall effects of monetary policy might be reasonably straightforward to predict, the timing of those effects is difficult to predict.

> **Monetary policy is capable of exerting expansionary and contractionary forces on the economy, but it operates with a time lag that is long and variable.**

Economists at the Bank of Canada estimate that it takes between 9 and 12 months for a change in monetary policy to have its main effect on real GDP, and a further 9 to 12 months for the policy to have its main effect on the price level (or the rate of inflation).

LESSONS FROM HISTORY 29-1

Two Views on the Role of Money in the Great Depression

In most people's minds, the Great Depression began with the stock market crash of October 1929. In the United States, Canada, and Europe, the decline in economic activity over the next four years was massive. From 1929 to 1933, annual real output fell by roughly 25 percent, one-quarter of the labour force was unemployed by 1933, the price level fell by more than 25 percent, and businesses failed on a massive scale. In the more than seven decades that have followed, no recession has come close to the Great Depression in terms of reduced economic activity, business failures, or unemployment.

The Great Depression has naturally attracted the attention of economists and, especially in the United States, these few years of experience have served as a kind of "retrospective laboratory" in which they have tried to test their theories.

The Basic Facts

The stock market crash of 1929, and other factors associated with a moderate downswing in business activity during the late 1920s, caused U.S. firms and households to want to hold more cash and fewer demand deposits. The banking system, however, could not meet this increased demand for liquidity (cash) without help from the Federal Reserve System (the U.S. central bank). As we saw in Chapter 27, because of the fractional-reserve banking system, commercial banks are never able to satisfy from their own reserves a large and sudden demand for cash—their reserves are always only a small fraction of total deposits.

The Federal Reserve had been set up to provide just such emergency assistance to commercial banks that were basically sound but were unable to meet sudden

demands by depositors to withdraw cash. However, the Federal Reserve refused to extend the necessary help, and successive waves of bank failures followed as a direct result. During each wave, hundreds of banks failed, ruining many depositors and thereby worsening an already severe depression. In the second half of 1931, almost 2000 U.S. banks were forced to suspend operations. One consequence of these failures was a sharp drop in the money supply; by 1933, M2 was 33 percent lower than it had been in 1929.

Competing Explanations

After the Great Depression was over, economists were able to examine the data and construct explanations for these dramatic events. To Monetarists, the basic facts seem decisive: To them, the fall in the money supply was clearly the major *cause* of the fall in output and employment that occurred during the Great Depression. Monetarists see the Great Depression as perhaps the single best piece of evidence of the strength of monetary forces and the single best lesson of the importance of monetary policy. In their view, the increased cash drain that led to the massive monetary contraction could have been prevented had the Federal Reserve quickly increased the level of cash reserves in the commercial banking system. In this case, the rise in cash reserves would have offset the increase in the cash drain, so that the money supply (currency plus bank deposits) could be maintained.

Keynesians argue that the fundamental cause of the Great Depression was a reduction in autonomous expenditure. They cite a large decline in housing construction (in response to a glut of housing), a decline in automobile purchases (as most first-time buying was

Destabilizing Policy?

The fact that monetary-policy actions taken today will not affect output and inflation until 1–2 years in the future means that the Bank of Canada must design its policy for what *is expected* to occur in the future rather than what *has already been observed*. To see why a monetary policy guided only by past and current events may be destabilizing, consider the following simple example. Suppose that on January 1 the Bank observes $Y < Y^*$ and concludes that an expansionary monetary policy is appropriate. It can reduce its target for the overnight rate at the next fixed announcement date (FAD), done and only replacement demand remained), and a reduction in consumption driven largely by pessimism caused by the stock market crash. Although Keynesians accept the argument that the Federal Reserve's behaviour was perverse and exacerbated an already bad situation, they do not attribute a pivotal role to the Federal Reserve or to the money supply. Instead, they see the fall in the money supply as a *result* of the decline in economic activity (through a reduced demand for loans and thus reduced bank lending) rather than as its cause.

Lessons from Canada's Experience

Canada can be used as a "control" in this retrospective laboratory, for the simple reason that Canada had broadly the same magnitude of economic collapse as did the United States, but *did not* have the same magnitude of bank failures. Unfortunately, Canada's experience is not able to resolve the disagreement—both sides of the debate can offer explanations of the Canadian experience consistent with their central arguments.

Keynesians look to Canada's experience to support their view that money was not central to the cause of the economic collapse in the United States. They point out that in Canada, where the central bank came to the aid of the banking system, bank failures were much less common during the Great Depression, and as a consequence, the money supply did not shrink drastically as it did in the United States. Thus, their argument is that since Canada did not escape the Great Depression but *did* escape the collapse in the money supply, money must not have been the central cause of the U.S. economic collapse.

Monetarists accept the point that Canada did not have a massive reduction in the money supply, but they argue that the economic contraction in the United States (which *was* caused by the collapse in the money supply)

spilled over into Canada, largely through a dramatic reduction in demand for Canadian goods. This spillover implies a large decline in export expenditure for Canada, and thus a decline in Canadian national income. Thus, Monetarists essentially argue that money in the United States was an important contributor to the economic decline in Canada.

During the Great Depression, bank failures were widespread in the United States but relatively uncommon in Canada. This difference in experience can be used to test hypotheses regarding the causes of the Great Depression. But considerable disagreement still remains.

For a discussion of these two views, and some attempts to discriminate between them, see Peter Temin, *Did Monetary Forces Cause the Great Depression?* (New York: Norton, 1976).

typically within a few weeks. By early February, the overnight interest rate will be reduced, as will the longer-term interest rates in the economy. The effects on aggregate demand, however, will not be felt in any significant way until late summer or early fall of that same year.

This policy action may turn out to be destabilizing, however. Some of the cyclical forces in the economy, unrelated to the Bank's actions, may have reversed since January, and by fall there may be a substantial inflationary output gap. However, since the effects of the monetary expansion that was initiated nine months earlier are just beginning to be felt, an expansionary monetary stimulus is adding to the existing inflationary gap.

If the Bank now applies the monetary brakes by raising interest rates, the output effects of this policy reversal will not be felt for another year or so. By that time, a contraction may have already set in because of the natural cyclical forces of the economy. Thus, the delayed effects of the monetary policy may turn a minor downturn into a major recession.

> **The long time lags in the effectiveness of monetary policy make monetary fine-tuning difficult; the policy may have a destabilizing effect.**

The Bank of Canada recognizes the possibility that if it responds to every shock that influences real GDP, then the overall effect of its policy may be to destabilize the economy rather than stabilize it. As a result, it is careful to assess the causes of the shocks that buffet the Canadian economy. It tries to avoid situations in which it responds to shocks that are believed to be short-lived and then must reverse its policy in the near future when the shocks disappear. In general, the Bank responds only to those shocks that are significant in magnitude and are expected to persist for several months or more.

Political Difficulties

Long lags in the workings of monetary policy also lead to some political criticism for the central bank.

Figure 29-6 shows a situation in which the current inflation rate is at the bottom of the Bank's 1–3 percent target band, but the expectation of future events suggests that inflation will be rising. This situation is often faced by the Bank when the economy is in the early stages of an economic recovery, as occurred in late 2009 and early 2010. At that time, the Canadian economy had been in recession for a year, and monetary policy had been very expansionary in an effort to stimulate the economy. But as real GDP began to grow and the existing recessionary gap began to narrow, the Bank needed to judge the appropriate time to begin tightening its policy in an attempt to keep inflation from rising above the 2-percent target.

What is the political problem? Remember that because of the time lags involved, any policy change that occurs today has no effect on real GDP for roughly nine months and the full effect on the price level (or the rate of inflation) does not occur for 18–24 months. If the economy is at point A in Figure 29-6, and inflation is expected to rise in the near future, then monetary policy must be changed *now* in order to counteract this future inflation. But this action could generate some criticism because the *current* inflation rate is low. In such situations, the Bank finds itself in the awkward position of advocating a tightening of monetary policy, in order to fight the expectation of future inflation, at a time when the *current* inflation rate suggests no need for tightening. But if the goal is to keep inflation within the target range, such *pre-emptive* monetary policy is necessary because of the unavoidable time lags.

FIGURE 29-6   Forward-Looking Monetary Policy

Since monetary policy works only with a considerable time lag, central-bank actions to keep inflation within its target range must be taken in advance of expected future events. Suppose the economy is currently at point A with inflation at the lower bound of the target range. If events in the near future are expected to cause inflation to rise sharply, then monetary policy must be tightened immediately to keep inflation within the desired range.

Time lags in monetary policy require that decisions regarding a loosening or tightening of monetary policy be forward-looking. This often leads to criticism of monetary policy, especially by those who do not recognize the long time lags.

29.4 Thirty Years of Canadian Monetary Policy

This section describes a few key episodes in recent Canadian monetary history. This is not done to teach history for its own sake, but because the lessons of past experience and past policy mistakes, interpreted through the filter of economic theory, provide our best hope for improving our policy performance in the future.

The OPEC oil-price shocks of 1973 and 1979–1980 led to reductions in GDP growth rates and increases in inflation in Canada—what came to be known as *stagflation*. At that time, the role of aggregate-supply shocks and their effect on macroeconomic equilibrium was not as well understood as it is today. The Bank of Canada's policy response involved considerable monetary expansion, and by 1980 the rate of inflation in Canada was more than 12 percent.

The Bank of Canada (and the U.S. Federal Reserve) then embarked on policies designed to reduce the growth rate of the money supply and eventually reduce the inflation rate. Unfortunately, at the same time innovations in the financial sector led to unexpected increases in the demand for money. The result was a much sharper increase in interest rates (see Figure 29-7) than was intended by the Bank of Canada and the

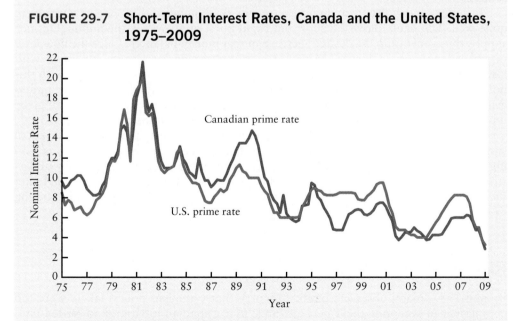

FIGURE 29-7   Short-Term Interest Rates, Canada and the United States, 1975–2009

(*Source:* Bank of Canada. Canadian rate is Series V122495; U.S. rate is Series V122148. Both are quarterly averages of monthly data.)

most serious recession since the 1930s. But the rate of inflation *did* fall, from more than 12 percent in 1980 to about 4 percent in 1984. This experience taught the Bank two important lessons:

1. Monetary policy can be *very* effective in reducing inflation.

2. Because of unexpected changes in money demand, monetary policy should focus more on interest rates than on the money supply.

As we saw earlier in this chapter, this second lesson is an important reason why the Bank now implements its policy by targeting the interest rate rather than by directly influencing the money supply.

Economic Recovery: 1983–1987

In early 1983, a sustained recovery began, and by mid-1987, real GDP had moved back toward potential. Much of the growth was centred in the export-oriented manufacturing industries in Ontario and Quebec. The first four years of the recovery saw cumulative real GDP growth of 15.7 percent.

> The main challenge for monetary policy in this period was to create sufficient liquidity to accommodate the recovery without triggering a return to the high inflation rates that prevailed at the start of the decade.

In other words, the Bank of Canada had to increase the money supply to *accommodate* the recovery-induced increase in money demand *without* increasing the money supply so much that it refuelled inflationary pressures.

In spite of much debate and uncertainty, the Bank handled this "re-entry" problem quite well. The Bank allowed a short but rapid burst of growth in the nominal money supply, thus generating the desired increase in real money balances. Once the new level of real balances was achieved, money growth was cut back to a rate consistent with low inflation (and for the underlying rate of growth in real income). The trick with this policy was that to avoid triggering expectations of renewed inflation, the Bank had to generate a one-shot increase in the *level* of the money supply without creating the impression that it was raising the long-term *rate of growth* of the money supply.

In late 1983 and early 1984, when growth in the money supply first started to surge, many voiced the fear that the Bank was being overly expansionary and was risking a return to higher inflation. As the re-entry problem came to be more widely understood and as inflationary pressures failed to re-emerge, these criticisms subsided, and the consensus appeared to be that the Bank had done a commendable job of handling the re-entry problem.

Rising Inflation: 1987–1990

By mid-1987, many observers began to worry that Canadian policymakers were too complacent in accepting the 4 percent range that Canadian inflation had settled into. Further, there was concern that inflationary pressures were starting to build—the money supply was growing quickly, real output growth was strong, unemployment was falling, and an inflationary gap was opening.

In 1987, many economists argued that if monetary policy was not tightened, Canada would experience gradually increasing inflation until once again a severe monetary restriction would be required to reduce the rate of inflation.

Inflation slowly crept upward. A monetary restriction designed to reduce inflation would obviously impose costs in the form of lower output and higher unemployment. Was the Bank prepared to inflict such costs, especially given that Canada had emerged from a deep recession only five years earlier?

In January 1988, Bank of Canada Governor John Crow announced that monetary policy would henceforth be guided less by short-term stabilization issues and more by the goal of long-term "price stability." Specifically, he said that "monetary policy should be conducted so as to achieve a pace of monetary expansion that promotes stability in the value of money. This means pursuing a policy aimed at achieving and maintaining stable prices."[2]

John Crow was the governor of the Bank of Canada from 1987 to 1994. In 1988 he announced that "price stability" would thenceforth be the Bank of Canada's objective.

Disinflation: 1990–1992

This explicit adoption of price stability as the Bank's only target set off a heated debate about the appropriate stance for monetary policy. The debate was fuelled by Crow's decision to give a high profile to his policy by repeatedly articulating and defending it in speeches and public appearances. He believed that this was necessary because expectations of continuing inflation had become entrenched. In his view, until the public believed that the Bank was serious about controlling inflation, whatever the short-term consequences, inflation could not be reduced. Some critics said that price stability was unobtainable. Others said the costs of reaching it would be too large in terms of several years of recessionary gaps. Supporters said that the long-term gains from having a stable price level would exceed the costs of getting there.

Despite the Bank's explicit policy of "price stability," the actual inflation rate increased slightly in the years immediately following John Crow's policy announcement, from about 4 percent in 1987 to just over 5 percent in 1990.

The controversy reached new heights when in 1990 the country (and much of the world) entered a sustained recession. Maintaining a tight monetary policy with high interest rates (see Figure 29-7) seemed perverse to many when the economy was already suffering from too little aggregate demand to sustain potential output.

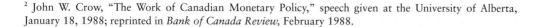

[2] John W. Crow, "The Work of Canadian Monetary Policy," speech given at the University of Alberta, January 18, 1988; reprinted in *Bank of Canada Review,* February 1988.

Furthermore, the high Canadian interest rates attracted foreign funds. Foreigners who wanted to buy Canadian bonds needed Canadian dollars, and their demands led to an appreciation of the Canadian dollar. This increased the price of Canadian exports while reducing the price of Canadian imports, putting Canadian export and import-competing industries at a competitive disadvantage and further increasing the unemployment that had been generated by the worldwide recession.

Inflation Targeting I: 1991–2000

In spite of heavy political pressure to lower interest rates, and of criticism from some economists who might have supported a move toward price stability in less depressed times, the Bank stood by its tight monetary policy. Indeed, in 1991, it formally announced *inflation-control targets* for the next several years. Beginning in 1992, inflation was to lie within the 3–5 percent range, with the range falling to 2–4 percent by 1993 and to 1–3 percent by the end of 1995.

As a result of the tight monetary policy, the inflation rate fell sharply, from about 5 percent in 1990 to less than 2 percent in 1992. For 1993 and 1994, inflation hovered around 2 percent. Furthermore, short-term nominal interest rates fell from a high of about 13 percent in 1990 to about 6 percent by the end of 1993. Recall that the nominal interest rate is equal to the real interest rate plus the rate of inflation. So this decline in nominal interest rates was the eventual result of the tight monetary policy that reduced inflation.

The Bank had succeeded in coming close to its target of price stability. Controversy continued, however, on two issues. First, was the result worth the price of a deeper, possibly more prolonged recession than might have occurred if the Bank had been willing to accept 3–4 percent inflation? Second, would the low inflation rate be sustainable once the recovery took the economy back toward potential output? If the inflation rate were to rise to 4 percent during the post-1993 recovery, then the verdict might well be that the cost of temporarily reducing the rate to below 2 percent was not worth the transitory gains.

Gordon Thiessen became the governor of the Bank of Canada in 1994 after inflation had hovered around 2 percent for about two years.

The debate over the Bank's emphasis on maintaining low inflation became centred on Governor John Crow, especially during the federal election campaign of 1993. Some called for the non-renewal of Crow's term as governor (which was scheduled to end in 1994) and his replacement with someone perceived to care more about the costs of fighting inflation. Others argued that the Bank's policy of "price stability" under Crow's stewardship was the right policy for the times and that the long-run benefits of maintaining low inflation would be worth the costs required to achieve it.[3]

In 1994, the minister of finance appointed Gordon Thiessen, the former senior deputy governor of the Bank, to be the new governor. With some irony, the minister of finance, whose party had been severe critics of Crow's policy while they were in opposition, affirmed the previous monetary policy of the Bank and urged the new governor to maintain the hard-won low inflation rate. The new governor agreed and extended the formal inflation target of 2 percent until 2001.

---

[3] For a very readable account of Canadian monetary policy from 1988 to 1993, see William Robson and David Laidler, *The Great Canadian Disinflation* (Toronto: C. D. Howe Institute, 1993).

For the next three years, the rate of inflation continued to hover between 1 and 2 percent. The main challenge for the Bank in the next few years was to keep inflation low while at the same time encouraging the economy to progress through what was viewed as a fragile recovery. Excessive stimulation of the economy would lead to the rise of inflation, which would sacrifice the hard-won gains achieved only a few years earlier. On the other hand, insufficient stimulation would itself be an obstacle to economic recovery.

Beginning in the summer of 1997, the economies of Thailand, Malaysia, Indonesia, and South Korea fell into serious recessions, thus beginning what is now known as the Asian Economic Crisis.[4] Since these countries are major importers of raw materials, their recessions led to a large decline in the world's demand for raw materials. As a result, the world price of raw materials fell by an average of about 30 percent in the subsequent year. Since Canada is a major producer and exporter of raw materials, this decline in the demand for raw materials was a negative aggregate demand shock for Canada. Working in the opposite direction, however, was the expansionary supply-side effect of lower raw materials prices for the many Canadian manufacturing firms that use raw materials as inputs. This positive supply shock was especially important for the United States, a major importer and user of raw materials. The impact of the Asian Crisis on the U.S. economy produced a third effect on Canada as the quickly growing U.S. economy increased its demand for Canadian goods and services.

In the spring of 1997, before the Asian Crisis had begun, the Canadian economy was growing and steadily closing a recessionary gap. The combination of forces created by the Asian Economic Crisis presented problems for the Bank of Canada and for the appropriate direction for monetary policy. Especially difficult was judging the relative strengths of the three separate effects. As it turned out, Canada's recessionary gap continued to shrink as the economy grew steadily. By 1999, the Asian economies were on their way to a healthy recovery.

Changes in stock-market values also created some challenges for the Bank of Canada in the 1990s. From 1994 through 1999, U.S. and Canadian stocks enjoyed unprecedented bull markets. The Dow Jones Industrial Average (an index of U.S. stock prices) increased from about 3500 in mid-1994 to about 11 000 in late 1999, an average annual increase of 26 percent. The Toronto Stock Exchange Index (now called the S&P/TSX), increased from roughly 4000 to 8000 over the same period, an average annual increase of 14 percent.

The concern for the Bank of Canada during this time was that the increase in wealth generated by these stock-market gains would stimulate consumption expenditures in what was already a steadily growing economy, thus increasing inflationary pressures. In December 1996, the chairman of the U.S. Federal Reserve, Alan Greenspan, warned market participants about their "irrational exuberance," a phrase that is now often quoted. Bank of Canada Governor Gordon Thiessen made similar remarks in Canada. Both central bankers were trying to dampen expectations in the stock market so that the stock-market gains, and thus the increases in wealth-induced spending, would not significantly contribute to inflationary pressures. But they had to be careful not to have their comments create a "crash" in the market that would have even more dramatic effects in the opposite direction.

As it turned out, the crash happened anyway. In both the United States and Canada, the stock markets had reached such levels that many commentators said it was only a matter of time before participants realized that stock prices no longer reflected the

---

[4] An important part of the cause of these recessions was the sudden collapse of their currencies, which were previously pegged in value to the U.S. dollar. We examine fixed and flexible exchange rates in detail in Chapter 35.

David Dodge was the governor of the Bank of Canada from 2001 to early 2008 and needed to steer monetary policy during a time of a strong appreciation of the Canadian dollar, driven partly by rising world commodity prices.

underlying values of the companies, at which point there would be massive selling and an inevitable crash. From the fall of 2000 to the spring of 2001, the major Canadian stock-market indexes fell by roughly 40 percent, driven to a large extent by huge reductions in the stock prices of high-tech firms. This stock-market decline is often referred to as the "dot-com" crash.

Inflation Targeting II: 2001–2007

David Dodge became the new governor of the Bank of Canada in the spring of 2001. During his tenure as governor, the Bank faced several significant policy challenges.

When the terrorist attacks in New York and Washington occurred on September 11, 2001, the stock markets took another dramatic plunge. By late in 2003, stock markets were still far below their pre-crash levels. The main challenge for monetary policy was to provide enough liquidity to the banking systems to prevent the economy from entering a recession. In both Canada and the United States, the central banks dramatically lowered their key interest rates over a period of several months.

From 2002 to 2005, the Bank of Canada's target for the overnight interest rate was 3 percentage points below its level from the summer of 2000. During this period, two external forces on the Canadian economy became apparent and presented a further challenge for the Bank of Canada. First, strong world economic growth, especially in China and India, contributed to a substantial increase in the world prices of oil and other raw materials. Given Canada's position as a major producer and exporter of these products, these price increases represented a significant positive external shock to aggregate demand. They also contributed to a substantial appreciation of the Canadian dollar, by more than 40 percent from 2002 to 2005. Taken by itself, this positive shock to Canadian aggregate demand created a justification for the Bank of Canada to tighten its monetary policy.

Working in the opposite direction was a second external shock, also contributing to an appreciation of the Canadian dollar. During the 2002–2005 period, partly in response to a large and growing U.S. current account deficit, the U.S. dollar was depreciating against the pound sterling and the euro. This "realignment" of the U.S. dollar also involved Canada and explained some part of the Canadian dollar's appreciation during that period. These exchange-rate changes, which were not themselves being caused by changes in the demand for Canadian goods and services, nonetheless tended to reduce Canadian net exports and aggregate demand, thus providing some justification for a loosening of Canadian monetary policy.

The problem for the Bank of Canada during this period was to determine the *relative* strength of these opposing forces and thus the appropriate *overall* direction for monetary policy. During the early part of this period, when Canadian real GDP was below potential, the Bank resisted tightening its policy, choosing instead to allow the commodity-price-driven expansion to close the existing output gap. By the summer of 2005, however, when the output gap appeared to be all but closed, the Bank began a series of increases in the target for the overnight interest rate, and by the summer of 2006 it had increased its target by two percentage points.

Throughout 2006 and 2007, world commodity prices continued their steep ascent and the effect on the Canadian economy was dramatic. Employment grew rapidly, real

GDP grew above the level of potential output, and serious concerns about inflation began to mount. During this period, the Bank of Canada continued to gradually raise its policy interest rate.

A related challenge for the Bank during this period involved regional and sectoral differences in economic performance within Canada. The strong growth in the prices of oil and raw materials naturally led to boom conditions in these sectors, which tend to be located in both Western and Atlantic Canada. However, these price increases harmed the profitability of many central Canadian manufacturing firms who used these products as important inputs. In addition, the appreciation of the Canadian dollar further challenged these firms, as foreign buyers reduced their demand for more expensive Canadian-made products.

Regional and sectoral differences highlight an inherent difficulty with monetary policy in a country as economically diverse as Canada. Because there must be a single monetary policy for the nation as a whole (as long as all parts of Canada continue to use the same currency), policy must be guided by the *average* level of economic activity in order to keep the *average* rate of inflation close to its target. But significant differences in economic activity across regions and/or sectors mean that many people will feel that monetary policy is being conducted inappropriately because economic activity in their specific region or sector is not the same as the national average.

Financial Crisis and Recession: 2007–Present

The next significant phase of Canadian monetary policy was determined largely by events taking place in other countries. From 2002 to 2006, U.S. housing prices had been rising unusually rapidly, but they began to slow their ascent in the middle of 2006. In 2007, these prices reached their peak and then collapsed, falling by more than 30 percent in many parts of the country. On a large scale, U.S. homeowners began "walking away" from their houses, whose market values had fallen below the total amount owing on the associated mortgages. In these situations, the financial institution holding the mortgage no longer receives regular mortgage payments from the homeowner and instead takes ownership of the vacated house.

For the many financial institutions that held the mortgages—or the mortgage-backed securities—the housing collapse led to a significant decline in the value of their assets. It soon became clear that millions of U.S. mortgages and mortgage-backed securities had been bought by financial institutions all over the world, and thus many large financial institutions in many countries were soon on the edge of insolvency and bankruptcy. What began as a collapse of U.S. housing prices soon became a global financial crisis.

Mark Carney became the new governor of the Bank of Canada in February 2008, just as the financial crisis was entering its most serious phase. With the collapse of major U.S. and U.K. financial institutions only a few months later, panic spread throughout the world's financial sector. It was unclear which institutions held large amounts of these "toxic" mortgage-backed securities and thus which institutions were in danger of going under. In this setting, the widespread fear of "counterparty risk" led to a virtual disappearance of short-term interbank lending. The flow of credit declined, and most lending that did take place was

Mark Carney became the Bank of Canada's governor in early 2008, amid a global financial crisis and the beginning of a significant economic recession.

transacted at much higher interest rates. Given the importance of credit in a market economy, restoring the flow of credit was essential to maintaining the level of economic activity.

In Canada, it soon became clear that Canadian banks were far less exposed to these "toxic" mortgage-backed securities than were the banks in the United States and much of Europe. As a result, there was no significant danger of a Canadian bank becoming insolvent during this episode. However, the globalized nature of financial markets implies that short-term credit markets in Canada are highly integrated with those in other countries, with the result that Canada also experienced a decline in interbank lending and a rise in short-term interest rates. As we discussed in *Applying Economic Concepts 29-1* on page 735, the Bank of Canada took two sets of actions during 2007–2008. First, it reduced its target for the overnight rate by more than 3.5 percentage points between the fall of 2007 and the end of 2008. Second, it eased the terms with which it was prepared to make short-term loans to financial institutions. Both sets of actions were designed to restore the flow of credit and reduce interest rates, thus helping to maintain the level of economic activity.

By late in 2008, however, it was clear that Canada would not be shielded from the global recession that was then beginning. The global financial crisis had a dramatic effect on the level of economic activity in the United States, the European Union, and many countries in Asia. With these economies experiencing recessions, there was a sharp decline in demand for Canada's exports. Canadian real GDP slowed sharply in late 2008 and began to fall in early 2009. The Bank of Canada's objective at this time was to provide as much monetary stimulus as was possible, complementing the large fiscal stimulus implemented by the Canadian government in its budget of 2009.

By the spring of 2009, however, the Bank of Canada was up against a wall—or, more literally, a floor. Having reduced its target for the overnight interest rate to 0.25 percent, it would not be able to reduce it further should that be necessary. It had reached what economists refer to as the "nominal interest rate floor." The Bank announced that, should further monetary stimulus be needed, it was prepared to embark on policies of either "quantitative easing" or "credit easing." Quantitative easing would involve the Bank directly purchasing government securities in a way that increases reserves in the banking system—a conventional open-market purchase of government bonds. Credit easing would involve the Bank purchasing private-sector bonds in an attempt to improve liquidity in specific segments of the financial market.

By early 2010, the Bank had not yet implemented these policies. But it did make a public commitment to keep its target for the overnight interest rate constant at 0.25 percent until such a time as the threat of rising inflation would require it to begin tightening its monetary policy.

Ⅹ myeconlab   ADDITIONAL TOPICS

With the success of many central banks in maintaining low and stable inflation, some economists have raised the concern that inflation may now be "too low," and that the economy may actually function more smoothly with slightly higher inflation. For more details about this contentious debate, look for **Can Inflation Be Too Low?** in the *Additional Topics* section of this book's MyEconLab.

www.myeconlab.com

Summary

29.1 How the Bank of Canada Implements Monetary Policy

- Monetary policy can be conducted either by setting the money supply or by setting the interest rate. But for a given negatively sloped M_D curve, both cannot be set independently.
- Because of its incomplete control over the money supply, as well as the uncertainty regarding both the slope and the position of the M_D curve, the Bank chooses to implement its policy by setting the interest rate.
- The Bank's policy instrument is the target it sets for the overnight interest rate. By offering to lend funds at a rate 25 basis points above this target (the bank rate) and to accept deposits on which it pays interest at 25 basis

points below the target, the Bank of Canada can control the actual overnight interest rate.
- Changes in the Bank's target for the overnight rate lead to changes in the actual overnight rate and also to changes in longer-term market interest rates. The various steps in the monetary transmission mechanism then come into play.
- The Bank of Canada conducts an expansionary monetary policy by reducing its target for the overnight interest rate. It conducts a contractionary monetary policy by raising its target for the overnight interest rate.

29.2 Inflation Targeting

- Many central banks have come to accept two propositions:

  1. High inflation is damaging to the economy.
  2. The long-run effects of monetary policy are mainly on the price level (or rate of inflation), and sustained inflation is ultimately generated by monetary policy.

  As a result, many central banks have adopted formal inflation targets.
- The Bank of Canada's formal inflation target is the rate of CPI inflation. It seeks to keep the annual inflation rate at 2 percent.

- In the short run, the Bank closely monitors the output gap. By tightening its policy during an inflationary gap (and loosening it during a recessionary gap), the Bank can keep the rate of inflation near 2 percent.
- The policy of inflation targeting helps to stabilize the economy. The Bank responds to positive shocks with a contractionary policy and responds to negative shocks with an expansionary policy.
- Two technical issues complicate the conduct of monetary policy:

  1. Volatile food and energy prices
  2. Changes in the exchange rate

29.3 Long and Variable Lags

- Though the Bank of Canada can change interest rates very quickly, it takes time for firms and households to change their expenditure. Even once those new plans are carried out, it takes time for the multiplier process to work its way through the economy, eventually increasing equilibrium national income.

- Long and variable lags in monetary policy lead many economists to argue that the Bank should not try to "fine-tune" the economy. Instead, it should respond only to shocks that are significant in size and persistent in duration.

29.4 Thirty Years of Canadian Monetary Policy

- In the early 1980s, the Bank of Canada embarked on a policy of tight money to reduce inflation. This policy contributed to the severity of the recession.
- A sustained economic recovery occurred from 1983 to 1987. The main challenge for monetary policy during this time was to create sufficient liquidity to accommodate the recovery without triggering a return to the

high inflation rates that prevailed at the start of the decade.
- In 1988, when inflation was between 4 and 5 percent, the Bank of Canada announced that monetary policy would henceforth be guided by the long-term goal of "price stability." By 1992, the Bank's tight money policy had reduced inflation to below 2 percent.

- Controversy concerned two issues. First, was the cost in terms of lost output and heavy unemployment worth the benefits of lower inflation? Second, could the low inflation rate be sustained?
- This controversy was partly responsible for the 1994 change in the Bank of Canada's governor, from John Crow to Gordon Thiessen. Despite this administrative change, the stated policy of price stability continued. By 2000, the rate of inflation had been around 2 percent for about seven years.
- Following the stock-market declines in 2000–2001 and the terrorist attacks in the United States in September 2001, the Bank of Canada and the U.S. Federal Reserve dramatically reduced their policy interest rates in an attempt to prevent a recession.

- In the 2002–2005 period, the main challenges for the Bank involved determining the relative strength of the two different forces leading to a substantial appreciation of the Canadian dollar. By summer of 2006, the Bank had increased its target for the overnight interest rate by two percentage points, to a level still below its previous peak in the summer of 2000.
- The onset of the global financial crisis led the Bank of Canada to implement policies designed to restore the flow of credit and also to reduce interest rates.
- By early 2009 the Canadian economy had been dragged into recession by a collapse in global demand. After the Bank reduced its target for the overnight rate to 0.25 percent, it announced that it was prepared to implement policies of "quantitative or credit easing," if necessary.

Key Concepts

Money supply vs. the interest rate
Overnight interest rate
The target overnight interest rate
The bank rate

Endogenous money supply
Open-market operations
Inflation targeting
CPI inflation vs. core inflation

The exchange rate and monetary
  policy
Lags in the effect of monetary policy

Study Exercises

myeconlab   SAVE TIME. IMPROVE RESULTS.

Visit MyEconLab to practise Study Exercises and prepare for tests and exams.
MyEconLab also offers a variety of other study tools to help you succeed.
www.myeconlab.com

1. Fill in the blanks to make the following statements correct.

   a. In general, there are two approaches to implementing monetary policy. The central bank can attempt to influence _____ directly or to influence _____ directly.

   b. The Bank of Canada chooses to implement its monetary policy by influencing the _____ directly. The Bank then uses _____ to accommodate the resulting change in money demand.

   c. The Bank of Canada does not try to influence the money supply directly because (1) the Bank cannot control the process of _____ carried out by the commercial banks; (2) the Bank is unsure about

   the change in _____ that would result from a change in the money supply; (3) the Bank is unsure of the position of the _____ curve at any given time.

2. Fill in the blanks to make the following statements correct.

   a. The interest rate that commercial banks charge each other for overnight loans is called the _____.

   b. The bank rate is _____ points above the target overnight interest rate. At this rate, the Bank stands ready to _____ to commercial banks. At a rate _____ points below the target, the Bank stands ready to _____ from commercial banks (and pay that rate as interest).

c. The Bank of Canada can change the amount of currency in circulation through _____. The Bank conducts these transactions to accommodate the changing demand for _____ by the commercial banks.

d. An expansionary monetary policy is one where the Bank of Canada _____ its target for the overnight interest rate. A contractionary monetary policy is one in which the Bank _____ its target for the overnight interest rate.

e. If the Bank of Canada wants to stimulate aggregate demand it can implement a(n) _____ monetary policy by _____ its target for the overnight interest rate. If the Bank wants to dampen aggregate demand it can implement a(n) _____ monetary policy by _____ its target for the overnight interest rate.

3. Fill in the blanks to make the following statements correct.

a. The long-run policy target for the Bank of Canada is the _____. The current target is to keep the inflation rate at _____ percent.

b. In the short run, the Bank of Canada closely monitors the _____.

c. It is not possible for the Bank of Canada to independently influence the following two variables: _____ and _____. The Bank of Canada conducts its policy by announcing a change in the _____. It then conducts the necessary _____ in order to make this rate an equilibrium in the money market.

d. The conduct of monetary policy is made more difficult because of lags. Two reasons for these time lags are

• _____

• _____

e. Economists have estimated that a change in monetary policy has an effect on real GDP after a period of _____ months and an effect on the price level after a period of _____ months.

f. Because of the long time lags involved in the execution of monetary policy, it is very possible that the policy may in fact have a _____ effect on the economy.

4. Read *Applying Economic Concepts 29-1* (page 735), which discusses the Bank of Canada's open-market operations and how these influence the amount of currency in circulation in the Canadian economy. Using simplified balance sheets like the ones shown below, suppose that a commercial bank uses $100 000 of excess cash reserves to purchase a government bond from the Bank of Canada.

a. What are the immediate effects on assets and liabilities for the commercial bank? Fill in the left-hand table.

b. What are the changes for the Bank of Canada? Fill in the right-hand table.

c. Explain what has happened to the amount of currency in circulation.

Commercial Bank		Bank of Canada	
Assets	Liabilities	Assets	Liabilities
Reserves	Deposits	Bonds	Commercial bank deposits
Bonds			Currency

5. In the text we stated that the Bank of Canada's long-run policy target is the rate of inflation.

a. What are the two propositions that have led many central banks to choose this long-run policy target?

b. How does the idea of long-run money neutrality relate to this choice of policy target?

c. The Bank of Canada closely monitors the level of real GDP and the output gap in the short run. How does it use this information in pursuit of its long-run policy of targeting the rate of inflation at 2 percent?

d. If monetary policy had sustained and systematic effects on real economic variables, do you think the Bank might choose a different long-run policy target? Explain.

6. The diagram below shows the demand for money and the supply of money.

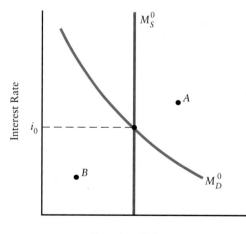

a. Explain why it is not possible for the Bank of Canada to set the money supply and the interest rate at point A or at point B.

b. In the diagram, draw a new money demand curve, M_D^1, to the right of M_D^0. Suppose the MD curve is shifting in unpredictable ways between M_D^0 and M_D^1. Why is a monetary policy that sets the interest rate more stable (and therefore preferable) to one that sets the money supply?

c. The Bank of Canada implements its monetary policy by setting the target for the overnight interest rate. If the Bank reduces its target, explain what happens to the amount of money in the economy. What is the role of open-market operations in the Bank's policy?

7. Milton Friedman was for many years a professor of economics at the University of Chicago and was the most influential Monetarist of his generation. He was known for accusing the Federal Reserve (the U.S. central bank) of following "an unstable monetary policy," arguing that although the Federal Reserve "has given lip service to controlling the quantity of money . . . it has given its heart to controlling interest rates."

a. Explain why, if the M_D function were approximately stable, targeting the growth rate in the money supply would produce a "stable" monetary policy. Show this in a diagram.

b. Explain why, if the M_D function moves suddenly and in unpredictable ways, targeting the money supply produces an "unstable" monetary policy. Show this in a diagram.

c. The Bank of Canada conducts its policy by setting short-term interest rates. What is the implication for this policy of an "unstable" M_D function?

8. Suppose it is mid-2007 and the stock market has been growing rapidly for the past five years. Some economists argue that the stock market has become "overvalued" and thus a "crash" is imminent.

a. How does a rising stock market affect aggregate demand? Show this in an *AD/AS* diagram.

b. For a central bank that is trying to keep real GDP close to potential, explain what challenges are posed by a rapidly rising stock market.

c. Suppose the stock market "crashes," falling suddenly by approximately 35 percent as it did in the fall of 2008. How does this affect aggregate demand? Show this in an *AD/AS* diagram.

9. Consider the relationship among exchange-rate changes, aggregate demand, and monetary policy. Assume we begin in a situation with real GDP equal to Y^*.

a. Suppose the world price for raw materials rises because of growing demand for these products. Given that Canada is a net exporter of raw materials, what is the likely effect on Canadian aggregate demand? Show this in an *AD/AS* diagram (assuming no change in the exchange rate).

b. Suppose instead that there is an increase in the demand by foreigners for Canadian financial assets such as government bonds. What is the direct effect on Canadian aggregate demand? Show this in an *AD/AS* diagram (assuming again no change in the exchange rate).

c. Both of the shocks described above are likely to cause an appreciation of the Canadian dollar on foreign-exchange markets. As the Canadian dollar appreciates, what are the effects on aggregate demand in part (a) and in part (b)? Show these "secondary" effects in your diagram and explain.

d. Given your answers to parts (a), (b), and (c), explain why the appropriate monetary policy response to a change in the exchange rate depends crucially on the *cause* of the exchange-rate change. What are the appropriate responses to each of the shocks (assuming they occur separately)?

Discussion Questions

1. It is often said that an expansionary monetary policy is like "pushing on a string." What is meant by this statement? How does this contrast with a contractionary monetary policy?

2. In 1988, the Bank of Canada announced that it was committed to achieving "price stability," but it did not commit itself to a particular target growth rate for any monetary aggregate that would be consistent with achieving its price stability target. Why do you think it failed to make such a commitment?

3. In the last few years, the path of CPI inflation has deviated from the path of core inflation several times (see Figure 29-5 on page 742). Why is core inflation less volatile than CPI inflation, and why might the Bank focus more on core inflation during some periods?

4. Suppose the Canadian economy has real GDP equal to potential and that nothing significant is expected to change in the near future. Then the Canadian dollar suddenly depreciates—apparently permanently—by 5 percent against the U.S. dollar. Explain why the appropriate response of monetary policy depends on the *cause* of the depreciation. In particular, make a distinction between

a. A depreciation caused by a reduction in demand for Canadian exports of raw materials; and

b. A depreciation caused by a reduction in demand for Canadian bonds that are now perceived as less attractive than U.S. bonds.

5. Consider a situation in which the Bank decides to lower its target for the overnight interest rate (an expansionary

monetary policy). But at the same time, there is an unpredicted reduction in the demand for money.

a. Explain why the money supply is said to be endogenous when the Bank implements its policy by setting the interest rate.

b. Following the Bank's expansionary policy, and the simultaneous reduction in money demand, what is the overall effect on the money supply? What does the answer depend on?

c. If the money supply were to fall in this case, why would we still call this an expansionary monetary policy?

6. During the financial crisis of 2007–2008, the Bank of Canada took extraordinary actions to inject liquidity into the banking system. As a result, the amount of reserves in the banking system increased significantly, even though the measures of the money supply increased only modestly. Discuss the motivations of the Bank of Canada during this period, the connection between reserves and the money supply, and the possible future effect on inflation from the large change in reserves.

Inflation and Disinflation

If you are a typical reader of this book, you were born around 1990. By the time you were old enough to notice some economic developments going on around you, it was almost the turn of the century. By that time, the rate of inflation in Canada was about 2 percent per year and had been at that level for almost a decade. Thus, unless you are older than the typical student taking a course in introductory economics, or you have come to Canada recently from a high-inflation country, inflation has not been a significant phenomenon in your life. It was not so long ago, however, that inflation was considered to be a serious problem in Canada (and many other countries as well). Even though high inflation in Canada is no longer a "headline" issue, understanding the process of inflation, and how it can be reduced, is central to understanding why the Bank of Canada is so committed to keeping inflation low.

FIGURE 30-1   Canadian CPI Inflation, 1965–2009

(*Source:* Based on authors' calculations using data from the Bank of Canada, www.bankofcanada.ca, Series PCPISA. For each month, the inflation rate is computed as the percentage change from the CPI 12 months earlier.)

Recall that **inflation** is a rise in the average level of prices—that is, a rise in the price level. Figure 30-1 shows the rate of CPI inflation in Canada since 1965 and shows what is often called the "twin peaks" of inflation. Rising from the mid-1960s, inflation peaked in 1974 at more than 12 percent, fell and then peaked again in 1981 at almost 13 percent, and then started its long but bumpy decline to its current level at around 2 percent, the midpoint of the Bank of Canada's official target band.

This bumpy path for the rate of inflation nicely illustrates one of the reasons that inflation is a problem for the economy. As we mentioned in Chapter 19, economists make the distinction between *anticipated* and *unanticipated* inflation, and we showed why unanticipated inflation is the more serious problem. If firms and workers have difficulty predicting what inflation will be, they have problems determining how wages and prices should be set. The result will be unexpected changes in real wages and relative prices as inflation ends up being different from what was expected. These inflation-induced changes in real wages and relative prices lead to changes in the allocation of resources. As you can imagine by looking at Figure 30-1, many of the changes in inflation between 1965 and 2009 were sudden and thus difficult to predict. To avoid this uncertainty in the economy, the Bank of Canada now strives to keep inflation both *low* and *stable*, near the official target of 2 percent. The result is an environment in which firms, workers, and households can more easily make plans for the future, secure in the knowledge that real wages, real interest rates, and relative prices will not be significantly affected by a volatile inflation rate.

What causes inflation? How can it be eliminated? And why are policies designed to reduce inflation so controversial? These are the central topics of this chapter.

inflation A rise in the average level of all prices. Usually expressed as the annual percentage change in the Consumer Price Index.

To compute the total inflation since the day of your birth to today, check out the "Inflation Calculator" at the Bank of Canada's website: **www.bankofcanada.ca.** *Click on "Monetary Policy" and then "Inflation."*

30.1 Adding Inflation to the Model

In the previous several chapters we examined the effects of shocks to aggregate demand and aggregate supply. In our macroeconomic model, *AD* and *AS* shocks influenced the values of both real GDP and the price level. Following these shocks, the economy's adjustment process always pushed the economy back toward the potential level of real GDP with a stable price level. In other words, any inflation that we have so far seen in our macroeconomic model was temporary—it existed only while the economy was adjusting toward its long-run equilibrium.

In this chapter we need to modify our model to explain how a *sustained* and *constant* inflation can exist. After all, even though inflation in Canada is very low, it still appears to be sustained and relatively constant at a rate of about 2 percent per year.

As we will soon see, one of the keys to understanding sustained inflation is to understand the role of *inflation expectations*. When combined with excess demand or excess supply, as reflected by the economy's output gap, such expectations give us a more complete understanding of why wages (and therefore prices) change. Let's begin our analysis by examining in more detail why wages change.

Why Wages Change

In Chapter 24, when we examined the economy's adjustment process, we saw that increases in wages led to increases in unit costs—because we maintained the assumption that technology (and thus productivity) was held constant. We continue with that assumption in this chapter. Thus, as wages and other factor prices rise, unit costs increase and the *AS* curve shifts up. Conversely, when wages and other factor prices fall, unit costs fall and the *AS* curve shifts down.

What are the forces that cause wages to change? The two main forces are the output gap and expectations of future inflation.[1] Much of what we discuss in the case of the output gap was first seen in Chapter 24, but the points are important enough to bear repeating.

---

[1] Wages may be affected by other forces that are associated with neither output gaps nor expectations of inflation, such as government guidelines, union power, and employers' optimism. Because there are many such forces that tend to act independently of one another, they may be regarded as random shocks and must be analyzed as separate causes for shifts in the *AS* curve.

Wages and the Output Gap In Chapter 24, we encountered three propositions about how changes in money wages were influenced by the output gap:

1. The excess demand for labour that is associated with an inflationary gap ($Y > Y^*$) puts upward pressure on money wages.

2. The excess supply of labour associated with a recessionary gap ($Y < Y^*$) puts downward pressure on money wages.

3. The absence of either an inflationary or a recessionary gap ($Y = Y^*$) means that demand forces do not exert any pressure on money wages.[2]

When real GDP is equal to Y^*, the unemployment rate is said to be equal to the NAIRU, which stands for the *non-accelerating inflation rate of unemployment*. The use of this particular name will be explained later in this chapter. Another name sometimes used in place of NAIRU is the *natural rate of unemployment*, but NAIRU is now the more common usage. It is designated by the symbol U^*.

The NAIRU is not zero. Instead, even when $Y = Y^*$, there may be a substantial amount of *frictional* and *structural* unemployment caused, for example, by the movement of people between jobs or between regions. When real output exceeds potential output ($Y > Y^*$), the unemployment rate will be less than the NAIRU ($U < U^*$). When real output is less than potential output ($Y < Y^*$), the unemployment rate will exceed the NAIRU ($U > U^*$).

We have assumed that wages react to various pressures of demand. These demand pressures can be stated either in terms of the relationship between actual and potential output or in terms of the relationship between the actual unemployment rate and the NAIRU. When $Y > Y^*$ (or $U < U^*$), there is an inflationary gap characterized by excess demand for labour, and wages are assumed to rise. Conversely, when $Y < Y^*$ (or $U > U^*$), there is a recessionary gap characterized by excess supply of labour, and wages are assumed to fall.

This relationship between the excess demand or supply of labour and the rate of change of money wages is represented by the Phillips curve, which we first discussed in Chapter 24.

Wages and Expected Inflation A second force that can influence wages is *expectations* of future inflation. Suppose both employers and employees expect 3 percent inflation next year. Workers will start negotiations from a base of a 3 percent increase in money wages, which would hold their *real wages* constant. Firms will also be inclined to begin bargaining by conceding at least a 3 percent increase in money wages because they expect that the prices at which they sell their products will rise by 3 percent. Starting from that base, workers may attempt to obtain some desired increase in their real wages. At this point, such factors as profits and bargaining power become important.

> **The expectation of some specific inflation rate creates pressure for money wages to rise by that rate.**

Practise with Study Guide
Chapter 30, Extension
Exercise 1.

The key point is that money wages can be rising even if no inflationary gap is present. As long as people *expect* prices to rise, their behaviour will put upward pressure

---

[2] As in Chapter 24, we are assuming that productivity is constant in our analysis in this chapter. Otherwise, output gaps would cause changes in wages *relative to productivity*.

rational expectations The theory that people understand how the economy works and learn quickly from their mistakes so that even though random errors may be made, systematic and persistent errors are not.

on money wages. Indeed, in every year since the Second World War, average nominal wages have increased in Canada, even though in some years there were notable recessionary gaps. The reason is that in every year the price level was expected to increase (and did, in fact, increase). Clarifying the distinction between these two separate forces on wages is an important objective of this chapter.

The central role for the *expectations* of future inflation suggests the importance of examining how firms and workers *form* their expectations. This has been a very active area of research within macroeconomics. *Applying Economic Concepts 30-1* discusses the formation of expectations and explains the important difference between *backward-looking* and *forward-looking* expectations.

APPLYING ECONOMIC CONCEPTS 30-1

How Do People Form Their Expectations?

The way in which firms and workers form their expectations about future inflation may have an important effect on that inflation. Generally, we can distinguish two main patterns: One is to look backward at past experience; the other is to look at current circumstances for a clue as to what may happen in the near future.

The first type of expectations are called *backward-looking*. People look at the past in order to predict what will happen in the future. The simplest possible form of such expectations is to expect the past to be repeated in the future. According to this view, if inflation has been 5 percent over the past year, people will expect it to be 5 percent next year. This expectation, however, is quite naïve. Everyone knows that the inflation rate does change, and therefore the past cannot be a perfectly accurate guide to the future.

A less naïve version has people revising their expectations in light of the mistakes that they made in estimating inflation in the past. For example, if you thought that this year's inflation rate was going to be 5 percent but it turned out to be only 3 percent, you might revise your estimate of next year's rate down somewhat from 5 percent.

Backward-looking expectations tend to change slowly because some time must pass before a change in the actual rate of inflation provides enough past experience to cause expectations to adjust.

The second main type of expectations are those that look to current economic conditions to estimate what is likely to happen in the future. One version of this type assumes that people look to the government's current macroeconomic policy to form their expectations of future inflation. They are assumed to understand how the economy works, and they form their expectations by predicting the outcome of the policies now being followed. In an obvious sense, such expectations are *forward-looking*.

A strong version of forward-looking expectations is called **rational expectations**. Rational expectations are not necessarily always correct; rather, the *rational expectations hypothesis* assumes that people make the best possible use of all the information available to them. One implication is that they will not continue to make persistent, systematic errors when forming their expectations. Thus, if the economic system about which they are forming expectations remains stable, their expectations will be correct *on average*. Sometimes next year's inflation rate will turn out to be above what people expected it to be; at other times, it will turn out to be below what people expected it to be. On average over many years, however, the actual rate will not, according to the rational expectations theory, be consistently under- or overestimated.

Forward-looking expectations can adjust quickly to changes in events. Instead of being based on past inflation rates, expected inflation is based on expected economic conditions and government policies.

Assuming that expectations are solely backward-looking seems overly naïve. People do look ahead and assess future possibilities rather than just blindly reacting to what has gone before. Yet the assumption of "fully rational" forward-looking expectations requires workers and firms to have a degree of understanding of the economy that few economists would claim to have. The actual process of wage setting probably combines forward-looking behaviour with expectations based on the experience of the recent past. Depending on the circumstances, expectations will sometimes tend to rely more on past experience and at other times more on present events whose effects are expected to influence the future.

Overall Effect on Wages We can now think of changes in money wages as resulting from two different forces:

$$\begin{array}{ccc} \text{Change in} \\ \text{money wages} \end{array} = \begin{array}{c} \text{Output-gap} \\ \text{effect} \end{array} + \begin{array}{c} \text{Expectational} \\ \text{effect} \end{array}$$

What happens to wages is the *net* effect of the two forces. Consider two examples. First, suppose both labour and management expect 3 percent inflation next year and are therefore willing to allow money wages to increase by 3 percent. Doing so would leave *real* wages unchanged. Suppose as well that there is a significant inflationary gap with an associated labour shortage. The excess demand for labour causes wages to rise by an additional 2 percentage points. The final outcome is that wages rise by 5 percent, the net effect of a 3 percent increase caused by expected inflation and a 2 percent increase caused by the excess demand for labour when $Y > Y^*$.

For the second example, assume again that expected inflation is 3 percent, but this time there is a recessionary gap. The associated high unemployment represents an excess supply of labour that exerts downward pressure on wage bargains. Hence, the output-gap effect now works to dampen wage increases, say, to the extent of 2 percentage points. Wages therefore rise only by 1 percent, the net effect of a 3 percent increase caused by expected inflation and a 2 percent *decrease* caused by the excess supply of labour when $Y < Y^*$.

From Wages to Prices

We saw in Chapters 23 and 24 that shifts in the *AS* curve depend on what happens to factor prices. We have just seen that output gaps and expectations of future inflation put pressure on wages to change and hence cause the *AS* curve to shift.

> The net effect of the two forces acting on wages—output gaps and inflation expectations—determines what happens to the *AS* curve.

If the net effect of the output-gap effect and the expectational effect is to raise wages, then the *AS* curve will shift up. This shift will cause the price level to rise—that is, the forces pushing up wages will be *inflationary*. On the other hand, if the net effect of the output-gap effect and the expectational effect is to reduce wages, the *AS* curve will shift down—the forces reducing wages will be *deflationary*.

Since anything that leads to higher wages will shift the *AS* curve up and lead to higher prices, we can decompose inflation caused by wage increases into two component parts: *output-gap inflation* and *expected inflation*. But because the *AS* curve can also shift for reasons unrelated to changes in wages, we must add a third element. Specifically, we must consider the effect of non-wage supply shocks on the *AS* curve and thus on the price level. The best example of a non-wage supply shock is a change in the prices of raw materials. We can then decompose actual inflation into its three component parts:

$$\begin{array}{c} \text{Actual} \\ \text{inflation} \end{array} = \begin{array}{c} \text{Output-gap} \\ \text{inflation} \end{array} + \begin{array}{c} \text{Expected} \\ \text{inflation} \end{array} + \begin{array}{c} \text{Supply-shock} \\ \text{inflation} \end{array}$$

For example, consider an economy that begins with real GDP equal to potential GDP and expectations of inflation are zero. In this case, the first two terms on the right-hand side are zero. But if an adverse supply shock then occurs, such as a significant increase in the price of imported raw materials, the *AS* curve shifts up and the price level rises.

Actual inflation will be positive. As we will see later in the chapter, such supply shocks are not uncommon, and they generate challenges for the Bank of Canada in its attempt to maintain low inflation.

Having discussed the component parts of inflation, we are now in a position to see how constant inflation can be included in our macroeconomic model.

Constant Inflation

*The Conference Board of Canada conducts a regular survey about people's expectations about inflation. See its website at **www.conferenceboard.ca**.*

Suppose the inflation rate is 2 percent per year and has been 2 percent for several years. This is what we mean by a *constant* inflation. In such a setting, people with backward-looking expectations about inflation will expect the actual level to continue into the future. Furthermore, in the absence of any announcements that the central bank will be attempting to alter its monetary policy, people with forward-looking expectations will expect the actual inflation rate to continue. Thus, for the economy as a whole, the expected rate of inflation will equal the actual rate of inflation.

> If inflation and monetary policy have been constant for several years, the expected rate of inflation will tend to equal the actual rate of inflation.

Suppose there are no supply shocks (we address these later in the chapter). Since actual inflation equals expected inflation, it immediately follows from the equation above that there can be *no* output gap—real GDP must equal its potential level, Y^*.

> In the absence of supply shocks, if expected inflation equals actual inflation, real GDP must be equal to potential GDP.

Figure 30-2 shows a constant inflation in the *AD/AS* diagram. What is causing this inflation? As we will see, such a constant inflation requires both the *expectations* of inflation (which shift the *AS* curve) and the continuing expansion of the money supply by the central bank (which shifts the *AD* curve). Let's see how this works.

Suppose both workers and employers expect 2 percent inflation over the coming years and that employers are therefore prepared to increase nominal wages by 2 percent per year. As wages rise by 2 percent, the *AS* curve shifts up by that amount. But in order for 2 percent to be the *actual* rate of inflation, the intersection of the *AS* and *AD* curves must be shifting up at the rate of 2 percent. This requires the *AD* curve to be shifting up at the same 2 percent rate—this *AD* shift is caused by the growth of the money supply. So in this case there is no output-gap inflation ($Y = Y^*$), and actual and expected inflation are equal. When the central bank increases the

FIGURE 30-2 Constant Inflation with No Supply Shocks

In the *AD/AS* model with no supply shocks, constant inflation is only possible when $Y = Y^*$. Expectations of a constant rate of inflation cause wages and thus the *AS* curve to shift upward at a uniform rate from AS_0 to AS_1 to AS_2. Monetary validation is causing the *AD* curve to shift upward at the same time from AD_0 to AD_1 to AD_2. As a result, real GDP remains at Y^* as the economy moves from equilibrium E_0 to E_1 to E_2 and so on. The constant inflation rate takes the price level from P_0 to P_1 to P_2. Wage costs are rising because of expectations of inflation, and these expectations are being validated by the central bank.

money supply at such a rate that the expectations of inflation end up being correct, it is said to be *validating* the expectations.

> **Constant inflation with $Y = Y^*$ occurs when the rate of monetary growth, the rate of wage increase, and the expected rate of inflation are all consistent with the actual inflation rate.**

The key point about constant inflation in our macro model is that there is no output-gap effect operating on wages. Wages rise at the expected rate of inflation. Expansions of the money supply validate those expectations.

Note that in this constant-inflation equilibrium, interest rates are being kept stable by two equal but offsetting forces. The central bank is increasing the money supply, which tends to push interest rates down. But at the same time, rising prices are increasing the demand for money and pushing interest rates up. In equilibrium, the monetary policy is just expansionary enough to accommodate the growing money demand, thus leaving interest rates unchanged. As we will see later in this chapter, in order to *reduce* the rate of inflation, the central bank must implement a contractionary monetary policy—by reducing the growth rate of the money supply sufficiently to raise interest rates.

Figure 30-2 can be used to analyze any constant (and positive) rate of inflation. It can also be used to analyze the case of *deflation*, a situation in which the price level is falling so that the inflation rate is negative. In this case, the AD and AS curves would be shifting down at a constant rate, keeping $Y = Y^*$. *Applying Economic Concepts 30-2* discusses deflation, the reasons that some people seem to fear its effect on the economy, and why these fears may be misplaced.

30.2 Shocks and Policy Responses

A constant rate of inflation is a special case in our macroeconomic model because the rising price level is not caused by an inflationary output gap. In many cases of inflation, however, inflationary pressure is initially created by an aggregate demand or supply shock. In this section we examine how AS and AD shocks affect inflation and the subsequent effects of the policy responses chosen by the central bank.

Before we do so, however, recall an assumption we made in Chapter 28 when we discussed the long-run effects of monetary policy. In that chapter we assumed the level of potential output to be independent of the path of real GDP. Thus, shocks that led to shifts in the AD or AS curves, and thus led to short-run changes in the level of real GDP, were assumed to have no influence on the level of potential output, Y^*.

We continue with that assumption in this chapter, but note that we can alternatively state the assumption in terms of the NAIRU, U^*. Specifically, we assume that the path of the actual unemployment rate does not affect the value of U^*, which is instead determined by various policy and institutional factors that we explore in detail in the next chapter. As in Chapter 28, the implication of this assumption is that, following AD or AS shocks, the economy's adjustment process eventually returns real GDP and unemployment to their unchanged levels of Y^* and U^*, respectively. As we first noted in Chapter 28, this assumption is controversial. In Western European countries, in particular, there is some empirical evidence to the contrary. But in Canada and the United States, the weight of evidence supports the assumption made in this book that Y^* and U^* are independent of the actual paths taken by Y and U.

Practise with Study Guide
Chapter 30, Short-Answer
Question 2.

Demand Shocks

demand inflation Inflation arising from an inflationary output gap caused, in turn, by a positive *AD* shock.

Any rightward shift in the *AD* curve that creates an inflationary output gap also creates what is called **demand inflation**. The shift in the *AD* curve could have been caused by a reduction in tax rates, by an increase in such autonomous expenditure items as investment, government, and net exports, or by an expansionary monetary policy.

Major demand-shock inflations occurred in Canada during and after the First and Second World Wars. In these cases, large increases in government expenditure without fully offsetting increases in taxes led to general excess demand ($Y > Y^*$). More generally, demand inflation sometimes occurs at the end of a strong upswing, as rising output causes excess demand to develop simultaneously in the markets for labour, intermediate goods, and final output. Demand inflation of this type occurred in Canada in 1989–1990 and to a lesser extent in 2003–2006.

APPLYING ECONOMIC CONCEPTS 30-2

Is Deflation a Problem?

We have discussed how inflation can be incorporated into our basic macroeconomic model. The model can also be used to discuss *deflation,* a situation in which the price level experiences an ongoing decline. For example, a deflation of 2 percent per year means that the price level is falling annually by 2 percent; in other words, deflation means a negative inflation rate.

Deflation is very rare; it has only been experienced a few times in the last century. During the Great Depression, the price level in Canada fell by approximately 25 percent between 1930 and 1933; and when the Japanese economy was growing very slowly in the early 2000s, the price level declined by about 1 percent per year.

In recent years, especially during the recession in 2008 and 2009, it was common to hear media discussion of the dangers of deflation and the need for central banks to take whatever actions were necessary to prevent it. The fear of deflation appears to stem from the belief that deflation causes a decline in economic activity, and this argument is usually based on the evidence drawn from the Great Depression, when real GDP fell by about 30 percent from 1929 to 1933.

How could deflation cause a decline in economic activity? A commonly heard argument is that when prices are falling, firms and consumers delay their spending because they know that prices will be lower in the future. The delay in spending leads to a leftward shift in the *AD* curve and, other things being equal, causes a decline in real GDP.

Economists who reject this line of argument usually make two observations, one about the historical evidence and the other about the proposed link from deflation to recession. First, while it is certainly true that there was significant deflation during the Great Depression, it was probably a *result* rather than a *cause* of the economic events. In this view, a combination of the stock-market crash, widespread bank failures, inappropriate monetary and fiscal policies, and a significant rise in protectionist trade policies caused a major decline in aggregate demand. This decline in turn caused a leftward shift of the *AD* curve, resulting in *both* a decline in real GDP and a decline in the price level (deflation).

The second point relates to the possibility that buyers delay their purchases because of deflation, and that this delay can cause a recession. How important can this effect be? If deflation were 25 percent per year, it is easy to imagine that many firms and consumers would delay some purchases—after all, a saving of 25 percent provides a significant incentive to wait. But this effect is almost absent when deflation is only 1 or 2 percent per year, as it was in Japan during the 1990s. And if this effect is absent, there is no fundamental danger associated with a small deflation.

Consider the opposite situation, that of prices rising by 1 or 2 percent annually. In this situation, do we expect firms and consumers to rush to purchase their products before prices rise, thereby pushing real GDP well above the economy's potential? The answer is no. When inflation is relatively constant at 1 or 2 or 3 percent per year, firms and consumers build it into their expectations, central banks build it into their policy decisions, and the economy can operate with real GDP equal to potential output, as we have shown in this chapter. The same would likely be true of deflation of 1 or 2 percent per year.

To begin our study of demand inflation, we make some simplifying assumptions. First, we assume that Y^* is constant. Second, we assume that there is no ongoing inflation. These two assumptions imply that our starting point is a stable long-run equilibrium, with constant real GDP and price level, rather than the long-run equilibrium with constant inflation as shown in Figure 30-2. We then suppose that this long-run equilibrium is disturbed by a rightward shift in the AD curve. This shift causes the price level and output to rise. It is important next to distinguish between the case in which the Bank of Canada validates the demand shock and the case in which it does not.

No Monetary Validation

Because the initial rise in AD takes output above potential, an inflationary gap opens up. The pressure of excess demand soon causes wages to rise, shifting the AS curve upward as shown in Figure 30-3. As long as the Bank of Canada holds the money supply constant, the rise in the price level moves the economy upward and to the left along the new AD curve, reducing the inflationary gap. Eventually, the gap is eliminated, and equilibrium is established at a higher but stable price level, with output at Y^*. In this case, the initial period of inflation is followed by further inflation that lasts only until the new long-run equilibrium is reached.

Monetary Validation

Suppose that after the demand shock created an inflationary gap, the Bank of Canada chose to attempt to sustain these "good economic times." It would then validate the demand shock by reducing its policy interest rate and allowing the money supply to increase. We illustrate this situation in Figure 30-4.

Two forces are now brought into play. Spurred by the inflationary gap, the increase in wages causes the AS curve to shift upward. Fuelled by the expansionary monetary policy, however, the AD curve shifts further to the right. As a result of both of these shifts, the price level rises, but real GDP remains above Y^*. Indeed, if the shift in the AD curve *exactly* offsets the shift in the AS curve, real GDP and the inflationary gap will remain constant.

> **Continued validation of a demand shock turns what would have been transitory inflation into sustained inflation fuelled by monetary expansion.**

In other words, the Bank of Canada could indeed choose to sustain the "good economic times" characterized by high output and low unemployment. But the result of this choice would be sustained inflation.

Supply Shocks

Any leftward shift in the AS curve that is *not* caused by excess demand in the markets for factors of production creates what is called **supply inflation**.

FIGURE 30-3   A Demand Shock with No Validation

A demand shock that is not validated produces temporary inflation, but the economy's adjustment process eventually restores potential GDP and stable prices. The initial long-run equilibrium is at P_0 and Y^*. A positive demand shock shifts AD_0 to AD_1, generating an inflationary gap. The excess demand puts upward pressure on wages, thus shifting AS_0 to AS_1. There is inflation as the economy moves from E_0 to E_1 to E_2, but at E_2 the price level is stable.

supply inflation Inflation arising from a negative AS shock that is not the result of excess demand in the domestic markets for factors of production.

FIGURE 30-4   A Demand Shock with Validation

Monetary validation of a positive demand shock causes the *AD* curve to shift further to the right, offsetting the upward shift in the *AS* curve and thereby leaving an inflationary gap despite the ever-rising price level. An initial demand shock moves the economy along the path of arrow ①, taking output to Y_1 and the price level to P_1. The resulting inflationary gap then causes the *AS* curve to shift upward. This time, however, the Bank of Canada validates the demand shock by increasing the money supply. As the money supply is increased, the *AD* curve shifts to the right. By the time the aggregate supply curve has reached AS_1, the aggregate demand curve has reached AD_2. The new equilibrium is at E_2. Output remains constant at Y_1, leaving the inflationary gap constant while the price level rises to P_2.

The persistent inflationary gap continues to push the *AS* curve upward, while the continued monetary validation continues to push the *AD* curve to the right. As long as this monetary validation continues, the economy moves along the vertical path of arrow ②.

An example of a supply shock is a rise in the costs of imported raw materials. Another is a rise in domestic wages not due to excess demand in the labour market. The rise in wages may occur, as we saw earlier, because of generally held expectations of future inflation. If both employers and employees expect inflation, money wages are likely to rise in anticipation of that inflation. These shocks cause the *AS* curve to shift upward.[3]

The initial effects of any negative supply shock are that the price level rises while output falls, as shown in Figure 30-5. As with the case of a demand shock, what happens next depends on how the Bank of Canada reacts. If the Bank allows the money supply to increase, it validates the supply shock; if it holds the money supply constant, the shock is not validated.

No Monetary Validation   The upward shift in the *AS* curve in Figure 30-5 causes the price level to rise and pushes output below Y^*, opening up a recessionary gap. Pressure mounts for money wages and other factor prices to fall. As wages and other factor prices fall, unit costs will fall. Consequently, the *AS* curve shifts down, increasing output while reducing the price level. The *AS* curve will continue to shift slowly downward, stopping only when real GDP is returned to Y^* and the price level is returned to its initial value of P_0. Thus, the period of inflation accompanying the original supply shock is eventually reversed until the initial long-run equilibrium is re-established.

A major concern in this case is the speed of the adjustment, which in earlier chapters was referred to as the second asymmetry of aggregate supply. If wages do not fall rapidly in the face of excess supply in the labour market, the adjustment back to potential output can take a long time. For example, suppose the original shock raised firms' costs by 6 percent. To reverse this shock and return real GDP to Y^*, firms' costs must fall by 6 percent. If money wages fell by only 2 percent per year, it would take three years to complete the adjustment.[4]

> Whenever wages and other factor prices fall only slowly in the face of excess supply, the recovery to potential output after a non-validated negative supply shock may take a long time.

Concern that such a lengthy adjustment will occur is often the motive that lies behind the strong pressure on the Bank of Canada to validate negative supply shocks.

---

[3] Recall our discussion in Chapter 24 of how some shocks affect *both* the *AD* and the *AS* curves. A rise in the price of oil is one example; since Canada is a producer and exporter of oil, a rise in the price of oil does represent a positive *AD* shock for Canada. In this discussion we confine ourselves to the effect of the *AS* shift.

[4] Nominal wages rarely fall because there is ongoing productivity growth that offsets the effect on wages of excess supply. But in this chapter we are holding productivity (and thus Y^*) constant so we can focus on the causes and consequences of inflation.

CHAPTER 30: INFLATION AND DISINFLATION   773

Monetary Validation   What happens if the Bank of Canada responds to the negative supply shock by lowering interest rates and allowing the money supply to increase, thus *validating* the shock? The monetary validation shifts the *AD* curve to the right and closes the output gap. As the recessionary gap is eliminated, the price level rises further, rather than falling back to its original value as it did when the supply shock was not validated. These effects are also illustrated in Figure 30-5.

> Monetary validation of a negative supply shock causes the initial rise in the price level to be followed by a further rise, resulting in a higher price level than would occur if the recessionary gap were relied on to reduce factor prices.

The most dramatic example of a supply-shock inflation came in the wake of the first OPEC oil-price shock. In 1974, the member countries of the Organization of the Petroleum Exporting Countries (OPEC) agreed to restrict output. Their action caused a three-fold increase in the price of oil and dramatic increases in the prices of many petroleum-related products, such as fertilizer and chemicals. The resulting increase in industrial costs shifted *AS* curves upward in all industrial countries. At this time, the Bank of Canada validated the supply shock with large increases in the money supply, whereas the Federal Reserve (the U.S. central bank) did not. As the theory predicts, Canada experienced a large increase in its price level but almost no recession, while the United States experienced a much smaller increase in its price level but a deeper recession.

FIGURE 30-5   A Supply Shock with and without Validation

Adverse supply shocks initially raise prices while lowering output. An adverse supply shock causes the *AS* curve to shift upward from AS_0 to AS_1, as shown by arrow ①. Equilibrium is established at E_1. If there is no monetary validation, the reduction in factor prices makes the *AS* curve shift slowly back down to AS_0. If there is monetary validation, the *AD* curve shifts from AD_0 to AD_1, as shown by arrow ②. Equilibrium is re-established at E_2 with output equal to potential output but with a higher price level, P_2.

Is Monetary Validation of Supply Shocks Desirable?   Suppose the Bank of Canada were to validate a negative supply shock and thus prevent what could otherwise be a protracted recession. Expressed in this way, monetary validation sounds like a good policy. Unfortunately, however, there is also a possible cost associated with this policy. The effect of the monetary validation is to extend the period of inflation. If this inflation leads firms and workers to expect *further* inflation, then point E_2 in Figure 30-5 will not be the end of the story. As expectations for further inflation develop, the *AS* curve will continue to shift upward. But if the Bank continues its policy of validation, then the *AD* curve will also continue to shift upward. It may not take long before the economy is in a *wage–price spiral*.

Once started, a wage–price spiral can be halted only if the Bank of Canada stops validating the expectational inflation initially caused by the supply shock. But the longer it waits to do so, the more firmly held will be the *expectations* that it will continue its policy of validating the shocks. These entrenched expectations may cause wages to continue rising even after validation has ceased. Because employers expect prices to rise, they go on granting wage increases. If expectations are entrenched firmly enough, the wage push can continue for quite some time, in spite of the downward pressure caused by the high unemployment associated with the recessionary gap.

For information on OPEC, see its website: **www.opec.org.**

Practise with Study Guide Chapter 30, Exercise 2.

A contract settlement that raises wages for a large number of workers will increase firms' costs and shift the AS curve upward, thus tending to reduce real GDP and raise the price level.

Because of this possibility, many economists argue that the wage–price spiral should not be allowed to begin. One way to ensure that it does not begin is to refuse to validate any supply shock.

> To some economists, caution dictates that negative supply shocks should never be validated, in order to avoid a wage–price spiral. Other economists are willing to risk validation in order to avoid the significant recessions that otherwise accompany the supply shock.

Accelerating Inflation

Consider a situation in which a demand or supply shock increases real GDP above Y^*. For example, a booming U.S. economy may lead to an increase in demand for Canadian goods, thus shifting Canada's AD curve to the right. Or a reduction in the world price of raw materials may reduce firms' costs and shift the Canadian AS curve downward. In both cases, the effect in Canada would be to increase real GDP above Y^*—unemployment is low, businesses are booming, and most people would describe this situation as "good economic times." As we saw in Chapter 29, as real GDP rises above Y^*, the Bank of Canada would normally begin to tighten its monetary policy in order to prevent inflation from rising above its formal target. Some people, however, might argue that the Bank of Canada should not "spoil the party" and instead should allow these boom conditions to continue. What would be the result if the Bank acted to maintain output above Y^*?

acceleration hypothesis
The hypothesis that when real GDP is held above potential, the persistent inflationary gap will cause inflation to accelerate.

What happens to the rate of inflation is predicted by the **acceleration hypothesis**, which says that when the central bank conducts its policy to hold the inflationary gap constant, the actual inflation rate will *accelerate*. The Bank of Canada may start by validating 2 percent inflation, but soon 2 percent will become expected, and given the demand pressure the inflation rate will rise to 3 percent and, if the Bank insists on validating 3 percent, the rate will become 4 percent, and so on, without limit. The process will end only when the Bank ends its policy of validation. Avoiding this possibility of gradually increasing inflation is one important reason that the Bank has adopted a formal (and unchanging) inflation target of 2 percent.

There are several steps in the reasoning behind the acceleration hypothesis. The first concerns the development of inflationary expectations.

Expectational Effects Recall our earlier discussion in this chapter about how actual inflation has three separate causes: output gaps, expectations, and non-wage supply shocks. It is restated here:

$$\frac{\text{Actual}}{\text{inflation}} = \frac{\text{Output-gap}}{\text{inflation}} + \frac{\text{Expected}}{\text{inflation}} + \frac{\text{Supply-shock}}{\text{inflation}}$$

To illustrate the importance of expectations in accelerating inflation, suppose the inflationary output gap creates sufficient excess demand to push up wages by 2 percent per year. As a result, the AS curve will also tend to be shifting upward at 2 percent per year.

When inflation has persisted for some time, however, people will likely come to expect that the inflation will continue. The expectation of 2 percent inflation will tend to push up wages by that amount *in addition to* the demand pressure. As the output-gap effect on wages is augmented by the expectational effect, the *AS* curve will begin to shift upward more rapidly. When expectations are for a 2 percent inflation and demand pressure is also pushing wages up by 2 percent, the overall effect will be a 4 percent increase in wages. Sooner or later, however, 4 percent inflation will come to be expected, and the expectational effect will rise to 4 percent. This new expectational component of 4 percent, when added to the output-gap component, will create an inflation rate of 6 percent. And so this cycle will go on. As long as there is excess demand arising from an inflationary output gap, and as long as actual inflation is equal to the output-gap effect plus the expectational effect, the inflation rate cannot stay constant because expectations will always be revised upward toward the actual inflation rate.

More Rapid Monetary Validation Required The second step in the argument is that if the Bank of Canada still wants to hold the level of output constant above Y^*, it must implement an expansionary monetary policy and allow the growth rate of the money supply to rise. This action is necessary because to hold real GDP constant, the *AD* curve must be shifted at an increasingly rapid pace to offset the increasingly rapid shifts in the *AS* curve, which are driven by the continually rising rate of expected inflation.

An Increasing Rate of Inflation The third step in the argument is that the rate of inflation must now be increasing because of the increasingly rapid upward shifts in both the *AD* and the *AS* curves. The rise in the actual inflation rate will in turn cause an increase in the expected inflation rate. This will then cause the actual inflation rate to increase, which will in turn increase the expected inflation rate, and so on. The net result is a *continually increasing rate of inflation.* Now we see the reason for the name NAIRU. If real GDP is held above Y^* (and thus the unemployment rate is below the NAIRU), the inflation rate tends to accelerate. The NAIRU is therefore the lowest level of sustained unemployment consistent with a *non-accelerating* rate of inflation.

> According to the acceleration hypothesis, as long as an inflationary output gap persists, expectations of inflation will be rising, which will lead to increases in the actual rate of inflation.

The tendency for inflation to accelerate is discussed further in *Extensions in Theory 30-1,* which examines how expected inflation affects the position of the Phillips curve.

Inflation as a Monetary Phenomenon

For many years, a debate among economists concerned the extent to which inflation is a monetary phenomenon. Does it have purely monetary causes—changes in the demand or the supply of money? Does it have purely monetary consequences—only the price level is affected? One slogan that states an extreme position on this issue was popularized many years ago by the late Milton Friedman: "Inflation is *everywhere* and *always* a monetary phenomenon." To consider these issues, let us summarize what we have learned already. First, look at the *causes* of inflation:

- *Cause 1:* On the demand side, anything that shifts the *AD* curve to the right will cause the price level to rise (demand inflation).

Practise with Study Guide
Chapter 30, Exercise 3.

- *Cause 2:* On the supply side, anything that shifts the *AS* curve upward will cause the price level to rise (supply inflation).
- *Cause 3:* Unless continual monetary validation occurs, the increases in the price level must eventually come to a halt.

The first two points tell us that a temporary burst of inflation need not be a monetary phenomenon. It need not have monetary causes, and it need not be accompanied by monetary expansion. The third point tells us that *sustained* inflation *must* be a monetary phenomenon. If a rise in prices is to continue indefinitely, it *must* be accompanied by a monetary policy that allows the money supply to continually increase. This is true regardless of the cause that set the inflation in motion.

Now, let us summarize the *consequences* of inflation, assuming that real GDP was initially at its potential level.

- *Consequence 1:* In the short run, demand inflation tends to be accompanied by an *increase* in real GDP above its potential level.
- *Consequence 2:* In the short run, supply inflation tends to be accompanied by a *decrease* in real GDP below its potential level.
- *Consequence 3:* When all costs and prices are adjusted *fully* (so that real GDP has returned to Y*), shifts in either the *AD* or the *AS* curve leave real GDP unchanged and affect only the price level.

EXTENSIONS IN THEORY 30-1

The Phillips Curve and Accelerating Inflation

As we first saw in Chapter 24, the Phillips curve describes the relationship between unemployment (or output) and the rate of change of wages. The Phillips curve was born in 1958 when Professor A. W. Phillips from the London School of Economics noted a relationship between unemployment and the rate of change of wages over a period of 100 years in the United Kingdom. Phillips was interested in studying the short-run behav-

iour of an economy subjected to cyclical fluctuations. In the years following Phillips's study, however, some economists treated the Phillips curve as establishing a long-term tradeoff between inflation and unemployment.

Suppose the government stabilizes output at Y_1 (and hence the unemployment rate at U_1), as shown by points *A* in the accompanying figures. To do this, it must validate the ensuing wage inflation, which is indicated by $\dot{W}_1$ in

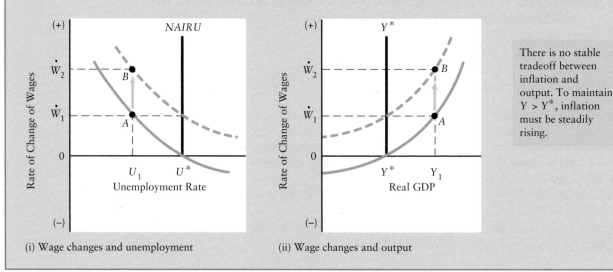

There is no stable tradeoff between inflation and output. To maintain $Y > Y^*$, inflation must be steadily rising.

(i) Wage changes and unemployment

(ii) Wage changes and output

The first two points tell us that inflation is not, in the short run, a purely monetary phenomenon. The third point tells us that inflation is a purely monetary phenomenon from the point of view of long-run equilibrium. There is still plenty of room for debate, however, on how long the short run will last. Most economists believe that the short run can be long enough for inflation to have major real effects on important economic variables, such as the distribution of wealth (which partly explains why most economists believe that keeping inflation low is desirable).

We have now reached three important conclusions:

- *Conclusion 1:* Without monetary validation, positive demand shocks cause inflationary output gaps and a temporary burst of inflation. The gaps are removed as rising factor prices push the *AS* curve upward, returning real GDP to its potential level but at a higher price level.
- *Conclusion 2:* Without monetary validation, negative supply shocks cause recessionary output gaps and a temporary burst of inflation. The gaps are eventually removed as factor prices fall, restoring real GDP to its potential and the price level to its initial level.
- *Conclusion 3:* Only with continuing monetary validation can inflation initiated by either supply or demand shocks continue indefinitely.

expectations-augmented Phillips curve The relationship between unemployment and the rate of increase of money wages that arises when the output-gap and expectations components of inflation are combined.

the figures. The government thus *appears* to be able to choose among particular combinations of (wage) inflation and unemployment, in which lower levels of unemployment are attained at the cost of higher rates of inflation.

In the 1960s, Phillips curves were fitted to the data for many countries, and governments made decisions about where they wanted to be on the tradeoff between inflation and unemployment. Then, in the late 1960s, in country after country, the rate of wage and price inflation associated with any given level of unemployment began to rise. Instead of being stable, the Phillips curves began to shift upward. The explanation lay primarily in the rise of inflation expectations.

It was gradually understood that the original Phillips curve concerned only the influence of the output gap and left out inflationary expectations. This was not unreasonable for Phillips's original curve, which was fitted mainly to nineteenth-century data where the price level was relatively constant. But in the inflationary period following the Second World War, this omission proved important and unfortunate. An increase in expected inflation shows up as an upward shift in the original Phillips curve that was drawn in Chapter 24. The importance of expectations can be shown by drawing what is called an **expectations-augmented Phillips curve,** as shown by the dashed Phillips curves here. The height of the Phillips curves above the axis at Y^* and at U^* show the expected inflation rate. These distances represent the amount that wages will rise even when

$Y = Y^*$ (or $U = U^*$) and there is neither excess demand nor excess supply in labour markets. The actual wage increase is shown by the augmented (dashed) curve, with the increase in wages exceeding expected inflation whenever $Y > Y^*$ ($U < U^*$) and falling short of expected inflation whenever $Y < Y^*$ ($U > U^*$).

Now we can see what was wrong with the idea of a stable inflation–unemployment tradeoff. Maintaining a particular output Y_1 or unemployment U_1 in the figures requires some inflation $\dot{W}_1$. And once this rate of inflation comes to be expected, people will demand that much just to hold their own. The Phillips curve will then shift upward to the position shown in the figures and the economy will be at point B. Now there is inflation $\dot{W}_2$ because of the combined effects of expectations and excess demand. However, this higher rate is above the expected rate ($\dot{W}_1$). Once this higher rate comes to be expected, the Phillips curve will shift upward once again.

As a result of the combination of output-gap inflation and expectational inflation, the inflation rate associated with any given positive output gap ($Y > Y^*$ or $U < U^*$) rises over time. This is the phenomenon of accelerating inflation that we discussed in the text.

The shifts in the Phillips curve are such that most economists agree that in the long run, when inflationary expectations have fully adjusted to actual inflation, there is no tradeoff between inflation and unemployment. In other words, the long-run Phillips curve is a vertical line above U^* (or Y^*).

EXTENSIONS IN THEORY 30-2

Is the NAIRU Like a Razor's Edge?

We have described the standard theory of inflation in which the only stable position for the economy is one in which unemployment is equal to the NAIRU and real GDP is equal to potential GDP, Y^*. According to this theory, the labour market is poised on a "razor's edge"; wages rise when unemployment is less than the NAIRU and wages fall when unemployment exceeds the NAIRU.

In recent years, however, this view has come under some criticism. For example, Canadian economist Lars Osberg and his colleagues from Dalhousie University were unable to find any unique value for the NAIRU in a careful empirical study of Canada's unemployment and inflation experience. Depending on the precise specification of the empirical model used, and the number of

years included in the statistical sample, they found that the estimated value for the NAIRU could lie within a range of several percentage points. When unemployment usually varies between a low of 6 percent and a high of 11 percent, a possible range of *several percentage points* indicates a very low degree of precision in the estimated NAIRU.

A glance at the accompanying figure for Canadian inflation and unemployment since 1984 shows no clear tendency for inflation to increase when unemployment is below some critical rate, nor to decrease when unemployment is above such a critical rate. If anything, there appear to be two distinct periods in the data. From 1984 to 1991, the unemployment rate varied between a high of 11.5 percent and a low of 7.5 percent, all while the

Canadian Inflation and Unemployment, 1984–2008

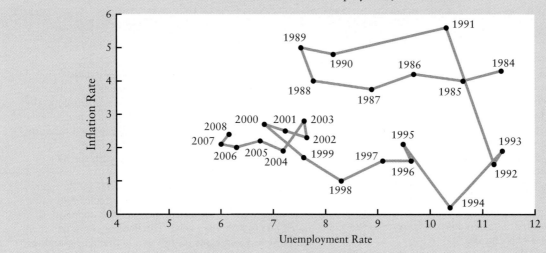

To put these conclusions differently, we can modify Friedman's statement slightly to represent the causes of inflation more accurately. While *AD* and *AS* shocks may lead to temporary inflation even in the absence of any actions by the central bank, *sustained* inflation can occur only if there is continual monetary validation by the central bank.

Sustained inflation is everywhere and always a monetary phenomenon.

We have been assuming in our macro model that wages rise when unemployment is less than the NAIRU ($Y > Y^*$) and that wages fall when unemployment exceeds the NAIRU ($Y < Y^*$). This assumption leads to the stark prediction that inflation can only be stable when unemployment exactly equals the NAIRU ($Y = Y^*$). In recent years, however, some economists have come to question this theory, believing instead that rate of inflation varied only slightly between 4 percent and 6 percent per year. Over the next 16 years, from 1992 until 2008, the unemployment rate fluctuated over a wider range, but inflation was generally less variable around a 2-percent average.

Several possible explanations for these data have been advanced, each of which may contribute something to the full explanation. First, when the public has confidence in the Bank of Canada's commitment to maintaining inflation at some given level, these expectations tend to remain constant as unemployment changes. Thus the influence of inflationary expectations on wages will be relatively insensitive to changes in the unemployment rate. In this case, we say that inflation expectations are "well anchored" because changes in the economic environment do not lead to significant changes in expectations. According to this view, for about a decade starting in 1984 the public had confidence in the Bank of Canada's commitment to keeping inflation in the 4–5 percent range. Then from 1992 onward, after the Bank of Canada had adopted its formal inflation target of 2 percent, the public once again believed that the Bank would carry out its stated objective. Thus the influence of inflation expectations on the path of wages was relatively invariant to large variations in the actual level of unemployment and real GDP; as a result, large swings in the unemployment rate were consistent with a relatively constant rate of inflation, as the figure shows.

A second explanation emphasizes the fact that most labour markets are not *auction markets* in which wages continually adjust to equate the demand and supply for labour. If employers have a reduced demand for workers, they usually respond by laying some workers off rather than by driving down wages. Instead of responding quickly to changes in excess demand or supplies in the labour market, wages tend to be set with longer-term conditions in mind. (We will say more about such long-term employment relationships in the next chapter.)

A third explanation is that the willingness of workers to push for higher wages (and in some situations to risk strikes) may depend on the nature of technological change. When technological change is creating good middle-wage jobs faster than it is destroying them, workers may be willing to push for higher wages whenever the labour market becomes relatively tight. This is a good description of the type of technological change that occurred between 1945 and the early 1970s, when factory jobs flourished, providing good wages for workers who did not have to be highly skilled. This may explain the appearance during this period of a well-defined Phillips curve with a razor's edge NAIRU. In contrast, the past three decades have seen technological change that destroys middle-wage manufacturing jobs while at the same time creating many high-wage jobs for highly trained and educated persons, as well as many low-wage jobs for the unskilled and uneducated. In this situation, workers who remain in manufacturing jobs may be reluctant to press for wage increases lest they be the next ones to lose their increasingly scarce, good jobs. In such an environment, even tight labour markets may not lead to substantial wage increases and hence there may not be a well-defined Phillips curve with its razor's edge NAIRU.

In summary, the description in our macro model of the wage-adjustment process has a certain compelling and valuable logic: Wages tend to rise when labour markets are tight and they tend to fall (although more slowly) when labour markets have excess supply. However, this relationship should be viewed as a general tendency rather than a strict, formulaic rule; there is unlikely to be a unique value of the NAIRU that acts as a "razor's edge" to determine wage adjustments.

the NAIRU is best viewed as a range rather than a unique, precise value. In this case, stable inflation would be consistent with a range of unemployment rates. *Extensions in Theory 30-2* explores this issue in greater detail.

30.3 Reducing Inflation

Suppose an economy has had a sustained and constant rate of inflation for several years. What must the central bank do to reduce the rate of inflation? What are the costs involved in doing so?

The Process of Disinflation

disinflation A reduction in the rate of inflation.

Disinflation means a reduction in the rate of inflation. In recent years, Canada has had two notable periods of disinflation—in 1981–1982 when inflation fell from more than 12 percent to 4 percent, and in 1990–1992 when inflation fell from 5 percent to less than 2 percent.

Reducing the rate of inflation takes time and involves major costs. The process begins when the Bank of Canada stops validating the ongoing inflation. It does this by raising its target for the overnight interest rate, which, in turn, raises longer-term market interest rates (and reduces the growth rate of the money supply). This action lowers real aggregate demand, reducing any existing inflationary gap. We will soon see, however, that it is usually necessary for the Bank to go further, creating a substantial recessionary gap that persists until the inflation is eliminated.

The process involves many costs. The recessionary gap hurts all who suffer in recessions, including the unemployed workers and the owners of firms who lose profits and risk bankruptcy. Unemployed resources mean lower output than would otherwise be produced. The temporary rise in interest rates hurts borrowers, including people with mortgages and firms with large loans. Among these groups who are most exposed and risk losing their wealth are young households with large mortgages and small firms that have taken on large debts to finance expansions.

Disinflation is thus a classic example of a policy that brings short-term pain for long-term gain. Inevitably, the question arises: Are the future benefits of lower inflation worth the immediate costs of reduced output and higher unemployment?

> **Reducing sustained inflation quickly incurs high costs for a short period of time; reducing it slowly incurs lower costs but for a longer period of time.**

The process of reducing sustained inflation can be divided into three phases. In the first phase, the monetary validation is stopped and any inflationary gap is eliminated. In the second phase, the economy still suffers from declining output and rising prices — *stagflation*. In the final phase, the economy experiences both increasing output and increasing prices, but the inflation then comes to an end. We now examine these three phases in detail.

The starting point for our analysis is an economy with an inflationary gap $(Y > Y^*)$ and rising inflation.[5]

Practise with Study Guide
Chapter 30, Exercise 1.

Phase 1: Removing Monetary Validation The first phase consists of tightening monetary policy by raising interest rates and thus reducing the growth rate of the money supply. This policy action slows the rate at which the AD curve is shifting upward. (An extreme case of monetary tightening in this setting is one where the Bank of Canada adopts a "cold-turkey approach"; interest rates are increased so much that the growth rate of the money supply is reduced to zero and the upward shift of the AD curve is halted abruptly. This extreme case is shown in part (i) of Figure 30-6.)

At this point, a controversy often breaks out—as it did in the early 1980s and early 1990s—over the effects that the increase in interest rates has on inflation. One group will point out that the rise in the interest rate increases business costs and that passing

---

[5] In the simpler case where the economy begins with $Y = Y^*$ and constant inflation, only the second and third phases are relevant.

on the extra costs through higher prices adds to inflation. They will condemn the Bank's tight monetary policy as inflationary. A second group will argue that rising interest rates are a necessary part of the disinflation policy.

The first group is correct in pointing out that the rise in interest rates may cause a one-time increase in the price level. The rise in interest costs may shift the AS curve upward, just as a rise in wage costs does. This rise in interest costs, however, has only a *one-time effect* on the price level. The first group is wrong, therefore, in asserting that the Bank's policy of driving up interest rates is contributing to a long-term increase in the rate of inflation. The second group is correct in saying that the rise in the interest rate is a necessary part of an anti-inflationary policy because the higher interest rate is necessary to reduce desired aggregate expenditure.

Suppose the Bank resists the pleas to hold down interest rates. It continues with its no-validation policy. The AD curve stops shifting, but under the combined influence of the present inflationary gap and expectations of continued inflation, wages continue to rise. Hence, the AS curve continues to shift upward. Eventually, the inflationary gap will be removed, as shown in part (i) of Figure 30-6.

If the excess demand from the inflationary output gap were the only influence on wages, the story would be ended. At $Y = Y^*$, there would be no upward demand pressure on wages and other factor prices. The AS curve would be stabilized, and real GDP would remain at Y^*. But it is usually not so simple.

Phase 2: Stagflation

As we explained earlier, wages depend not only on current excess demand but also on inflation expectations. Once inflation expectations have been established, it is not always easy to get people to revise them downward, even in the face of announced changes in monetary policies. Hence, the AS curve continues to shift upward, causing the price level to continue to rise and output to fall. The combination of increased inflation and a reduction in output (or its growth rate) is called **stagflation**. This is phase 2, shown in part (ii) of Figure 30-6.

> **Expectations can cause inflation to persist even after its original causes have been removed. What was initially a demand and expectational inflation because of an inflationary gap becomes a pure expectational inflation.**

stagflation The simultaneous increase in inflation and reduction in output (or its growth rate) that is caused by an upward shift of the AS curve.

The ease with which the Bank of Canada can end such an inflation depends on how easy it is to change these expectations of continued inflation. This change is more difficult to the extent that expectations are backward-looking and easier to the extent that expectations are forward-looking.

To the extent that people look mainly to past inflation rates to determine their expectations of the future, they will be slow to change their expectations. As the actual inflation rate falls below the expected rate, a long time will be required for the downward adjustment to take place. The longer a given rate has persisted, the more firmly will people expect that rate to persist.

To the extent that expectations are forward-looking, people will take notice of the Bank's announced changes in policy and revise their expectations of future inflation downward in the light of the new policy. If people fully understand the Bank's policies as soon as they are implemented, if they have full confidence that the Bank will stick to its policies, if they know exactly how much time will be required for the Bank's policies to have effect, and if they adjust their expectations exactly in line with this knowledge, there is little need for any recessionary gap to develop. Once the inflationary gap has been removed, expectations will immediately be revised downward, so there will then be no pressure on wages to rise because of either demand or expectational forces. In Figure 30-6, Y would not fall below Y^* because

FIGURE 30-6   Eliminating a Sustained Inflation

(i) Phase 1: Removing the inflationary gap

(ii) Phase 2: Stagflation

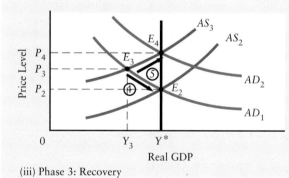

(iii) Phase 3: Recovery

(i) Phase 1: The elimination of a sustained inflation begins with a monetary tightening to remove the inflationary gap. The initial position is one where fully validated inflation is taking the economy along the path shown by arrow ①. When the curves reach AS_1 and AD_1, the central bank adopts a tight monetary policy, which halts the growth of the money supply, thus stabilizing aggregate demand at AD_1. Due to the output gap and inflation expectations, wages continue to rise, taking the AS curve leftward. The economy moves along arrow ②, with output falling and the price level rising. When aggregate supply reaches AS_2, the inflationary gap is removed, output is Y^*, and the price level is P_2.

(ii) Phase 2: Expectations and wage momentum lead to stagflation, with falling output and continuing inflation. The economy moves along the path shown by arrow ③. The driving force is now the AS curve, which continues to shift because inflation expectations cause wages to continue rising. The recessionary gap grows as output falls. Inflation continues, but at a diminishing rate. If wages stop rising when output has reached Y_3 and the price level has reached P_3, the stagflation phase is over, with equilibrium at E_3.

(iii) Phase 3: After expectations are reversed, recovery takes output to Y^*, and the price level is stabilized. There are two possible scenarios for recovery. In the first, the recessionary gap causes wages to fall (slowly), taking the AS curve back to AS_2 (slowly), as shown by arrow ④. The economy retraces the path originally followed in part (ii) back to E_2. In the second scenario, the central bank increases the money supply sufficiently to shift the AD curve to AD_2. The economy then moves along the path shown by arrow ⑤. This restores output to potential at the cost of further temporary inflation that takes the price level to P_4. Potential output and a stable price level are now achieved.

the AS curve would stop shifting upward at AS_2. The inflation would be eliminated at almost no cost.

> **How long inflation persists after the inflationary gap has been removed depends on how quickly expectations of continued inflation are revised downward.**

The importance of expectations explains why the Bank of Canada and other central banks emphasize their precise objectives in their many public speeches. In 1990–1991, the Bank's governor, John Crow, gave many speeches in an effort to convince the public that the Bank would stick to its newly adopted inflation target. This communications strategy was an attempt to reduce inflationary expectations and thus slow the upward shift of Canada's *AS* curve. And today, the governor of the Bank of Canada regularly speaks publicly about the Bank's 2-percent inflation target and about the importance of achieving it. Such public communications help to "anchor" inflation expectations at the 2-percent target.

If the *AS* curve does continue to shift upward, causing *Y* to fall below *Y**, the emerging recessionary gap has two effects. First, unemployment rises and the output-gap effect begins to put downward pressure on wages. Second, the continuing expectations of inflation tend to raise wages further. The overall effect on wages and thus the *AS* curve is a combination of the output-gap effect and the expectational effect. When the recessionary gap is still new, the expectational effect is likely to outweigh the output-gap effect; wages will continue rising and the *AS* curve will continue to shift upward. But as the extent of excess supply deepens, and inflation itself begins to moderate, the output-gap effect will eventually come to offset the expectational effect; wages

The main cost of disinflation is the reduction in economic activity that is a necessary part of the process. Increases in unemployment and plant closures are typical.

will stop rising and the *AS* curve will stop shifting upward. At this point the stagflation phase is over. Inflation has come to a halt, but a large recessionary gap now exists.

Phase 3: Recovery The final phase is the return to potential output. When the economy comes to rest at the end of the stagflation, the situation is exactly the same as when the economy is hit by a negative supply shock. The move back to potential output can be accomplished in either of two ways. First, the recessionary gap can be relied on to reduce factor prices, thereby shifting the *AS* curve downward, reducing prices but increasing real GDP. Second, an expansionary monetary policy can shift the *AD* curve upward, increasing both prices and real GDP. These two possibilities are illustrated in part (iii) of Figure 30-6.

Some economists worry about relying on the *AS* curve to shift downward to return the economy to potential output. Their concern is primarily that it will take too long for wages to fall sufficiently to shift the *AS* curve—though output will eventually return to potential, the long adjustment period will be characterized by high unemployment. These economists have a preference for a monetary expansion to get output back to potential.

Other economists worry about a temporary burst of monetary expansion because they fear that expectations of inflation may be rekindled when the Bank's monetary expansion shifts the *AD* curve to the right. And if inflationary expectations *are* revived, the Bank will then be faced with a tough decision—either it must let another recession develop to break these new inflation expectations, or it must validate the inflation to reduce unemployment. In the latter case, the Bank is back where it started, with validated inflation on its hands—and diminished credibility.

The Cost of Disinflation

The foregoing discussion of the process of disinflation highlights the cost of disinflation.

The cost of disinflation is the loss of output that is generated in the process.

As we said earlier, the size and duration of the recession depends to a large extent on how quickly inflation expectations are revised downward as the disinflation continues. If expectations are mainly backward-looking and thus slow to adjust to the changes in policy, the recession will be deep and protracted. Conversely, if expectations are mainly forward-looking and thus quick to adjust to changes in policy, the recession may be mild and of short duration.

But *how costly* is the process of disinflation? Economists have derived a simple measure of the cost of disinflation based on the depth and length of the recession and on the amount of disinflation. This measure is called the **sacrifice ratio** and is defined as the cumulative loss of real GDP caused by a given disinflation (expressed as a percentage of potential GDP) divided by the number of percentage points by which inflation has fallen. For example, the 1990–1992 disinflation in Canada reduced inflation by roughly four percentage points. Suppose the cumulative loss of real GDP caused by that disinflation was equal to $80 billion and that potential GDP at the time was equal to $800 billion. The cumulative loss of output would then have been 10 percent of potential output. The sacrifice ratio would therefore have been 10/4 = 2.5. The interpretation of this number is that it "costs" 2.5 percent of real GDP for each percentage point of inflation that is reduced.

The numbers in the previous example are hypothetical, but typical estimates of the sacrifice ratio for many developed countries range between 2 and 4. Figure 30-7 illustrates the time paths of real GDP and inflation following a disinflation and shows how to compute the sacrifice ratio. Note an important assumption that is implicit whenever measuring the sacrifice ratio in this way. The assumption is that all changes in the path of real GDP are *caused by* the disinflation.

sacrifice ratio The cumulative loss in real GDP, expressed as a percentage of potential output, divided by the percentage-point reduction in the rate of inflation.

Conclusion

Throughout the history of economics, inflation has been recognized as a harmful phenomenon. The high inflation rates that Canada experienced in the 1970s and early 1980s (see Figure 30-1 on page 736) were also experienced in many developed countries. In the past 30 years these countries have learned much about the causes of inflation, the policies required to reduce it, and the costs associated with doing so.

In particular, Canada and several other countries have adopted formal inflation-targeting regimes, which have been successful at keeping inflation low and stable. An important aspect of inflation targeting is to keep the *expectations* of inflation low. As we have seen in this chapter, keeping inflation expectations low is crucial to keeping actual inflation low.

In recent years, some commentators have argued that the dangers of inflation have been eliminated, that inflation is now "dead." Central to these arguments is the view that greater international competition through the process of globalization will keep inflationary pressures at bay. Yet, whatever forces globalization might bring, it remains true that *sustained* inflation is a monetary phenomenon. Unless central banks are committed to keeping inflation low and stable, damaging inflation remains a potential threat to the economy.

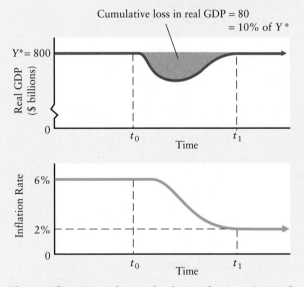

FIGURE 30-7   The Cost of Disinflation: The Sacrifice Ratio

The sacrifice ratio is larger the deeper the recession and the longer it takes real GDP to return to potential. In this example, the economy begins with $Y = Y^*$ and inflation of 6 percent. At t_0, the disinflation begins. A recessionary gap opens up and inflation falls only slowly. By t_1, real GDP has returned to Y^* and inflation has been reduced by four percentage points. In this figure, the cumulative loss of real GDP is 10 percent of Y^* and inflation has fallen by four percentage points. The sacrifice ratio is therefore 10/4 = 2.5, indicating that it costs 2.5 percent of GDP to reduce inflation by one percentage point.

Summary

30.1 Adding Inflation to the Model   (LO) ❶ ❷

- Sustained price inflation will be accompanied by closely related growth in wages and other factor prices such that the *AS* curve is shifting upward. Factors that influence shifts in the *AS* curve can be divided into two main components: output gaps and expectations. Random supply-side shocks will also exert an influence.
- Inflationary output gaps tend to cause wages to rise; recessionary output gaps tend to cause wages to fall.
- Expectations of inflation tend to cause wage increases equal to the expected price-level increases. Expectations can be backward-looking, forward-looking, or some combination of the two.
- With a constant rate of inflation and no supply shocks, expected inflation will eventually come to equal actual inflation. This implies that there is no output-gap effect on inflation—that is, real GDP equals its potential level.
- Constant inflation of 2 percent per year is shown graphically in the macroeconomic model by the *AD* and *AS* curves shifting up by 2 percent per year, keeping real GDP equal to Y^*.

30.2 Shocks and Policy Responses   (LO) ❸ ❹

- The initial effects of positive demand shocks are a rise in the price level and a rise in real GDP. If the inflation is unvalidated, output tends to return to its potential level while the price level rises further (as the *AS* curve shifts upward). Monetary validation allows demand inflation to proceed without reducing the inflationary gap (*AD* curve continues to shift upward).
- The initial effects of negative supply shocks are a rise in the price level and a fall in real GDP. If inflation is unvalidated, output will slowly move back to its potential level as the price level slowly falls to its pre-shock level (*AS* curve slowly shifts down). Monetary valida-tion allows supply inflation to continue in spite of a persistent recessionary gap (*AD* curve shifts up with monetary validation).
- If the Bank of Canada tries to keep real GDP constant at some level above Y^*, the actual inflation rate will eventually accelerate. In our macro model, in the absence of supply shocks, constant inflation is only possible when there are no demand pressures on inflation—that is, when $Y = Y^*$.
- Aggregate demand and supply shocks have temporary effects on inflation. But sustained inflation is a monetary phenomenon.

30.3 Reducing Inflation   (LO) ❺ ❻

- The process of ending a sustained inflation can be divided into three phases.
  1. Phase 1 consists of ending monetary validation and allowing the upward shift in the *AS* curve to remove any inflationary gap that does exist.
  2. In Phase 2, a recessionary gap develops as expecta-tions of further inflation cause the *AS* curve to con-tinue to shift upward even after the inflationary gap is removed.
  3. In Phase 3, the economy returns to potential output, sometimes aided by a one-time monetary expansion that raises the *AD* curve to the level consistent with potential output.
- The cost of disinflation is the recession (output loss) that is created in the process. The sacrifice ratio is a measure of this cost and is calculated as the cumulative loss in real GDP (expressed as a percentage of Y^*) divided by the reduction in inflation.

Key Concepts

Temporary and sustained inflation
The NAIRU
Forward-looking and
 backward-looking expectations

Expectational, output-gap, and
 supply-shock pressures on inflation
Monetary validation of demand and
 supply shocks

Expectations-augmented Phillips curve
Accelerating inflation
Disinflation
Sacrifice ratio

Study Exercises

1. Fill in the blanks to make the following statements correct.

   a. The term NAIRU stands for the _____.
   b. Unemployment is said to be equal to the NAIRU when GDP is equal to _____.
   c. Changes in money wages result from two different effects: the _____ effect and the _____ effect. Both of these effects cause the _____ curve to shift.
   d. The *AS* curve shifts up when money wages _____ and also shifts up with a negative _____ shock.
   e. Actual inflation can come from any of its three component parts. They are _____, _____, and _____.
   f. If the rate of inflation is constant at 6 percent and actual GDP equals potential GDP, then we can say that the central bank is _____ inflation expectations. That is, the central bank is permitting a(n) _____ in the money supply such that the expected and actual inflation rates are equal at _____ percent.

2. Fill in the blanks to make the following statements correct.

   a. Suppose the economy is initially at potential GDP (*Y**) and then there is a sudden increase in the demand for Canadian exports. The *AD* curve shifts to the _____ and opens a(n) _____ gap.
   b. With an inflationary gap, the economy is operating where GDP is above _____. In an effort to maintain the output gap, the Bank of Canada may choose to validate the inflation by _____ the interest rate and allowing the money supply to _____. The actual inflation rate will _____.
   c. The alternative policy response to an inflationary gap is to not validate the inflation. The _____ curve stops shifting upward. The _____ curve shifts upward due to rising wages caused by _____. Real GDP eventually returns to _____ at a higher _____.

   d. Economists say that sustained inflation is a _____ phenomenon.
   e. Reducing a sustained inflation requires that monetary _____ be stopped. Inflation will persist, however, until _____ of continued inflation are revised downward.
   f. The cost of disinflation is the cost of the _____ that is generated in the process.

3. The table below shows several macroeconomic situations, each with a given amount of excess demand (or supply) for labour and a level of inflation expectations. Both are expressed in percentage per year. For example, in Case A excess demand for labour is pushing wages up by 4 percent per year, and expected inflation is pushing wages up by 3 percent per year.

Case	Excess Demand	Inflation Expectations	Total Wage Change	AS Shift
A	+4	+3	___	___
B	+4	0	___	___
C	0	+3	___	___
D	3	0	___	___
E	3	+4	___	___

   a. For each case, identify whether there is an inflationary or a recessionary output gap.
   b. For each case, what is the total effect on nominal wages? Fill in the third column.
   c. For each case, in which direction is the *AS* curve shifting (up or down)? Fill in the last column.

4. This exercise requires you to compute inflationary expectations based on a simple formula, and it will help you to understand why backward-looking expectations adjust slowly to changes in economic events. Suppose that the *actual* inflation rate in year t is denoted Π_t. *Expected* inflation for year $t+1$ is denoted Π^e_{t+1}. Now, suppose that workers and firms form their expectations according to

   $$\Pi^e_{t+1} = \theta\Pi^T + (1-\theta)\Pi_t \qquad \text{(with } 0 < \theta < 1)$$

where Π^T is the central bank's announced *inflation target*. This simple equation says that people's expectations for inflation at $t + 1$ are a weighted average of last year's actual inflation rate and the central bank's currently announced target. We will use this equation to see how the size of determines the extent to which expectations are backward-looking. Consider the table below, which shows the data for a reduction in actual inflation from 10 percent to 2 percent.

Year (t)	Π_t	Π^T	Π^e_{t+1}
1	10	2	——
2	9	2	——
3	6	2	——
4	3	2	——
5	2	2	——
6	2	2	——
7	2	2	——
8	2	2	——

a. Assume that θ is equal to 0.1. Compute expected inflation for each year and fill in the table.
b. On a scale diagram, plot the time path of actual inflation, expected inflation, and the inflation target.
c. Now assume that θ equals 0.9. Repeat parts (a) and (b).
d. Which value of θ corresponds to more backward-looking expectations? Explain.

e. Given the different speed of adjustment of inflationary expectations, predict which disinflation is more costly in terms of lost output—the one with θ = 0.1 or with θ = 0.9. Explain.

5. The diagram below shows an *AD/AS* diagram. The economy is in long-run equilibrium with real GDP equal to Y^* and the price level is stable at P_0.

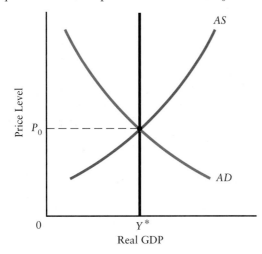

a. Suppose the central bank announces that it will implement an expansionary monetary policy that will shift the *AD* curve up by 5 percent. Show the likely effect of this announcement on the *AS* curve.
b. Does the shift of the *AS* curve in part (a) depend on whether workers and firms believe the central bank's announcement? Explain.
c. In a new *AD/AS* diagram, show how a sustained and constant inflation of 5 percent is represented.
d. In the absence of any supply shocks, explain why a constant inflation is only possible when real GDP is equal to s^*.

6. The diagram below shows an *AD/AS* diagram. Suppose the economy experiences a positive aggregate demand shock—say an increase in the demand for Canada's exports. This increases real GDP to Y_1.

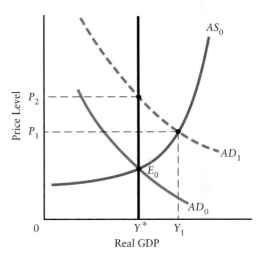

a. Explain what happens if the Bank of Canada does not react to the shock. Show this in the diagram.
b. Now suppose the Bank decides to maintain real GDP at Y_1—that is, it decides to validate the shock. Explain how this is possible, and show it in a diagram.
c. What is the effect on inflation from the policy in part (b)? Is inflation constant or is it rising? Explain.

7. The diagram below shows an *AD/AS* diagram. Suppose the economy experiences a negative aggregate supply shock—say, an increase in wages driven by a major union settlement. This reduces real GDP to Y_1.

a. Explain what happens if the Bank of Canada does not react to the shock. Show this in the diagram.
b. Now suppose the Bank decides to offset the shock's effect on real GDP—that is, it validates the

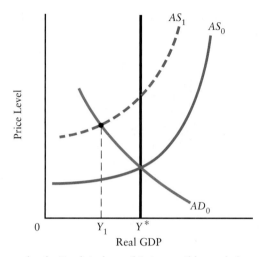

shock. Explain how this is possible, and show it in a diagram.

c. What danger do many economists see in validating such supply shocks? What is the alternative?

8. The table below shows some data on various disinflations. In each case, assume that potential GDP is equal to $900 billion.

   a. In each case, compute the sacrifice ratio.
   b. Explain why the sacrifice ratio can be expected to be smaller when expectations are more forward looking.
   c. Explain why the sacrifice ratio can be expected to be smaller when central-bank announcements are more credible.

Case	Reduction Inflation	Cumulative GDP Loss	Sacrifice Ratio
A	5 percentage points	$100 billion	____
B	2	30	____
C	6	60	____
D	8	80	____

Discussion Questions

1. Why might the cost of disinflation vary from one inflationary period to another? Are there reasons to think the cost might be higher the longer inflation has persisted? What might the Bank of Canada do to reduce the cost?

2. What sources of inflation are suggested by each of the following quotations?

   a. A newspaper editorial in Manchester, England: "If American unions were as strong as those in Britain, America's inflationary experience would have been as disastrous as Britain's."
   b. An article in *The Economist*: "Oil price collapse will reduce inflation."
   c. A Canadian newspaper article in June 2009: "Tensions in Iran fuel an oil-driven inflation."
   d. A newspaper headline in October 2008: "Bank's fast growth of money will spur inflation."

3. Discuss the apparent conflict between the following views. Can you suggest how they might be reconciled using aggregate demand and aggregate supply analysis?

   a. "A rise in interest rates is deflationary, because ending entrenched inflation with a tight monetary policy usually requires that interest rates rise steeply."

   b. "A rise in interest rates is inflationary, because interest is a major business cost and, as with other costs, a rise in interest will be passed on by firms in the form of higher prices."

4. What is the relationship between the sacrifice ratio and the central bank's credibility?

   a. Explain why a more credible policy of disinflation reduces the costs of disinflation.
   b. Explain how you think the Bank of Canada might be able to make its disinflation policy more credible.
   c. Can the Bank's policy responses to negative supply shocks influence the credibility it is likely to have when trying to end a sustained inflation? Explain.

5. Suppose you are the governor of the Bank of Canada and that inflation has been high and roughly constant for a number of years. You have two policy choices: You can continue to validate the ongoing inflation, or you can attempt to eliminate the sustained inflation. Outline the issues involved when making this choice. List and explain the costs of ongoing inflation, and also the costs of a potential disinflation. Explain how you make your policy decision.

6. In January 1991, the federal government introduced the Goods and Services Tax (GST). If you were to

suppose that the GST was a *new* tax (in fact, it replaced an existing tax), what would be the effect on the *AS* curve? Is the introduction of the GST (or an increase in its rate) inflationary? Does it increase inflation permanently?

7. In the summer of 2006, a time when U.S. inflation was rising and output was above potential, a story in *The Globe and Mail* reported that the release of strong employment-growth data for the United States led to a plunge in prices on the U.S. stock market.

   a. Explain why high employment growth would lead people to expect the U.S. central bank to tighten its monetary policy.
   b. Explain why higher U.S. interest rates would lead to lower prices of U.S. stocks.
   c. How would you expect this announcement to affect Canada?

31

Unemployment Fluctuations and the NAIRU

When the level of economic activity changes, so do the levels of employment and unemployment. When real GDP increases in the short run, employment usually rises and unemployment falls. Conversely, when real GDP falls in the short run, employment falls and unemployment rises. Figure 31-1 shows the course of the unemployment rate in Canada over the past few decades. Recall from Chapter 19 that the unemployment rate is the percentage of the labour force that is unemployed. It is clear that the unemployment rate has followed a cyclical path, rising during the recessions of 1981–1982, 1991–1992, and 2009, and falling during the expansions of the late 1980s and late 1990s. In this chapter we examine theories designed to explain these short-run fluctuations.

In addition to examining short-run fluctuations in the unemployment rate, economists also study the concept of the NAIRU—the rate of unemployment that exists when real GDP is equal to potential output, Y^*. At points A, B, C, and D in Figure 31-1, real GDP was approximately equal to potential output, and thus the unemployment rates then were approximately equal to the NAIRU. We will see in this chapter several reasons why the NAIRU might change over time and thus offer some explanations for the gradual decline in the NAIRU apparent in the figure, from about 8 percent in 1977 (point A) to approximately 6 percent in 2007 (point D).

We begin by examining some basic facts about employment and unemployment.

31.1 Employment and Unemployment

Look back at Figure 19-3 on page 482, which shows the path of employment and the labour force in Canada since 1960. The most striking feature of part (i) of the figure is that, when viewed over the long term, the growth in employment has approximately matched the growth in the labour force. Also notice in part (ii) of Figure 19-3, and also in Figure 31-1, that the unemployment rate displays considerable short-run fluctuations. These two characteristics of the labour force—long-term growth in employment but short-term fluctuations in the unemployment rate—are common to most developed countries.

> Over the span of many years, increases in the labour force are more or less matched by increases in employment. Over the short term, however, the unemployment rate fluctuates considerably because changes in the labour force are not exactly matched by changes in employment.

Changes in Employment

The level of employment in Canada has increased dramatically over the past few decades. In 1959, there were approximately 5 million employed Canadians. By 2008, total employment was 17.1 million. The actual level of employment, of course, is determined both by the demand for labour and by the supply of labour. How have the two "sides" of the Canadian labour market been changing?

On the supply side, the labour force has expanded virtually every year since the end of the Second World War. The causes have included a rising population, which boosts entry into the labour force of people born 15 to 25 years previously; increased labour force participation by various groups, especially women; and net immigration of working-age persons.

FIGURE 31-1   Canadian Unemployment Rate, 1976–2009

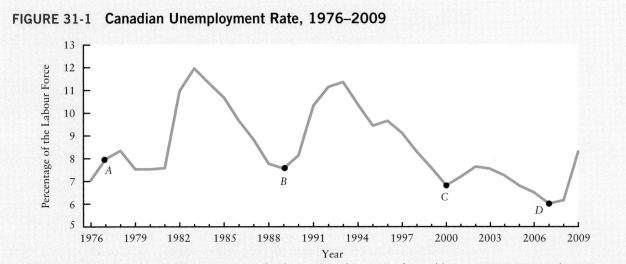

(*Source:* Data from Statistics Canada, CANSIM database, annual average of monthly series V2062815. Labour Force Information, cat. no. 71-001-XIE.)

On the demand side, many existing jobs are eliminated every year, and many new jobs are created. Economic growth causes some sectors of the economy to decline and others to expand. Jobs are lost in the sectors that are contracting and created in sectors that are expanding. Furthermore, even in relatively stable industries, many firms disappear and many new ones are set up. The net increase in employment is the difference between all the jobs that are created and all those that are lost.

> In most years, enough new jobs are created both to replace old jobs that have been eliminated and to provide jobs for the growing labour force. The result is a net increase in employment in most years.

In a typical year in Canada, the level of employment increases by about 230 000 workers, an annual growth rate of roughly 1.3 percent.

Changes in Unemployment

In the early 1980s, worldwide unemployment rose to high levels. The unemployment rate remained high in many advanced industrial countries and only began to fall, and even then very slowly, during the latter half of the decade. Canadian experience reflected these international developments rather closely. From a high of more than 12 percent in 1983, the Canadian unemployment rate fell to 7.5 percent in 1989, a point that many economists at the time thought was close to the Canadian NAIRU (see point *B* in Figure 31-1).

With the onset of another recession in the early 1990s, the unemployment rate then rose through 1990 and 1991, reaching 11.3 percent by 1992. During the next few years, the unemployment rate fell only slowly as the Canadian recovery was weak; by early 1994 the unemployment rate was still more than 10 percent. But the speed of the Canadian recovery quickened and unemployment began to drop. By early 2000, after five years of healthy economic recovery, the unemployment rate was 6.8 percent. Following the large stock-market decline in late 2000, together with the decline in confidence associated with the 2001 terrorist attacks in New York and Washington, the Canadian and U.S. economies slowed, and unemployment increased. Recovery was rapid, however, and by the summer of 2008 Canadian real GDP was at or above its potential, and the unemployment rate had fallen to below 6 percent, the lowest it had been in more than 30 years.

> During periods of rapid economic growth, the unemployment rate usually falls. During recessions or periods of slow growth, the unemployment rate usually rises.

Flows in the Labour Market

As we have just observed, many existing jobs are eliminated every year, as industries contract and firms either shrink or close down altogether. Similarly, new jobs are continually being created, as other industries expand and new firms are born. The public's and the media's focus on the labour market, however, tends to be on the overall level of employment and unemployment rather than on the amount of *job creation* and *job destruction*. This focus can often lead us to the conclusion that few changes are occurring in the labour market when in fact the truth is exactly the opposite.

For example, the Canadian unemployment rate was roughly constant at 6.1 percent from 2007 to 2008. Does this mean no jobs were created during the year? Or that the Canadian labour market was stagnant during this period? No. In fact, workers were finding jobs at the rate of roughly 400 000 *per month*. At the same time, however, other workers were leaving jobs or entering the labour force at roughly the same rate. This tremendous number of flows *out of unemployment* was being approximately matched by the number of flows *into unemployment*. The net result was that total unemployment changed only slightly.

For data on current employment and unemployment in Canada, see Statistics Canada's website: **www.statcan.gc.ca.** Click on "Canadian Statistics" and then type in "unemployment."

> **The amount of activity in the labour market is better reflected by the flows into and out of unemployment than by the overall unemployment rate.**

By looking at the *gross flows* in the labour market, we are able to see economic activity that is hidden when we look just at changes in the overall level of employment and unemployment (which is determined by *net* flows). Indeed, these gross flows are typically so large that they dwarf the net flows. See *Applying Economic Concepts 31-1* for more discussion of the gross flows in the Canadian labour market, and how these gross-flows data can be used to compute the average length of unemployment spells.

Practise with Study Guide Chapter 31, Additional Multiple-Choice Questions 1–8.

myeconlab ADDITIONAL TOPICS

A number of problems are associated with the measurement of unemployment, some of which relate to how "actively" people currently not working are searching for a job. For a detailed discussion of some of these problems, as well as an illustration of why they are important for understanding the gap between U.S. and Canadian unemployment rates, look for **Understanding the Canada–U.S. Unemployment Gap** in the *Additional Topics* section of this book's MyEconLab.

www.myeconlab.com

Consequences of Unemployment

To most people, unemployment is seen as a social "bad," just as output is seen as a social "good." But this does not mean *all* unemployment is bad, just as we know that not all output—such as noise or air pollution—is good. Indeed, we will see later in this chapter that some unemployment is socially desirable as it reflects the necessary time spent searching to make appropriate matches between firms and workers.

We examine two costs of unemployment. The first is the associated loss in output. The second is the harm done to the individuals who are unemployed.

Lost Output Every person counted as unemployed is willing and able to work and is seeking a job but has yet to find one. Hence, the unemployed are valuable resources who are currently not producing output. The output that is not produced, but potentially could be, is a loss for society. Once an unemployed person regains employment, however, output rises again and this loss goes away. But nothing makes up for the *past*

APPLYING ECONOMIC CONCEPTS 31-1

Stocks and Flows in the Canadian Labour Market

In most reports about changes in unemployment, both in Canada and abroad, emphasis is typically on the changes in the *stock* of unemployment—that is, on the number of people who are unemployed at a particular point in time. But as we said in the text, the focus on the stock of unemployment can often hide much activity in the labour market, activity that is revealed by looking at *gross flows* in the labour market.

What Are Labour-Market Flows?

The first figure in this box shows the difference between stocks and flows in the labour market. The blue circles represent the number of individuals at the end of each month (the *stocks*) in each possible "state"—employment (*E*), unemployment (*U*), and *not* in the labour force (*N*). The six red arrows represent the monthly *flows* of individuals among the various states. For example, arrow ① shows the monthly flow of individuals from *E* to *U*. These individuals begin the month in *E* (employed), leave their jobs sometime during the month, and end the month as unemployed individuals, in *U*. Arrow ③ shows the flow from *N* to *U*—these individuals are new entrants to the labour force during the month and begin their labour-force experience as unemployed individuals.

In the second figure, three series of data are shown for Canada from 1976 to 2003—a period that includes the major recessions of 1981 and 1991. (Unfortunately, Statistics Canada has stopped publishing these data, so more recent data are not available.) The top line is the stock of unemployment—the actual *number* of people unemployed at a specific point in time. During the severe recession of the early 1980s, unemployment peaked at approximately 1.7 million people and then fell during the recovery until 1989. With the onset of the next recession in 1990–1991, unemployment rose again, reaching nearly 1.8 million in 1992.

The two lower lines show *gross flows* in the labour market. (These flows data are not available for 1997 and 1998, which explains the break in the lines at that point.) The orange line shows the monthly flow into unemployment, corresponding to the sum of the flows in arrows ① and ③ in the first figure. This flow into unemployment represents:

- workers losing jobs through layoffs or plant closure
- workers quitting jobs to search for different jobs
- new entrants to the labour force searching for jobs

The monthly flow into unemployment varies between approximately 300 000 and 500 000 individuals *per month*.

The green line shows the monthly flow out of unemployment, corresponding to the sum of the flows in arrows ② and ④ in the first figure. This outflow represents:

- unemployed individuals finding new jobs
- unemployed individuals becoming discouraged and leaving the labour force

The monthly flow out of unemployment is roughly the same size as the monthly inflow, 300 000–500 000 individuals per month.

What is the connection between the flows and the stocks in the labour market? Whenever the flows into unemployment exceed the flows out of unemployment, the stock of unemployment rises. Conversely, whenever the flows out of unemployment exceed the flows into unemployment, the stock of unemployment falls.

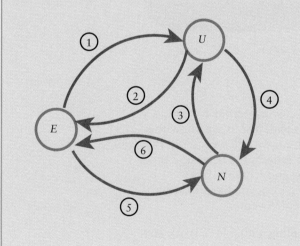

Using Flows Data

There are two reasons why looking at flows can be very useful when we think about the labour market. First, they show the tremendous amount of activity in the labour market even though the stock of unemployment may not be changing significantly. For example, between 1991 and 1992 the stock of unemployment in Canada varied between 1.4 million and 1.6 million persons. But during that two-year period, roughly 400 000 persons *per month* either became unemployed or ceased being unemployed. This number reflects the massive amount of regular turnover that exists in the Canadian labour market—turnover that is the essence of what economists call *frictional unemployment*.

The second reason that looking at flows is useful is that the relationship between the flows and the stock can tell us something about the amount of time the average unemployed person spends unemployed. If U_S is the stock of unemployment, and U_O is the monthly outflow from unemployment, then one simple estimate of the average duration of an unemployment spell is

$$\text{Average duration of} \atop \text{unemployment spell} = \frac{U_S}{U_O}$$

Consider the situation in 1999, at the peak of the business cycle. At that time, the stock of unemployment was approximately 1 million people and the outflow from unemployment was at a rate of approximately 400 000 persons per month. Thus, the average unemployed person in 1999 could expect to leave unemployment in about 2.5 months (1 000 000 people/400 000 people per month = 2.5 months). In contrast, in 1992, at the depth of the previous recession, the expected duration of an unemployment spell was more than 3.5 months (1 600 000/450 000 = 3.6).

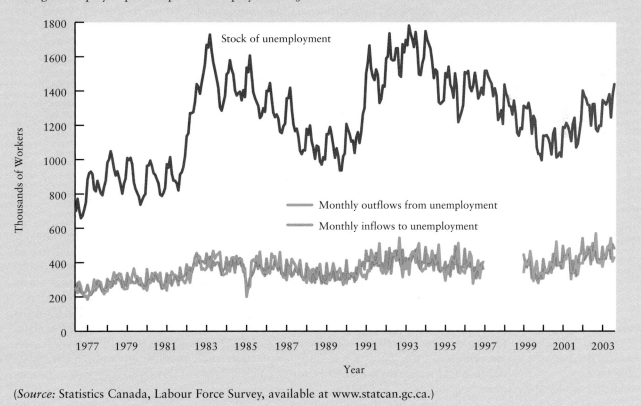

(*Source:* Statistics Canada, Labour Force Survey, available at www.statcan.gc.ca.)

loss that existed while the worker was unemployed. In other words, the loss of output that accompanies unemployment is lost forever. In a world of scarcity with many unsatisfied wants, this loss represents a serious waste of resources.

Personal Costs   For the typical Canadian worker, being unemployed for long periods of time is very unusual. Most spells of unemployment are short; in 2007, the OECD estimated that only 7.5 percent of Canadian unemployment spells lasted 12 months or longer. In other words, the vast majority of unemployed workers find new jobs in just a few months. Moreover, many workers experiencing temporary unemployment have access to the employment insurance program that provides some income during their spell of unemployment.

But this does not mean there are no problems associated with unemployment, especially for those relatively few workers who are unemployed for long periods of time. The effects of long-term unemployment, in terms of the disillusioned who have given up trying to make it within the system and who contribute to social unrest, should be a matter of serious concern to the "haves" as well as the "have-nots." The loss of self-esteem and the dislocation of families that often result from situations of prolonged unemployment are genuine tragedies.

The general case for concern about high unemployment has been eloquently put by Princeton economist Alan Blinder:

> A high-pressure economy provides opportunities, facilitates structural change, encourages inventiveness and innovation, and opens doors for society's underdogs. . . . All these promote the social cohesion and economic progress that make democratic mixed capitalism such a wonderful system when it works well. A low-pressure economy slams the doors shut, breeds a bunker mentality that resists change, stifles productivity growth, and fosters both inequality and mean-spirited public policy. All this makes reducing high unemployment a political, economic, and moral challenge of the highest order.[1]

31.2 Unemployment Fluctuations

It is clear from Figure 31-1 on page 791 that the unemployment rate fluctuates considerably over relatively short periods of time. Over the years, economists have debated the sources of these fluctuations. One group of economists, who are often referred to as *New Keynesians,* emphasize the distinction between the unemployment that exists when real GDP is equal to Y^*, and unemployment that is due to deviations of real GDP from Y^*. The former, as we saw in Chapter 19, is called the NAIRU, and is made up of frictional and structural unemployment. The latter is often called **cyclical unemployment**, which falls (or rises) as real GDP rises above (or falls below) Y^*. As we will soon see, New Keynesians argue that such cyclical unemployment exists because real wages do not quickly adjust to clear labour markets in response to shocks of various kinds.

Practise with Study Guide
Chapter 31, Exercise 1.

cyclical unemployment
Unemployment not due to frictional or structural factors; it is due to deviations of GDP from Y^*.

---

[1] A. S. Blinder, "The Challenge of High Unemployment," *American Economic Review* 78 (1988), 2:1.

The second group, often called *New Classical* economists, has a different view of short-run fluctuations in unemployment. In their models, real wages adjust immediately to clear labour markets, and as a result real GDP is always equal to Y^*. (As we saw in Chapter 24, if the economy's adjustment process operates very quickly, real GDP returns to Y^* very soon after any *AD* or *AS* shock.) In the New Classical perspective, the unemployment rate does fluctuate, but only because of changes in the amount of frictional or structural unemployment. For the New Classical economists, there is no cyclical unemployment whatsoever.

A central difference between the two schools of thought regards the *nature* of unemployment. For New Keynesians, workers who are suffering cyclical unemployment are normally presumed to be *involuntarily* unemployed—they are willing to work at the going wage but are unable to find appropriate jobs. In contrast, for New Classical economists, all unemployment is deemed to be *voluntary*—workers are unemployed only because they choose not to work or not to accept available job offers.

We now explore in more detail the New Classical and New Keynesian theories of unemployment fluctuations.

New Classical Theories[2]

Two major characteristics of New Classical models are that agents continuously optimize and markets continuously clear. In such models, there can be no involuntary unemployment. These theories then seek to explain unemployment as the outcome of voluntary decisions made by individuals who are choosing to do what they do, including spending some time out of employment.

The New Classical theory explains fluctuations in employment and real wages as having one of two causes. First, as shown in part (i) of Figure 31-2, changes in technology that affect the *marginal product* of labour will lead to changes in the demand for labour. If these technological shocks are sometimes positive and sometimes negative, they will lead to fluctuations in the level of employment and real wages. Second, as shown in part (ii) of Figure 31-2, changes in the willingness of individuals to work will lead to changes in the supply of labour and thus to fluctuations in the level of employment and real wages. In both cases, however, note that the flexibility of real wages results in a *clearing* of the labour market. In this setting, whatever unemployment exists cannot be involuntary and must be caused by either frictional or structural causes, the two components of the NAIRU.

> New Classical theory assumes that labour markets always clear. People who are not working are assumed to have voluntarily withdrawn from the labour market for one reason or another. There is no involuntary unemployment.

There are two problems with this New Classical view of labour markets. First, empirical observation is not consistent with the fluctuations in real wages predicted by New Classical theory. In Canada and other developed economies, employment tends to be quite volatile over the business cycle, whereas real wages tend to show

---

[2] The label "New Classical" is used because many of the arguments put forward by this group of economists are essentially more detailed and precise versions of arguments that would have been very familiar to the Classical economists, from Adam Smith and David Ricardo to Alfred Marshall.

FIGURE 31-2   Employment and Wages in a New Classical Labour Market

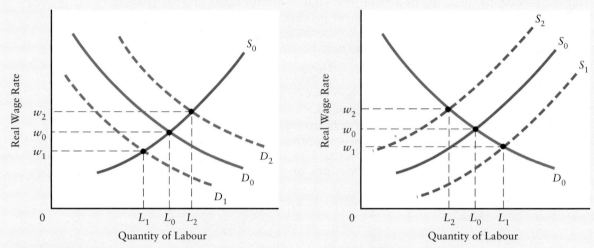

(i) Demand shifts   (ii) Supply shifts

In a New Classical labour market, there is no involuntary unemployment. The figure shows a perfectly competitive market for one type of labour. In part (i), the demand curves D_1, D_0, and D_2 are the demands for this market corresponding to low, medium, and high values for the marginal product of labour. As demand rises from D_1 to D_0 to D_2, real wages rise from w_1 to w_0 to w_2, and employment rises from L_1 to L_0 to L_2. In part (ii), the supply of labour fluctuates from S_1 to S_0 to S_2, and wages fluctuate from w_1 to w_0 to w_2. In both parts, the labour market always clears and there is no involuntary unemployment.

little cyclical variation. The second problem is that the New Classical theory predicts no involuntary unemployment whatsoever, a prediction that many economists argue is unsupported by empirical observation. (Many unemployed workers who are nonetheless actively searching for a job would be shocked to find out that some economists view them as *voluntarily* unemployed!)

Extensions in Theory 31-1 examines New Classical theory in more detail and explains why many economists, though rejecting its explanations of the economy in the short run, believe that it contains valuable insights about the economy's long-run behaviour.

New Keynesian Theories[3]

Many of the economists who reject the New Classical approach argue that most people, despite reading market signals correctly, nonetheless react in ways that do not cause markets to clear at all times. These economists—many of whom refer to themselves as New Keynesians—believe that many people are involuntarily unemployed in the sense that *they would accept an offer of work in jobs for which they are trained, at the going wage rate, if such an offer were made.* These economists concentrate their efforts on

---

[3] The label "New Keynesian" is used because many of the arguments put forward by these economists are closely related to ideas famously argued by John Maynard Keynes in *The General Theory of Employment, Interest and Money* (1936).

EXTENSIONS IN THEORY 31-1

A Closer Look at New Classical Theory

New Classical theory attempts to explain cyclical fluctuations in the context of models in which wages and prices adjust very quickly to shocks. These models contrast sharply with the models we have discussed in this book in which fluctuations in output arise largely because wages and prices adjust only gradually to shocks. If wages and prices were able to adjust instantly to all shocks, output would always be equal to potential output—there would never be inflationary or recessionary gaps. The complete and immediate flexibility of wages and prices is therefore a distinguishing feature of New Classical macro theory.

Key Propositions and Criticisms

The view of the business cycle found in New Classical models is that short-run fluctuations in real GDP are caused by fluctuations in potential output, Y^*. In this view, unemployment is always equal to the NAIRU, and it is the NAIRU itself that fluctuates. Thus, the explanation of cyclical fluctuations that arises in New Classical models is based on the role of supply shocks originating from sources such as oil price changes, technical progress, and changes in tastes. Monetary factors typically play no role in these models.

The New Classical approach is controversial. The major claims in its favour include the following:

1. It has been able to demonstrate that an economy subject to technological and taste shocks (but without aggregate demand fluctuations) has fluctuations that are similar to those in the actual economy.
2. It suggests that an integrated approach to understanding cycles and growth may be appropriate, as both reflect forces that affect the level of potential output. The distinction it makes is that some shocks are temporary (and hence have cyclical effects) whereas others are permanent (and therefore affect the economy's long-term growth).
3. It provides useful insights into how shocks, regardless of their origin, spread over time to the different sectors of the economy.

Critics of the New Classical approach express concern about its assumptions of individuals' behaviour.

They are also skeptical about an approach that ignores monetary issues. For example, they point out that New Classical models are unable to provide insights into the short-term correlation between money and output that is at the heart of the traditional macro model and for which a considerable amount of empirical evidence exists, in Canada as well as many other countries. Recessions that have their origins in financial markets, such as the major global recession of 2008–2009, cannot easily be explained by the New Classical theories.

Policy Implications

Because the New Classical approach gives no role to aggregate demand in influencing business cycles, it provides no role for stabilization operating through monetary and fiscal policies. Indeed, the models predict that the use of such demand-management policies can be *harmful*. Thus many New Classical economists would oppose the fiscal stimulus provided by both the Canadian and U.S. governments in an attempt to mitigate the worst effects of the major recession that began in 2008.

At the heart of the New Classical theory is the proposition that cycles represent *efficient* responses to the shocks that are hitting the economy. Policymakers may mistakenly interpret cyclical fluctuations as deviations from potential output caused by shifts in either the *AD* or the *AS* curves. The policymakers may try to stabilize output and thereby distort the maximizing decisions made by households and firms. This distortion will in turn cause the responses to the real shocks (as opposed to nominal, monetary shocks) to be inefficient.

Economists disagree about how well New Classical models explain short-run fluctuations. However, since the New Classical approach emphasizes the importance of markets always clearing in response to changes in technology or other shocks, many economists who view New Classical models as a poor description of the economy in the short run believe that many of the New Classical insights are important when thinking about the behaviour of the economy in the long run.

FIGURE 31-3   Unemployment and Sticky Wages in a New Keynesian Labour Market

When the wage rate does not change enough to equate quantity demanded with quantity supplied, there will be unemployment in slumps and labour shortages in booms. When demand is at its normal level D_0, the market is cleared with wage rate w_0, employment is L_0, and there is no involuntary unemployment. In a recession, demand falls to D_1, but the wage falls only to w_1'. As a result, L_1 of labour is demanded and L_1' is supplied. Employment is determined by the quantity demanded at L_1. The remainder of the supply for which there is no demand, L_1L_1', is involuntarily unemployed. In a boom, demand rises to D_2, but the wage rate rises only to w_2'. As a result, the quantity demanded is L_2', whereas only L_2 is supplied. Employment rises to L_2, which is the amount supplied. The rest of the demand cannot be satisfied, making excess demand for labour of L_2L_2'.

explaining why wages do not quickly adjust to eliminate involuntary unemployment. If wages do not respond quickly to shifts in supply and demand in the labour market, quantity supplied and quantity demanded may *not* be equated for extended periods of time. Labour markets will then display unemployment during recessions and excess demand during booms, as shown in Figure 31-3.

New Keynesian theories start with the observation that wages do not change every time demand or supply shifts. When unemployed workers are looking for jobs, they do not knock on employers' doors and offer to work at lower wages than are being paid to current workers; instead, they answer help-wanted ads and hope to get the jobs offered but are often disappointed. Nor do employers, seeing an excess of applicants for the few jobs that are available, go to the current workers and reduce their wages until there is no one who is looking for a job; instead, they pick and choose until they fill their needs and then hang a sign saying "No Help Wanted."

There are several possible reasons why wages do not quickly adjust to all shocks in the labour market.

Long-Term Employment Relationships

One set of theories is based on the advantages to both workers and employers of relatively long-term and stable employment relationships. Workers want job security in the face of fluctuating demand. Employers want workers who understand the firm's organization, production, and marketing plans. Under these circumstances, both parties care about things in addition to the wage rate, and wages are somewhat insensitive to fluctuations in current economic conditions. Wages are, in effect, regular payments to workers over an extended employment relationship rather than a device for fine-tuning the current supplies of and demands for labour. Given this situation, the tendency is for employers to "smooth" the income of employees by paying a steady wage and letting profits and employment fluctuate to absorb the effects of temporary increases and decreases in demand for the firm's product.

A number of labour-market institutions work to achieve these results. For example, many long-term contracts provide for a schedule of wages over a period of several years. Similarly, employee benefits, such as pensions and supplementary health insurance, tend to bind workers to particular employers. Another example is pay that rises with years of service. This helps to bind the employee to the company, whereas seniority rules for layoffs bind the employer to the long-term worker.

In many labour markets in which long-term relationships are important, the wage rate does not fluctuate to clear the market continuously.

Menu Costs and Wage Contracts A typical large firm sells dozens of differentiated products and employs many different types of labour. Changing prices and wages in response to every minor fluctuation in demand is a costly and time-consuming activity. Many firms therefore find it optimal to keep their price lists (*menus*) constant for significant periods of time. Since large firms are often operating in imperfectly competitive markets, they have some discretion over price. Hence, firms often react to small changes in demand by holding prices constant and responding with changes in output and employment. If many firms behave this way, output and employment will respond to changes in aggregate demand. In other words, the amount of involuntary unemployment will fluctuate over the business cycle.

The Canadian evidence is consistent with the existence of sluggish price adjustment by firms, especially those in manufacturing industries. Such "price stickiness" was a central feature of Keynesian economics; today, much of the New Keynesian perspective is based on the idea that sticky prices are a result of firms' optimal responses to adjustment costs.

Wages tend to be inflexible in the short term because wage rates are generally set only occasionally. Wages are set often on an annual basis; in some unionized contracts wages are set for up to three years. Such inflexibility of wages implies that changes in aggregate demand and supply will tend to cause changes in the amount of involuntary unemployment.

The quick adjustment of wages to excess demands and supplies is not a characteristic of labour markets in which employees and firms have long-term relationships, such as in the health-care sector.

> Costs associated with changing prices and wages lead firms and workers to make such changes only infrequently. As a result, many prices and wages are slow in adjusting to shocks.

Efficiency Wages The idea of *efficiency wages* forms the core of another strand of New Keynesian thinking about why wages do not quickly adjust to clear labour markets. For any of a number of reasons, employers may find that they get more output per dollar of wages paid—that is, a more efficient workforce—when they pay labour somewhat more than the minimum amount that would induce workers to work for them.

Suppose it is costly for employers to monitor workers' performance on the job so that some workers will be able to shirk duties with a low probability of being caught. Given prevailing labour-market institutions, it is generally impossible for employers to levy fines on employees for shirking on the job since the employees could just leave their jobs rather than pay the fines. So firms may instead choose to pay a wage premium—an efficiency wage—to the workers, in excess of the wage that the workers will get elsewhere in the labour market. With such a wage premium, workers will be reluctant to shirk because if they get caught and laid off, they will then lose this wage premium.

How does this relate to involuntary unemployment? The wage premium paid to prevent workers from shirking means that the quantity of labour supplied may exceed the quantity demanded by firms, thereby creating involuntary unemployment. Wages do not fall to clear the labour market because firms would rather pay a high wage to motivated workers than a lower wage to workers who would then shirk their duties. The result is involuntary unemployment for some workers.

> Efficiency-wage theory predicts that firms may find it profitable to pay high enough wages so that working is a clearly superior alternative to being laid off. Involuntary unemployment results.

Union Bargaining The final New Keynesian theory to be considered assumes that those already employed ("insiders") have more say in wage bargaining than those currently not employed ("outsiders"). Employed workers are often represented by a union, which negotiates the wage rate with firms. The union will generally represent the interests of the insiders but will not necessarily reflect the interests of the outsiders. Insiders will naturally want to bid up wages even though to do so will harm the employment prospects of the outsiders. Hence, this theory generates an outcome to the bargaining process between firms and unions in which the wage is set higher than the market-clearing level, just as with efficiency wages. The consequence is some involuntary unemployment.

In addition to explaining the existence of involuntary unemployment, this theory adds one important insight regarding international differences in unemployment. In some countries, unions bargain at the level of the firm; in others they bargain at the level of the whole industry or the whole economy. Where bargaining is decentralized, as in Canada and the United States, the union can push for higher wages for the insiders without worrying about the effects on outsiders or on the rest of the economy. However, where bargaining is more centralized, as in much of Western Europe, the effects on the rest of the economy become partially internalized into the bargaining process, because union negotiators are bargaining on behalf of a larger group of workers, rather than just those currently employed.

This theory leads to the following predictions. Decentralized bargaining with strong unions will lead to higher-than-market-clearing wages, and higher unemployment as the outsiders are excluded from jobs. In contrast, more centralized bargaining will produce an outcome closer to the market-clearing outcome, so unemployment will be lower. In situations in which unionization is low or unions are weak, the outcome will be close to the market-clearing outcome. This analysis may partly explain why unemployment is relatively high in EU countries (where unions are strong and bargaining is decentralized), lower in Scandinavia (where unions are also strong but bargaining is centralized), and even lower in Canada and the United States (where the extent of unionization is much lower and thus even decentralized wage bargaining affects only a small portion of the economy).

> **In labour markets with powerful unions, wages are set in a bargaining process. If unions act in the interests of the current "insiders," wages will be high and involuntary unemployment will exist. If unions act in the interests of all workers, wages and involuntary unemployment will both be lower.**

Convergence of Theories?

We have examined two classes of theories of unemployment fluctuations. In the New Classical theories, wages and prices adjust instantly to clear markets and so real GDP is always equal to potential GDP. Unemployment fluctuates, but it is always equal to the NAIRU, U^*. Using the terminology we introduced earlier, there is no *cyclical* unemployment in New Classical models; all unemployment is either frictional or structural. In contrast, New Keynesian models emphasize the gradual adjustment of wages and prices and thus the existence of periods in which real GDP is either above or below potential GDP. In these models, unemployment fluctuates around the value of U^*—that is, U does not always equal U^*. Cyclical unemployment fluctuates over the business cycle. Table 31-1 provides a summary of the key assumptions and predictions of these two classes of theories.

TABLE 31-1   Summary of New Classical and New Keynesian Theories

	New Classical Theory	New Keynesian Theory
	Key Assumptions	
Market clearing	Wages and price are perfectly flexible; all markets are continuously clearing.	Wages and prices are slow to adjust; markets are not continuously clearing.
	Key Predictions	
Unemployment	U is always equal to the NAIRU. There is no cyclical or involuntary unemployment; all unemployment is voluntary.	U often deviates from the NAIRU. Unemployment has both voluntary and involuntary components.
Role of AD shocks	AD shocks do not cause changes in output because the AS curve adjusts instantly to bring Y back to Y^*.	AD shocks cause changes in output because the AS curve adjusts only gradually to bring Y back to Y^*.
Changes in Y^* and the NAIRU	Shocks to technology and preferences lead to changes in both Y^* and the NAIRU.	Shocks to technology and preferences lead to changes in both Y^* and the NAIRU.

Note, however, that the contrast between New Classical and New Keynesian models is sharper in the short run than the long run. In the short run, the extent of wage and price flexibility, and thus the extent to which real GDP deviates from potential output, is a major distinguishing point between these two classes of models. In the long run, however, most economists agree that real GDP tends to return to its potential level, Y^*, and that Y^* grows more or less continually for reasons including population growth, capital accumulation, and technological change.

Both New Classical economists and New Keynesians agree that in the long run the unemployment rate tends toward U^*.

Let's restate the difference between New Keynesian and New Classical models another way. In New Keynesian models there is a meaningful difference between the short run and the long run that is determined by the degree of wage and price flexibility. In New Classical models, however, wages and prices adjust instantly, so there is no similar distinction between the short run and the long run. But since *both* classes of models agree that wages and prices tend to be flexible in the long run, they have the same predictions regarding the long-run effects of policy.

For example, New Keynesians argue that a monetary expansion will raise real GDP above Y^* and reduce U below U^*. In the long run, however, output will tend to return to Y^*, U will return to U^*, and the main long-run effect of the monetary expansion will be a higher price level. New Classical economists agree on this predicted long-run effect, but they argue that the short-run real effects on output and unemployment will either be absent or be of much shorter duration since wages and prices adjust very quickly.

New Keynesians and New Classical economists agree that the actual unemployment rate will tend toward the NAIRU in the long run. Our next job is to understand why the NAIRU changes. We turn to this topic now.

Practise with Study Guide
Chapter 31, Short-Answer
Questions 1–3.

31.3 What Determines the NAIRU?

The NAIRU is composed of frictional and structural unemployment. Our interest is in why the NAIRU changes over time and in the extent to which economic policy can affect it.

Frictional Unemployment

frictional unemployment
Unemployment that results from the turnover in the labour market as workers move between jobs.

As we saw in Chapter 19, **frictional unemployment** results from the normal turnover of labour. One source of frictional unemployment is young people who enter the labour force and look for jobs. Another source is people who leave their jobs. Some may quit because they are dissatisfied with the type of work or their working conditions; others may be fired because of incompetence or laid off because their employers go out of business. Whatever the reason, they must search for new jobs, which takes time. Persons who are unemployed while searching for jobs are said to be frictionally unemployed or in *search unemployment*.

> The normal turnover of labour causes frictional unemployment to persist, even if the economy is at potential output.

How "voluntary" is frictional unemployment? Some of it is clearly voluntary. For example, a worker may know of an available job but may not accept it so she can search for a better one. Some of it is also involuntary, such as when a worker gets laid off and cannot find *any* job offer for a period of weeks, even though he may be actively searching. *Extensions in Theory 31-2* shows that the distinction between voluntary and involuntary unemployment is not always as clear as it might at first seem.

Structural Unemployment

structural unemployment
Unemployment caused by a mismatch in skills, industry, or location between available jobs and unemployed workers.

Structural unemployment is defined as a mismatch between the current structure of the labour force—in terms of skills, occupations, industries, or geographical locations—and the current structure of firms' demand for labour. Since changes in the structure of the demand for labour are occurring continually in any modern economy, and since it takes time for workers to adjust, some amount of structural unemployment always exists.

Natural Causes Changes that accompany economic growth shift the structure of the demand for labour. Demand might rise in such expanding areas as British Columbia's Lower Mainland or northern Alberta but might fall in parts of Ontario and Quebec. Demand rises for workers with certain skills, such as computer programming and electronics engineering, and falls for workers with other skills, such as stenography, assembly line work, and middle management. To meet changing demands, the structure of the labour force must change. Some existing workers can retrain and some new entrants can acquire fresh skills, but the transition is often difficult, especially for already experienced workers whose skills become economically obsolete.

Increases in international competition can also cause structural unemployment. As the geographical distribution of world production changes, so does the composition of

EXTENSIONS IN THEORY 31-2

Voluntary Versus Involuntary Unemployment

Frictional unemployment is *involuntary* if the job seeker has not yet found a job for which his or her training and experience are suitable, even when such jobs exist somewhere in the economy. Frictional unemployment is *voluntary* if the unemployed person is aware of available jobs for which he or she is suited but is searching for better options. But how should we classify an unemployed person who refuses to accept a job at a lower skill level than the one for which she is qualified? What if she turns down a job for which she is trained because she hopes to get a higher wage offer for a similar job from another employer?

In one sense, people in search unemployment are voluntarily unemployed because they could almost always find *some* job, no matter how poorly paid or inappropriate to their training; in another sense, they are involuntarily unemployed because they have not yet succeeded in finding the job that they believe exists and for which they feel they are suited at a rate of pay that they believe is attainable.

Workers do not have perfect knowledge of all available jobs and rates of pay, and they may be able to gain information only by searching the labour market. Facing this uncertainty, they may find it sensible to refuse a first job offer, for the offer may prove to be a poor one in light of further market information. But too much search—for example, holding off while being supported by others in the hope of finding a job better than a job for which one is really suited—is an economic waste. Thus, search unemployment is a grey area: Some of it is useful, but too much can be wasteful.

Some search unemployment is desirable because it gives unemployed people time to find an available job that makes the best use of their skills.

How long it pays for people to remain in search unemployment depends on the economic costs of being unemployed. By lowering the costs of being unemployed, employment insurance tends to increase the amount of search unemployment. This may or may not increase economic efficiency, depending on whether or not it induces people to search beyond the point at which they acquire new and valuable information about the labour market.

---

production and of labour demand in any one country. Labour adapts to such shifts by changing jobs, skills, and locations, but until the transition is complete, structural unemployment exists.

> Structural unemployment will increase if there is either an increase in the pace at which the structure of the demand for labour is changing or a decrease in the pace at which labour is adapting to these changes.

Following the Canada–U.S. Free Trade Agreement in 1989 and the North American Free Trade Agreement (NAFTA) in 1994, there were significant shifts of economic activity within Canada. For example, the textiles industry, much of which was located in Quebec, contracted; at the same time there was an expansion of the high-tech industry, much of which was located in the Ottawa Valley. The types of workers released from the textiles industry, however, were not exactly what were required in the expanding high-tech industry. This type of mismatch in skills and locations contributed to structural unemployment during the early 1990s.

Structural unemployment also increased during the 2002–2008 period in response to the dramatic increase in the world price of oil. The demand for labour increased sharply in the petroleum-producing regions of Alberta, Saskatchewan, and Newfoundland. At the same time, many jobs were lost in the manufacturing heartland of Ontario and Quebec because the rising price of oil significantly increased firms' costs. Some of

Increases in the world price of oil between 2002 and 2008 led to a reduction in manufacturing activity in Central Canada and economic expansions in oil-producing regions of the country, such as the Alberta oil sands shown here. Structural unemployment was created until workers could move from Eastern and Central Canada to Alberta.

For information on Canada's Employment Insurance program, see the website for Human Resources and Social Development Canada: **www.hrsdc.gc.ca.**

the displaced workers could find jobs relatively quickly in expanding firms in other regions or sectors, but for most workers this transition was slow. Structural unemployment was the result.

Policy Causes Government policies can influence the speed with which labour markets adapt to changes. Some countries, including Canada, have adopted policies that *discourage* movement among regions, industries, and occupations. These policies (which may be desirable for other reasons) tend to reduce the rate at which unemployed workers are matched with vacant jobs, and thus tend to raise the amount of structural unemployment.

For two related reasons, the employment-insurance (EI) program contributes to structural unemployment. First, the Canadian EI system ties workers' benefits to the regional unemployment rate in such a way that unemployed workers can collect EI benefits for more weeks in regions where unemployment is high than where it is low. The EI system therefore encourages unemployed workers to remain in high-unemployment regions rather than encouraging them to move to regions where employment prospects are more favourable. Second, workers are eligible for employment insurance only if they have worked for a given number of weeks in the previous year—this is known as the *entrance requirement*. In some cases, however, these entrance requirements are very low and thus seasonal workers are encouraged to work for a few months and then collect employment insurance and wait for the next season, rather than finding other jobs during the off season.

Finally, labour-market policies that make it difficult or costly for firms to fire workers also make employers more reluctant to hire workers in the first place. Such policies, which are very common in the European Union, reduce the amount of turnover in the labour market and are believed to be an important contributor to the amount of long-term unemployment in those countries. In Germany, Italy, and Belgium, for example, the labour laws impose very high costs on firms whenever workers are laid off. In those countries, approximately 50 percent of all unemployment spells last for *longer* than 12 months.

The Frictional–Structural Distinction

As with many distinctions, the one between frictional and structural unemployment is not precise. In a sense, structural unemployment is really long-term frictional unemployment. Consider, for example, what would happen if there were an increase in world demand for Canadian-made car parts but at the same time a decline in world demand for Canadian-assembled cars. This change would require labour to move from one sector (the car-assembly sector) to another (the car-parts manufacturing sector). If the reallocation were to occur quickly, we would call the unemployment *frictional*; if the reallocation were to occur slowly, we would call the unemployment *structural*.

In practice, structural and frictional unemployment cannot be separated. But the two of them, taken together, *can* be separated from cyclical unemployment. Specifically, when real GDP is at its potential level, the *only* unemployment (by definition) is the NAIRU, which comprises frictional and structural unemployment. For example, real GDP in Canada was approximately equal to potential GDP in 2007. At that time, the unemployment rate was 6 percent, and thus the NAIRU was approximately 6 percent. In contrast, two years later in 2009 after the onset of the most recent recession, the unemployment rate was about 8.5 percent. If the underlying frictions and structural change in the economy were unchanged over those two years, we could conclude that in 2009, 2.5 percentage points of the actual unemployment rate was due to cyclical factors and the rest was due to frictional and structural factors.

Why Does the NAIRU Change?

In general, the NAIRU can rise for two reasons. First, the economy may be subjected to *more* shocks requiring an adjustment of the labour force between sectors or regions. Second, the *ability* of the labour force to adjust to any given shock may decline. In either case, the amount of frictional or structural unemployment will rise, and the NAIRU will therefore increase.

We now examine several specific causes of changes in the NAIRU.

Young workers have higher unemployment rates than do older workers. As the share of younger workers in the labour force decreases, so will the economy's NAIRU.

Demographic Shifts Because young people usually try several jobs before settling into one for a longer period of time, young or inexperienced workers have more labour-market turnover and therefore higher unemployment rates than experienced workers. The proportion of inexperienced workers in the labour force rose significantly as the baby-boom generation of the 1950s entered the labour force in the 1970s and 1980s. This trend had the effect of increasing the NAIRU during the 1970s and 1980s. But as the baby-boom generation aged, and the fraction of young workers in the labour force declined in the late 1990s and early 2000s, the opposite effect was observed and tended to reduce the NAIRU.

A second demographic trend relates to the labour-force participation of women. During the 1960s and 1970s women tended to have higher unemployment rates than men. Since this was true at all points of the business cycle, the higher unemployment was higher frictional and structural unemployment. Thus, when female labour-force participation rates increased dramatically in the 1960s and 1970s, the NAIRU naturally increased. In recent years, however, female unemployment rates have dropped below the rates for men, and so continued increases in female participation will, if anything, tend to decrease the NAIRU.

> **Greater labour-force participation by groups with high unemployment rates increases the NAIRU.**

See Figure 31-4 for Canadian unemployment rates for various demographic groups in 2008. Notice especially the significantly higher unemployment rates for youth of both sexes. These data form the basis for the often-heard view that while overall unemployment may be at acceptable levels, youth unemployment may be a serious problem. However, to the extent that this higher youth unemployment is due to greater turnover (much of which is voluntary), there may not be a serious problem.

FIGURE 31-4   Canadian Unemployment Rates by Demographic Groups, 2008

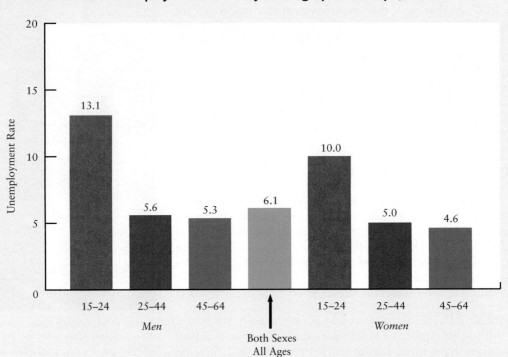

Unemployment is unevenly spread among different groups in the labour force. In 2008, when the overall unemployment rate was 6.1 percent, the unemployment rates for youths (of both sexes) were considerably higher.

(*Source:* These data are available on Statistics Canada's website, www.statcan.gc.ca, by searching for "labour force." "Labour force characteristics by age and sex (estimates)"; http://www40.statcan.gc.ca/l01/cst01/labor20a-eng.htm.)

Hysteresis   Some models of unemployment show that the NAIRU can be influenced by the current rate of unemployment. Such models get their name from the Greek word *hysteresis,* meaning "lagged effect."

One mechanism that can lead to hysteresis arises from the importance of experience and on-the-job training. Suppose a recession causes a significant group of new entrants to the labour force to encounter unusual difficulty obtaining their first jobs. As a result, this unlucky group will be slow to acquire the important skills that workers generally learn in their first jobs. When demand increases again, this group of workers will be at a disadvantage relative to workers with normal histories of experience, and the unlucky group may take longer to find jobs and thus have unemployment rates that will be higher than average. Hence, the NAIRU will be higher than it would have been had there been no recession.

Another force that can cause such effects is emphasized by commentators in the European Union, which has a more heavily unionized labour force than does either Canada or the United States. In times of high unemployment, people who are currently employed ("insiders") may use their bargaining power to ensure that their own status is maintained and prevent new entrants to the labour force ("outsiders") from competing effectively. For this reason, high unemployment—whatever its initial cause—will tend to become "locked in." If outsiders are denied access to the labour market, their unemployment will fail to exert downward pressure on wages, and the NAIRU will tend to rise.

Globalization and Structural Change

The ongoing process of globalization, especially since the mid-1970s, has increased the rate at which labour is being reallocated across regions and sectors in the Canadian economy. While most economists argue that the growing integration of Canada in the global economy generates net benefits for Canada, they also recognize a downside. One unfortunate consequence is that Canadian labour markets are increasingly affected by changes in demand and supply conditions elsewhere in the world. As Canadian labour markets require more frequent and larger adjustments to economic events occurring in other parts of the world, the NAIRU will tend to increase.

Policy and Labour-Market Flexibility

We mentioned briefly how policies can affect structural unemployment. It is worthwhile emphasizing again the important role that government policy can have on the NAIRU.

One important cause of unemployment is *inflexibility* in the labour market. If wages are inflexible, shocks to labour demand or supply can cause unemployment. If workers are unable or unwilling to move between regions or between industries, changes in the structure of the economy can cause unemployment. If it is costly for firms to hire workers, firms will find other ways of increasing output (such as switching to more capital-intensive methods of production). In general, since the economy is always being buffeted by shocks of one sort or another, the less flexible is the labour market, the higher structural unemployment will be.

> **Any government policy that reduces labour-market flexibility is likely to increase the NAIRU.**

Consider employment insurance (EI) as an example of a policy that reduces labour-market flexibility. EI provides income support to eligible unemployed workers and thus reduces the costs to the worker of being unemployed. This income support will typically lead the worker to search longer for a new job and thus increase frictional unemployment. This longer search may be desirable since by reducing the cost of unemployment the worker is able to conduct a thorough search for a job that is an appropriate match for his or her specific skills. On the other hand, if the EI system is so generous that workers have little incentive to accept reasonable jobs—instead holding out for the "perfect" job—then the increase in unemployment generated by the EI system will be undesirable.

In general, however, the basic message should be clear. The more generous is the employment insurance system, the less motivated unemployed workers will be to accept a new job quickly. This reduction in labour-market flexibility will increase the NAIRU.

A second example concerns policies designed to increase job security for workers. In most Western European countries, firms cannot lay off workers without showing cause, which can lead to costly delays and even litigation. When firms do lay workers off, they are required either to give several months' notice before doing so or, in lieu of such notice, are required to make severance payments equal to several months' worth of pay. In Italy, for example, a worker who has been with the firm for 10 years is guaranteed either 20 months' notice before termination or a severance payment equal to 20 months' worth of pay.

Such job-security provisions greatly reduce the flexibility of firms. But this inflexibility on the part of the firms is passed on to workers. Any policy that forces the firm to incur large costs for laying off workers is likely to lead the same firm to be very hesitant about hiring workers in the first place. Given this reduction in labour-market flexibility, such policies are likely to increase the NAIRU.

Such mandated job security is relatively rare in Canada and the United States. Its rarity contributes to the general belief among economists that North American labour markets are much more flexible than those in Europe. Many economists see this as the most important explanation for why unemployment rates in Canada and the United States are significantly below the unemployment rates in Europe and have been for more than two decades.

31.4 Reducing Unemployment

Practise with Study Guide
Chapter 31, Exercises 2 and 3.

In the remainder of this chapter we briefly examine what can be done to reduce unemployment. Other things being equal, all governments would like to reduce unemployment. The questions are "Can it be done?" and "If so, at what cost?"

Cyclical Unemployment

We do not need to say much more about cyclical unemployment because its control is the subject of stabilization policy, which we have studied in several earlier chapters. A major recession that occurs because of negative *AD* or *AS* shocks can be countered by monetary and fiscal policies to reduce cyclical unemployment.

There is room for debate, however, about *how much* the government can and should do in this respect. Advocates of stabilization policy call for expansionary fiscal and monetary policies to reduce cyclical unemployment (and increase output) during recessionary gaps, at least when they last for sustained periods of time. Advocates of a hands-off approach say that normal market adjustments can be relied on to remove recessionary gaps and that government policy, no matter how well intentioned, will only make things worse. They call for setting simple rules for monetary and fiscal policy that would make discretionary stabilization policy impossible.

Whatever may be argued in principle, however, policymakers have not yet agreed to abandon stabilization measures in practice. In the recession that began in most countries in 2008, for example, governments were quite aggressive in their implementation of expansionary fiscal and monetary policies in an attempt to dampen the recession's effects on falling output and rising unemployment.

Frictional Unemployment

The turnover in the labour market that causes frictional unemployment is an inevitable part of the functioning of the economy. Some frictional unemployment is a natural part of the learning process for young workers. New entrants to the labour force (many of whom are young) have to try several jobs to see which is most suitable, and this leads to a high turnover rate among the young and hence high frictional unemployment.

Employment insurance is one method of helping people cope with unemployment. It has reduced significantly the human costs of the bouts with unemployment that are inevitable in a changing society. Nothing, however, is without cost. Although employment insurance alleviates the suffering caused by some kinds of unemployment, it also contributes to search unemployment, as we have already observed. As with any policy, a rational assessment of the value of employment insurance requires a balancing of its undoubted benefits against its undoubted costs. Many Canadians believe that when this calculation is made, the benefits greatly exceed the costs, although many also recognize the scope for reform of certain aspects of the program.

Many provisions have been added over the years to the employment insurance scheme to focus it more on people in general need and to reduce its effect of raising the unemployment rate. For example, workers must be actively seeking employment in order to be eligible for EI. Also, workers who voluntarily quit their jobs (without cause) are not eligible to collect EI. In recent years, the benefits received by eligible unemployed workers have been reduced, thus decreasing the likelihood that job seekers will reject early job offers. These changes have contributed to a decline in the amount of frictional unemployment.

For two of the most widely used job-match websites, go to www.monster.ca or www.workopolis.ca.

Structural Unemployment

The reallocation of labour among occupations, industries, skill categories, and regions that gives rise to structural unemployment is an inevitable part of a market economy. Much of this required reallocation is driven by technological change, which occurs in different ways and at different paces in various parts of the economy. Ever since the beginning of the Industrial Revolution in the late eighteenth century, workers have resisted the introduction of new techniques that replace the older techniques at which they were skilled. Such resistance is understandable. New techniques often destroy the value of the knowledge and experience of workers skilled in the displaced techniques. Older workers may not even get a chance to start over with the new technique. Employers may prefer to hire younger persons who will learn the new skills faster than older workers who are set in their ways of thinking. From society's point of view, new techniques are beneficial because they are a major source of economic growth. From the point of view of the workers they displace, however, new techniques can be an unmitigated disaster.

There are two basic approaches to reducing structural unemployment: Try to resist the changes that the economy experiences or accept the changes and try to assist the necessary adjustments. Throughout history, both approaches have been tried.

Resisting Change
Over the long term, policies aimed at maintaining employment levels in declining industries run into increasing difficulties. Agreements to hire unneeded workers raise costs and can hasten the decline of an industry threatened by competitive products. An industry that is declining because of economic change becomes an increasingly large burden on the public purse as economic forces become less and less favourable to its success. Sooner or later, public support is withdrawn, and it is followed by a precipitous decline.

As we assess these remedies for structural unemployment, it is important to realize that although they are not viable in the long run for the entire economy, they may be the best alternatives for the affected workers during their lifetimes.

> There is often a genuine conflict between the private interest of workers threatened by structural unemployment, whose interests lie in preserving existing jobs, and the social interest served by reallocating resources to where they are most valuable.

Assisting Adjustment A second general approach to dealing with structural change is to accept the decline of specific industries and the loss of specific jobs that go with them and to try to reduce the cost of adjustment for the workers affected. A number of policies have been introduced in Canada to ease the adjustment to changing economic conditions.

One such policy is publicly subsidized education and retraining schemes. The public involvement is motivated largely by imperfections in capital markets that make it difficult for workers to borrow funds for education, training, or retraining. A major component of labour-market policies is a system of loans and subsidies for higher education.

Another policy is motivated by the difficulty in obtaining good information about current and future job prospects. In recent years, the development of the Internet has greatly improved the flow of this type of information. Human Resources and Skills Development Canada (HRSDC), for example, operates an Internet-based service to speed up and improve the quality of matches between firms and workers. This national Job Bank allows firms (or workers) to specify certain characteristics and skills and then match these characteristics with workers (or firms) on the "other side" of the labour market.

To learn more about the national Job Bank, go to Service Canada's website: **www.jobbank.gc.ca.**

> **Policies to increase retraining and to improve the flow of labour-market information will tend to reduce the amount of structural unemployment.**

The choice between designing policies to "resist change" or "assist adjustment" was apparent early in 2009 when the Canadian and U.S. governments were faced with the probable collapse of Chrysler and General Motors. The desperate financial position of these storied auto companies was partly due to the deep global recession, but it was also partly due to business practices that over several years had proven to be unsuccessful. If the governments did nothing to help the auto companies, their collapse would lead to thousands of job losses in the auto and auto-parts sectors. If instead the governments decided to provide financial assistance to the troubled companies, there was a real possibility that the assistance would only delay the companies' inevitable collapse, but at great cost to taxpayers.

In the end, the governments coordinated their actions and made large financial contributions to the firms in exchange for partial ownership. In addition, both companies were required to restructure their businesses and provide credible plans for how their firms would compete effectively against their domestic and foreign rivals. The next few years will be interesting ones in the North American auto sector.

---

myeconlab ADDITIONAL TOPICS

Politicians often claim that government-provided financial assistance to specific sectors or firms can "create" many jobs. Most economists, however, argue that the success of such policies in increasing the total number of jobs depends on the state of the economy, specifically the level of current GDP relative to potential GDP. For more information, look for **Does Government Support of Specific Industries Really Create Jobs?** in the *Additional Topics* section of this book's MyEconLab.

w w w . m y e c o n l a b . c o m

Conclusion

Over the years, unemployment has been regarded in many different ways. Harsh critics see it as proof that the market system is badly flawed. Reformers regard it as a necessary evil of the market system and a suitable object for government policy to reduce its incidence and its harmful effects. Others see it as overblown in importance and believe that it does not reflect any real inability of workers to obtain jobs if they really want to work.

Most government policy follows a middle route. Fiscal and monetary policies generally seek to reduce at least the most persistent of recessionary gaps, and a host of labour-market policies are designed to reduce frictional and structural unemployment. Such social policies as employment insurance seek to reduce the sting of unemployment for the many who are thought to suffer from it for reasons beyond their control.

As global economic competition becomes more intense and as new knowledge-driven methods of production spread, the ability to adjust to economic change will become increasingly important. Countries that succeed in the global marketplace, while also managing to maintain humane social welfare systems, will be those that best learn how to deal with changes in the economic landscape. This will mean avoiding economic policies that inhibit change while adopting social policies that reduce the human cost of adjusting to change. This is an enormous challenge for future Canadian economic and social policies.

Summary

31.1 Employment and Unemployment   LO ❶

- Canadian employment and the Canadian labour force increased along a strong upward trend throughout the twentieth century. The unemployment rate fluctuates significantly over the course of the business cycle.
- Looking only at the level of employment or unemployment misses a tremendous amount of activity in the labour market as individuals flow from unemployment to employment or from employment to unemployment. In recent years in Canada, approximately 400 000 people *per month* flowed between employment and unemployment. This level of gross flows reflects the turnover that is a normal part of any labour market.

- It is useful to distinguish among several types of unemployment: cyclical unemployment, which is associated with output gaps; frictional unemployment, which is a result of normal labour-market turnover; and structural unemployment, which is caused by the need to reallocate resources among occupations, regions, and industries as the structure of demand and supply changes.
- Together, frictional unemployment and structural unemployment make up the NAIRU. The actual unemployment rate is equal to the NAIRU when real GDP is equal to Y^*.

31.2 Unemployment Fluctuations   LO ❷

- There is a long-standing debate among economists regarding the causes of unemployment fluctuations.
- New Classical theories look to explanations that allow the labour market to be cleared continuously by perfectly flexible wages and prices. Such theories can explain cyclical variations in employment but predict no involuntary unemployment.
- New Keynesian theories have focused on the long-term nature of employer–worker relationships in which wages tend to respond only a little, and employment

tends to respond a lot, to changes in the demand and supply of labour. More recent New Keynesian theories have examined the possibility that it may be efficient for employers to pay wages that are above the level that would clear the labour market (efficiency wages).
- This debate applies only to the short-run behaviour of the economy. Both classes of models, for example, predict that in the long run, monetary expansions or contractions have few effects on output, employment, or unemployment.

31.3 What Determines the NAIRU?

- The NAIRU will always be positive because it takes time for labour to move between jobs both in normal turnover (frictional unemployment) and in response to changes in the structure of the demand for labour (structural unemployment).
- Because different workers have different sets of skills and because different firms require workers with different sets of skills, some unemployment—resulting from workers searching for appropriate job matches with employers—is socially desirable.

- Anything that increases the rate of turnover in the labour market, or the pace of structural change in the economy, will likely increase the NAIRU.
- Employment insurance also increases the NAIRU by encouraging workers to continue searching for an appropriate job. Policies that mandate job security increase the costs to firms of laying off workers. This makes them reluctant to hire workers in the first place and may increase the NAIRU.

31.4 Reducing Unemployment

- Cyclical unemployment can be reduced by using monetary or fiscal policies to close recessionary gaps.
- Frictional and structural unemployment can be reduced by making it easier to move between jobs and by raising the cost of staying unemployed (e.g., by reducing employment insurance benefits).

- In a growing, changing economy populated by people who want to change jobs for many reasons, it is neither possible nor desirable to reduce unemployment to zero.
- Policies that assist workers in retraining and in moving between jobs, regions, or industries may be the most effective way to deal with the various shocks that buffet the economy.

Key Concepts

Gross flows in the labour market
Cyclical, frictional, and structural
   unemployment
New Classical and New Keynesian
   theories of unemployment

Long-term employment relationships
Efficiency wages
Hysteresis
The components of the NAIRU

Determinants of the NAIRU
Policies to reduce the NAIRU
Labour-market flexibility

Study Exercises

1. Fill in the blanks to make the following statements correct.

   a. The overall unemployment rate in Canada is not a good indicator of the level of *activity* in the labour market because _____.

   b. *Gross* flows in the labour market are much _____ than net flows in the labour market.

   c. In a typical month in Canada, _____ workers flow in each direction between unemployment and employment.

   d. Cyclical unemployment exists when real GDP is _____ than potential GDP. When real GDP is equal to potential GDP, then all unemployment is either _____ or _____.

   e. New Classical theories assume that the labour market always _____ with flexible _____ and that any unemployment that does exist is _____.

   f. New Keynesian theories assume that wages do not instantly _____ to clear the market. A recessionary gap can persist and result in unemployment that is _____.

g. The New Classical and New Keynesian theories both assume that, in the long run, wages and prices _____ and the unemployment rate will revert to the _____, as any _____ gap is closed.

2. Fill in the blanks to make the following statements correct.

a. The NAIRU is composed of _____ unemployment and _____ unemployment. The NAIRU is always _____ than zero.

b. If there are 1000 loggers in British Columbia who are unemployed, and 1000 vacant positions for call-centre operators in New Brunswick, we say that this unemployment is _____.

c. Suppose the NAIRU in June 2009 was 6.0 percent. If the actual unemployment rate was 8.2 percent, we can conclude that _____ percentage points are due to _____ factors and the remaining _____ percentage points are due to _____ and _____ factors.

d. Suppose the government increased the number of weeks that an unemployed worker can collect employment-insurance benefits from 12 weeks to 16 weeks. The NAIRU is likely to _____ because of an increase in the amount of _____ unemployment.

e. Countries with greater labour-market flexibility are likely to have _____ unemployment rates than countries in which policies inhibit flexibility.

f. Cyclical unemployment can be reduced by closing a(n) _____ gap by using _____ and _____ policies.

3. The following table shows the pattern of real GDP, potential GDP, and the unemployment rate for several years in Cycleland.

Year	Real GDP (billions of dollars)	Potential GDP (billions of dollars)	Unemployment Rate (%)
2001	790	740	6.3
2002	800	760	6.5
2003	780	780	6.8
2004	750	800	8.2
2005	765	810	8.4
2006	790	830	8.4
2007	815	850	8.0
2008	845	870	7.5
2009	875	890	7.2
2010	900	900	6.8
2011	930	920	6.7

a. On a scale diagram, draw the path of real GDP and potential GDP (with time on the horizontal axis).

b. On a separate diagram (below the first one) show the path of the unemployment rate.

c. For which years is it possible to determine the value of the NAIRU?

d. Does the NAIRU change over the 10-year period? Provide one reason that the NAIRU could increase.

4. The diagram below shows a simple AD/AS diagram. The economy begins in long-run equilibrium at E_0 with real GDP equal to Y^*.

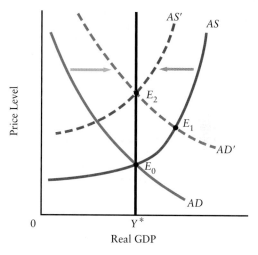

a. At E_0, the unemployment rate is 8 percent. What type of unemployment is this?

b. A positive aggregate demand shock now shifts the AD curve to AD'. At E_1 the unemployment rate is only 6.5 percent. Is there cyclical unemployment at E_1?

c. Describe the economy's adjustment process to E_2.

d. What is the unemployment rate at E_2? What kind of unemployment exists at E_2?

5. The diagram below shows a simple AD/AS diagram. The economy begins in long-run equilibrium at E_0 with real GDP equal to Y^*.

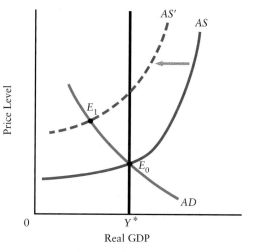

a. At E_0, the unemployment rate is 6 percent. What type of unemployment is this?

b. A negative aggregate supply shock now shifts the AS curve to AS'. At E_1 the unemployment rate is 7.5 percent. Is there cyclical unemployment at E_1? How much?

c. If monetary and fiscal policy do not react to the shock, describe the economy's adjustment process to its new long-run equilibrium.

d. What is the unemployment rate at the economy's new long-run equilibrium? What kind of unemployment exists there? Explain.

6. The diagram below shows a perfectly competitive labour market. The initial equilibrium is with wage w^* and employment L^*.

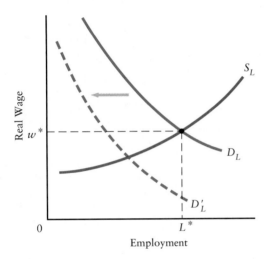

a. Suppose the demand for labour decreases to D_L'. If wages are perfectly flexible, what is the effect on wages and employment? Show this in the diagram.

b. Is there any involuntary unemployment in part (a) after the shock?

c. Now suppose wages can only adjust half as much as in part (a)—that is, wages are sticky. What is the effect on wages and employment in this case? Show this in the diagram.

d. Is there any involuntary unemployment in part (c) after the shock? How much?

Discussion Questions

1. Interpret the following statements from newspapers in terms of types of unemployment.

a. "Recession hits local factory; 1800 workers laid off."

7. Consider an economy that begins with real GDP equal to potential. There is then a sudden increase in the prices of raw materials, which shifts the AS curve upward.

a. Draw the initial long-run equilibrium in an AD/AS diagram.

b. Now show the immediate effect of the supply shock in your diagram.

c. Suppose wages and prices in this economy adjust instantly to shocks. Describe what happens to unemployment in this economy. Explain.

d. If wages and prices adjust only slowly to shocks, what happens to unemployment? Explain.

e. In parts (c) and (d), is Y always equal to Y^* (and U always equal to U^*)? Explain why a key difference between New Keynesian and New Classical theories of unemployment involves the degree of wage and price flexibility.

8. The table below shows the percentage of the labour force accounted for by youths (15–24 years old) and older workers (25 years and older) over several years. Suppose that, because of their lower skills and greater turnover, youths have a higher unemployment rate than older workers (see Figure 31-4 on page 808).

| | Percentage of Labour Force | |
Year	Youths	Older Workers
1	20	80
2	21	79
3	22	78
4	23	77
5	25	75
6	27	73
7	29	71
8	31	69

a. Suppose that in Year 1 real GDP is equal to potential GDP, and the unemployment rate among older workers is 6 percent but is 14 percent among youths. What is the economy's NAIRU?

b. Now suppose that for the next eight years real GDP remains equal to potential and that the unemployment rates for each group remain the same. Compute the value of the NAIRU for each year.

c. Explain why the NAIRU rises even though output is always equal to potential.

b. "Of course, I could take a job as a dishwasher, but I'm trying to find something that makes use of my high school education," says a local teenager in our survey of the unemployed.

c. "Retraining is the best reaction to the increased use of robots."

d. "Uneven growth: Alberta booms while Ontario sputters."

2. Discuss the following views. Is it possible that both views are right? Explain.

a. "Canadian workers should resist the automation that is destroying their jobs," says a labour leader.

b. "Given the fierce foreign competition faced by Canadian firms, it's a case of automate or die," says an industrialist.

3. "No one needs to be out of work if he or she really wants a job; just look at the Help Wanted signs in many fast-food businesses and retail shops." Does the existence of the unfilled vacancies suggested in the quotation imply that there need be no cyclical unemployment as long as workers are not excessively fussy about the kinds of jobs they will take?

4. What differences in approach toward the problem of unemployment are suggested by the following facts?

a. In 2009, the Canadian and U.S. governments gave billions of dollars of financial assistance to GM and Chrysler to protect auto-sector jobs.

b. Sweden has for many years been a pioneer in spending large sums to retrain and to relocate displaced workers.

5. The Canadian government, in its 2009 federal budget, significantly increased its spending on bridges, sewers, and roads in order to fight the coming recession and protect jobs. What do you think of such a policy to "create jobs"? Is such a policy equally likely to create jobs during a recession as when the economy is already operating at potential output? Explain.

6. Consider two hypothetical countries. In Country A, 20 percent of the labour force is unemployed for half the year and employed for the other half; the remaining 80 percent of the labour force is never unemployed. In Country B, 100 percent of the labour force is unemployed for 10 percent of the year and employed for the other 90 percent of the year. Note that both countries have an overall unemployment rate of 10 percent. Discuss which of these countries seems to have the more serious unemployment problem, and explain why.

7. There is a great deal of debate over the appropriate level of generosity for Canada's employment insurance program.

a. Explain what problem can be caused by having an EI system that is too generous.

b. Explain what problem can be caused by having an EI system that is not generous enough.

c. If EI generosity were reduced and the NAIRU declined as a result, is this necessarily a desirable outcome?

Government Debt and Deficits

Until the mid-1990s, no single measure associated with the federal government was the focus of more attention and controversy than the size of the government's annual budget deficit and its accumulated level of debt. Some people argued that the debt was an economic time bomb, waiting to explode and cause serious harm to our living standards. Others argued that the only real danger posed by debt was from the dramatic policy changes proposed to reduce it.

By 2002, after two decades of debate about debt and deficits, the focus shifted to what the governments—federal and provincial—should do with their actual and projected budget surpluses. Just as earlier debates raged over the harmful effects of high government budget deficits, debates raged then about whether governments that are facing budget surpluses should increase spending, reduce taxes, or use the surpluses to reduce the outstanding stock of government debt.

By 2009, with the onset of economic recession, the federal government then announced a return to significant budget deficits, in part caused by the recession-induced decline in tax revenues and in part caused by an intentional increase in spending designed to stimulate the struggling economy. Debate then turned to the most appropriate set of fiscal policies for the government to implement.

In this chapter, we examine various issues surrounding government debt, deficits, and surpluses. We begin by considering the simple arithmetic of government budgets. This tells us how the deficit or surplus in any given year is related to the outstanding stock of debt. We then explore why deficits and debt matter for the performance of the economy—as well as what changes we can expect over the near future if Canadian governments are successful in returning to either balanced budgets or budget surpluses.

32.1 Facts and Definitions

There is a simple relationship between the government's expenditures, its tax revenues, and its borrowing. This relationship is summarized in what economists call the government's *budget constraint*.

The Government's Budget Constraint

As is true for any individual's expenditures, government expenditures must be financed either by income or by borrowing. The difference between individuals and governments, however, is that governments typically do not earn income by selling products or labour services; instead, they earn income by levying taxes. Thus, all government expenditure must be financed either by tax revenues or by borrowing. This point is illustrated by the following simple equation, which is called the government's *budget constraint*:

$$\text{Government expenditure} = \text{Tax revenue} + \text{Borrowing}$$

We divide government expenditure into two categories. The first is purchases of goods and services, G. The second is the interest payments on the outstanding stock of debt; this is referred to as **debt-service payments** and is denoted $i \times D$, where i is the interest rate and D is the stock of government debt (which has accumulated over time from the government's past borrowing). A third category of government spending is *transfers* to individuals and firms (such as employment-insurance benefits and industrial subsidies) but, as we did in earlier chapters, we include transfers as part of T, which is the government's *net tax revenue* (tax revenue minus transfers). The government's budget constraint can therefore be rewritten as

$$G + i \times D = T + \text{Borrowing}$$

or, subtracting T from both sides,

$$(G + i \times D) - T = \text{Borrowing}$$

This equation simply says that any excess of total government spending over net tax revenues must be financed by government borrowing.

The government's annual **budget deficit** is the excess of government expenditure over tax revenues in a given year. From the budget constraint just given, this annual deficit is exactly the same as the amount borrowed by the government during the year. Since the government borrows by issuing bonds and selling them to lenders, borrowing by the government increases the stock of **government debt**. Since D is the outstanding stock of government debt, ΔD is the *change* in the stock of debt during the course of the year. The budget deficit can therefore be written as

$$\text{Budget deficit} = \Delta D = (G + i \times D) - T$$

> **The government's annual budget deficit is the excess of expenditure over tax revenues in a given year. It is also equal to the change in the stock of government debt during the year.**

debt-service payments Payments that represent the interest owed on a current stock of debt.

budget deficit Any shortfall of current revenue below current expenditure.

government debt The outstanding stock of financial liabilities for the government, equal to the accumulation of past budget deficits.

Notice two points about budget deficits. First, a change in the size of the deficit requires a change in the level of expenditures *relative* to the level of tax revenues. For a given level of tax revenues, a smaller deficit can come about only through a reduction in government expenditures; conversely, for a given level of expenditures, a smaller deficit requires an increase in tax revenues. Second, since the budget deficit is equal to the amount of new government borrowing, the stock of government debt will rise whenever the budget deficit is positive. Even a drastic reduction in the size of the annual budget deficit is therefore not sufficient to reduce the outstanding stock of government debt; the stock of debt will fall only if the budget deficit becomes *negative*. In this case, there is said to be a **budget surplus.**

budget surplus Any excess of current revenue over current expenditure.

> **A budget deficit increases the stock of debt; a budget surplus reduces it.**

primary budget deficit
The difference between the government's overall budget deficit and its debt-service payments.

The Primary Budget Deficit
Government expenditure comprises purchases of goods and services (G), and debt-service payments ($i \times D$). Since at any point in time the outstanding stock of government debt—determined by *past* government borrowing—cannot be influenced by current government policy, the debt-service component of total expenditures is beyond the control of the government. In contrast, the other components of the government's budget are said to be *discretionary* because the government can choose to change the levels of G or T. To capture the part of the budget deficit that is attributable to discretionary expenditures and revenues, the government's **primary budget deficit** is defined as the difference between government purchases of goods and services and net tax revenues:

$$\text{Primary budget deficit} = G - T$$

The government's primary budget deficit shows the extent to which tax revenues are able to finance the *discretionary* part of total expenditure. Another name for discretionary expenditure is the government's *program spending.*

Because of the need to make debt-service payments, there are often large differences between the government's overall budget deficit (or surplus) and its primary budget deficit (or surplus). In the 2005–2006 fiscal year, for example, the Canadian government had about $221 billion in tax revenues and only $213 billion in expenditures. The overall surplus in that year was therefore $8 billion. But of the $213 billion in expenditures, $179 billion were discretionary or program expenditures and $34 billion were debt-service payments. Thus, while tax revenues exceeded total expenditures by $8 billion (the overall budget surplus), they exceeded *discretionary* expenditures by $42 billion ($221B – $179B). The primary budget surplus was therefore $42 billion.

By the 2009–2010 fiscal year, however, the onset of economic recession had changed the numbers considerably. Total tax revenues were approximately $217 billion, while program spending had increased to $242 billion and debt-service charges were $31 billion. The overall budget deficit was therefore $56 billion and, after subtracting the debt-service payments, the primary deficit was $25 billion.

For the most recent federal budget forecasts, see the website for the Department of Finance: ***www.fin.gc.ca.***

> **The primary budget surplus or deficit shows the extent to which tax revenues can cover the government's program spending; it is equal to the overall deficit minus debt-service payments.**

Deficits and Debt in Canada

Federal Government   In a growing economy, many macroeconomic variables, such as the levels of government expenditure and tax revenue, tend also to grow. As a result, rather than looking at the absolute size of the government deficit or debt, economists focus on government debt and deficits in relation to the overall size of the economy. Some budget deficits that would be unmanageable in a small country like New Zealand might be quite acceptable for a larger country like Canada, and trivial for a huge economy like the United States. Similarly, a government budget deficit that seemed crushing in Canada in 1910 might appear trivial in 2010 because the size of the Canadian economy is many times larger now than it was then.

The path of federal budget deficits since 1962 is shown in Figure 32-1. The top panel shows total federal spending and total federal tax revenues as percentages of GDP. The bottom panel shows the total federal budget deficit as a percentage of GDP. Large and persistent budget deficits began in the mid-1970s. Throughout the 1980s and early 1990s, the average budget deficit was over 5 percent of GDP. In the mid-1990s, the federal government embarked on a successful policy of deficit reduction and by 1998 reported its first budget surplus in almost 20 years. The federal budget was then continually in surplus until the 2008–2009 fiscal year, at which point the budget returned to a small deficit.

As we saw in the previous section, a deficit implies that the stock of government debt is rising. Thus, the persistent deficits that began in the 1970s have their counterpart in a steadily rising stock of government debt. Figure 32-2 shows the path of Canadian federal government debt since 1940. At the beginning of the Second World War, the stock of federal debt was equal to about 45 percent of GDP. The enormous increase in the debt-to-GDP ratio over the next five years reflects wartime borrowing used to finance military expenditures. From 1946 to 1974, however, there was a continual decline in the debt-to-GDP ratio. The economy was growing quickly during this period. But equally important was that the federal government in the post-war years typically ran significant budget surpluses. These two factors explain the dramatic decline in the debt-to-GDP ratio between 1946 and 1974.

By 1974 the federal debt was only 14 percent of GDP. The large and persistent budget deficits beginning in the mid-1970s, however, along with a general

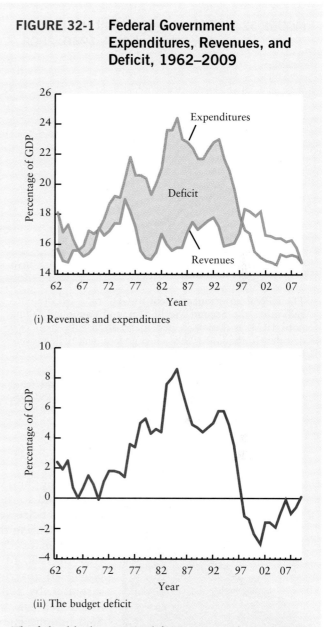

FIGURE 32-1 Federal Government Expenditures, Revenues, and Deficit, 1962–2009

(i) Revenues and expenditures

(ii) The budget deficit

The federal budget was in deficit every year between 1971 and 1997. From 1998 to 2008 there were budget surpluses. The budget returned to deficit in 2009. Part (i) shows revenues and expenditures as a percentage of GDP. Part (ii) shows the budget deficit (or surplus) as a percentage of GDP.

(*Source:* Based on data from the Department of Finance, *Fiscal Reference Tables*, October 2009, Tables 4 and 8, pp. 12, 16, http://fin.gc.ca/frt-trf/2009/frt0901-eng.asp#tbl4. Reproduced with the permission of the Minister of Public Works and Government Services, 2010.)

FIGURE 32-2   Federal Government Net Debt as Percentage of GDP, 1940–2008

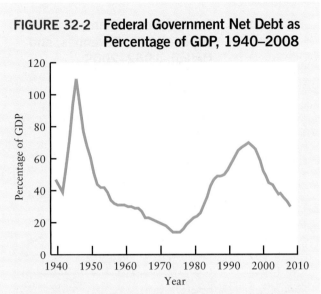

The federal government's debt-to-GDP ratio fell dramatically after the Second World War and continued falling until 1975. It then increased markedly for the next two decades. In the late 1990s when government deficits were reduced and the economy was in a healthy recovery, the debt-to-GDP ratio began to fall.

(*Source:* Based on authors' calculations using data from Statistics Canada, CANSIM database, Series V151548, and Series V498086.)

slowdown in the rate of economic growth, led to a significant upward trend in the debt-to-GDP ratio. The ratio climbed steadily from 1979 to 1996, when it peaked at more than 69 percent of GDP. Then, with the significant reductions in the deficit beginning in 1996, the debt-to-GDP ratio began to fall. By 2009, the federal government's stock of debt was $459 billion, just 28.6 percent of GDP, the lowest it had been since the early 1980s.

Provincial Governments   Canadian provincial governments are responsible for a significant fraction of total government revenues and expenditures. In many countries, sizable regional governments either do not exist, as in the United Kingdom and New Zealand, or are often required to run balanced budgets, as is the case for about two-thirds of the 50 states in the United States. In contrast, the size of Canadian provincial governments—measured by their spending and taxing powers relative to that of the federal government—means that an examination of government debt and deficits in Canada would not be complete without paying attention to the provincial governments' fiscal positions.

When examining the size and effects of budget deficits or surpluses, it is important to consider all levels of government—federal, provincial, territorial, and municipal.

The Canadian government ran very large budget deficits to finance Canada's participation in the Second World War. As a result, Canada's debt increased to 110 percent of GDP by 1946.

During the 1970s, the provincial governments were running budget deficits and so the stock of provincial government debt was increasing. But the deficits were small enough for the debt not to be growing relative to GDP. During the 1980s and early 1990s, however, provincial deficits grew dramatically. The provincial debt grew from roughly 4 percent of GDP in 1980 to 25 percent in 1998. In the subsequent decade, most provincial governments eliminated their deficits and some had budget surpluses. By 2009, however, economic recession had driven them back into deficit—the combined provincial and territorial deficit in 2009 was $8.3 billion. The total provincial and territorial debt at that time was about 15 percent of GDP.

32.2 Two Analytical Issues

Before we can discuss some of the macroeconomic effects of budget deficits and surpluses, we must examine two analytical issues: deficits and the stance of fiscal policy; and changes in the debt-to-GDP ratio.

The Stance of Fiscal Policy

In Chapters 22 and 24 we examined *fiscal policy*, which is the use of government spending and tax policies. We noted there that changes in expenditure and taxation normally lead to changes in the government's budget deficit or surplus. Thus, it is tempting to view changes in the government's budget deficit as reflecting changes in fiscal policy. For example, we could interpret an increase in the deficit as indicating an expansionary fiscal policy, since the rise in the deficit is associated with either an increase in government expenditures or a decrease in tax revenue (or both). Was the dramatic rise in the Canadian federal budget deficit between 2008 and 2010 *purely* the result of fiscal policy?

No. In general, only some changes in the budget deficit are due to discretionary changes in the government's expenditure or taxation policies. Other changes have nothing to do with explicit changes in policy, but instead are the result of changes in the level of economic activity that are outside the influence of government policy. If our goal is to judge the stance of fiscal policy, however, it is only the changes in the deficit *caused by changes in policy* that are relevant.

www.

For macroeconomic data that are comparable across countries, see the OECD's website: **www.oecd.org**.

The Budget Deficit Function   To see why the budget deficit can rise or fall even when there is no change in fiscal policy, recall the equation defining the government's budget deficit.

$$\text{Budget deficit} = (G + i \times D) - T$$

As we first discussed in Chapter 22, the level of net tax revenues typically depends on the level of national income, even with unchanged policy. For example, as income rises the level of revenue raised through income taxation also rises. Furthermore, as income rises there are typically fewer transfers (such as welfare or employment insurance) made to the private sector. Thus, net taxes, *T*, increase when national income increases. In contrast, the level of government purchases and debt-service payments can be viewed as more or less independent of the level of national income, at least over short periods of time. Thus, with no changes in expenditure or taxation policies, the budget deficit will tend to increase in recessions and fall in booms. That is, there is a negative relationship between national income and the government's budget deficit.

> For a given set of expenditure and taxation policies, the budget deficit rises as real GDP falls and falls as real GDP rises.

Figure 32-3 plots this basic relationship, which is called the **budget deficit function**. When the government determines its expenditure and taxation polices, it determines the *position* of the budget deficit function. A more expansionary fiscal policy

FIGURE 32-3   The Budget Deficit Function

For given government purchases and debt-service payments, there is a negative relationship between real GDP and the government budget deficit. *G* and *iD* are assumed to be independent of the level of real GDP. In contrast, a rise in real GDP leads to higher tax revenues and lower transfers, and thus to higher net tax revenue, *T*. Thus, the budget deficit falls as real GDP increases. Therefore, even with unchanged fiscal policies, changes in real GDP will lead to changes in the budget deficit.

A more expansionary fiscal policy implies an increase in spending or a reduction in taxes at *any level of real GDP* and thus an upward shift of the budget deficit function. A more contractionary fiscal policy shifts the budget deficit function down.

budget deficit function
A relationship that plots, for a given fiscal policy, the government's budget deficit as a function of the level of real GDP.

shifts the budget deficit function up. A more contractionary fiscal policy shifts the budget deficit function down. In contrast, a change in the level of real GDP in the absence of any policy change will represent a *movement along* the budget deficit function. Thus, for a given set of policies, the budget deficit will decrease when Y rises and increase when Y falls.

> Fiscal policy determines the position of the budget deficit function. Changes in real GDP lead to movements along a given budget deficit function.

The Cyclically Adjusted Deficit   We have said that a more expansionary fiscal policy will shift the budget deficit function up, whereas a more contractionary policy will shift it down. Therefore, *if we could hold real GDP constant,* an increase in the deficit would reveal a fiscal expansion, whereas a decrease in the deficit would reveal a fiscal contraction. While we cannot actually hold GDP constant in practice, we can accomplish the same thing by measuring what the budget deficit would be at a specific level of GDP. The **cyclically adjusted deficit (CAD)** does just this; it measures the deficit as if real GDP were equal to Y^*. Changes in the CAD then reveal changes in the stance of fiscal policy, as illustrated in Figure 32-4. The cyclically adjusted deficit is sometimes called the *structural deficit* because its emphasis is on the *structure* of fiscal policy, separate from the current position of the economy in the business cycle.

cyclically adjusted deficit (CAD) An estimate of what the government budget deficit would be if real GDP were equal to Y^*; sometimes called a structural deficit.

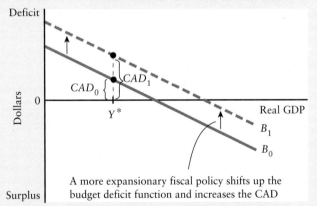

FIGURE 32-4   The Cyclically Adjusted Deficit and Changes in Fiscal Policy

A more expansionary fiscal policy shifts up the budget deficit function and increases the CAD

A more expansionary fiscal policy increases the cyclically adjusted deficit; a more contractionary fiscal policy reduces it. Initially, fiscal policy gives rise to the budget deficit function B_0. Changes in real GDP will change the actual budget deficit, but the CAD is the deficit that would exist if real GDP were equal to Y^*. With the budget deficit function B_0, the cyclically adjusted deficit is CAD_0.

Now suppose that fiscal policy becomes more expansionary because of greater spending or a reduction in tax rates. The budget deficit function shifts upward to B_1 and the cyclically adjusted deficit rises to CAD_1. The increase in the CAD reveals the expansionary change in fiscal policy. Conversely, a more contractionary fiscal policy would shift the budget deficit function down and reduce the CAD.

> An expansionary change in fiscal policy increases the cyclically adjusted deficit; a contractionary change in fiscal policy reduces the cyclically adjusted deficit.

Figure 32-5 shows the cyclically adjusted deficit in Canada and plots it together with the actual budget deficit. Both are expressed as percentages of GDP and represent the combined budget deficits of all levels of government. Unlike the actual budget deficit, which can be precisely measured, the cyclically adjusted deficit can only be estimated. The reason is that its value depends on the value of potential GDP, Y^*, which itself is not directly observable and hence must be estimated. Note from Figure 32-5 that the actual deficit is larger than the cyclically adjusted deficit during times of recessionary gaps, such as 1981–1985 and 1991–1998 (and likely 2010–2012 as well). This relationship reflects the fact that during these periods actual GDP is less than potential GDP, and thus actual tax revenues are less than they would be if output were equal to potential. Conversely, the actual budget deficit is less than the cyclically adjusted deficit during periods of inflationary gaps, such as 1986–1989 and 2000, reflecting the fact that during these periods actual GDP is greater than potential and thus tax revenues are greater than they would be if output were equal to potential. In years where the actual deficit is approximately equal to the cyclically adjusted deficit, such as 1985, 1990, 1999, and 2004–2007, real GDP is approximately equal to potential.

Changes in the expansionary or contractionary stance of fiscal policy are shown by the *changes* in the cyclically adjusted deficit. For example, the dramatic rise in Canada's cyclically adjusted deficit from 1982 to 1985 reveals a considerable fiscal expansion; the more gradual decline from 1985 to 1994 reveals a moderate fiscal contraction. From 1994 to 2000, the very substantial fiscal contraction, at both federal and provincial levels, led to the sharp decline in the cyclically adjusted deficit. Since 2000, the combined government sector has had an actual and a cyclically adjusted budget surplus of about 1 percent of GDP, and the stance of fiscal policy has not changed markedly. What is not shown in Figure 32-5 (because the official data were not yet available as this book went to press) is the substantial increase in the actual budget deficit in 2009 to approximately 3 percent of GDP. Most of this rise in the deficit reflected a

FIGURE 32-5   The Actual and Cyclically Adjusted Deficit, Combined Government, 1981–2007

The difference between the actual budget deficit and the cyclically adjusted budget deficit reveals the level of output compared to potential. The changes in the cyclically adjusted deficit show changes in the stance of fiscal policy. The actual budget deficit is above the cyclically adjusted budget deficit when output is below potential; the actual deficit is less than the cyclically adjusted deficit when output is above potential. An increase in the cyclically adjusted deficit reveals a fiscal expansion; a decrease reveals a fiscal contraction.

(*Source:* Based on data from the Department of Finance, *Fiscal Reference Tables*, September 2007, Table 46, p. 51, http://fin.gc.ca/frt-trf/2007/frt07_e.pdf. Reproduced with the permission of the Minister of Public Works and Government Services, 2010.)

decline in real GDP as the economy went into recession. But Canadian governments also increased their spending and reduced some taxes so that the cyclically adjusted deficit also increased but only by about 1 percentage point of GDP.

Practise with Study Guide
Chapter 32, Exercise 2.

Changes in the Debt-to-GDP Ratio

In order to gauge the importance of government deficits and debt, they should be considered relative to the size of the economy. This is why economists often discuss the federal government's debt-to-GDP ratio rather than the absolute amount of government debt. Here we examine the link between the overall budget deficit, the primary budget deficit, and changes in the debt-to-GDP ratio.

With a little algebra, it is possible to write a simple expression that relates the government's primary budget deficit to the change in the debt-to-GDP ratio. (To see the complete derivation of this equation, see *Extensions in Theory 32-1.*) The equation is

Practise with Study Guide
Chapter 32, Exercise 4.

$$\Delta d = x + (r - g) \times d$$

EXTENSIONS IN THEORY 32-1

Changes in the Debt-to-GDP Ratio

This box derives the simple equation in the text describing the change in the debt-to-GDP ratio. Let d be the debt-to-GDP ratio and let Δd be the amount by which d changes annually. Since d is a ratio, its change over time depends on the change in the numerator relative to the change in the denominator. That is, the debt-to-GDP ratio will increase if the stock of debt grows more quickly than GDP; it will decrease if the stock of debt grows less quickly than GDP. Representing the percentage change in d as $\Delta d/d$, we have*

$$\frac{\Delta d}{d} = \frac{\Delta D}{D} - \frac{\Delta \text{GDP}}{\text{GDP}}$$

Think about each of these terms separately. As you will recall from the first section of this chapter, the change in the stock of debt, ΔD, is equal to the amount of new government borrowing—that is, it is equal to the budget deficit. From the government's budget constraint, the deficit is equal to $(G - T + i \times D)$. The second term in the equation above is the growth rate of nominal GDP. Note that the growth rate of nominal GDP depends on both the rate of growth of real output and the rate of inflation. If we let g be the rate of growth of real GDP and π be the rate of inflation, then $g + \pi$ is the growth rate of nominal GDP.

We therefore rewrite the previous expression to get

$$\frac{\Delta d}{d} = \frac{G - T + i \times D}{D} - (g + \pi)$$

Now we multiply both sides by d to get an expression for the absolute change in the debt-to-GDP ratio:

$$\Delta d = \frac{G - T + i \times D}{D} \times d - (g + \pi) \times d$$

Since d is equal to D/GDP, our equation can be simplified:

$$\Delta d = \frac{G - T + i \times D}{\text{GDP}} - (g + \pi) \times d$$

Now recall that $(G - T)$ is the primary budget deficit. Let x be this primary budget deficit as a percentage of GDP and express the debt-service payments also as a percentage of GDP. This gives

$$\Delta d = x + i \times d - (g + \pi) \times d$$

Finally, recall that the real interest rate is equal to the nominal interest rate minus the rate of inflation,

$$r = i - \pi$$

We now combine terms to get

$$\Delta d = x + (r - g) \times d$$

which is the equation shown in the text.

_____

* For any variable X that is equal to the ratio of two other variables, Y/Z, the percentage change in X is closely approximated by the percentage change in Y minus the percentage change in Z. The lower are the rates of change of Y and Z, the better is this approximation.

where d is the debt-to-GDP ratio, x is the government's primary budget deficit as a percentage of GDP, r is the real interest rate on government bonds, g is the growth rate of real GDP, and Δd is the *change* in the debt-to-GDP ratio.

This simple equation shows two separate forces, each of which tend to increase the debt-to-GDP ratio. First, if the real interest rate exceeds the growth rate of real GDP (if r exceeds g), the debt-to-GDP ratio will rise for the simple reason that the debt accumulates at a faster rate than GDP grows. Second, if the government has a *primary* budget deficit (if x is positive), the debt-to-GDP ratio will rise because the government is incurring new debt to finance its program spending.

Let's use some recent numbers for Canada to interpret this equation. In the 2008–2009 fiscal year, the federal government had a primary budget surplus of

1.8 percent of GDP, so x was -0.018. The real interest rate on government bonds, r, was about 1.7 percent, or 0.017, while the annual growth rate of real GDP was about 1.0 percent, 0.01. Finally, the government's outstanding stock of debt at the start of the fiscal year was about 30 percent of GDP, 0.30. Putting this information together, we see that Δd was

$$\begin{aligned} \Delta d &= -0.018 + (0.017 - 0.01) \times (0.30) \\ &= -0.018 + 0.0021 \\ &= -0.016 \end{aligned}$$

which means that the government's debt-to-GDP ratio fell by 1.6 percentage points during the 2008–2009 fiscal year. Furthermore, the real interest rate was above the growth rate of GDP that year, and so without the primary surplus the debt-to-GDP ratio would otherwise have increased.

In recent federal budgets, the government has announced its goal of further reducing the debt-to-GDP ratio. What is necessary for this objective to be met? First, continuing primary budget surpluses are helpful. Second, a real interest rate that is less than the growth rate of real GDP is helpful. If both of these occur, then the debt ratio will definitely fall; if only one of these two occurs, then the overall effect on the debt ratio will depend on the relative size of the two effects.

Practise with Study Guide
Chapter 32, Exercise 3.

> **If the real interest rate on government debt is approximately equal to the growth rate of real GDP, reductions in the debt-to-GDP ratio require the government to run primary budget surpluses.**

---

myeconlab **ADDITIONAL TOPICS**

This simple equation can be used to identify the various causes of the accumulation of Canada's federal debt and to illustrate some useful policy lessons regarding debt reduction. For more details, look for **What Caused the Build-Up of Canada's Public Debt?** in the *Additional Topics* section of this book's MyEconLab.

www.myeconlab.com

32.3 The Effects of Government Debt and Deficits

Let's now examine why we should care about the size of the government deficit (or surplus) and its debt. We begin with the important idea that deficits may *crowd out* private-sector activity and thereby may harm future generations by reducing the economy's growth rate. The opposite idea is equally important—that budget surpluses may *crowd in* private-sector activity and therefore may be beneficial to future generations by increasing the economy's growth rate. In this section, we pose the issue as the effects of budget deficits. At the end of the section we review the arguments by discussing the effects of budget surpluses, which have recently been relevant in Canada.

Before beginning our analysis, we must be clear about an assumption in our macro model. As we saw earlier in this chapter, when the government increases its budget deficit, it necessarily increases its borrowing. This increase in borrowing is a reduction in the government's saving. In our model, we make the assumption that any reduction in the government's saving has only small effects on the amount of saving by the private sector—with the result that *national* saving falls along with government saving. Thus, we assume in our model that an increase in the government's budget deficit leads to a reduction in national saving. We make this assumption because it is consistent with the bulk of empirical evidence on this issue.

In our model, we assume that an increase in the government's budget deficit leads to a decrease in national saving. Alternatively, a reduction in the budget deficit leads to an increase in national saving.

✗ myeconlab   ADDITIONAL TOPICS

The relationship between the government's budget deficit and national saving has been actively debated for many years. Central to this debate is the extent to which consumers and taxpayers are forward looking, and care about future tax changes. For more details on this debate, look for **Budget Deficits and National Saving** in the *Additional Topics* section of this book's MyEconLab.

www.myeconlab.com

Do Deficits Crowd Out Private Activity?

It is useful to make the distinction between an economy that is *closed* to international trade in goods, service, and assets and one that is *open* to such trade. We consider the two cases separately.

Investment in Closed Economies   We know from Chapter 26, in which we examined the relationship between saving and investment, that in a closed economy saving must exactly equal investment. The only way that a closed economy can save is to accumulate physical capital. Suppose in a closed economy there is an increase in the budget deficit, and thus a reduction in government saving, brought about either by an increase in government spending or a reduction in taxes. This reduction in government saving is assumed to lead to a similar reduction in national saving. As we saw in Chapter 26, the decrease in the supply of national saving will lead to an excess demand for loanable funds and thus to an increase in the interest rate. As the real interest rate increases, those components of aggregate demand that are sensitive to the interest rate—investment in particular—will fall. The result is what is called the **crowding out** of domestic investment and other interest-sensitive expenditures; it is shown in Figure 32-6.

Practise with Study Guide Chapter 32, Extension Exercise E1.

crowding out The offsetting reduction in private expenditure caused by the rise in interest rates that follows an expansionary fiscal policy.

If a government budget deficit leads to a reduction in national saving, real interest rates will rise and private investment will be crowded out.

Net Exports in Open Economies There is a second effect in an open economy when financial capital is internationally mobile. Consider once again the possibility that the Canadian government increases its budget deficit either by increasing spending or by reducing taxes. What is the effect of the reduction in national saving in an open economy, like Canada's?

As real interest rates rise in Canada, foreigners are attracted to the higher-yield Canadian assets and thus foreign financial capital flows into Canada. But since Canadian dollars are required in order to buy Canadian interest-earning assets, this capital inflow increases the demand for Canadian dollars in the foreign-exchange market and thus leads to an appreciation of the Canadian dollar.

This appreciation makes Canadian goods more expensive relative to foreign goods, inducing an increase in imports and a reduction in exports, thereby reducing Canada's net exports. In an open economy like Canada's, therefore, a rise in the government deficit leads to an appreciation of the currency and to a crowding out of net exports.

In an open economy, the government budget deficit attracts foreign financial capital and appreciates the domestic currency. The result is a crowding out of net exports.

Do Deficits Harm Future Generations?

In a closed economy, a rise in the government deficit pushes up interest rates and crowds out domestic investment. In an open economy, a rise in the government deficit also appreciates the currency and crowds out net exports. In both cases, there may be a cost to future generations. Economists call this cost the *long-term burden of government debt.* Such a burden will be present if the private expenditure that is

FIGURE 32-6   The Crowding Out of Investment

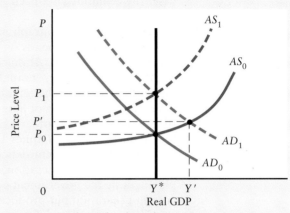

(i) Aggregate demand and supply

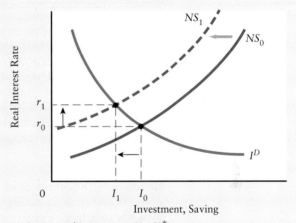

(ii) Saving and investment $(Y = Y^*)$

For a closed economy whose real GDP equals potential, an increase in the budget deficit will cause a reduction in national saving, an increase in the interest rate, and a reduction in investment. Consider a closed economy that is in long-run equilibrium at Y^* and P_0 in part (i). Suppose the government increases its spending or reduces its taxes, thus increasing the budget deficit. Either policy raises aggregate demand and shifts AD_0 to AD_1. The new short-run equilibrium is at Y' and P', but the adjustment process will then cause factor prices to rise, shifting the AS curve from AS_0 to AS_1. The new long-run equilibrium will be at Y^* and P_1.

The effect of this change on saving and investment can be seen in part (ii), which shows the market for loanable funds in the long run, with real GDP equal to Y^*. The increase in the government's budget deficit reduces national saving and shifts NS_0 to NS_1. The equilibrium real interest rate rises and the amount of investment falls from I_0 to I_1.

crowded out would have added more to the economy's productive capacity than what is added by the government's expenditure financed by the budget deficit. In this case, the economy's reduced productive capacity implies a lower future growth rate of potential GDP.

The previous paragraph suggests that whether government budget deficits harm future generations depends on the nature of the government goods and services being financed by the deficit. At one extreme, the government borrowing may finance a project that generates a substantial return to future generations, and thus the future generations may be made better off by today's budget deficit. An example might be the government's financing of long-term medical research projects that generate a return in the distant future. Another example is the government's financing of a new highway that reduces transport times for people and products for many years. At the other extreme, the government deficit may finance some government program that benefits mainly the current generation, and thus future generations may be harmed. An example might be the government's financing of cultural or sporting events that benefit the current generation but produce little or no benefits for future generations.

The concern that deficits may be inappropriately placing a burden on future generations has led some economists to advocate the idea of *capital budgeting* by the government. Under this scheme, the government would essentially classify each of its expenditures as either consumption or investment; the former would be spending that mostly benefits the current generation while the latter would be spending that mostly benefits future generations.

With capital budgeting, government deficits could be used to minimize the undesirable redistributions of income between generations. For example, the government might be committed to borrowing no more in any given year than the expenditures classified as investments. In this way, future generations would receive benefits from current government spending that are approximately equivalent to the future taxes they will pay.

> **Government budget deficits represent taxes that must be paid by future generations. Whether these future generations are harmed by the current budget deficit depends to a large extent on the nature of the government spending financed by the deficit.**

Does Government Debt Hamper Economic Policy?

The costs imposed on future generations by government debt are very real. Unfortunately, the fact that these costs sometimes occur in the very distant future often leads us to ignore their importance. But other problems associated with the presence of government debt are more immediately apparent. In particular, government debt may make the conduct of monetary and fiscal policy more difficult.

Monetary Policy   To see how a large stock of government debt can hamper the conduct of monetary policy, consider a country that has a high debt-to-GDP ratio and that has a real interest rate above the growth rate of GDP. As we saw previously, the debt-to-GDP ratio will continue to grow in this situation unless the government starts running significant primary budget *surpluses*. But such primary surpluses require either increases in taxation or reductions in program spending, both of which are politically unpopular. If such primary surpluses look unlikely to be achieved in the near future, both foreign and domestic creditors may come to expect the government to put pressure on the central bank to purchase—or *monetize*—an increasing portion of its deficit. Such monetization means that the money supply is increasing and will eventually be reflected in higher inflation. Any ensuing inflation would erode the real value of the bonds held by creditors. Such fears of future debt monetization will lead to expectations of future inflation and thus will put upward pressure on nominal interest rates and on some prices and wages. Thus, even in the absence of any actions by the central bank to increase the rate of growth of the money supply, a large government debt may lead to the *expectation* of future inflation, thus hampering the task of the central bank in keeping inflation and inflationary expectations low.

Budget deficits used to finance investment projects may not harm future generations because the future generations will benefit from the investment.

In December 1995, before the federal government had been successful in reducing its large annual budget deficits and thus slowing the rise of the debt-to-GDP ratio, the governor of the Bank of Canada at the time, Gordon Thiessen, appeared before the House of Commons Standing Committee on Public Accounts. His comments to that committee expressed this view that high levels of government debt generate concerns on the part of creditors.

> *We would probably all agree . . . that our society needs to sort out its views about acceptable levels of taxation and the size of government, and those views can influence the amount of debt our society can afford to carry. However, when you reach a high debt-to-GDP ratio, what is sustainable is also very much influenced by the willingness of investors in financial markets to hold your debt.*
>
> *I do not mean to imply that financial markets might suddenly decide to stop lending to Canadian governments. What happens, as recent experience has shown, is that at very high levels of debt, there may be an increasing nervousness among lenders so that they would only continue to hold Canadian government debt at much higher interest rates.[1]*

Fiscal Policy In Chapter 22 we saw that fiscal policy could potentially be used to stabilize aggregate demand and thereby stabilize real GDP. For example, in a booming economy, the government might reduce spending or increase tax rates to reduce inflationary pressures. Or during a recession, the government might reduce tax rates and increase spending in an attempt to stimulate aggregate demand, as it did in 2009 and 2010. Having cyclically adjusted budget deficits in recessions and cyclically adjusted budget surpluses in booms is one way of implementing *counter-cyclical fiscal policy.*

How does the presence of government debt affect the government's ability to conduct such counter-cyclical fiscal policy? Perhaps the easiest way to answer this question is to recall the equation that describes the change in the debt-to-GDP ratio:

$$\Delta d = x + (r - g) \times d$$

This equation shows that the *change* in the debt-to-GDP ratio (Δd) depends on the *level* of the debt-to-GDP ratio (d). For example, if the real interest rate exceeds the growth rate of real GDP, so that $r - g$ is positive, the increase in the debt-to-GDP ratio (Δd) will be higher if d is already high than if it is low (for any given value of x).

[1] Comments by Gordon Thiessen in the *Bank of Canada Review*, Winter 1995–1996.

With this relationship in mind, consider the dilemma faced during a recession by a government that is considering an expansionary fiscal policy. Such an expansionary fiscal policy would increase the primary budget deficit and therefore increase x. On the one hand, the short-run benefits of a fiscal expansion in terms of raising the level of real GDP seem clear; on the other hand, the same government may be wary of taking actions that lead to large increases in the debt-to-GDP ratio.

If the stock of outstanding government debt is small relative to the size of the economy, the government has a great deal of flexibility in conducting counter-cyclical fiscal policy. The small value of d implies that d will be rising only slowly in the absence of a primary deficit. Thus, the government may be able to increase the primary deficit—either by increasing program spending or by reducing tax rates—without generating a large increase in the debt-to-GDP ratio. But the government has significantly less flexibility if the stock of outstanding government debt is already very large. In this case, the high value of d means that even in the absence of a primary budget deficit, d will be increasing quickly. Thus, any increase in the primary deficit brought about by the counter-cyclical fiscal policy runs the danger of generating increases in the debt-to-GDP ratio that may be viewed by creditors as unsustainable. As the previous quote from Gordon Thiessen suggests, such perceptions of unsustainability may lead to an increase in the real interest rate on government debt, which exacerbates the problem by driving d up even faster.

The idea that a large and rising stock of government debt could "tie the hands" of the government in times when it would otherwise want to conduct counter-cyclical fiscal policy was brought to the fore of Canadian economic policy by the late Douglas Purvis of Queen's University (and a co-author of this textbook for many years). Purvis argued in the mid-1980s that Canadian government deficits must be brought under control quickly so that the debt would not accumulate to the point where the government would have no room left for fiscal stabilization policy. These warnings were not heeded. By the onset of the next recession in 1991, the federal government had added roughly $200 billion to the stock of debt and the debt-to-GDP ratio was just less than 70 percent. Predictably, the government felt unable to use discretionary fiscal policy to reduce some of the effects of the recession.

However, by 2008, after the federal debt-to-GDP ratio had fallen to less than 30 percent as a result of more than a decade of fiscal restraint and rapid economic growth, the setting had changed significantly. When the Canadian economy entered recession late in 2008, the Conservative government recognized that Canada's past fiscal prudence gave it the needed flexibility to design an aggressively counter-cyclical fiscal policy. The federal budget of 2009 announced large spending increases and tax reductions that were predicted to result in budget deficits that would increase the debt-to-GDP ratio by roughly 3 percentage points over the next two years. The government was careful, however, to indicate clearly its intentions of returning the debt-to-GDP ratio to its previously announced target of 25 percent. The need for short-term fiscal stimulus was tempered by the recognition of the importance of long-term fiscal prudence.

Notice that during our analysis of the effects of government deficits and debt, we never mentioned *who* buys the bonds issued by the government. In particular, we have made no distinction between government bonds held by Canadians and those held by foreign residents. However, we often hear the claim that foreign-held debt is a serious problem because the government's debt-service payments leave the country, whereas government debt held by domestic residents is not a problem because it is just money "we owe to ourselves." *Applying Economic Concepts 32-1* investigates this issue and explains why it may be irrelevant *who* holds the government debt.

APPLYING ECONOMIC CONCEPTS 32-1

Is Foreign-Held Debt a Problem?

In 2008 about one-quarter of the federal government's debt was held outside Canada. Thus, of the $33 billion in interest payments made on the government debt in 2008, roughly $8 billion was paid to foreigners. This fact has led many commentators in the popular press to suggest that Canada "reclaim" its national debt and keep these "lost" interest payments. These observers seem to believe that if more of the Canadian government debt were held within Canada, then Canada would be a richer country.

How do we "reclaim" the debt? The federal government simply has to issue new debt to Canadians and use the proceeds of this borrowing to redeem (to buy back) existing debt held by foreigners. By so doing, the fraction of government debt held by Canadians would be increased and the fraction held by foreigners decreased. Advocates of this proposal argue that the result would be higher Canadian income in the long run as fewer interest payments are sent to foreign creditors.

Proponents of this view fail to recognize the importance of an *integrated* world capital market and the fact that government bonds are only one type of asset held by creditors. Suppose the federal government issued $1 billion of new "Canadians-only" bonds to Canadians and used the proceeds to redeem an equal amount of existing foreign-held federal government debt. Two questions must be addressed: (1) What would make Canadians buy such bonds? and (2) What would happen to Canada's net foreign indebtedness as a result? We deal with these two issues in turn.

In order to convince Canadians to buy $1 billion worth of these new bonds, these same Canadians must somehow be convinced to divert $1 billion from some other use. For example, they could give up $1 billion worth of consumption to buy these bonds or they could sell $1 billion worth of their holdings of private corporate bonds to buy these new government bonds. In the first case, the reduction in consumption implies an increase in private saving. But it is difficult to see why Canadians would be prepared to increase their private saving simply in response to a change in the ownership of the federal government debt. What *might* convince them to increase their saving is if these new bonds

offered a rate of return greater than that of other assets available on the market. But, in this case, it is hard to see how the federal government could improve its fiscal position by issuing new high-interest-rate bonds to raise funds used to redeem existing lower-interest-rate bonds.

Suppose, then, that these new "Canadians-only" bonds are *not* successful in increasing the amount of total private saving. Instead, the issuance of these bonds simply leads some Canadians to sell $1 billion of their holdings of private corporate debt so they can purchase the new bonds. The government then takes the $1 billion raised by the selling of the new bonds and redeems $1 billion worth of foreign-held debt. The total amount of government debt is unchanged, but less of the government debt is held by foreigners. The story does not end there, however. Recall that Canadians were able to buy these new government bonds only by selling off some of their current holdings of private corporate debt. But with an unchanged pool of Canadian savings, these corporate bonds *must* then be bought by foreigners. Thus, total private corporate debt is unchanged, but *more* of it is held by foreigners. While it is true that the federal government has $1 billion less foreign-held debt, the private sector has $1 billion *more* foreign-held debt. And, though the government will now be making fewer interest payments to foreign creditors, the Canadian economy as a whole—the private plus public sectors—will be making the same interest payments to foreigners as before. Thus, the issuing of "Canadians-only" bonds, and the reduction in foreign-held government debt, has no effect on the stream of income available to domestic residents.

Is there some way for the Canadian economy to reduce its foreign indebtedness? Yes, but with a highly integrated global capital market like the one that exists today, schemes like Canadians-only bonds will not work. The only way that the Canadian economy can reduce its indebtedness to foreign creditors is to increase its national saving rate. This requires either an increase in private saving or an increase in public saving (that is, an increase in the government's budget surplus), or both.

With the arrival of the global economic recession of 2008–2009, Finance Minister Jim Flaherty implemented a significant fiscal expansion that contributed to a large increase in the federal budget deficit.

Recent Budget Surpluses

We have been discussing the effects of government debt and deficits on the economy. As we saw earlier, government deficits were an important part of the Canadian economic environment for more than 20 years, from the early 1970s to the mid-1990s. But by 1998, after several years of deficit fighting, the federal government had its first surplus in more than 20 years, and most of the provinces had also eliminated their budget deficits. For the next several years, the federal government had modest budget surpluses. This period was also one of rapid economic growth. The combination of the surpluses and the fast-growing economy led to a dramatic decline in the debt-to-GDP ratio. From its peak of almost 70 percent in 1996, the debt-to-GDP ratio fell below 50 percent in 2001, fell below 40 percent by 2005, and was just below 30 percent in 2008. Even with the budget deficits planned for the 2009–2011 period, the debt-to-GDP ratio was still forecast to return to roughly 30 percent by approximately 2015.

To analyze the economic effects of budget surpluses, we need only to reverse the arguments that we have developed in this chapter. After all, an increase in the budget surplus is just the same as a reduction in the budget deficit. But it will be useful to review and summarize these arguments. If the Canadian federal and provincial governments were to have budget surpluses, our economic theory tells us what to expect:

- The rise in the government budget surplus would raise the level of national saving.
- The rise in national saving would create an excess supply of loanable funds, thus putting downward pressure on interest rates. The result would be a "crowding in" of investment.
- The budget surplus would also lead to a "crowding in" of net exports.
- As the surpluses continue, the stock of government debt would be falling. Combined with a growing economy, this would make the debt-to-GDP ratio fall relatively sharply.
- The lower debt-to-GDP ratio would reduce bondholders' fears of future monetization and thus reduce interest rates on government debt.
- The lower debt-to-GDP ratio would restore the government's flexibility to use counter-cyclical fiscal policy if the economy enters another recession.

32.4 Formal Fiscal Rules?

After more than two decades of persistent budget deficits in Canada, and then several years of budget surpluses, the nature of political debate about fiscal policy shifted considerably. Whereas during the mid-1980s there was active political debate about whether deficits were a problem, and what costs would be involved in reducing them, by 2007 all major political parties in Canada stressed the importance of avoiding budget deficits. The onset of economic recession in 2008 changed the debate again. As the severity of the recession became clearer, all political parties argued the need for fiscal measures to stimulate the economy, but at the same time emphasized the importance of returning to a balanced budget (or surplus) as soon as the economy showed signs of a solid recovery.

In some quarters, there is support for the idea that legislation should be amended to make balanced budgets a legal requirement. Would such legislation be desirable? We examine two related but slightly different proposals.

Annually Balanced Budgets?

Balancing the budget on an annual basis would be extremely difficult to achieve. The reason is that a significant portion of the government budget is beyond the short-term control of the government, and a further large amount is hard to change quickly. For example, the entire debt-service component of government expenditures is determined by past borrowing and thus cannot be altered by the current government. In addition, as we saw in our discussion of the cyclically adjusted deficit, changes in real GDP that are beyond the control of the government lead to significant changes in tax revenues (and transfer payments) and thus generate significant changes in the budget deficit or surplus.

Even if it were possible for the government to control its spending and revenues perfectly on a year-to-year basis, it would probably be *undesirable* to balance the budget every year. We saw earlier in this chapter that government tax revenues (net of transfers) tend to fall in recessions and rise in booms. In contrast, the level of government purchases is more or less independent of the level of real GDP. As a result, fiscal policy contains a built-in stabilizer as we first saw in Chapter 24; in recessions, the increase in the budget deficit stimulates aggregate demand whereas in booms the budget surplus reduces aggregate demand.

But things would be very different with an annually balanced budget. With a balanced budget, government expenditures would be *forced* to adjust to the changing level of tax revenues. In a recession, when tax revenues naturally decline, a balanced budget would require either a *reduction* in government expenditures or an *increase* in tax rates, thus generating a major *destabilizing* force on real GDP. Similarly, as tax revenues naturally rise in an economic boom, a balanced budget would require either an increase in government expenditures or a reduction in taxes, thus risking an overheating of the economy.

> An annually balanced budget would accentuate the swings in real GDP and thus undermine other stabilization policies being followed.

Cyclically Balanced Budgets?

One alternative to the extreme policy of requiring an annually balanced budget is to require that the government budget be balanced over the course of a full economic cycle. Budget deficits would be permitted in recessions as long as they were matched by surpluses in booms. In this way, the built-in stabilizers could still perform their important role, but there would be no persistent build-up of government debt. In principle, this is a desirable treatment of the tradeoff between the short-run benefits of deficits and the long-run costs of debt.

Despite its appeal, the idea of cyclically balanced budgets has its problems as well. Perhaps the most important problem with a cyclically balanced budget is an operational

Practise with Study Guide Chapter 32, Extension Exercise E2.

For some forecasts and analysis of the government's fiscal options, see the Royal Bank's website: **www.rbc. com.** *Go to "economics."*

one. In order to have a law that requires the budget to be balanced over the business cycle, it is necessary to be able to *define* the cycle precisely. But there will always be disagreement about what stage of the cycle the economy is currently in, and thus there will be disagreement as to whether the current government should be increasing or reducing its deficit. Compounding this problem is the fact that politicians will have a stake in the identification of the cycle. Those who favour increased deficits will argue that this year is an unusually bad year and thus an increase in the deficit is justified; deficit "hawks," in contrast, will always tend to find this year to be unusually good and thus a time to run budget surpluses.

A second problem is largely political. Suppose one government runs large deficits for a few years during a recession and then gets replaced in an election. Would the succeeding government then be bound to run budget surpluses after the recovery? What one government commits itself to in one year does not necessarily restrict what it (or its successor) does in the next year.

> Balancing the budget over the course of the business cycle is in principle a desirable means of reconciling short-term stabilization with long-term fiscal prudence. The difficulty in precisely defining the business cycle, however, suggests that governments could best follow this as an approximate guide rather than as a formal rule.

Allowing for Growth

A further problem with any policy that requires a balanced budget—whether over one year or over the business cycle—is that the emphasis is naturally on the overall budget deficit. But, as we saw earlier in this chapter, what determines the change in the debt-to-GDP ratio is the growth of the debt *relative* to the growth of the economy. With a growing economy, it is possible to have positive overall budget deficits—and thus a growing debt—and still have a falling debt-to-GDP ratio. Thus, to the extent that the debt-to-GDP ratio is the relevant gauge of a country's debt problem, focus should be placed on the debt-to-GDP ratio rather than on the budget deficit itself.

> Some economists view a stable (or falling) debt-to-GDP ratio as the appropriate indicator of fiscal prudence. Their view permits a budget deficit such that the stock of debt grows no faster than GDP.

By this standard, the budgets of the last several years have been "prudent" because they have led to a growth rate in the stock of debt smaller than the growth rate of real GDP, and thus a reduction in the debt-to-GDP ratio. For example, in 1996, the debt-to-GDP ratio reached its recent maximum of 70 percent. Significant fiscal contractions, combined with healthy economic growth, led to a decline in the debt-to-GDP ratio to 50 percent by 2001, less than 40 percent by 2005, and less than 30 percent by 2008. The budget deficits of 2010 and 2011 led to a modest increase in the debt ratio, but the government continues to aim for 25 percent. It currently appears that this target could be reached within several years, but only with some modest budget surpluses in the near future.

Summary

32.1 Facts and Definitions

- The government's budget deficit is equal to total government expenditure minus total government revenue. Since the government must borrow to finance any shortfall in its revenues, the annual deficit is equal to the annual increase in the stock of government debt. Whenever the deficit is positive, the stock of government debt is growing.

- The primary budget deficit is equal to the excess of the government's program spending over total tax revenues.
- Large and persistent budget deficits beginning in the 1970s increased the stock of debt so that by 1996 the federal government net debt was equal to 70 percent of GDP. By 2008, after several years of fiscal contraction, the federal debt-to-GDP ratio was just below 30 percent.

32.2 Two Analytical Issues

- Since taxes (net of transfers) tend to rise when real GDP rises, the overall budget deficit tends to rise during recessions and fall during booms. This tendency makes the budget deficit a poor measure of the stance of fiscal policy.
- The cyclically adjusted deficit is the budget deficit that would exist with the current set of fiscal policies if real GDP were equal to potential GDP. Changes in the cyclically adjusted deficit reflect changes in the stance of fiscal policy.

- The change in the debt-to-GDP ratio from one year to the next is given by

$$\Delta d = x + (r - g) \times d$$

where d is the debt-to-GDP ratio, x is the primary deficit as a percentage of GDP, r is the real interest rate on government bonds, and g is the growth rate of real GDP.

32.3 The Effects of Government Debt and Deficits

- In a closed economy, an increase in the budget deficit leads to a reduction in national saving and a rise in real interest rates. This increase in interest rates reduces the amount of investment and leads to a reduction in the growth rate of potential output.
- In an open economy, an increase in the budget deficit also pushes up interest rates and attracts foreign financial capital. This leads to a currency appreciation and a reduction in net exports.
- In either open or closed economies, the long-term burden of government debt is a redistribution of resources away from future generations and toward current generations.

- A large debt-to-GDP ratio may lead creditors to expect increases in inflation, as the government attempts to finance deficits through the creation of money. Such increases in inflationary expectations hamper the conduct of monetary policy.
- A large debt-to-GDP ratio also limits the extent to which the government can conduct counter-cyclical fiscal policy without risking large increases in the debt-to-GDP ratio that may be viewed by creditors as unsustainable.

32.4 Formal Fiscal Rules?

- Since tax revenues (net of transfers) naturally rise as real GDP increases, legislation requiring an annually balanced budget forces either expenditures to rise or tax rates to fall during booms. This produces destabilizing fiscal policy.
- Cyclically balanced budgets, in principle, permit the short-run benefits of deficits to be realized without

incurring the long-run costs of debt accumulation. Implementation of this policy is difficult, however, since the precise identification of the business cycle is very controversial.
- In a growing economy, it is more sensible to focus on changes in the debt-to-GDP ratio than on balancing the budget over some specific horizon.

Key Concepts

Government's budget constraint
Primary budget deficit
The relationship between deficits and
the national debt

Debt-service payments
Debt-to-GDP ratio
Crowding out of investment
Crowding out of net exports

Long-term burden of the debt
Annually balanced budget
Cyclically balanced budget

Study Exercises

myeconlab SAVE TIME. IMPROVE RESULTS.

Visit MyEconLab to practise Study Exercises and prepare for tests and exams.
MyEconLab also offers a variety of other study tools to help you succeed.
www.myeconlab.com

1. Fill in the blanks to make the following statements correct.

   a. The government's budget constraint shows that government expenditures must be equal to the sum of _____ and _____.

   b. The government's annual budget deficit is the excess of total _____ over total _____ in a given year.

   c. If the government's total budget deficit is $20 billion and its debt-service payments are $18 billion, then its _____ is $2 billion. If the total budget deficit is $20 billion and its debt-service payments are $26 billion, then its _____ is $6 billion.

   d. In recent years, Canada has had a series of _____ and the debt-to-GDP ratio has been _____.

2. Fill in the blanks to make the following statements correct.

   a. When there is no change in the government's fiscal policy it is still possible for the budget deficit to fall because _____.

   b. For a given set of fiscal policies, the budget deficit _____ as real GDP rises and _____ as real GDP falls.

   c. The cyclically adjusted deficit is the budget deficit that would exist if real GDP equalled _____ and the government's _____ were at their current levels.

   d. Suppose the real interest rate is 2 percent and the growth rate of real GDP is 1.5 percent. If the government wants to stabilize the debt-to-GDP ratio, then it is necessary to have a _____.

3. Fill in the blanks to make the following statements correct.

   a. In a closed economy, when the government borrows to finance the deficit, interest rates will _____ and some private investment will be _____.

   b. In an open economy, when the government borrows to finance the deficit, interest rates will _____, the Canadian dollar will _____, and net exports will _____.

   c. The long-term burden of government debt is the reduced _____ for future generations.

   d. Suppose a law was passed that required the government to balance its budget each year. Fiscal policy would then have a _____ effect.

   e. A cyclically balanced budget is difficult to implement because it is difficult to identify the _____.

4. The table below shows government spending data over eight years in Debtland. All figures are in billions of dollars. The symbols used are as defined in the text.

Year	G (1)	T (2)	iD (3)	Budget Deficit (4)	Primary Budget Deficit (5)	Stock of Debt (6)
2004	175	175	25	—	—	—
2005	180	180	26	—	—	—
2006	185	185	27	—	—	—
2007	188	190	26	—	—	—
2008	185	195	25	—	—	—
2009	185	200	24	—	—	—
2010	180	205	23	—	—	—
2011	175	210	22	—	—	—

a. Compute Debtland's budget deficit in each year and complete column 4 in the table. (Since we are computing the deficit, a negative number indicates a surplus.)

b. Compute Debtland's primary budget deficit in each year and complete column 5 in the table.

c. Suppose the initial stock of debt (in 2003) was $400 billion. Noting that the deficit in 2004 adds to the existing stock of debt, what is the stock of debt by the end of 2004?

d. Compute the stock of debt for each year and complete column 6 in the table.

e. Suppose you know that Debtland's debt-to-GDP ratio was the same in 2011 as in 2003. By what percentage did GDP grow between 2003 and 2011?

5. The figure below shows the budget deficit function for a country.

a. Explain why the budget deficit function is downward sloping.

b. If the government increases its level of purchases (G), what happens to the budget deficit at any level of real GDP? Show this in the diagram.

c. If the government increases its level of net tax revenues (T), what happens to the deficit at any level of real GDP? Show this in the diagram.

d. Explain why a rise in the actual budget deficit does not necessarily reflect a change in fiscal policy.

How would a fiscal expansion appear in the diagram? A fiscal contraction?

6. In the late 1990s, the U.S. government was slightly ahead of the Canadian government in reducing its budget deficit. The following table shows the actual budget deficit and the cyclically adjusted deficit (both as a percentage of GDP) for the United States from 1989 to 1997.

Year	Actual Deficit	CAD
1989	2.8	2.9
1990	3.9	3.2
1991	4.6	3.4
1992	4.7	3.7
1993	3.9	3.7
1994	3.0	2.8
1995	2.3	2.6
1996	1.4	1.6
1997	0.3	1.0

a. On a scale diagram (with the year on the horizontal axis), graph the actual deficit and the cyclically adjusted deficit.

b. From 1990 to 1994, the actual budget deficit is above the CAD. Explain why.

c. From 1995 to 1997, the actual budget deficit is below the CAD. Explain why.

d. Identify the periods when U.S. fiscal policy was expansionary.

e. Identify the periods when U.S. fiscal policy was contractionary.

f. Look back at Figure 32-5 on page 825. How does the stance of U.S. fiscal policy over this period compare with Canada's?

7. The following table shows hypothetical data from 1999 to 2005 that can be used to compute the change in the debt-to-GDP ratio. The symbols used are as defined in the text.

Year	x (1)	r (2)	g (3)	d (4)	Δd (5)
2004	0.03	0.045	0.025	0.70	___
2005	0.02	0.04	0.025	___	___
2006	0.01	0.035	0.025	___	___
2007	0.00	0.035	0.025	___	___
2008	−0.01	0.03	0.025	___	___
2009	−0.02	0.03	0.025	___	___
2010	−0.03	0.025	0.025	___	___

a. Remember from the text that the change in the debt-to-GDP ratio (Δd) during a year is given by $\Delta d = x + (r - g) \times d$. Compute Δd for 2004.

b. Column 4 is the debt-to-GDP ratio. Note that d in 2005 is equal to d from 2004 plus Δd in 2005. Compute d in 2005.

c. Using the same method, compute d and Δd for each year, and complete columns 4 and 5.

d. Plot d in a scale diagram with the year on the horizontal axis. What discretionary variable was most responsible for the observed decline in d?

e. Note that as the primary deficit (x) falls between 2004 and 2010, there is also a downward trend in the real interest rate. Can you offer an explanation for this?

8. The diagram below shows an *AD/AS* diagram. The economy begins at E_0 with output equal to Y^*. Suppose the government in this closed economy increases G and finances it by running a deficit (borrowing). The *AD* curve shifts to the right.

a. How does the interest rate at E_1 compare with that at E_0? Explain.

b. Given your answer to part (a), how does investment at E_1 compare with investment at E_0?

c. Explain the economy's adjustment toward E_2. What happens to the interest rate and investment?

d. What is the long-run effect of the fiscal expansion on the growth rate of Y^*?

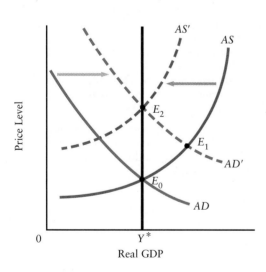

9. The diagram below shows an *AD/AS* diagram. The economy begins at E_0 with output equal to Y^*. Suppose the government in this closed economy decreases its budget deficit by increasing T (and keeping G unchanged), thus causing the *AD* curve to shift to the left.

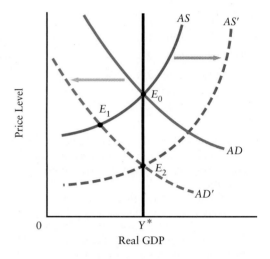

a. How does the interest rate at E_1 compare with that at E_0? Explain.

b. Given your answer to part (a), how does investment at E_1 compare with investment at E_0?

c. Explain the economy's adjustment toward E_2. What happens to the interest rate and investment?

d. What is the long-run effect of the government deficit on the growth rate of Y^*?

e. Comparing the short-run and the long-run effects of this policy, what dilemma does the government face in reducing its deficit?

Discussion Questions

1. Evaluate each of the following proposals to "control the deficit" in order to avoid the long-run burden of the debt.

   a. Maintain a zero cyclically adjusted deficit.
   b. Keep the debt-to-GDP ratio constant.
   c. Limit government borrowing in each year to some fixed percentage of national income in that year.

2. Judith Maxwell, a noted Canadian economist, has warned that "when interest rates are higher than the economic growth rate, the ratio of debt to GDP acquires dangerous upward momentum." Discuss why this is so. How does the primary deficit enter the analysis?

3. In the late 1990s, the minister of finance announced that expenditures would rise, yet he still predicted that the budget surplus would increase. Explain how these statements should be interpreted.

4. Paul Martin was the federal minister of finance from 1993 to 2002 and is credited with reducing Canada's budget deficit during that period. He stressed the importance of using very conservative forecasts for economic growth. Explain the role of forecasts and why Martin chose to use conservative ones.

5. A government official recently exclaimed, "The prime minister's policies are working! Lower interest rates combined with staunch fiscal policy have reduced the deficit significantly." What do interest rates have to do with government spending and taxes when it comes to deficit management?

6. The Canadian federal budget moved from a surplus of $9.6 billion in the 2007–2008 fiscal year to a small deficit of $1.1 billion the next year, and a large deficit of roughly $35 billion in 2009–2010.

   a. Suppose real GDP was at potential in each of the first two years. What can you conclude about the cause of the change in the budget deficit? Show this change in a diagram of the budget deficit function.
   b. Suppose from 2008–2009 to 2009–2010, two things happened. Real GDP fell and the government implemented an expansionary fiscal policy. Show these two separate events in a diagram of the budget deficit function.

33

The Gains from International Trade

LEARNING OBJECTIVES

In this chapter you will learn

❶ why the gains from trade depend on the pattern of comparative advantage.

❷ how factor endowments and climate can influence a country's comparative advantage.

❸ about the law of one price.

❹ why countries export some goods and import others.

Trade between peoples and nations has been going on throughout human history, and humans have gone to great lengths and endured severe hardship in order to reap the benefits of trade. Centuries ago, for example, the inhabitants of remote islands in Southeast Polynesia travelled the open ocean in canoes for days at a time to trade oyster shells, volcanic glass, basalt, and food items with inhabitants of other, distant islands.

Today, the required activities for trade may be far less demanding, but the transactions themselves are no less important. Canadian consumers buy cars from Germany, Germans take holidays in Italy, Italians buy spices from Africa, Africans import oil from Kuwait, Kuwaitis buy Japanese cameras, and the Japanese buy Canadian lumber. *International trade* refers to the exchange of goods and services that takes place across international boundaries.

The founders of modern economics were concerned with foreign trade problems. The great eighteenth-century British philosopher and economist David Hume (1711–1776), one of the first to work out the theory of the price system, developed his concepts mainly in terms of prices in foreign trade. Adam Smith (1723–1790), in *The Wealth of Nations,* attacked government restriction of international trade. David Ricardo (1772–1823) developed the basic theory of the gains from trade that is studied in this chapter. The repeal of the Corn Laws—tariffs on the importation of grains into the United Kingdom—and the transformation of that country during the nineteenth century from a country of high tariffs to one of complete free trade were to some extent the result of arguments by economists whose theories of the gains from international trade led them to condemn tariffs.

FIGURE 33-1   The Growth in World Trade, 1950–2007

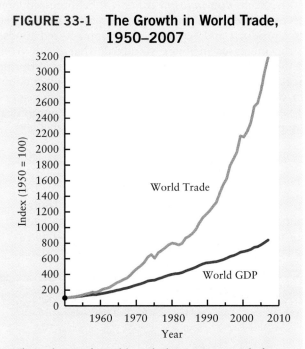

The volume of world trade has grown much faster than world GDP over the past six decades. The figure shows the growth of real GDP and the volume of trade since 1950. Both are expressed as index numbers, set equal to 100 in 1950. Real world GDP has increased more than seven times since 1950; world trade volume has increased 30 times.

(*Source:* World Trade Organization, *International Trade Statistics 2008*, www.wto.org. Go to "Resources" and select "Trade Statistics." Then click on "International Trade Statistics, 2008" and go to "Selected Long-Term Trends." Choose Chart II.1, p. 37. © 2008 World Trade Organization. www.wto.org/english/res_e/statis_e/its2008_e/its2008_e.pdf. Used with permission.)

FIGURE 33-2   Canadian Exports and Imports of Goods by Industry, 2008

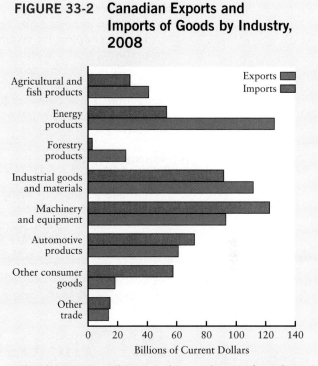

Canada exports and imports large volumes of goods in most industries. The data show the value of goods exported and imported by industry in 2008 (trade in services is not shown). The total value of goods exported was $490 billion; the total value of goods imported was $443 billion.

(*Source:* These data are available on Statistics Canada's website: www.statcan.gc.ca. Search for "International trade" or "Canada's merchandise exports" http://statcan.gc.ca/pub/65-208-x/2008000/tbl/t2-eng.htm, "Canada's merchandise imports" http://statcan.gc.ca/pub/65-208-x/2008000/tbl/t3-eng.htm.)

International trade is becoming increasingly important, not just for Canada but for the world as a whole. As Figure 33-1 shows, the volume of world trade has grown much faster than has world real GDP over the past six decades. Since 1950, the world's real GDP has increased by more than seven times, an average annual growth rate of 3.7 percent. Over the same period, however, the volume of world trade has increased by more than 30 times, an average annual growth rate of 6.1 percent.

Figure 33-2 shows some data for Canadian trade in 2008. The figure shows the value of Canadian exports and imports of goods in several broad industry groupings. There are three important points to note from the figure. First, international trade is very important for Canada. In 2008, Canada exported $490 billion and imported more than $440 billion in goods—if we added trade in services, each of these values would be higher by about $80 billion; each flow (exports and imports) amounts to about 35 percent of GDP. Second, exports and imports are roughly the same size, so that the *volume* of trade is much larger than the *balance* of trade—the value of exports minus the value of imports. Third, in most of the industry groupings there are significant

For information on world trade, see the World Trade Organization's website: **www.wto.org.**

amounts of both imports and exports. Such *intra-industry trade* will be discussed later in the chapter. Canada does not just export resource products and import manufactured goods; it also imports many resource products and exports many manufactured goods.

In this chapter, we examine the increases in living standards that result from international trade. We find that the source of the gains from trade lies in differing cost conditions among geographical regions. World income is maximized when countries specialize in the products in which they have the lowest opportunity costs of production. These costs are partly determined by natural endowments (geographical and climatic conditions), partly by public policy, and partly by historical accident.

> ### ✗ myeconlab ADDITIONAL TOPICS
>
> Canada trades with many countries, but most of our trade is with the United States, and the fraction of our total trade with the United States has been increasing in recent years. For more information on the location of Canada's trade, look for **Who Are Canada's Trading Partners?** in the *Additional Topics* section of this book's MyEconLab.
>
> www.myeconlab.com

33.1 The Gains from Trade

open economy An economy that engages in international trade.

closed economy An economy that has no foreign trade.

An economy that engages in international trade is called an **open economy**; one that does not is called a **closed economy**. A situation in which a country does no foreign trade is called one of *autarky*.

Although politicians often regard foreign trade differently from domestic trade, economists from Adam Smith on have argued that the causes and consequences of international trade are simply an extension of the principles governing trade between domestic firms and individuals. What are the benefits of trade among individuals, among groups, among regions, or among countries?

Interpersonal, Interregional, and International Trade

To begin, consider trade among individuals. Without trade, each person would have to be self-sufficient: Each would have to produce all the food, clothing, shelter, medical services, entertainment, and luxuries that he or she consumed. Because most individuals are not particularly good at producing such a large range of products, a world of individual self-sufficiency would be a world with extremely low living standards.

Trade among individuals allows people to specialize in activities they can do well and to buy from others the goods and services they cannot easily produce. A good doctor who is a bad carpenter can provide medical services not only for her own family but also for a good carpenter without the training or the ability to practise medicine. Thus, trade and specialization are intimately connected.

> **Without trade, everyone must be self-sufficient; with trade, people can specialize in what they do well and satisfy other needs by trading.**

The same principle applies to regions. Without interregional trade, each region would be forced to be self-sufficient. With trade, each region can specialize in producing products for which it has some natural or acquired advantage. Prairie regions can specialize in growing grain, mountain regions in mining and forest products, and regions with abundant power can specialize in manufacturing. Cool regions can produce wheat and other crops that thrive in temperate climates, and hot regions can grow such tropical crops as bananas, sugarcane, and coffee. The living standards of the inhabitants of all regions will be higher when each region specializes in products in which it has some natural or acquired advantage and obtains other products by trade than when all regions seek to be self-sufficient.

This same basic principle also applies to countries. A national boundary is a political invention and rarely delimits an area that is naturally self-sufficient. Countries, like regions and individuals, can gain from specialization. More of some goods are produced domestically than residents want to consume, while residents would like to consume more of other goods than is produced domestically. International trade is necessary to achieve the gains that international specialization makes possible.

> With trade, each individual, region, or country is able to concentrate on producing goods and services that it produces efficiently while trading to obtain goods and services that it does not produce efficiently.

gains from trade The increased output attributable to the specialization according to comparative advantage that is made possible by trade.

Specialization and trade go hand in hand because there is no incentive to achieve the gains from specialization without being able to trade the goods produced for goods desired. Economists use the term **gains from trade** to embrace the results of both.

Illustrating the Gains from Trade

Our discussion of individuals, regions, and countries emphasized the *differences* in their abilities to produce various products. In what follows we focus on trade between countries and, in order to focus on the differences across countries, we assume that within each country the average cost of production of any good is independent of *how much* of that good is produced. That is, we are making the assumption of *constant costs*. Our next example involves only two countries and two products, but the general principles also apply to the case of many countries and many products.

Practise with Study Guide Chapter 33, Exercise 1.

Absolute Advantage   One region is said to have an **absolute advantage** over another in the production of good *X* when an equal quantity of resources can produce more *X* in the first region than in the second. Or, to put it differently, if it takes fewer resources to produce one unit of good *X* there than in another country. Table 33-1 shows an example. The two "countries" are Canada and the European Union (EU) and the two goods are wheat and cloth. The table shows the *absolute cost* of producing one unit of wheat and one unit of cloth in each country. The absolute cost is the dollar cost of the labour, capital, and other resources required to produce the goods. Thus, the country that can produce a specific good with fewer resources can produce it at a lower absolute cost.

In Table 33-1, the absolute resource cost for both wheat and cloth is less in Canada than in the EU. Canada is therefore said to have an *absolute advantage* over the EU in the production of both wheat and cloth. Canada has an absolute advantage over the EU in producing these goods because it is a more efficient producer—it takes less labour and other resources to produce the goods in Canada than in the EU.

absolute advantage The situation that exists when one country can produce some commodity at lower absolute cost than another country.

TABLE 33-1   Absolute Costs and Absolute Advantage

	Wheat (kilograms)	Cloth (metres)
Canada	$1 per kilogram	$5 per metre
EU	$3 per kilogram	$6 per metre

Absolute advantage reflects the differences in absolute costs of producing goods between countries. The numbers show the dollar cost of the total amount of resources necessary for producing wheat and cloth in Canada and the EU. Note that Canada is a lower-cost producer than the EU for both wheat and cloth. Canada is therefore said to have an absolute advantage in the production of both goods.

comparative advantage
The situation that exists when a country can produce a good with less forgone output of other goods than can another country.

The situation in Table 33-1 is hypothetical, but it is encountered often in the real world. Some countries, because they have access to cheap natural resources or better-trained workers or more sophisticated capital equipment, are low-cost producers for a wide range of products. Does this mean that high-cost countries stand no chance of being successful producers in a globalized world of international trade? Will the low-cost countries produce everything, leaving nothing to be done by high-cost countries? The answer is no. As we will see immediately, the gains from international trade do *not* depend on the pattern of absolute advantage.

Comparative Advantage   The great English economist David Ricardo (1722–1823) was the first to provide an explanation of the pattern of international trade in a world in which countries had different costs. His theory of *comparative advantage* is still accepted by economists as a valid statement of one of the major sources of the gains from international trade. A country is said to have a **comparative advantage** in the production of good X if the cost of producing X *in terms of forgone* output of other goods is lower in that country than in another. Thus, the pattern of comparative advantage is based on *opportunity costs* rather than absolute costs. Table 33-2 illustrates the pattern of comparative advantage in the Canada–EU example. The opportunity cost in Canada for one kilogram of wheat is computed by determining how much cloth must be given up in Canada in order to produce an additional kilogram of wheat. From Table 33-1, the absolute costs of wheat and cloth were $1 per kilogram and $5 per metre, respectively. Thus, in order to produce one extra kilogram of wheat, Canada must use resources that could have produced one-fifth of a metre of cloth. So the opportunity cost of one kilogram of wheat is 0.2 metres of cloth. By exactly the same reasoning, the opportunity cost of one metre of cloth in Canada is 5.0 kilograms of wheat. These opportunity costs are shown in Table 33-2.

Even though a country may have an absolute advantage in all goods (as Canada does in Table 33-1), it *cannot* have a comparative advantage in all goods. Similarly, even though a country may be inefficient in absolute terms and thus have no absolute advantage in any goods (as is the case for the EU in Table 33-1) it *must* have a comparative advantage in some good. In Table 33-2, Canada has a comparative advantage in the production of wheat because Canada must give up less cloth to produce one kilogram of wheat than must be given up in the EU. Similarly, the EU has a comparative advantage in the production of cloth because the EU must give up less wheat in order to produce one metre of cloth than must be given up in Canada.

TABLE 33-2   Opportunity Costs and Comparative Advantage

	Wheat (kilograms)	Cloth (metres)
Canada	0.2 m of cloth	5.0 kg of wheat
EU	0.5 m of cloth	2.0 kg of wheat

Comparative advantages reflect opportunity costs that differ between countries. The first column shows the opportunity cost of a kilogram of wheat in terms of the amount of cloth that must be given up. The second column shows the opportunity cost of a metre of cloth in terms of the amount of wheat that must be given up. Canada has a comparative advantage in wheat production because it has a lower opportunity cost for wheat than does the EU. The EU has a comparative advantage in cloth because its opportunity cost for cloth is lower than that in Canada.

The gains from specialization and trade depend on the pattern of comparative, not absolute, advantage.

In our example, total world wheat production can be increased if Canada devotes more resources to the production of wheat and fewer resources to the production of cloth. Similarly, total world cloth production can be increased if the EU devotes more resources to the production of cloth and fewer to wheat. In the extreme case, Canada could *specialize* by producing *only* wheat and the EU could specialize by producing only cloth. Such reallocations of resources increase total world output because each country is specializing in the production of the good in which it has the lowest opportunity cost. The gains from specialization along the lines of comparative advantage are shown in Table 33-3.

> **World output increases if countries specialize in the production of the goods in which they have a comparative advantage.**

Not *any* pattern of specialization, however, is beneficial for the world. In our example, if Canada were to specialize in cloth and the EU in wheat, total world output would *fall*. To see this, note that in order to produce one extra metre of cloth in Canada, five kilograms of wheat must be sacrificed (see Table 33-2). Similarly, in order to produce four extra kilograms of wheat in the EU, two metres of cloth must be sacrificed. Thus, if each country produced these additional units of the "wrong" good, total world output of wheat would fall by one kilogram and total output of cloth would fall by one metre.

> **Specialization of production *against* the pattern of comparative advantage leads to a decline in total world output.**

We have discussed comparative advantage in terms of opportunity costs. We can also illustrate it by considering the two countries' production possibilities boundaries. Recall from Chapter 1 the connection between a country's production possibilities boundary and the opportunity costs of production. The slope of the production possibilities boundary indicates the opportunity costs. The existence of different opportunity costs across countries implies comparative advantages that can lead to gains from trade. Figure 33-3 illustrates how two countries can both gain from trade when they have different opportunity costs in production and those opportunity costs are independent of the level of production. An alternative diagrammatic illustration of the gains from trade appears in *Extensions in Theory 33-1*, where the production possibilities boundary is concave (which means that the opportunity cost for each good is higher when more of that good is being produced).

The conclusions about the gains from trade arising from international differences in opportunity costs are summarized below.

1. Country A has a comparative advantage over Country B in producing a product when the opportunity cost of production in Country A is lower. This implies, however, that it has a comparative *dis*advantage in some other product(s).

2. The opportunity cost of product X is the amount of output of other products that must be sacrificed in order to increase the output of X by one unit.

TABLE 33-3   The Gains from Specialization

Changes from each country producing more units of the product in which it has the lower opportunity cost

	Wheat (kilograms)	Cloth (metres)
Canada	+5.0	−1.0
EU	−4.0	+2.0
Total	+1.0	+1.0

Whenever opportunity costs differ between countries, specialization can increase the world's production of both products. These calculations show that there are gains from specialization given the opportunity costs of Table 33-2. To produce five more kilograms of wheat, Canada must sacrifice 1.0 m of cloth. To produce two more metres of cloth, the EU must sacrifice 4.0 kg of wheat. Making both changes increases world production of both wheat and cloth.

Practise with Study Guide
Chapter 33, Exercise 4 and
Extension Exercises E1 and E2.

FIGURE 33-3   The Gains from Trade with Constant Opportunity Costs

(i) Canada   (ii) European Union

International trade leads to specialization in production and increased consumption possibilities. The purple lines in parts (i) and (ii) represent the production possibilities boundaries for Canada and the EU, respectively. In the absence of any international trade, these also represent each country's consumption possibilities.

The difference in the slopes of the production possibilities boundaries reflects differences in comparative advantage, as shown in Table 33-2. In each part the opportunity cost of increasing production of wheat by the same amount (measured by the distance *ba*) is the amount by which the production of cloth must be reduced (measured by the distance *bc*). The relatively steep production possibilities boundary for Canada thus indicates that the opportunity cost of producing wheat in Canada is less than that in the European Union.

If trade is possible at some relative prices between the two countries' opportunity costs of production, each country will specialize in the production of the good in which it has a comparative advantage. In each part of the figure, the slope of the green line shows the relative prices at which trade takes place. Production occurs in each country at *S* (for specialization); Canada produces only wheat, and the EU produces only cloth.

Consumption possibilities for each country are now given by the green line that passes through *S*. Consumption possibilities are increased in both countries; consumption may occur at some point, such as *d*, that involves a combination of wheat and cloth that was not attainable in the absence of trade.

3. When opportunity costs for all products are the same in all countries, there is no comparative advantage and there is no possibility of gains from specialization and trade.

4. When opportunity costs differ in any two countries and both countries are producing both products, it is always possible to increase production of both products by a suitable reallocation of resources within each country.

Though the concepts of comparative advantage and specialization are relatively straightforward, it is helpful to work through numerical examples to solidify your understanding. *Applying Economic Concepts 33-1* provides two examples and works through the computations of absolute and comparative advantage.

The Gains from Trade with Variable Costs

So far, we have assumed that opportunity costs are the same whatever the scale of output, and we have seen that there are gains from specialization and trade as long

The Gains from Trade More Generally

Examining the gains from trade is relatively easy in the case where each country's production possibilities boundary is a straight line. What happens in the more realistic case where the production possibilities boundary is concave? As this box shows, the same basic principles of the gains from trade apply to this more complex case.

International trade leads to an expansion of the set of goods that can be consumed in the economy in two ways:

1. By allowing the bundle of goods consumed to differ from the bundle produced

2. By permitting a profitable change in the pattern of production

Without international trade, the bundle of goods produced must be the same as the bundle consumed. With international trade, the consumption and production bundles can be altered independently to reflect the relative values placed on goods by international markets.

Fixed Production

In each part of the figure, the purple curve is the economy's production possibilities boundary. In the absence of international trade, the economy must consume the same bundle of goods that it produces. Thus, the production possibilities boundary is also the consumption possibilities boundary. Suppose the economy produces and consumes at point a, with x_1 of good X and y_1 of good Y, as in part (i) of the figure.

Next suppose that with production point a, good Y can be exchanged for good X internationally. The consumption possibilities are now shown by the line tt drawn through point a. The slope of tt indicates the quantity of Y that exchanges for a unit of X on the international market—that is, the relative price of X in terms of Y.

Although production is fixed at point a, consumption can now be anywhere on the line tt. For example,

the consumption point could be at b. This could be achieved by exporting y_2y_1 units of Y and importing x_1x_2 units of X. Because point b (and all others on line tt to the right of a) lies outside the production possibilities boundary, there are potential gains from trade. Consumers are no longer limited by their own country's production possibilities. Let us suppose that they prefer point b to point a. They have achieved a gain from trade by being allowed to exchange some of their production of good Y for some quantity of good X and thus to consume more of good X than is produced at home.

Variable Production

There is a further opportunity for the expansion of the country's consumption possibilities: With trade, production may be altered in response to international prices. The country may produce the bundle of goods that is most valuable in world markets. That is represented by the bundle d in part (ii). The consumption possibilities boundary is shifted to the line $t't'$ by changing production from a to d and thereby increasing the country's degree of specialization in good Y. For every point on the original consumption possibilities boundary tt, there are points on the new boundary $t't'$ that allow more consumption of both goods—for example, compare points b and f. Notice also that, except at the zero-trade point d, the new consumption possibilities boundary lies *everywhere above the production possibilities boundary*.

The benefits of moving from a no-trade position, such as point a, to a trading position, such as points b or f, are the *gains from trade* to the country. When the production of good Y is increased and the production of good X decreased, the country is able to move to a point, such as f, by producing more of good Y, in which the country has a comparative advantage, and trading the additional production for good X.

(i) Fixed production

(ii) Variable production

APPLYING ECONOMIC CONCEPTS 33-1

Two Examples of Absolute and Comparative Advantage

Example #1

Argentina and Brazil can both produce fish and leather. The table shows the total resource cost, in dollars, of producing one kilogram of each good in both countries.

	Fish (kg)	Leather (kg)
Argentina	$2	$5
Brazil	$3	$4

Absolute Advantage Argentina is the more efficient producer of fish since its total resource cost ($2) is less than Brazil's ($3), and so it has the absolute advantage in producing fish. Brazil has the absolute advantage in producing leather.

Comparative Advantage To know the pattern of comparative advantage, we must compute the *opportunity costs of production*. In Argentina, producing one more kilogram of leather requires using $5 of resources—the amount that could have been used to produce 2½ kg of fish. Thus, producing 1 kg of leather involves giving up 2½ kg of fish. In Brazil, however, one extra kilogram of leather only requires a sacrifice of 1⅓ kg of fish. Since Brazil has the lower opportunity cost for leather (it gives up the least fish), it has the comparative advantage in leather production.

The opportunity cost for fish production *must* be the inverse of that for leather. In Argentina, one extra kilogram of fish "costs" 0.4 kg of leather. In Brazil, one extra kilogram of fish "costs" 0.75 kg of leather. Since Argentina has the lower opportunity cost of fish, it has the comparative advantage in fish production.

Specialization If Argentina and Brazil were to trade with each other, total production would be increased if each country specialized in the production of the good in which it has the comparative advantage. Argentina should produce fish and buy its leather from Brazil; Brazil should produce leather and buy its fish from Argentina.

Example #2

Switzerland and Austria can both produce glass and chocolate. Each country has 1000 units of identical resources, which we will call "labour." The table shows the maximum amount of each good that each country could produce if it devoted all resources to the production of that good.

	Glass (tonnes)	Chocolate (kg)
Austria	5 000	400 000
Switzerland	4 000	200 000

Absolute Advantage Each unit of labour in Austria can produce 5 tonnes of glass or 400 kg of chocolate. The identical unit of labour in Switzerland can produce only 4 tonnes of glass or 200 kg of chocolate. Switzerland is less efficient than Austria in the production of both goods; Austria therefore has the absolute advantage in *both* goods.

Comparative Advantage Once again, we need to know the opportunity costs of production. In Austria, producing one extra tonne of glass requires giving up 80 kg (= 400 000/5000) of chocolate. In Switzerland, producing one extra tonne of glass "costs" 50 kg (= 200 000/4000) of chocolate. Switzerland has the lower opportunity cost for glass and thus has the comparative advantage in glass production. It follows that Austria *must* have the comparative advantage in the production of chocolate. Austria's opportunity cost of 1 kg of chocolate is 1/80 tonne of glass whereas Switzerland's opportunity cost of 1 kg of chocolate is 1/50 tonne of glass.

Specialization If the two countries engaged in international trade, total output would be maximized if Austria specialized in the production of chocolate and Switzerland specialized in the production of glass.

as there are differences in opportunity costs across countries. If costs vary with the level of output, or as experience is acquired via specialization, *additional* gains are possible.

Economies of Scale In many industries, production costs fall as the scale of output increases. The larger the scale of operations, the more efficiently large-scale machinery can be used and the more a detailed division of tasks among workers is possible. Small countries (such as Switzerland, Belgium, and Israel) whose domestic markets are not large enough to exploit economies of scale would find it prohibitively expensive to become self-sufficient by producing a little bit of everything at very high cost.

One of the important lessons learned from patterns of world trade since the Second World War has concerned imperfect competition and product differentiation. Virtually all of today's manufactured consumer goods are produced in a vast array of differentiated product lines. In some industries, many firms produce different items in this array; in others, only a few firms produce the entire array. In either case, they may not exhaust all available economies of scale. Thus, an increase in the size of the market, even in a large economy, may allow the exploitation of some previously unexploited scale economies in individual product lines.

These possibilities were first dramatically illustrated when the European Common Market (now known as the European Union) was set up in the late 1950s. Economists had expected that specialization would occur according to the theory of comparative advantage, with one country specializing in cars, another in refrigerators, another in fashion and clothing, another in shoes, and so on. This is not the way it worked out. Instead, much of the vast growth of trade was in *intra-industry* trade—that is, trade of goods or services within the same broad industry. Today, one can buy French, English, Italian, and German fashion goods, cars, shoes, appliances, and a host of other products in London, Paris, Berlin, and Rome. Ships loaded with Swedish furniture bound for London pass ships loaded with English furniture bound for Stockholm, and so on.

The same increase in intra-industry trade happened with Canada–U.S. trade over successive rounds of tariff cuts that were negotiated after the Second World War, the most recent being those associated with the 1989 Canada–U.S. Free Trade Agreement, and its 1994 expansion into the North American Free Trade Agreement (NAFTA), which included Mexico. In several broad industrial groups, including automotive products, machinery, textiles, and forestry products, both imports and exports increased in each country. What free trade in Europe and North America did was to allow a proliferation of differentiated products, with different countries each specializing in different subproduct lines. Consumers have shown by their expenditures that they value this enormous increase in the range of choice among differentiated products, and producers have gained economies by being able to operate at a larger scale.

Wine is a good example of an industry in which there is much intra-industry trade. Canada, for example, imports wine from many countries but also exports Canadian-made wine to the same countries.

In industries with significant scale economies, small countries that do not trade will have low levels of output and therefore high costs. With international trade, however, small countries can produce for the large global market and thus produce at lower costs. International trade therefore allows small countries to reap the benefits of scale economies.

Learning by Doing   The discussion so far has assumed that costs vary with the *level* of output. But they may also vary with the *accumulated experience* in producing a product over time.

learning by doing The reduction in unit costs that often results as workers learn through repeatedly performing the same tasks. It causes a downward shift in the average cost curve.

Early economists placed great importance on a concept that is now called **learning by doing**. They believed that as countries gained experience in particular tasks, workers and managers would become more efficient in performing them. As people acquire expertise, costs tend to fall. There is substantial evidence that such learning by doing does occur. It is particularly important in many of today's knowledge-intensive high-tech industries. The distinction between this phenomenon and economies of scale is illustrated in Figure 33-4. It is one more example of the difference between a movement along a curve and a shift of the curve.

The opportunity for learning by doing has an important implication: Policymakers need not accept current comparative advantages as given. Through such means as education and tax incentives, they can seek to develop new comparative advantages. Moreover, countries cannot complacently assume that their existing comparative advantages will persist. Misguided education policies, the wrong tax incentives, or policies that discourage risk taking can lead to the rapid erosion of a country's comparative advantage in particular products and industries.

FIGURE 33-4   Economies of Scale Versus Learning by Doing

Specialization may lead to gains from trade through scale economies, learning by doing, or both. Consider a country that wants to consume the quantity Q_0. Suppose it can produce that quantity at an average cost per unit of c_0. Suppose further that the country has a comparative advantage in producing this product and can export the quantity Q_0Q_1 if it produces Q_1. This may lead to cost savings in two ways.

First, the increased level of production of Q_1 compared with Q_0 permits it to move along its cost curve from a to b, thereby reducing costs per unit to c_1. This is an economy of scale.

Second, as workers and management become more experienced, they may be able to produce at lower costs. This is learning by doing and it shifts the cost curve from $LRAC$ to $LRAC'$. At output Q_1, costs per unit fall to c_2. The movement from a to b' incorporates both economies of scale and learning by doing.

Sources of Comparative Advantage

David Ricardo's analysis taught us that the gains from trade arise from the pattern of comparative advantage. However, his analysis did not explain the *sources* of a country's comparative advantage. Why do comparative advantages exist? Since a country's comparative advantage depends on its opportunity costs, we could also ask: Why do different countries have different opportunity costs?

Different Factor Endowments The traditional answer to this question was provided early in the twentieth century by two Swedish economists, Eli Heckscher and Bertil Ohlin. Ohlin was subsequently awarded the Nobel Prize in economics for his work in the theory of international trade. Their explanation for international differences in opportunity costs is now incorporated in the Heckscher-Ohlin model. According to their theory, the international cost differences that form the basis for comparative advantage arise because factor endowments differ across countries. This is often called the *factor endowment theory of comparative advantage.*

To see how this theory works, consider the prices for various types of goods in countries *in the absence of trade.* A country that is well endowed with fertile land but has a small population (like Canada) will find that land is cheap but labour is expensive. It will therefore produce land-intensive agricultural goods cheaply and labour-intensive goods, such as machine tools, only at high cost. The reverse will be true for a second country that is small in size but possesses abundant and efficient labour (like Japan). As a result, the first country will have a comparative advantage in agricultural production and the second in goods that use much labour and little land.

> According to the Heckscher-Ohlin theory, countries have comparative advantages in the production of goods that use intensively the factors of production with which they are abundantly endowed.

For example, Canada is abundantly endowed with forests relative to most other countries. According to the Heckscher-Ohlin theory, Canada has a comparative advantage in goods that use forest products intensively, such as newsprint, paper, raw lumber, and wooden furniture. In contrast, relative to most other countries, Canada is sparsely endowed with labour. Thus, Canada has a comparative disadvantage in goods that use labour intensively, such as cotton or many other textile products.

Canada is extremely well endowed with forests. It is no surprise, therefore, that it has a comparative advantage in a whole range of forestry products.

Different Climates   The factor endowment theory provides only part of the entire explanation for the sources of comparative advantage. One additional influence comes from all those natural factors that can be called *climate* in the broadest sense. If you combine land, labour, and capital in the same way in Nicaragua and in Iceland, you will not get the same output of most agricultural goods. Sunshine, rainfall, and average temperature also matter. If you seek to work with wool or cotton in dry climates, you will get different results from when you work in damp climates. (You can, of course, artificially create any climate you want in a factory, but it costs money to create what is freely provided elsewhere.)

> Climate affects comparative advantage.

Of course, if we consider "warm weather" a factor of production, then we could simply say that countries like Nicaragua are better endowed with that factor than countries like Iceland. In this sense, explanations of comparative advantage based on different climates are really just a special case of explanations based on factor endowments.

Human Capital   Acquired skills, what economists call *human capital*, matter greatly in determining comparative advantage. Beginning in the late nineteenth century, Germany had an excellent set of trade schools that were attended by virtually every male who did not go on to higher education. As a result, Germany had a strong comparative advantage in many consumer goods that required some skill to produce, such as electric razors, cake mixers, and blenders. The people of Persia (now Iran) produced carpets of high quality over the centuries, and from childhood their workers developed skills in carpet making that few others could match. So they had a comparative advantage in high-quality carpets and some related commodities.

Early on, Americans developed the skills necessary to mass-produce goods of reasonable quality made from standardized parts. So the United States developed a comparative advantage in many products made with mass-production techniques. One early set of products made in this way was firearms. Rifles and pistols were mass-produced and assembled from standardized parts. This allowed U.S. firms to produce their firearms at much lower costs than in other countries where similar weapons were made one at a time by craftsmen. One of these, the Colt six-shooter, blazed its way into fame in the nineteenth century in the American "Wild West."

Acquired Comparative Advantage This last mentioned source of comparative advantage makes it clear that many comparative advantages are *acquired*. Further, they can change. Thus, comparative advantage should be viewed as being *dynamic* rather than static. Many new industries are seen to depend more on human capital than on fixed physical capital or natural resources. The skills of a computer designer, a video game programmer, or a sound mix technician are acquired by education and on-the-job training. Natural endowments of energy and raw materials cannot account for Silicon Valley's leadership in computer technology, for Canada's prominence in communications technology, for Taiwan's excellence in electronics, or for Switzerland's prominence in private banking.

If comparative advantage can be acquired, it can also be *lost*. If firms within one country fail to innovate and adopt the latest technologies available in their industry, but competing firms in other countries are aggressively innovating and reducing their production costs, the first country will eventually lose whatever comparative advantage it once had in that industry. In recent years, for example, pulp and paper mills in Canada have been closing, driven out of the industry by Scandinavian firms that more aggressively pursue improvements in productivity.

With today's growing international competition, no country's comparative advantages are secure unless its firms innovate and keep up with their foreign competitors and its education system produces workers, managers, and innovators with the requisite skills.

myeconlab **ADDITIONAL TOPICS**

The race between firms for innovation and productivity improvements is often used as an illustration for how countries also "compete" against one another in terms of international trade. Many observers appear to adopt this view when they argue that productivity growth in the developing world harms living standards in the developed countries. Is this argument correct? Look for **Does Third-World Growth Harm First-World Prosperity?** in the *Additional Topics* section of this book's MyEconLab.

www.myeconlab.com

Contrasting Views? This modern view is in sharp contrast with the traditional assumption that cost structures based largely on a country's natural endowments lead to a given pattern of international comparative advantage. The traditional view suggests that a government interested in maximizing its citizens' material standard of living should encourage specialization of production in goods for which it *currently* has a comparative advantage. If all countries followed this advice, each would have been specialized in a relatively narrow range of distinct products. The British would have produced engineering products, Canadians would have produced resource-based primary products, Americans would have been farmers and factory workers, Central Americans would have been banana and coffee growers, and so on.

There are surely elements of truth in both extreme views. It would be unwise to neglect resource endowments, climate, culture, social patterns, and institutional arrangements. But it would also be unwise to assume that all advantages are innate and immutable.

To some extent, these views are reconciled by the theory of human capital, which is a topic we discussed in Chapter 14. Comparative advantages that depend on human capital are consistent with traditional Heckscher-Ohlin theory. The difference is that this type of capital is acquired through conscious decision making relating to such matters as education and technical training.

33.2 The Determination of Trade Patterns

Comparative advantage has been the central concept in our discussion about the gains from trade. If Canada has a comparative advantage in lumber and Italy has a comparative advantage in shoes, then the total output of lumber and shoes can be increased if Canada specializes in the production of lumber and Italy specializes in the production of shoes. With such patterns of specialization, Canada will naturally export lumber to Italy and Italy will export shoes to Canada.

It is one thing to discuss the *potential* gains from trade if countries specialized in the production of particular goods and exported these to other countries. But do *actual* trade patterns occur along the lines of comparative advantage? In this section of the chapter we use a simple demand-and-supply model to examine why Canada exports some products and imports others. We will see that comparative advantage, whether natural or acquired, plays a central role in determining actual trade patterns.

There are some products, such as coffee and mangoes, that Canada does not produce (and will probably never produce). Any domestic consumption of these products must therefore be satisfied by imports from other countries. At the other extreme, there are some products, such as nickel or potash, of which Canada is one of the world's major suppliers, and demand in the rest of the world must be satisfied partly by exports from Canada. Finally, there are some products, such as houses and cement, that are so expensive to transport that every country produces approximately what it consumes.

Our interest in this section is with the vast number of intermediate cases in which Canada is only one of many producers of an internationally traded product, as with beef, oil, copper, wheat, lumber, and newsprint. Will Canada be an exporter or an importer of such products? And what is the role-played by comparative advantage?

*For data on Canadian trade by industry and by country, go to Statistics Canada's website at **www.statcan. gc.ca.** and search for "trade."*

The Law of One Price

Whether Canada imports or exports a product for which it is only one of many producers depends to a great extent on the product's price. This brings us to what economists call the *law of one price*.

> The law of one price states that when a product is traded throughout the entire world, the prices in various countries will differ by no more than the cost of transporting the product between countries. Aside from differences caused by these transport costs, there is a single world price.

Many basic products—such as copper wire, steel pipe, iron ore, and computer RAM chips—fall within this category. The world price for each good is the price that equates the quantity demanded worldwide with the quantity supplied worldwide. The world price of an internationally traded product may be influenced greatly, or only slightly, by the demand and supply coming from any one country. The extent of one country's influence will depend on how important its quantities demanded and supplied are in relation to the worldwide totals.

The simplest case for us to study arises when the country, which we will take to be Canada, accounts for only a small part of the total worldwide demand and supply. In this case, Canada does not itself produce enough to influence the world price significantly. Similarly, Canadian purchases are too small a proportion of worldwide demand to affect the world price in any significant way. Producers and consumers in Canada thus face a world price that they cannot influence by their own actions.

In this case, the price that rules in the Canadian market must be the world price (adjusted for the exchange rate between the Canadian dollar and the foreign currency). The law of one price says that this must be so. What would happen if the Canadian domestic price diverged from the world price? If the Canadian price were below the world price, no supplier would sell in the Canadian market because higher profits could be made by selling abroad. The absence of supply to the Canadian market would thus drive up the Canadian price. Conversely, if the Canadian domestic price were above the worldwide price, no buyer would buy from a Canadian seller because lower prices are available by buying abroad. The absence of demand on the Canadian market would thus drive down the Canadian price.

The Pattern of Foreign Trade

Let us now see what determines the pattern of international trade in such circumstances.

An Exported Product   To determine the pattern of Canadian trade, we first show the Canadian domestic demand and supply curves for some product, say, lumber. This is done in Figure 33-5. The intersection of these two curves tells us what the price and quantity would be *if there were no foreign trade*. Now compare this no-trade price with the world price of that product.[1] If the world price is higher, the actual price in Canada will exceed the no-trade price. In this situation there will be an excess of Canadian supply over Canadian demand. Domestic producers want to sell Q_2 units of lumber but domestic consumers want to buy only Q_1 units. If Canada were a closed economy, such excess supply would drive the price down to p_d. But in an open economy with a world price of p_w, this excess supply is exported to Canada's trading partners.

> Countries export products whose world price exceeds the price that would exist domestically if there were no foreign trade.

Export Development Canada is a Crown corporation devoted to improving Canada's export prospects. For information about Canada's exports, check out its website: **www.edc.ca**.

Practise with Study Guide Chapter 33, Exercise 5.

---

[1] If the world price is stated in terms of some foreign currency (as it often is), the price must be converted into Canadian dollars by using the current exchange rate between the foreign currency and Canadian dollars.

What is the role of comparative advantage in this analysis? We have said that Canada will export lumber if the world price exceeds Canada's no-trade price. Note that in a competitive market the price of the product reflects the product's marginal cost, which in turn reflects the opportunity cost of producing the product. That Canada's no-trade price for lumber is lower than the world price reflects the fact that the opportunity cost of producing lumber in Canada is less than the opportunity cost of producing it in the rest of the world. Thus, by exporting goods that have a low no-trade price, Canada is exporting the goods for which it has a comparative advantage.

> **Countries export the goods for which they are low-cost producers. That is, they export goods for which they have a comparative advantage.**

An Imported Product

Now consider some other product—for example, computer RAM chips. Once again, look first at the domestic demand and supply curves, shown this time in Figure 33-6. The intersection of these curves determines the no-trade price that would rule if there were no foreign trade. The world price of RAM chips is below the Canadian no-trade price so that, at the price ruling in Canada, domestic demand is larger and domestic supply is smaller than if the no-trade price had ruled. The excess of domestic demand over domestic supply is met by imports.

> **Countries import products whose world price is less than the price that would exist domestically if there were no foreign trade.**

Again, this analysis can be restated in terms of comparative advantage. The high Canadian no-trade price of RAM chips reflects the fact that RAM chips have a higher opportunity cost in Canada than elsewhere in the world. This high cost means that Canada has a comparative disadvantage in RAM chips. So Canada imports goods for which it has a comparative disadvantage.

> **Countries import the goods for which they are high-cost producers. That is, they import goods for which they have a comparative disadvantage.**

FIGURE 33-5   An Exported Good

Exports occur whenever there is excess supply domestically at the world price. The domestic demand and supply curves are D and S, respectively. The domestic price in the absence of foreign trade is p_d, with Q_d produced and consumed domestically. The world price of p_w is higher than p_d. At p_w, Q_1 is demanded while Q_2 is supplied domestically. The excess of the domestic supply over the domestic demand is exported.

FIGURE 33-6   An Imported Good

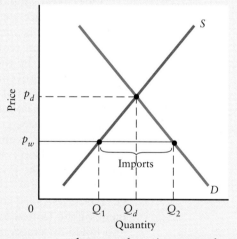

Imports occur whenever there is excess demand domestically at the world price. The domestic demand and supply curves are D and S, respectively. The domestic price in the absence of foreign trade is p_d, with Q_d produced and consumed domestically. The world price of p_w is less than p_d. At the world price Q_2 is demanded, whereas Q_1 is supplied domestically. The excess of domestic demand over domestic supply is satisfied through imports.

Is Comparative Advantage Obsolete?

It is sometimes said that the theory of comparative advantage is nearly 200 years old, and things have changed so much since then that the theory must surely be obsolete.

Contrary to such assertions, comparative advantage remains an important economic concept. At any one time—because comparative advantage is reflected in international relative prices, and these relative prices determine what goods a country will import and what it will export—the operation of the price system will result in trade that follows the current pattern of comparative advantage. For example, if Canadian costs of producing steel are particularly low relative to other Canadian costs, Canada will export steel at international prices (which it does). If Canada's costs of producing textiles are particularly high relative to other Canadian costs, Canada will import textiles at international prices (which it does). Thus, there is no reason to change the view that Ricardo long ago expounded: *Current comparative advantage is a major determinant of trade under free-market conditions.*

What has changed, however, is economists' views about the *determinants* of comparative advantage. It now seems that current comparative advantage may be more open to change by private entrepreneurial activities and by government policy than used to be thought. Thus, what is obsolete is the belief that a country's current pattern of comparative advantage, and hence its current pattern of imports and exports, must be accepted as given and unchangeable.

The theory that comparative advantage determines trade flows is not obsolete, but the theory that comparative advantage is completely determined by forces beyond the reach of decisions made by private firms and by public policy has been discredited.

One caveat should be noted. It is one thing to observe that it is *possible* for governments to influence a country's pattern of comparative advantage. It is quite another to conclude that it is *advisable* for them to try. The case in support of a specific government intervention requires that (1) there is scope for governments to improve on the results achieved by the free market, (2) the costs of the intervention be less than the value of the improvement to be achieved, and (3) governments will actually be able to carry out the required interventionist policies (without, for example, being sidetracked by considerations of electoral advantage).

In many cases, governments have succeeded in creating important comparative advantages. For example, the Taiwanese government virtually created that nation's electronics industry and then passed it over to private hands in which it became a world leader. The government of Singapore created a computer-parts industry that became a major world supplier. However, there are also many examples in which governments failed in their attempts to create comparative advantage. The government of the United Kingdom tried to create a comparative advantage in computers and failed miserably, wasting much public money in the process. The government of Ireland tried to create a comparative advantage in automobile production and failed to create more than a modest, unprofitable industry that eventually disappeared. The world is strewn not only with spectacular successes, which show that it can be done, but also with abject failures, which show that the attempt to do so is fraught with many dangers.

One other comment should be made regarding the relevance of the concept of comparative advantage. For understanding international trade in copper wire, lumber, oil, bananas, coffee, textiles, and many other relatively simple products, the concept of comparative advantage is very useful. In some manufacturing industries, however, where products have dozens or perhaps hundreds of components, the determinants of trade flows are more complex than the theory of comparative advantage suggests. For example, it is difficult to see why Canada might have a comparative advantage in the production of automobile transmissions but not in automobile brake systems or air-conditioning systems. Yet, the automobile sector is perhaps the best example of an industry in which a firm's "supply chain" includes products made by several other firms in several countries. *Applying Economic Concepts 33-2* discusses how the forces of globalization and economies of scale have led to the development of complex global supply chains.

The Terms of Trade

terms of trade The ratio of the average price of a country's exports to the average price of its imports.

We have seen that world production can be increased when countries specialize in the production of the goods for which they have a comparative advantage and then trade with one another. We now ask: How will these gains from specialization and trade be shared among countries? The division of the gain depends on what is called the **terms of trade**, which relate to the quantity of imported goods that can be obtained per unit of goods exported. The terms of trade are measured by the ratio of the price of exports to the price of imports.

A rise in the price of imported goods, with the price of exports unchanged, indicates a *fall in the terms of trade*; it will now take more exports to buy the same quantity of imports. Similarly, a rise in the price of exported goods, with the price of imports unchanged, indicates a *rise in the terms of trade*; it will now take fewer exports to buy the same quantity of imports. Thus, the ratio of these prices measures the amount of imports that can be obtained per unit of goods exported.

The terms of trade can be illustrated with a country's production possibilities boundary, as shown in Figure 33-7. The figure shows the hypothetical case in which Canada can produce only wheat and cloth. As we saw earlier, the slope of Canada's production possibilities boundary shows the relative opportunity costs of producing the two goods in Canada. A steep production possibilities boundary indicates that only a small amount of cloth must be given up to get more wheat; thus cloth is relatively costly and wheat is relatively cheap. A flatter production possibilities boundary indicates that a larger amount of cloth must be given up to get more wheat; thus cloth is relatively cheap and wheat is relatively expensive. Thus, the slope of the production possibilities boundary in Figure 33-7 shows the relative price of cloth (in terms of wheat) that Canada faces in the absence of international trade.

FIGURE 33-7   An Improvement in the Terms of Trade

A rise in the relative price of exports is a terms-of-trade improvement and expands consumption opportunities

Changes in the terms of trade lead to changes in a country's consumption possibilities. The hypothetical production possibilities boundary is shown for Canada. With international trade at relative prices T_0, Canada specializes in the production of wheat, producing at point S, but is able to consume at a point like A. It pays for its imports of cloth with its exports of wheat.

If the price of wheat rises relative to the price of cloth, production remains at S but the line T_1 shows Canada's new consumption possibilities. Consumption can now take place at a point like B where consumption of both wheat and cloth has increased. The increase in the terms of trade makes Canada better off because of the increase in consumption possibilities.

APPLYING ECONOMIC CONCEPTS 33-2

Comparative Advantage and Global Supply Chains

The discussion of comparative advantage developed in this chapter applies easily to many products with one or even a few components. One can sensibly speak of national comparative advantages for whole products, such as Costa Rica for bananas, Canada for lumber, Chile for copper, Korea for steel, and Saudi Arabia for oil.

For many manufactured products, however, and even for some resource-based products and service industries, production is carried out in complex and integrated "global supply chains," with a product's several different components being produced in different countries and often by different firms. In this world of "integrative trade," it is no longer clear where some products are "made," even though one could easily determine where each of the product's many components is produced. This method of decentralized production has several causes. First, the existence of scale economies provides an incentive for individual firms to reduce their costs by concentrating the production of each individual component in a different specialized large factory. Second, differences in national wage rates for various types of labour provide an incentive for these production facilities to be located in different countries. Third, the current very low costs of communication and transportation make it possible to coordinate supply chains globally and ship parts and final

products anywhere at low cost. (If fuel becomes expensive enough to make transport costs a significant part of total costs, it will become economic to do much more production closer to final markets than it has been over the last few decades.)

Consider three examples. The famous iPod sold by Apple clearly says "Made in China" on the box, but most of the value from its design occurs in the United States, many electronic components come from Korea and Japan, and only the iPod's final assembly occurs in China. Apple chooses to locate assembly in China, using components manufactured elsewhere, because by doing so it can maximize its product quality and minimize costs.

Bombardier jet aircraft designed and assembled in Canada also involve global supply chains. Fuselage parts come from Japan, the wings are produced in Northern Ireland, engines are imported from the United States, and the avionics are engineered in the United States but sourced from Asian suppliers. Bombardier adopts this business model because costs can be reduced and quality maximized by using specialty suppliers at each link in the global supply chain.

Such global supply chains even exist for some products that appear to have few "components," such as fish. For example, a Canadian firm may hire a Chilean trawler to fish in the Indian Ocean, land its

Practise with Study Guide
Chapter 33, Exercise 3.

If, through international trade, Canada has access to different relative prices, Canada will be led to specialize in the production of one good or the other. In Figure 33-7, we show a case in which the world relative price of cloth is lower than the relative price Canada would have if it did not trade. (This lower *world* relative price of cloth reflects the fact that other countries can produce cloth more cheaply than Canada.) Faced with a lower relative price of cloth, Canada ends up specializing in the production of the relatively high-priced product (wheat), and importing the relatively low-priced product (cloth). This point of specialization is point S in Figure 33-7.

The *green* lines in the figure show alternative values of the world relative prices—that is, alternative values for Canada's terms of trade. A rise in the terms of trade indicates a fall in the relative price of cloth (or a rise in the relative price of wheat). This increase in the terms of trade is shown as an upward rotation of the green line from T_0 to T_1. A reduction in the terms of trade is shown as a downward rotation in the green line, from T_1 to T_0.

It should be clear from Figure 33-7 why changes in the terms of trade are important. Suppose the international relative prices are initially given by T_0. Canada specializes in catch in Malaysia where it is frozen, and then send it to China for further processing before it is finally sold to Japanese wholesalers. This supply chain could operate in two different ways. First, the Canadian firm could manage the entire process but leave ownership to the individual firms at each stage of the supply chain. In this case, the Canadian firm is providing management expertise and would earn a return that in the data appears as a Canadian export of services. Alternatively, the Canadian firm could own the product but merely hire the services of the required firms at each stage of the supply chain. In this case, the return to the Canadian firm would be significantly higher because of the need to manage the various risks involved in production, such as unexpected swings in prices, natural disasters, and human error.

There are three implications for how we think about international trade in the presence of integrated global supply chains. First, we should not view countries as having comparative advantages in entire products but rather in the specific productive activities that take place along the global supply chain. China may not have a comparative advantage in "producing" consumer electronics but may have one in assembling them. Canada may not have a comparative advantage in "producing" jet aircraft but may have one in designing them.

Second, these comparative advantages may not be long-lasting because they are sensitive to changes in the economic environment. For example, significant changes in national corporate tax rates, exchange rates, and wages for factory workers will generally change the optimal location for the production of a product's various components.

Third, traditional data on international trade does not capture the extent of integration in global supply chains. The iPod assembled in China and exported to the United States appears simply as a Chinese export; but the significant value generated by the U.S.-based design team may appear in no trade statistics whatsoever. It follows that the measured flow of a country's exports of some products does not necessarily correspond closely with the level of local economic activity (production and employment) actually generated by those products. Even in Canada's resource sector, the domestic content of exports is not 100 percent, although it is typically more than 75 percent, meaning that up to one-quarter of the value of the final exported product comes from imported inputs. In most manufacturing industries, however, the domestic content of exports is 50 percent or lower, and in the automobile industry it is only 35 percent.

The presence of such highly integrated global supply chains indicates the importance of two-way trade in Canadian manufacturing: Access to low-price and high-quality imports is as crucial to the Canadian economy as is our access to world markets where we can sell our intermediate and final products.

the production of wheat (point S) but consumes at some point like A, where it finances imports of cloth with exports of wheat. Now suppose there is a shift in world demand toward wheat and away from cloth, and this leads to an increase in the relative price of wheat. The terms of trade increase to T_1 and, with unchanged production at point S, Canada can now afford to consume at a point like B where consumption of both wheat and cloth has increased.

A rise in a country's terms of trade is beneficial because it expands the country's consumption possibilities.

Conversely, a reduction in the price of a country's exports (relative to the price of its imports) is harmful for a country. In Figure 33-7, this is shown as a change of the terms of trade from T_1 to T_0. Even though production may remain unchanged, the range of goods available to be consumed falls, and this reduction in consumption possibilities leads to an overall loss of welfare.

How do we measure the terms of trade in real economies? Because international trade involves many countries and many products, we cannot use the simple ratio of

FIGURE 33-8   Canada's Terms of Trade, 1961–2008

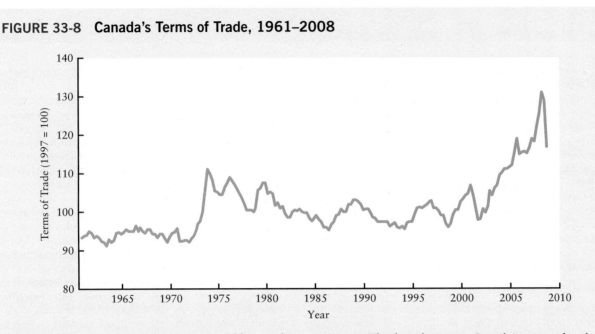

Canada's terms of trade have been quite variable over the past 50 years. The data shown are Canada's terms of trade—the ratio of an index of Canadian export prices to an index of Canadian import prices. As the relative prices of lumber, oil, wheat, electronic equipment, textiles, fruit, and other products change, the terms of trade naturally change.

(*Source:* Statistics Canada, CANSIM database, Series V1997754 and V1997751 and authors' calculations.)

the prices of two goods as in Figure 33-7. The basic principle, however, is the same. A country's terms of trade are computed as an index number:

$$\text{Terms of trade} = \frac{\text{Index of export prices}}{\text{Index of import prices}} \times 100$$

A rise in the index is referred to as a *favourable* change in a country's terms of trade (sometimes called a terms of trade *improvement*). A decrease in the index of the terms of trade is called an *unfavourable* change (or a terms of trade *deterioration*). For example, the sharp rise in oil prices in the 1970s led to large unfavourable shifts in the terms of trade of oil-importing countries. When oil prices fell sharply in the mid-1980s, the terms of trade of oil-importing countries changed favourably. The converse was true for oil-exporting countries.

Canada's terms of trade since 1961 are shown in Figure 33-8. As is clear, the terms of trade are quite variable, reflecting frequent changes in the relative prices of different products. Note the dramatic increase (improvement) in Canada's terms of trade in the early 1970s, reflecting the large increase in oil prices caused by OPEC's output restrictions. Since Canada is a net exporter of oil, its terms of trade improve when the price of oil increases. An even larger increase occurred in the 2002–2008 period, when the world prices of most commodities, especially energy-related commodities, increased sharply.

Summary

33.1 The Gains from Trade

- Country A has an *absolute* advantage over Country B in the production of a specific product when the absolute resource cost of the product is less in Country A than in Country B.
- Country A has a *comparative* advantage over Country B in the production of a specific good if the forgone output of other goods is less in Country A than in Country B.
- Comparative advantage occurs whenever countries have different opportunity costs of producing particular goods. World production of all products can be increased if each country transfers resources into the production of the products for which it has a comparative advantage.
- Trade allows all countries to obtain the goods for which they do not have a comparative advantage at a lower

opportunity cost than they would face if they were to produce all products for themselves; specialization and trade therefore allow all countries to have more of all products than they could have if they tried to be self-sufficient.
- A nation that engages in trade and specialization may also realize the benefits of economies of large-scale production and of learning by doing.
- Classical theory regarded comparative advantage as largely determined by natural resource endowments that are difficult to change. Economists now believe that some comparative advantages can be acquired and consequently can be changed. A country may, in this view, influence its role in world production and trade.

33.2 The Determination of Trade Patterns

- The law of one price says that the national prices of tradable goods must differ by no more than the costs of transporting these goods between countries. After accounting for these transport costs, there is a single world price.
- Countries will export a good when the world price exceeds the price that would exist in the country if there were no trade. The low no-trade price reflects a low opportunity cost and thus a comparative advantage in that good. Thus, countries export goods for which they have a comparative advantage.
- Countries will import a good when the world price is less than the price that would exist in the country if

there were no trade. The high no-trade price reflects a high opportunity cost and thus a comparative disadvantage in that good. Thus, countries import goods for which they have a comparative disadvantage.
- The terms of trade refer to the ratio of the prices of goods exported to the prices of those imported. The terms of trade determine the quantity of imports that can be obtained per unit of exports.
- A favourable change in the terms of trade—a rise in export prices relative to import prices—is beneficial for a country because it expands its consumption possibilities.

Key Concepts

Interpersonal, interregional, and international specialization
Absolute advantage and comparative advantage
Opportunity cost and comparative advantage

The gains from trade: specialization, scale economies, and learning by doing
The sources of comparative advantage

Factor endowments
Acquired comparative advantage
The law of one price
The terms of trade

Study Exercises

1. Fill in the blanks to make the following statements correct.

   a. The "gains from trade" refers to the increased _____ caused by specialization and trade.
   b. Suppose Argentina can produce one kilogram of beef for $2.50 and Brazil can produce one kilogram of beef for $2.90. Argentina is said to have a(n) _____ in beef production over Brazil. The gains from trade do *not* depend on _____.
   c. Comparative advantage is based on _____ rather than absolute costs.
   d. It is possible for a country to have a comparative advantage in some good and a(n) _____ in none.
   e. If all countries specialize in the production of goods for which they have a comparative advantage, then world output will _____.
   f. If opportunity costs are the same in all countries, there is no _____ and no possibility of _____.

2. Fill in the blanks to make the following statements correct.

   a. Such a product as coffee beans is cheaply transported and is traded around the world. The law of _____ tells us that it will tend to have _____ worldwide price.
   b. If the domestic price of copper wire in Canada (in the absence of trade) is $20 per unit and the world price is $24 per unit, then Canada will have an excess _____, which it will then _____. The opportunity cost of producing copper wire in Canada is _____ than the opportunity cost of producing it in the rest of the world.
   c. Canada will import goods for which it has an excess _____ at the world price. In the absence of trade, the _____ price of these goods would be less than the _____ price.
   d. A rise in Canada's terms of trade means that the average price of Canada's _____ has risen compared with the average price of Canada's _____. This change is referred to as a terms of trade _____.

   e. The terms of trade determine the quantity of _____ that can be obtained per unit of _____.

3. The following diagram shows the production possibilities boundary for Arcticland, a country that produces only two goods, ice and fish. Labour is the only factor of production.

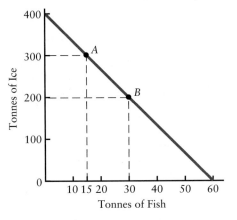

   a. Beginning at any point on Arcticland's production possibilities boundary, what is the opportunity cost of producing 10 more tonnes of fish?
   b. Beginning at any point on Arcticland's production possibilities boundary, what is the opportunity cost of producing 100 more tonnes of ice?

4. The following table shows the production of wheat and corn in Brazil and Mexico. Assume that both countries have one million acres of arable land.

	Brazil	Mexico
Wheat	90 bushels per acre	50 bushels per acre
Corn	30 bushels per acre	20 bushels per acre

   a. Which country has the absolute advantage in wheat? In corn? Explain.
   b. What is the opportunity cost of producing an extra bushel of wheat in Brazil? In Mexico? Which

country has the comparative advantage in wheat production? Explain.

c. Which country has the comparative advantage in corn production? Explain.

d. Explain why one country can have an absolute advantage in both goods but cannot have a comparative advantage in both goods.

e. On a scale diagram with wheat on the horizontal axis and corn on the vertical axis, draw each country's production possibilities boundary.

f. What is shown by the slope of each country's production possibilities boundary? Be as precise as possible.

5. The following diagrams show the production possibilities boundaries for Canada and France, both of which produce only two goods, wine and lumber.

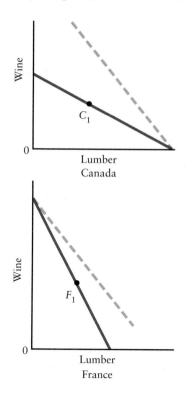

a. Which country has the comparative advantage in lumber? Explain.

b. Which country has the comparative advantage in wine? Explain.

c. Suppose Canada and France are initially not trading with each other and are producing at points C_1 and F_1, respectively. Suppose when trade is introduced, the free-trade relative prices are shown by the slope of the dashed line. Show in the diagrams which combination of goods each country will now produce.

d. In this case, what will be the pattern of trade for each country?

6. The following diagrams show the Canadian markets for newsprint and machinery, which we assume to be competitive.

a. Suppose there is no international trade. What would be the equilibrium price and quantity in the Canadian newsprint and machinery markets?

b. Now suppose Canada is open to trade with the rest of the world. If the world price of newsprint is higher than the price of newsprint from part (a), what will happen to the levels of domestic production and consumption? Explain.

c. If the world price of machinery is lower than the price of machinery from part (a), what happens to the levels of domestic consumption and production? Explain.

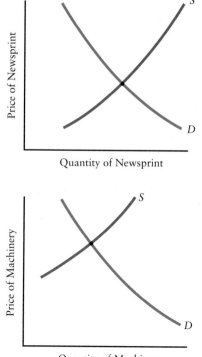

7. The table below shows indexes for the prices of imports and exports over several years for a hypothetical country.

Year	Import Prices	Export Prices	Terms of Trade
2005	90	110	___
2006	95	87	___
2007	98	83	___
2008	100	100	___
2009	102	105	___
2010	100	112	___
2011	103	118	___

a. Compute the terms of trade in each year for this country and fill in the table.

b. In which years do the terms of trade improve?

c. In which years do the terms of trade deteriorate?

d. Explain why a terms of trade "improvement" is good for the country.

8. For each of the following events, explain the likely effect on Canada's terms of trade. Your existing knowledge of Canada's imports and exports should be adequate to answer this question.

a. A hurricane damages much of Brazil's coffee crop.

b. OPEC countries succeed in significantly restricting the world supply of oil.

c. Several new large copper mines come into production in Chile.

d. A major recession in Southeast Asia reduces the world demand for pork.

e. Russia, a large producer of wheat, experiences a massive drought that reduces its wheat crop by more than 30 percent.

Discussion Questions

1. Adam Smith saw a close connection between the wealth of a nation and its willingness "freely to engage" in foreign trade. What is the connection?

2. When the North American Free Trade Agreement (NAFTA) was being negotiated in the early 1990s, there was a great deal of debate. One critic argued that "it can't be in our interest to sign this deal; Mexico gains too much from it." What does the theory of the gains from trade have to say about that criticism?

3. One product innovation that appears imminent is the electric car. However, development costs are high and economies of scale and learning by doing are both likely to be operative. As a result, there will be a substantial competitive advantage for those who develop a marketable product early. What implications might this have for government policies toward North American automobile manufacturers' activities in this area? Should the Canadian or U.S. governments encourage joint efforts by Chrysler, Ford, and GM, even if this appears to lessen competition among them?

4. Studies of Canadian trade patterns have shown that industries with high wages are among the largest and fastest-growing export sectors. One example is the computer software industry. Does this finding contradict the principle of comparative advantage?

5. Predict what each of the following events would do to the terms of trade of the importing country and the exporting country, other things being equal.

a. A blight destroys a large part of the coffee beans produced in the world.

b. The Koreans cut the price of the steel they sell to Canada.

c. General inflation of 4 percent occurs around the world.

d. Violation of OPEC output quotas leads to a sharp fall in the price of oil.

6. Are there always benefits to specialization and trade? When are the benefits greatest? Under what situations are there *no* benefits from specialization and trade?

34

Trade Policy

Conducting business in a foreign country is not always easy. Differences in language, in local laws and customs, and in currency often complicate transactions. Our concern in this chapter, however, is not with these complications but with government policy toward international trade, which is called **trade policy.** At one extreme is a policy of free trade—that is, an absence of any form of government interference with the free flow of international trade. Any departure from free trade designed to protect domestic industries from foreign competition is called **protectionism.**

We begin by briefly restating the case for free trade and then go on to examine various valid and invalid arguments that are commonly advanced for some degree of protection. We then explore some of the methods commonly used to restrict trade, such as tariffs and quotas. Finally, we examine the many modern institutions designed to foster freer trade on either a global or a regional basis. In particular, we discuss the North American Free Trade Agreement (NAFTA) and the World Trade Organization (WTO).

LEARNING OBJECTIVES

In this chapter you will learn

1 the various situations in which a country may rationally choose to protect some industries.

2 the most common fallacious arguments in favour of protection.

3 the effects of a tariff or quota on imported goods.

4 why trade-remedy laws are sometimes just thinly disguised protection.

5 the distinction between trade creation and trade diversion.

6 the main features of the North American Free Trade Agreement.

trade policy A government's policy involving restrictions placed on international trade.

protectionism Any government policy that interferes with free trade in order to protect domestic firms and workers from foreign competition.

tariff A tax applied on imports of goods or services.

non-tariff barriers (NTBs) Restrictions other than tariffs designed to reduce imports.

34.1 Free Trade or Protection?

Today, most governments accept the proposition that a relatively free flow of international trade is desirable for the health of their individual economies. But heated debates still occur over trade policy. Should a country permit the *completely* free flow of international trade, or should it sometimes seek to protect its local producers from foreign competition? If some protection is desired, should it be achieved by tariffs or by non-tariff barriers? **Tariffs** are taxes designed to raise the price of imported goods. **Non-tariff barriers (NTBs)** are devices other than tariffs designed to reduce the flow of imports; examples are import quotas and customs procedures that are deliberately more cumbersome than necessary.

The Case for Free Trade

The gains from trade were presented in Chapter 33. Comparative advantages arise whenever countries have different opportunity costs. Free trade encourages all countries to specialize in producing products in which they have a comparative advantage. This pattern of specialization maximizes world production and hence maximizes average world living standards (as measured by the world's per capita GDP).

Free trade does not necessarily make *everyone* better off than they would be in its absence. For example, reducing an existing tariff often results in individual groups receiving a smaller share of a larger world output so that they lose even though the average person gains. If we ask whether it is *possible* for free trade to improve everyone's living standards, the answer is yes because the larger total value of output that free trade generates could, at least in principle, be divided up in such a way that every individual is better off. If we ask whether free trade always does so in practice, however, the answer is, not necessarily.

> Free trade makes the country as a whole better off, even though it may not make every individual in the country better off.

In today's world, a country's products must stand up to international competition if they are to survive. Over even as short a period as a few years, firms that do not develop new products and new production methods fall seriously behind their foreign competitors. If one country protects its domestic firms by imposing a tariff, those firms are likely to become complacent about the need to adopt new technologies, and over time they will become less competitive in international markets. As the technology gap between domestic and foreign firms widens, the tariff wall will provide less and less protection. Eventually, the domestic firms will succumb to foreign competition. Meanwhile, domestic living standards will fall relative to foreign ones.

Given that any country can be better off by specializing in those goods in which it has a comparative advantage, one might wonder why most countries of the world continue in some way to restrict the flow of trade. Why do tariffs and other barriers to trade continue to exist two centuries after Adam Smith and David Ricardo stated the case for free trade? Is there a valid case for some protection?

The Case for Protection

Two kinds of arguments for protection are commonly heard. The first concerns objectives *other than* maximizing national income; the second concerns the desire to increase one country's national income, possibly at the expense of the national incomes of other countries.

Objectives Other than Maximizing National Income

A country's national income may be maximized with free trade and yet it may still be rational to oppose free trade because of other policy objectives.

ADVANTAGES OF DIVERSIFICATION. For a very small country, specializing in the production of only a few products—though dictated by comparative advantage—might involve risks that the country does not want to take. One such risk is that technological advances may render its basic product obsolete. Another risk, especially for countries specialized in producing a small range of agricultural products, is that swings in world prices lead to large swings in national income. Everyone understands these risks, but there is debate about what governments can do about it. The pro-tariff argument is that the government can encourage a more diversified economy by protecting domestic industries that otherwise could not compete with their foreign rivals. Opponents argue that governments, being naturally influenced by political motives, are poor judges of which industries can be protected in order to produce diversification at a reasonable cost.

Countries whose economies are based on the production of only a few goods face risks from fluctuations in world prices. For this reason, protection to promote diversification may be viewed as desirable.

PROTECTION OF SPECIFIC GROUPS. Although specialization according to comparative advantage will maximize *average* per capita GDP, some specific groups may have higher incomes under protection than under free trade. Of particular interest in Canada and the United States has been the effect that greater international trade has on the incomes of unskilled workers.

Consider the ratio of skilled workers to unskilled workers. There are plenty of both types throughout the world. Compared with much of the rest of the world, however, Canada has more skilled and fewer unskilled people. When trade is expanded because of a reduction in tariffs, Canada will tend to export goods made by its abundant skilled workers and import goods made by unskilled workers. (This is the basic prediction of the *factor endowment theory* of comparative advantage that we discussed in Chapter 33.) Because Canada is now exporting more goods made by skilled labour, the domestic demand for such labour rises. Because Canada is now importing more goods made by unskilled labour, the domestic demand for such labour falls. This specialization according to comparative advantage raises average Canadian living standards, but it will also tend to raise the wages of skilled Canadian workers relative to the wages of unskilled Canadian workers.

If increasing trade has these effects, then reducing trade by erecting protectionist trade barriers can have the opposite effects. Protectionist policies may raise the incomes of unskilled Canadian workers, giving them a larger share of a smaller total GDP. The conclusion is that trade restrictions can improve the earnings of one group whenever the restrictions increase the demand for that group's services. This is done, however, at the expense of a reduction in *overall* national income and hence the country's average living standards.

This analysis is important because it reveals both the grain of truth and the dangers that lie behind the resistance to trade liberalization (i.e., freer trade) on the part of some labour groups and some organizations whose main concern is with the poor.

> Social and distributional concerns may lead to the rational adoption of protectionist policies. But the cost of such protection is a reduction in the country's average living standards.

Economists cannot say that it is irrational for a society to sacrifice average living standards in order to protect specific groups. But economists can do three things when presented with such arguments for adopting protectionist measures. First, they can ask if the proposed measures really do achieve the ends suggested. Second, they can calculate the cost of the measures in terms of lowered average living standards. Third, they can see if there are alternative means of achieving the stated goals at lower cost in terms of lost national income.

Maximizing National Income Next we consider several arguments for the use of tariffs when the stated objective is to maximize a country's national income.

TO IMPROVE THE TERMS OF TRADE. Tariffs can be used to change the terms of trade in favour of a country that makes up a large fraction of the world demand for some product that it imports. By restricting its demand for that product through a tariff, it can force down the price that foreign exporters receive for that product. The price paid by domestic consumers will probably rise but as long as the increase is less than the tariff, foreign suppliers will receive less per unit. For example, a 20 percent U.S. tariff on the import of Canadian softwood lumber might raise the price paid by U.S. consumers by 12 percent and lower the price received by Canadian suppliers by 8 percent (the difference between the two prices being received by the U.S. Treasury). This reduction in the price received by the Canadian suppliers of a U.S. import is a terms-of-trade improvement for the United States (and a terms-of-trade deterioration for Canada).

Note that not all countries can improve their terms of trade by levying tariffs on imported goods. A *necessary* condition is that the importing country has *market power*—in other words, that its imports represent a large proportion of total world demand for the good in question, so that its restrictive trade policies lead to a decline in the world price of its imports. Small countries, like Canada, are not large enough importers of any good to have a significant effect on world prices. For small countries, therefore, tariffs cannot improve their terms of trade.

> Large countries can sometimes improve their terms of trade by levying tariffs on some imported goods; small countries cannot.

TO PROTECT INFANT INDUSTRIES. The oldest valid arguments for protection as a means of raising living standards concern economies of scale or learning by doing. It is usually called the **infant industry argument**. An infant industry is nothing more than a new, small industry. If such an industry has large economies of scale or the scope for learning by doing, costs will be high when the industry is small but will fall as the industry grows. In such industries, the country that first enters the field has a tremendous advantage. A developing country may find that in the early stages of development, its industries are unable to compete with established foreign rivals. A trade restriction may protect these industries from foreign competition while they "grow up." When they are large enough, they will be able to produce as cheaply as foreign rivals and thus be able to compete without protection.

Practise with Study Guide Chapter 34, Extension Exercise E1.

infant industry argument
The argument that new domestic industries with potential for economies of scale or learning by doing need to be protected from competition from established, low-cost foreign producers so that they can grow large enough to achieve costs as low as those of foreign producers.

Most of the now industrialized countries developed their industries initially under quite heavy tariff protection. (In Canada's case, the National Policy of 1876 established a high tariff wall behind which many Canadian industries developed and thrived for many years.) Once the industrial sector was well developed, these countries moved to reduce their levels of protection, thus moving a long way toward freer trade. Electronics in Taiwan, automobiles in Japan, commercial aircraft in Europe (specifically the consortium of European governments that created Airbus), and shipbuilding in South Korea are all examples in which protection of infant industries was successful. In each case, the national industry, protected by its home government, developed into a major player in the global marketplace.

One practical problem with this argument for protection is that some infants "never grow up." Once the young firm gets used to operating in a protected environment, it may resist having that protection disappear, even though all economies of scale may have been achieved. This is as much a political problem as an economic one. Political leaders must therefore be careful before offering protection to infant industries because they must recognize the political difficulties involved in removing that protection in the future. The countries that were most successful in having their protected industries eventually grow up and succeed in fierce international competition were those, such as Taiwan and South Korea, that ruthlessly withdrew support from unsuccessful infants within a specified time period.

TO EARN ECONOMIC PROFITS IN FOREIGN MARKETS. Another argument for protectionist policies is to help create an advantage in producing or marketing some product that is expected to generate economic profits through its sales to foreign consumers. If protection of the domestic market, which might include subsidizing domestic firms, can increase the chance that one of the domestic firms will become established and thus earn high profits, the protection may pay off. The economic profits earned in foreign markets may exceed the cost to domestic taxpayers of the protection. This is the general idea behind the concept of *strategic trade policy.*

Opponents of strategic trade policy argue that it is nothing more than a modern version of age-old and faulty justifications for tariff protection. Once all countries try to be strategic, they will all waste vast sums trying to break into industries in which there is no room for most of them. Domestic consumers would benefit most, they say, if their governments let other countries engage in this game. Consumers could then buy the cheap, subsidized foreign products and export traditional non-subsidized products in return. The opponents of strategic trade policy also argue that democratic governments that enter the game of picking and backing winners are likely to make more bad choices than good ones. One bad choice, with all of its massive development costs written off, would require that many good choices also be made in order to make the equivalent in profits that would allow taxpayers to break even overall.

An ongoing dispute between Canada and Brazil illustrates how strategic trade policy is often difficult to distinguish from pure protection. The world's two major producers of regional jets are Bombardier, based in Montreal, and Embraer SA, based in Brazil. For several years, each company has accused its competitor's government of using illegal subsidies to help the domestic company sell jets in world markets. Brazil's Pro-Ex

For many years, Canada and Brazil have been in a trade dispute centred on each country's alleged support of aerospace manufacturers. Canada's Bombardier and Brazil's Embraer both receive considerable financial assistance from their respective federal governments. Taxpayers in each country foot the bill.

program provides Embraer's customers with low-interest loans with which to purchase Embraer's jets. Export Development Canada (EDC) provides similar loans to Bombardier's customers. In addition, the Canadian government's Technology Partnerships program subsidizes research and development activities in high-tech aerospace and defence companies. As the leading Canadian aerospace company, Bombardier benefits significantly from this program.

In 1999, the World Trade Organization (WTO) ruled that both the Brazilian and the Canadian governments were using illegal subsidy programs to support their aerospace firms. Both countries, however, naturally view their respective programs as necessary responses to the other country's subsidization. Many economists believe that an agreement to eliminate both programs would leave a "level playing field," while saving Brazilian and Canadian taxpayers a considerable amount of money. As of 2009, however, both countries continue to support their respective aerospace firms and both sets of taxpayers continue to foot the bill.

*For a list and discussion of many ongoing trade disputes, see the WTO's website: **www.wto.org.***

Fallacious Arguments for Protection

We have seen that free trade is generally beneficial for a country overall even though it does not necessarily make every person better off. We have also seen that there are some situations in which there are valid arguments for restricting trade. For every valid argument, however, there are many fallacious arguments—many of these are based, directly or indirectly, on the misconception that in every transaction there is a winner and a loser. Here we review a few arguments that are frequently heard in political debates concerning international trade.

Keep the Money at Home   This argument says that if I buy a foreign good, I have the good and the foreigner has the money, whereas if I buy the same good locally, I have the good and our country has the money, too. This argument is based on a common misconception. It assumes that domestic money actually goes abroad physically when imports are purchased and that trade flows only in one direction. But when Canadian importers purchase Japanese goods, they do not send dollars abroad. They (or their financial agents) buy Japanese yen and use them to pay the Japanese manufacturers. They purchase the yen on the foreign-exchange market by giving up dollars to someone who wants to use them for expenditure in Canada. Even if the money did go abroad physically—that is, if a Japanese firm accepted a bunch of Canadian $100 bills—it would be because that firm (or someone to whom it could sell the dollars) wanted them to spend in the only country where they are legal tender—Canada.

Canadian currency ultimately does no one any good except as purchasing power in Canada. It would be miraculous if Canadian money could be exported in return for real goods. After all, the Bank of Canada has the power to create as much new Canadian money as it wants (at almost zero direct cost). It is only because Canadian money can buy Canadian products and Canadian assets that others want it.

Protect Against Low-Wage Foreign Labour   This argument says that the products of low-wage countries will drive Canadian products from the market, and the high Canadian standard of living will be dragged down to that of its poorer trading partners. For example, if Canada imports cotton shirts from India, higher-cost Canadian textile firms may go out of business and Canadian workers may be laid off. Arguments of this sort have swayed many voters over the years.

As a prelude to considering this argument, think what the argument would imply if taken out of the international context and put into a local one, where the same principles govern the gains from trade. Is it really impossible for a rich person to gain by trading with a poor person? Would the local millionaire be better off if she did all her own typing, gardening, and cooking? No one believes that a rich person gains nothing by trading with those who are less rich.

Why, then, must a rich group of people lose when they trade with a poor group? "Well," some may say, "the poor group will price its goods too cheaply." Does anyone believe that consumers lose from buying in discount stores or supermarkets just because the prices are lower there than at the old-fashioned corner store? Consumers gain when they can buy the same goods at a lower price. If Chinese, Mexican, or Indian workers earn low wages and the goods they produce are sold at low prices, Canadians will gain by obtaining imports at a low cost in terms of the goods that must be exported in return. The cheaper our imports are, the better off we are in terms of the goods and services available for domestic consumption.

As we said earlier in this chapter, *some* Canadians may be better off if Canada places high tariffs on the import of Chinese goods. In particular, if the Chinese goods compete with goods made by unskilled Canadian workers, then those unskilled workers will be better off if a Canadian tariff protects their firms and thus their jobs. But Canadian income overall—that is, average per capita real income—will be higher when there is free trade.

Exports Are Good; Imports Are Bad   Exports create domestic income; imports create income for foreigners. Surely, then, it is desirable to encourage exports by subsidizing them and to discourage imports by taxing them. This is an appealing argument, but it is incorrect.

Exports raise GDP by adding to the value of domestic output and income, but they do not add to the value of domestic consumption. The standard of living in a country depends on the level of consumption, not on the level of income. In other words, income is not of much use except that it provides the means for consumption.

If exports really were "good" and imports really were "bad," then a fully employed economy that managed to increase exports without a corresponding increase in imports ought to be better off. Such a change, however, would result in a reduction in current standards of living because when more goods are sent abroad but no more are brought in from abroad, the total goods available for domestic consumption must fall.

The living standards of a country depend on the goods and services consumed in that country. The importance of exports is that they provide the resources required to purchase imports, either now or in the future.

Create Domestic Jobs   It is sometimes said that an economy with substantial unemployment, such as Canada during the early 1990s, provides an exception to the case for freer trade. Suppose tariffs or import quotas reduce the imports of Japanese cars, Korean textiles, German kitchen equipment, and Polish vodka. Surely, the argument goes, this will create more employment in Canadian industries producing similar products. This may be true but it will also *reduce* employment in other industries.

The Japanese, Koreans, Germans, and Poles can buy from Canada only if they earn Canadian dollars by selling their domestically produced goods and services to Canada (or by borrowing dollars from Canada).[1] The decline in their sales of cars, textiles, kitchen equipment, and vodka will decrease their purchases of Canadian lumber, cars, software, banking services, and holidays. Jobs will be lost in Canadian export industries and gained in industries that formerly faced competition from imports. The major long-term effect is that the same amount of total employment in Canada will merely be redistributed among industries. In the process, living standards will be reduced because

---

[1] They can also get dollars by selling to other countries and then using their currencies to buy Canadian dollars. But this intermediate step only complicates the transaction; it does not change its fundamental nature. Other countries must have earned the dollars by selling goods to Canada or borrowing from Canada.

employment expands in inefficient import-competing industries and contracts in efficient exporting industries.

A country that imposes tariffs in an attempt to create domestic jobs risks starting a "trade war" with its trading partners. Such a trade war can easily leave every country worse off, as world output (and thus income) falls significantly. An income-reducing trade war followed the onset of the Great Depression in 1929 as many countries increased tariffs to protect their domestic industries in an attempt to stimulate domestic production and employment. Most economists agree that this trade war made the Great Depression worse than it otherwise would have been. *Lessons from History 34-1*

LESSONS FROM HISTORY 34-1

Trade Protection and Recession

With the onset of the Great Depression in 1929, governments in many countries responded to internal political pressures to protect domestic jobs. In the United States, Congress passed the Smoot-Hawley Tariff Act in June 1930, legislation that raised tariffs on hundreds of different imported products. At the time, a petition against the legislation was signed by 1028 economists who argued that such tariffs would be costly for America and would initiate a "tariff war" between the United States and its trading partners, thereby worsening the economic situation.

In retrospect, the economists were clearly correct. Dozens of countries protested the increase in U.S. tariffs but then retaliated by increasing their own tariffs. Here in Canada, Liberal Prime Minister Mackenzie King raised tariffs on imported U.S. products and lowered them on imports from the rest of the British Empire. Confident that he would earn the public's support for his aggressive actions, he promptly called a federal election. But the Conservatives under R.B. Bennett argued that the Liberal actions were far too timid, and the voters apparently agreed. The Liberals were soundly defeated, Bennett became prime minister, and Canadian tariffs on U.S. products were raised even further.

Economists today agree that the widespread increase in tariffs in the 1930s contributed significantly to a reduction in trade flows and made the economic situation worse. In January of 1929, before the onset of the Depression, the volume of world trade was $5.3 billion. Four years later, at the depth of the Depression, world trade had collapsed to $1.8 billion, a reduction of 66 percent. The net effect, instead of increasing employment in any country, was to shift jobs from efficient export industries to inefficient domestic industries, supplying local markets in place of imports.

When the most recent global recession began in the fall of 2008, driven largely by the global financial crisis that had started a year earlier, world leaders were mindful of this important lesson from the Great Depression. When meeting in Washington, D.C., to coordinate their policy responses, the leaders of the world's largest developed and developing countries (the G20 group of countries) publicly committed to not raising any tariffs for at least one year.

Despite this commitment, however, protectionist measures soon emerged. In the United States, the fiscal stimulus package passed by Congress included a "buy America" clause requiring that any funds from the package not be spent on imported construction materials. Similar kinds of protection were built in to the fiscal stimulus packages in China and some European countries. Canada and other major trading nations were understandably concerned by these actions and soon began threatening their own retaliatory measures. The Canadian government went to great lengths to argue that U.S. trade protection would not only hurt Canada but would also hurt the United States by raising prices for American consumers, thus making economic recovery more difficult.

While the lessons from history were being forgotten by some political leaders, a few prominent voices were arguing the dangers of increased trade protection. The World Bank issued a report in March 2009 indicating that in the previous four months world leaders had proposed or implemented 78 different protectionist measures. The president of the World Bank urged leaders to rethink these policies: "Leaders must not heed the siren-song of protectionist fixes, whether for trade, stimulus packages or bailouts. . . . Economic isolationism can lead to a negative spiral of events such as those we saw in the 1930s, which made a bad situation much, much worse."

discusses this relationship between tariffs and recession and how it has resurfaced in the economic policies proposed to counteract the global recession that began in late 2008.

34.2 Methods of Protection

We now go on to explore two specific protectionist policies. Both cause the price of the imported good to rise and the quantity demanded by domestic consumers to fall. They differ, however, in how they achieve these results.

Practise with Study Guide Chapter 34, Exercise 1.

Tariffs

A tariff, also called an *import duty*, is a tax on imported goods. For example, consider a Canadian firm that wants to import cotton T-shirts from India at $5 per shirt. If the Canadian government levies a 20 percent tariff on imported cotton shirts, the Canadian firm pays $5 to the Indian exporter *plus* $1 (20 percent of $5) in import duties to the Canada Revenue Agency. The immediate effect of a tariff is therefore to increase the domestic price of the T-shirt to $6. This price increase has important implications for domestic consumers as well as domestic producers. The effect of a tariff is shown in Figure 34-1.

The initial effect of the tariff is to raise the domestic price of the imported product above its world price by the amount of the tariff. Imports fall. As a result, foreign producers sell less and must transfer resources to other lines of production. The price received on domestically produced units rises, as does the quantity produced domestically. On both counts, domestic producers earn more. However, the cost of producing the extra production at home exceeds the price at which it could be purchased on the world market. Thus, the benefit to domestic producers comes at the expense of domestic consumers. Indeed, domestic consumers lose on two counts: First, they consume less of the product because its price rises, and second, they pay a higher price for the amount that they do consume. This extra spending ends up in two places: The extra that is paid on all units produced at home goes to domestic producers, and the extra that is paid on units still imported goes to the government as tariff revenue.

The overall loss to the domestic economy from levying a tariff is best seen in terms of the changes in consumer and producer surplus. Before the tariff,

FIGURE 34-1   The Deadweight Loss of a Tariff

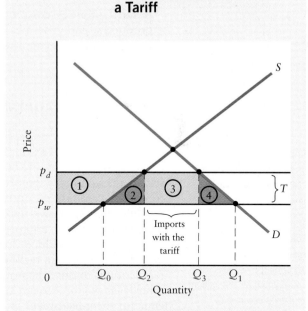

A tariff imposes a deadweight loss for the importing country. Before the tariff, the price in the domestic economy is the world price, p_w. Imports are Q_0Q_1. With a tariff of T per unit, the domestic price rises to p_d. Domestic consumption falls to Q_3, and consumer surplus falls by areas ① + ② + ③ + ④. Domestic production rises to Q_2 and producer surplus increases by area ①. Imports fall to Q_2Q_3, and the government collects tariff revenue equal to area ③. The sum of areas ② and ④ represents the deadweight loss of the tariff.

consumer surplus was equal to the entire area below the demand curve and above the price line at p_w. After the tariff, the price increase leads to less consumption and less consumer surplus. The loss of consumer surplus is the sum of the areas ①, ②, ③, and ④ in Figure 34-1. As domestic producers respond to the higher domestic price by increasing their production and sales, they earn more producer surplus, equal to area ①. Finally, the taxpayers gain the tariff revenue equal to area ③. This is simply a redistribution of surplus away from consumers toward taxpayers. In summary:

$$\begin{array}{ll} \text{Loss of consumer surplus} & = ① + ② + ③ + ④ \\ \text{Gain of producer surplus} & = ① \\ \underline{\text{Gain of tariff revenue} \qquad\qquad = ③ \qquad\qquad\qquad\qquad} \\ \text{Net loss in surplus} & = ② + ④ \end{array}$$

The overall effect of the tariff is therefore to create a deadweight loss to the domestic economy equal to areas ② plus ④. Domestic consumers are worse off, while domestic firms and taxpayers are better off. But the net effect is a loss of surplus for the economy as a whole. This is the overall cost of levying a tariff.

> A tariff imposes costs on domestic consumers, generates benefits for domestic producers, and generates revenue for the government. But the overall net effect is negative; a tariff generates a deadweight loss for the economy.

Quotas and Voluntary Export Restrictions (VERs)

The second type of protectionist policy directly restricts the quantity of an imported product. A common example is the **import quota,** by which the importing country sets a maximum quantity of some product that may be imported each year. Another measure is the **voluntary export restriction (VER),** an agreement by an exporting country to limit the amount of a product that it sells to the importing country.

Figure 34-2 shows that a quantity restriction and a tariff have similar effects on domestic consumers and producers—they both raise domestic prices, increase domestic production, and reduce domestic consumption. But a direct quantity restriction is actually *worse* than a tariff for the importing country because the effect of the quantity restriction is to raise the price received by the foreign suppliers of the good. In contrast, a tariff leaves the foreign suppliers' price unchanged and instead generates tariff revenue for the government of the importing country.

> Import quotas and voluntary export restrictions (VERs) impose larger deadweight losses on the importing country than do tariffs that lead to the same level of imports.

import quota A limit set on the quantity of a foreign commodity that may be imported in a given time period.

voluntary export restriction (VER) An agreement by an exporting country to limit the amount of a good exported to another country.

Practise with Study Guide Chapter 34, Exercise 2.

Canada, the United States, and the European Union have used VERs extensively, and the EU makes frequent use of import quotas. Japan has been pressured into negotiating several VERs with Canada, the United States, and the EU in order to limit sales of some of the Japanese goods that have had the most success in international competition. For example, in 1983, the United States and Canada negotiated VERs whereby the Japanese government agreed to restrict total sales of Japanese cars to these two countries for three years. When the agreements ran out in 1986, the Japanese continued to restrict their automobile sales by unilateral voluntary action. Japan's readiness to restrict its exports to North America reflects the high profits that Japanese automobile producers were making under the system of VERs, as explained in Figure 34-2. In recent years, such VERs have become less important because Japan's major automobile producers, Honda and Toyota, both have established manufacturing plants in Canada.

Tariffs Versus Quotas?

The dispute that raged for several years between Canada and the United States over Canadian softwood lumber (spruce, pine, fir, cedar) exports illustrates an important distinction between tariffs and quotas. The United States protected its softwood lumber industry in two ways:

- by imposing tariffs on imports of Canadian softwood lumber
- by pressuring Canadian governments to place export quotas on Canadian softwood lumber shipments to the United States

Analysis of Figures 34-1 and 34-2 reveals that the choice between tariffs and quotas matters greatly for Canadian producers.

In the case of a U.S. tariff on imported Canadian softwood lumber, Figure 34-1 illustrates the U.S. market. An import tariff raises the domestic price for U.S. lumber users and also increases the profits of U.S. lumber producers. Canadian lumber producers are harmed because there is less demand for their product at the unchanged world price. Area ③ in the figure represents U.S. tariff revenue collected on the imports of Canadian lumber—revenue that accrues to the United States government.

Figure 34-2 illustrates the U.S. market for softwood lumber when a quota is placed on the level of Canadian exports (U.S. imports). As with the tariff, the restricted supply of Canadian lumber to the U.S. market drives up the price to U.S. users and also raises profits for U.S. producers. But with a quota there is an important difference: The higher price in the U.S. market is received by the Canadian lumber producers, as shown by area ③ in the figure.

While a tariff and quota may lead to the same reduced volume of exports, the tariff permits some surplus to be captured by the importing country, whereas the quota allows some surplus to be captured by the exporting country (area ③ in both cases). In the U.S.–Canadian softwood lumber dispute, both tariffs and quotas were used. And while both systems were to be preferred *overall* by a system of free trade, Canada had

FIGURE 34-2   The Deadweight Loss of an Import Quota

An import quota drives up the domestic price and imposes a deadweight loss on the importing country. With free trade, the domestic price is the world price, p_w. Imports are $Q_0 Q_1$. If imports are restricted to only $Q_2 Q_3$ (through either quotas or VERs), the domestic price must rise to the point where the restricted level of imports just satisfies the domestic excess demand—this occurs only at P_d. The rise in price and reduction in consumption reduces consumer surplus by areas ① + ② + ③ + ④. Domestic producers increase their output as the domestic price rises, and producer surplus increases by area ①. Area ③ does not accrue to the domestic economy; instead this area represents extra producer surplus for the foreign firms that export their product to this country. The net effect of the quota or VER is a deadweight loss for the importing country of areas ② + ③ + ④. Import quotas are therefore worse than tariffs for the importing country.

an interest in imposing quotas on Canadian lumber exporters rather than having the same export reduction accomplished by a U.S. tariff.

> **myeconlab ADDITIONAL TOPICS**
>
> The trade dispute regarding Canada's softwood-lumber exports to the United States raged for almost 20 years. By 2006, a new agreement had been approved by the Canadian and U.S. governments. For details about the history, politics, and economics of this trade dispute, look for **The Continuing Saga of Softwood Lumber** in the *Additional Topics* section of this book's MyEconLab.
>
> **w w w . m y e c o n l a b . c o m**

Trade-Remedy Laws and Non-tariff Barriers

As tariffs in many countries were lowered over the years since the Second World War, countries that wanted to protect domestic industries began using, and often abusing, a series of trade restrictions that came to be known as non-tariff barriers (NTBs). The original purpose of some of these barriers was to remedy certain legitimate problems that arise in international trade and, for this reason, they are often called *trade-remedy laws*. All too often, however, such laws are misused and over time become potent means of simple protection.

Dumping Selling a product in a foreign country at a lower price than in the domestic market is known as **dumping**. For example, if U.S.-made cars are sold for less in Canada than they are sold for in the United States, the U.S. automobile firms are said to be *dumping*. Dumping is a form of price discrimination studied in the theory of monopoly (see Chapter 10). Most governments have antidumping duties designed to protect their own industries against what is viewed as unfair foreign pricing practices.

dumping The practice of selling a commodity at a lower price in the export market than in the domestic market for reasons unrelated to differences in costs of servicing the two markets.

> Dumping, if it lasts indefinitely, can be a gift to the receiving country. Its consumers get goods from abroad at lower prices than they otherwise would.

Dumping is more often a temporary measure, designed to get rid of unwanted surpluses, or a predatory attempt to drive competitors out of business. In either case, domestic producers complain about unfair foreign competition. In both cases, it is accepted international practice to levy *antidumping duties* on foreign imports. These duties are designed to eliminate the discriminatory elements in their prices.

Unfortunately, antidumping laws have been evolving over the past three decades in ways that allow antidumping duties to become barriers to trade and competition rather than to provide redress for genuinely unfair trading practices.

Several features of the antidumping system that is now in place in many countries make it highly protectionist. First, any price discrimination between national markets is classified as dumping and is subject to penalties. Thus, prices in the producer's domestic market become, in effect, minimum prices below which no sales can be made in foreign markets, whatever the nature of demand in the domestic and foreign markets. Second, many countries' laws calculate the "margin of dumping" as the difference between the price that is charged in that country's market and the foreign producer's average cost. Thus, when there is a global slump in some industry so that the profit-maximizing price for all producers is below average cost, foreign producers can be convicted of dumping. This gives domestic producers enormous protection whenever the market price falls temporarily below average cost. Third, law in the United States (but not in all other countries) places the onus of proof on the accused. Facing a charge of dumping, a foreign producer must prove that the charge is unfounded. Fourth, U.S. antidumping duties are imposed with no time limit, so they often persist long after foreign firms have altered the prices that gave rise to them.

> Antidumping laws were first designed to permit countries to respond to predatory pricing by foreign firms. More recently, they have been used to protect domestic firms against any foreign competition.

Countervailing Duties   Countervailing duties, which are commonly used by the U.S. government but much less so elsewhere, provide another case in which a trade-remedy law can become a covert method of protection. The countervailing duty is designed to act as a means of creating a "level playing field" on which fair international competition can take place. Privately owned domestic firms rightly complain that they cannot compete against the seemingly bottomless purses of foreign governments. Subsidized foreign exports can be sold indefinitely at prices that would produce losses in the absence of the subsidy. The original object of countervailing duties was to counteract the effect on price of the presence of such foreign subsidies.

If a domestic firm suspects the existence of such a subsidy and registers a complaint, its government is required to make an investigation. For a countervailing duty to be levied, the investigation must determine, first, that the foreign subsidy to the specific industry in question does exist and, second, that it is large enough to cause significant injury to competing domestic firms.

There is no doubt that countervailing duties have sometimes been used to counteract the effects of foreign subsidies. Many governments complain, however, that countervailing duties are often used as thinly disguised protection. At the early stages of the development of countervailing duties, only subsidies whose prime effect was to distort trade were possible objects of countervailing duties. Even then, however, the existence of equivalent domestic subsidies was not taken into account when decisions were made to put countervailing duties on subsidized imports. Thus, the United States levies some countervailing duties against foreign goods even though the foreign subsidy is less than the domestic (U.S.) subsidy. This does not create a level playing field.

Softwood lumber (spruce, pine, and fir) is extensively used in North America for the framing of houses and small buildings. For many years, the United States levied countervailing duties on Canadian softwood lumber exports, alleging that Canadian provinces unfairly subsidized production. In 2006, the Canadian and U.S. governments reached an agreement to end the dispute.

Over time, the type of subsidy that is subject to countervailing duties has evolved until almost any government program that affects industry now risks becoming the object of a countervailing duty. Because all governments, including most U.S. state governments, have programs that provide direct or indirect assistance to industry, the potential for the use of countervailing duties as thinly disguised trade barriers is enormous.

The best-known example in Canada of a U.S. countervailing duty is the 27-percent duty imposed between 2001 and 2005 on U.S. imports of Canadian softwood lumber. The U.S. justification for the duty was that Canadian provincial governments allegedly provided a subsidy to domestic lumber producers by charging artificially low *stumpage fees*—the fees paid by the companies to cut trees on Crown land. In 2006, the U.S. government agreed to eliminate the countervailing duty but only if restrictions were placed on Canadian lumber exports. Thus, a tariff was replaced by a combination of an export quota and an export tax.

34.3 Current Trade Policy

In the remainder of the chapter, we discuss trade policy in practice. We start with the many international agreements that govern current trade policies and then look in a little more detail at the NAFTA.

Before 1947, in the absence of any international agreement, any country was free to impose tariffs on its imports. However, when one country increased its tariffs, the action often triggered retaliatory actions by its trading partners. The 1930s saw a high-water mark of world protectionism as each country sought to raise its employment and output by raising its tariffs. The end result was lowered efficiency, less trade, but no more employment or income. Since the end of the Second World War, much effort has been devoted to reducing tariff barriers, both on a multilateral and on a regional basis.

The GATT and the WTO

One of the most notable achievements of the post–Second World War era was the creation of the General Agreement on Tariffs and Trade (GATT) in 1947. The principle of the GATT was that each member country agreed not to make unilateral tariff increases. This prevented the outbreak of "tariff wars" in which countries raised tariffs to protect particular domestic industries and to retaliate against other countries' tariff increases. The GATT has since been replaced by the World Trade Organization (WTO), which continues the work of the GATT.

The Uruguay Round   The Uruguay Round—the final round of trade agreements under the GATT—was completed in 1994 after years of negotiations. It reduced world tariffs by about 40 percent. A significant failure of these negotiations was the absence of an agreement to liberalize trade in agricultural goods. The European Union and Canada both resisted an agreement in this area. The EU's Common Agricultural Policy (CAP) provides general support for most of its agricultural products, many of which are exported. The EU's position as a subsidized exporter causes major harm to agricultural producers in developing countries whose governments are too poor to compete with the EU in a subsidy war. Canada, which has free trade in many agricultural commodities, was concerned about maintaining its "supply management" over a number of industries including poultry, eggs, and dairy products. These schemes are administered by the provinces, which restrict domestic production and thus push domestic prices well above world levels. The federal government made such high domestic prices possible by imposing import quotas for these products at the national level.

Canada, the EU, and a number of other countries that lavishly protect some or all of their domestic agricultural producers were finally forced to agree to a plan to end all import quotas on agricultural products. In a process called "tariffication," these quotas were replaced by "tariff equivalents"—tariffs that restrict trade by the same amount as the quotas did. For example, a quota that restricted imports of some products to no more than 100 000 units per month and resulted in an increase in the domestic price by 20 percent was replaced by a tariff on that imported product of 20 percent. In the case of the Canadian poultry, egg, and dairy industries, some of the tariff equivalents were as high as *several hundred percent*, which illustrates the restrictiveness of the Canadian policy. The hope among countries that are pushing for freer trade in agricultural commodities is that pressure will build to reduce these very high tariffs over the next few decades.

International trade negotiations sometimes generate considerable grass-roots opposition. There is some opposition to the reduction of tariffs in developed countries and some controversy regarding the appropriate way to address the concerns of developing countries.

Despite the failure to achieve free trade in agricultural products, the Uruguay Round was generally viewed as a success. Perhaps its most significant achievement was the creation of the World Trade Organization (WTO) to replace the GATT. An important part of the WTO is its formal dispute-settlement mechanism. This mechanism allows countries to take cases of alleged trade violations—such as illegal subsidies or tariffs—to the WTO for a formal ruling, and obliges member countries to follow the ruling. The WTO's dispute-settlement mechanism is thus a significant step toward a "rules-based" global trading system.

The Doha Round Agriculture also plays a central role in the current round of trade negotiations, which began in Doha, Qatar, in 2000. Many issues were discussed and negotiated over the next several years, ranging from competition policy to antidumping and from environmental policies to electronic commerce. But one of the most contentious issues is agriculture. The WTO member governments claim to be committed to reducing export subsidies and other forms of government support to agriculture. Movements in this direction will naturally cause political friction within the developed economies that currently protect and support their agricultural producers, especially the United States and the European Union, which provide (by far) the most support to their farmers. A failure to reduce agricultural support in the developed countries, however, will increase the political frictions that already exist between developed and developing nations. For the many developing countries that have natural comparative advantages in agricultural products and that cannot afford to compete in a "subsidy war" with the developed countries, the liberalization of trade in agricultural products is crucial. They see the Doha round as central to their economic development.

Several sets of meetings were held for the Doha round, but little progress was made. By 2007, it appeared that the Doha round was all but dead. When the global financial crisis occurred in 2008 and quickly turned into a major global recession, most countries understandably turned their attention to stimulating domestic growth; international trade negotiations were not an immediate priority. As this book went to press in late 2009, it was still unclear how much attention will be devoted to restarting the Doha round.

Protests About the WTO   Despite the successes of the WTO, it has its critics. In December 1999, trade ministers from the WTO member countries met in Seattle to set the agenda for what would become the Doha Round of trade negotiations. The Seattle meetings were delayed and interrupted by massive protests from environmental and labour groups, among others, who argued that the WTO's process of negotiating trade agreements pays insufficient attention to environmental and labour standards, especially in the developing countries. Many WTO officials and trade ministers, including those from the developing countries, recognized the importance of environmental and labour issues but questioned the wisdom of formally including these concerns in trade agreements. Reaching agreement on trade issues among the 155 (and growing) member countries of the WTO is difficult enough—it would be almost impossible if the issues were bundled with the even more contentious environmental and labour issues. The result would be an overall agreement that achieved very little in terms of either trade liberalization, environmental protection, or establishing labour standards. Instead, many trade officials argued that the existing International Labour Organization should be strengthened and a separate international organization like the WTO should be created to promote environmental issues. These organizations could then push ahead to achieve in their respective domains the same success that the GATT achieved over 50 years of negotiations.

Some of the protesters against the WTO process argue that paying greater attention to environmental and labour issues will improve the living standards in developing countries, where such standards typically fall far behind those in developed economies. One of the interesting ironies of the negotiations, however, is that the governments of the developing countries are among the strongest *opponents* of including environmental and labour issues in trade negotiations. They feel that developed countries would use stringent environmental and labour standards as a means of preventing imports from developing countries, thus protecting their own industries.

As it turned out, the work program for the Doha Round included very little on environmental issues and nothing on labour standards. Apparently, the view of the Doha negotiators was that many trade issues could usefully be discussed without getting embroiled in the very contentious but important environmental and labour issues. Perhaps the *next* round of WTO talks will include these broader issues.

In any event, it seems a safe bet that these tensions between trade policy and environmental/labour policies will continue. At some point, further progress on trade liberalization will require that environmental and labour issues be addressed. Either domestic political pressures will push individual member countries to insist that these issues be included within the WTO negotiations, or other organizations like the WTO will be developed or strengthened to address the concerns. Whatever approach is followed, it appears that these will surely continue to be hot policy issues in the twenty-first century.

Applying Economic Concepts 34-1 addresses some of the often-heard criticisms of the WTO and argues that, as imperfect as the institution may be, it holds out much promise for continued progress in trade liberalization.

*For more information on the WTO, see its website at **www.wto.org**.*

APPLYING ECONOMIC CONCEPTS 34-1

Should the WTO Be Abolished?

Globalization protesters often direct their wrath at the World Trade Organization. Extremists argue that all institutions supporting globalization should be abolished. Other critics admit that globalization is inevitable but say that the WTO is so faulty in providing a rules-based system that it does more harm than good.

Supporters of the WTO argue that it is the best hope for poor countries that would be most oppressed in a lawless world in which rich countries, particularly the United States and members of the European Union, could behave as they wanted. Rather than allowing the poorer countries to flounder in a lawless world, the WTO provides a rules-based regime and has a dispute-settlement function that has heard more than 300 cases. Even if the rich countries do exert undue power over the negotiations, at least the WTO meetings provide a forum for poor nations to speak out and broker alliances. The alternative—no voice in a no-rules system—would be much worse.

Critics often respond that while the existence of the dispute-settlement mechanism may be beneficial, the enforcement of those settlements is undermined by disparities in economic power. Nations with large economies can use trade sanctions against small nations, but the small nation that attempts the same often inflicts the most harm on its own economy. Supporters of the WTO agree that this *is* a major defect, but the dispute-settlement mechanism has accomplished much, and to discard it because of imperfect enforcement would be a great loss. What is needed is *reform*—with larger economies agreeing to graduated enforcement mechanisms, including stiffer penalties for themselves.

Critics also claim that the WTO is a failure because it does not permit the imposition of trade sanctions against countries that pollute their own environments or exploit their own workers. But the poorest countries, many of whom are strong WTO supporters, fear that advanced countries would use environmental and labour standards written into the body of trade agreements as disguised non-tariff barriers. To the poorer countries it would be "policy imperialism" to argue that they should be forced to accept the standards of environmental and labour protection that the rich countries can only now afford. Nonetheless, environmental and labour protections are being written into some new trade agreements, and it remains to be seen if they will work beneficially or harmfully—or not at all.

Critics also complain that the WTO is undemocratic. In response, supporters point out that it is representatives of sovereign nations, usually elected ones, who conduct the negotiations, and that any agreements must be ratified by respective national parliaments before they come into effect. It is unlikely that any organization able to achieve agreement among 155 member-country governments could be any more democratic while still being effective.

Finally, some critics claim that the WTO is simply a tool for those who advocate a doctrinaire form of laissez-faire capitalism. It is true that some WTO supporters believe that unfettered free markets can meet all social requirements. A far larger number of supporters, however, believe that the market system needs government involvement if it is to meet societal needs for justice and growth. The vast majority of supporters agree that most, if not all, trade restrictions are harmful and that the WTO, with its mission of continued trade liberalization, can create significant benefits to rich and poor countries alike.

Regional Trade Agreements

Regional agreements seek to liberalize trade over a much smaller group of countries than the WTO membership. Three standard forms of regional trade-liberalizing agreements are *free trade areas, customs unions,* and *common markets.*

A **free trade area (FTA)** is the least comprehensive of the three. It allows for tariff-free trade among the member countries, but it leaves each member free to establish its own trade policy with respect to other countries. As a result, members must maintain customs points at their common borders to make sure that imports into the free trade area do not all enter through the member that is levying the lowest tariff on each item. They must also agree on *rules of origin* to establish when a good is made in a member country and hence is able to pass tariff-free across their borders, and when it is imported from outside the FTA and hence is subject to tariffs when it crosses borders within the FTA. The three countries in North America formed a free-trade area when

free trade area (FTA) An agreement among two or more countries to abolish tariffs on trade among themselves while each remains free to set its own tariffs against other countries.

they created the NAFTA in 1994. In recent years, Canada has signed bilateral free-trade agreements with Israel, Chile, Costa Rica, Peru, Colombia, and Jordan.

A **customs union** is a free trade area in which the member countries agree to establish a common trade policy with the rest of the world. Because they have a common trade policy, the members need neither customs controls on goods moving among themselves nor rules of origin. Once a good has entered any member country it has met the common rules and regulations and paid the common tariff and so it may henceforth be treated the same as a good that is produced within the union. An example of a customs union is Mercosur, an agreement linking Argentina, Brazil, Paraguay, and Uruguay.

A **common market** is a customs union that also has free movement of labour and capital among its members. The European Union is by far the most successful example of a common market. Indeed, the EU is now moving toward a full *economic union* in which all economic policies in the member countries are harmonized. The adoption of the euro as the EU's common currency in 1999 was a significant step in this direction.

Trade Creation and Trade Diversion

A major effect of regional trade liberalization is to redirect the flow of trade. Economists divide these effects into two categories: *trade creation* and *trade diversion*. These concepts were first developed by Jacob Viner, a Canadian-born economist who taught at the University of Chicago and Princeton University in the first half of the twentieth century.

Trade creation occurs when producers in one member country find that they can export products to another member country that previously were produced there because of tariff protection. For example, when the North American Free Trade Agreement (NAFTA) eliminated most cross-border tariffs among Mexico, Canada, and the United States, some U.S. firms found that they could undersell their Canadian competitors in some product lines, and some Canadian firms found that they could undersell their U.S. competitors in other product lines. As a result, specialization occurred, and new international trade developed among the three countries.

> Trade creation represents efficient specialization according to comparative advantage.

Trade diversion occurs when exporters in one member country *replace* foreign exporters as suppliers to another member country. For example, trade diversion occurs when U.S. firms find that they can undersell competitors from the rest of the world in the Canadian market, not because they are the cheapest source of supply, but because their tariff-free prices under NAFTA are lower than the tariff-burdened prices of imports from other countries. This effect is a gain to U.S. firms and Canadian consumers of the product. U.S. firms get new business and therefore they clearly gain. Canadian consumers buy the product at a lower, tariff-free price from the U.S. producer than they used to pay to the third-country producer (with a tariff), and so they are also better off. But Canada as a whole is worse off as a result of the trade diversion. Canada is now buying the product from a U.S. producer at a higher price with no tariff. Before the agreement, it was buying from a third-country producer at a lower price (and collecting tariff revenue).

> From the global perspective, trade diversion represents an inefficient use of resources.

One argument *against* regional trade agreements is that the costs of trade diversion may outweigh the benefits of trade creation. While recognizing this possibility, many economists believe that regional agreements, especially among only a few countries, are much easier to negotiate than multilateral agreements through the WTO. In addition,

customs union A group of countries who agree to have free trade among themselves and a common set of barriers against imports from the rest of the world.

common market A customs union with the added provision that labour and capital can move freely among the members.

trade creation A consequence of reduced trade barriers among a set of countries whereby trade within the group is increased and trade with the rest of the world remains roughly constant.

trade diversion A consequence of reduced trade barriers among a set of countries whereby trade within the group replaces trade that used to take place with countries outside the group.

regional agreements may represent effective *incremental* progress in what is a very lengthy process of achieving global free trade.

The North American Free Trade Agreement

The NAFTA dates from 1994 and is an extension of the 1989 Canada–U.S. Free Trade Agreement (FTA). It established a free trade area, as opposed to a customs union; each member country retains its own external trade policy, and rules of origin are needed to determine when a good is made within North America and thus allowed to move freely among the members.

National Treatment   The fundamental principle that guides the NAFTA is that of *national treatment*. The principle of national treatment is that individual countries are free to establish any laws they want, with the sole proviso that these laws must not discriminate on the basis of nationality. For example, Canada can have tough environmental laws, but it must enforce these laws equally on *all* firms located in Canada, independent of their nationality. In addition, Canada can have strict product standards, but it must enforce these equally on domestically produced and imported goods. The idea of national treatment is to allow a maximum of policy independence while preventing national policies from being used as trade barriers.

Other Major Provisions   There are several other major provisions in the NAFTA. First, all tariffs on trade between the United States and Canada were eliminated by 1999 and Canada–Mexico and Mexico–U.S. tariffs were phased out by 2010. Also, a number of non-tariff barriers were eliminated or restricted.

Second, the agreement guarantees national treatment of foreign investment once it enters a country while permitting each country to screen a substantial amount of inbound foreign investment before it enters.

Third, all existing measures that restrict trade and investment that are not explicitly removed by the agreement are "grandfathered," a term referring to the continuation of a practice that predates the agreement and would have been prohibited by the terms of the agreement were it not specifically exempted. This is probably the single most important departure from free trade under the NAFTA. Under it, a large collection of restrictive measures in each of the three countries is given indefinite life. An alternative would have been to "sunset" all these provisions by negotiating dates at which each would be eliminated. From the point of view of long-term trade liberalization, even a 50-year extension would have been preferable to an indefinite exemption. In Canada, the main examples are supply-managed agricultural products and the cultural industries (both of which may be liberalized over time as a result of WTO negotiations).

Fourth, trade in most non-governmental services is liberalized by giving service firms the right of establishment in all member countries and the privilege of national treatment. There is also a limited opening of the markets in financial services to entry from firms based in the NAFTA countries.

Finally, a significant minority of government procurement is opened to cross-border bids. But a large part of such purchases are exempt from the NAFTA provisions. This was the loophole that allowed the U.S. Congress to stipulate that some of the purchases outlined in its fiscal stimulus package of 2009 had to be made in the United States rather than imported from the cheapest suppliers within the NAFTA area—the "buy American" clause that was mentioned earlier.

Dispute Settlement   From Canada's point of view, by far the biggest setback in the negotiations for the Canada–U.S. FTA was the failure to obtain agreement on a common

For information about the NAFTA, go to the website for the NAFTA Secretariat: **www.nafta-sec-alena.org.**

regime for countervailing and antidumping duties. In view of that failure, no significant attempt was made to deal with this issue in the subsequent NAFTA negotiations. The U.S. Congress had been unwilling to abandon the unilateral use of these powerful weapons.

In the absence of such a multilateral regime, a NAFTA dispute-settlement mechanism was created. Under it, the justifications required for the levying of antidumping and countervailing duties are subject to review by a panel of Canadians, Americans, and Mexicans. This international review replaces appeal through the domestic courts. The panel has the power to suspend any duties until it is satisfied that the domestic laws have been correctly and fairly applied.

The establishment of the dispute-settlement mechanism in NAFTA was path breaking: For the first time in its history, the United States agreed to submit the administration of its domestic laws to *binding* scrutiny by an international panel that often contains a majority of foreigners.

Practise with Study Guide
Chapter 34, Exercise 3.

Results   The Canada–U.S. FTA aroused a great debate in Canada. Indeed, the Canadian federal election of 1988 was fought almost entirely on the issue of free trade. Supporters looked for major increases in the security of existing trade from U.S. protectionist attacks and for a growth of new trade. Detractors predicted a flight of firms to the United States, the loss of many Canadian jobs, and even the demise of Canada's political independence.

By and large, however, both the Canada–U.S. FTA and the NAFTA agreements worked out just about as expected by their supporters. Industry restructured in the direction of greater export orientation in all three countries, and trade creation occurred. The flow of trade among the three countries increased markedly, but especially so between Canada and the United States. As the theory of trade predicts, specialization occurred in many areas, resulting in more U.S. imports of some product lines from Canada and more U.S. exports of other goods to Canada. In 1988, before the Canada–U.S. FTA took effect, Canada exported $85 billion in goods to the United States and imported $74 billion from the United States. By 2008, the value of Canada–U.S. trade had more than quadrupled—Canadian exports of goods to the United States had increased to $370 billion and imports from the United States had increased to $280 billion. (Note that these figures exclude trade in services; with services included, the increase in Canada–U.S. trade between 1988 and 2008 would be even larger.)

It is hard to say how much trade diversion there has been and will be in the future. The greatest potential for trade diversion is with Mexico, which competes in the Canadian and U.S. markets with a large number of products produced in other low-wage countries. Southeast Asian exporters to the United States and Canada have been worried that Mexico would capture some of their markets by virtue of having tariff-free access denied to their goods. Most estimates predict, however, that trade creation will dominate over trade diversion.

Most transitional difficulties were initially felt in each country's import-competing industries, just as theory predicts. Such an agreement as the NAFTA brings its advantages by encouraging a movement of resources out of protected but inefficient import-competing industries, which decline, and into efficient export industries, which expand because they have better access to the markets of other member countries. Southern Ontario and parts of Quebec had difficulties as some traditional exports fell and labour and capital were shifting to sectors where trade was expanding. By the late 1990s, however, Southern Ontario was booming again and its most profitable sectors were those that exported to the United States.

There were also some pleasant surprises resulting from free trade. Two Canadian industries that many economists expected to suffer from the FTA and the NAFTA were

APPLYING ECONOMIC CONCEPTS 34-2

Canadian Wine: A Free-Trade Success Story

Before the Canada–U.S. FTA was signed in 1989, great fears were expressed over the fate of the Canadian wine industry, located mainly in Ontario and British Columbia. It was heavily tariff protected and, with a few notable exceptions, concentrated mainly on cheap, low-quality products. Contrary to most people's expectations, rather than being decimated, the industry now produces a wide variety of high-quality products, some of which have won international competitions.

The nature of the pre-FTA protection largely explains the dramatic turnaround of the Canadian wine industry once the FTA took effect. First, Canadian wine producers had been protected by high tariffs on imported wine but were at the same time required by law to produce wine by using only domestically grown grapes. The domestic grape growers, however, produced varieties of grapes not conducive to the production of high-quality wines, and with a captive domestic market, they had little incentive to change their behaviour. Thus, Canadian wine producers concentrated their efforts on "hiding" the attributes of poor-quality grapes rather than enhancing the attributes of high-quality grapes. The result was low-quality wine.

The second important aspect of the protection was that the high Canadian tariff was levied on a per unit rather than on an *ad valorem* basis. For example, the tariff was expressed as so many dollars per litre rather than as a specific percentage of the price. Charging a tariff by the litre gave most protection to the low-quality wines with low value per litre. The higher the per-litre value of the wine, the lower the percentage tariff protection. For example, a $5-per-litre tariff would have the following effects. A low-quality imported wine valued at $5 per litre would have its price raised to $10, a 100 percent increase in price, whereas a higher-quality imported wine valued at $25 per litre would have its price increased to $30, only a 20 percent increase in price.

Responding to these incentives, the Canadian industry concentrated on low-quality wines. The market for these wines was protected by the nearly prohibitive tariffs on competing low-quality imports and by the high prices charged for high-quality imports. In addition, protection was provided by many hidden charges that the various provincial governments' liquor monopolies levied in order to protect local producers.

When the tariff was removed under the FTA, the incentives were to move up-market, producing much more value per hectare of land. Fortunately, much of the Canadian wine-growing land in the Okanagan Valley in B.C. and the Niagara Peninsula in Ontario is well suited for growing the grapes required for good wines. Within a very few years, and with some government assistance to grape growers to make the transition from low-quality to high-quality grapes, Canadian wines were competing effectively with imported products in the medium-quality range. B.C. and Ontario wines do not yet reach the quality of major French wines in the $50–$70 (per bottle) range, but they compete very effectively in quality with wines in the $15–$25 range and sometimes even higher up the quality scale.

The success of the wine industry is a good example of how tariffs can distort incentives and push an industry into a structure that makes it dependent on the tariff. Looking at the pre-FTA industry, very few people suspected that it would be able to survive, let alone become a world-class industry.

winemaking and textiles. Yet both of these industries prospered as Canadian firms improved quality, productivity, and benefited from increased access to the huge U.S. market. *Applying Economic Concepts 34-2* discusses the success of the Canadian wine industry after the tariffs on wine were eliminated.

Finally, the dispute-settlement mechanism seems to have worked well. A large number of disputes have arisen and have been referred to panels. (Interested readers can read updated accounts of settled and ongoing disputes on the website for the Department of Foreign Affairs and International Trade at **www.dfait.gc.ca**.) Panel members have usually reacted as professionals rather than as nationals. Most cases have been decided on their merits; allegations that decisions were reached on national rather than professional grounds have been rare.

Summary

34.1 Free Trade or Protection?   (LO) ❶ ❷

- The case for free trade is that world output of all products can be higher under free trade than when protectionism restricts regional specialization.
- Trade protection may be advocated to promote economic diversification or to provide protection for specific groups. The cost of such protection is lower average living standards.
- Protection can also be urged on the grounds that it may lead to higher living standards for the protectionist country than would a policy of free trade. Such a result might come about by using market power to influence the terms of trade or by developing a dynamic comparative advantage by allowing inexperienced or uneconomically small industries to become efficient enough to compete with foreign industries.
- Some fallacious protectionist arguments are that (a) mutually advantageous trade is impossible because one trader's gain must always be the other's loss; (b) buying abroad sends our money abroad, while buying at home keeps our money at home; (c) our high-paid workers must be protected against the competition from low-paid foreign workers; and (d) imports are to be discouraged because they reduce national income and cause unemployment.

34.2 Methods of Protection   (LO) ❸ ❹

- A tariff raises the domestic price of the imported product and leads to a reduction in the level of imports. Domestic consumers lose and domestic producers gain. The overall effect of a tariff is a deadweight loss for the importing country.
- A quota (or voluntary export restriction) restricts the amount of imports and thus drives up the domestic price of the good. Domestic consumers lose and domestic producers gain. The overall effect is a *larger* deadweight loss than with a tariff because, rather than the importing country collecting tariff revenue, foreign producers benefit from a higher price.
- Antidumping and countervailing duties, although providing legitimate restraints on unfair trading practices, are often used as serious barriers to trade.

34.3 Current Trade Policy   (LO) ❺ ❻

- The General Agreement on Tariffs and Trade (GATT), under which countries agreed to reduce trade barriers through multilateral negotiations and not to raise them unilaterally, has greatly reduced world tariffs since its inception in 1947.
- The World Trade Organization (WTO) was created in 1995 as the successor to GATT. It has 155 member countries and contains a formal dispute-settlement mechanism.
- Regional trade-liberalizing agreements, such as free trade areas and common markets, bring efficiency gains through trade creation and efficiency losses through trade diversion.
- The North American Free Trade Agreement (NAFTA) is the world's largest and most successful free trade area, and the European Union is the world's largest and most successful common market.
- NAFTA is based on the principle of "national treatment." This allows Canada, the United States, and Mexico to implement whatever social, economic, or environmental policies they choose providing that such policies treat foreign and domestic firms (and their products) equally.

Key Concepts

Free trade and protectionism
Tariffs and import quotas
Voluntary export restrictions (VERs)
Countervailing and antidumping
    duties

The General Agreement on Tariffs and
    Trade (GATT)
The World Trade Organization (WTO)
Common markets, customs unions,
    and free trade areas

Trade creation and trade diversion
Non-tariff barriers
The North American Free Trade
    Agreement (NAFTA)

Study Exercises

1. Fill in the blanks to make the following statements correct.

   a. The _____ argument provided the rationale for Canada's National Policy of 1876. A high tariff wall allowed many Canadian industries to develop where they may not have been able to compete otherwise.

   b. Advertisements that encourage us to "buy Canadian" are promoting a(n) _____ argument for protection. The reason is that money spent on imported goods must ultimately be spent on _____ goods and services anyway.

   c. Fallacious arguments for protection usually come from a misunderstanding of the gains from _____ or from the misbelief that protection can increase total _____.

2. Fill in the blanks to make the following statements correct.

   a. A tariff imposed on the import of leather shoes will cause a(n) _____ in the domestic price. Total quantity of leather shoes sold in Canada will _____. Domestic (Canadian) production of leather shoes will _____ and the quantity of shoes imported will _____.

   b. The beneficiaries of the tariff described above are _____ because they receive a higher price for the same good and _____ because they receive tariff revenue. The parties that are clearly worse off are _____ because they now pay a higher price for the same good, and _____ because they sell less in the Canadian market.

   c. The overall effect of a tariff on the importing country is a(n) _____ in welfare. The tariff creates a(n) _____ loss for the economy.

   d. Suppose an import quota restricted the import of leather shoes into Canada to 20 000 pairs per year when the free trade imported amount was 40 000 pairs. The domestic price will _____, total quantity sold in Canada will _____, and domestic production will _____.

   e. The beneficiaries of the quota described above are _____ and _____ because they both receive a higher price in the Canadian market. The party that is clearly worse off is _____ because they are now paying a higher price.

   f. The overall effect of an import quota on the importing country is a(n) _____ in welfare. The quota imposes a(n) _____ loss for the economy.

3. Fill in the blanks to make the following statements correct.

   a. A regional trade agreement, such as the NAFTA, or a common market, such as the European Union, allows for _____, whereby trade within the group of member countries is increased.

   b. A regional trade agreement, such as the NAFTA, or a common market, such as the European Union, also results in _____, whereby trade within the group of member countries replaces trade previously done with other _____.

   c. The fundamental principle that guides the NAFTA is the principle of _____, which means that any member country can implement the policies of its choosing, as long as _____ and _____ firms are treated equally.

4. Canada produces steel domestically and also imports it from abroad. Assume that the world market for steel is competitive and that Canada is a small producer, unable to affect the world price. Since Canada imports steel, we know that in the absence of trade, the Canadian equilibrium price would exceed the world price.

   a. Draw a diagram showing the Canadian market for steel, with imports at the world price.

   b. Explain why the imposition of a tariff on imported steel will increase the price of steel in Canada.

   c. Who benefits and who is harmed by such a tariff? Show these effects in your diagram.

5. The diagram below shows the Canadian market for leather shoes, which we assume to be competitive. The world price is p_w. If the Canadian government imposes a tariff of t dollars per unit, the domestic price then rises to $p_w + t$.

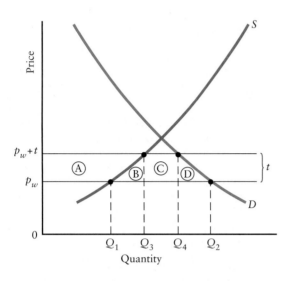

a. What quantity of leather shoes is imported before the tariff is imposed? After the tariff?
b. What is the effect of the tariff on the Canadian production of shoes? Which areas in the diagram show the increase in domestic producer surplus?
c. Which areas in the diagram show the reduction in domestic consumer surplus as a result of the higher Canadian price?
d. The Canadian government earns tariff revenue on the imported shoes. Which area in the diagram shows this tariff revenue?
e. What is the overall effect of this tariff on the economy? Which area in the diagram shows the deadweight loss?

6. Use the diagram from Question 5 to analyze the effects of imposing an import quota instead of a tariff to protect domestic shoe producers. Draw the diagram as in Question 5 and answer the following questions.

a. Explain why an import quota of Q_3Q_4 raises the domestic price to $p_w + t$.
b. With import quotas, the Canadian government earns no tariff revenue. Who gets this money now?
c. Is the import quota better or worse than the tariff for Canada as a whole? Explain.

7. Under pressure from the Canadian and U.S. governments in the early 1980s, Japanese automobile producers agreed to restrict their exports to the North American market. After the formal agreement ended, the Japanese producers decided unilaterally to continue restricting their exports. Carefully review Figure 34-2 on page 877 and then answer the following questions.

a. Explain why such voluntary export restrictions (VERs) are "voluntary."
b. Explain why an agreement to export only 100 000 cars to North America is better for the Japanese producers than a North American tariff that results in the same volume of Japanese exports.
c. Who is paying for these benefits to the Japanese producers?

8. Go to Statistics Canada's website: **www.statcan.gc.ca**. Go to "Summary tables," type in "exports and imports," and answer the following questions.

a. For the most recent year shown, what was the value of Canada's exports to the United States? To the European Union?
b. For the same year, what was the value of Canada's imports from the United States? From the European Union?
c. Compute what economists call the "volume of trade" (the sum of exports and imports) between Canada and the United States. How has the volume of trade grown over the past five years? Has trade grown faster than national income?

9. The table below shows the prices *in Canada* of cotton towels produced in the United States, Canada, and Malaysia. Assume that all cotton towels are identical.

Producing Country	Canadian Price (in $) Without Tariff	Canadian Price (in $) With 20% Tariff
Canada	4.75	4.75
United States	4.50	5.40
Malaysia	4.00	4.80

a. Suppose Canada imposes a 20 percent tariff on imported towels from any country. Assuming that Canadians purchase only the lowest-price towels, from which country will Canada buy its towels?
b. Now suppose Canada eliminates tariffs on towels from all countries. Which towels will Canada now buy?
c. Canada and the United States now negotiate a free-trade agreement that eliminates all tariffs between the two countries, but Canada maintains the 20 percent tariff on other countries. Which towels now get imported into Canada?
d. Which of the situations described above is called trade creation and which is called trade diversion?

Discussion Questions

1. In the early 1990s, many Canadians opposed Canada's entry into the NAFTA on the grounds that Canadian firms could not compete with the goods produced by cheap Mexican labour. Comment on the following points in relation to the above worries:

    a. "Mexicans are the most expensive cheap labour I have ever encountered"—statement by the owner of a Canadian firm that is moving back to Canada from Mexico.

    b. The theory of the gains from trade says that a high-productivity, high-wage country can gain from trading with a low-wage, low-productivity country.

    c. Technological change is rapidly reducing labour costs as a proportion of total costs in many products; in many industries that use high-tech production methods this proportion is already well below 20 percent.

2. Should Canada trade with countries with poor human rights records? If trade with China is severely restricted because of its lack of respect for human rights, who will be the gainers and who the losers? Argue the cases that this policy will help, and that it will hinder, human rights progress in China.

3. Import quotas and voluntary export restrictions are often used instead of tariffs. What real difference, if any, is there among quotas, voluntary export restrictions (VERs), and tariffs? Explain why lobbyists for some import-competing industries (cheese, milk, shoes) support import quotas while lobbyists for others (pizza manufacturers, soft drink manufacturers, retail stores) oppose them. Would you expect labour unions to support or oppose quotas?

4. During the 1990s, many foreign automobile producers built production and assembly facilities in Canada. What are some advantages and disadvantages associated with shifting production from, for example, Japan to Canada? Are these cars still considered "imports"? What has been happening to the definitions of "foreign made" and "domestic made"?

5. Consider a mythical country called Forestland, which exports a large amount of lumber to a nearby country called Houseland. The lumber industry in Houseland has convinced its federal government that it is being harmed by the low prices being charged by the lumber producers in Forestland. You are an advisor to the government in Forestland. Explain who gains and who loses from each of the following policies.

    a. Houseland imposes a tariff on lumber imports from Forestland.

    b. Forestland imposes a tax on each unit of lumber exported to Houseland.

    c. Forestland agrees to restrict its exports of lumber to Houseland.

    d. Which policy is likely to garner the most political support in Houseland? In Forestland?

6. In 1999, the Canadian government imposed antidumping duties of up to 43 percent on hot-rolled steel imports from France, Russia, Slovakia, and Romania. The allegation was that these countries were dumping steel into the Canadian market.

    a. Who benefits from such alleged dumping? Who is harmed?

    b. Who benefits from the imposition of the antidumping duties? Who is harmed?

    c. Is Canada as a whole made better off by the imposition of the duties? Explain.

7. In 2009, the Canadian government lobbied the U.S. congress to remove a "buy American" clause from an early version of its U.S.$787 billion fiscal-stimulus package. The clause stated that all funds used for infrastructure spending must be spent on U.S.-made supplies and materials. Why would the Canadian government complain?

35

Exchange Rates and the Balance of Payments

In 1973, it cost only 96 Canadian cents to purchase one U.S. dollar. Almost three decades later, in 2001, the Canadian dollar had depreciated so much that it then cost over $1.55 Canadian to purchase one U.S. dollar. This 30-year depreciation of the Canadian dollar was neither smooth nor steady. During the late 1980s, the Canadian dollar appreciated by more than 10 percent; during the late 1990s, it depreciated just as much. Then, between 2002 and 2007, the Canadian dollar appreciated sharply against the U.S. dollar; at its peak in 2007 it cost only 90 cents Canadian to purchase one U.S. dollar. By 2009 the Canadian dollar had depreciated again, until the price of one U.S. dollar was $1.15 Canadian. What explains these dramatic movements in the exchange rate?

In this chapter we examine what determines the exchange rate, why it changes, and the effects these changes have on the economy. The discussion will bring together material on three topics studied elsewhere in this book: the theory of supply and demand (Chapter 3), monetary policy and inflation (Chapters 29 and 30), and international trade (Chapter 33).

We begin by examining a country's balance of payments—the record of transactions in goods, services, and assets with the rest of the world. After introducing terms, we see why the balance of payments is defined in such a way that it *always* balances.

35.1 The Balance of Payments

Statistics Canada documents transactions between Canada and the rest of the world. The record of such transactions is made in the **balance of payments accounts**. For computing Canada's balance of payments, each transaction, such as the exports or imports of goods, or the international purchase or sales of assets, is classified according to whether the transaction generates a *payment* or a *receipt* for Canada.

Table 35-1 shows the major items in the Canadian balance of payments accounts for 2008. Transactions that represent a receipt for Canada, such as the sale of a product or asset to foreigners, are recorded in the balance of payments accounts as a *credit* item. Transactions that represent a payment for Canada, such as the purchase of a product or asset from foreigners, are recorded as a *debit* item.

There are two main categories to the balance of payments: the *current account* and the *capital account*. We examine each account in turn.

The Current Account

The **current account** records transactions arising from trade in goods and services. It also includes net investment income earned from foreign asset holdings. The current account is divided into two main sections.

The first section, called the **trade account**, records payments and receipts arising from the import and export of goods, such as computers and cars, and services, such as legal or architectural services. (Tourism constitutes a large part of the trade in services.) Canadian imports of goods and services require a payment to foreigners and thus are entered as debit items on the trade account; Canadian exports of goods and services generate a receipt to Canada and thus are recorded as credit items.

The second section, called the **capital-service account**, records the payments and receipts that represent income on assets. When a firm located in Canada, for example, pays dividends to foreign owners, the payments to foreigners are a debit item in Canada's balance of payments. In contrast, when Canadians earn income from their foreign-located investments, these receipts for Canada are recorded as credit items.

As shown in Table 35-1, Canadian exports of goods and services were $560 billion in 2008, and Canadian imports of goods and services were $536 billion. The trade account had a surplus of $24 billion—in other words, in 2008 Canada sold $24 billion more worth of goods and services to the world than it bought from the world. But in terms of the capital-service account, things were the other way around. The table shows that Canadians paid $16 billion more to foreigners in investment income than they received from foreigners. The current account balance (the sum of the trade and capital-service accounts) had a surplus of $7.7 billion.

The Capital Account

The **capital account** records international transactions in assets, including bonds, shares of companies, real estate, and factories. The purchase of foreign assets by Canadians is treated just like the purchase of foreign goods. Since purchasing a foreign asset requires a payment from Canadians to foreigners, it is entered as a debit item in the Canadian capital account. Note that when Canadians purchase foreign assets, financial capital is leaving Canada and going abroad, and so this is called a *capital outflow.* In

balance of payments accounts A summary record of a country's transactions with the rest of the world, including the buying and selling of goods, services, and assets.

current account The part of the balance of payments accounts that records payments and receipts arising from trade in goods and services and from interest and dividends that are earned by capital owned in one country and invested in another.

trade account In the balance of payments, this account records the value of exports and imports of goods and services.

capital-service account In the balance of payments, this account records the payments and receipts that represent income on assets (such as interest and dividends).

capital account The part of the balance of payments accounts that records payments and receipts arising from the purchase and sale of assets.

TABLE 35-1   Canadian Balance of Payments, 2008 (billions of dollars)

CURRENT ACCOUNT	
Trade Account	
Merchandise exports	+489.9
Service exports	+70.5
Merchandise imports	−443.0
Service imports	−93.0
Trade balance	+24.0
Capital-Service Account	
Net investment income (including unilateral transfers)	−16.3
Current Account balance	+7.7
CAPITAL ACCOUNT	
Net change in Canadian investments abroad [capital outflow (−)]	−102.7
Net change in foreign investments in Canada [capital inflow (+)]	+97.3
Official Financing Account	
Changes in official international reserves [increases (−)]	−1.7
Capital Account Balance	−7.1
Statistical Discrepancy	+0.6
Balance of Payments	0.0

The overall balance of payments always balances, but the individual components do not have to. In 2008, Canada had an overall trade surplus (including trade in goods and services) of $24.0 billion. There was a deficit of $16.3 billion on the capital-service account. There was thus a $7.7 billion surplus on the current account. There was a deficit on the capital account of $7.1 billion because the trading of assets internationally resulted in a net outflow of capital. The statistical discrepancy entry of $0.6 billion compensates for the inability to measure some items accurately. The current account plus the capital account (plus the statistical discrepancy) is equal to the balance of payments—which is always zero.

(*Source:* Statistics Canada; search for "balance of payments, 2008." Table 1: Balance of payments, http://www.statcan.gc.ca/daily-quotidien/090828/t090828a1-eng.htm.)

contrast, the sale of Canadian assets to foreigners generates a receipt for Canada, and thus is entered as a credit item in the Canadian capital account. When Canadians sell assets to foreigners, financial capital is entering Canada from abroad, and so this is called a *capital inflow.*

As shown in Table 35-1, in 2008, Canadians increased their holdings of assets abroad by $102.7 billion, resulting in a capital outflow of that amount. At the same time, foreigners increased their holdings of assets in Canada by $97.3 billion, resulting in a capital inflow of that amount. Though not shown in the table, the capital account distinguishes between *direct investment* and *portfolio investment.* The former involves the purchase or sale of assets that alter the legal control of those assets, such as when a controlling interest of a company is purchased. The latter involves transactions in assets that do not alter the legal control of the assets, such as when a minority of a company's shares is purchased.

One part of the capital account shows the government's transactions in its official foreign-exchange reserves. This *official financing account* is included as part of the capital account because official reserves are *assets* rather than goods or services. If the government increases its reserves, it does so by purchasing foreign-currency assets, and this is recorded as a debit item in the official financing account. If the government instead reduces its reserves, it sells some foreign-currency assets, and this transaction would be recorded as a credit item in the official financing account. In 2008, the Government of Canada increased its official reserves by $1.7 billion.

In 2008, the overall capital account had a deficit of $7.1 billion, meaning that there was a net capital outflow of this amount from Canada to the rest of the world. In other words, Canadian households, firms, and governments, taken together, increased their net holdings of foreign assets by $7.1 billion in 2008.

The Balance of Payments Must Balance

The current account balance represents the difference between the payments and receipts from international transactions in goods and services. The capital account balance is the difference between payments and receipts from international transactions in assets. The balance of payments is the sum of current account and capital account balances. In any given period (usually a year) the *current account plus the capital account must equal zero.* In other words, the balance of payments is always equal to zero. In algebraic terms, we can write

$$\text{Balance of payments} = CA + KA = 0$$

where CA is the current account balance and KA is the capital account balance. Note that this is an *identity*—the accounting system used for the balance of payments defines transactions in such a way that $CA + KA = 0$. But this accounting system is based on some economic logic. Let's consider an example that illustrates the logical connection between the current and capital accounts.

Consider a year in which Canadian households, firms, and governments, taken together, purchase \$100 billion in goods and services from the rest of the world. During the same year, Canadians sell \$150 billion of goods and services to the rest of the world. Exports are \$150 billion and imports are \$100 billion, so Canada has a current account surplus of \$50 billion, $CA = \$50$ billion. (We suppose for simplicity that the capital-service account is zero.) The meaning of this \$50 billion surplus is that Canadians now have claims on foreigners equal to \$50 billion—that is, foreigners owe Canadians \$50 billion. What does Canada do with these claims?

There are *only* two possibilities. The first is that Canadians use these \$50 billion in claims to purchase \$50 billion in additional goods and services from the rest of the world. In this case, Canada's imports rise to \$150 billion and the current account is now in balance ($CA = 0$). Since there have been no transactions in assets, the capital account is also in balance ($KA = 0$). It is clear now that $CA + KA = 0$.

The only other possibility is that Canadians use these \$50 billion in claims to purchase assets from foreigners—a capital outflow from Canada. They could purchase land, bonds, corporate shares, or factories. But whatever they purchase, the capital account will now be in deficit by \$50 billion ($KA = -\$50$ billion). In this case, the current account surplus of \$50 billion is exactly offset by the capital account deficit of \$50 billion. Once again we have $CA + KA = 0$.

Any surplus on the current account must be matched by an equal deficit on the capital account. A current account surplus thus implies a capital outflow. The balance of payments is always zero.

Notice that the opposite situation is also possible and that the balance of payments again sums to zero. Suppose Canadians purchase \$75 billion more in goods and services from the rest of the world than they sell—so Canada has a current account deficit of \$75 billion, $CA = -\$75$ billion. (We continue to assume that the capital-service account is zero.) The rest of the world now has claims of this amount on Canadians, meaning that Canadians owe \$75 billion to foreigners. These claims must be used either to purchase more Canadian goods and services or more Canadian assets. If foreigners purchase \$75 billion in additional Canadian goods and services, Canada's current account is balanced ($CA = 0$) and we again have $CA + KA = 0$. If foreigners choose instead to purchase \$75 billion in Canadian assets, then Canada's capital account will be in surplus by \$75 billion—a capital inflow. In this case, the current account will be in deficit ($CA = -\$75$ billion) and the capital account will be in surplus ($KA = \$75$ billion), but again we see that $CA + KA = 0$.

Any deficit in the current account must be matched by an equal surplus in the capital account. A current-account deficit thus implies a capital inflow. The balance of payments is always zero.

For balance of payments statistics for many countries, see the IMF's website: www.imf.org.

Let's go back and review the actual numbers from Table 35-1. In 2008, Canada had a current account surplus of $7.7 billion. From these net exports of goods and services, Canadian firms and households therefore accumulated $7.7 billion in new claims on foreigners in that year. With these claims, Canadians then purchased the same amount (aside from the statistical discrepancy) in foreign assets, and so there was a capital outflow, or a capital account deficit. The balance of payments, as always, was in balance.

That the balance of payments always sums to zero is important. This result is not based on assumptions about behaviour or any other theoretical reasoning—it is an *accounting identity*. Many people nonetheless find balance of payments accounting confusing. *Applying Economic Concepts 35-1* discusses an individual student's balance of payments with the rest of the world and illustrates why an individual's balance of payments must always balance.

A Balance of Payments Deficit?

Unless further qualified, the term "balance of payments deficit" does not make sense since the balance of payments must always balance. But such a term is nonetheless often used in the press and even by some economists. What does this mean? Most often the term is used carelessly—a balance of payments deficit is mentioned when what is actually meant is a current account deficit.

There are also occasions when people speak of a country as having a balance of payments deficit or surplus when they are actually referring to the balance of all accounts *excluding* the official financing account. In other words, they are referring to the combined balance on current and capital accounts, *excluding* the changes in the government's foreign-currency reserves. For example, consider a year in which the Government of Canada sells $5 billion of its foreign-currency reserves. This transaction is a credit item in the official financing account (part of Canada's capital account). It must be the case that *all other* items in the current and capital accounts *combined* sum to an overall deficit. In this case, some people might say that Canada's balance of payments "deficit" is being financed by the government's sale of foreign-currency reserves. But when we use the terms properly, we know that Canada's balance of payments, as always, is balanced.

> A "balance of payments deficit" probably refers to a situation in which the government is selling official foreign-currency reserves. A "balance of payments surplus" refers to a situation in which the government is buying official foreign-currency reserves. In both cases, as always, the balance of payments is actually in balance.

Summary

This brings us to the end of our discussion of the balance of payments. Keep in mind that this is just an exercise in accounting. Though at times you may find it difficult to keep the various credits and debits in the various accounts straight in your mind, remember that the structure of the accounting system is quite simple. Here is a brief review:

Practise with Study Guide
Chapter 35, Short-Answer
Question 1.

1. The current account shows all transactions in goods and services between Canada and the rest of the world (including investment income and transfers).

A Student's Balance of Payments with the Rest of the World

Many students find a country's balance of payments confusing, especially the idea that the balance of payments *must always* balance. Why, they often ask, can't Canada export more goods and services to the world than it imports and at the same time have a net sale of assets to the rest of the world? The connection between the current-account transactions and the capital-account transactions is not always obvious.

Perhaps the easiest way to see this connection is to consider an individual's "balance of payments" with the rest of the world. Of course, most individuals would not normally compute their balance of payments, but by doing so we can recognize the everyday concepts involved and also see the necessary connection between any individual's "current account" and "capital account." The reason that Canada's balance of payments must always balance is exactly the same reason that an individual's balance of payments must always balance.

The table shows the balance of payments for Stefan, a university student. Stefan is fortunate in several respects. First, his parents are able to provide some of the funds needed to finance his education. Second, he has a summer job that pays well. Third, he was given some Canada Savings Bonds when he was born that provide him with some interest income every year.

Stefan's Balance of Payments

Current Account (Income and Expenditure)	
Labour income ("exports")	+$10 000
Purchase of goods and services ("imports")	−$17 000
Interest income	+$ 500
Transfers (from his parents)	+$10 000
Current Account Balance	+ $ 3 500

Capital Account (Changes in Assets) (− denotes an increase)	
Financial Assets	
Purchase of mutual funds	−$1 500
Increase in savings account deposits	−$2 000
Capital Account Balance	−$3 500
BALANCE OF PAYMENTS	$0

The top part of the table shows Stefan's income and expenditures for a single year. This is his current account. The bottom part shows the change in Stefan's assets over the same year. This is his capital account. (Note that, for Stefan as well as for any country, the capital account does not show the overall stock of assets—it only shows the *changes* in the stock of assets during the year.)

Let's begin with his current account. Stefan has a good summer job that earns him $10 000 after taxes. This $10 000 represents Stefan's "exports" to the rest of the world—he earns this income by selling his labour services to a tree-planting company. Over the year, however, he spends $17 000 on tuition, books, clothes, groceries, and other goods and services. These are Stefan's "imports" from the rest of the world. Stefan clearly has a "trade deficit" equal to $7000—he "imports" more than he "exports."

There are two other sources of income shown in Stefan's current account. First, he earns $500 in interest income. Second, his parents give him $10 000 to help pay for his education—a *transfer* in the terminology of balance of payments accounting. The interest income and transfer together make up Stefan's "capital-service account"—Stefan has a surplus of $10 500.

Stefan's overall current account shows a surplus of $3500. This means he receives $3500 more than he spends on goods and services. But where does this $3500 go?

Now let's consider Stefan's capital account, the bottom part of the table. The $3500 surplus on current account *must* end up as increases in Stefan's assets. He invests $1500 in a mutual fund and he also increases his savings-account deposits by $2000. In both cases he is purchasing assets—he buys units in a mutual fund and he also "buys" a bank deposit. Since Stefan must make a payment to purchase these assets, each appears as a debit item in his capital account. Stefan's capital account balance is a deficit of $3500.

Finally, note that Stefan's current account and capital account *must* sum to zero. There is no way around this. Any surplus of income over expenditures (on current account) must show up as an increase in his assets (or a decrease in his debts) on his capital account. Conversely, any excess of expenditures over income must be financed by reducing his assets (or by increasing his debts). Stefan's balance of payments *must* balance.

What is true for Stefan is true for any individual and also true for any accounting unit you choose to consider. Saskatoon's balance of payments with the rest of the world must balance. Saskatchewan's balance of payments with the rest of the world must balance. Western Canada's balance of payments with the rest of the world must balance. And so must Canada's, and any other country's.

2. The capital account shows all transactions in assets between Canada and the rest of the world. Part of the capital account shows the change in the government's holding of foreign-currency reserves.

3. All transactions involving a payment from Canada appear as debit items. All transactions involving a receipt to Canada appear as credit items.

4. The balance of payments—the sum of the current account and the capital account—must, by definition, always be zero.

We now go on to explore how exchange rates are determined in the foreign-exchange market. We will see that a knowledge of the various categories in the balance of payments will help in our understanding of why changes in exchange rates occur.

35.2 The Foreign-Exchange Market

Money is vital in any sophisticated economy that relies on specialization and trade. Yet money as we know it is a *national* matter. If you live in Argentina, you earn pesos and spend pesos; if you operate a business in Austria, you borrow euros and pay your workers in euros. The currency of a country is acceptable within the border of that country, but usually it will not be accepted by firms and households in another country. Just try buying your next pair of jeans in Canada with British pounds sterling or Japanese yen.

> Trade between countries normally requires the exchange of the currency of one country for that of another.

exchange rate The number of units of domestic currency required to purchase one unit of foreign currency.

The exchange of one currency for another is called a *foreign-exchange transaction*. The **exchange rate** is the rate at which one currency exchanges for another. In Canada's case, the exchange rate is the Canadian-dollar price of one unit of foreign currency. For example, in July 2009, the price of one U.S. dollar was 1.15 Canadian dollars. Thus, the Canada–U.S. exchange rate was 1.15.

Note that in the news media the exchange rate is usually expressed in the opposite way—as the number of U.S. dollars that it takes to buy one Canadian dollar. So instead of reporting that the Canadian–U.S. exchange rate in July 2009 was 1.15, the press would say that the Canadian dollar was "worth" 86.9 U.S. cents (1/1.15 = 0.869).

We can choose to define the Canada–U.S. exchange rate either way: as the Canadian-dollar price of one U.S. dollar or as the U.S.-dollar price of one Canadian dollar. But we must choose one method and stick to it; otherwise, our discussions will quickly become very confusing. In this book we *always* define the exchange rate in the way Canadian economists usually do—as the Canadian-dollar price of one unit of foreign currency. This definition makes it clear that foreign currency, like any good or service, has a price expressed in Canadian dollars. In this case, the price has a special name—the exchange rate.

appreciation A fall in the exchange rate—the domestic currency has become more valuable so that it takes fewer units of domestic currency to purchase one unit of foreign currency.

An **appreciation** of the Canadian dollar means that the Canadian dollar has become more valuable so that it takes fewer Canadian dollars to purchase one unit of foreign currency. For example, if the Canadian dollar appreciates against the U.S. dollar from 1.15 to 1.04, it takes 11 fewer Canadian cents to purchase one U.S. dollar. Thus, an appreciation of the Canadian dollar implies a *fall* in the exchange rate.

Conversely, a **depreciation** of the Canadian dollar means that the Canadian dollar has become less valuable so that it takes more Canadian dollars to purchase one unit of foreign currency. Thus, a depreciation of the Canadian dollar means a *rise* in the exchange rate.

> **An appreciation of the Canadian dollar is a fall in the exchange rate; a depreciation of the Canadian dollar is a rise in the exchange rate.**

We now go on to build a simple theory of the foreign-exchange market. This will allow us to analyze the determinants of the exchange rate. To keep things simple, we use an example involving trade between Canada and Europe, and thus we examine the determination of the exchange rate between the two currencies: the Canadian dollar and the euro. But, in this example, Europe is just a shorthand for "the rest of the world" and the euro is just a shorthand for "all other currencies." (It would be more natural to think in terms of Canada–U.S. trade since 80 percent of Canadian trade is with the United States, but this quickly becomes confusing because both countries' currencies are called the dollar.)

> **Because Canadian dollars are traded for euros in the foreign-exchange market, it follows that a demand for euros implies a supply of Canadian dollars and that a supply of euros implies a demand for Canadian dollars.**

For this reason, a theory of the exchange rate between dollars and euros can deal either with the demand and supply of dollars or with the demand and supply of euros; both need not be considered. We will concentrate on the demand, supply, and price of euros. Thus, the market we will be considering (in general terms) is the foreign-exchange market—the "product" is foreign exchange (euros in our case) and the "price" is the exchange rate (the Canadian-dollar price of euros).

We develop our example in terms of the demand and supply analysis first encountered in Chapter 3. To do so, we need only to recall that in the market for foreign exchange, transactions that generate a receipt for Canada in its balance of payments represent a *supply* of foreign exchange. Foreign exchange is being supplied by the foreigners who need Canadian funds to purchase Canadian goods or assets. Conversely, transactions that are a payment from Canada in the balance of payments represent a *demand* for foreign exchange. Foreign exchange is being demanded by the Canadians who are purchasing foreign goods or assets. In what follows we make the (realistic) assumption that the Bank of Canada makes no transactions in the foreign-exchange market. Later we discuss the role of central bank transactions.

The Supply of Foreign Exchange

Whenever foreigners purchase Canadian goods, services, or assets, they supply foreign currency to the foreign-exchange market and demand, in return, Canadian dollars with which to pay for their purchases. Thus, the supply of foreign exchange (and the associated demand for Canadian dollars) arises from Canada's sales of goods, services, and assets to the rest of the world.

Canadian Exports One important source of supply of foreign exchange is foreigners who wish to buy Canadian-made goods and services. A French importer of lumber is such a purchaser; an Austrian couple planning a vacation in Canada is another; the

depreciation A rise in the exchange rate—the domestic currency has become less valuable so that it takes more units of domestic currency to purchase one unit of foreign currency.

Trade between countries that use different currencies requires that currencies also be exchanged; this takes place in foreign-exchange markets where exchange rates—the price of one currency in terms of another—are determined.

Hungarian government seeking to buy Canadian engineering services is a third. All are sources of supply of foreign exchange, arising out of international trade. Each potential buyer wants to sell its own currency in exchange for Canadian dollars that it can then use to purchase Canadian goods and services.

Asset Sales: Capital Inflows   A second source of supply of foreign exchange comes from foreigners who want to purchase Canadian assets, such as government or corporate bonds, real estate, or shares in a Canadian firm. To buy Canadian assets, holders of foreign currencies must first sell their foreign currency and buy Canadian dollars. As we saw earlier in the chapter, when Canadians sell assets to foreigners, we say there is a *capital inflow* to Canada.

Reserve Currency   Firms, banks, and governments often accumulate and hold foreign-exchange reserves, just as individuals maintain savings accounts. These reserves may be in several different currencies. For example, the government of Poland may decide to increase its reserve holdings of Canadian dollars and reduce its reserve holdings of euros; if it does so, it will be a supplier of euros (and a demander of Canadian dollars) in foreign-exchange markets.

The Total Supply of Foreign Exchange   The supply of foreign exchange (or the demand for Canadian dollars) by holders of foreign currencies is the sum of the supplies for all the purposes just discussed—for purchases of Canadian exports, for capital inflow to Canada, and for the purchase of Canadian dollars to add to currency reserves.

Furthermore, because people, firms, and governments in all countries purchase goods and assets from many other countries, the demand for any one currency will be the aggregate demand of individuals, firms, and governments in a number of different countries. Thus, the total supply of foreign exchange (or the demand for Canadian dollars) may include Germans who are offering euros, Japanese who are offering yen, Argentinians who are offering pesos, and so on. For simplicity, however, we go back to our two-country example and use only Canada and Europe.

The Supply Curve for Foreign Exchange   The supply of foreign exchange on the foreign-exchange market is represented by a positively sloped curve, such as the one shown in Figure 35-1. This figure plots the Canadian-dollar price of euros (the exchange rate) on the vertical axis and the quantity of euros on the horizontal axis. Moving up the vertical axis, more dollars are needed to purchase one euro—the dollar is depreciating. Moving down the vertical axis, fewer dollars are needed to purchase one euro—the dollar is appreciating.

Why is the supply curve for foreign exchange positively sloped? Consider the supply of foreign exchange derived from foreign purchases of Canadian exports. If the

Canadian dollar depreciates (moving up the vertical axis), it takes fewer euros to purchase one Canadian dollar. Thus, for a given Canadian-dollar price of the product, the euro price has fallen. European consumers will therefore buy more of the cheaper Canadian goods and will thus supply more foreign exchange for this purpose. In the opposite case, when the dollar appreciates (moving down the vertical axis), the euro price of Canadian exports rises. European consumers will buy fewer Canadian goods and thus supply less foreign exchange.[1]

Similar considerations affect other sources of supply of foreign exchange. When the Canadian dollar depreciates (a higher exchange rate), Canadian securities and other assets become attractive purchases, and the quantity purchased by foreigners will rise. With this rise, the amount of foreign exchange supplied to pay for the purchases will increase.

> The supply curve for foreign exchange is positively sloped when it is plotted against the exchange rate; a depreciation of the Canadian dollar (a rise in the exchange rate) increases the quantity of foreign exchange supplied.

The Demand for Foreign Exchange

The demand for foreign exchange arises from all international transactions that represent a payment in Canada's balance of payments. What sorts of international transactions generate a demand for foreign exchange (and a supply of Canadian dollars)? They are the same sort of transactions we just discussed, but this time they are moving in the opposite direction—Canadians, rather than foreigners, are doing the purchasing. Canadians seeking to purchase foreign products will be supplying Canadian dollars and demanding foreign exchange for this purpose. Canadians may also seek to purchase foreign assets. If they do, they will supply Canadian dollars and demand foreign exchange. Similarly, a country with reserves of Canadian dollars may decide to sell them in order to demand some other currency.

The Demand Curve for Foreign Exchange When the Canadian dollar depreciates against the euro, the Canadian-dollar price of European goods rises. Because

FIGURE 35-1 The Foreign-Exchange Market

The demand for foreign exchange is negatively sloped, and the supply of foreign exchange is positively sloped, when plotted against the exchange rate, measured as the Canadian-dollar price of one unit of foreign currency. The demand for foreign exchange is given by the blue line D. It represents the sum of transactions on both current and capital accounts that require payments to foreigners. The supply of foreign exchange is given by the red line S. It represents the sum of transactions on both current and capital accounts that represent receipts from foreigners.

In this example, the equilibrium value of the exchange rate is $1.50—it takes 1.50 Canadian dollars to purchase one euro.

---

[1] We have assumed here that the foreign price elasticity of demand for Canadian exports is greater than 1, so that a price change leads to a proportionately larger change in quantity demanded. This is a common assumption in the analysis of international trade. In the case of Canada (and other small countries) it is common to go further and make the "small open economy" assumption—that the country faces *given world prices* for both its exports and its imports. In this case, the foreign price elasticity of demand for exports is infinite. This means, for example, that Canadians can sell all the oil or wheat they produce at the going world prices of those commodities.

it takes more dollars to buy the same European good at an unchanged euro price, Canadians will buy fewer of the now more expensive European goods. The amount of foreign exchange being demanded by Canadians in order to pay for imported European goods will fall.[2] In the opposite case, when the Canadian dollar appreciates, European goods become cheaper, more are sold, and more dollars are spent on them. Thus, more foreign exchange will be demanded to pay for the extra imports. This same argument applies in exactly the same way to the purchases of foreign assets. Figure 35-1 shows the demand curve for foreign exchange.

> The demand curve for foreign exchange is negatively sloped when it is plotted against the exchange rate; an appreciation of the Canadian dollar (a fall in the exchange rate) increases the quantity of foreign exchange demanded.

35.3 The Determination of Exchange Rates

The demand and supply curves in Figure 35-1 do not include official financing transactions (the demands for or supplies of foreign exchange by the Bank of Canada). To complete our analysis, we must incorporate the role of official financing transactions. We need to consider three important cases:

1. When the central bank makes no transactions in the foreign-exchange market, there is said to be a purely **flexible exchange rate**.

2. When the central bank intervenes in the foreign-exchange market to "fix" the exchange rate at a particular value, there is said to be a **fixed exchange rate** or *pegged exchange rate*.

3. Between these two "pure" systems is a variety of possible intermediate cases, including the *adjustable peg* and the *managed float*. In the **adjustable peg system**, central banks fix specific values for their exchange rates, but they explicitly recognize that circumstances may arise in which they will change that value. In a **managed float**, the central bank seeks to have some stabilizing influence on the exchange rate but does not try to fix it at some publicly announced value.

Most industrialized countries today operate a mostly flexible exchange rate. It is mostly market determined but the central bank sometimes intervenes to offset short-run fluctuations. The countries of the European Union (EU) had a system of fixed exchange rates (relative to one another's currencies) between 1979 and 1999. In

flexible exchange rate An exchange rate that is left free to be determined by the forces of demand and supply on the free market, with no intervention by central banks.

fixed exchange rate An exchange rate that is maintained within a small range around its publicly stated par value by the intervention in the foreign-exchange market by a country's central bank.

adjustable peg system A system in which exchange rates are fixed in the short term but are occasionally changed in response to changes in economic events.

managed float A situation in which the central bank intervenes in the foreign-exchange market to smooth out some of the large, short-term fluctuations in a country's exchange rate, while still leaving the market to determine the exchange rate in the longer term.

---

[2] As long as the price elasticity of demand for imports is greater than 1, the fall in the volume of imports will exceed the rise in price, and hence fewer dollars will be spent on them. This condition (and the one in the previous footnote on page 901) is related to a famous long-standing issue in international economics, called the *Marshall-Lerner condition*. In what follows, we take the standard approach of assuming that both the price elasticity of demand for imports and the price elasticity of the demand for Canadian exports exceeds 1. This guarantees that the slopes of the curves are as shown in Figure 35-1.

1999 the EU introduced a common currency—the euro—that was adopted by most of the EU member countries (an important exception being the United Kingdom). Thus, they now have no exchange rates for national currencies within the EU but the single common currency has a flexible exchange rate relative to countries outside the EU. The United States, Japan, the United Kingdom, Australia, and most other major industrialized countries have flexible exchange rates with relatively small amounts of foreign-exchange intervention by their central banks.

Canada alternated between a system of fixed exchange rates and flexible exchange rates (with limited intervention) throughout most of the period following the Second World War. In contrast, most other countries pegged their currencies to the U.S. dollar under the Bretton Woods system. Canada has had a flexible exchange rate since 1970. Later in the chapter we examine the issues involved in choosing between a flexible and fixed exchange-rate system. For now, let's explore how the various systems operate.

Flexible Exchange Rates

We begin with an exchange rate that is set in a freely competitive market, with no intervention by the central bank. Like any competitive price, the exchange rate fluctuates as the conditions of demand and supply change.

Suppose the current exchange rate is so high (say, e_1 in Figure 35-2) that the quantity of foreign exchange supplied exceeds the quantity demanded. There is thus an excess supply of foreign exchange (and an excess demand of Canadian dollars). This excess supply of foreign exchange, just as in our analysis in Chapter 3, will cause the price of foreign exchange (the exchange rate) to fall. As the exchange rate falls—an appreciation of the Canadian dollar—the euro price of Canadian goods rises, and this leads to a reduction in the quantity of foreign exchange supplied. Also, as the exchange rate falls, the Canadian-dollar price of European goods falls, and this fall leads to an increase in the quantity of

FIGURE 35-2 Fixed and Flexible Exchanges Rates

Excess supply of foreign exchange

Exchange Rate (Canadian-dollar price of euros)

e_1

E

e_0

e_2

S

D

Excess demand for foreign exchange

0

Quantity of Foreign Currency (euros)

In the absence of central bank intervention, the exchange rate adjusts to clear the foreign-exchange market. The demand for and supply of foreign exchange are as in Figure 35-1 on page 901. If official financing is zero, there is a purely flexible exchange rate. It will adjust to equate the demand and supply of foreign exchange; this occurs at E with an exchange rate of e_0.

If the exchange rate is higher than that, say at e_1, the supply of foreign exchange will exceed the demand. The exchange rate will fall (the dollar will appreciate) until it reaches e_0, where balance is achieved at E. If the exchange rate is below e_0, say at e_2, the demand for foreign exchange will exceed the supply. The exchange rate will rise (the dollar will depreciate) until it reaches e_0, where balance is achieved at E.

In the case of a fixed exchange rate, the central bank uses its official financing transactions to meet the excess demands or supplies that arise at the fixed value of the exchange rate. For example, if it chooses to fix the exchange rate at e_1, there will be an excess supply of foreign exchange. The central bank will purchase foreign exchange (and sell dollars) to meet the excess supply and keep the exchange rate constant. Alternatively, if the central bank chooses to fix the exchange rate at e_2, there will be an excess demand for foreign exchange. The central bank will sell foreign exchange (and buy dollars) to meet the excess demand and keep the exchange rate constant.

foreign exchange demanded. Thus, the excess supply of foreign exchange leads to a fall in the exchange rate, which in turn reduces the amount of excess supply. Where the two curves intersect, quantity demanded equals quantity supplied, and the exchange rate is at its equilibrium value.

Practise with Study Guide
Chapter 35, Exercise 2.

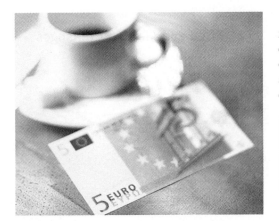

In 1999, 11 countries of the European Union adopted a common currency—the euro. By 2009, when 16 countries had adopted the currency, the price of one euro was 1.62 Canadian dollars.

What happens when the exchange rate is below its equilibrium value, such as at e_2 in Figure 35-2? The quantity of foreign exchange demanded will exceed the quantity supplied. With foreign exchange in excess demand, its price will naturally rise, and as it does the amount of excess demand will be reduced until equilibrium is re-established.

> A foreign-exchange market is like other competitive markets in that the forces of demand and supply lead to an equilibrium price at which quantity demanded equals quantity supplied.

Recall that we have been assuming that there is no official financing by the central bank. We now consider a system of fixed exchange rates in which official financing plays a central role in the analysis.

Fixed Exchange Rates

Practise with Study Guide
Chapter 35, Exercise 3.

If the central bank chooses to fix the exchange rate at a particular value, its official financing transactions must offset any excess demand or supply of foreign exchange that arises at that exchange rate. These transactions are described in Figure 35-2.

The gold standard that operated for much of the nineteenth century and the early part of the twentieth century was a fixed exchange-rate system. The Bretton Woods system, established by international agreement in 1944 and operated until the early 1970s, was a fixed exchange-rate system that provided for circumstances under which exchange rates could be adjusted. It was thus an adjustable peg system; the International Monetary Fund (IMF) has its origins in the Bretton Woods system, and one of its principal tasks was approving and monitoring exchange-rate changes. The European Exchange Rate Mechanism (ERM), which existed from 1979 to 1999, was also a fixed exchange-rate system for the countries in the European Union; their exchange rates were fixed to one another but floated as a block against the U.S. dollar and other currencies. As mentioned earlier, this system of separate currencies with fixed exchange rates was replaced in 1999 when most of the countries of the EU adopted a common currency—the euro.

Applying Economic Concepts 35-2 examines how a fixed exchange-rate system operates. It shows why a central bank that chooses to fix its exchange rate must give up some control of its foreign-exchange reserves. We now go on to study the workings of a flexible exchange-rate system, the system used in Canada and most industrialized countries.

*For information on the European Central Bank, see its website: **www.ecb.int.***

Changes in Flexible Exchange Rates

What causes exchange rates to vary? The simplest answer to this question is changes in demand or supply in the foreign-exchange market. Anything that shifts the demand curve for foreign exchange to the right or the supply curve for foreign exchange to the left leads to a rise in the exchange rate—a depreciation of the Canadian dollar. Conversely, anything that shifts the demand curve for foreign exchange to the left or the supply curve for foreign exchange to the right leads to a fall in the exchange rate—an appreciation of the Canadian dollar. These points are nothing more than a restatement

APPLYING ECONOMIC CONCEPTS 35-2

Managing Fixed Exchange Rates

This box provides some details on how a central bank operates a regime of fixed exchange rates. Though Canada has a flexible exchange rate (with very rare foreign-exchange intervention by the Bank of Canada), we will imagine a situation in which the Bank of Canada pegs the Canadian–U.S. exchange rate. The accompanying figure shows the *monthly* demand for and supply of foreign exchange (U.S. dollars).

Suppose the Bank of Canada fixed the exchange rate between the narrow limits of, say, C$1.10 to C$1.15 to the U.S. dollar. The Bank then stabilizes the exchange rate in the face of seasonal, cyclical, and other fluctuations in demand and supply, entering the market to prevent the rate from going outside the permitted band. At the price of $1.10, the Bank offers to buy any amount of U.S. dollars; at the price of $1.15, the Bank offers to sell any amount of U.S. dollars. When the Bank buys U.S. dollars, its foreign-exchange reserves rise; when it sells U.S. dollars, its foreign-exchange reserves fall.

We make the following observations:

1. If the demand curve cuts the supply curve in the range 1.10 to 1.15, as D_0 does in the accompanying figure, the Bank need not intervene in the market.

2. If the demand curve shifts to D_1, there is an excess demand for U.S. dollars that the Bank must satisfy. The Bank sells U.S. dollars from its reserves to the extent of Q_4Q_1 per month in order to prevent the exchange rate from rising above 1.15.

3. If the demand curve shifts to D_2, there is an excess supply of U.S. dollars that the Bank must satisfy. The Bank buys U.S. dollars to the extent of Q_2Q_3 per month in order to prevent the exchange rate from falling below 1.10.

If, on average, the demand and supply curves intersect in the range 1.10 to 1.15, the Bank's foreign-exchange reserves will be relatively stable, with the Bank buying U.S. dollars when the demand is abnormally low and selling them when the demand is abnormally high. Over a long period, however, the average level of reserves will be fairly stable.

If conditions change, the Bank's foreign-exchange reserves will rise or fall more or less continuously. For example, suppose the average level of demand becomes D_1, with fluctuations on either side of this level. The average drain on the Bank's foreign-exchange reserves will then be Q_4Q_1 *per month*. But this situation cannot continue indefinitely because the Bank has only a limited amount of foreign-exchange reserves. In this situation, there are two alternatives: The Bank can change the fixed exchange rate so that the band of permissible prices straddles the new equilibrium price, or govern-

ment policy can try to shift the curves so that the intersection is in the band 1.10 to 1.15. To accomplish this goal, the government must restrict demand for foreign exchange: It can impose import quotas and foreign-travel restrictions, or it can seek to increase the supply of U.S. dollars by encouraging Canadian exports.

Thailand in 1997 provides an example of an exchange rate fixed at a level that led to a persistent excess demand for foreign exchange. Thailand's central bank had fixed the value of its currency, the baht, to the U.S. dollar. When an excess demand for foreign currency developed in Thailand, the central bank began to deplete its stock of foreign-exchange reserves as it purchased the baht in an attempt to support its external value. By July of 1997, however, the central bank's stock of foreign-exchange reserves had been depleted to such an extent that it could no longer fix the exchange rate. With an excess demand for foreign exchange and a central bank that could no longer fix the exchange rate, depreciation was the natural result. The baht depreciated dramatically and Thailand then moved away from a fixed exchange-rate system.

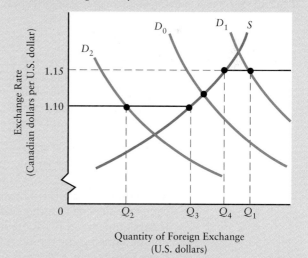

Quantity of Foreign Exchange
(U.S. dollars)

China currently fixes its exchange rate at a level that results in a persistent excess supply of foreign exchange (and excess demand for Chinese currency). The Chinese yuan is permitted to fluctuate in a very narrow band around 6.8 yuan to the U.S. dollar. This exchange rate is above what would otherwise be the free-market equilibrium, and as a result there is a significant excess supply of foreign currency. To prevent the yuan from appreciating, the Chinese central bank purchases foreign-exchange reserves every month. In recent years, these purchases have led to an enormous accumulation of foreign-exchange reserves in China.

FIGURE 35-3   Changes in a Flexible Exchange Rate

(i) Demand shifts   (ii) Supply shifts

An increase in the demand for foreign exchange or a decrease in the supply will cause the Canadian dollar to depreciate (the exchange rate to rise); a decrease in the demand or an increase in supply will cause the dollar to appreciate (the exchange rate to fall). The initial demand and supply curves are D_0 and S_0. Equilibrium is at E_0 with an exchange rate of e_0. An increase in the demand for foreign exchange from D_0 to D_1 in part (i), or a decrease in the supply of foreign exchange from S_0 to S_1 in part (ii), will cause the dollar to depreciate. In both parts, the new equilibrium is at E_1, and the dollar depreciation is shown by the rise in the exchange rate from e_0 to e_1. Conversely, a decrease in the demand for foreign exchange or an increase in the supply of foreign exchange will cause the dollar to appreciate.

of the laws of supply and demand, applied now to the market for foreign exchange; they are illustrated in Figure 35-3.

What causes the shifts in demand and supply that lead to changes in exchange rates? There are many causes, some transitory and some persistent. Let's look at several of the most important ones.

A Supply-Side Increase in the Domestic Price of Exports   Suppose some event on the supply side of the paper market results in an increase in the Canadian-dollar price of Canadian paper. For example, the government may impose a new pollution tax on paper producers. What this will do to the supply of foreign exchange depends on the price elasticity of foreign demand for the Canadian product. If foreign demand for Canadian paper is elastic, perhaps because other countries supply the same product in world markets, the total amount spent on Canadian paper will decrease and hence less foreign exchange will be supplied to purchase Canadian paper. Thus, the supply curve for foreign exchange will shift to the left. The reduction in the supply of foreign exchange will cause an increase in the exchange rate: The Canadian dollar will depreciate. This is illustrated in part (ii) of Figure 35-3. If the demand is inelastic (say, because Canada is the only country that produces this particular kind of paper), then more will be spent and the supply of foreign exchange to pay the bigger bill will increase. The increase in the supply of foreign exchange will cause a reduction in the exchange rate: The Canadian dollar will appreciate.

A Rise in the Foreign Price of Imports   Suppose the euro price of European automobiles increases sharply. Suppose also that Canadian consumers have an elastic demand for European cars because they can easily switch to Canadian-made substitutes. Consequently, they spend fewer euros for European automobiles than they did before and hence demand less foreign exchange. The demand curve for foreign exchange shifts to the left, and the Canadian dollar will appreciate. If the demand for European cars were inelastic, total spending on them would rise, and the demand for foreign exchange would shift to the right, leading to a depreciation of the Canadian dollar. This is illustrated in part (i) of Figure 35-3.

Changes in Overall Price Levels
Suppose that instead of a change in the price of a specific product, such as cars or paper, there is a change in *all* prices because of general inflation. We consider separate cases, each corresponding to a different pattern of Canadian inflation relative to foreign inflation.

EQUAL INFLATION IN BOTH COUNTRIES.
Suppose inflation is running at 5 percent in both Canada and Europe. In this case, the euro prices of European goods and the dollar prices of Canadian goods both rise by 5 percent. At the *existing* exchange rate, the dollar prices of European goods and the euro prices of Canadian goods will each rise by 5 percent, and hence the relative prices of imports and domestically produced goods will be unchanged in both countries. Since there is no reason to expect a change in either country's demand for imports at the original exchange rate, the inflation in the two countries leaves the equilibrium exchange rate unchanged.

INFLATION IN ONLY ONE COUNTRY.
What will happen if there is inflation in Canada while the price level remains stable in Europe? The dollar price of Canadian goods will rise, and they will become more expensive in Europe. This increase will cause the quantity of Canadian exports, and therefore the amount of foreign exchange supplied by European importers, to decrease. Thus, the supply curve for foreign exchange shifts to the left.

At the same time, European goods in Canada will have an unchanged Canadian-dollar price, while the price of Canadian goods sold in Canada will increase because of the inflation. Thus, European goods will be more attractive compared with Canadian goods (because they have become relatively cheaper), and thus more European goods will be bought in Canada. At any exchange rate, the amount of foreign exchange demanded to purchase imports will rise. Thus, the demand curve for foreign exchange shifts to the right.

Canadian inflation that is unmatched in Europe will therefore cause the supply curve for foreign exchange to shift to the left and the demand curve for foreign exchange to shift to the right. As a result, the equilibrium exchange rate *must* rise—there is a depreciation of the Canadian dollar relative to the euro.

INFLATION AT UNEQUAL RATES.
The two foregoing examples are, of course, just limiting cases of a more general situation in which the rate of inflation is different in the two countries. The arguments can readily be extended when we realize that it is the *relative* inflation in two countries that determines whether home goods or foreign goods look more or less attractive. If country A's inflation rate is higher than country B's, country A's exports are becoming relatively expensive in B's markets while imports from B are becoming relatively cheap in A's markets. This causes A's currency to depreciate relative to B's.

> Other things being equal, if Canada has higher inflation than other countries, the Canadian dollar will be depreciating relative to other currencies. If Canada has lower inflation than other countries, the Canadian dollar will be appreciating.

Capital Movements
Capital flows can exert strong influences on exchange rates. For example, an increased desire by Canadians to purchase European assets

(a capital outflow from Canada) will shift the demand curve for foreign exchange to the right, and the dollar will depreciate. In contrast, a desire by foreigners to increase their holdings of Canadian assets will shift the supply curve for foreign currency to the right and cause the Canadian dollar to appreciate.

Practise with Study Guide
Chapter 35, Exercise 4.

SHORT-TERM CAPITAL MOVEMENTS. An important motive for short-term capital flows is a change in interest rates. International traders hold transaction balances just as do domestic traders. These balances are often lent out on a short-term basis rather than being left idle. Naturally, the holders of these balances will tend to lend them, other things being equal, in markets in which interest rates are highest. Thus, if one country's short-term interest rate rises above the rates in other countries (say, because that country undertakes a contractionary monetary policy), there will tend to be a large inflow of short-term capital into that country in an effort to take advantage of the high rate. This inflow of financial capital will increase the demand for the domestic currency and cause it to appreciate. If the short-term interest rate should fall in one country (say, because of a monetary expansion in that country), there will tend to be a shift of financial capital away from that country, and its currency will tend to depreciate. We saw this basic relationship between interest rates, capital flows, and the exchange rate in Chapter 28 when we discussed the monetary transmission mechanism in an open economy.

Currencies are traded and exchange rates are determined in sophisticated foreign-exchange markets in which thousands of currency traders all over the world transact with one another. Economic and political events influence their buying and selling decisions, and thus influence exchange rates.

Changes in Canadian monetary policy lead to changes in interest rates and thus to international flows of financial capital. A contractionary monetary policy in Canada will lead to a rise in Canadian interest rates, a capital inflow, and an appreciation of the Canadian dollar. An expansionary monetary policy in Canada will lead to a reduction in Canadian interest rates, a capital outflow, and a depreciation of the Canadian dollar.

A second motive for short-term capital movements is speculation about the *future value* of a country's exchange rate. If foreigners expect the Canadian dollar to appreciate in the near future, they will rush to buy assets that pay off in Canadian dollars, such as Canadian stocks or bonds; if they expect the Canadian dollar to depreciate in the near future, they will be reluctant to buy or to hold Canadian securities.

LONG-TERM CAPITAL MOVEMENTS. Long-term capital movements are largely influenced by long-term expectations about another country's profit opportunities and the long-run value of its currency. A French firm would be more willing to purchase a Canadian factory if it expected that the dollar profits would buy more euros in future years than the profits from investment in a French factory. This could happen if the Canadian firm earned greater profits than the French firm, with exchange rates remaining unchanged. It could also happen if the profits were the same but the French firm expected the Canadian dollar to appreciate relative to the euro.

Structural Changes

An economy can undergo structural changes that alter the equilibrium exchange rate. *Structural change* is an all-purpose term for a change in cost structures, the invention of new products, changes in preferences between products, or anything else that affects the pattern of comparative advantage. Consider three examples.

Suppose the reluctance of firms in one country to adopt technological innovations results in that country's products not improving as rapidly as those produced in other countries. Consumers' demand will shift slowly away from the first country's products and toward those of its foreign competitors. This shift will cause a gradual depreciation in the first country's currency because fewer people want to buy that country's goods and thus fewer people want to buy that country's currency. For this reason, a country with faster productivity growth than other countries tends to experience an appreciation of its currency.

A second example relates to the discovery of valuable mineral resources. Prominent examples are the development of natural gas in the Netherlands in the early 1960s, the development of North Sea oil in the United Kingdom in the 1970s, and the recent discovery of large diamond deposits in the Northwest Territories. If firms in one country make such a discovery and begin selling these resources to the rest of the world, the foreign purchasers must supply their foreign currency in order to purchase the currency of the exporting country. The result is an appreciation of the currency of the exporting country.

> **Anything that leads to changes in the pattern of trade, such as changes in costs or changes in demand, will generally lead to changes in exchange rates.**

A final example of particular relevance to Canada relates to changes in demand for a country's exports. For many countries, including Canada, the prices of the goods that it sells to other countries are determined in world markets. Examples include commodities such as oil, copper, pulp, lumber, wheat, coffee, cocoa, zinc, tin, aluminum, and gold. Changes in the world demand for or supply of these commodities typically have significant effects on exchange rates. For example, if there is a reduction in the world demand for these products there will be an accompanying reduction in demand for the currencies of those countries that export these products. Their currencies will depreciate. Similarly, increases in the world price of these commodities will lead to an appreciation of the currencies in countries that export them. For this reason, the Canadian dollar is often referred to as a "commodity currency" because there is a strong correlation between changes in world commodity prices and changes in the Canadian exchange rate. In the 2002–2007 period, large increases in the world prices of energy and other raw materials were an important factor in the sharp appreciation of the Canadian dollar. But these same prices declined sharply in 2008 as the world entered a significant recession, and the commodity-price decline contributed to a significant depreciation of the Canadian dollar.

The Volatility of Exchange Rates

We have discussed several variables that can lead to changes in the exchange rate, including changes in relative prices, changes in interest rates, and changes in the pattern of trade. Since these variables are changing at different times by different amounts and often in different directions, it should not be surprising that exchange rates are constantly changing. Indeed, exchange rates are one of the most volatile of all macroeconomic variables. One reason for this volatility that we have not yet discussed is that foreign-exchange traders, when they are deciding whether to buy or sell foreign currency, respond to all sorts of "news" that they think will influence economic conditions, both currently and in the future. Since such news is constantly becoming available, the exchange rate is continuously changing as this new information leads traders to change their demand and supply decisions. *Applying Economic Concepts 35-3* discusses in more detail how news affects the volatility of exchange rates.

ⓧ myeconlab   ADDITIONAL TOPICS

Economists have long noticed that exchange rates tend to be more volatile than any of the variables we have been discussing. For a brief discussion of a famous theory in which the expectations of future exchange-rate changes play a central role, look for **Expectations and Exchange-Rate Overshooting** in the *Additional Topics* section of this book's MyEconLab.

www.myeconlab.com

35.4 Three Policy Issues

Practise with Study Guide
Chapter 35, Extension Exercise 1.

This chapter has so far explained how the balance of payments accounts are constructed and how exchange rates are determined. It is now time to use this knowledge to explore some important policy issues. We examine three issues commonly discussed in the media. As we will see, these media discussions are not always as well informed as they could be. We pose the three policy issues as questions:

1. Is a current account deficit "bad" and a surplus "good"?

2. Is there a "correct" value for the Canadian dollar?

3. Should Canada fix its exchange rate with the U.S. dollar?

Current Account Deficits and Surpluses

Figure 35-4 shows the path of Canada's current account balance (as a percentage of GDP) since 1961. In most years, Canada has a significant trade surplus since it exports more goods and services to the world than it imports. But because it makes more investment payments (both interest and dividends) to foreigners than it receives from foreigners, it has a deficit on the capital-service portion of the current account. During most of the 1960–1995 period, Canada had an overall current account deficit of 2 or 3 percent of GDP. In the past few years, however, Canada's trade surplus has increased by more than the capital-service deficit, and the result has been a significant turnaround in the current account balance. From 2000 to 2008, Canada had a current account surplus of 1–2 percent of GDP.

As we have learned, Canada's balance of payments are defined in such a way that they must always balance, so during the 1960–1995 period the current account deficits were matched by capital account surpluses of the same size. During these years, Canada was selling more assets to the rest of the world—both bonds and equity—than it was buying from the rest of the world. Similarly, the recent current account surpluses

News and the Exchange Rate

Foreign-exchange markets are different from markets for consumer goods in that the vast bulk of trading takes place between professional foreign-exchange traders working for banks, mutual-fund companies, and pension funds. These traders do not meet one another face to face. Rather, they do their transactions over the telephone or the computer, and the other party to the transaction could be anywhere in the world. The structure of this market has one interesting implication: Exchange rates respond to news. Let's see why this is and what this means.

Deals done by professional traders are all on a large scale, typically involving sums no smaller than $1 million and often very much larger. Each trader tends to specialize in trades between a small number of currencies, say the Canadian and the U.S. dollars, or the U.S. dollar and the Japanese yen. But the traders for all currencies for each bank sit close together in a trading room so they can hear what is going on in the other markets. When a big news event breaks, anywhere in the world, this will be shouted out simultaneously to all traders in the room.

Each trader is also faced with several computer screens and many buttons that connect him or her quickly by telephone to other traders. Speed of transaction can be very important if you are dealing with large amounts of money in a market that is continuously changing the prices quoted. The most recent price quotes from around the world appear on the screens. However, contracts are agreed over the telephone (and are recorded in case of a disagreement) and the paperwork follows within two days.

As exchange rates are closely related to expectations and to interest rates, the foreign-exchange traders have to keep an eye on all major news events affecting the economic environment. Since all the players in the foreign-exchange markets are professionals, they are well informed, not just about what has happened but also about forecasts of what is likely to happen. Accordingly, the exchange rate at any point in time reflects not just history but also current expectations of future events.

As soon as some future event comes to be expected—such as the central bank's plans to tighten monetary policy—it will be reflected in the current exchange rate. Events expected to happen soon will be given more weight than those events expected to happen in the more distant future. The fact that expectations of future events are incorporated quickly into the exchange rate has an interesting implication: The only component in today's news that will cause the exchange rate to change is what was *not expected* to happen. Economists attribute the unforecastable component of news to a random error. It is random in the sense that it has no detectable pattern and it is unrelated to the information available before it happened.

Some events are clearly unforecastable, like an earthquake in Japan or a head of state having a heart attack. Others are the production of economic statistics for which forecasts have generally been published. In the latter case it is the deviation of announced figures from their forecast value that tends to move exchange rates.

Exchange rates are therefore moved by news. And since much news is random and unpredictable, many changes in exchange rates will tend to be random. Some people, observing the volatility of exchange rates, conclude that foreign-exchange markets are inefficient. However, with well-informed professional traders who have forward-looking expectations, new information is rapidly transmitted into prices. The volatility of exchange rates, therefore, largely reflects the volatility of relevant, but unexpected, events around the world.

Current news events, the announcements made by public officials, and the expectation of future events play a large role in determining whether currency traders decide to buy or sell foreign exchange. The frequency and randomness of news releases partly explain why exchange rates tend to be so volatile.

FIGURE 35-4   Canada's Current Account Balance, 1961–2008

(*Source:* Statistics Canada, CANSIM database, Series V113713 expressed as a percentage of nominal GDP, Series V498086.)

were matched by capital account deficits, meaning that in recent years Canada was buying more assets from foreigners than we were selling to foreigners.

It is common for TV anchors to report negatively on a rise in the current account deficit and positively on its decline. But are current account deficits really a problem? Should we be celebrating Canada's current account surpluses when they occur? We address this issue in three parts.

Mercantilism   Many people argue that a current account deficit is undesirable because it means that Canada is buying more goods and services from the world than it is selling to the world. Central to this view is the belief that exports are "good" and imports are "bad." We discussed this belief, and argued why it was incorrect, in Chapter 34 when we explored some of the fallacious arguments for trade protection.

As a carryover from a long-discredited eighteenth-century doctrine called *mercantilism,* a current account surplus is sometimes called a "favourable balance," and a current account deficit is sometimes called an "unfavourable balance." Mercantilists, both ancient and modern, believe that a country's gains from trade arise only from having a "favourable" balance of trade—that is, by exporting more goods and services than it imports. But this belief misses the central point of comparative advantage that we explored in Chapter 33—that countries gain from trade because trade allows each country to specialize in the production of those products in which its opportunity costs are low. The gains from trade have *nothing* to do with whether there is a trade deficit or a trade surplus.

Lessons from History 35-1 discusses the doctrine of mercantilism. The lesson to be learned is that the gains from trade depend on the *volume* of trade (imports plus exports) rather than the *balance* of trade. There is nothing inherently bad about having a current account deficit and nothing inherently good about having a current account surplus.

LESSONS FROM HISTORY 35-1

Mercantilism, Then and Now

Media commentators, politicians, and much of the general public often appear to believe that a nation should export more than it imports and thereby secure a current account surplus. They appear to believe that the benefits derived from international trade are measured by the size of that surplus.

This view is related to the *exploitation doctrine* of international trade: One country's surplus is another country's deficit. Hence, one country's gain, judged by its surplus, must be another country's loss, judged by its deficit.

People who hold such views today are echoing an ancient economic doctrine called *mercantilism*. The mercantilists were a group of economists who preceded Adam Smith. They judged the success of trade by the size of the trade balance. In many cases, this doctrine made sense in terms of their objective, which was to use international trade as a means of building up the political and military power of the state, rather than as a means of raising the living standards of its citizens. A current account surplus allowed the nation (then and now) to acquire assets. (In those days, the assets took the form of gold. Today, they are mostly claims on the currencies of other countries.) These assets could then be used to pay armies, to purchase weapons from abroad, and to finance colonial expansions.

If the objective is to promote the welfare and living standards of ordinary citizens, however, the mercantilist focus on the balance of trade makes no sense. The principle of comparative advantage shows that average living standards are maximized by having individuals, regions, and countries specialize in the things they produce comparatively best and then trading to obtain the things they produce comparatively worst. With specialization, domestic consumers get access to products they want at the lowest possible prices, while domestic firms are able to sell their products at higher prices than would otherwise be possible. The more specialization takes place, the more trade occurs and thus the more average living standards increase.

For the country as a whole, therefore, the gains from trade are to be judged by the *volume* of trade rather than by the *balance* of trade. A situation in which there is a large volume of trade even though each country has a zero balance of trade can thus be regarded as satisfactory. Furthermore, a change in policy that results in an equal increase in both exports and imports will generate gains because it allows for specialization according to comparative advantage, even though it causes no change in either country's trade balance.

International Borrowing If Canada has a current account deficit, it also has a capital account surplus. It is a net seller of assets to the rest of the world. These assets are either bonds, in which case Canadians are borrowing from foreigners, or they are shares in firms (equities), in which case Canadians are selling their capital stock to foreigners.

It follows that the question "Should Canada have a current account deficit?" is the same as the question "Should Canadians be net sellers of assets to foreigners?" It is not immediately clear that the answer to this question should be no. It is true that by selling bonds to foreigners, Canadians increase their indebtedness to foreigners and will eventually have to redeem the bonds and pay interest. And by selling income-earning equities to foreigners, Canadians give up a stream of income that they would otherwise have. But, in both cases, they get a lump sum of funds that can be used for any type of consumption or investment. Is it obviously "better" to have a lower debt or a higher future income stream than to have a lump sum of funds right now? If it were better, no family would ever borrow money to buy a house or a car, and no firm would ever borrow money to build a factory.

A country that has a current account deficit is either borrowing from the rest of the world or selling its ownership of some of its capital assets to the rest of the world. This is not necessarily undesirable.

To argue that it is undesirable for Canada to have a current account deficit is to argue that Canadians as a whole should not borrow from (or sell assets to) the rest of the world. But surely the wisdom of borrowing depends on *why* Canadians are borrowing. It is therefore important to know *why* there is a current account deficit.

Causes of Current Account Deficits   There are several possible causes of a current account deficit. This can be seen most clearly by recalling some national-income accounting from Chapter 20. Recall that GDP is equal to the sum of actual consumption, investment, government purchases, and net exports,

$$GDP = C_a + I_a + G_a + NX_a$$

where the subscript "*a*" denotes *actual* expenditure rather than desired expenditure. Next, note that GNP is equal to GDP plus the net investment income received from abroad, which we call R.

$$GNP = GDP + R = C_a + I_a + G_a + NX_a + R$$

Note that the current account balance is simply the trade balance, NX_a, plus the net investment income, R. We denote the actual current account balance CA_a. If CA_a is positive, there is a current account surplus; if CA_a is negative, there is a current account deficit. The equation now becomes

$$GNP = C_a + I_a + G_a + CA_a \tag{35-1}$$

Now consider how a given amount of GNP that accrues to households can be spent. There are only three ways to dispose of income. It can be consumed, saved, or paid in taxes. That is,

$$GNP = C_a + S_a + T_a \tag{35-2}$$

By equating Equations 35-1 and 35-2, and by omitting the "*a*" subscripts for simplicity, we derive an interesting relationship among national saving, investment, and the current account balance:

$$C + I + G + CA = C + S + T$$
$$\Rightarrow CA = S + (T - G) - I$$

This last equation says that the current account balance in any year is exactly equal to the excess of national saving, $S + (T - G)$, over domestic investment I. If Canadians (and their governments) decide to save more than is needed to finance the amount of domestic investment, where do the excess funds go? They are used to acquire foreign assets, and thus Canada has a current account surplus ($CA > 0$). In contrast, if Canadians do not save enough to finance the amount of domestic investment, the balance must be financed by foreign funds. Thus, Canada has a current account deficit ($CA < 0$). Finally, we can re-arrange this equation very slightly to get

$$CA = (S - I) + (T - G) \tag{35-3}$$

which says that the current account balance is equal to the excess of private saving over investment plus the government budget surplus.

Equation 35-3 shows three separate reasons for any given increase in the current account deficit (a fall in CA). First, a reduction in private saving, other things being equal, will lead to a rise in the current account deficit. Second, a rise in domestic investment, other things being equal, will increase the current account deficit. Finally, other things being equal, a rise in the government's budget deficit (a fall in the budget surplus) will raise the current account deficit. This third case is often referred to as a situation of *twin deficits*. That is, a rise in the government's budget deficit will also have the effect (if S and I remain constant) of increasing the current account deficit.

An increase in the level of investment, a decrease in the level of private saving, and an increase in the government's budget deficit are all possible causes of an increase in a country's current account deficit.

A boom in domestic investment, other things being equal, will lead to an increase in the current account deficit. But there is little that is undesirable about this situation.

In the end, it makes little sense to discuss the desirability of a change in the current account deficit without first knowing the *cause* of the change. Knowing the cause is crucial to knowing whether the change in the current account deficit is undesirable. The following two examples illustrate this important point.

First, suppose business opportunities in Canada are very promising and, as a result, there is an increase in the level of private-sector investment. Most people would consider such an investment boom desirable because it would increase current output and employment and, by increasing the country's capital stock, it would also increase the level of potential output in the future. But as is clear from Equation 35-3, other things being equal, the immediate effect of the rise in Canadian investment is an increase in the Canadian current account deficit. The current account deficit increases because, in the absence of increased domestic saving, the increase in domestic investment can only take place if it is financed by a capital inflow from other countries. This capital inflow represents a rise in Canada's current account deficit (or capital account surplus). In this case, however, it would be difficult to argue that the increase in Canada's current account deficit is undesirable as it simply reflects a boom in domestic business opportunities.

For a second example, suppose the domestic economy begins to slow and households and firms become pessimistic about the future. In such a situation, we expect households to increase their saving and firms to reduce their investment, thus increasing the value of $(S - I)$. As the economy slows we would also expect the government's net tax revenues to fall, thus decreasing the value of $(T - G)$. But it is possible that the first effect dominates the second effect, thus leading to an increase in the current account surplus. Is the increase in Canada's current account surplus desirable? Most people would probably agree that the onset of a recession as just described is surely undesirable, involving a loss of output and employment.

A country's current account deficit can increase for a number of reasons. Whether the rise in the current account deficit is desirable depends on its underlying cause. A rise in the current account deficit may reflect a positive economic development; a decline in the current account deficit may reflect a negative economic development.

Is There a "Correct" Value for the Canadian Dollar?

From the summer of 1997 to the end of 1999, the external value of the Canadian dollar fell from about 72 to 65 U.S. cents. It was common to hear financial commentators discuss how the Canadian dollar was "undervalued." Retailers selling imported products and firms using imported supplies complained that the weak Canadian dollar was undermining their business. Opposite statements were heard between 2002 and 2008 when, as a result of high world prices for raw materials, the Canadian dollar appreciated enormously. At the time, some financial commentators argued that the Canadian dollar was "overvalued." Canadian firms in the tourist-oriented hospitality industry and those exporting manufactured products complained that the strong Canadian dollar was damaging their business. In both cases, the observers appeared to believe that there was some "correct" value for the Canadian dollar. Is there?

As we saw in the previous section, a country that chooses to use a flexible exchange rate has its exchange rate determined by competitive forces in the foreign-exchange market. In Canada, and other countries as well, fluctuations in exchange rates have many causes. Some changes may be good for Canada, such as a worldwide shortage of wheat that drives up the world price of wheat, a major Canadian export. Others may be bad for Canada, such as the discovery of new copper deposits in Chile that drives down the price of copper, also a major Canadian export. But the various supply and demand forces are coming together in the foreign-exchange market to determine the equilibrium value of the exchange rate. Changes in this value may reflect positive or negative events for Canada, but it is difficult to think of this equilibrium value as being either "too high" or "too low."

> With a flexible exchange rate, the market determines the value of the exchange rate. With respect to the forces of demand and supply, the equilibrium exchange rate is the "correct" exchange rate.

Saying that the current equilibrium exchange rate is the "correct" rate in no way suggests that this "correct" rate is constant. Indeed, foreign-exchange markets are so large, with so many participants in so many countries, each responding to a slightly different set of events and expectations, that the equilibrium exchange rate is constantly changing. In other words, as various forces lead to frequent changes in the demand for and supply of the Canadian dollar in foreign-exchange markets, the "correct" value of the Canadian exchange rate is constantly changing.

Some economists accept that the current exchange rate, as determined by the foreign-exchange market, is indeed the correct rate, but they make a distinction between the immediate value of the exchange rate and its long-run value. These economists argue that, whereas various shocks may cause the exchange rate to rise or fall in the short run, there does exist some "fundamental" level to which it will eventually return. This brings us to the theory of *purchasing power parity*.

purchasing power parity (PPP) The theory that over the long term, the exchange rate between two currencies adjusts to reflect relative price levels.

Purchasing Power Parity   The theory of **purchasing power parity (PPP)** holds that over the long term, the value of the exchange rate between two currencies depends on the two currencies' relative purchasing power. The theory holds that a currency will tend to have the same purchasing power when it is spent in its home country as it would have if it were converted to foreign exchange and spent in the foreign country. Another way to say the same thing is that the price of *identical baskets of goods* should be the same in the two countries when the price is expressed in the same currency. If we let P_C and P_E be the price levels in Canada and Europe, respectively, and let e be the price of euros in terms of Canadian dollars (the exchange rate), then the theory of purchasing power parity predicts the following equality in the long run:

$$P_C = e \times P_E \qquad (35\text{-}4)$$

This equation simply says that if a basket of goods costs 1000 euros in Europe and the exchange rate is 1.6 (that is, 1.6 Canadian dollars per euro), then that same basket of goods should cost 1600 dollars in Canada (1.6 × 1000 = 1600).

> **According to the theory of purchasing power parity, the exchange rate between two countries' currencies is determined by the relative price levels in the two countries.**

For The Economist's *Big Mac Index, which uses the idea of PPP, see its website:* **www.economist.com.**

The idea behind PPP is a simple one. Suppose that Equation 35-4 did *not* hold—specifically, suppose that P_C was greater than $e \times P_E$, so that Canadian-dollar prices in Canada exceeded the Canadian-dollar prices of the same goods in Europe. In this case, people would increase their purchases of the cheaper European goods and reduce their purchases of the expensive Canadian goods. These actions would have the effect of depreciating the Canadian dollar (a rise in *e*); this depreciation would continue until the equality was re-established.

The *PPP exchange rate* is the value of the exchange rate that makes Equation 35-4 hold. That is, the PPP exchange rate (between the Canadian dollar and the euro) is defined to be

$$e^{PPP} \equiv P_C/P_E \qquad (35\text{-}5)$$

Note that the PPP exchange rate is itself not constant. If inflation is higher in Canada than in Europe, for example, P_C will be rising faster than P_E and so the PPP exchange rate will be rising. Conversely, if inflation is lower in Canada than in Europe, P_C will be rising more slowly than P_E and the PPP exchange rate will be falling.[3]

A Caveat About PPP   Should we expect the *actual* exchange rate to equal the PPP exchange rate? The theory of purchasing power parity predicts that if the actual exchange rate (*e*) does not equal the PPP exchange rate (e^{PPP}), then demands and supplies of Canadian and European goods will change until the equality holds. Thus, the theory of PPP predicts that the actual exchange rate will eventually equal the PPP exchange rate.

Figure 35-5 shows the path of the actual Canadian–U.S. exchange rate and the PPP exchange rate since 1981. It is clear from the figure that there are long periods of time over which the actual exchange rate deviates significantly from the PPP exchange rate. Why is this the case? Is there something wrong with the theory of purchasing power parity?

Recall from Equation 35-4 that P_C and P_E were defined as the prices of *identical baskets of goods* in Canada and Europe, respectively. Given that the goods are the same, the argument that the prices should (eventually) be equated across the two countries is sensible—if the prices are not equated across the two countries, there would be an incentive to purchase in the cheaper country rather than in the more expensive country, and this would lead to changes in the exchange rate until Equation 35-4 *did* hold.

---

[3] For a very readable review of the PPP theory and its empirical testing, see R. Lafrance and L. Schembri, "Purchasing Power Parity: Definitions, Measurement, and Interpretation," *Bank of Canada Review,* Autumn, 2002.

FIGURE 35-5　Actual and PPP Exchange Rates, 1981–2009

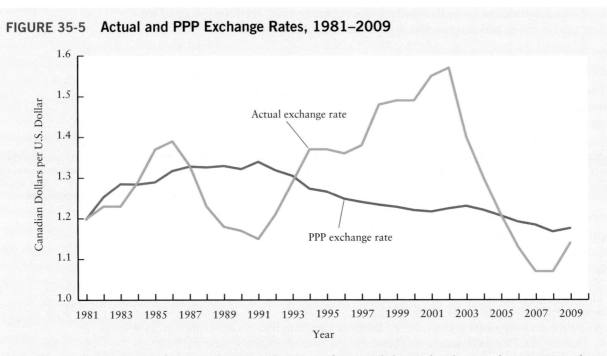

The actual exchange rate deviates from the PPP exchange rate for extended periods. The Canada–U.S. PPP exchange rate is the ratio of Canadian to U.S. price indices. This PPP exchange rate increased during the 1980s when Canadian inflation was above that in the United States; it declined over the next 20 years when Canadian inflation was lower than in the United States. The actual Canada–U.S. exchange rate has fluctuated more dramatically and shows little tendency to track the PPP exchange rate.

(*Source:* Canadian CPI is from the Bank of Canada, Series PCPISA, annual average. U.S. CPI is from U.S. Bureau of Labor Statistics: www.bls.gov. Exchange rate is from Statistics Canada, CANSIM database, Series V37432, annual average.)

One problem, however, when we apply the theory of purchasing power parity to *national price indices,* such as the Consumer Price Index or the implicit GDP deflator, is that the two baskets of goods are typically *not* the same—for two reasons.

DIFFERENT COUNTRIES PRODUCE DIFFERENT GOODS.　Suppose we apply the theory of PPP to the Canada–Europe exchange rate and we use the GDP deflators from the two countries as the measures of prices. Recall from Chapter 20 that the GDP deflator is an index of prices of goods *produced within the country.* But Canada and Europe clearly produce very different goods. The price of forest products will have a large weight in the Canadian GDP deflator but less weight in the European GDP deflator; in contrast, the price of wine will have a much larger weight in the European GDP deflator than in the Canadian GDP deflator.

The implication of these differences for the theory of PPP is important. As long as changes in the *relative* prices of goods occur, such as a change in the price of forest products relative to wine, then P_C (the Canadian GDP deflator) will change relative to P_E (the European GDP deflator) *even though the prices of individual goods might be equated across the two countries.* Thus, differences in the structure of the price indices between two countries mean that using a PPP exchange rate computed on the basis of Equation 35-5 will be misleading. In other words, in the presence of changing relative prices, there is no reason to expect the actual exchange rate to equal the PPP exchange rate.

NON-TRADED GOODS ARE IMPORTANT.   The previous discussion emphasized that the *baskets* of goods across two countries might differ even though the products in the baskets were the same. But even if Canada and Europe produced exactly the same range of goods, so that the various weights in the GDP deflators were the same, there is another reason why the basket of goods in Canada differs from the basket of goods in Europe. Some of the goods produced in Canada are *non-traded goods,* such as haircuts, restaurant meals, and many other services. Non-traded goods are also produced in Europe. But, since non-traded goods cannot be traded (by definition), there is nothing that will force their prices to be equal across the two countries. If haircuts are more expensive in Paris than in Toronto (as they are), we do not expect people to shift their consumption of haircuts away from Paris toward Toronto, and thus we should not expect the actual exchange rate to move to make Equation 35-4 hold.

The conclusion of this discussion is that we must be very careful in selecting the price indices we use when we apply the theory of purchasing power parity. We know that countries have different patterns of production and thus have different structures to their national price indices. Thus, in the presence of changes in relative prices of various products, the national price indices can change in ways that will not lead to changes in the exchange rate. Similarly, the presence of non-traded goods implies that some differences in prices across countries will not lead to changes in the location of demand and thus changes in the exchange rate.

> Changes in relative prices and the presence of non-traded goods imply that purchasing power parity need not hold—not even in the long run.

Should Canada Have a Fixed Exchange Rate?

In recent years, some economists have suggested that Canada peg the value of its currency to the U.S. dollar. Advocates of a fixed Canadian exchange rate see this policy as a means of avoiding the significant fluctuations in the Canadian–U.S. dollar exchange rate that would otherwise occur—fluctuations such as the 10 percent depreciation that occurred between 1997 and 1999 and the 60 percent appreciation that occurred between 2002 and 2007. They argue that exchange-rate fluctuations generate uncertainty for importers and exporters and thus increase the costs associated with trade.

Others have gone further in suggesting that Canada actually abandon its currency altogether and simply adopt the U.S. dollar. They point to the European Union, which introduced the euro as its common currency in 1999. If a common currency is acceptable to most of Europe, why should Canada and the United States be any different?

These are contentious suggestions that have attracted a great deal of public attention in recent years. We examine this issue by comparing the main benefits of flexible and fixed exchange rates. Whereas flexible exchange rates dampen the effects on output and employment from external shocks to the economy, fixed exchange rates reduce the uncertainty faced by traders.

⟨Ⅹ myeconlab⟩ ADDITIONAL TOPICS

The debate over fixed and flexible exchange rates is closely related to the issue of whether a group of countries is best served by a common currency or instead by separate currencies for each country. For more information, look for **What Is an Optimal Currency Area?** in the *Additional Topics* section of this book's MyEconLab.

Flexible Exchange Rates as "Shock Absorbers"   For most of the years following the Second World War, Canada has used a flexible exchange rate. Even when most other major countries chose to peg the value of their currencies to the U.S. dollar (and to gold) under the Bretton Woods system, Canada usually chose a flexible exchange rate (there were a few short periods in which Canada fixed its exchange rate). For all of its history Canada's economy has been heavily reliant on the export of resource-based products, the prices of which are determined in world markets and are often highly variable from year to year. Changes in these prices constitute changes in Canada's terms of trade and, as we saw earlier in this chapter, changes in a country's terms of trade are an important reason why exchange rates are so variable.

That the exchange rate adjusts in response to shocks is actually the main advantage of a flexible (rather than fixed) exchange rate. A flexible exchange rate acts as a "shock absorber," dampening the effects on the country's output and employment from external shocks. To understand how this happens, consider a simple example.

Suppose a reduction in world demand leads to a reduction in the world prices of raw materials, which are major Canadian exports. When world demand for raw materials declines, there is a reduction in demand for Canadian exports and an accompanying reduction in demand for Canadian dollars (or a reduction in the supply of foreign exchange) in the foreign-exchange market. The effect on Canadian real GDP is shown in part (ii) of Figure 35-6 by the leftward shift of the AD curve. The effect in the foreign-exchange market is shown in part (i) by the leftward shift of the supply curve for foreign exchange. Consider the effect of this shock in two different situations. In the first, the Bank of Canada maintains a fixed exchange rate; in the second, the Bank of Canada allows the exchange rate to be freely determined by demand and supply.

If the Bank of Canada fixes the exchange rate at e_0, the reduction in the supply of foreign exchange from S_0 to S_1 leads to an excess demand for foreign currency. To keep the exchange rate fixed at e_0, the Bank must sell sufficient foreign-exchange reserves to satisfy the excess demand. But the negative shock to aggregate demand still occurs and thus output and employment in Canada fall, as shown in part (ii) of Figure 35-6. Canadian wages will eventually fall and the AS curve will eventually shift downward, returning real GDP to the level of potential output. But the closing of the recessionary gap may be slow and painful.

If Canada instead has a flexible exchange rate, the reduction in the world prices of raw materials will lead to a reduction in the supply of foreign exchange and thus to a depreciation of the Canadian dollar. The exchange rate will increase from e_0 to e_1. The AD curve will shift to the left, reducing Canada's GDP, just as in the fixed-exchange-rate case. The sectors of the Canadian economy producing raw materials will still be in recession, for there has been a reduction in demand for these products. But the overall Canadian downturn will be dampened by the depreciation of the Canadian dollar. Other exporting sectors of the Canadian economy will actually *expand* as a result of the depreciation because their products are now more competitive in world markets. Thus, as shown in part (ii) of Figure 35-6, the leftward shift of the AD curve will not be as large as in the case of the fixed exchange rate. The overall result is that, with a flexible exchange rate, the deterioration in Canada's terms of trade leads to a less severe Canadian recession than if Canada had a fixed exchange rate.

One of the advantages of flexible exchange rates is that, in response to shocks to the terms of trade, the exchange rate can act as a shock absorber, dampening the effects of the shock on output and employment.

The Asian Crisis of 1997–1998 provides an excellent example of how Canada's flexible exchange rate dampened the effects of a negative external shock. When the

FIGURE 35-6   Flexible Exchange Rates as a Shock Absorber

(i) Foreign-exchange market   (ii) *AD* and *AS*

Flexible exchange rates adjust to terms of trade shocks and thus dampen the effect on output and employment. The economy begins with the exchange rate equal to e_0 in part (i) and GDP equal to Y^* in part (ii). A reduction in the world's demand for Canadian exports causes a reduction in the supply of foreign exchange, shifting S_0 to S_1 in part (i).

With a fixed exchange rate, the Bank of Canada maintains the exchange rate at e_0, satisfying the excess demand for foreign exchange by selling its foreign-currency reserves. The reduction in the demand for Canada's exports is a negative aggregate demand shock. AD_0 shifts to the left to AD_1 in part (ii), causing GDP to fall to Y_1. The recessionary gap eventually pushes wages down, the *AS* curve shifts downward over time, and the economy moves along AD_1 to Y^*. The adjustment, however, may be protracted.

With a flexible exchange rate, the Bank of Canada allows the Canadian dollar to depreciate. The exchange rate rises to e_1 in part (i). The reduction in demand for Canadian exports still causes the *AD* curve to shift to the left in part (ii), but the shift is dampened by the depreciation of the dollar, which makes Canadian products more competitive in world markets. The *AD* curve shifts only to AD_2 and so GDP falls only to Y_2. There is still a recession, but smaller than in the case with a fixed exchange rate.

Asian countries of Malaysia, Indonesia, Thailand, and South Korea experienced their large recessions in 1997 and 1998, their demand for many raw materials declined sharply. As they are major users of raw materials, the effect was felt on world markets. The average prices of raw materials fell by roughly 30 percent from the summer of 1997 to the end of 1998. Many of these raw materials, of course, are important exports for Canada, and so the decline in their world prices implied a terms-of-trade deterioration for Canada.

Especially hard hit was British Columbia's forestry sector, in which output fell dramatically in many paper and lumber mills because of the lack of sales in Asia. As expected, there was also a significant depreciation of the Canadian dollar, just as described in Figure 35-6. But as the Canadian dollar depreciated, the Canadian manufacturing sector, concentrated mainly in Ontario and Quebec, was given a large boost. The 10 percent depreciation of the Canadian dollar meant that Canadian machinery, furniture, telecommunications equipment, and a whole range of other products were now more competitive in world markets. Thus, the boom in the Central Canadian manufacturing sector offset to some extent the significant recession that was going on in British Columbia. If Canada had had a fixed exchange rate, the 10 percent depreciation would not have occurred. But the initial shock from the Asian Crisis would still have taken place. The net result would have been lower output and higher unemployment than actually occurred.

A few years later, between 2002 and 2007, the opposite forces were at work, and once again Canada's flexible exchange rate acted as a shock absorber. Because of strong global economic growth, especially in China and India, world prices for energy and other raw materials increased significantly. This was a positive shock to Canadian aggregate demand, and the price increase caused an improvement in Canada's terms of trade and an appreciation of the Canadian dollar by more than 60 percent. During this period the energy and commodity-producing sectors of the Canadian economy were booming. At the same time, however, the appreciation of the Canadian dollar tended to reduce activity in the central Canadian manufacturing sector, thus dampening the overall effect of the positive shock on the Canadian economy.

Note that having a fixed exchange rate does not prevent a country from being subjected to shocks from the rest of the world. Some advocates of fixed exchange rates seem to think that by fixing the value of a country's currency, the country is shielding itself from undesirable fluctuations. But shocks to a country's terms of trade will always occur. As long as there are changes in the demand for and supply of various products around the world, there will also be changes in a country's terms of trade. What Figure 35-6 shows, however, is that by fixing the exchange rate and thus avoiding the fluctuations in the value of the currency, the effects of the shock merely show up as increased volatility in output and employment.

> A country will always experience shocks in its terms of trade. A flexible exchange rate absorbs some of the shock, reducing the effect on output and employment. A fixed exchange rate simply redistributes the effect of the shock—the exchange rate is smoother but output and employment are more volatile.

Trade, Transaction Costs, and Uncertainty

Despite the benefits of international trade, there are costs involved in exporting and importing goods and services. The *transaction costs* of international trade involve the costs associated with converting one currency to another, as must be done either by the importer or by the exporter of the product that is traded. For example, if you have an import–export business in Canada and want to import some bicycles from Japan, you will probably have to purchase Japanese yen at a bank or foreign-exchange dealer and, with those yen, pay the Japanese seller for the bicycles. Even if the Japanese seller accepts Canadian dollars for the bicycles, and this often is the case, he will be required to convert those Canadian dollars into yen before he can use that money in Japan to pay his workers or pay for other costs of production.

> The greater is the volume of trade between two countries, the higher are the aggregate transaction costs associated with international trade.

Such transaction costs exist even if trade takes place between two countries with fixed exchange rates. For example, if the Bank of Canada pegged the value of the Canadian dollar to the U.S. dollar, any trade between the two countries would still require the costly conversion of one currency to the other. Thus, the existence of transaction costs cannot be used as an argument in favour of fixed exchange rates and against flexible exchange rates. As long as there are two currencies, the transaction costs must be borne by one party or the other. These transaction costs could be avoided only if the two countries shared a common currency.

Many economists believe, however, that the volatility of flexible exchange rates generates another type of cost for importers and exporters. Specifically, the unpredictability of the exchange rate leads to *uncertainty* about the profitability of any specific international transaction or investment. Such uncertainty, given risk-averse firms, can be expected to lead to a smaller volume of international trade and foreign direct investment and thus to fewer benefits from such trade.

On the investment side, if a firm is going to invest substantial amounts of its capital in building facilities to produce goods mainly for sale in a foreign country, it bears the uncertainty of not knowing what the exchange rate will be when its investment eventually comes online. This uncertainty may make firms unwilling to make investments they otherwise would make to take advantage of a Canadian comparative advantage in certain goods.

For example, suppose a Canadian appliance manufacturer enters into a contract to purchase a specified amount of steel from a Japanese producer for a specified yen price in one year's time. In this case, the Japanese producer bears no *foreign-exchange risk* because the price is specified in yen. But the Canadian appliance manufacturer bears considerable risk. If the yen depreciates relative to the dollar over the coming year, fewer Canadian dollars will be required to pay for the steel. But if the yen appreciates relative to the dollar over the coming year, more Canadian dollars will be required to pay for the steel. The Canadian buyer therefore faces a risk in terms of the Canadian-dollar cost of the steel. If the firm is *risk averse*, meaning simply that it would be prepared to pay a cost to avoid the risk, the presence of the risk may lead to fewer international transactions of this type. Perhaps to avoid the foreign-exchange risk, the Canadian buyer will decide instead to buy Canadian-made steel, even though it may be slightly more expensive or not quite the right type that is needed.

> **If the presence of foreign-exchange risk leads to less international trade, there will be a reduction in the gains from trade.**

Many of the people who advocate Canada's move to a fixed exchange rate point to the avoidance of this foreign-exchange risk as the main benefit. They argue that if the Canadian dollar were pegged in value to the U.S. dollar, both importers and exporters would face less uncertainty on the most important part of their trade—that between Canada and the United States. With the greater certainty, they argue, would come greater trade flows and thus an increase in the overall gains from trade.

But many economists disagree. While accepting the basic argument regarding the risks created by flexible (and volatile) exchange rates, they note that importers and exporters already have the means to avoid this uncertainty. In particular, traders can participate in *forward markets* in which they can buy or sell foreign exchange *in the future* at prices specified today. For example, the Canadian appliance manufacturer could enter into a contract to purchase the required amount of yen in one year's time at a price specified today. In this case, no matter what happened to the yen–dollar exchange rate in the intervening year, the uncertainty regarding the Canadian-dollar price of the steel would be entirely eliminated.

Monetary Policy   One final point should be noted about the choice between flexible and fixed exchange rates. If the Bank of Canada chooses to allow the exchange rate to fluctuate in response to shocks, it can focus its monetary policy on the control of inflation. In other words, it can adjust its monetary policy—sometimes tightening and other times loosening—to keep inflation close to the stated 2-percent target. But if the Bank chooses instead to fix the exchange rate, it is not *also* able to control inflation.

As we saw in Chapter 29, the Bank of Canada has only one policy instrument, its target for the overnight interest rate. If the Bank must intervene in the foreign-exchange market to keep the exchange rate fixed—sometimes buying foreign exchange and other times selling it—these transactions will influence the Canadian money supply directly and thus influence Canadian interest rates. But these changes in interest rates may not be consistent with the Bank's policy objective of keeping inflation close to the 2-percent target.

> **If the Bank of Canada chooses to fix the exchange rate, it cannot also conduct its policy to keep inflation at 2 percent. The Bank of Canada has only one policy instrument.**

Summing Up

So, should Canada give up its flexible exchange rate and instead peg the value of the Canadian dollar to the U.S. dollar? Advocates of this policy emphasize the foreign-exchange risk faced by importers, exporters, and investors, and the gains from increased trade that would result from a fixed exchange rate. Opponents to the policy emphasize the shock-absorption benefits from a flexible exchange rate and the benefits of having monetary policy directed at controlling inflation.

This debate will surely go on for a while, partly because it is difficult to quantify the costs and benefits of a flexible exchange rate. Economists on both sides of the debate understand and accept the logic of the arguments from the other side. But researchers have so far been unable to determine how much of a shock is absorbed by a flexible exchange rate, and thus to estimate how much more volatile output and employment would be with a fixed exchange rate. Similarly, it is very difficult to estimate just how much more trade would take place if the foreign-exchange risk faced by traders were eliminated by means of a fixed exchange rate. Without convincing empirical evidence supporting the move to a fixed exchange rate, however, the status quo will probably remain. It is probably safe to assume that Canada will continue to have a flexible exchange rate, at least for the next several years.

Summary

35.1 The Balance of Payments

- Actual transactions among Canadian firms, households, and governments and those in the rest of the world are reported in the balance of payments accounts. In these accounts, any transaction that represents a receipt for Canada (Canadians sell goods or assets to foreigners) is recorded as a credit item. Any transaction that represents a payment from Canada (Canadians purchase goods or assets from foreigners) is recorded as a debit item.
- Categories in the balance of payments accounts are the trade account, the capital-service account, the current account (which is equal to the trade account plus the capital-service account), and the capital account (which includes the official financing account).
- If all transactions are recorded in the balance of payments, the sum of all credit items necessarily equals the sum of all debit items. Thus, the balance of payments must always balance.
- A country with a current account deficit must also have a capital inflow—a capital account surplus. A country with a current account surplus must also have a capital outflow—a capital account deficit.

35.2 The Foreign-Exchange Market

- The exchange rate between the Canadian dollar and some foreign currency is defined as the number of Canadian dollars required to purchase one unit of the foreign currency. A rise in the exchange rate is a depreciation of the Canadian dollar; a fall in the exchange rate is an appreciation of the Canadian dollar.

- The supply of foreign exchange (or the demand for Canadian dollars) arises from Canadian exports of goods and services, capital flows into Canada, and the desire of foreign banks, firms, and governments to use Canadian dollars as part of their reserves.
- The demand for foreign exchange (or the supply of Canadian dollars to purchase foreign currencies) arises from Canadian imports of goods and services, capital flows from Canada, and the desire of holders of Canadian dollars to decrease the size of their holdings.
- A depreciation of the Canadian dollar lowers the foreign price of Canadian exports and increases the amount of foreign exchange supplied (to purchase Canadian exports). Thus, the supply curve for foreign exchange is positively sloped when plotted against the exchange rate.
- A depreciation of the Canadian dollar raises the dollar price of imports from abroad and hence lowers the amount of foreign exchange demanded to purchase foreign goods. Thus, the demand curve for foreign exchange is negatively sloped when plotted against the exchange rate.

35.3 The Determination of Exchange Rates   🔟 ❸ ❹

- When the central bank does not intervene in the foreign exchange market, there is a purely flexible exchange rate. Under fixed exchange rates, the central bank intervenes in the foreign-exchange market to maintain the exchange rate at an announced value. To do this, the central bank must hold sufficient stocks of foreign-exchange reserves.
- Under a flexible, or floating, exchange rate, the exchange rate is determined by supply of and demand for the currency.
- The Canadian dollar will appreciate in foreign-exchange markets if there is an increase in the supply of foreign exchange (an increase in the demand for Canadian dollars) or if there is a reduction in the demand for foreign exchange (a reduction in the supply of Canadian dollars). The opposite changes will lead to a depreciation of the Canadian dollar.
- Changes in the exchange rate are caused by changes in such things as the rate of inflation in different countries, capital movements, structural conditions, and expectations about the future exchange rate.

35.4 Three Policy Issues   🔟 ❹ ❺ ❻

- The view that current account deficits are undesirable is usually based on the mercantilist notion that exports are "good" and imports are "bad." But the gains from trade have nothing to do with the balance of trade—they depend on the volume of trade.
- From national income accounting, the current account balance is given by

$$CA = (S - I) + (T - G)$$

- An increase in investment, a decrease in saving, and an increase in the government budget deficit can each be the cause of a rise in the current account deficit.
- With a flexible exchange rate, supply and demand in the foreign-exchange market determine the "correct" value of the exchange rate. But this "correct" value is constantly changing as market conditions vary.
- The theory of purchasing power parity (PPP) predicts that exchange rates will adjust so that the purchasing power of a given currency is the same in different countries. That is, the prices of identical baskets of goods will be equated in different countries (when expressed in the same currency).
- If price indices from different countries are used as the basis for computing the PPP exchange rate, differences in the structure of price indices across countries, together with the presence of non-traded goods, can be responsible for persistent deviations of the actual exchange rate from this measure of the PPP exchange rate.
- An important benefit of a flexible exchange rate is that it acts as a shock absorber, dampening the effects on output and employment from shocks to a country's terms of trade.
- An important benefit of fixed exchange rates is that they reduce transaction costs and foreign-exchange risk faced by importers and exporters.

Key Concepts

Balance of payments accounts
Current and capital accounts
Changes in official reserves
Foreign exchange and exchange rates
Appreciation and depreciation

Sources of the demand for and supply
　of foreign exchange
Fixed and flexible exchange rates
Mercantilist views on the balance of
　trade and volume of trade

Purchasing power parity
PPP exchange rate
Flexible exchange rates as shock
　absorbers
Foreign-exchange risk

Study Exercises

1. Fill in the blanks to make the following statements correct.

   a. If a wine shop in Alberta buys a case of wine from Chile, the transaction is recorded as a(n) _____ in the _____ account, which is a subsection of the _____ account.

   b. If a Canadian receives dividend payments from a firm in Britain, the transaction is recorded as a(n) _____ in the _____ account, which is a subsection of the _____ account.

   c. If a German pension-fund manager purchases a B.C. Hydro bond, the transaction is recorded as a(n) _____ in the _____ account. If a Canadian sells her ownership stake in a newspaper chain to an American, the transaction is recorded as a(n) _____ in the _____ account.

   d. The sum of the current account and the capital account is known as the _____ and must *always* equal _____.

2. Fill in the blanks to make the following statements correct.

   a. A depreciation of the Canadian dollar means that it takes _____ Canadian dollars to purchase one unit of foreign currency, and there has been a(n) _____ in the exchange rate. An appreciation of the Canadian dollar means that it takes _____ Canadian dollars to purchase one unit of foreign currency, and there has been a(n) _____ in the exchange rate.

   b. Suppose a newscaster tells us that the Canadian dollar is valued at 89.6 U.S. cents. In this case, we say the Canadian–U.S. exchange rate is _____, meaning that it takes _____ Canadian dollars to buy one U.S. dollar.

   c. The exchange rate is determined at the intersection of the _____ curve for foreign exchange and the _____ curve for foreign exchange. An exchange rate above this level means an excess _____ foreign exchange, which is also an excess _____ Canadian dollars. The exchange rate will _____ and the Canadian dollar will _____.

   d. If there is a rise in foreign GDP, and foreign demand for Canadian goods increases, there will be a(n) _____ in supply of foreign currency. The Canadian dollar will _____.

   e. An increase in Canadian prices relative to foreign prices will cause a(n) _____ in the demand for foreign exchange, and a(n) _____ in the supply of foreign exchange. The exchange rate will _____ and the Canadian dollar will therefore _____.

3. Fill in the blanks to make the following statements correct.

   a. If the exchange rate is determined by the equality of supply and demand for foreign exchange and the central bank makes no foreign-exchange transactions, we say there is a(n) _____ exchange rate.

   b. If the central bank buys and sells foreign exchange in an effort to maintain the exchange rate at a specific value, we say we have a(n) _____ exchange rate.

c. If the central bank pegs the exchange rate above its free-market equilibrium level, there will be a(n) _____ foreign exchange and the central bank will _____ foreign currency.

d. If the central bank pegs the exchange rate below its free-market equilibrium level, there will be a(n) _____ foreign exchange and the central bank will _____ foreign currency.

4. The table below shows Tess's financial details for 2010. Answer the following questions about her "balance of payments."

Tess's Financial Details, 2010	
Income from babysitting	$2 500
Income from newspaper route	3 500
Gift from grandparents	1 000
Interest from bank deposits	150
Expenditure on coffee and pastry	1 000
Expenditure on tuition	3 500
Purchase of mutual funds	1 200
Bank balance at end of year	3 500
Increase in bank balance during the year	1 450

a. What is Tess's "trade balance"? Explain.

b. What is Tess's overall current account balance? Explain.

c. What is Tess's capital account balance? Explain.

d. There is one (and only one) piece of information shown above that is not needed to compute Tess's balance of payments. What is it? Explain why it is not needed.

5. The diagram below shows the demand for foreign currency (the supply of Canadian dollars) and the supply of foreign currency (the demand for Canadian dollars). The equilibrium exchange rate is e^*. Assume that Canada has a purely flexible exchange rate.

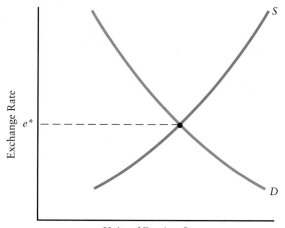

Units of Foreign Currency

a. Show in the diagram the effect of a general inflation in Canada (when there is no inflation in the rest of the world). Explain.

b. Show what happens to the exchange rate if there is a large increase in foreign demand for Canadian telecommunications equipment. Explain.

c. Show the effect of an increase in Canadian investors' demand for Japanese government bonds. Explain.

6. The diagram below shows the demand for foreign currency (the supply of Canadian dollars) and the supply of foreign currency (the demand for Canadian dollars). The equilibrium exchange rate is e^*.

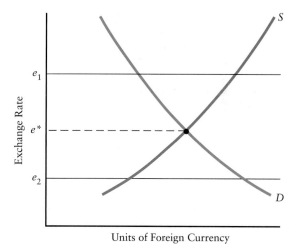

Units of Foreign Currency

a. Suppose the Bank of Canada decides to fix the exchange rate at e_1. What must the Bank do to accomplish its goal? How do the Bank's actions show up in the balance of payments accounts?

b. In part (a), explain why some people would call this a "a balance of payments surplus" even though the balance of payments is in balance.

c. Now suppose the Bank of Canada decides to fix the exchange rate at e_2. What must the Bank do to accomplish this goal? How do the Bank's actions show up in the balance of payments accounts?

d. With the exchange rate fixed at e_2, explain why some people would call this a "balance of payments deficit" even though the balance of payments is in balance.

7. Suppose the Canadian economy is at potential output with a stable price level. There is then an upturn in the world demand for construction materials, especially lumber.

a. Draw a diagram of the foreign-exchange market. Assuming that Canada has a flexible exchange rate, show the likely effect on Canada's exchange rate.

b. Explain the Bank of Canada's participation in the foreign-exchange market if Canada has a fixed exchange rate.

c. Now draw an *AD/AS* diagram for the Canadian economy. What is the likely effect of the shock on Canadian GDP under the conditions in part (a)?

d. On the same *AD/AS* diagram from part (c), show the effect of the shock on Canadian GDP under the conditions of part (b).

e. Explain how a flexible exchange rate acts as a shock absorber, insulating the economy from both positive and negative shocks.

8. Every few months, *The Economist* publishes its "Big Mac Index." Using the current exchange rates, it compares the U.S.-dollar price of Big Macs in several countries. It then concludes that countries in which the Big Mac is cheaper (in U.S. dollars) than in the United States have "undervalued" currencies. Similarly, countries with Big Macs more expensive than in the United States have "overvalued" currencies. The table below shows data from February 2009. (Data from **www.economist.com**.) It shows the domestic-currency prices of Big Macs in various countries. It also shows the exchange rate, expressed as the number of units of domestic currency needed to purchase one U.S. dollar.

Country	Domestic Currency Price	Exchange Rate	U.S. Dollar Price
Canada	$4.16 (Cdn.)	1.24	$___
Australia	$3.45 (Aus.)	1.57	$___
U.S.A.	$3.54	1.00	$___
Japan	290 yen	89.80	$___
Euro area	3.42 euros	0.78	$___
U.K.	2.29 pounds	0.69	$___

a. For each country, use the exchange rate provided to convert the domestic-currency price to the U.S.-dollar price. The price in terms of the currency for any country *i* is $P_i = e \times P_{U.S.}$.

b. By the logic used in *The Economist*, which currencies are overvalued and which are undervalued relative to the U.S. dollar?

c. Are Big Macs traded goods? If not, does this present a problem for *The Economist*? Explain.

d. Which of the following goods do you think would be a better candidate for this exercise? Explain your choice.

(i) cement

(ii) diamonds

(iii) fresh fruit

(iv) computer RAM chips

9. A former Canadian prime minister once suggested that Canada should try to have balanced trade, industry by industry.

a. Do you think this makes sense? Explain.

b. How about the idea of balanced trade, country by country? Explain whether this makes sense.

Discussion Questions

1. What is the probable effect of each of the following on the exchange rate of a country, other things being equal?

a. The quantity of oil imports is greatly decreased, but the expenditure on imported oil is higher because of price increases.

b. The country's inflation rate falls much lower than that of its trading partners.

c. Rising labour costs of the country's manufacturers lead to a worsening ability to compete in world markets.

d. The government greatly expands its gifts of food and machinery to developing countries.

e. A major boom occurs with rising employment.

f. The central bank raises interest rates sharply.

g. More domestic oil is discovered and developed.

2. Canada's trade surplus with the United States (or the U.S. trade deficit with Canada) has been the cause of considerable concern to some U.S. politicians. Many economists, however, argue that U.S. policymakers should not be concerned with reducing the U.S. trade deficit with Canada primarily because there is no reason to expect a balance between any two countries. Comment on the need for policies to address the U.S. trade deficit with Canada.

3. Outline the reasoning behind the following recent newspaper headline: "Loonie plunges as Bank of Canada lowers rates."

4. "Under a flexible exchange rate system, no country need suffer unemployment, for if its prices are low enough, there will be more than enough demand to

keep its factories and farms fully occupied." The evidence suggests that flexible exchange rates have not generally eliminated unemployment. Can you explain why? Can changing exchange rates ever cure unemployment?

5. After the Canadian dollar had appreciated significantly over the previous few years, a letter to *The Globe and Mail* said that "the economy of this once wonderful country is in the sewer and the politicians keep on tinkering, not knowing how to fix it." The letter proposed a 20 percent depreciation of the Canadian dollar and argued that the immediate effects would be (among other things)

  - a dramatic rise in exports
  - a dramatic fall in imports
  - a large net inflow of new foreign investment

What do you think of the proposal? What would the Bank of Canada have to do to achieve a 20 percent depreciation of the Canadian dollar? If such a depreciation were to take place, is it possible for it to have the effects claimed by the author of the letter? Explain.

6. Many commentators are perplexed when they observe a depreciation of the Canadian dollar but not a reduction in the Canadian current account deficit. Explain why there is not a precise relationship between the value of the dollar and the current account balance. Give one example of an event that would give rise to each of the following:

  a. Appreciation of the Canadian dollar and a fall in Canada's current account surplus
  b. Depreciation of the Canadian dollar and a fall in Canada's current account surplus

Challenges Facing the Developing Countries

36w

www.MyEconLab.com

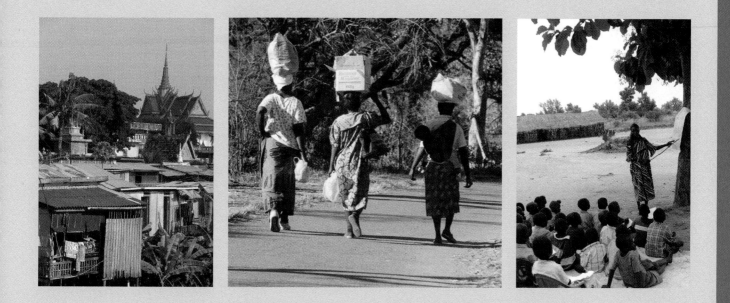

myeconlab

ADDITIONAL CHAPTER ONLINE

The chapter **Challenges Facing the Developing Countries** can be found on the MyEconLab.

www.myeconlab.com

Mathematical Notes

1. Because one cannot divide by zero, the ratio $\Delta Y/\Delta X$ cannot be evaluated when $\Delta X = 0$. However, as ΔX *approaches* zero, the ratio $\Delta Y/\Delta X$ increases without limit:

$$\lim_{\Delta X \to 0} \frac{\Delta Y}{\Delta X} = \infty$$

Therefore, we say that the slope of a vertical line (when $\Delta X = 0$ for any ΔY) is equal to infinity. (p. 40)

2. Many variables affect the quantity demanded. Using functional notation, the argument of the next several pages of the text can be anticipated. Let Q^D represent the quantity of a commodity demanded and

$$T, \overline{Y}, N, \hat{Y}, p, p_j$$

represent, respectively, tastes, average household income, population, income distribution, the commodity's own price, and the price of the jth other commodity.

The demand function is

$$Q^D = D(T, \overline{Y}, N, \hat{Y}, p, p_j), \qquad j = 1, 2, \ldots, n$$

The demand schedule or curve is given by

$$Q^D = d(p) \,\bigg|\, T, \overline{Y}, N, \hat{Y}, p_j$$

where the notation means that the variables to the right of the vertical line are held constant.

This function is correctly described as the demand function with respect to price, all other variables being held constant. This function, often written concisely as $Q^D = d(p)$, shifts in response to changes in other variables. Consider average income: if, as is usually hypothesized, $\partial Q^D/\partial \overline{Y} > 0$, then increases in average income shift $Q^D = d(p)$ rightward and decreases in average income shift $Q^D = d(p)$ leftward. Changes in other variables likewise shift this function in the direction implied by the relationship of that variable to the quantity demanded. (p. 49)

3. Quantity demanded is a simple and straightforward but frequently misunderstood concept in everyday use, but it has a clear mathematical meaning. It refers to the dependent variable in the demand function from note 2:

$$Q^D = D(T, \overline{Y}, N, \hat{Y}, p, p_j)$$

It takes on a specific value whenever a specific value is assigned to each of the independent variables. The value of Q^D changes whenever the value of any independent variable is changed. Q^D could change, for example, as a result of a change in any one price, in average income, in the distribution of income, in tastes, or in population. It could also change as a result of the net effect of changes in all of the independent variables occurring at once.

Some textbooks reserve the term *change in quantity demanded* for a movement along a demand curve, that is, a change in Q^D as a result *only* of a change in p. They then use other words for a change in Q^D caused by a change in the other variables in the demand function. This usage is potentially confusing because it gives the single variable Q^D more than one name.

Our usage, which corresponds to that in more advanced treatments, avoids this confusion. We call Q^D *quantity demanded* and refer to any change in Q^D as a *change in quantity demanded*. In this usage it is correct to say that a movement along a demand curve is a change in quantity demanded, but it is incorrect to say that a change in quantity demanded can occur *only because of* a movement along a demand curve (because Q^D can change for other reasons, for example, a *ceteris paribus* change in average household income). (p. 56)

4. Similar to the way we treated quantity demanded in note 2, let Q^S represent the quantity of a commodity supplied and

$$C, X, p, w_i$$

represent, respectively, producers' goals, technology, the product's price, and the price of the ith input.

The supply function is

$$Q^S = S(C, X, p, w_i), \qquad i = 1, 2, \ldots, m$$

The supply schedule or curve is given by

$$Q^S = s(p) \,\bigg|\, C, X, w_i$$

This is the supply function with respect to price, all other variables being held constant. This function, often written concisely as $Q^S = s(p)$, shifts in response to changes in other variables. (p. 58)

5. Equilibrium occurs where $Q^D = Q^S$. For *specified values of all other variables,* this requires that

$$d(p) = s(p) \qquad [5.1]$$

Equation 5.1 defines an equilibrium value of p; hence, although p is an *independent* or *exogenous* variable in each of the supply and demand functions, it is an *endogenous* variable in the economic model that imposes the equilibrium condition expressed in Equation 5.1. Price is endogenous because it is assumed to adjust to bring about equality between quantity demanded and quantity supplied. Equilibrium quantity, also an endogenous variable, is determined by substituting the equilibrium price into either $d(p)$ or $s(p)$.

Graphically, Equation 5.1 is satisfied only at the point where the demand and supply curves intersect. Thus, supply and demand curves are said to determine the equilibrium values of the endogenous variables, price and quantity. A shift in any of the independent variables held constant in the d and s functions will shift the demand or supply curves and lead to different equilibrium values for price and quantity. (p. 64)

6. The axis reversal arose in the following way. Alfred Marshall (1842–1924) theorized in terms of "demand price" and "supply price," these being the prices that would lead to a given quantity being demanded or supplied. Thus,

$$p^D = d(Q) \qquad [6.1]$$
$$p^S = s(Q) \qquad [6.2]$$

and the condition of equilibrium is

$$d(Q) = s(Q)$$

When graphing the behavioural relationships expressed in Equations 6.1 and 6.2, Marshall naturally put the independent variable, Q, on the horizontal axis.

Leon Walras (1834–1910), whose formulation of the working of a competitive market has become the accepted one, focused on quantity demanded and quantity supplied *at a given price.* Thus,

$$Q^D = d(p)$$
$$Q^S = s(p)$$

and the condition of equilibrium is

$$d(p) = s(p)$$

Walras did not use graphical representation. Had he done so, he would surely have placed p (his independent variable) on the horizontal axis.

Marshall, among his other influences on later generations of economists, was the great popularizer of graphical analysis in economics. Today, we use his graphs, even for Walras's analysis. The axis reversal is thus one of those historical accidents that seem odd to people who did not live through the "perfectly natural" sequence of steps that produced it. (p. 64)

7. The definition in the text uses finite changes and is called *arc elasticity.* The parallel definition using derivatives is

$$\eta = \frac{dQ}{dp} \cdot \frac{p}{Q}$$

and is called *point elasticity.* Further discussion appears in the Appendix to Chapter 4. (p. 79)

8. The propositions in the text are proved as follows. Letting *TE* stand for total expenditure, we can write

$$TE = p \cdot Q$$

It follows that the change in total expenditure is

$$dTE = Q \cdot dp + p \cdot dQ \qquad [8.1]$$

Multiplying and dividing both terms on the right-hand side of Equation 8.1 by $p \cdot Q$ yields

$$dTE = \left[\frac{dp}{p} + \frac{dQ}{Q} \right] \cdot (p \cdot Q)$$

Because dp and dQ are opposite in sign as we move along the demand curve, dTE will have the same sign as the term in brackets on the right-hand side that dominates—that is, on which percentage change is largest.

A second way of arranging Equation 8.1 is to divide both sides by dp to get

$$\frac{dTE}{dp} = Q + p \cdot \frac{dQ}{dp} \qquad [8.2]$$

From the definition of point elasticity in note 7, however,

$$Q \cdot \eta = p \cdot \frac{dQ}{dp} \qquad [8.3]$$

which we can substitute into Equation 8.1 to obtain

$$\frac{dTE}{dp} = Q + Q \cdot \eta = Q \cdot (1 + \eta) \qquad [8.4]$$

Because η is a negative number, the sign of the right-hand side of Equation 8.4 is negative if the absolute value of η exceeds unity (elastic demand) and positive if it is less than unity (inelastic demand).

Total expenditure is maximized when dTE/dp is equal to zero. As can be seen from Equation 8.4, this occurs when elasticity is equal to -1. (p. 83)

9. The distinction made between an incremental change and a marginal change is the distinction for the function $Y = Y(X)$ between $\Delta Y/\Delta X$ and the derivative dY/dX. The latter is the limit of the former as ΔX approaches zero. We shall meet this distinction repeatedly—in this chapter in reference to marginal and incremental *utility* and in later chapters with respect to such concepts as marginal and incremental *product, cost,* and *revenue.* Where Y is a function of more than one variable—for example, $Y = f(X, Z)$—the marginal relationship between Y and X is the partial derivative $\partial Y/\partial X$ rather than the total derivative, dY/dX. (p. 121)

10. The hypothesis of diminishing marginal utility requires that we can measure utility of consumption by a function

$$U = U(X_1, X_2, \ldots, X_n)$$

where $X_1, \ldots, X_n$ are quantities of the n goods consumed by a household. It really embodies two utility hypotheses: first,

$$\partial U/\partial X_i > 0$$

which says that the consumer can get more utility by increasing consumption of the commodity; second,

$$\partial^2 U/\partial X_i^2 < 0$$

which says that the utility of *additional* consumption of some good declines as the amount of that good consumed increases. (p. 122)

11. Because the slope of the indifference curve is negative, it is the absolute value of the slope that declines as one moves downward to the right along the curve. The algebraic value, of course, increases. The phrase *diminishing marginal rate of substitution* thus refers to the absolute, not the algebraic, value of the slope. (p. 140)

12. The relationship between the slope of the budget line and relative prices can be seen as follows. In the two-good example, a change in expenditure (ΔE) is given by the equation

$$\Delta E = p_C \cdot \Delta C + p_F \cdot \Delta F \qquad [12.1]$$

Expenditure is constant for all combinations of F and C that lie on the same budget line. Thus, along such a line we have $\Delta E = 0$. This implies

$$p_C \cdot \Delta C + p_F \cdot \Delta F = 0 \qquad [12.2]$$

and thus

$$\Delta C/\Delta F = -p_F/p_C \qquad [12.3]$$

The ratio $\Delta C/\Delta F$ is the slope of the budget line. It is negative because, with a fixed budget, one must consume less C in order to consume more F. In other words, Equation 12.3 says that the negative of the slope of the budget line is the ratio of the absolute prices (i.e., the relative price). Although prices do not show directly in Figure 6A-3, they are implicit in the budget line: Its slope depends solely on the relative price, while its position, given a fixed money income, depends on the absolute prices of the two goods. (p. 143)

13. *Marginal product,* as defined in the text, is really *incremental* product. More advanced treatments distinguish between this notion and marginal product as the limit of the ratio as ΔL approaches zero. Marginal product thus measures the rate at which total product is changing as one factor is varied and

is the partial derivative of the total product with respect to the variable factor. In symbols,

$$MP = \frac{\partial TP}{\partial L}$$

(p. 160)

14. We have referred specifically both to diminishing *marginal* product and to diminishing *average* product. In most cases, eventually diminishing marginal product implies eventually diminishing average product. This is, however, not necessary, as the accompanying figure shows.

   In this case, marginal product diminishes after v units of the variable factor are employed. Because marginal product falls toward, but never quite reaches, a value of m, average product rises continually toward, but never quite reaches, the same value. (p. 161)

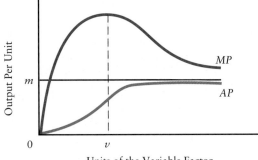

Units of the Variable Factor

15. Let Q be the quantity of output and L the quantity of the variable factor. In the short run,

$$TP = Q = f(L) \qquad [15.1]$$

We now define

$$AP = \frac{Q}{L} = \frac{f(L)}{L} \qquad [15.2]$$

$$MP = \frac{dQ}{dL} \qquad [15.3]$$

We are concerned with the relationship between AP and MP. Where average product is rising, at a maximum, or falling is determined by its derivative with respect to L:

$$\frac{d(Q/L)}{dL} = \frac{L \cdot (dQ/dL) - Q}{L^2} \qquad [15.4]$$

This may be rewritten

$$\frac{1}{L} \cdot \left[\frac{dQ}{dL} - \frac{Q}{L} \right] = \frac{1}{L} \cdot (MP - AP) \qquad [15.5]$$

Clearly, when MP is greater than AP, the expression in Equation 15.5 is positive and thus AP is rising. When MP is less than AP, AP is falling. When they are equal, AP is neither rising nor falling. (p. 162)

16. The text defines *incremental cost*. Strictly, marginal cost is the rate of change of total cost with respect to output, Q. Thus,

$$MC = \frac{dTC}{dQ}$$

From the definitions, $TC = TFC + TVC$. Fixed costs are not a function of output. Thus, we may write $TC = Z + f(Q)$, where $f(Q)$ is total variable costs and Z is a constant. From this we see that $MC = df(Q)/dQ$. MC is thus independent of the size of the fixed costs. (p. 164)

17. This point is easily seen if a little algebra is used:

$$AVC = \frac{TVC}{Q}$$

but note that $TVC = L \cdot w$ and $Q = AP \cdot L$, where L is the quantity of the variable factor used and w is its cost per unit. Therefore,

$$AVC = \frac{L \cdot w}{AP \cdot L} = \frac{w}{AP}$$

Because w is a constant, it follows that AVC and AP vary inversely with each other, and when AP is at its maximum value, AVC must be at its minimum value. (p. 167)

18. A little elementary calculus will prove the point:

$$MC = \frac{dTC}{dQ} = \frac{dTVC}{dQ} = \frac{d(L \cdot w)}{dQ}$$

If w does not vary with output,

$$MC = \frac{dL}{dQ} \cdot w$$

However, referring to note 15 (Equation 15.3), we see that

$$\frac{dL}{dQ} = \frac{1}{MP}$$

Thus,

$$MC = \frac{w}{MP}$$

Because w is fixed, MC varies negatively with MP. When MP is at a maximum, MC is at a minimum. (p. 167)

19. Strictly speaking, the marginal rate of substitution refers to the slope of the tangent to the isoquant at a particular point, whereas the calculations in Table 8A-1 refer to the average rate of substitution between two distinct points on the isoquant. Assume a production function

$$Q = Q(K, L) \qquad [19.1]$$

Isoquants are given by the function

$$K = I(L, \overline{Q}) \qquad [19.2]$$

derived from Equation 19.1 by expressing K as an explicit function of L and Q. A single isoquant relates to a particular level of output, $\overline{Q}$. Define Q_K and Q_L as an alternative, more compact notation for $\partial Q/\partial K$ and $\partial Q/\partial L$, the marginal products of capital and labour. Also, let Q_{KK} and Q_{LL} stand for $\partial^2 Q/\partial K^2$ and $\partial^2 Q/\partial L^2$, respectively. To obtain the slope of the isoquant, totally differentiate Equation 19.1 to obtain

$$dQ = Q_K \cdot dK + Q_L \cdot dL$$

Then, because we are moving along a single isoquant, set $dQ = 0$ to obtain

$$\frac{dK}{dL} = -\frac{Q_L}{Q_K} = MRS$$

Diminishing marginal productivity implies $Q_{LL} < 0$ and $Q_{KK} < 0$, and hence, as we move down the isoquant of Figure 8A-1, Q_K is rising and Q_L is falling, so the absolute value of MRS is diminishing. This is called the *hypothesis of a diminishing marginal rate of substitution*. (p. 192)

20. Formally, the problem is to choose K and L in order to maximize

$$Q = Q(K, L)$$

subject to the constraint

$$p_K \cdot K + p_L \cdot L = C$$

To do this, form the Lagrangean,

$$\mathcal{L} = Q(K, L) - \lambda(p_K \cdot K + p_L \cdot L - C)$$

where λ is called the Lagrange multiplier.

The first-order conditions for this maximization problem are

$$Q_K = \lambda \cdot p_K \qquad [20.1]$$
$$Q_L = \lambda \cdot p_L \qquad [20.2]$$
$$p_K \cdot K + p_L \cdot L = C \qquad [20.3]$$

Dividing Equation 20.1 by Equation 20.2 yields

$$\frac{Q_K}{Q_L} = \frac{p_K}{p_L}$$

That is, the ratio of the marginal products, which is -1 times the MRS, is equal to the ratio of the factor prices, which is -1 times the slope of the isocost line. (p. 195)

21. Marginal revenue is mathematically the derivative of total revenue with respect to output, dTR/dQ. Incremental revenue is $\Delta TR/\Delta Q$. However, the term *marginal revenue* is used loosely to refer to both concepts. (p. 202)

22. For notes 22 through 24, it is helpful first to define some terms. Let

$$\pi_n = TR_n - TC_n$$

where π_n is the profit when Q_n units are sold.

If the firm is maximizing its profits by producing Q_n units, it is necessary that its profits be at least as large as the profits at output zero. That is,

$$\pi_n \geq \pi_0 \qquad [22.1]$$

The condition says that profits from producing must be greater than profits from not producing. Condition 22.1 can be rewritten as

$$TR_n - TVC_n - TFC_n \geq TR_0 - TVC_0 - TFC_0 \qquad [22.2]$$

However, note that by definition

$$TR_0 = 0 \qquad [22.3]$$

$$TVC_0 = 0 \qquad [22.4]$$

$$TFC_n = TFC_0 = Z \qquad [22.5]$$

where Z is a constant. By substituting Equations 22.3, 22.4, and 22.5 into Condition 22.2, we get

$$TR_n - TVC_n \geq 0$$

from which we obtain

$$TR_n \geq TVC_n$$

This proves Rule 1.

On a per-unit basis, it becomes

$$\frac{TR_n}{Q_n} \geq \frac{TVC_n}{Q_n} \qquad [22.6]$$

where Q_n is the number of units produced.

Because $TR_n = Q_n \cdot p_n$, where p_n is the price when n units are sold, Condition 22.6 may be rewritten as

$$p_n \geq AVC_n$$

(p. 204)

23. Using elementary calculus, we may prove Rule 2.

$$\pi_n = TR_n - TC_n$$

each of which is a function of output Q. To maximize π, it is necessary that

$$\frac{d\pi}{dQ} = 0 \qquad [23.1]$$

and that

$$\frac{d^2\pi}{dQ^2} < 0 \qquad [23.2]$$

From the definitions,

$$\frac{d\pi}{dQ} = \frac{dTR}{dQ} - \frac{dTC}{dQ} = MR - MC \qquad [23.3]$$

From Equations 23.1 and 23.3, a necessary condition for attaining maximum π is $MR - MC = 0$, or $MR = MC$, as is required by Rule 2. (p. 205)

24. To prove that for a negatively sloped demand curve, marginal revenue is less than price, let $p = p(Q)$. Then

$$TR = p \cdot Q = p(Q) \cdot Q$$

$$MR = \frac{dTR}{dQ} = Q \cdot \frac{dp}{dQ} + p$$

For a negatively sloped demand curve, dp/dQ is negative, and thus MR is less than price for positive values of Q. (p. 227)

25. The equation for a downward-sloping straight-line demand curve with price on the vertical axis is

$$p = a - b \cdot Q$$

where $-b$ is the slope of the demand curve. Total revenue is price times quantity:

$$TR = p \cdot Q = a \cdot Q - b \cdot Q^2$$

Marginal revenue is

$$MR = \frac{dTR}{dQ} = a - 2 \cdot b \cdot Q$$

Thus, the MR curve and the demand curve are both straight lines, and the (absolute value of the) slope of the MR curve ($2b$) is twice that of the demand curve (b). (p. 227)

26. The marginal revenue produced by the factor involves two elements: first, the additional output that an extra unit of the factor produces and, second, the change in price of the product that the extra output causes. Let Q be output, R revenue, and L the number of units of the variable factor hired. The contribution to revenue of additional labour is $\partial R/\partial L$. This, in turn, depends on the contribution of the extra labour to output $\partial Q/\partial L$ (the marginal product of the factor) and $\partial R/\partial Q$ (the firm's marginal revenue from the extra output). Thus,

$$\frac{\partial R}{\partial L} = \frac{\partial Q}{\partial L} \cdot \frac{\partial R}{\partial Q}$$

We define the left-hand side as marginal revenue product, MRP. Thus,

$$MRP = MP \cdot MR$$

(p. 309)

27. The proposition that the marginal labour cost is above the average labour cost when the average is rising is essentially the same proposition proved in note 15. Nevertheless, let us do it again, using elementary calculus.

The quantity of labour supplied depends on the wage rate: $L^s = f(w)$. Total labour cost along the supply curve is $w \cdot L^s$. The average cost of labour is $(w \cdot L^s) / L^s = w$. The marginal cost of labour is

$$\frac{d(w \cdot L^s)}{dL^s} = w + L^s \cdot \frac{dw}{dL^s}$$

Rewrite this as

$$MC = AC + L^s \cdot \frac{dw}{dL^s}$$

As long as the supply curve slopes upward, $dw/dL^s > 0$; therefore, $MC > AC$. (p. 341)

28. In the text, we define *MPC* as an incremental ratio. For mathematical treatment, it is sometimes convenient to define all marginal concepts as derivatives: $MPC = dC/dY_D$, $MPS = dS/dY_D$, and so on. (p. 524)

29. The basic relationship is

$$Y_D = C + S$$

Dividing through by Y_D yields

$$\frac{Y_D}{Y_D} = \frac{C}{Y_D} + \frac{S}{Y_D}$$

and thus

$$1 = APC + APS$$

Next, take the first difference of the basic relationship to get

$$\Delta Y_D = \Delta C + \Delta S$$

Dividing through by ΔY_D gives

$$\frac{\Delta Y_D}{\Delta Y_D} = \frac{\Delta C}{\Delta Y_D} + \frac{\Delta S}{\Delta Y_D}$$

and thus
$$1 = MPC + MPS$$

(p. 525)

30. The total expenditure over all rounds is the sum of an infinite series. If we let A stand for autonomous expenditure and z for the marginal propensity to spend, the change in autonomous expenditure is ΔA in the first round, $z \cdot \Delta A$ in the second, $z^2 \cdot \Delta A$ in the third, and so on. This can be written as

$$\Delta A \cdot (1 + z + z^2 + \ldots + z^n)$$

If z is less than 1, the series in parentheses converges to $1/(1 - z)$ as n approaches infinity. The total change in expenditure is thus $\Delta A/(1 - z)$. In the example in the box, $z = 0.80$; therefore, the change in total expenditure is

$$\frac{\Delta A}{1 - z} = \frac{\Delta A}{0.2} = 5 \cdot \Delta A$$

(p. 538)

31. This is based on what is called the "rule of 72." Any sum growing at the rate of X percent per year will double in approximately $72/X$ years. For two sums growing at the rates of X percent and Y percent per year, the *difference* between the two sums will double in approximately $72/(X - Y)$ years. (pp. 629, 639)

32. The time taken to break even is a function of the *difference* in growth rates, not their *levels*. Thus, if 4 percent and 5 percent or 5 percent and 6 percent had been used in the example, it still would have taken the same number of years. To see this quickly, recognize that we are interested in the ratio of two exponential growth paths:

$$\frac{e^{r_1 t}}{e^{r_2 t}} = e^{(r_1 - r_2)t}$$

(p. 642)

33. A simple example of a production function is $GDP = z(LK)^{1/2}$. This equation says that to find the amount of GDP produced, multiply the amount of labour by the amount of capital, take the square root, and multiply the result by the constant z. This production function has positive but diminishing marginal returns to either factor. This can be seen by evaluating the first and second partial derivatives and showing the first derivatives to be positive and the second derivatives to be negative.

For example,

$$\frac{\partial GDP}{\partial K} = \frac{z \cdot L^{1/2}}{2 \cdot K^{1/2}} > 0$$

and

$$\frac{\partial^2 GDP}{\partial K^2} = -\frac{z \cdot L^{1/2}}{4 \cdot K^{3/2}} < 0$$

(p. 650)

34. The production function GDP = $z(LK)^{1/2}$ displays contant returns to scale. To see this, multiply both L and K by the same constant, θ, and see that this multiplies the whole value of GDP by θ:

$$z(\theta L \cdot \theta K)^{1/2} = z(\theta^2 \cdot LK)^{1/2} = \theta z(LK)^{1/2} = \theta \cdot \text{GDP}$$

(p. 652)

35. This is easily proved. The banking system wants sufficient deposits (D) to establish the target ratio (v) of deposits to reserves (R). This gives $R/D = v$. Any change in D of size ΔD has to be accompanied by a change in R of ΔR of sufficient size to restore v. Thus, $\Delta R/\Delta D = v$, so $\Delta D = \Delta R/v$ and $\Delta D/\Delta R = 1/v$. This can be shown also in terms of the deposits created by the sequence in Table 27-7. Let v be the reserve ratio and $e = 1 - v$ be the excess reserves per dollar of new deposits. If X dollars are initially deposited in the system, the successive rounds of new deposits will be $X, eX, e^2X, e^3X, \ldots$. The series

$$X + eX + e^2X + e^3X + \ldots$$
$$= X \cdot [1 + e + e^2 + e^3 + \ldots]$$

has a limit of $X \cdot \dfrac{1}{1 - e}$

$$= X \cdot \dfrac{1}{1 - (1 - v)} = \dfrac{X}{v}$$

This is the total new deposits created by an injection of \$$X$ of new reserves into the banking system. For example, when $v = 0.20$, an injection of \$100 into the system will lead to an overall increase in deposits of \$500. (p. 690)

36. Suppose that the public wishes to hold a fraction, c, of deposits in cash, C. Now suppose that X dollars are injected into the system. Ultimately, this money will be held either as reserves by the banking system or as cash by the public. Thus, we have

$$\Delta C + \Delta R = X$$

From the banking system's reserve behaviour, we have $\Delta R = v \cdot \Delta D$, and from the public's cash behaviour, we have $\Delta C = c \cdot \Delta D$. Substituting into the above equation, we get the result that

$$\Delta D = \dfrac{X}{v + c}$$

From this we can also relate the change in reserves and the change in cash holdings to the initial injection:

$$\Delta R = \dfrac{v}{v + c} \cdot X$$

$$\Delta C = \dfrac{c}{v + c} \times X$$

For example, when $v = 0.20$ and $c = 0.05$, an injection of \$100 will lead to an increase in reserves of \$80, an increase in cash in the hands of the public of \$20, and an increase in deposits of \$400. (p. 692)

Photo Credits

Timeline
of Great
Economists

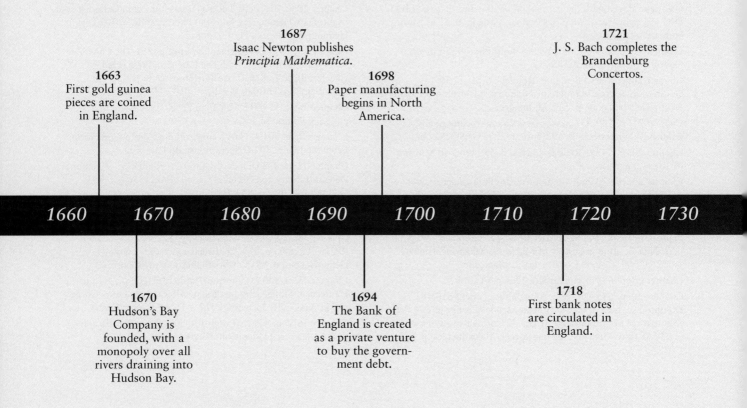

1663
First gold guinea
pieces are coined
in England.

1687
Isaac Newton publishes
Principia Mathematica.

1698
Paper manufacturing
begins in North
America.

1721
J. S. Bach completes the
Brandenburg
Concertos.

1660   1670   1680   1690   1700   1710   1720   1730

1670
Hudson's Bay
Company is
founded, with a
monopoly over all
rivers draining into
Hudson Bay.

1694
The Bank of
England is created
as a private venture
to buy the govern-
ment debt.

1718
First bank notes
are circulated in
England.

A D A M   S M I T H   (1723–1790)

Adam Smith was born in 1723 in the small Scottish town of Kirkcaldy. He is perhaps the single most influential figure in the development of modern economics, and even those who have never studied economics know of his most famous work, *The Wealth of Nations,* and of the terms *laissez-faire* and the *invisible hand,* both attributable to Smith. He was able to describe the workings of the capitalist market economy, the division of labour in production, the role of money, free trade, and the nature of economic growth. Even today, the breadth of his scholarship is considered astounding.

Smith was raised by his mother, as his father had died before his birth. His intellectual promise was discovered early, and at age 14 Smith was sent to study at Glasgow and then at Oxford. He then returned to an appointment as professor of moral philosophy at University of Glasgow, where he became one of the leading philosophers of his day. He lectured on natural theology, ethics, jurisprudence, and political economy to students who travelled from as far away as Russia to hear his lectures.

In 1759, Smith published *The Theory of Moral Sentiments,* in which he attempted to identify the origins of moral judgment. In this early work, Smith writes of the motivation of self-interest and of the morality that keeps it in check. After its publication, Smith left his post at the University of Glasgow to embark on a European tour as the tutor to a young aristocrat, the Duke of Buccleuch, with whom he travelled for two years. In exchange for this assignment Smith was provided with a salary for the remainder of his life. He returned to the small town of his birth and spent the next 10 years alone, writing his most famous work.

An Inquiry into the Nature and Causes of the Wealth of Nations was published in 1776. His contributions in this book (generally known as *The Wealth of Nations*) were revolutionary, and the text became the foundation of much of modern economics. It continues to be reprinted today. Smith rejected the notion that a country's supply of gold and silver was the measure of its wealth—rather, it was the real incomes of the people that determined national wealth. Growth in the real incomes of the country's citizens—that is, economic growth—would result from specialization in production, the division of labour, and the use of money to facilitate trade. Smith provided a framework for analyzing the questions of income growth, value, and distribution.

Smith's work marked the beginning of what is called the Classical period in economic thought, which continued for the next 75 years. This school of thought was centred on the principles of natural liberty (laissez-faire) and the importance of economic growth as a means of bettering the conditions of human existence.

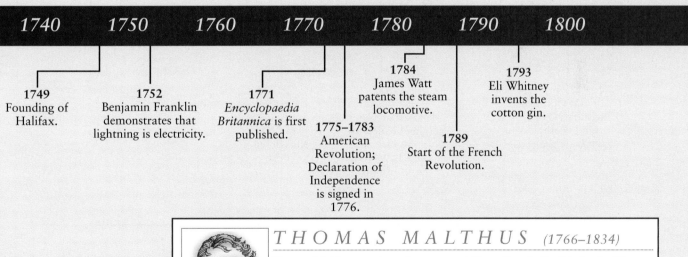

1740	1750	1760	1770	1780	1790	1800

1749
Founding of Halifax.

1752
Benjamin Franklin demonstrates that lightning is electricity.

1771
Encyclopaedia Britannica is first published.

1775–1783
American Revolution; Declaration of Independence is signed in 1776.

1784
James Watt patents the steam locomotive.

1789
Start of the French Revolution.

1793
Eli Whitney invents the cotton gin.

T H O M A S   M A L T H U S   (1766–1834)

Thomas Malthus was born into a reasonably well-to-do English family. He was educated at Cambridge and from 1805 until his death he held the first British professorship of political economy in the East India Company's college at Haileybury. In 1798 he published *An Essay on the Principle of Population as It Affects the Future Improvement of Society,* which was revised many times in subsequent years until finally he published *A Summary View of the Principle of Population* in 1830.

It is these essays on population for which Malthus is best known. His first proposition was that population, when unchecked, would increase in a geometric progression such that the population would double every 25 years. His second proposition was that the means of subsistence (i.e. the food supply) cannot possibly increase faster than in arithmetic progression (increasing by a given number of units every year). The result would be population growth eventually outstripping food production, and thus abject poverty and suffering for the majority of people in every society.

Malthus's population theory had tremendous intellectual influence at the time and became an integral part of the Classical theory of income distribution. However, it is no longer taken as a good description of current or past trends.

DAVID RICARDO (1772–1823)

David Ricardo was born in London to parents who had immigrated from the Netherlands. Ricardo's father was very successful in money markets, and Ricardo himself had earned enough money on the stock exchange that he was very wealthy before he was 30. He had little formal education, but after reading Adam Smith's *The Wealth of Nations* in 1799, he chose to divide his time between studying and writing about political economy and increasing his own personal wealth.

Ricardo's place in the history of economics was assured by his achievement in constructing an abstract model of how capitalism worked. He built an analytic "system" using deductive reasoning that characterizes economic theorizing to the present day. The three critical principles in Ricardo's system were (1) the theory of rent, (2) Thomas Malthus's population principle, and (3) the wages-fund doctrine. Ricardo published *The Principles of Political Economy and Taxation* in 1817, which dominated Classical economics for the following half-century.

Ricardo also contributed the concept of comparative advantage to the study of international trade. Ricardo's theories regarding the gains from trade had some influence on the repeal of the British Corn Laws in 1846—tariffs on the importation of grains into Great Britain—and the subsequent transformation of that country during the nineteenth century from a country of high tariffs to one of completely free trade.

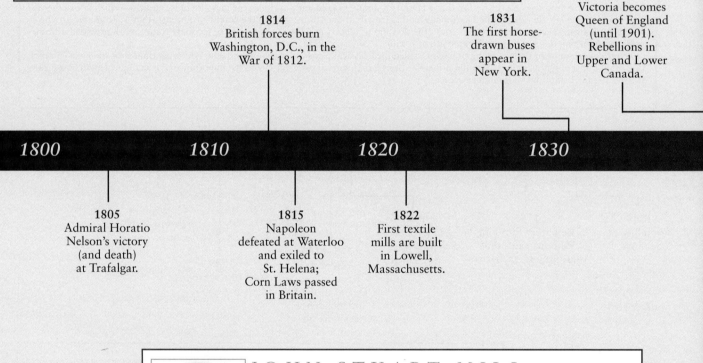

1814
British forces burn
Washington, D.C., in the
War of 1812.

1831
The first horse-
drawn buses
appear in
New York.

1837
Victoria becomes
Queen of England
(until 1901).
Rebellions in
Upper and Lower
Canada.

1800   1810   1820   1830

1805
Admiral Horatio
Nelson's victory
(and death)
at Trafalgar.

1815
Napoleon
defeated at Waterloo
and exiled to
St. Helena;
Corn Laws passed
in Britain.

1822
First textile
mills are built
in Lowell,
Massachusetts.

JOHN STUART MILL (1806–1873)

John Stuart Mill, born in London, was the son of James Mill, a prominent British historian, economist, and philosopher. By age 12 he was acquainted with the major economics works of the day, and at 13 he was correcting the proofs of his father's book, *Elements of Political Economy*. J. S. Mill spent most of his life working at the East India Company—his extraordinarily prolific writing career was conducted entirely as an aside. In 1848 he published his *Principles of Political Economy*, which updated the principles found in Adam Smith's *The Wealth of Nations* and which remained the basic textbook for students of economics until the end of the nineteenth century. In *Principles*, Mill made an important contribution to the economics discipline by distinguishing between the economics of production and of distribution. He pointed out that economic laws had nothing to do with the distribution of wealth, which was a societal matter, but had everything to do with production.

Previous to Mill's *Principles* was his *System of Logic* (1843), which was the century's most influential text on logic and the theory of knowledge. His essays on ethics, contemporary culture, and freedom of speech, such as *Utilitarianism* and *On Liberty*, are still widely studied today.

KARL MARX (1818–1883)

Karl Marx was born in Trier, Germany (then part of Prussia), and studied law, history, and philosophy at the universities of Bonn, Berlin, and Jena. Marx travelled between Prussia, Paris, and Brussels, working at various jobs until finally settling in London in 1849, where he lived the remainder of his life. Most of his time was spent in the mainly unpaid pursuits of writing and studying economics in the library of the British Museum. Marx's contributions to economics are intricately bound to his views of history and society. *The Communist Manifesto* was published with Friedrich Engels in 1848, his *Critique of Political Economy* in 1859, and in 1867 the first volume of *Das Kapital*. (The remaining volumes, edited by Engels, were published after Marx's death.)

For Marx, capitalism was a stage in an evolutionary process from a primitive agricultural economy toward an inevitable elimination of private property and the class structure. Marx's "labour theory of value," whereby the quantity of labour used in the manufacture of a product determined its value, held the central place in his economic thought. He believed that the worker provided "surplus value" to the capitalist. The capitalist would then use the profit arising from this surplus value to reinvest in plant and machinery. Through time, more would be spent for plant and machinery than for wages, which would lead to lower profits (since profits arose only from the surplus value from labour) and a resulting squeeze in the real income of workers. Marx believed that in the capitalists' effort to maintain profits in this unstable system, there would emerge a "reserve army of the unemployed." The resulting class conflict would become increasingly acute until revolution by the workers would overthrow capitalism.

1859
Charles Darwin publishes *On the Origin of Species*.

1846
Britain repeals the Corn Laws.

1867
British North America Act establishes the Dominion of Canada. Alfred Nobel invents dynamite.

1840   1850   1860   1870

1844
Electric telegraph opens between Washington and Baltimore.

1861–1865
The U.S. Civil War; Abraham Lincoln is assassinated in 1865.

1869
Opening of the Suez Canal.

1840
Act of Union unites Upper and Lower Canada.

LEON WALRAS (1834–1910)

Leon Walras was born in France, the son of an economist. After being trained inauspiciously in engineering and performing poorly in mathematics, Walras spent some time pursuing other endeavours, such as novel writing and working for the railway. Eventually he promised his father he would study economics, and by 1870 he was given a professorship in economics in the Faculty of Law at the University of Lausanne in Switzerland. Once there, Walras began the feverish activity that eventually led to his important contributions to economic theory.

In the 1870s, Walras was one of three economists to put forward the marginal utility theory of value (simultaneously with William Stanley Jevons of England and Carl Menger of Austria). Further, he constructed a mathematical model of general equilibrium using a system of simultaneous equations that he used to argue that equilibrium prices and quantities are uniquely determined. Central to general equilibrium analysis is the notion that the prices and quantities of all commodities are determined simultaneously because the whole system is interdependent. Walras's most important work was *Elements of Pure Economics*, published in 1874. In addition to all of Walras's other accomplishments in economics (and despite his early poor performance in mathematics!), we today regard him as the founder of mathematical economics.

Leon Walras and Alfred Marshall are regarded by many economists to be the two most important economic theorists who ever lived. Much of the framework of economic theory studied today is either Walrasian or Marshallian in character.

CARL MENGER *(1840–1921)*

Carl Menger was born in Galicia (then part of Austria), and he came from a family of Austrian civil servants and army officers. After studying law in Prague and Vienna, he turned to economics and in 1871 published *Grundsatze der Volkswirtschaftslehre* (translated as *Principles of Economics*), for which he became famous. He held a professorship at the University of Vienna until 1903. Menger was the founder of a school of thought known as the "Austrian School," which effectively displaced the German historical method on the continent and which survives today as an alternative to mainstream Neoclassical economics.

Menger was one of three economists in the 1870s who independently put forward a theory of value based on marginal utility. Prior to what economists now call the "marginal revolution," value was thought to be derived solely from the inputs of labour and capital. Menger developed the marginal utility theory of value, in which the value of any good is determined by individuals' subjective evaluations of that good. According to Menger, a good has some value if it has the ability to satisfy some human want or desire, and *utility* is the capacity of the good to do so. Menger went on to develop the idea that the individual will maximize total utility at the point where the last unit of each good consumed provides equal utility—that is, where marginal utilities are equal.

Menger's emphasis on the marginal utility theory of value led him to focus on consumption rather than production as the determinant of price. Menger focused only on the demand for goods and largely ignored the supply. It would remain for Alfred Marshall and Leon Walras to combine demand and supply for a more complete picture of price determination.

| **1871**
The Great Fire destroys much of Chicago. | **1876**
Alexander Graham Bell founds Bell Telephone Co. | **1880**
Thomas Edison invents the electric light bulb. | **1885**
The last spike is driven on the Canadian Pacific Railway. Louis Riel is hanged. |

1870   *1875*   *1880*   *1885*

ALFRED MARSHALL *(1842–1924)*

Alfred Marshall was born in Clapham, England, the son of a bank cashier, and was descended from a long line of clerics. Marshall's father, despite intense effort, was unable to steer the young Marshall into the church. Instead, Marshall followed his passion for mathematics at Cambridge and chose economics as a field of study after reading J. S. Mill's *Principles of Political Economy*. His career was then spent mainly at Cambridge, where he taught economics to John Maynard Keynes, Arthur Pigou, Joan Robinson, and countless other British theorists in the "Cambridge tradition." His *Principles of Economics*, published in 1890, replaced Mill's *Principles* as the dominant economics textbook of English-speaking universities.

Marshall institutionalized modern marginal analysis, the basic concepts of supply and demand, and perhaps most importantly the notion of economic equilibrium resulting from the interaction of supply and demand. He also pioneered partial equilibrium analysis—examining the forces of supply and demand in a particular market provided that all other influences can be excluded, *ceteris paribus*.

Although many of the ideas had been put forward by previous writers, Marshall was able to synthesize the previous analyses of utility and cost and present a thorough and complete statement of the laws of demand and supply. Marshall refined and developed microeconomic theory to such a degree that much of what he wrote would be familiar to students of this textbook today.

It is also interesting to note that although Alfred Marshall and Leon Walras were simultaneously expanding the frontiers of economic theory, there was almost no communication between the two men. Though Marshall chose partial equilibrium analysis as the appropriate method for dealing with selected markets in a complex world, he did acknowledge the correctness of Walras's general equilibrium system. Walras, on the other hand, was adamant (and sometimes rude) in his opposition to the methods that Marshall was putting forward. History has shown that both the partial and the general equilibrium approaches to economic analysis are required for understanding the functioning of the economy.

THORSTEIN VEBLEN (1857–1929)

Thorstein Veblen was born on a farm in Wisconsin to Norwegian parents. He received his Ph.D. in philosophy from Yale University, after which he returned to his father's farm because he was unable to secure an academic position. For seven years he remained there, reading voraciously on economics and other social sciences. Eventually, he took academic positions at the University of Chicago, Stanford University, the University of Missouri, and the New School for Social Research (in New York). Veblen was the founder of "institutional economics," the only uniquely North American school of economic thought.

In 1899, Veblen published *The Theory of the Leisure Class*, in which he sought to apply Charles Darwin's evolutionism to the study of modern economic life. He examined problems in the social institutions of the day, and savagely criticized Classical and Neoclassical economic analysis. Although Veblen failed to shift the path of mainstream economic analysis, he did contribute the idea of the importance of long-run institutional studies as a useful complement to short-run price theory analysis. He also reminded the profession that economics is a *social* science, and not merely a branch of mathematics.

Veblen remains most famous today for his idea of "conspicuous consumption." He observed that some commodities were consumed not for their intrinsic qualities but because they carried snob appeal. He suggested that the more expensive such a commodity became, the greater might be its ability to confer status on its purchaser.

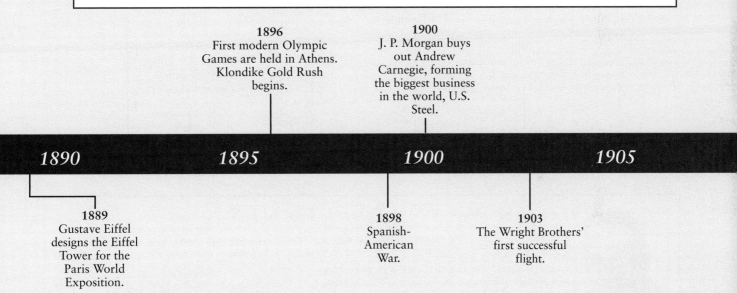

1896
First modern Olympic
Games are held in Athens.
Klondike Gold Rush
begins.

1900
J. P. Morgan buys
out Andrew
Carnegie, forming
the biggest business
in the world, U.S.
Steel.

1890   **1895**   **1900**   **1905**

1889
Gustave Eiffel
designs the Eiffel
Tower for the
Paris World
Exposition.

1898
Spanish-
American
War.

1903
The Wright Brothers'
first successful
flight.

VILFREDO PARETO (1848–1923)

Vilfredo Pareto was an Italian, born in Paris, and was trained to be an engineer. Though he actually practised as an engineer, he would later succeed Leon Walras to the Chair of Economics in the Faculty of Law at the University of Lausanne.

Pareto built upon the system of general equilibrium that Walras had developed. In his *Cours d'économie politique* (1897) and his *Manuel d'économie politique* (1906) Pareto set forth the foundations of modern welfare economics. He showed that theories of consumer behaviour and exchange could be constructed on assumptions of ordinal utility, rather than cardinal utility, eliminating the need to compare one person's utility with another's. Using the indifference curve analysis developed by F. Y. Edgeworth, Pareto was able to demonstrate that total welfare could be increased by an exchange if one person could be made better off without anyone else becoming worse off. Pareto applied this analysis to consumption and exchange, as well as to production. Pareto's contributions in this area are remembered in economists' references to *Pareto optimality* and *Pareto efficiency*.

JOSEPH SCHUMPETER (1883–1950)

Joseph Schumpeter was born in Triesch, Moravia (now in the Czech Republic). He was a university professor and later a Minister of Finance in Austria. In 1932, he emigrated to the United States to avoid the rise to power of Adolf Hitler. He spent his remaining years at Harvard University.

Schumpeter, a pioneering theorist of innovation, emphasized the role of the entrepreneur in economic development. The existence of the entrepreneur meant continuous innovation and waves of adaptation to changing technology. He is best known for his theory of "creative destruction," where the prospect of monopoly profits provides owners the incentive to finance inventions and innovations. One monopoly can replace another with superior technology or a superior product, thereby circumventing the entry barriers of a monopolized industry. He criticized mainstream economists for emphasizing the static (allocative) efficiency of perfect competition—a market structure that would, if it could ever be achieved, retard technological change and economic growth.

Schumpeter's best known works are *The Theory of Economic Development* (1911), *Business Cycles* (1939), and *Capitalism, Socialism and Democracy* (1943).

1912
Titanic sinks on her
maiden voyage, killing
1513 people.

1914
Opening of the
Panama Canal.
First World War
begins.

1918
Treaty of Versailles ends
First World War.

1908
Henry Ford introduces
the Model T.

1917
Bolshevik Revolution
in Russia brings
V. I. Lenin to power.

1905   **1910**   **1915**   **1920**

JOHN MAYNARD KEYNES (1883–1946)

John Maynard Keynes was born in Cambridge, England. His parents were both intellectuals, and his father, John Neville Keynes, was a famous logician and writer on economic methodology. The young Keynes was educated at Eton and then at Kings College, Cambridge, where he was a student of Alfred Marshall and Arthur Pigou. His career included appointments to the Treasury in Britain during both World Wars, a leading role in the establishment of the International Monetary Fund (through discussions at Bretton Woods, New Hampshire, in 1944), and editorship of the *Economic Journal* from 1911 to 1945, all in addition to his academic position at Kings College.

Keynes published extensively during his life but his most influential work, *The General Theory of Employment, Interest, and Money,* appeared in 1936. This book was published in the midst of the Great Depression when the output of goods and services had fallen drastically, unemployment was intolerably high, and it had become clear to many that the market would not self-adjust to achieve potential output within an acceptable period of time. Fluctuations in economic activity were familiar at this point, but the failure of the economy to recover rapidly from this depression was unprecedented. Neoclassical economists held that during a downturn both wages and the interest rate would fall low enough to induce investment and employment and cause an expansion. They believed that the persistent unemployment during the 1930s was caused by inflexible wages and they recommended that workers be convinced to accept wage cuts.

Keynes believed that this policy, though perhaps correct for a single industry, was not correct for the entire economy. Widespread wage cuts would reduce the consumption portion of aggregate demand, which would offset any increase in employment. Keynes argued that unemployment could be cured only by manipulating aggregate demand, whereby increased demand (through government expenditure) would increase the price level, reduce real wages, and thereby stimulate employment.

Keynes's views found acceptance after the publication of his *General Theory* and had a profound effect on government policy around the world, particularly in the 1940s, 1950s, and 1960s. As we know from this textbook, Keynes's name is attached to much of macroeconomics, from much of the basic theory to the Keynesian short-run aggregate supply curve and the Keynesian consumption function. His contributions to economics go well beyond what can be mentioned in a few paragraphs—for, in effect, he laid the foundations for modern macroeconomics.

EDWARD CHAMBERLIN (1899–1967)

Edward Chamberlin was born in La Conner, Washington, and received his Ph.D. from Harvard University in 1927. He became a full professor at Harvard in 1937 and stayed there until his retirement in 1966. He published *The Theory of Monopolistic Competition* in 1933.

Before Chamberlin's book (which appeared more or less simultaneously with Joan Robinson's *The Economics of Imperfect Competition*), the models of perfect competition and monopoly had been fairly well worked out. Though economists were aware of a middle ground between these two market structures and some analysis of duopoly (two sellers) had been presented, it was Chamberlin and Robinson who closely examined this problem of imperfect markets.

Chamberlin's main contribution was explaining the importance of product differentiation for firms in market structures between perfect competition and monopoly. Chamberlin saw that though there may be a large number of firms in the market (the competitive element), each firm created for itself a unique product or advantage that gave it some control over price (the monopoly element). Specifically, he identified items such as copyrights, trademarks, brand names, and location as monopoly elements behind a product. Though Alfred Marshall regarded price as the only variable in question, Chamberlin saw both price and the product itself as variables under control of the firm in monopolistically competitive markets.

1927
Charles Lindbergh flies *Spirit of St. Louis* nonstop from New York to Paris.

1929
Stock market crashes (October 29). Beginning of Great Depression.

1933
Adolf Hitler becomes German Chancellor.

1939
Germany invades Poland; Second World War begins.

1940
Unemployment Insurance begins as national program in Canada.

1925　　　*1930*　　　*1935*　　　*1940*

1922
The Soviet Union is formed; Joseph Stalin named Secretary General of the Communist Party.

FRIEDRICH AUGUST VON HAYEK (1899–1992)

Friedrich von Hayek was born in Vienna and studied at the University of Vienna, where he was trained in the Austrian tradition of economics (a school of thought originating with Carl Menger). He held academic positions at the London School of Economics and the University of Chicago. He returned to Europe in 1962 to the University of Freiburg in what was then West Germany and the University of Salzburg in Austria. He was awarded the Nobel Prize in Economics in 1974.

Hayek contributed new ideas and theories in many different areas of economics, but he is perhaps best known for his general conception of economics as a "coordination problem." His observation of market economies suggested that the relative prices determined in free markets provided the signals that allowed the actions of all decision makers to mesh—even though there was no formal planning taking place to coordinate these actions. He emphasized this "spontaneous order" at work in the economy as the subject matter for economics. The role of knowledge and information in the market process became central to Hayek, an idea that has grown in importance to the economics profession over the years.

Hayek's theory of business cycles provided an example of the breakdown of this coordination. A monetary disturbance (e.g., an increase in the money supply) would distort the signals (relative prices) by artificially raising the return to certain types of economic activity. When the disturbance disappeared, the boom caused by these distorted signals would be followed by a slump. Although Hayek's business-cycle theory was eclipsed by the Keynesian revolution, his emphasis on economics as a coordination problem has had a major influence on contemporary economic thought.

Hayek was also prominent in advocating the virtues of free markets as contributing to human freedom in the broad sense as well as to economic efficiency in the narrow sense. His *The Road to Serfdom* (1944) sounded an alarm about the political and economic implications of the then-growing belief in the virtues of central planning. His *Constitution of Liberty* (1960) is a much deeper philosophical analysis of the forces, economic and otherwise, that contribute to the liberty of the individual.

MILTON FRIEDMAN *(1912–2006)*

Milton Friedman completed graduate studies in economics at the University of Chicago and at Columbia University, where he received his Ph.D. in 1946. Most of Friedman's academic career was spent as a professor at the University of Chicago, and after retiring in 1977 he was a senior research fellow at the Hoover Institution at Stanford University. Friedman is best known as one of the leading proponents of Monetarism and for his belief in the power of free markets. His work greatly influenced modern macroeconomics.

Friedman made his first significant mark on the profession with the publication of *The Theory of the Consumption Function* in 1957. There he developed the permanent income hypothesis, and argued that consumption depends on long-run average income rather than current disposable income, as it does in Keynesian analysis. This was an early example of a macroeconomic theory that emphasized the importance of forward-looking consumers. In 1963, he co-authored with Anna Schwartz his most influential book, *A Monetary History of the United States, 1867–1960*, where they presented evidence in support of the monetarist view that changes in the supply of money can cause dramatic fluctuations in the level of economic activity. Although this view was seriously challenged by subsequent research, Friedman helped the profession to understand the power of and the limitations of monetary policy.

Capitalism and Freedom (1962) and *Free to Choose* (1980), the latter co-written with his wife, Rose Friedman, are part of Friedman's attempts to communicate his ideas about economics and, in particular, the power of the free market, to a mass audience of non-economists. Both books became international bestsellers, and these books, in addition to his writing for newspapers and magazines, made Milton Friedman one of the most famous modern economists. He was awarded the Nobel Prize in Economics in 1976.

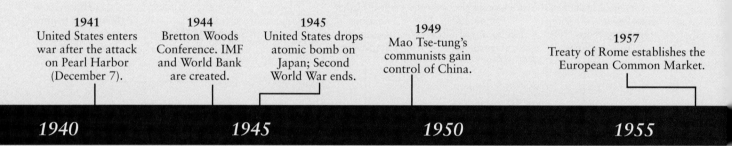

1941
United States enters war after the attack on Pearl Harbor (December 7).

1944
Bretton Woods Conference. IMF and World Bank are created.

1945
United States drops atomic bomb on Japan; Second World War ends.

1949
Mao Tse-tung's communists gain control of China.

1957
Treaty of Rome establishes the European Common Market.

1940　　*1945*　　*1950*　　*1955*

JOHN KENNETH GALBRAITH *(1908–2006)*

John Kenneth Galbraith was born on a farm in Southeastern Ontario, to a family of Scottish-Canadian farmers. He began his undergraduate education at the Ontario Agricultural College in Guelph in 1926 where he studied agricultural economics and animal husbandry. He moved to California to study at the University of California at Berkeley and completed a Ph.D. in agricultural economics in 1934. Galbraith was hired by Harvard University in 1934 and, aside from his government and diplomatic postings, remained on staff there until his death.

Galbraith was heavily influenced by the ideas of John Maynard Keynes, Thorstein Veblen, and the "institutional" school of economics. He rejected the technical and mathematical approach of Neoclassical economics. Instead he emphasized the interplay of economics, politics, culture, and tradition, a combination that does not lend itself well to mathematical modelling. He was much more of a "political economist" in the style of the nineteenth century than a theoretical economist of the late twentieth century.

His most famous book was *The Affluent Society* (1958), where he argued that the United States had become obsessed with overproducing consumer goods and instead should be making large public investments in highways, education, and other public services. His expression "private opulence and public squalor" became well known, and many would agree is even more relevant today than it was when he wrote the words over 50 years ago. In a later book, *The New Industrial State* (1967), Galbraith argued that very few U.S. industries fit economists' model of perfect competition, and that the economy was dominated by large, powerful firms. In general, Galbraith continued to write about topics that he believed the economics profession had neglected—topics such as advertising, the separation of corporate ownership and management, oligopoly, and government and military spending.

Because of Galbraith's desire to focus on the interplay of economics, politics, and society, he was often criticized (or ignored) by mainstream economists. But he was undeterred. And while many economists disagreed with his approach and some of his political views, he was widely recognized as a gifted and insightful writer and speaker.

KENNETH ARROW *(b. 1921)*

Kenneth Arrow was born and educated in New York City. He began graduate work at Columbia University and received an M.A. in mathematics in 1941. Over the following ten years, after Arrow had completed his Ph.D. course work, he served in the U.S. Army Air Corps during the Second World War and held various research jobs while searching for a dissertation topic. His dissertation, which earned him his Ph.D. from Columbia in 1951, subsequently became a classic in economics, *Social Choice and Individual Values* (1951). Kenneth Arrow is currently Professor, Emeritus, at Stanford University.

In his 1951 book Arrow presented his "Impossibility Theorem," which we encounter in Chapter 16 of this book. His conclusion that it is not possible to construct a set of voting rules for making public choices that is simultaneously democratic and efficient has led to decades of work by economists, philosophers, and political scientists in the field of social choice theory.

Arrow also made significant contributions in other areas of economics. In 1954 (with Gerard Debreu) he constructed a mathematical model of an economy with many individual, inter-related markets, and proved the existence of a theoretical general market-clearing equilibrium. Arrow's work in the economics of uncertainty was also a major contribution. In *Essays in the Theory of Risk-Bearing* (1971), he introduced the concepts of moral hazard and adverse selection (among other ideas about risk), which we also encounter in Chapter 16 of this book. Arrow was one of the first economists to develop the idea of "learning by doing" which has played an important role in modern theories of economic growth.

Arrow was awarded the Nobel Prize in 1972 (jointly with British economist John Hicks) and in 2004 was awarded the National Medal of Science, the United States' highest scientific honour.

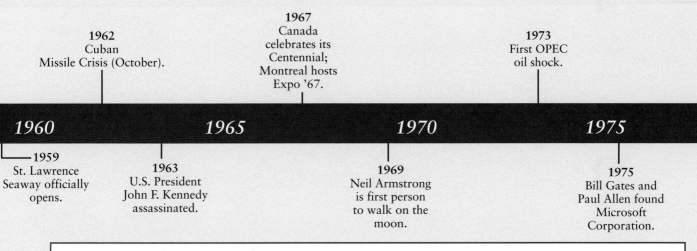

1962
Cuban
Missile Crisis (October).

1967
Canada
celebrates its
Centennial;
Montreal hosts
Expo '67.

1973
First OPEC
oil shock.

1960   *1965*   *1970*   *1975*

1959
St. Lawrence
Seaway officially
opens.

1963
U.S. President
John F. Kennedy
assassinated.

1969
Neil Armstrong
is first person
to walk on the
moon.

1975
Bill Gates and
Paul Allen found
Microsoft
Corporation.

PAUL SAMUELSON *(1915–2009)*

Paul Samuelson was born in Gary, Indiana, the son of a drugstore owner. He received his Ph.D. in economics in 1941 from Harvard University and spent his academic career at the Massachusetts Institute of Technology (MIT), where he is currently Institute Professor of Economics, Emeritus.

Samuelson is generally regarded as one of the greatest economic theorists of the twentieth century. While still a graduate student at Harvard, Samuelson wrote most of *Foundations of Economic Analysis* (1947), which was path-breaking at the time and used mathematical analysis and constrained optimization techniques to shed insight into economic behaviour. He systematized economic theory into a more rigorous mathematical discipline, which has had enormous effects on the way economics is studied today.

Though Samuelson has made major contributions to many branches of economics, three are particularly notable. First, he showed how the central predictions of demand theory could be tested using the "revealed preferences" of consumers from observed market behaviour. Second, in international trade theory, he made important contributions in the analysis of the gains from trade and the effects of tariff protection on the distribution of income. Third, most familiar to readers of this book, he is credited with introducing the 45°-line model of short-run national income determination. This diagram, encountered throughout Chapters 21 and 22 of this book, has become the standard tool for teaching the Keynesian theory of national-income determination in the short run. Samuelson's work has also provided valuable insights in other areas of economics, including government taxation and expenditure, capital theory, and theories of economic growth.

Samuelson is also well known for his famous introductory economics textbook, *Economics,* first published in 1948, which provided a systematic treatment of both micro- and macroeconomics in a way that had not been presented before. In general, he is credited with raising the level of scientific and mathematical analysis in economics. Samuelson was awarded the Nobel Prize in Economics in 1970, and was the first American scholar to receive this honour.

Index

Key terms and their page references are in boldface. *f* denotes a figure, *t* denotes a table, and *n* denotes a footnote.